D0938739

MEDICAL ORTHODOXY
AND THE
FUTURE OF PSYCHOANALYSIS

Library
I.U.P.
ndiana, Pa.

131.34   Ei 88m

MEDICAL ORTHODOXY
AND THE
FUTURE OF PSYCHOANALYSIS

by

K. R. EISSLER

International Universities Press, Inc., New York

Copyright 1965, by International Universities Press, Inc.

Library of Congress Catalog Card Number: 65-18721

A000004596271

Manufactured in the United States of America
by Hallmark Press, New York

Table of Contents

Preface

On rereading the manuscript, I asked myself whether this is an angry book. Except perhaps for the last appendix, I believe it is not—although in some places it may sound like one. I do not know whether the grievances and defects of our time are grosser and more revolting than those of previous centuries, and therefore I do not know whether they should or should not be accepted as unavoidable, or perhaps understood rather than castigated. At any rate, my critique deals only with the fringes of what the historian will later on surely have to discuss as the 'black record' of our century. Nevertheless, it behooves everyone living in these times to call attention to defects that his particular professional position permits him to observe—defects that may have been overlooked or insufficiently stressed by others. Although in most instances he will, for obvious reasons, lay too much stress on such defects, still it seems to me that he cannot evade his duty to set forth an uncompromising criticism—narcissistically as he may overvalue it—of what he perceives from his particular vantage point.

But, with perhaps one exception, I did not follow Goethe's advice: "One ought always to counterbalance the day's separate perversities (topsy-turvinesses) by the weight of great world-historical [events]. [*Den einzelnen Verkehrtheiten des Tages sollte man immer nur grosse weltgeschichtliche Massen entgegensetzen.*]"

In earlier times, discussions were conducted with greater vigor and passion than seems to suit the *fin de siècle* atmosphere that has begun to

· vii ·

spread, as the second millennium of our civilization draws to a close. I could have been more sarcastic—and thus more offensive perhaps—than I have permitted myself to be. I regret that good manners have prevented me from calling a spade a spade more often, particularly in the last appendix where I am dealing with three among the many who are wasting their talents spreading untruths about Freud. The misrepresentation of psychoanalysis is bad enough, yet it may justify itself by the difficulty of grasping what is, as a whole, in flux, in many areas insufficiently defined, and at times even contradictory. Nevertheless, misrepresentations with regard to Freud's life and character that could easily have been avoided, if the available sources had been studied with even a modicum of objectivity, deserve a far more bitter reply than I have in any case allowed myself to indulge in.

When, many years ago, I reviewed a book critically, the author criticized me in turn for the "unconstructiveness" of my criticism. Ever since then, I have been plagued by the question of what it is that makes criticism constructive or unconstructive. I have not made much progress toward finding an answer to that question, but I am inclined to suspect that the more piercing the criticism is, the less 'constructive' it will seem to some to be. Since in what follows criticism is quite prevalent, I here wish to express the hope that it will prove to be not altogether 'unconstructive.'

I also want to add that I have deliberately omitted from my discussion of the problem of lay analysis most questions of such practical matters as the need for fully trained analysts to work as teachers, social workers, nurses, as well as in other professional areas—as was done occasionally in some European countries. Such combinations of professional tasks have proven to be fruitful, not only for psychoanalysis in general, but also to the primary field in which these analysts have been working.

I would have preferred to give this book an accusatory title such as "Futile Remarks on Lay Analysis and Other Subjects." Since this was considered too chilling as a title, I had to drop it. In view of man's predilection for occupying his mind with futile matters, that title might even have had an attraction for many readers. Be that as it may, the reader will note that in the text itself my remarks have to do with subjects about most of which everyone concerned has already made up his mind, so that discussion of them is truly futile in our times.

I am above all indebted to Mr. Harold Collins for his painstaking editorial work. He has devoted much of his time and great effort to the production of a readable manuscript, and has also suggested many changes of substance, almost all of which I have incorporated to the benefit of the final product. I am deeply grateful for the extraordinary conscientiousness with which Mr. Collins has dealt with many complexities of the manuscript. I also owe to Mr. Collins the index.

Mrs. Irene Azarian was kind enough to go through the manuscript editorially. Generously, she did not spare time in an effort to eradicate troublesome mistakes that had persisted until then.

Prof. Frank A. Beach most generously advised me on sleeping habits in the animal kingdom.

Miss Liselotte Bendix, our Institute librarian, has been most kind and patient in providing me with literature. I am grateful for her endurance. She has also done me a great service in helping me uncover one of those not so infrequent misquotations with which the envious try to deprecate Freud.

I owe thanks to Professor Boring's kind reply to a historical question I raised.

Mr. Ernst Federn was kind enough to read the manuscript, inasmuch as it refers directly to lay analysis. Aside from a few bibliographical references, I found it impossible to incorporate the many astute and pertinent comments he had to make. I am glad to hear that he will publish his ideas on lay analysis; they are in some respects superior to mine, and would have partially lost their merits if I had tried to work them into my own manuscript.

I am grateful to Miss Mona M. Karff who has made valuable suggestions with regard to questions of style.

Mr. Masud R. Khan lent me his expert advice on editorial matters, and I owe to him the final title of the book.

I am indebted also to Dr. Heinz Kohut for valuable editorial advice with regard to the last appendix. It might perhaps have been wiser to incorporate all of his (sometimes rather critical) suggestions. No doubt, the changes I owe to him stood that section in good stead.

Mr. Eugene Langston kindly advised me on a detail of American-Japanese relations.

I owe particular thanks to Prof. Le Corbeiller for his gracious reply to an inquiry regarding his paper of 1947. His epitome of the laws of cultural growth, which he was generous enough to send me, was delightful to read and most instructive.

Professor Otto Maenchen was kind enough to convey to me his critical remarks upon my hypothesis regarding an aspect of Japanese history. I also owe him some bibliographical references and guidance in the intricacies of the spelling of Japanese names.

Professor Saul Rosenzweig was kind enough to give me permission to cite an important, as yet unpublished discovery of his regarding the correct dating of a paper by Freud.

Dr. Angela Sanchez de Selke kindly went through the entire manuscript, and I am indebted to her for a number of suggestions, which I was able to use most profitably.

Last but not least, I must express my gratitude to Dr. A. Kagan, to whom psychoanalysis owes so much in this country, for accepting a manuscript so controversial as this. Whether by so doing he will prove to have been of service or disservice to the growth of psychoanalysis, the reader will have to decide.

It is because of the manuscript's controversial nature that I have to forgo the pleasure of expressing my thanks to colleagues and friends with whom I had the privilege of discussing many issues dealt with in this book. Since the first draft goes back to 1948, the reader can easily imagine from how many people I have received constructive criticism and valuable stimulation.

In view of the comprehensive scope of the topics, there was hardly any limit to the literature that I could have cited. The proper selection from abundance requires the sort of skill which I should not be at all surprised to find myself lacking, so that I probably owe apologies to a goodly number of authors.

Among the many reasons which have made me procrastinate with submitting the manuscript for publication, I am all too aware of one: shortcomings of mine, which have become particularly patent to me in my discussions of psychosomatic medicine and of Pavlov's objective psychology. I do not want to ask the reader for forbearance. Although I, myself, am quite fond of the Roman proverb *ex pede Herculem* and do not hesitate to cite it, I ask the reader not to reject the whole, merely because he may have found in it many errors of detail. In view of the far-reaching consequences inherent in the subject matter—consequences which ought to be of concern to everyone who is seriously interested in the future of psychology—the principal issue should not be lost to view behind any flaws in my discussion of it, no matter how many these may be.

K. R. E.

New York, Christmas Eve, 1963.

MEDICAL ORTHODOXY
AND THE
FUTURE OF PSYCHOANALYSIS

Introduction

The limitations of the historical period in which one is living should arouse greater interest than they commonly do. When man pursues his interest in what mankind has already accomplished or what it will yet accomplish, he usually finds reason—unless he has a particularly strong optimistic bent—to bemoan the all too many *shortcomings* that he is forced to observe. Yet he seldom turns his attention to the *boundaries on thought and action* characteristic of his own, or any other historical period, which make these shortcomings inescapable.

That such boundaries do exist, there can be no doubt. Yet one may well doubt whether man is able to recognize or acknowledge the limitations imposed by his time or the causes of those limitations. The paradox that is so characteristic of man, and only of man, still remains—that the very act of recognizing and acknowledging these limitations may be sufficient to make him capable of transcending them.

I cannot flatter myself with the thought that, in discussing some problems of our own time, I have set my sights on such a high goal, not to speak of having made a single step toward it. In what follows the introduction, I am only expressing—with one or two exceptions—opinions with which a minority by and large agrees, and the majority disagrees. It is quite evident—indeed, certain—that on these matters the majority will win out. Even if my opinions were presented in a more persuasive way and with more convincing arguments than I am capable of, there is not much chance that, with regard to the questions I have taken up here, anything will be changed in existing practice or, for that matter, in the distribution of opinion. My emphasis upon the problem of lay analysis— that is, upon the fact that it is only to graduates of medical schools that adequate psychoanalytic training is available—may appear to be addressed to a rather peripheral—one might even say esoteric—issue, of little relevance to the grave problems that civilization is facing.

In social actuality, this problem may, indeed, seem to be a trifle; nevertheless, much, perhaps very much, may hinge upon the stand that society takes in this matter—if two premises of mine are correct. One is that solutions based upon insights that have been gained through the use of scientific methods are more promising, contain less risk of failure, and therefore prove to be more effective, than those gained by any other method. The other is that psychoanalysis (in the meaning that Freud gave to the term) comes closest to the truth among the wide variety of present-day psychologies. The first premise will be accepted by many; there are few who will not doubt the latter. Yet if it too is correct, then the problem of lay analysis is of the greatest concern, as I shall try to show.

The fate of Freud's psychoanalysis in our time is quite remarkable. In his autobiographical sketch, Freud (1925d, p. 54) records, with an implicit but justified pride, the fact that the first World War passed without damage to the psychoanalytic movement. Alas, the same cannot be said of World War II, from which psychoanalysis did not emerge without deep injuries. Totally excluded from cultural life in the vast area on the other side of the world, reduced to a precarious existence in the Catholic countries of the West, it flourishes almost solely in the English-speaking countries, and especially in North America. Curiously enough, it is precisely there that its success may be its undoing. It has been popularized to an unheard-of degree, and almost every group of that composite whole that is socially covered by the term 'psychoanalysis' in the United States has selected one particular aspect of human existence, converted it into an absolute and, by denial, exaggeration and falsification, succeeded in degenerating even the little good, if any, that may still lie somewhere at the bottom of a heap of nonsense.

Here Bouillenne's (1962) characterization of "Man, the Destroying

Biotype" may come handily to mind. In most significant areas of nature, the jungle law of 'eat or be eaten' is dominant. One reason, probably, why we love flowers so much is that, for most of them, that dreadful principle does not prevail. I have read that, in some instances at least, when plants are competing for limited sources of nourishment, the outcome is not that the stronger species suppresses the weaker but that all of them grow smaller. What a lovely way of solving conflicts! When organisms developed means of locomotion, they certainly gave up acting with such wisdom; now we are discovering that man, even though he is by no means forced to do so through indomitable necessities of self-preservation, nevertheless in the service of that supreme law is devouring so much of his environment, and so quickly, that after a while nothing may be left. Thus the paradoxical eventuality looms that man's acquisition of mastery over a great multitude of natural processes may lead, if only by its direct effects within the area of food-getting, to gradual starvation, even to his extinction as a species.

Yet this destructiveness seems to have been indispensable to cultural growth—for man is not only a destroying biotype, but also a destroying sociotype.[1] In order to create new art, he has had to destroy ancient art. One may speculate that, if he were less destructive, the Roman Forum and most Roman palaces (or the Acropolis in its sublime beauty) would still stand unscathed, for man would have built a medieval Rome adjoining either of them (most certainly, he would not have built modern Rome with Sacconi's much cursed Vittoriano).

Indeed, every lover of art would prefer this solution—which, for obvious reasons, would have been impossible. Yet, aside from these obvious reasons, there is probably a psychological one also at work. In order to create new art, one has to destroy the old; new culture grows on the debris of what preceded it. In our times, this destructive process has been slowed down, although not halted. Ancient Egyptian temples are to be inundated in the near future; old churches are still becoming the victims of city planning; and the rumor does not die down that entire ancient quarters in Rome will be felled.

By and large, we may say that, aside from the (not inconsiderable!) effects of war damage, in our historical period, more of ancient art has been unearthed, restored and thereby preserved than has been destroyed;

[1] Cf. Freud (1933a, p. 152) about the internalization of aggression: "It is like a carrying-over into the region of the mind of the dilemma—eat or be eaten—which dominates the organic world."

simultaneously, however, one is forced to note that the artistic impulse has become greatly weakened. Our time is tolerant of, and nondestructive toward, the whole of preceding art, chiefly because art has moved to the periphery and no longer elicits strong emotions. It is only a slight exaggeration to say that man now destroys art to a far lesser extent than he did before, because he is far less moved by it. This, of course, does not include his *intellectual* interest in art. Hand in hand with the non-selective preservation of all preceding works of art goes eclecticism.

The tendency of our century is toward an *understanding* of all forms in which art has manifested itself up to now, without *rejection* of any forms of these manifestations. Modern man is expected to approach primitive art with the same awe as he would feel for Michelangelo's Pietà: that is to say, art can never be ugly, because it is *always* the carrier of something human and thus always meaningful. It is up to the sophistication, knowledgeability and empathic talents of the beholder to discover that human element; the aesthetic, formal elements then follow—automatically.

So far as I know, there has never before been a time in which some or even the majority of art forms would not have been vigorously rejected as ugly, barbaric or primitive, and enthusiasm concentrated on one or very few styles. Yet in this way those styles that were not regarded as "acceptable" were either ignored or destroyed, or their validity as artistic manifestation was denied—all of which is part of the destructiveness of the sociotype.

In psychology today, the sociocultural situation is more complicated. Its eclectic side is rather apparent. The modern psychoanalyst is supposedly bound to acknowledge the warrantability of every last claim and approach that sprouts in the ill-defined area of psychoanalysis. Even though it constituted progress when the West at last made it official—as some great minds had been asserting for a long time—that every religion, in so far as it deters man from cruel acts and promotes unselfishness, has its own rightful position (this too was achieved only after the fervor of the religious impulse became strangely weakened), nevertheless it is lamentable that an equivalent principle of intellectual tolerance should be introduced into science.

No epistemological discourse is necessary here concerning the 'relativity' of scientific theory—which does not rule out a firm statement of what conclusions are to be drawn from the facts so far known. Opposition to, and refutation of, what is plainly wrong are, however, regarded as intolerance, dogmatism, or some other kind of archaism. The only critical trend that is considered proper with regard to Freud—and is consistently encountered in the literature—is the one that shows Freud to be wrong—either wholly or, preferably, in some significant area of his theories.

The tendency to 'disprove' Freud, or to disagree with him—a tendency which emerges with increasing clarity as time progresses—is of the greatest significance. One may perhaps be tempted to think that, in this instance, the destroying sociotype has, after all, a beneficial effect, in that it prepares the field for a new genius—a process comparable to that which was described earlier with regard to the emergence of a new period in the history of art. I myself doubt the existence of constructive potentialities in what is now being done to Freud's work. I do not think it can in any way be compared with ploughing and decomposing the sod, so as to prepare for a new sowing.

I will have a few words to say later on what makes psychoanalysis (I use the term with few exceptions in the sense in which Freud understood it) so extremely vulnerable. I want now to emphasize my belief that Freud's work, his methodology, the prerequisites that have to be fulfilled, in order to live up to the standards that he introduced—in short, the task he outlined for psychology—are a burden too great to be borne by the average person, no matter how great his psychological endowment may be. Freud now seems to have been too humble or too modest, when he countered Stefan Zweig's doubt that "psycho-analysis can be practiced by average human beings" by comparing this objection with the early claim that a microscopist or surgeon had "to possess very special and rare qualifications" (S. Freud, 1873-1939, p. 403). After all, psychoanalysis is now about sixty years old, or a little older, and how many have been able to produce a reconstruction of childhood history that can rival Freud's case history of the Wolf Man?

In whatever way psychoanalytic technique may have changed since, the reconstruction of the first quinquennium remains the fountainhead of analysis. It is well known that many analysts have resolved (in their own minds) the difficulty inherent in this by simply denying the importance and necessity of such reconstruction. Yet I think that Freud understated the difficulty—the actual hardship, in fact—involved in carrying out an analysis. To be sure, there are certainly a number of analysts—how small that number is will never be known—who, in their practice, do satisfy the frame of reference created by Freud, as far as that is humanly possible.

The growth of science, however, clearly requires more than mere practice; for to perceive the essentially new in the huge mass of material garnered in each analysis is a great art, which Freud clearly possessed. As to the skill in microscopy, to which Freud referred in his exchange with Zweig, that has become routinized to such an extent that a large number of scientists have been able to make brilliant discoveries through it. But it seems that patience is incompatible with basic characteristics of the destroying bio- or sociotype: man's ambition drives him on to produce works that may make their impact on him and his habitat as 'original.' Accustomed by the stupendous rise of the natural sciences to the attainment almost daily of the most surprising discoveries, he looks for the same sort of thing in the field of psychology.

The aping of the natural sciences by the mental sciences (Gillispie, 1960, p. 163) has always been pronounced. There was a time when a psychiatrist could boast that he was static—a boast for which today he would expect to be stoned, and which could only be the content of a psychoanalyst's nightmare. Then followed a time when a psychoanalytic paper was considered of subordinate importance, unless the term 'dynamic' was thrown in at least half a dozen times. Now it is the term 'structure' that must be at the center. I do not, of course, doubt the significance of the dynamic and structural aspects. I am only speaking out against the notion of the magic effects of words, and against an attitude that amounts to equating scientific standards with terminology which purports to realize them (as if the mere use of such terms by itself lifted a paper to the point of filling those requirements).

The tendency to imitation of the natural sciences is partly responsible for the hostility—latent or manifest, as the case may be—against Freud. It seems to many to be impossible for the body of Freud's theories to remain valid for a longer time than do theories within the field of the contemporary natural sciences, where they are replaced more or less rapidly. Yet a study of the history of science does not confirm this viewpoint.

At the inception of a science, it takes quite a while for it to get off the ground. The growth of Copernicus's theory was impeded for about a century (Gillispie, 1960, p. 19). At the present time, the acceleration inherent in the development of a science has reached unbelievable heights among the natural sciences; yet psychoanalysis is still beset with troubles of its first post-Copernican century, and no whistling in the wilderness will relieve it of historical necessity. Le Corbeiller (1947) has demonstrated quite convincingly the various phases of the growth of a science or of a group of sciences, their eventually reaching a growth phase that follows an exponential curve and then gradually levels off to a plateau. I am certain that psychology, as far off as this time ever may be, will also one day enter its phase of exponential growth. That it has not yet reached that phase only a very opinionated person will deny.

Right now, if the truth is to be faced, one must admit that there is very little chance that the student of the human psyche, by applying the psychoanalytic technique, could make an essential advance beyond Freud's work. The pain of acknowledging this may be severe, and it will probably be vigorously denied, for many scientists are forced to maintain illusions in order to keep up their creative output. The question, of course, to which the correct answer is of such great importance, is whether the concerted effort to undermine Freud's psychoanalysis and replace it with 'improvements' will not end in leading psychology astray and greatly reduce the chances of gaining deeper insights. In other words, will the effect of man, the destructive sociotype, be in this instance constructive, —as has so often happened in the field of art—or will it cause regressions, to undo which will later take much effort and time?

One must also consider whether or not the range of insights that can be gained by means of the psychoanalytic method has been essentially exhausted. It is at least conceivable that Freud was powerful enough to extract from the psychoanalytic situation all the knowledge that can be obtained through the method of free association. One has to distinguish here, of course, between molar and molecular knowledge. It seems very likely that, with the introduction and pursuit of ego psychology, Freud went to the limits of psychoanalytic molar investigation. Only in the realm of the dream, wit and apraxia has Freud produced complete molecular surveys of psychic phenomena. In other areas, he at least laid enough of a basis so that molecular research could proceed further. If reason were the sole determinant for the analyst, he would focus his efforts on filling the gaps left by Freud, and revise the molar part only as that became necessary in the light of new molecular findings. But reason rarely prevails in human affairs. Freud (1926a) was probably quite right when he asserted in the form of a question: "But have you ever found that men do anything but confuse and distort what they get hold of?" (p. 193).

The productive effect of new techniques is unquestionable. It can be seen clearly in the development of art and music; but it is especially true of science. The invention of the microscope, for example, introduced a fundamentally new era into biology. Freud, too, was favored by the emergence of a new technique: hypnosis. Following Breuer, he fitted it to his purposes; and then quickly replaced it with an even better one: free association. It is possible that a new technique will be required, to give psychology a boost equal to the one it obtained when hypnosis and free association were placed at its service.[2] It is my personal belief that this boost may come one day from electrophysiology, refinements in which may be carried to unimaginable subtleties and depths. No doubt this is a fantasy, however, and at present anyone eager to learn about the mind's structure cannot do better than to make use of the technique that Freud evolved.

It is easy to see that, within the field of psychoanalysis, as it exists in social reality, where it is torn in different directions by innumerable and obnoxious efforts at 'improvement,' there remains one area of relative wisdom and rationality—that of psychoanalytic ego psychology.[3] With the triad of papers *The Ego and the Id* (1923a), *Inhibition, Symptom and Anxiety* (1926c) and *The Anatomy of the Mental Personality* (1933a, pp. 82-112), Freud made a turn that is characteristic of the accomplishments of genuis—namely, the synthesis of work that, under less propitious conditions, would have had to be distributed among several people. It reminds me of Goethe, who was the greatest among the *Sturm und Drang* poets, the classicists, and the romantics and high romantics (Korff, 1923-1958). His achievements in each period alone would have been sufficient to secure his position as Germany's greatest poet.

Similarly, Freud's achievement during the cathartic phase would have brought eminence to him; and it would not have reduced his claim to fame if another genius had evolved catharsis into free association and written *The Interpretation of Dreams*. Yet, as is well known, he went even further and created the psychoanalytic psychology of ego and superego. Thus, it is historically and practically correct, for those who are the

[2] It seems to me that it is in the field of applied psychoanalysis that the greatest prospect now lies of making far-reaching discoveries about the psychology of man.

[3] As may be expected, many analysts would object to this statement. How far apart psychoanalysts may be in evaluating psychoanalytic theory and practice can be seen in the case of Glover. He criticized Hartmann's basic text of 1939 severely—and, I think, quite unjustifiedly—(Glover 1961), almost depriving him of the status of a psychoanalytic theoretician. In 1964, however, in dealing with Alexander, most of whose writings of about the last two and a half decades (as far as I have been able to read them) impressed me almost as the acme of what an analyst should not think and do in practice (see later), Glover accorded him a status almost of eminence in psychoanalysis.

true inheritors to evolve still further the concluding section of his life work, which he not only initiated but carried forward himself for quite a distance. And indeed substantial advancement has been made in that area.

When I now turn to the concept of ego autonomy (Hartmann, 1939, 1950, 1952, 1955; Rapaport, 1951b, 1958), which holds a pivotal position in psychoanalytic ego psychology, I do not discuss it in the way this concept is usually defined in current literature, and I beg the reader to keep this in mind. That the ego is an independent variable, and that it—or its equivalent—already held this position in Freud's cathartic phase, one cannot doubt; but in order to assign autonomy to the ego, more is needed than this—or so, at least, it seems to me. I shall therefore discuss autonomy on a broader basis and express some of the doubts I harbor about the possibilities of viewing the ego as an autonomous organization.

In Freud's work, the ego holds two different positions; or perhaps it would be better to say that two different aspects are given different emphases, depending on the range of problems that were of central interest to Freud at the particular moment. When Freud was writing, he had "to blind myself artificially to focus all the light on one dark spot" (S. Freud, 1873-1939, p. 312)—a procedure which endows almost every one of his papers with its absolute power to be convincing. But his genius made him constantly shift around "the dark spot" (or the illuminating beam of light). This led not only to the synthesis of an extraordinarily wide range of problems, but also to the awareness of differences of aspect with regard to one and the same object, depending on the angle from which it was viewed.

Thus, in *The Ego and the Id,* one aspect of the ego and its relation to the drives was at the core of Freud's concern; he illustrated it by the metaphor of "a man on horseback, who has to hold in check the superior strength of the horse" (1923a, p. 25), adding that "the rider tries to do so with his own strength, while the ego uses borrowed forces," and further, that the man on horseback is often "obliged to guide it where it wants to go."

Another important analogy is used to illustrate the effectiveness of one of the ego's most important functions—namely, the securing of a postponement of motor discharges by means of the interposition of thinking processes between the perceptual and motor spheres. This power to delay, Freud (1923) continues, is "like that of a constitutional monarch, without whose sanction no law can be passed, but who hesitates long before imposing his veto on any measure put forward by Parliament" (p. 55). The meaning of the analogy is rendered unambiguous by the introductory remark that even this power of the ego is more form than fact.

Yet, only three years later, Freud was to introduce a new trend into ego psychology. This move was altogether characteristic of him, and testifies to the fact that his genius, which was closely attuned to the complexities of reality, never permitted psychoanalysis to grow stale through the monotonous repetition of emphasis upon a single limited aspect. In a now famous programmatic statement at the end of the second section of his *Inhibition, Symptom and Anxiety*, Freud vigorously turned against the use of psychoanalytic findings as a means of developing *Weltanschauungen*, for the description of the ego's potential defeat in its endeavors to meet the complexity of its multiple tasks had had the effect of producing a corresponding *Weltanschauung* among many analysts.

The ego is, after all, not impotent *vis-à-vis* the drives, Freud says now, but exerts great power over them by means of repression. When a drive is repressed, its gratification is inhibited; this means that an excitatory process is blocked that would otherwise have taken place. In view of this effect, Freud properly speaks of the ego's *überraschende Machtentfaltung*, which means literally a "surprising unfolding of power" (cf. Freud 1926c, p. 97); by producing anxiety, the ego can instantaneously initiate repression. To illustrate this, the analogy of the political minority is now introduced: "Let us imagine a country in which a certain small faction objects to a proposed measure, the passage of which would have the support of the masses. This minority obtains command of the press and by its help manipulates the supreme arbiter, 'public opinion,' and so succeeds in preventing the measure from being passed" (Freud, 1926c, p. 92). The manipulation of public opinion would then stand for the production of anxiety, by means of which the defeat of the measure, which would stand for repression, is obtained.

Thus we have here three separate and successive analogies: the horseback rider and the horse; the constitutional monarch and parliament; the minority and the masses. Only the last was intended to reflect the ego's relative strength. Yet a closer scrutiny of these analogies may deprive them of their initial power to be convincing; for example, since most horseback riders are in command of their horses, *this* analogy would serve better to illustrate the ego's strength.[4] If Freud had not introduced the

[4] Dr. Strachey (Freud, 1923a, p. 25 n.2) calls attention to one of Freud's dreams (1900, pp. 229-231) from which the subjective background of this analogy can be

second analogy with the qualification of "form and fact," it might likewise have been used to illustrate the ego's strength, for the constitutional monarch has constitutional powers to overrule parliament directly, while manipulation of public opinion is a rather precarious measure, of dubious effect, for it may easily recoil and lead to naught.[5] I do not know whether I am right in saying that the analogies foreshadow to a certain extent propositions of the subsequent phase, for in his *New Introductory Lectures* of 1933 more is again heard about the ego's weaknesses.

Concomitantly with these shifts in the evaluation of ego strength and ego weakness,[6] there occurred shifts in Freud's views and theories regarding the vexing problem of anxiety, for he recognized anxiety as the initiator of repression.

Up to 1926, anxiety aside from reality anxiety was by and large viewed as an impediment or burden to man; but in *Inhibition, Symptom and Anxiety* it is put into a position of what might almost be called eminent superiority. Whereas as late as 1923, anxiety was still being equated with a "flight-reflex" (1923a, p. 57), by 1926 "the function of producing the anxiety effect according to its need" had been allocated to the ego (1926c, p. 162); at one point, Freud even speaks of "the intentional reproduction of anxiety as a signal of danger" (1933a, p. 138). This kind of anxiety is described as being produced on the ego's "own initiative" (1926c, p. 162), and thus it is contrasted with the appearance of automatic, involuntary, newly formed anxiety. The transition from the latter to the former, which is made possible by the maturation of the ego, is of course a focal problem of psychoanalytic research (cf. 1926c, p. 138). The reader can hardly finish Freud's 1926 treatise on anxiety without getting the impression that the ego, once endowed with the efficacy of the anxiety signal, is strong and well prepared to navigate the treacherous waters, with their dangerous undercurrents and backflows. Rarely has a

---

learned. At a time when Freud's power of locomotion was severely impeded by "the most unbearable pain with every step I took," he, who had never learned to ride, dreamed he was riding a horse. In this dream, the insecurity of a number of situations was vigorously denied. The joke of the Sunday horseman who has to ride to where his horse wants to go appears as early as 1898 (S. Freud, 1887-1902, p. 258).

[5] As a matter of fact, Freud had used a similar analogy to illustrate the ego's weakness. In *The Ego and the Id* (1923a, p. 56), he had written: "In its position midway between the id and reality, it [the ego] only too often yields to the temptation to become sycophantic, opportunist and lying, like a politician who sees the truth but wants to keep his place in popular favour."

[6] For the Janus-like aspects of these concepts, see Nunberg (1939). For a different approach to the problem of ego strength, see Hartmann (1939, p. 15f.).

signal functioned simultaneously as both weapon and tool with equal efficiency.

Nevertheless, in his *New Introductory Lectures* Freud once again presents what may be called a new trend, which may possibly be regarded as a synthesis of the two that I have just dealt with in somewhat cursory form. The strength of the ego and its assets is set forth; at the same time, its weaknesses are acknowledged, and the horseback rider analogy is reinstituted (Freud, 1933a, p. 108): "On the whole, the ego has to, carry out the intention of the id." At one point, anxiety is referred to as a sign of weakness: "When the ego is forced to acknowledge its weakness, it breaks out into anxiety" (p. 109). Nevertheless, while repeating the assertion of the ego's weakness in relation to the id, Freud (without any "intention of withdrawing this assertion") also reasserts that the ego exerts an influence on the processes in the id by means of the anxiety signal (p. 128). Indeed, without the anxiety signal, the ego would have to either tolerate the breakthrough of what could be a highly dangerous drive, or submit to a full-fledged anxiety attack. It thus gains in many respects from its possession of the short-lasting and more or less harmless anxiety signal.

Nevertheless, it may be countered that the ego is forced to stoop here to the employment of a technique that is archaic, in the last analysis of questionable value (for the repressed drive may still cause unforeseeable damage to the ego), and generally not worthy of an organization already endowed with reason—at least potentially, even if it does not always actually use it. Freud remarked on techniques that would stand the ego in better stead: he spoke of the ego's mastery of drives (*Triebbeherrschung*), which apparently cannot be achieved by the anxiety signal, but only "through the mental representative of the instinct becoming subordinated to a larger organization, and finding its place in a coherent unity" (1933a, p. 107).

Later, Freud (1937a, p. 326) called this the 'taming' of the instinct. That is to say, "it is brought into harmony with the ego and becomes accessible to the influence of the other trends in the ego, no longer seeking for independent satisfaction." Such effects can never be achieved by anxiety signals, but only by mastery or taming. The ego shows its full force only when it achieves mastery, but how often does man achieve mastery as a permanent solution? In most instances, man must resign himself to the anxiety signal and to repression, which—beneficial as they may prove themselves to be under propitious conditions—do not seem to testify to true autonomy.

I have not set forth anything new here; nevertheless, it may be useful to recall some of the facts mentioned, before the question is raised once again: what is really the ego's autonomy compared with that of the drives? One is immediately reminded of the psychobiological fact of sleep, in which the ego is forced to surrender almost all its prerogatives and to expose itself to external dangers that not too infrequently conjoin to inflict grave damage on just such an occasion,[7] whereas the drives maintain their activity, do their work, and seek their satisfactions. And the strongest ego, braced as it may be for successful coping with internal and external dangers, finally succumbs to death—which in turn, according to Freud, is the final consummation of a drive satisfaction.

Sleep and death are psychobiological facts that may have to be looked at as inherently infringing gravely upon ego autonomy or, at least, severely limiting its extent (Rapaport, 1958; Hartmann, 1959). Furthermore, the ego has a store of quite surprising functions, anticipation of the future being not the least among them. Its ability to project itself into the future, to unravel with approximate accuracy the effects of an action and the probabilities of future events, should be, one would think, an outstanding protective device against dangers and a means for the facilitation of ego-syntonic and reality-syntonic action. Despite this important endowment, one only relatively rarely observes the ego to be ready to bow to necessities beyond the immediate future—not to speak of its unwillingness to abandon its eternal bent toward wishful thinking, at times when man should be accepting historical necessities and objectively evaluating the society in which he is living.[8]

It is in the historical process that the ego's frailty and infirmity—one might almost say, its futility—are perceived with particular distinctness. Among the endless number of instances of this sort that one may cite on the occasion when man's involvement in the historical process is brought up, Leonidas—rightly or wrongly—comes to my mind. He saved Greece

[7] Prof. Frank A. Beach has been kind enough to inform me that at present no general rules can be formulated concerning the correlation between external danger and sleep in the animal kingdom. It seems that, in general, animals are protected during sleep by a number of different mechanisms, which vary from species to species (see Hediger, 1959). It would be interesting if it turned out that the dangers to man brought about by sleep have no evolutionary antecedents.

[8] For a psychoanalytic investigation of rational and irrational actions, see Hartmann (1947).

at the cost of his life. But where is the Athens, where is the Sparta he rescued? And would he have endured Thermopylae had he known that the Peloponnesian War would follow only fifty years later? Might not the Persians, after all, have become the willing disciples of Greek culture, and thus safeguarded Greek superiority far better than it was safeguarded, after their elimination from Europe?

At any rate, despite his own efforts, man still remains little more than a pawn in the course of history. Yet no argument can alter the fact that, through the evolvement of the ego, evolution has led to the emergence of a structure endowed with incomparable capabilities for adjustment. Nevertheless, this achievement must always be seen in its right proportion, for each step of differentiation, as is well known, simultaneously establishes—in addition to improved adaptability—a locus of vulnerability (Hartmann, 1939, p. 48f.). At the time when *homo sapiens* has become extinct, some lower forms of life will still go on existing. Differentiation, although it may be of great survival value to the individual, does not necessarily serve this purpose for the species (cf. Hartmann, 1939, p. 27).

Depressing as the image of man may seem to be, when his history is figuratively compressed into a short span of time—for then human life is reduced to a chain of jumps from the womb to the grave—an entirely different view arises when one beholds the accumulation of cultural achievements that have found concrete realization in a variety of media. In some of these man-made objects, the ego's inherent weaknesses are not visible. In whatever respect their creators' egos may have failed, the products of the great Greek genius—as well as those of the simple Athenian craftsman—shine forth in sublime beauty, emblems of man's greatness, despite the frailty that any particular artist's own life story may demonstrate only too convincingly. Consequently, a psychology that sets out to deal seriously with the question of ego autonomy has to take up the problem of creativity, for it is in the creative act—which leads to a materialization of a part of the self—that the ego comes at all close to what may be described as autonomy.

To be sure, during the course of a psychoanalytic inquiry, one has the opportunity to make observations on the subject's creativity; yet an examination of the psychoanalytic literature will show that man's creativity still remains essentially an enigma. This is not true, to the same degree, of the triad—drive demand, defense, symptom compromise—which, although still rich in unsolved problems, is understood psychoanalytically, at least in approximation. It may be worth while pausing for a moment here to consider a limitation that is imposed upon the psychoanalytic method of inquiry.

The analyst has the opportunity to observe the subject's ego in its daily struggle with id, superego and reality. The search for an understanding of this struggle leads far back into the subject's early infancy and has as its outcome the grasp of a substantial part of the subject's personality. Yet Freud has called attention to the fact that not all the areas of the personality that would fall legitimately within the analyst's orbit are actually drawn into the psychoanalytic process, for only a limited range of the subject's conflicts actually become activated during the course of the psychoanalytic exploration (Freud, 1937a, p. 318f.). For good reasons, Freud warned against any artificial excitation of those problem areas that remain moot during the course of a psychoanalysis (*ibid.*, p. 333f.).

Let us call the representation of an activated defense mechanism and the representation of the content against which the defense is directed a 'plan.'[9] Let us define it in more general terms as the representation of a configuration that includes both activated stimulus and activated response. The stimulus may be a drive demand, a superego request, a reality task, while the response may be anxiety, rage, a neurotic symptom, a poem or merely a thought.

We can then say that the analyst observes, during the years of his inquiry into the daily experiences of the subject, a multitude and variety of plans. He may succeed in reducing this huge mass to one or a few common denominators; yet he knows that he cannot ever become acquainted with all of the subject's plans, if for no other reason than that he can ascertain the subject's development only as far as the biological phase that the subject has reached at the time of the psychoanalytic inquiry. He is therefore not in a position to gauge the full scope of the ego's resourcefulness in meeting all the tasks inherent in human life, some of which the subject will still have to meet after the termination of treatment. In order to even approximate the full record of the ego's potential, a study has to be made of the subject's life history from birth to death (cf. Hartmann and Kris, 1945; Hartmann, 1959). Just as the thinkers have asserted, as far back as in ancient times, that the decision as to

[9] Miller et al. (1960, p. 16) define 'plan' as follows: "A Plan is any hierarchical process in the organism that can control the order in which a sequence of operations is to be performed." I also take the differentiation of plan and metaplan, presently to be discussed, from Miller et al. However, I am using the authors' terms in a way different from theirs.

whether a man lives happily or not could be made only after his death, so too does the psychologist know that, in order for us to estimate what a man really was, the whole history of his life must be on record.[10]

From the viewpoint of the psychology of the id, this implies that some drive wish, some repressed content, may make itself noticeable only in old age. Indeed, a self may so ingeniously conceal the secrets of the repressed that, on occasion, the truth will come to the fore only in the succeeding generation; it may even happen, although very rarely, that a parent will harbor a wish that is so deeply repressed that its only consequence is the stimulation of an acting out in his progeny.[11] In other words, it is not easy to make a *total* survey of id demands in the course of a psychoanalytic inquiry; and it is an even more complicated task to establish the full range of ego responses, ego assets and ego deficiencies, since solutions and responses may evolve in old age, that may seem quite new. A final evaluation of the self is possible only on the basis of full knowledge of how the self responded to the total variety of stresses it had to meet.

Indeed, it must be admitted that this full knowledge will be obtainable only in rare instances, for that external combination of circumstances, which would bring out the self's total potentialities, may never come about. There is a story that illustrates what is meant here. A man comes to Heaven and asks St. Peter if he can meet the greatest strategic mind that ever lived. He is taken to a person of whom he has never heard, and who has lived a very trivial, uneventful life. When he complains about having been fooled, because he was led neither to Caesar nor to Napoleon nor their like, St. Peter counters that this unknown man actually *was* the most brilliant strategic mind, he just never had the opportunity to show it. (The analyst, of course, is greatly interested in such potentials, whether they are creative or pathological; but experience shows that, in their totality, they are not available during the course of a psychoanalytic inquiry.)

I suggest that we call the full scope of these potentialities the 'meta-

[10] Yet the establishment of an accurate record of a life history—let us say of a historical personality—requires experience in historical methodology. I do not here go into the fact that, in order to produce the sort of record that would live up to psychoanalytic requirements and specifications, more is required than the expertise of the historian. I merely stress at this point the fact that historical methodology is indispensable if one is to obtain a life history of any sort.

[11] One may almost be inclined to make a comparison between the appearance in the progeny of that which is deeply repressed in the parent, and the Mendelian laws of inheritance.

plan,' and the factors involved in their realization the ego's strategy; tactics will similarly be correlated with the ego's plans. Yet the metaplan should be regarded as more than the accumulation of all the individual plans, whether latent or manifest. In observing the patient's tactics during the course of daily observations, one sees that a number of smaller plans fit well into a single supraordinated plan. During the progress of the psychoanalytic inquiry, we may finally succeed in ascertaining a single common denominator—or a few—underlying the great variety of plans observed. I suggest, however, that we would probably change our final estimate of each of these denominators, once the metaplan were known. Freud reported a thought-provoking example of a successfully treated patient who, twelve or fourteen years after the termination of treatment, had to undergo a hysterectomy; this trauma initiated a new phase of— at this juncture, incurable—psychopathology (Freud, 1937a, p. 323). The fact that the patient had been strong enough to endure a number of severe stresses after termination, yet broke down under the impact of a hysterectomy, plainly brings to light a new factor, which cannot but affect the observations made, and the conclusions drawn during the previous psychoanalytic inquiry.

There is no doubt that psychoanalysis has gained its deepest insights in situations in which the ego can be observed in a relative failure (A. Freud, 1936). This is quite clear in the case of the neurotic symptom and apraxia; but the dream—which, for a long time, has been the main source of information—is also an evidence of failure since, in dreaming, the ego is not able to fulfill its wish to sleep.

In his inquiry into the psychology of jokes (or wit), however, Freud turned toward a field in which the ego does not fail, but on the contrary produces a configuration that has to be evaluated positively, and is actually sought by the self as a desirable goal. It may be significant that the decisive mechanism of joke formation is today viewed in terms derived from clinical psychopathology, and is thus characterized as a "regression in the service of the ego" (Kris). I wonder whether it would indicate any significant change in our view if we were to look at a mechanism that is indispensable (if the self is to reach its goal at all) as a progression, since here the ego, as a matter of fact, exerts a direct influence upon the repressed. It controls it and, as Kris has so admirably described it (1952, *passim*), forces it to carry out a piece of ego-syntonic work.

In general, the use of the archaic for purposes of cultural achievement should not be regarded as a regression. I consider sleep to be a true regression in the service of the ego, for in sleep the ego relinquishes controls and exposes itself to dangers; yet in wit formation no such relinquishment occurs, and the repressed is harnessed for an ego purpose. The regression in sleep, and what is called 'regression' in wit formation or art in general, are essentially different in their function and valence. In order to grasp a metaplan, the progressions of which the self is capable must be particularly well understood; the neurosis is not only man's privilege, but also his creativity.

Here is, no doubt, the most serious weakness of ego psychology. Although Freud did make a beginning, his effort has carried us in this area the least distance toward understanding; and, so long as our present knowledge of the ego is not complemented by insight into the nature of the creative process, ego psychology has not yet solved one of its more important tasks.

Cultural products—the materializations of man's creativity—are, for the psychoanalyst, of twofold interest. Usually it is the psychological path leading to the creation of a particular value that challenges his biographical ingenuity, thus fulfilling—at least in part—the program that Dilthey outlined:

> The highest understanding of a [literary] artist would be obtained, if one could point to the totality of those circumstances inside and outside of him, under which there arises that modification of his external and internal experiences and insights that determines his productions, and if one could grasp the cohesiveness that gives form, through this modification, to motif, plot, characters and means of representation [of literary works] [Dilthey, 1905, p. 127; translation mine].

It would be interesting to determine to what extent psychoanalysis has lived up to Dilthey's demands, in what respects it has failed, and what have been the reasons for that failure. However, cultural productions might also be used in a different way—and Dilthey did use them for such purposes—namely, in order to learn something from them about the structure of the personality.

If one studies a text like Otto Ernst's *Das Heilige* (I could suggest any number of others), in which one of the best phenomenological analyses of the irrational religious feeling is given, one may quickly become aware —without necessarily sharing the author's belief that he has described an objective reality existing outside the human mind—that an experiential modality is here presented which the analyst would probably never encounter clinically in the complex form in which Ernst presented it. To be sure, Freud made a beginning by scrutinizing the primitive taboo; but Ernst presented the phenomenon in its completeness. It would be one of the tasks of ego psychology to infer from the phenomenological description the structural elements that are its prerequisites.

It is possible that a new avenue might thus be opened for the study of ego autonomy. Here I want to add only a few thoughts on the complex problem of the relationship between ego autonomy and cultural product. The majority of cultural products probably does not testify to the creator's autonomy; more often than not, they are the outcome of imitation, in which tradition imposes upon the self some quite unoriginal tactics. The analyst's attention has, of course, often been drawn to instances in which the self—during the creative act—has been serving predominantly id impulses (Kris, 1946), very much to the detriment of the final product and its quality. Yet, curiously enough, at the very moment when the self has succeeded in creating quite original values, and of the highest quality, it often denies responsibility and spontaneity, and asserts that it has acted as the medium for an outside force (Kris, 1939). Nevertheless, it seems to me that, in those rare instances of extraordinary creativity which we single out by the term 'genius,' the ego succeeds, during the act of creation, in truly using id and superego demands (and satisfying them) for the fulfillment of its own purposes.[12] In other words, in some creative acts id and superego become the ego's servants, and the deepest conflicts become the soil out of which ego-syntonic achievements grow. A primary aim of the ego is thereby realized through the subservience of those provinces that usually impose their aims upon the ego.

Be that as it may, the genius, who materializes the maximum potential inherent in the human species, and is therefore its most significant representative, occurs so rarely that it is questionable whether or not he should be referred to in a general discussion of ego autonomy.

It seems to me, however, that Freud alluded to the relationship between creativity and what is now called ego autonomy, when he cited Heine's verses (which read, in prose translation): "Illness was no doubt the final cause of the whole urge to create. By creating, I could recover; by creating, I became healthy" (Freud, 1914b, p. 85, n. 3).[13]

[12] See Kris in Loomie et al. (1958, p. 50f.), where this is shown for id impulses.
[13] Heine attributes these words to God; Freud quotes them in discussing the necessity to love, so that illness may not occur; yet they seem most appropriate to a characterization of man and his functional relationship to the objects of his creativity.

The relationship of the drives to the id, and of the perceptions to the ego—that is the relationship of man's talents to his creativity. Consequently, the first step must be a psychological understanding of talent, which would certainly lead to a psychology of creativity.[14]

Yet a brief deliberation will show that, whatever the psychoanalyst who has been trained in medicine, biology and pathology may be able to contribute to a psychology of endowment, he also needs, not only the findings obtained in many a nonmedical field, but the active co-operation of scholars who are experts in what may be called 'the humanities.' For almost all of these deal constantly with the products of man's talents, with their investigation, classification and history, whereas at no point in his medical studies has the physician ever dealt with anything that is comparable with or equivalent to a 'cultural product.' Creativity obviously has some connections with biological procreation; but the study of the latter will hardly serve as adequate preparation for an understanding of the former. If psychoanalytic ego psychology is to become fully productive, it will have to open the academic doors to laymen.

I have chosen 'cultural products' as an example, because it is here that the shortcomings and inevitable failures of the analyst whose preparatory studies have been limited to medical training become so glaringly obvious. I could equally well have selected perception, or any other field of general psychology. Through the way in which psychoanalytic ego psychology has progressed, the psychology of perception has acquired a dignity comparable to that of the drive. If the logic of scientific procedure were to be adhered to, the psychoanalyst would have to investigate which part or parts of academic psychology stand the psychoanalytic test (cf. Hartmann, 1939, p. 17). And, if the issue is viewed thus abstractly, it may be said that the whole areas included under academic psychology and the humanities should be regarded as parts of psychoanalysis.

In the chapters which follow, I have not pursued the matter in that light. But I thought it appropriate to stress a viewpoint that takes on new significance, in terms of the phase in which psychoanalysis now finds itself. The main danger which, in my opinion, psychoanalytic ego psychology faces today is a rationalistic trend.

Freud seems to have been aware that the study of the ego in the state of anxiety and defense against it (what I would call the 'ego tactics') leads to a one-sided result. At least, this is how I interpret him when he

[14] Cf. Hartmann (1939, p. 21), "For psychology, both conflict and achievement are indispensable points of view."

says that, in the study of the circumstances under which anxiety arises, he had to view the ego's behavior in defense in a mode of "rational transfiguration" (*in rationeller Verklärung*) (Freud, 1926c, p. 146).

Indeed, in studying the basic theoretical model underlying that phase of Freud's ego psychology which is represented in *Inhibition, Symptom and Anxiety,* one may feel strongly inclined to utilize Leibniz's famous concept of 'pre-established harmony,' whereas the basic models of the previous phases would warrant, as far as the ego-id relationship is concerned, the characterization of a 'pre-established *dis*harmony.'

Of course, similar antinomies of pre-established harmony and disharmony—depending on the facet examined and the angle of vision—are encountered when the relationship of mind and body or of the sexes is scrutinized. With all due apology for the teleological implications of the formulation, it may be said that nature has outdone itself in artistry in its fitting together of mind and body, or of male and female. They seem to be made for each other, masterpieces of 'fitting in,' one unthinkable without the other—both splendid examples of pre-established harmony. Yet experience has shown that it is precisely within the orbit of such harmonies that the gravest conflicts burgeon: the mind too frequently turning against the body, and the body becoming the source of mental pain and even despair; the sexes, almost as if they had been destined by nature for enmity, turning against each other, so that 'the battle of the sexes' becomes a hackneyed motto. Here, too, then, the pre-established harmony changes into a pre-established disharmony.

This antinomy seems most significant, however, of human existence in its totality; and when Freud (1940a) conjectured that "the *individual* dies of his internal conflict but that the *species* dies of its unsuccessful struggle against the external world" (when changes outstrip the species' adaptiveness) (p. 23, italics by Freud), he was formulating the pre-established disharmony between ego and id—another essential characteristic of man. That Freud, with his masterly flair for the conflicting, could also think in terms of what I have tentatively referred to as 'pre-established disharmony,' testifies anew to the comprehensiveness of his theoretical range.

One of the many tasks that ego psychology is called upon to fulfill is to unravel the complex relationship between these two aspects of pre-established harmony and pre-established disharmony. With some degree of simplification, one might tentatively suggest that the study of plan and tactics—the analyst's lot in his daily clinical work—may create a propensity for viewing the ego in that "rational transfiguration" which Freud speaks of. If this were so, one might go further and deduce that preoccupation with the ego's metaplan and strategy may lead one to stress instead the ego's weakness and failure.

One can refer here to a very common disorder. The depression of the aged is clinically well known. More often than not, even the very productive and active person does not escape it. It has many reasons, which vary from person to person; nevertheless, it seems possible to detect one common denominator: regret for the deficit in the realization of what was latently potential in the self. This proportion between the sum total of actually realized love, pleasure, joy, achievement or whatever, toward which a person had been consciously and unconsciously striving on the one hand, and what, on the other hand, could have been potentially activated, yet in fact remained unused, a fallow principal—this proportion is an all-too-well justified causative agent of the sense of depression. One feels inclined to repeat with Freud (1917d): "We only wonder why a man has to be ill before he can become accessible to a truth of this kind" (p. 246).

The metaplan would, of course, contain the potentially realizable, and thus permit a final accounting of the degree to which the potential autonomy had been realized. For it seems to me that only under the rarest of conditions does that autonomy become a real fact—perhaps only in the genius who, despite frequent protestations to the contrary, had made himself relatively independent of both his external and internal milieu, in so far as he has integrated both, and formed out of them his own, superbly original world.

Yet the measure of autonomy to be expected in the ordinary man is much less than that which may occur in the genius, who is an atypical, and in the long run improbable, mutation-like product of nature. What one can see in the aging of the average man is a gradual weakening of the defenses. Insidiously, the repressed gains entry into the fabric of the ego, and undermines its original aims. Old loyalties are imperceptibly broken—often without those in the environment even being aware of that fact. Freud (1939) described personalities in whom a deeply repressed identification of early childhood emerges on the surface, propelled by biological forces: "in the end [it] again comes to light" (p. 198). Consequently, in order to evaluate the ego's strength, what is needed is a picture of its resilience under the impact of all the biological stresses entailed in living. If we pursue the ego's strategy and derive therefrom its metaplan, we may discover that what seemed to be autonomy was in reality only pretense and illusion.

It is even possible that deepened knowledge may reveal the ego's final defeat to be the reflection of a basic law inherent in man's status as a part of nature.

I recently came across the following observation which sounds like the strongest disavowal of ego autonomy:

> We are born mad, acquire morality and become stupid and unhappy. Then we die. This, the natural history of man under domestication, is so little agreeable to our self-love and so vexing in its apparently rigid sequence under a variety of forms and changes in the patterns of civilization, that mankind has invariably found it helpful to find a refuge in myths to relieve its perplexity and to mitigate its unhappiness [Eder, 1962, p. 81].

Those who have penetrated furthest into the thicket of man's mind—such writers as Shakespeare or Dostoyevsky—would agree with Eder; many a passage from Freud's writings could be set alongside his, to confirm it. Yet man is more than the quotation indicates, even though he is also mad. Incredible man—who, armed with a handful of alphabetical symbols and digits, has conquered the world, formulating the deepest insights into the structure of reality, and constructing, in machines and by other means, his own additions to it. Perhaps man would not have been so superbly creative, were he not at bottom also mad. The madness, the creativity and the destructiveness as a bio- and sociotype form a triad of trends that supplement each other.

If any one of these components were missing, it would no longer be man but a different species—possibly more pleasant, but also surely more boring. Yet the full range of man's madness, creativity, and destructiveness cannot be fathomed by the study of plans and ego tactics. Only a grasp of the metaplan and the comprehensive strategy will reveal them in their full force. Of course, we also get an inkling of the metaplan in our own daily work; yet we never do know how much is left undetected, and therefore do not grasp its full range.

It seems warranted to surmise that what Freud has called the rational transfiguration may narrow down the full scope of ego psychology and restrict it to the study of tactics, thereby causing it to lose sight of the comprehensive panorama—unless doors are thrown open, and the cultural man, with the full spectrum of all his cultural activities and many acts of madness, is also given full entrance into the arena of ego psychology.

The present trend in ego psychology is one in which the ego comes out on top of itself. The madness which is inherent in human existence, and to which Freud alluded when he said that the dream is a psychosis (even though a short-lasting one), is no longer felt in ego psychology. This was probably necessary, for only through molecular investigation and microscopic closeness to the subject is it possible to gain certain insights. Yet the surface of the world appears quite different, depending on whether it is viewed for the purpose of producing the map of a small locale or that of the entire world—not to speak of how it appears when the world is viewed in the context of the universe. Each of these views and maps is, of course, correct and valid in its own right. All the crushing magnificence of Mount Everest to one who stands at its foot does not negate the fact that it is merely a small hill when viewed from afar, and nothing at all, when viewed from still further away. If the ego is put into a more universal context, one has to admit the existence of comparable limitations, and acknowledge a frailty that seems so strongly to gainsay the possibilities of autonomy or its like.

My proposals regarding the differentiation of plan and metaplan would require clinical exemplification, if they are not to lead to a purely speculative model, which one may accept or reject, in accordance with views that would then smack of metaphysics. I have found myself here on the horns of a dilemma, since clinical experience, by my own definition, leads only under exceptional conditions to the grasp of a metaplan, and no such good fortune had come my way. I was therefore thinking of abandoning the whole matter when, in a fortunate moment, it dawned on me that there already exists a literary masterpiece, which seems to confirm my idea—so much so that I even started to suspect that I might have unconsciously derived the whole idea from it (although, to the best of my knowledge, this was not the case).

When I now adduce evidence, not from clinical experience, but from the ending of Goethe's *Faust* (at least with regard to Faust's earthly days, not his apotheosis in Heaven), this suits my whole intent all the better, in so far as this is an introduction to a discourse on lay analysis, and medical students are in general not 'burdened' with the interpretation of *Faust*. Furthermore, this would not be the first time that insight into man has been gained from the study of what a great poet has discovered in his observation of mankind and then reproduced in poetic transfiguration.

It seems to me that the full meaning of the ending of *Faust* is not always fully explicated in the exegeses of the literary historian, and therefore a detailed presentation seems in order.

The play starts with a wager between the Lord and Mephisto, with Faust's soul as the stakes: it will belong to the Devil, if he succeeds in corrupting him. The Lord predicts that a good man, even "in his dark urge" (*in seinem dunklen Drange*), will remain conscious of the right way. The primary wager between God and Devil has several subtle aspects, a discussion of which is unnecessary in this context. In psychoanalytic terminology, it can be described basically in the following way: will the id or the superego ultimately win out in man?—that is to say, will the ethical quality of the end product, and not the ethical values of accumulated single acts, be decisive with regard to the outcome of the wager?[15]

This primary wager is set off against the secondary and more specific wager between Mephisto and Faust, in which Faust declares that he will readily surrender to the Devil, if he should ever say of a moment that it is so beauteous that it ought to abide.

This secondary wager is actually won by Mephisto, for Faust, shortly before his death, confesses that one moment has been of such marvelous exquisiteness that he wished it to abide. But it is a moment, as we shall presently see, that bears very clearly the superego's stamp, so that Mephisto has in effect *lost* his primary bet with the Lord. Quite consistently, then, Goethe let the death and interment scenes be followed by Faust's heavenly apotheosis. All the turbulent and fantastic events through which Mephisto has tried to corrupt Faust are of no significance here, for the way in which Faust has been dealing with them belongs to ego tactics, and only the analysis of the end result counts in this particular context.

As the tragedy draws to an end, Faust puts a new demand to Mephisto. He does not desire any greater power or glory, nor does he seek gratification within the sensual sphere; instead, he is driven toward bold *enterprise and achievement*. Seeing the fruitless onslaughts of the ocean against the shores of the continent, he has arrived at the idea of wresting land from the sea, in order "to exclude the imperious sea from the shore, to narrow the borders of the moist [liquid] breadth [*Das herrische Meer vom Ufer auszuschliessen, Der feuchten Breite Grenzen zu verengen*]" (verses 10229 and 10230).

He receives the shores as a fief from the Emperor—his reward for having

---

15 It is noteworthy that Goethe seems to break here with the medieval concept of ethics, and adheres instead to an amazingly 'modern' developmental point of view.

rescued the empire from anarchy. Faust now has the opportunity to realize his project of draining the ocean and reclaiming soil for purposes of colonization.

The fifth and last act of *Faust* (Part II) starts with the Philemon and Baucis episode. These two are a kind of paraphrase of their Greek prototypes—a kindly, gentle, and aged couple, who love the little plot of land on which they have decided to end their days. Not far from their cabin stands Faust's palace, on reclaimed soil. As far as the eye can reach, Faust can see, as he stands on the palace roof, land that is his own, land that *he* has wrested from the destructive ocean. Only one low hill is not his: on it stands the old couple's cabin, and a little church. They do not accept Faust's offer to give this up in return for a far larger country seat, which Faust offers them as compensation.

When Mephisto returns from seafaring, with twenty ships loaded with treasures collected for Faust, his master, now greatly aged, shows no appreciation, but instead commands him to remove Philemon and Baucis. The sound of the bells in the little church irks him; it reminds him over and over again of the limits of his possessions and power. Mephisto carries out Faust's command; in his attempt to dispossess the couple, their cabin is burned down, and Philemon and Baucis die. Blinded by the exhalation of Care (*Sorge*), Faust calls his thralls to go to work and complete his plan. Instead, Mephisto approaches with the Lemures, who will dig Faust's grave.

Faust, however, takes the clinking of the gravediggers' spades to be the sound of his bondsmen, at work in his fight against the ocean. A marsh, with its poisonous exhalations, endangers what has so far been achieved; when this last obstacle has been removed, then space will be opened for millions. Faust has a vision of how people will live in this vast area—not in absolute security, but in active freedom. He ardently desires to witness that future moment when he will "stand with free folk on free soil [*Auf freiem Grund mit freiem Volke stehn*]" (verse 11580). To such a moment he might well say, "Abide indeed, you are too beauteous." In the presentiment of such bliss, he enjoys the supreme moment of his existence; and with these very words, he dies.

Thus Mephisto has won his wager with Faust. Yet it is clear also that Mephisto has lost his wager with the Lord, since Faust had found fulfillment in the full integration of the superego in a twofold way: the *realization* of a social act that is *projected into the future*. It is a particularly subtle point, showing his profound insight into man, that Goethe let Faust—the incarnation of the impatient, tempestuous personality, who is incapable of waiting—experience the fulfillment of his existence, not in a moment of bliss *contained in the here and now,* but in a moment that *carries the stamp of the future.*

It is this orientation toward the eventual that provides the full flavor of the superego, for only a self that has integrated a fully developed superego is capable of projecting itself so unreservedly into the future that a future moment can provide the bliss 'reserved by nature' for the present. Thus it seems that Goethe's ultimate wisdom coincided with what so many other philosophers had said before him: that it is man's ability to rise above sensual pleasure and *find fulfillment in social action* that makes him different from the beast.

I myself lay stress, in this context, on the *creative* act. Faust would not have found his fulfillment in Christian charity; he was more narcissistic than Christian ethics permits. He dies in the illusion that even "the trace of my earthly days cannot perish for aeons [*Es kann die Spur von meinen Erdentagen nicht in Äonen untergehn*]." True charity is not divested of its creative aspect, but falters when it is carried through with the intention of creating imperishable traces. For true charity requires the total abandonment of narcissism. In his last moments, Faust looks forward to a world shaped in accordance with *his* idea; however ideal this may be, it rests on the expectation of his placing an imperishable imprint of the self upon the world—the rightful expectation of genius.

To what extent some details of this episode had grown out of Goethe's own life may be gathered from a consideration of his own pet project —out of which he had anticipated the same results as Faust, and to which he had also devoted years of planning, care and great energy. This was the opening of the Ilmenau silver mines, heartbreakingly thwarted over and over again by the incessant incursion of ground water which the technical means of Goethe's times could not bring under control.

Yet creativity as ultimate fulfillment is set in Goethe's tragedy against a background of the utmost gruesomeness, for Faust, hearing the clinking of the gravediggers' spades, takes that as a signal that his consummate achievement is on the verge of being realized, when in reality his 'great work' will never reach the light of day. I think that no greater moment of 'dramatic irony' has ever been created.

It is only against this background that one can grasp the gigantic conception of the play, for here the solace found in creativity transcends the cheapness of a homily. The inner necessity for man to posit values

(*Wertsetzung*) is shown with one stroke to be a consummate illusion, for it is at the very moment when Faust, for the first and last time, fully trusted in and surrendered to a value, that he became the victim of a grievous deception—which might even be called the pinnacle of self-deception.

Thus we come to the second factor I mentioned earlier—the ego's unavoidable madness. Only a creature who posits values—and the act of positing values is more than just preference of pleasure and rejection of pain—can be considered human. We do not yet know for certain *why* human life can develop *only* within the framework of value-positing, but it is an indisputable fact that the necessity of positing values is as inherent to human life as the existence of drives. Human life, we know, cannot be imagined without the momentum of drives; but an existence without values would, after a certain age, have to be called 'subhuman.' Furthermore, however clearly modern man may have recognized the relativity of values, however extensively he may have integrated that truth, if *values* per se are psychologically represented in man as only something relative, than he is the victim of a deep disturbance. The full evolvement of personality *requires absolute value representation,* such as Faust undertook in his last moments.

Since it is out of the question that the aged poet could have introduced this element coincidentally with falling victim to a basic self-deception merely for purposes of dramatic effect, I take it that, in this incident (which may be called a sort of 'poetic injustice'), he who, perhaps more than anyone else, believed in values, created values, so to speak lived in and by values,[16] left the message that, in positing values, man *is* mad. When we consider that roughly one third of the last act is taken up, directly or indirectly, with the Philemon and Baucis episode, I think we would be correct in finding here a stress on "Man, the Destructive Biotype," whose constitutional aggressiveness and destructiveness are quantitatively beyond what can be mastered by the self, and must therefore lead far beyond the limits of self-preservation, to acts of sheer wantonness.[17]

[16] Cf. Dilthey (1905, p. 160), who says of Goethe that, in his recorded conversation, one notices "an unshakeable, heartening belief in the valuable and meaningful context of the world [*Ein unerschütterlicher beglückender Glaube an den wertvollen und bedeutsamen Zusammenhang der Welt*]."

[17] When one considers Freud's (1933a) statement that "we have to destroy other things and other people, in order not to destroy ourselves, in order to protect ourselves from the tendency to self-destruction" (p. 144f.), then one may interpret Faust's destruction of the two old people as a last-ditch defense against the approach of death.

Goethe seems to let us know here that, as much as man strives of necessity toward the fulfillment of his creative urges, so he is also bound to destroy. And this destruction was shown to be as real as Faust's expectation of the disappearance of the last marsh was shown to be an illusion.

One final point. At no earlier moment in the play can there be detected any signal to the listener that Faust, the man who is insatiably thirsting for knowledge and driven to search for the primal causes, will in his last moments fall victim to illusion; yet, self-deception is not alien to him, for looking back one feels: "Yes, this is Faust, entirely Faust!" The same holds true of his fulfillment in creativity, which a perspicacious mind might perhaps have anticipated, as well as his wanton destruction of Philemon and Baucis, not so surprising in the light of preceding events. These too are Faust—and entirely Faust! Do we discover here plan and metaplan, as I have outlined them earlier? May we consider the play up to the fifth act as showing the ego in its tactics, while the last scene, when Faust is dying, by the introduction of an *essential* element, alone makes it possible for us to grasp the *full groundwork* of Faust's personality? It thus illustrates what I have set forth under the perhaps ill-chosen term 'metaplan,' not to speak of what it may mean in terms of Goethe's own 'metaplan,' that by the form he gave to the last moments of his own literary self-incarnation, he pronounced an outlook such as can hardly be found in any of his previous creations.[18]

[18] It is tempting to compare Shakespeare's last play, The Tempest, with Faust (Part II). Shakespeare had already presented, in a large number of the most brutal instances, man's madness in positing values; this may have been among the many reasons why his last message was a conciliatory one. The famous verses, "We are such stuff/ As dreams are made on, and our little life/ Is rounded with a sleep" can be interpreted as referring to the human folly that lies at the bottom of value-positing. Similarly, Gonzago's 'commonwealth' speech (which follows Montaigne) has overtones of Faust's predeath vision. There are many profound strands connecting the two literary works, which I will not pursue. For the biographical background to Shakespeare's Tempest, see Sachs (1919).

1

Notes on the History of Lay Analysis

The birth of psychoanalysis may be likened to Athena's springing forth fully armed from the head of Zeus. I do not intend by this comparison to imply that psychoanalysis made its appearance complete and fully accoutered, but to emphasize that it was the product of one brain alone, that of Sigmund Freud. He created it single-handed, at first in solitude, later in the company of an ever-increasing number of pupils and collaborators. This makes it possible to trace with particular exactitude the history of this branch of science.

On the basis of an observation made by his fatherly friend, the famous Josef Breuer, as well as his own enriching clinical experience under Charcot at the Salpêtrière in Paris, Freud made, during the last decade of the nineteenth century, the initial discoveries from which he evolved what is known today as psychoanalysis. How he went about it in the beginning he has himself many times recounted, and one can still watch him at work as one reads the *Studies on Hysteria* (Breuer and Freud, 1893-1895), with their exact case presentations and detailed accounts of treatment procedure. The original hypnotic procedure was later replaced by the simplest conversation imaginable: the patient lying on a couch and saying everything that went through his mind, Freud sitting behind him and from time to time offering an interpretation. Brought into being out of the desire to cure patients whose diseases no one had previously known how to treat effectively, psychoanalysis quickly proved to be an instrument demanding respect for much more than its therapeutic value: it emerged as a means through which psychology could become an effective discipline.

To his own surprise, Freud had discovered a method by which he was able to harvest a bounty of psychological insights. Man's mind could at last be investigated in a reliable and scientific way. The poet's or the artist's intuitive knowledge of man was replaced with rational, scientific insight; nor was it any longer necessary to rely on speculative or metaphysical deductions. This became evident with Freud's first major contribution to the field of mental science, *The Interpretation of Dreams* (1900). Here a psychological phenomenon, the dream, an ever-present element in the inventory of the personality, was given a scientific explanation. This explanation required certain assumptions regarding the structure of the mind, and thus Freud's treatise ends with the by now famous seventh chapter, which sets forth a general theory of the mind.

Freud's discoveries at first sounded implausible; they did not square with any view of man's nature theretofore advanced. Since, moreover, his findings not only contradicted the traditional and time-honored theories, but flew in the face of established religious, ethical, and moral convictions, it was inevitable that he should be rejected, and even at times vilified. As is no less frequently the case, however, the genius also found followers. Freud, who had suffered profoundly from his rebuffs and isolation, welcomed the support of those who were attracted by the far-reaching implications of his new psychology. Of course, his contact with these supporters had to be organized in some fashion; at the outset, the simplest mode seemed the best. Weekly meetings were held, for the first eight years, in the waiting room of Freud's office, and after that in a small auditorium rented for the purpose (Jones, 1953-1957, Vol. 2, p. 9f.). These were the beginnings of what are today the local psychoanalytic societies in most European capitals and many of the larger cities of the United States; the latter societies in turn are organized into a national organization, the American Psychoanalytic Association, and all of them together into the International Psycho-Analytic Association.

In the days of these early meetings, no one seems to have cared particularly about the previous education or the current profession of those who participated. Since the new psychology was somewhat esoteric, it was apparently taken for granted that it would arouse serious interest only among the sophisticated and well educated. Thus men of all varieties of learning gathered around Freud, and it is improbable that this group regarded psychoanalysis as a medical specialty.[1]

As time went on, not only did the number of Freud's followers increase, but also the theory became more and more complicated. Concomitantly, organizational and administrative aspects gained in importance, until such giant organizations as the American Psychoanalytic Association evolved, with its semiannual national meetings, its numerous committees, its strict membership requirements, and its quarterly *Journal*. Administration is, of course, also top-heavy in the local societies, and what was once the loosest possible association of like-minded people interested in or dedicated to the growth of the new psychology became a firmly knit, solidified organization, to acquire membership in which is a most difficult task, requiring, under optimal conditions, at least ten years of graduate work.

In earlier days, nearly everyone who wanted to conduct an analysis was likely to be able to do so. He familiarized himself with Freud's writings—and went ahead. As matters went, most of those who were interested in doing so were physicians. But this was rather a situational effect, and not the outcome of plan and intent, as can be seen from the number of nonmedical members in some of the early societies. The *Correspondenzblatt,* through which members were informed about matters of general interest, in its first issue, in July 1910, listed the members of the local Viennese Society. We find among them fifteen physicians and seven nonmedical members. How many of the latter engaged in practice is not known. Jones (1953-1957, Vol. 3, p. 290) believes there were only two lay analysts, Pfister and Hug-Hellmuth, before the First World War. I rather doubt this; but the actual number is irrelevant in this context, for *any of the lay members could have analyzed if he had chosen to do so.* There was no objection or mental reservation or doubt, in those early years, as far as I know, on the question of whether any person who was familiar with Freud's writings and had accepted his technique as suitable might apply them in practice. How many were aware then that an issue lay hidden that, for a while, would threaten the homogeneity of psychoanalytic organizations? Everyone seemed to

[1] To be sure, the first psychoanalytic periodical, *Zentralblatt für Psychoanalyse,* had the subtitle *Medizinische Monatsschrift für Seelenkunde* (Medical Monthly Journal for Psychology) but the editorial board had a heavy sprinkling of laymen.

take it for granted that the practice of psychoanalysis did not require the acquisition of a specific body of knowledge *aside from the understanding of psychoanalysis proper*.[2] Would that situation—too sane and peaceful to endure, I almost feel driven to add—have continued unchanged indefinitely, if it had not been for an extraneous and completely unforeseen event of only local importance?

I have always thought so, but from Jones's chapter on lay analysis (1953-1957, Vol. 3, pp. 287-301) it is clear that the issue had been smoldering for some time before it exploded.[3] The issue must already have been regarded as serious in 1925, for A. A. Brill, president of the New York Psychoanalytic Society at that time, published an article in a New York newspaper, expressing his disapproval of lay analysis (Jones, 1953-1957, Vol. 3, p. 292). According to Jones, in the autumn of the same year, he even expressed a determination to break relations with Freud over the matter.[4] The bone of contention was the question of American lay people who had been trained in Vienna and started to practice in the United States upon their return. The question also came up, in this connection, of whether a member who moved to another country had a right to membership in the new place.

The event, however, that led to Freud's booklet on *The Question of Lay Analysis* (1926a), and thus to a public discussion of the whole issue, was the threat of court action by a patient against a most promising member of the Viennese Psychoanalytic Society, a prominent nonmedi-

[2] Freud's first reference to lay analysis, possibly the first reference to this subject at all, can be found in Freud's introduction to Pfister's *Psychoanalytic Method* (Freud, 1913d, p. 330f.). In it, Freud expresses himself unreservedly as in favor of it. "The practice of psycho-analysis calls much less for medical training than for psychological instruction and a free human outlook."

[3] For how long a time the idyllic picture I have drawn of the peaceful co-operation of physicians and lay people in the early period was valid cannot be determined. The trend seems to have shifted both toward and away from lay analysis, probably depending on the local situation. The Dutch Society had apparently admitted only physicians from its inception, for its annual report to the International Psycho-Analytical Association in 1921 announces that, from that year on, lay people would be permitted to attend Society meetings and become associate members (Meijer, 1922), whereas up to then only physicians had the right of membership and attendance.

[4] How strong "the fear of lay analysis exhibited by medical men was at that time can be seen from the fact that it forced Ferenczi during his stay in the United States (1926-1927) "to hold two separate courses, one for laymen and the other for a medical audience" (Bryan, 1927). For an important document that gives evidence regarding the feeling of the British group about lay analysis, see the report signed by Jones, Strachey, and Rickman (1927).

cal analyst, an outstanding scholar and a pupil of Freud's, the writer of psychoanalytic texts of great merit.[5] The analyst was exonerated; no trial took place; the patient was to all appearance untrustworthy, to say the least. Yet subsequently, discussion, argument, discord, almost open hostility, broke out around the question of whether or not lay people should be permitted to conduct analysis.

The battle seems to be over, at least on this side of the Atlantic.[6] Lay people may occasionally, at best, be elected honorary members of the American Psychoanalytic Association, but they are not permitted to become regular members. Since the few outstanding lay analysts who took refuge from Europe in this country will have no successors, there will come a time when all the adequately trained psychoanalysts in the United States will be physicians. No argument against this prospect is likely to be of any avail: the fact that many of the local groups in the United States were set up by lay analysts, who analyzed and trained the charter members; that among the most renowned analysts we find a substantial number of lay analysts; that some of the most frequently cited texts had been written by lay analysts; that the present high level of psychoanalytic development would be—as is generally acknowledged —unthinkable without the past and present contribution of lay analysts —all this does not count. There will come a day when there will be no lay analysis in this country, and other countries seem ready to follow suit.

Such an end situation has not come into being all at once. The tide of battle ebbed and flowed for a while before lay analysis suffered its final defeat. Of the period when lay analysis was still an issue, I want

[5] It is no indiscretion if I record that it was Dr. Theodor Reik who played this cata-lytic role in Freud's writing of the book. (Cf. S. Freud, 1873-1939, p. 356f., for a letter written on behalf of Dr. Reik. See also Freud 1926d, for an additional remark regarding his relationship to Dr. Reik.)

[6] I must make a reservation here. The law of the country does not seem to prohibit the practice of psychoanalysis by nonmedical therapists, as can be seen from the fact that there are societies in some states that train lay people as psychoanalysts. However, there seems to be agreement among the experts that the training given by most of the fifteen approved Training Institutes of the American Psychoanalytic Association is un-rivaled in quality. It is by no means an exaggeration to say that anyone who is refused training in one of these institutions has lost the opportunity of becoming a qualified psychoanalyst. (For a survey of bona fide psychoanalytic training in the United States, see Lewin and Ross, 1960.) Therefore, my discussion, in so far as it pertains to the United States, is concerned not with governmental restrictions, but only with those that are established by psychoanalytic groups per se. In Europe the matter is different; in some countries, groups favorably inclined toward lay analysis are limited in their training by the law of the country.

to say a few words before turning to a discussion of the text that Freud wrote in June and July of 1926 (it was published in September of that same year) on the subject of lay analysis (cf. Strachey 1959, p. 180).

In the United States, a strong feeling against lay analysis seems to have developed shortly after psychoanalysis got its first footing. As far as I have been able to gather from the available sources and informants, this hostility was well founded. The new psychology suffered terrible abuse at the hands of some extremely unscrupulous practitioners; the disrepute in which psychoanalysis stood at that time can hardly be imagined at present, when psychoanalytic societies are officially accorded a place of dignity and respect by the organized medical profession. In those years it was utterly impossible for an outsider to get an even remotely objective impression of what psychoanalysis was, since it was advertised and assertedly practiced by people of such low standing that, on the face of it, it deserved to be rejected. In such a situation, it was an act of wisdom to draw a line of distinction between genuine and spurious psychoanalysis. The shortest and most promising step that offered itself to conscientious practitioners, however, seems to have been that of separating themselves conspicuously from the quasiprofessional 'rabble,' by forming societies consisting exclusively of *physicians* who had been trained in psychoanalysis.

To be sure, some members of the medical profession were indulging freely in wild analysis, but it was apparently regarded as easier to counteract the evil consequences of their activity than of that which resulted from similar wild analysis by lay persons. Even so, the New York Psychoanalytic Society in 1929 temporarily permitted the practice of lay analysis—if it was restricted to children. Details of the sometimes acrimonious dispute between the Americans and those Europeans who were against any compromise on the question of lay analysis are recorded in Jones's (1953-1957) biography of Freud; they are not pertinent in this context. After many attempts at finding a compromise, a split in the International Psycho-Analytical Association was avoided by permitting each component society to regulate the matter on its own terms.[7]

[7] In the United States, as has been said, lay analysts are ineligible for national membership. In England, Switzerland, Holland, Germany, and the Scandinavian countries, on the contrary, lay analysis seems to be accepted by the respective societies. In France, there is a court decision in favor of it; however, a superior court has since reversed that decision. Circumstances make it appear probable that lay analysis will gradually be officially prohibited in most of the leading psychoanalytic centers.

In view of the fabulous success that the American Psychoanalytic Association has achieved in this country, its decision with regard to lay analysis may appear to be fully justified. That the same success might very well have been achieved without the exclusion of lay analysis will be denied by most; probably very few would hold that the present curtailment of lay analysis, and its impending total disappearance, has caused and will cause any significant damage not outweighed by the success thus far recorded.

It is high time, therefore, to review—at least cursorily—Freud's views on this subject.

The discussion was opened by Freud in *The Question of Lay Analysis*. In this little-read book, Freud (1926a) was for the most part following—at least to all external appearances—the course of a series of discussions that he had held with a higher civil servant or government official, whose decision would have a bearing on the legal position of lay analysis in Austria. Freud calls him the "impartial person" in the book,[8] describing him in the Postscript as "a man to whom I had myself talked about Reik's case and for whom I had, at his request, written a confidential opinion on the subject"[9] (Freud, 1927a, p. 251). As the book reveals, Freud did not succeed in persuading the official to accept his views.

The bulk of Freud's discourse is taken up with a splendid exposition of psychoanalysis. It is obvious that the implicit function of this part is to convince the "impartial person" that psychoanalysis is unrelated to medicine, and cannot with any justification be regarded as a medical specialty—in other words, that psychoanalysis is psychology. Yet eventually Freud had to grapple explicitly with the problem (Chapters VI and VII), and to substantiate his conviction that the practice of psychoanalysis should not be kept exclusively in the hands of physicians. There is a special interest for the American reader in his conclusions, for from

---

[8] The subtitle of Freud's book was: *Conversations with an Impartial Person.*

[9] Freud's memorandum has not been found yet. (Only recently I have been informed of a paragraph in a letter written by Freud to Abraham in 1924, in which he makes a few remarks of relevance to our subject matter. From these remarks it is evident that it was Arnold Durig [1872-1961], who was full Professor of Physiology at the University of Vienna and also an official [*Obersanitätsrat*] at the State Department of Health [*Gesundheitsamt*], at whose request Freud wrote the memorandum on lay analysis. Knowledge of Freud's letter reached me too late to permit me to do justice to the problems that are raised by it. Curiously, when I wrote Professor Durig in 1954, inquiring into the connections he may have had with matters of lay analysis, he seemed to have forgotten his own involvement, and replied that he had had none.)

scarcely any other section of Freud's writings will he get a similar impression of outdatedness.[10]

One of Freud's basic ideas was that the definition of 'quackery' should be changed. According to Austrian law, anyone who treats patients without possessing a medical diploma is a quack, whereas Freud insisted on regarding as a quack "anyone who undertakes a treatment without possessing the knowledge and capacities necessary for it" (1926a, p. 230). By taking the question out of the context of legalistic definitions, and posing instead the criterion of knowledge as against ignorance, without any consideration of the possession or nonpossession of an official diploma, Freud gave the whole discussion an unforeseen turn, as a result of which a substantial number of physicians could well fall under suspicion of quackery.[11] Indeed, if in Freud's time a physician practiced psychotherapy, or undertook a psychoanalytic treatment, merely on the basis of possessing a license which actually entitled him legally to use all available treatment methods, he would more than likely have been engaging in an activity for which he was not prepared and in which he was not competent, so that he would have been a 'quack,' in the literal sense of the word. This is often true even now, and many leaders in medical education would presumably agree officially with that position. To be sure, they might not follow Freud when he argued that anyone, including laymen, should, if adequately trained, be permitted to practice psychoanalysis; but the attitude of casualness and indifference toward the problems involved in the treatment of neuroses, so common among physicians in earlier years, is no longer encountered in official discussions of the subject.

[10] Cf. Freud: "This question of [lay analysis] has its limitations both in time and place" (1926a, p. 183). Freud added that he was publishing the tract only in connection with the Austrian situation. The outdatedness does not, of course, characterize the exposition of psychoanalytic theory.

[11] Already in 1925, in view of the increasing application psychoanalysis had found in education and child rearing, Freud (1925d) wrote: "It is no longer possible to restrict the practice of psycho-analysis to doctors and to exclude laymen from it. In fact, a doctor who has not been through a special training is, in spite of his diploma, a layman in analysis, and a non-doctor who has been suitably trained can, with occasional reference to a doctor, carry out the analytic treatment not only of children but also of neurotics" (p. 70). The problem appears today in a different form, which Freud could not have foreseen. The term 'psychoanalysis' has become so popular that many a physician who earns his livelihood by psychotherapy believes that he has to call his therapeutic method 'psychoanalysis,' if he wishes to maintain a sufficient number of patients. Thus many psychiatrists who are in fact applying psychotherapy, but not psychoanalysis, still designate their technique by the latter term, which should be reserved for the well-defined method proposed by Freud.

Freud continues the application of his definition of quackery to an aspect of medical training. This training was the very opposite of what was needed by way of preparation for psychoanalysis: the student's attention was absorbed by the study of objectively ascertainable facts, such as are taught in physics, anatomy, and the various branches of medicine. The problem of life was reduced to the interplay of physical forces. The psychic aspect of organic life was neglected, for the study of the higher mental functions was regarded as belonging to psychology and philosophy. Training in psychiatry in the broad sense, Freud goes on, does not overcome this limitation, for psychiatry seeks the physical causes of mental disturbance, approaching it in the same spirit as medicine approaches all other diseases (p. 230).

This may sound as if Freud was objecting to medical training for being one-sided—which was not the case at all. He acknowledged the great merit of medical training, asserting that its merit lies precisely in its single-facetedness, just as all sciences are single-faceted. But what is right about methods developed to permit insight into objective facts is not necessarily right in the field of therapeutics. Clinical dealings with the neurotic patient make it apparent that the psychic aspect of life is not to be omitted. Medical education does not contribute anything that enables the physician to cure the neuroses. Medicine may one day find biological means of treatment, but that day is far off. Neurotic syndromes still remain inaccessible to medical therapeutics (p. 231).

Even worse, medical schools send forth physicians with a wrong orientation regarding the neuroses. They are prone to attach little significance to neurotic manifestations; they feel no respect for research within the psychological area. The attitude they have adopted is that, while something has to be done, since neurotics are patients, tedious preparation is unnecessary; the main thing is not to give up experimenting with something new. The existing training facilities for psychoanalysis are not respected in the universities, says Freud, and it is improbable that physicians who intend to specialize in psychotherapy will avail themselves of any of them (p. 232).

The reader of today will feel able to counter many of these assertions. In the United States, the psychoanalytic training institutes are held in high respect. Indeed, for a while, there were psychiatric hospitals that made previous training at a psychoanalytic institute a prerequisite to residency. The position of psychiatry has also changed essentially in the American universities. Whereas classical psychiatry is hardly taught at

all, the student is speedily introduced to the foundations of psychoanalysis; even entire groups of internal disorders are viewed in some
departments as of psychic or psychosomatic origin; in most medical
schools every student has to work for a time at a psychiatric outpatient
clinic and on psychiatric wards, where he familiarizes himself with psychotherapeutic techniques, most of which are derivatives of Freud's
psychoanalysis. Psychiatry has lost its isolation in the medical curriculum, and the young physician who enters psychoanalytic training in
order to become proficient in a subspecialty is not making a new start;
he is continuing a course of instruction begun during his student years.
His position seems to be no different from that of those who set out to
specialize in ophthalmology, or in any other branch of medicine. Some
universities have incorporated their own psychoanalytic training institutes; those without university affiliation enjoy the same respect, if not
more, since they have been in existence longer than the former, and
have an experienced teaching staff at their disposal that can draw on a
tradition evolved since the years when Freud wrote his tract.[12]

Freud thought that the medical curriculum was sufficiently onerous
to make it unwise to burden it further with the teaching of the treatment of neuroses. But the medical profession in this country did not
respond to this idea in the way that Freud had outlined in general
terms. The future physician gladly extends his interest to the psychic
forces on whose optimal interplay the well-being of body and mind depends. To be sure, there are still physicians who behave as most did
during the first quarter of the twentieth century, and as Freud so
penetratingly described. But in the three or four decades that have since
passed, the medical situation has changed so profoundly that this part
of Freud's reasoning seems to be no longer pertinent.

Freud drew further arguments from the area of legislative action. He
believed that the moment was most inopportune to erect legal barriers
to lay analysis. Any law that did so would be one-sided, since it would
prevent excellently endowed lay persons from practicing analysis, while
leaving the ill-trained physician free to do so. Such a law would not
provide an authority to decide what psychoanalysis was, what kind of
training it required, and under what conditions it might be practiced.

[12] Psychoanalytic education in this country has recently found its lasting documentation in the splendid presentation by Bertram D. Lewin and Helen Ross (1960). A comparison of their text with Freud's comments on the relationship between medicine and
psychoanalysis will hardly reveal any common denominator.

In merely forbidding lay analysis, it would be purely negative—and un-enforceable besides, for external reasons. No instruments are used in an analysis and no drugs administered; a simple conversation flows back and forth between analyst and patient. How would the law determine exactly what procedure actually constituted a psychoanalytic treatment? Freud thought that legislative interference with the development of psychoanalysis would yield only disadvantages, in view of the newness of the field, the paucity of what was known about it outside of a few small groups, and the mixed evaluation it had received at the hands of official science. The public itself should decide by whom it wanted to be treated; the spread of information was the only step necessary at that time.

These considerations, although not invalidated by the passage of time, have their place only in the historic setting which brought them forth. The reader will recall that the Austrian Government had considered the possibility of forbidding lay analysis by law. In the United States, a large measure of freedom obtains: there are institutions that provide training for lay analysts, and as far as I know there is in most States no legal barrier to the lay practice of analysis. Consequently, this aspect of Freud's discussion is likewise inapplicable to the present situation.

Despite his strong feeling in favor of lay analysis, Freud did not hesitate to acknowledge that the medical analyst has certain advantages, although most of them are apparent rather than real. Since physical factors may give rise to symptoms almost indistinguishable from those of psychogenic etiology, and since a neurosis may be the precursor of severe mental disease, every patient must be examined by a medical analyst before being treated by a lay analyst. This requirement is, however, no valid argument against lay analysis as such. Once a favorable diagnosis has been arrived at, the patient can properly be taken over by the lay analyst. By the same token, the fact that, during so long a period as psychoanalysis entails, physical disease may often prove to be a complication does not, in Freud's judgment (p. 243f.), invalidate lay analysis. In such a situation, both medically trained and lay analysts are equally under the necessity of seeking the advice of a medical specialist for their patients.

One consideration that may tip the scales somewhat in favor of having analysis practiced by physicians is that the diagnostic interview prior to treatment may appear to be a detour that should, if possible, be avoided. Jones made a strong point in favor of the medically trained analyst by reporting, from his own experience, having gained the impression—later confirmed—of cancer of the colon in a patient who, during treatment, presented symptoms of seemingly psychogenic origin (Jones, 1927a, p. 193).

Freud's argument that the curricula of medical schools of his time were unsuitable for the future analyst in that much that was of no use to psychotherapy was taught, and much that was of great use to it omitted, applies no less to the curricula of all other university divisions (cf. Reich, 1927, p. 254). There were—and for that matter are—no colleges in existence for the training of the future lay analyst.[13] Again Freud's argument does not seem to weigh especially heavily in favor of lay analysis.

Yet how would the reader evaluate Freud's arguments concerning psychoanalysis proper? He turns against the prospect of analysis being swallowed up by medicine, and finding "its last resting place in a textbook of psychiatry under the heading 'Methods of Treatment'" (Freud 1926a, p. 248); he further turns against the prospect of psychoanalytic therapy destroying the science of psychoanalysis (1927a, p. 254). I think that no analyst would disagree with Freud that such eventualities ought to be avoided at all costs. But is this what has actually happened? After all, what Freud foresaw has not yet taken place,[14] and the opponent of lay analysis may justify his view by pointing to the failure of Freud's prediction that medical analysis would necessarily lead to such debasement of psychoanalysis.

It is evident that Freud felt strongly against the suppression or prohibition of lay analysis. There is, however, one passage that may give one reason to suspect that at heart he may perhaps have been on the side of the medically trained psychoanalyst. In a discussion on lay analysis in the *International Journal of Psycho-Analysis* (Jones, Strachey, and Rickman, 1927) Freud was misunderstood as having been of the opinion that physicians "were in general incompetent to practice analysis"[15] (Freud 1927a, p. 257). This was by no means what Freud had in

[13] In 1926 Freud thought that a college of psychoanalysis was perhaps no more than an ideal—but an ideal which must be realized. I think that it has become feasible since then (cf. Kubie, 1954).

[14] In a letter written in 1938, and to be quoted presently, Freud did declare that in this country one of his predictions had come true.

[15] It was Reich (1927, p. 253) who had drawn this conclusion.

mind.[16] In order to correct the misunderstanding, he wrote: "The idea probably arose from my having been led to declare in the course of my observations . . . that untrained medical analysts were even more dangerous than laymen" (1927a, p. 257). This sentence is surprising, for Freud had taken great pains earlier to explain that lay analysts as such are not dangerous at all, but only those, from whatever discipline, who were inadequately trained in analysis. What Freud had in mind is clear, but his wording may induce some to conclude that he, perhaps unconsciously, thought that there was a danger inherent in lay analysis, or that he felt apprehensive about the possibility that the future of psychoanalysis might be entrusted exclusively to a generation of lay analysts, as a consequence of the strong stand he had taken in their behalf. Furthermore, Freud introduces the passage in which he expresses himself favorably—although with some reservations—about medically trained psychoanalysts, with a delightful anecdote containing a skeptically defensive note on women. "Women are the best thing we have of the kind," replied a man to someone who complained that women were weak and troublesome. "I am bound to admit," Freud goes on, "that so long as schools such as we desire for the training of analysts are not yet in existence, people who have had a preliminary education in medicine are the best material for future analysts" (1927a, p. 257).

Is Freud here retracting some of the salient points that he had raised earlier? Perhaps. Yet, no one can read what Freud wrote on the topic without being impressed by the intensity of his feeling in favor of lay analysis, and he maintained that same view to his last days. Jones reproduces a letter that Freud wrote during the last year of his life, in which he says that he would insist on his views then even more than before, "in the face of the obvious American tendency to turn psychoanalysis into a mere housemaid of psychiatry" (Jones 1953-1957, Vol. 3, p. 300f.). Thus he was apparently not favorably impressed by the development that psychoanalysis had taken in this country. However, in the two decades since his death, psychoanalysis has made a notable upswing in the United States, an upswing without its like in any other country. One can only guess what Freud's comment would have been if he had lived to observe the present psychoanalytic situation in this country.

[16] Freud had stated *expressis verbis* that physicians who had received training in a psychoanalytic training institution would, of course, always be welcome, and he added, with what sounded like pride: "Four-fifths of those whom I recognize as my pupils are in any case doctors" (1926a, p. 229).

The summary I have given of the last two sections of Freud's book is extremely cursory. It falls far short of doing justice to the wit, penetration, variety, and complexity of the arguments presented. Yet Freud himself was avowedly dissatisfied with it. Thus, on July 6, 1926, he wrote to Ferenczi: "Shallow stuff with some cutting remarks, which because of my bad mood at present are rather bitter" (Jones, 1953-1957, Vol. 3, p. 292). Jones refers to it as a little book hastily put together; in his review, he says that Freud's main argument "contains nothing new, it omits much of importance, and it is unmistakably partial" (1927a, p. 92). He regrets that Freud dealt so extensively with the local Viennese authorities, but "glossed over, simplified, or left altogether unmentioned" technical aspects of the problem (p. 86).[17]

Freud's book was followed by an extended discussion of the problem by medical and lay analysts, which was published in English and German (Jones, Strachey, Rickman, 1927). If one reads that discussion today, one is struck by the fact that, although it might be expected that some objectivity would have been attained since 1927, the problem has so far not found a satisfactory solution. One feels inclined to assume that, if the debate were reopened today, it would once again be largely emotional, and would consist by and large of a repetition of the same arguments used then.

As to the earlier discussion: in addition to Freud, twenty-five analysts (twenty physicians and five lay analysts) participated. Of these, seven were in favor of lay analysis without reservation; five in favor, but with reservations covering a wide range; eleven opposed it; for two, it was impossible to determine to which group they belonged. There were also statements from the New York and the Hungarian Societies (one analyst incorporated in his contribution the final opinion of the Viennese Society); the former expressed itself unreservedly against, the latter for, lay psychoanalysis. It may also be worth mentioning that one analyst who had taken a qualified favorable view of lay analysis became opposed to it—after he emigrated to the United States.

The negative attitude of some analysts does not show up immediately in their remarks. A few introduce their contribution with a statement of agreement with Freud; only during the course of their discussion

[17] The book on lay analysis is infrequently cited, and seems to have been read so rarely that far-reaching innovations (to be pointed out later) which are to be found in it have, as far as I know, remained generally unnoticed. A leading analyst, well known for his erudition and his command of the psychoanalytic literature, once told me that it was the only publication of Freud's he had never read.

does it turn out that they are opposed to granting lay analysts the right to carry on therapeutic analyses. The desire to remain in agreement with Freud can readily be assumed in these instances, and may at times be responsible for the difficulty of determining a particular analyst's opinion.

What seems to have worried some of the discussants was their impression that Freud favored the idea that the future of psychoanalysis should be in the hands of lay analysts, or at least that he wanted a majority of psychoanalysts to be lay people—in short, that he did not care at all for the presence of physicians in psychoanalytic societies.

As far as I can judge, this was far from Freud's thinking, although some of his statements may lead to such a conclusion if taken literally. Yet if the situation in which Freud found himself is considered, this impression can easily be corrected. Four fifths of his followers were physicians, and most of the analysts with whom he maintained the closest contact were medical men. Furthermore, the so-called 'Committee,' a kind of inner circle or 'old guard,' a group of the most reliable and steadfast analysts who functioned as a sort of watchdog committee, consisted of four physicians and two lay analysts (Jones 1953-1957, Vol. 2, pp. 152-167). The threat was not the loss of medical analysts but of lay analysts, and Freud was therefore justly motivated in mustering all his arguments against any trend toward putting psychoanalysis exclusively into the hands of the medical men, which would inevitably lead to psychoanalysis being regarded as a medical specialty. When he spoke against medical analysts he did not have in mind, I am certain, the faithful service that psychoanalysis had received from the majority of those physicians who for years had made their lifework the growth and flourishing of psychoanalysis. I suppose he looked upon them as atypical among medical men, as indeed they were, since they were a tiny percentage of a large professional group that seemed to be bound to tradition with iron bands, and unwilling even to entertain the possibility that the claims of psychoanalysis might be correct. Freud, I am confident, did not have these select few in mind but was rather envisioning a time when psychotherapy would become a widespread medical specialty, and the teaching of some form of psychoanalysis within the academic surroundings would be entirely turned over to the medical profession, more or less without the control of the psychoanalytic institutions.

Some writers have contended that Freud was one-sided or biased, that some of the criticisms he leveled against medicine, its teaching, and its representatives could also have been leveled against the humanities.

Something will be said about this later, but at this point I cannot agree with the contention that Freud betrayed his bias by not raising a parallel argument against the humanities. What Freud was concerned with at that moment was the question of whether or not psychoanalysis was to be handed over to the physicians. Had the question been whether or not it should be surrendered to the representatives of the humanities, Freud would no doubt have written on that question in a vein that might easily have earned him the reputation of being biased in favor of medicine, as against the humanities. Little as he liked the idea of psychoanalysis becoming simply a medical specialty, he would have liked it just as little if psychoanalysis had been on its way toward a niche in one of the many departments of the university faculty of philosophy.

In concluding this brief examination of the 1927 discussion, I cannot forego calling attention to a few statements, some of them quite curious, that one finds in that discussion. Müller-Braunschweig (1927, p. 236) surmised that it was because he was not a qualified medical practitioner that he rarely had patients with intercurrent organic diseases; he explained this as arising from the patient's feeling that it was even less likely that a lay analyst would occupy himself with the body than that a medical analyst would.

Van Ophuijsen (1927, p. 280) found it "indisputable that a relatively large number of lay analysts understands analysis better and employs it more skillfully than very many medical analysts." Nevertheless, he thought that this did not prove that lay persons should be permitted to practice psychoanalysis.

Glover (1927, p. 218) thought that a lay organization would have to meet the dangers of religious healing. He stated also that the argument is invalid that medical teaching is capable of ruining the psychological touch of a prospective analyst, for the student who would be ruined by such influence would never have made a good medical analyst anyway.

A good many more statements could be cited that would likely strike the reader as highly questionable, and at times even nonsensical—such as the assertion that an analysis cannot be conducted without knowledge of the parasitic worms and of the symptoms they cause.[18]

At any rate, emotion clearly played a greater role in the 1927 deliberations than is ordinarily conducive to correct thinking, and I doubt that its role has even now been sufficiently reduced to ensure a more fruitful

---

[18] The discussant who made this point is said to have later become the victim of paranoid psychosis.

discussion.[19] Nevertheless, as will be seen later, I regard one aspect of the problem as important enough to warrant risking even the pitfall of possible distortion because of emotional involvement.

Neither the participants in the discussion, nor Jones in his review of Freud's book, referred to two substantive propositions that Freud raised, which were highly consequential and, as far as I know, original. The first—which was, to be sure, not germane to the question of lay analysis —described the ego in terms that included constitutional factors in its history, whereas up to then the ego had been held to be the resultant of the impingement of external factors (Freud, 1926a, p. 242).[20] The second, and more important, was the statement (p. 248) that therapy of the neuroses was one of several *applications* of psychoanalysis, a remark Freud enlarged upon in the postscript (1927a, p. 252), which was not available to the discussants. We shall see later that the implications of this seemingly inconsequential remark are surprisingly far-reaching. Nevertheless, I do not think that if anyone had thought this remark through to its logical conclusion, that would have changed the course of the debate in any essential way. Freud's book, which constituted in effect a warning and a plea, remained unheeded by the majority of his followers[21]; the idea of lay analysis was a stillbirth, the first complex idea of Freud's to be disregarded by the majority of his own followers. Whether this was to prove decisively good or bad for the development of psychoanalysis remains to be seen.

Although the reference to history in the title of this chapter would

[19] How little progress has been made in finding agreement with regard to lay analysis can be learned from the symposium on "The Problem of Medical and Lay Psychotherapy" (1950).

[20] In 1937 Freud elaborated upon this question more explicitly (1937a, p. 343; cf. Hartmann 1950, p. 79).

[21] After the debate of 1927, it occasionally happened that a medically trained psychoanalyst took a stand in favor of lay analysis. Paul Federn (1928, pp. 76, 80, 81; 1943, p. 134f.) was one of them, among those who were close to Freud. In this country, Muriel Gardiner was one of the exceptions. In her paper of 1960, she spoke unreservedly for lay analysis, and recently, in a biographical sketch (1962), she presented most touchingly the woes she suffered on her way to becoming a medically trained analyst. Her paper poignantly sets forth personal experiences which can be well used as illustrations of some of my theoretical points, and will have greater power of conviction than theory ever could. Szasz (1959) discussed the equivalent problem within the framework of medical psychotherapy. He argues against the stand taken by medical organizations concerning the independent nonmedical psychotherapist. His article is commendable, because it contains much detail regarding the history of the problem in this country, and many subtle arguments in favor of psychotherapy as a nonmedical field. However, it is not predominantly psychoanalytically oriented, and leads to some conclusions that might be debatable in terms of psychoanalytic theory.

provide sufficient reason for going back to preanalytic times, I refrain from doing so. It would probably be futile to argue in favor of lay analysis on the ground that for millennia emotional diseases were treated by nonmedical men, and in many instances with outstanding success. Such an argument would be unlikely to convince those in whom there is the deeply rooted idea that, since therapy in general is exclusively the function of the medical profession, the therapy of the neuroses must also be theirs. I shall take the opportunity later to consider some of the sociological implications of this state of affairs.

I wish to close this chapter with a general statement. From the historical study, one obtains the impression that the question of lay analysis is more than merely a matter of administration or organization. Behind what may appear to the outsider as a cut-and-dry issue of bureaucracy, there rest differences of conception, outlook, almost, one might say, of philosophy, which make the question of lay analysis—however academic it may be at present in the United States—a very worthwhile subject of inquiry on theoretical grounds.

For obvious reasons, a comparison (which I hesitate to make, for it may be easily misunderstood and turned against psychoanalysis) with religious issues, say of the Christian churches, comes to mind. Such was the controversy between Homoiousianism and Homoousianism, which to the outsider may even seem to be nothing but a quibble about a letter; yet it covered vast differences of doctrine.

2

The Two Psychologies

Whoever feels strongly in favor of lay analysis and regrets that Freud's tract on that subject had little, if any, effect on the organization of psychoanalysis, and is still relatively little read, may feel prompted, in writing on this topic himself, to prove deductively—as Freud did—that the structure of psychoanalysis is such as to make medical knowledge and training unnecessary. Although it is apparent that to pursue the same line of thought once again would be redundant, I shall set forth one aspect of psychoanalysis as I see it, which may facilitate the trend of the discussion.

What follows may perhaps be easily refuted—but only if the simplification of very complicated situations for the sake of constructing basic models is regarded as inadmissible. There are two kinds of psychology; they differ essentially with regard to their fundamental conception of their subject matter. One kind investigates the psyche as if it were a medium of an *outside* pattern of forces: man and his functions are dealt with as if they were strictly, or almost strictly, limited to *reactions* to external stimuli or objects. Thus, the mind is investigated as a kind of repository of reactions to its environment. The other kind of psychology, in its investigations, approaches the psyche as a system. In placing these concepts of medium and system at the center, I am following Fritz Heider (1926, 1930), who employed these same concepts in his analysis of the structure of reality, and of the relationship between reality and the functioning of the perceptive apparatus. Figure 1 (drawn from Heider, 1930, p. 47) serves as an example.

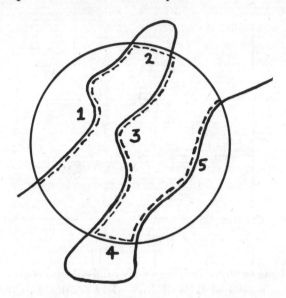

Let us assume that an iron ball has been attached by an invisible thread to a given point on a horizontal plane. At full length, that invisible thread determines the greatest distance (represented by the circle in Figure 1) to which the ball can go, in any direction on that plane, from its point of attachment. A magnet is then moved, above the ball, along a path shown by the continuous (irregular) line in Figure 1. The ball will simultaneously follow the path shown by the dotted line in the same figure. In this process, the movement of the magnet is a *core* event, *internally* conditioned, while the movement of the ball is *externally* conditioned, *enforced* upon it by the magnet's movement. In parts 1, 3, and 5, the movement of the ball is purely *medial*, strictly following the movement of the magnet; yet parts 2 and 4 reveal that the ball is not in fact a *pure medium*, but—because of the invisible thread—constitutes a *system* in itself.

Heider was concerned with showing the importance of differentiating between core (system) and medial events in the psychology of perception. My intent is to apply these concepts of medium and system to such ·

entire areas of psychology as academic psychology and psychoanalysis. In my opinion, the essential difference between these two psychologies lies in the fact that, while academic psychology is basically directed toward the examination of medial events, what psychoanalysis investigates is the systemic event. That this is so can be seen from the fact that, for a long time, the chief interest in academic psychology has been in questions of sensation, perception, and learning (K. Lewin, 1926, p. 294f.), whereas that of psychoanalysis has been in the instinctual drives and psychic constellations (such as dream, apraxia, and neurosis), all of which are characterized by phenomena that obviously lie outside the medial range and are instead the more or less direct manifestations of system properties.

By and large, the following views have obtained for a long time in academic psychology. It has been held that external stimuli reach sense organs, enforcing changes in them that are, in general, strictly related to these stimuli. It has further been held that these changes in the sense organs are forwarded by the nerves and tracts to the cerebral cortex, there effecting a sensation or perception that is in turn correlated with the original stimuli. The aspect of greatest interest to the academic psychologist has been the correlation between external stimuli and the ensuing changes in the sense organs. The eye was viewed as a camera, and the picture produced on the retina by the stimuli was compared with the picture left on a photographic film after exposure.

Thus the variety of perceptions and sensations became a congeries of traces left on the mind by the impact of the world outside, the mind itself being viewed primarily as a medium to receive and retain that impact. The underlying idea was that the more the perceptive media were able to eliminate their individual mode of functioning—their arbitrariness, if you will—outside of or beyond their function of receiving and forwarding messages, the better they served their purpose: just as a slave is the more useful to his master, the less his individual needs and desires keep him from being completely absorbed in obedience, or as a hypnotized medium perceives and feels more perfectly in accordance with the commands of the hypnotist, the more he has been (temporarily) deprived of his individuality.[1]

[1] It is of interest to take note of the beginnings of the psychology of perception in Western civilization. No more instructive quotation could be cited in this context than that from Boring's text of 1942 (p. 4f.): "The Greeks also had a theory of perception that still *haunts the present*. Empedocles (ca. 440-ca. 435 B.C.) supposed that objects give off from their surfaces or pores effluvia, which act upon the senses to furnish knowl-

How far this concept of psychic functions as media went can be observed quite clearly in the initial views of the psychology of thinking. The thinking process was taken to be (again with due apology for simplification) a chain of associations. The question of which association would follow which stimulus was thought to depend solely on which associations had been combined with which stimulus the largest number of times. Let us say the experience *rose* was combined x times with *red* and y times with *beautiful*; if x is greater than y, and there has been no other experience that has followed the experience *rose* a greater number of times than x, then the next association will undoubtedly be *red*. That is to say, thinking is the medium of the largest number of previous experiences, which means that it is correlated with percentages of accidental events in the outer world.

The effort of academic psychology to find series of medially related events is unmistakable.[2] Perception is clearly the most suitable area of investigation for a medially oriented psychology; but I am not prepared to say whether it was its prolonged preoccupation with the psychology of perception that gave academic psychology its medial flavor, or whether it was sociohistoric factors to begin with that caused psychologists to approach the psychic functions as if they were media.[3]

Contrary to this medial approach, the initial and central concept of psychoanalysis has been that of the instinctual drive, which is regarded as originating in a psychobiological unit more or less independently of the external world, and as the manifestation of properties inherent in a system. I therefore call psychoanalysis a system psychology. Of course, such sharply defined distinctions do not actually exist. The medial view of perception could not be consistently maintained. Afterimages, for example, are not responses to external stimuli, but demonstrate—at least to a minimal degree—the system character of sense organs. The functioning of the sense organs exhibits a number of other deviations from

edge of the outer world. Democritos (ca. 460-ca. 370 B.C.) and Epicuros (ca. 341-270 B.C.) described these projections as faint images, simulacra or eidola of the objects which, being *conducted to the mind*, give it acquaintance with the objects which they represent." (Italics mine).

[2] Cf. Hebb (1949, p. 4): "Now the tradition in psychology has long been a search for the property of the stimulus which by itself determines the ensuing response, at any given stage of learning."

[3] It is of historical interest to consider the impetus that academic psychology received in the middle of the nineteenth century from the controversy about differences in the observation of stellar events. Man's failure to serve as an ideal medium in a task that involved perceiving and recording opened new avenues of research. (Cf. "The Personal Equation," in Boring, 1929, pp. 134-153.)

the behavior of a supposedly pure medium. Gestalt psychology, for example, has effectively demonstrated that almost all perceptions quite definitely show the earmarks of a system factor, and do not follow the principle of the camera.[4] Further research in the psychology of thinking has also demonstrated the untenability of the basic principle of association psychology.

Yet, one gets the impression that academic psychology has never quite rid itself of its original disposition to regard psychology as a science of media.[5] This is at first glance quite understandable, since we usually try to solve scientific problems by modifying existing concepts, rather than by establishing a new set.

This can be exemplified by reference to Figure 1. Someone investigating parts 1, 3, and 5 of the ball's path will at first describe the ball as a medium of the magnet. If he then becomes aware of parts 2 and 4 of the path, he will probably add an auxiliary hypothesis, without relinquishing the main one already set up. Thus the central concept—that of medium—will continue to influence all subsequent observations and conclusions. Nevertheless, it is very difficult to regard the drives as media; the fact that academic psychology has not succeeded in producing an even half-way satisfactory psychology of drives confirms the view that academic psychology is inherently a medial psychology.

In psychoanalysis, to be sure, we encounter the reverse of the process just described. Once concepts of a systemic nature—such as drive, conflict, repression—had been evolved in Freud's early investigation of the neuroses, psychoanalysis continued from then on to adhere to the character of its earliest hypotheses. As a matter of fact, all later theories, which were necessitated by new observations, had the consequence mainly of re-emphasizing man's systemic nature.

Even perception, which seems most strikingly to fulfill the pattern of an almost ideally medial function, is presented by Freud as a systemic one. Thus Freud wrote:

. . . cathectic innervations are sent out and withdrawn in rapid periodic impulses from within into the completely pervious system Pcpt.-Cs. So

[4] Gestalt psychology, however, has centered its attention on the inner dynamics of the perceptive apparatus, a system factor which in psychoanalytic psychology would take no more than a peripheral position.

[5] However far academic psychology may have moved from the early static, atomic psychology, even such modern texts as Heider's papers and Osgood's (1953) comprehensive text show that it has not yet outgrown its essentially medial outlook. I think that the same impression would also be derived from a reading of Boring's (1929) classical text.

long as that system is cathected in this manner, it receives perceptions (which are accompanied by consciousness) and passes the excitation on to the unconscious mnemic systems; but as soon as the cathexis is withdrawn, consciousness is extinguished and the functioning of the system comes to a standstill. It is as though the unconscious stretches out feelers, through the medium of the system Pcpt.-Cs., towards the external world and hastily withdraws them as soon as they have sampled the excitations coming from it [Freud, 1925a, p. 231].

Here perception is viewed as an activity by means of which the unconscious takes hold of, and temporarily incorporates, a part of the external world. No clearer proof than this terse statement of Freud's need be adduced to demonstrate the rigor with which psychoanalysis insists on a systemic approach. Yet it must also be acknowledged that psychoanalysis has not yet succeeded in creating a satisfactory and comprehensive psychology of perception and thinking.

In carrying the idea of man as an *agens effectuans* so far that even perception is deprived of its medial character, Freud was following an ancient occidental tradition, which I wish to illustrate by the following quotation from Cicero, who was of the Platonic school:

We do not even now distinguish with our eyes the things we see; for there is no perception in the body, but, as is taught, not only by natural philosophers but also by the experts of medicine, who have seen the proofs openly disclosed, there are, as it were, passages bored from the seat of the soul to eye and ear and nose. Often, therefore, we are hindered by absorption in thought or by some attack of sickness, and though eyes and ears are open and uninjured, we neither see nor hear, so that it can be readily understood that it is the soul which both sees and hears, and not those parts of us which serve as windows to the soul, and yet the mind can perceive nothing through them, unless it is active and attentive [Cicero, *Tusculan Disputations,* I, p. 20].

Here we see Cicero vigorously repudiating the idea that perception is merely a medial function. I want to reemphasize the psychoanalytic view by referring to another quotation from Freud, who wrote (1925b, p. 238): "Perception is not a purely passive matter. The ego periodically sends out small amounts of cathexis into the perceptual system, by means of which it samples the external stimuli, and then after every such tentative advance it draws back again."[6]

[6] See also Freud (1920a, p. 28): "They [sense organs] may perhaps be compared with feelers which are all the time making tentative advances towards the external world and then drawing back from it."

Cicero uses the following quotation from Plato's *Phaedrus* in his *Tusculan Disputations* (I, p. 23; italics mine):

> Since it is clear, then, that that which is self-moving is eternal, who is there to say that this property has not been bestowed on souls? *For everything which is set in motion by impulse from the outside is soulless; what on the other hand has soul is stirred by movement from within and its own.*

The italicized portion of this quotation clearly states that what is medium cannot be regarded as part of the truly human world; whatever is to be attributed to the human cosmos must carry the earmarks of system or core events—a truly individualistic and personalistic viewpoint.

In Chapter 25 of the first of his five Disputations, Cicero also rejects the idea of the medial character of memory. Rhetorically, he asks: "Or do we think that like wax the soul has marks impressed upon it and that memory consists of the traces of things registered in the mind?" Whatever may be the metaphysical character of Cicero's reasoning, it is noteworthy that we encounter in him views regarding the systemic nature of man that go almost beyond Freud's rigorous theories.

For Freud did not deny the medial nature of certain apparatuses. This becomes evident in his speculation regarding the evolution of consciousness. The constant exposure of the surface layers of the living organism to external stimuli would have led, he thought, to a permanent modification of that layer: "A crust would thus be formed which would at last have been so thoroughly 'baked through' by stimulation that it would present the most favourable possible conditions for the reception of stimuli and become incapable of any further modification" (Freud, 1920a, p. 261). That is to say, such a layer would have become the ideal medium.

Yet, in general, the medial aspect (or, better, the study of medial functions) was of little concern to Freud. For this neglect, if one wishes to call it that, psychoanalysis has been severely chided, as I shall presently show. But first I want to say that the pertinent and even, I dare say, the most pertinent things about man may be explicated without one's first reaching a satisfactory theory about medial functions. If man were understood as a system, in the sense in which I am here using that term, the particulars about the medial functions would not—in principle—remain undetected for a long time. However, this does not work the other way. Even when everything has become known about medial functions, as far as their capacities to fulfill their tasks as media are concerned, man will still remain an enigma.

If one wants to know how the particular aspect of the problem I am concerned with appears to the academic psychologist, one may turn to Hebb's presidential address of 1960, in which he gives a summary of the present state of psychology and its prospect. For obvious reasons, psychoanalysis is given only a little room in that address. Yet it is acknowledged to be a valid psychology—which, however, is separated from academic psychology by the existence of "a genuine discontinuity" (Hebb, 1960, p. 736). This discontinuity seems to him to be explained by the many shortcomings for which he reproaches psychoanalysis.

Hebb may be right in claiming that psychoanalysis has shown no real interest "in the problem of learning, of sensation and perception, of concept formation, of the nature of mind or the validity of introspective data." Recent developments[7] have shown that Freud's work contains the germs of more far-reaching insights into these very subjects than might have been anticipated; yet Hebb is right in that an explicit and focal interest in those areas has been missing. When he makes the same claim about the mechanics of behavior, I do not go along with him.

The address becomes most interesting, however, when Hebb turns to an outline of what he envisions as the second phase of the "revolution" that has taken place in American psychology since the end of the last century. The first phase was devoted to the extirpation of animism by the rigorous application of the S-R formula; now it is time to investigate behavioristically the mediating processes. Although concepts such as mind and consciousness are, he admits, ill-defined and crudely conceived, still every science, along with the "molecularly precise" terms, uses "molar and grossly defined" ones (Hebb, 1960, p. 739).

It is the necessity of the experimental psychologist "to deal with the 'I' or 'ego'" that the author seems to put in the center of his exposition. Hallucinations produced under the impact of sense deprivation, pathology of the body image, and allied subjects are viewed as the proper subjects of research, if we wish to obtain adequate insight into the psychology of the mediating processes. Thus psychopathology is drawn into the legitimate orbit of the academic psychologist. The realization of such a program—indeed, its very existence—is a belated justification of the superiority of Freud's approach—namely, that psychopathology is the

7 See, particularly, Hartmann 1939.

fountainhead of insight into man's personality. Only this approach can protect the psychologist against falling into the irrelevances of a medial psychology (although, in itself, it is not an absolute protection). Some misguided psychologist, who started his training in the atmosphere of the rigorously insisted-upon S-R formula, may yet succeed in 'resolving' even hallucinations and phantom limbs into medial processes. Whether academic psychology will be able to steer away from such a pitfall remains to be seen.

It sounds ominous when one hears Hebb saying, in referring to the basic division of the personality made in psychoanalytic theory, that "an analogy is made with a conflict of three agents, operating on an upper and lower level, but without detail concerning the nature of their existence or their mode of operation. In short, the analogy is still analogy" (Hebb, 1960, p. 736).[8]

If such a view should persist, despite experimental studies in the psychopathology of the self, the second phase of the American psychological revolution will not have achieved its optimal results, for the discontinuity between academic psychology and psychoanalysis will still remain a historical fact, if not to the benefit of the latter then certainly to the disadvantage of the former.

In the light of overwhelming clinical evidence, psychoanalysis does, indeed, adhere to the theory that the human personality consists of three provinces—ego, id, and superego—which represent three different groups of "core events" (once again to use Heider's terminology). These core events may stand (singly or as groups) in a great variety of relations to one another. Thus man is a system, the parts of which are in more or less constant inner conflict. Furthermore, according to psychoanalysis, in each time cross-section the past of that system is more or less represented, and has its full share in determining how the system deals with the present. So far, no other scientific psychology has been evolved that can match the consistency and rigor with which Freud pursued the investigation of man's personality as a system. It is this systemic nature of psychoanalysis that I find to be its most characteristic feature.

[8] I dare say that this exegesis upon psychoanalysis proves that "the genuine discontinuity with academic theory" is not to be explained solely in terms of psychoanalytic shortcomings, but rather by the genuine difference of conceptualization in the two fields. It is not, indeed, Freud's fault, nor is it that of psychoanalysis, that genuine theory strikes the outsider as "analogy." From the psychoanalytic vantage point, the theory of "cell assembly" (Hebb, 1949), like all other neurophysiological theorizing about problems of ego psychology, appears to be no more than thinking in analogies, which does not truly reach the dignity of a psychological theory.

3

The Psychoanalytic Situation

Thus far, I have set forth in abstract terms one aspect of psycho-analysis, which I believe to be essential in so far as it distinguishes psychoanalysis significantly from all other psychologies, and particularly from the varieties of academic psychology. I shall now proceed to examine the basic psychoanalytic situation. Once again, I shall try to be as abstract and general as possible, so as to be able to distinguish among essentials, and thus facilitate proper classification.

The psychoanalytic situation is unique in several ways. One of its characteristic features is its restriction to two persons: observer and subject. It does not allow the presence of any third party at all (Freud, 1926a, p. 185), not even in the form of a written record. The subject is provided with the opportunity for maximum freedom of verbalization with regard to his ideation, as well as his feelings, impulses, and sensations—in brief, with regard to everything he becomes sufficiently conscious of to articulate. The only restriction is upon his muscular system: he is not to put his physical impulses into action as long as he is part of the psychoanalytic situation. The kinetic sphere is limited to expressive movements, to automatisms, to all those innervations that lie outside the sphere of action in the narrower sense. The psychoanalytic situation is, in short, designed for maximum verbalization[1] along with minimum action.

In order to set in motion the process of verbalization, the subject is asked to assume a supine position, and to say everything and anything that comes to his mind—the important as well as the unimportant, the pleasing as well as the disgusting, the desirable as well as the repulsive —all the time without trying to pursue any particular aim.

The analyst, in order not to interfere in any way with this flow of free associations, is posted behind the subject. If my earlier remarks about the two psychologies are now recalled, the rationale inherent in the structure of this situation will be quickly recognized.[2] Since psychoanalysis is intent on studying the system properties of personality, the subject must be brought into a situation in which all stimuli are excluded such as may tend to render him a medium. The analytic situation is therefore kept relatively free of stimulations that would impose upon the subject any 'relevant obligation' to respond to. The physical environment of the analyst's office becomes routine, societal barriers and stimulations both fall away, and the analyst's discretion and confidentiality are offered as the guaranties for full freedom of communication. The subject is made aware from the start that no particular information is expected from him. Thus, neither any stimulus to react to, nor any appeal

[1] Since it is not my purpose in this presentation to offer an exposition of psychoanalysis, I am using such a general term as 'verbalization' to cover, in this context, a wider area than that usually assigned to it. Both the relevance and the importance of the emotional processes involved in these verbalizations are well known, and the processes have often been investigated. Yet they must themselves be verbalized, if the goal of psychoanalysis is to be fully reached. To avoid any unnecessary misunderstanding, I should therefore add that I understand maximum verbalization as including maximum insight.

[2] As with all great inventions and discoveries, the structure Freud gave to the psychoanalytic situation grew out of the genius's whole personality, and was not merely a utilitarian means to a utilitarian end. Thus Freud (1913b) gave, as one of the reasons for advising the patient's horizontal position during treatment, the following: "I cannot put up with being stared at by other people for eight hours a day (or more)" (p. 134). Yet, in order to understand fully the rationale of this arrangement, one must also read Freud's beautiful description of the vista that the method of free association opened up to him (Freud, 1925d, p. 40f.). This avowed coincidence of personal motive and discovery is now used by some to ridicule the 'paraphernalia' of Freud's technique, and to imply that, since such a setup was a rationalization of a personal idiosyncrasy, present-day analysts, in still following Freud's original arrangement, are in effect continuing as a ritual what was for Freud himself no more than a subjective defense. Fromm uses this sort of argument (1959, p. 107f.); yet the results of Fromm's technique themselves reveal how a change in what may strike the observer as a mere technical detail of almost trivial importance may in fact end the systemic nature of a psychology and destroy the very essence of the science of systemic psychology. (For a biological factor relevant to the arrangement that Freud instituted, see Klein, 1956, pp. 160-164.)

to activate a medial function is present, as far as that can be achieved in a natural setting. Whatever the subject reveals, therefore, will of necessity contain a reference to a system property. Since the subject is not guided by external demands, and his only 'obligation' is to verbalize the total contents of his mind without restraint or restriction, the associations he produces are called 'free.'[3]

Yet it soon becomes evident that the subject's verbalizations can be grouped into two classes. One includes reports that enrich our knowledge about the reality in which he is living, his past history, his feelings, his wishes, and so on. The other group includes manifestations of those forces that in any way interfere with the reporting process—that is, which delay, falsify, or conceal the subject's possible communications. This second group of data reveal to the analyst the subject's defense mechanisms, which stand in the way of his obtaining the subject's whole history and thus complete insight into the structure of the subject's personality. To be sure, these defense mechanisms are also part of that structure and must therefore be studied as carefully as the rest, for if their effect cannot be eliminated, insight into the total personality will be greatly impeded. Therefore, the psychoanalytic situation must be structured in such a way that the whole range of defense mechanisms also becomes available for observation—a result which Freud achieved by the shift from hypnosis to free association.

In order to eliminate the pathological effect of these defensive devices, their nature—that is, their mode of operation, their history, and their functions—must be demonstrated to the subject through interpretation. More often than not, it is also necessary to reconstruct from the subject's free associations, as exactly as possible, against what these defense mechanisms are employed. The analyst's interpretation of the subject's defenses, and his reconstruction of what is being warded off by them, on the one hand, and, on the other hand, the subject's new insight into his techniques for warding off, as well as into the contents of what is being warded off—these lead to new understanding and knowledge on the part of both analyst and subject.

As can well be imagined, the task of verbalizing anything and everything that presents itself to consciousness is not easy, and it is even less

[3] From the analytic point of view, of course, they are not free, as Freud frequently demonstrated. Their sequence and interconnection are determined, although by links that are so far unknown to the subject, and must be discovered by the analyst. Precisely these connections are the system properties of the psychoanalytic subject.

easy to expand the area to be covered by free association. Thus, even under ideal conditions, part of the subject's relevant history will be left unverbalized—that is, will not be recalled, but may remain reconstruction. Events of the first year or years of life, for example, can be remembered only under unusual circumstances, and many relevant events are so deeply repressed that they literally defy the psychoanalytic process.[4]

What may seem to have been set forth here as a relatively simple matter is in reality a most difficult one. A large number of technical problems are involved, such as the choice and timing of interpretation, their proper sequence and validation, etc. The ideal goal of the psychoanalytic situation may therefore be summed up as the total verbalization by the subject of all those psychic phenomena which present themselves to his mind, and the extension of that same area to include the total personality. Total verbalization, as well as total extension of the area drawn into the psychoanalytic situation, are never actually attained, to be sure; they can be approached asymptotically only.[5] The analyst's behavior—for example, his interference or noninterference with the psychoanalytic situation—is determined by his effort to achieve a maximum approximation of these two goals. In any particular situation, the actual approach should reflect this long-range view. Any interference by the psychoanalyst with the psychoanalytic situation, even though it may be of high immediate value in terms of symptomatic recovery, is to be excluded, if it will impair or indirectly delay the final approximation—the maximum verbalization of which the subject is capable.

I should now like to discuss a hypothetical situation, which seems to me to be of crucial significance. Let us assume that a psychologist wishes to study the structure of the human personality, in order to shape —on the basis of his own observations—the requisite theories and hypotheses. He turns, for that purpose, to an analyst. The latter, in keeping with his own views, will advise the inquirer to look for a subject who is ready to communicate his free associations to an observer for about an hour a day over a long period of time. The inquirer will further be told that the record thus gathered will not speak for itself, but will

[4] Yet such reconstructions can be validated, and their scientific value approaches that of actual recollections (cf. Freud, 1937b).

[5] My presentation is here following schematic lines. The goal of analysis, of course, can never be the removal of the defense mechanisms but their taming, that is to say, their being harnessed to work for the good of the self. The functioning of the psychic apparatus requires an optimal pressure by the repressed, which is an essential factor in the maintenance of vital feelings.

require periodic scrutiny and discussion in order for him to be able to form constructs, hypotheses, and theories necessary for the explanation of the observational data. He must therefore return after a while with the material he has collected, from which—he will be assured—convincing conclusions concerning the subject's personality structure will be drawn.

It may well happen that the psychologist does return after a time, only to report disappointment over his failure in carrying out the experiment. He may give the following report:

After some search, I did find an intelligent person who seemed quite suited for this undertaking. He was a thirty-two-year-old white male, Protestant, a successful businessman who had worked his way up from the lower middle class to some wealth, was married, and had two children. He is a conscientious, hard-working, reliable person and, when I told him of my purpose, he expressed a real interest in what might turn up during the course of the investigation. Having been almost completely engaged in the pursuit of his career until then, he looked forward to this opportunity for daily relaxation and for gradually becoming familiar with the inner workings of his mind. He therefore kept his appointments scrupulously, and proceeded just as I had requested. He showed the same reliability and consistency of effort for which he is known in his business dealings, and seemed to demonstrate the same sense of responsibility that he shows toward his family and his friends. Nevertheless, the content of his communications did not in any way bring me closer to an understanding of his personality.

First of all, he rarely told me anything of his past; he did not even speak much of his childhood. All his free associations centered on his plans for the future, his worries about his family and his friends, the obstacles he met with in his present undertakings, and the pleasure he had gained from recent successes. He was consistently preoccupied with the reality by which he is now surrounded and which offers him opportunities to act. To act, to achieve, to be active were the only dimensions of his life in which he seemed interested. I inquired about his feelings; he did not have much to report. He feels affection for his wife, his children, his friends; he gets annoyed or angry when reality frustrates his efforts to improve his professional situation; he is worried and sad when one of the children is sick.

I hoped that his dreams, as I have been told, would bring to light the material I was searching for. Yet, when he came for his hour, his recollection of the preceding night's dreams had usually faded away. In an effort to accommodate me, he would even write his dreams down soon after awakening; but he was unable to associate them with anything relevant except perhaps a few trivial events of the preceding day.

The analyst is likely to listen incredulously to this report, recalling the valuable insights he himself has obtained by the use of this same method. He may even feel inclined to make the researcher's lack of experience responsible for this 'failure.' However, upon examining the notes and records that the researcher put down after each hour, he may discover that the latter has proceeded in a quite adequate way. He did not antagonize the patient by pressing too hard, or by giving premature interpretations; where it seemed that a resistance developed, he tried to overcome it properly, etc. The analyst will have to admit that, in his own practice, he has never had to deal with such a situation. The reason for the curious outcome here must be—he may be forced to conclude—that, in so far as a human being responds adequately to external stimuli, or when his personality is structured in a reality-adequate way, he is, in effect, not analyzable. For he is not and cannot become drawn into the observation of purely inner processes—and especially those from or about his past; instead, he is more or less preoccupied with his present and future actions, since thinking is, as Freud says, a "trial action," or the rehearsal of an action (*Probehandeln*).

One may even feel inclined to say that, in so far as a personality *behaves* in a reality-adequate way—that is to say, is not neurotic—it cannot be analyzed. Yet that would be untrue in two respects: first, what is called 'reality-adequate behavior' may itself be neurotic, since society does not evaluate or describe behavior in psychological terms, but in terms of its utility or suitability. Secondly, it is quite conceivable that, in a subject, the conflict tension, even though not of neurotic quality, nevertheless may be sufficient to create a disposition favorable to psychoanalytic inquiry. In any case, if we dispense with theoretical subtleties and restrict ourselves to empirical approximations, one is quite justified in saying that those who, on a statistical basis, are called 'normal' are not promising subjects for psychoanalysis. Anna Freud (1936, pp. 3-10) has described the conditions of upset equilibrium that are the precondition for the possibility of learning about a subject's personality structure and thus of giving an interpretation.

The psychoanalytic psychologist can make scientific statements about seemingly one-dimensional configurations only after having observed them in a state in which the component functions were in discord or working at loggerheads. When, under the impact of interpretations, or of any other factor, the state of disharmony among the component functions has been discontinued, and their smooth interplay has been established or re-established, then the psychologist has been afforded the dual opportunity of studying: first, the nature of the component functions; secondly, the factors which make possible their smooth interplay. In other words, the psychoanalyst cannot examine the *terminus ad quem* unless the pathway leading to it from the *termini a quo* is known.

Freud took this for granted in his essay on lay analysis. He wrote: "For reasons which can easily be understood, neurotic human beings offer far more instructive and accessible material than normal ones" (1927a, p. 254). I would go beyond that. In so-called "normalcy" (surely a fictitious concept), id, superego, and the ego functions that organize reality seem to work in unison; the personality thus appears to be one-dimensional. 'Free association' will under such circumstances become reduced to an experimental mode of action (*Probehandeln*): it will become a thinking about the means that will make possible the attainment of reality-adequate goals. Man then appears the way society wishes him to appear, and the analyst gets an image of him only as a societal medium.[6]

One must conclude that the situation in which psychological research (and here I mean, of course, research in system psychology) can best be undertaken is that in which a neurotic subject submits to the psychoanalytic process.[7]

Therefore, after having scrutinized the above-mentioned record of a 'normal' person, the analyst would have to tell the would-be researcher to be sure to start the next instance of his investigation with a neurotic person. Such a record will give him ample opportunity to gain insight and to form constructs, theories, and hypotheses regarding the structure

[6] This remark should not be taken merely as a theoretical one. I have often had occasion to talk with subjects who, for reasons outside of their own need, should have been familiarized with the unconscious background of their actions. These were people who considered themselves normal, and who were rather successful in their dealings with reality. Almost every time my attempts had to be given up. Of course, instances should also be mentioned here of those who, under the same conditions, have of their own choice turned to an analyst and, having discovered, in the course of one or a few conversations, the many disharmonies and inconsistencies of which they had been unaware, soon prove to be excellent subjects of psychoanalysis.

[7] Nothing would be easier than to enumerate the many instances in which the general principle I have set forth has been invalidated. Since a detailed presentation of the scientific potential of psychoanalysis would be outside the area of this paper, it is unnecessary, for the trend of thought I am trying to convey, to go beyond that which is valid in principle.

of the personality. At the same time, however, the researcher will have become entangled in something that is disapproved by the American Psychoanalytic Association, and in some places is even prohibited by law, for he will now have become a lay analyst.

The hypothetical case I have introduced implies the absolute conjunction in psychoanalysis of research with what, from the practical point of view, is called therapy. As a matter of fact, it is only when this conjunction is actually present that one should speak of psychoanalysis *in sensu strictiori*. Freud wrote:

> Psychoanalysis from the beginning has constituted a point of union between healing and research. Knowledge brought therapeutic success. It was impossible to treat a patient without learning something new, it was impossible to gain fresh insight without perceiving its beneficent results. Our analytic procedure is the only one in which this precious conjunction is assured [Freud, 1927a, p. 256].

Freud did not assert that treatment and research are identical in the psychoanalytic situation; he spoke of a "point of union" (the word *Junktim* which Freud used is perhaps stronger than "point of union," but it does not signify identity). However, it is my conviction that, considering others among Freud's definitions of psychoanalysis, the conclusion becomes inescapable that no logical separation can be established between research and treatment in the psychoanalytic situation.[8]

This is a unique and extremely far-reaching array of conditions which is not found in any other field of medicine, and is not even comparable with anything encountered in any other science. If anyone were to set out, on the one hand, to find out everything he could about the structure of a specific personality, its genesis and its dynamics; or if, on the other hand, he were to undertake to cure that same subject of his neurotic symptomatology—for both purposes he would have to proceed in identical ways, and an outsider would not be able to determine at any point in the process which of the two goals was being pursued. In psychoanalysis, to cure and to gain knowledge require identical processes.

The scientific researcher, solely interested in gaining knowledge, and

---

[8] In his *New Lectures*, Freud said that, in psychoanalysis, "understanding and cure go almost hand in hand" (1933a, p. 198). The German original, in fact, uses stronger language than the standard English translation; it says: "almost coincide" (*beinahe zusammenfallen*). In the same context, Freud writes of "the underlying identity subsisting between pathological and so-called normal process," a statement which, in my opinion, also substantiates the principal conclusion I am drawing.

the physician, solely interested in the restoration of the patient's health —both, if they want to carry the potential of the psychoanalytic situation to its asymptotic maximum, can proceed in no other way than to analyze and interpret the subject's defensive apparatus, to draw further areas of ego, id, and superego into the psychoanalytic process, to uncover the past and present effects which reality, id, and superego have had upon the ego, and thus to reconstruct the whole history of the personality. For researcher and physician, interpretation would be the only tool they could operate with.

When I state that to cure and to obtain knowledge are identical processes, whose knowledge do I mean—the observer's or the subject's? The fact that this knowledge is of concern to both subject and observer once again constitutes a unique combination of circumstances. The observer can obtain knowledge only in so far as the subject goes through the same process. Clinically, one finds that, when the observer gathers considerable knowledge regarding the subject, but does not convey it to the subject; or, when the subject, despite this conveyance, does not integrate the knowledge, then the whole process—whether it be therapy or investigation—comes to a standstill, and the observer must remain content with the partial knowledge attained, which may be quite far from the potential maximum.

This relationship is such, indeed, that a considerable discrepancy between the observer's and the subject's knowledge at any point of the investigation may often be regarded as an unfavorable omen, presaging an unsatisfactory conclusion to the undertaking.[9]

The ideal situation would be a sequence of the following processes: (1) a step forward in the gathering of knowledge by the observer; followed by (2) the conveyance of this new piece of knowledge to the subject; in turn, followed by (3) the discovery and elimination of the obstacles in the way of the subject's integration of this knowledge; which process simultaneously paves the way to (4) gaining still further knowledge about the subject's personality. After the conclusion of this integrative process, the same sequence would be repeated with a new observation. Clinical reality, of course, never follows this ideal type; all kinds of variations are encountered, which do not need to be described here.

A further statement is in order, concerning the term "knowledge."

[9] In contrast to this view, cf. Freud: "We avoid telling him [the patient] at once things that we have often discovered quite early, or we avoid telling him the whole of what we think we have discovered" (1940a, p. 71; cf. also 1926a, p. 220).

Knowledge generally refers to an intellectual content which corresponds with the truth. Thus, for example, if someone says that in 1492 Columbus set foot upon an island which he then called San Salvador, we say that he possesses knowledge of the discovery of America. Such correspondence between fact and idea, however, would not suffice by itself to denote knowledge in psychoanalytic parlance, in which the term means more than this in two respects. First, knowledge, from the psychoanalytic viewpoint, must not be isolated from the subject's previous knowledge but must be in maximum associative connection with *all* systems of the personality, including both the unconscious and the preconscious; or, to turn to the structural aspect, knowledge, in order to meet the psychoanalytic requirements, has to be represented *in all three provinces* (ego, superego, and id), in a way that is characteristic of each province. *All* the implications inherent in an intellectual content must come to the subject's awareness.[10] Second, the previous reference to knowledge (about Columbus) does not take into account the emotional reverberations evoked in the subject's mind with regard to this knowledge. He may like, hate, or be totally indifferent to his own knowledge of the discovery of America. Knowledge, as the term is used in the psychoanalytic situation, is evaluated primarily in terms of the emotional reverberations of the particular content. Indifference to knowledge is tantamount to the absence of knowledge, in the psychoanalytic situation; here knowledge must include the integration of the full meaning of a content, a process which is regularly accompanied by an array of feelings.

Interpretations which have the most consequential effects upon the subject are often described by him as having been experienced like a revelation, comparable to the opening of a new horizon, which offers a new prospect for the future precisely because his past life now appears in a new light. Such a synthesis of knowledge with its corresponding emotions is one of the most difficult and delicate of tasks, and it is because of their failure to complete it that a good many analyses come to naught. Yet not only must the knowledge conveyed to the subject not remain isolated and devoid of emotion, but the observer himself must not fall into the pitfall either of intellectualization or of emotional overcathexis. The observer's psychic processes optimal to the course of investigation

[10] Cf. Freud (1916-1917): "Knowledge is not always the same as knowledge: there are different sorts of knowledge, which are far from equivalent psychologically . . . The knowledge must rest on an internal change in the patient. . . ." (p. 281).

are very difficult to describe. Suffice it to say that they do not involve solely intellectual or ideational processes.

Thus the psychoanalytic situation, when it is subjected to logical analysis, and when all factors of a historical, societal—or, as one may say, fortuitous or accidental—nature are removed, appears to be one of pure research, and one cannot escape being a scientist, if he is a psychoanalyst. Like M. Jourdain, who spoke prose for forty years without knowing that he did, an analyst might think of himself as merely a simple practitioner, solely interested in the welfare of his patients; yet if he carries the psychoanalytic situation to its potential maximum, he is bound to become— not *un médecin,* perhaps, but *un homme de science, malgré lui.*[11] If a practitioner in general medicine were to keep a record of everything relevant that occurred in his practice, this might be of interest to the sociologist or the statistician, but only very rarely for medical research. Should a practicing analyst, however, even one devoid of any research interest, keep an equivalent record, it would contain—*malgré lui*—a wealth of new scientific data.

I cannot agree with Freud when he speaks of cases which are "quite uninteresting scientifically" (1927a, p. 255).[12] This seems to me hardly conceivable in the light of the present status of psychoanalytic research. I rather think that Freud's view cited earlier, with regard to the union of healing and research, holds true of all instances in which psychoanalysis has accomplished its goal; and I would be inclined to believe that the "scientifically uninteresting" case is merely one in which the analytic process has fallen short of its maximum potential. (To be sure, clinical considerations may make an approximation to this potential inadvisable in particular instances, but such instances have no relevance in this context.)

Here it is appropriate to quote from an early paper by Freud (1912a)

[11] It is necessary to add a qualification here. Sarton once wisely remarked that Leonardo da Vinci cannot be called a predecessor of Copernicus solely on the ground that he once wrote, "The sun does not move." "A man of science must prove, or at least explain clearly, what he has in mind." (Sarton, 1955, p. 219f.) Likewise, the 'discoveries' that the therapeutically motivated analyst indifferent to research makes are not truly part and parcel of science in the narrower meaning; for as long as they are not elaborated or put into context—that is to say, organized—they are of no real consequence. Nevertheless, this reservation, important as it is, does not contravene my previous metaphor.

[12] In a paper which Freud wrote only two years earlier, a passage can be found whose interpretation leads to a view different from the one just quoted. Considering the need to analyze early childhood in each instance of analysis, Freud had this to say: "Indeed, analysts may feel assured, I think, that there is no risk of their work becoming mechanical, and so losing its interest, during the next few decades" (1925e, p. 248).

which, by its double-barreled argument, both confirms and seems to refute my view: "One of the claims," Freud writes, "of psychoanalysis to distinction is . . . that in its execution research and treatment *coincide* [italics mine]; nevertheless, after a certain point, the technique required for the one opposes that required for the other. It is not a good thing to work on a case scientifically while treatment is still proceeding—to piece together its structure, to try to foretell its further progress, and to get a picture from time to time of the correct state of affairs, as scientific interest would demand" (p. 114).[13] Here Freud clearly puts forward a position of the ultimate opposition between treatment and science, very much in contrast with my thesis of their consistent identity. Yet this difference has to do with a phase in the history of psychoanalytic practice during which many a question of method had not yet been clarified.

Up to now, I have scarcely spoken of techniques. Research and treatment do coincide, objectively; granted. But what would be the effect on the subject, Freud asks, if the analyst proceeded in the way scientists commonly do, and wrote down his observations as soon as he made them, etc.? Psychoanalytic research has its own methodology, which is essentially different from that of other fields of science. Indeed, an analyst's preoccupation with the objectively true sequence of events—namely, that in analyzing a subject, he will make a new discovery in his field—may serve to prevent him from ever reaching the very goal he has in mind. How the analyst must proceed in order to bring about the subject's maximum verbalization is a technical question. Yet, whatever the answer may be, it will not ever negate the fact that the analytic situation is, in essence, research.

To be sure, even an analyst who is especially interested in research may analyze patients with whom he cannot achieve any scientific advance; but this, in my opinion, may occur not because the analysis of the subject is inherently unproductive, but perhaps because our sight is not sharp enough, so that what is uniquely individual in that particular personality —the very ensemble of facts never before observed, and for that very reason of considerable scientific interest—is not truly perceived. Therefore it can be said that a psychoanalysis which is properly conducted and

13 Two years earlier Freud (1910d) had made a sharp distinction between science and practice by introducing his address at the Second Psychoanalytic Congress with an "appeal to your medical, not to your scientific interest" (p. 141). Cf. also Freud (1913f): "The cases of illness which come under a psycho-analyst's observation are of course of unequal value in adding to his knowledge" (p. 193). In this passage Freud speaks later of cases from which the psychoanalyst learns nothing.

takes a successful course will lead to a series of scientific discoveries, whether these be recognized or unrecognized by the analyst who has conducted the analysis.

However, in my effort to show the identity of therapy and research, I have so far neglected an observation which is of far-reaching significance for this question. Repeated experience has shown—at least when psychoanalysis is conducted in the way that Freud seems to have had in mind, so that it serves to convey maximum knowledge to the subject as well as to the analyst—that the less the observer is motivated by a therapeutic intent, and the more he is impelled by the motive of gaining knowledge about the structure of the subject's personality, the greater seems to be the probability that the maximum potential in the psychoanalytic situation will be actualized. There is no logical reason I know of for this fact; it is based merely on empirical observation.

The therapist who raises the question, "What do I have to do to *remove* this symptom?" will arrive—if he remains within the psychoanalytic orbit—at answers in no way fundamentally different from those he would come to if he asked himself, "What do I have to do to *gain knowledge of the reasons* for the existence of this symptom?" Nevertheless, one can observe in clinical reality that it is the very therapeutic intent, curiously enough, that often becomes the barrier to the patient's recovery. In the psychological intimacy that surrounds observer and subject in the psychoanalytic situation, the observer's motives have an effect upon the subject even when they are not verbalized.[14]

As a matter of fact, the most significant deviations from Freud's technique within the official school of psychoanalysis seem to have arisen among those psychoanalysts who are primarily, often almost solely, motivated by therapy, and who therefore have lost sight of that total system to whose investigation psychoanalysis is devoted. (It is truly amazing to see how little the *will* to cure by itself helps in matters of the human mind.)

Freud was aware of this paradoxical effect of the therapeutic motive. He wrote, when setting forth how he happened, so to speak, to become an analyst: "I scarcely think, however, that my lack of genuine medical

[14] I do not want to make any blanket generalizations as to the superiority of the research attitude. In my opinion, it is almost certainly superior for the analysis of neurotics. There are, however, borderline cases and acute schizophrenics to whom the therapist ought to convey an awareness of his determination and ability to help. Yet, even in these instances, the therapist's overt expression should serve only as a part of his technique, and must not replace his own inner attitude of seeking explanations.

temperament has done much damage to my patients. For it is not greatly to the advantage of patients if their doctor's therapeutic interest has too marked an emotional emphasis. They are best helped if he carries out his task coolly and keeping as closely as possible to the rules" (Freud, 1927a, p. 254).[15] Yet I believe that, even in the absence of overcathexis of the therapeutic intent, the mere fact of the therapist's wanting to *cure* the patient, rather than to convey *insight*, may be of disservice to patients who are more than usually sensitive, and who therefore present us with better than usual evidence for the validation of this proposition. With them, apparently, a consistent attitude of 'What are the reasons for . . . ?' is therapeutically more effective than one of 'How should I treat . . . ?'

The best motivation and the most appropriate attitude for dealing practically with the psychoanalytic situation is the constant search for the causes of observed data. I have obtained surprising clinical results with patients whom I have told, at the proper time, that they do not need to feel under any obligation with regard to their recovery, and that they may continue their analyses even should they decide not to recover. I have said this, of course, with a 'therapeutic twinkle' in my eye, but it seems to be suitable in some instances as a way of relieving the patient of the pressure which arises as soon as he develops the impression that it has become his 'duty,' so to speak, to recover.

Quite generally, I think, the therapeutic aspect of psychoanalysis is misunderstood. Psychoanalysis is not some sort of therapeutic agent comparable to those used in internal medicine. According to Freud, it is not the function of psychoanalysis to ensure the subsidence of the symptoms, under all circumstances; it is rather its function to ensure the ego's freedom of choice. The *motives* for the choice that the patient finally makes must be revealed to him; but the *responsibility* for that choice rests in the patient's self, once it has acquired freedom through the psychoanalytic process. This seems, at least, to have been Freud's approach, to judge from a note in which he discussed alternative techniques by which to eliminate a certain malignant symptom. He opposed the use of one technique that was therapeutically more promising because it would be irreconcilable with the basic principles of psychoanalysis. "After all," he wrote, "analysis does not set out to abolish the possibility of morbid reactions, but to give the patient's ego *freedom* to choose one way or the

---

[15] The standard English translation of the last eight words may give cause for misunderstanding. A literal translation of the original *"möglichst korrekt"* would be: "as accurately as possible."

other" (Freud, 1923a, p. 72n., italics by Freud). In this instance, clearly, the psychoanalytic situation was not for Freud primarily a therapeutic one, in the narrower sense of the word.

It may be that the commands of the Hippocratic tradition must remain unfulfilled here; a principle seems to have been brought to light that does not exist in regard to other medical specialties, and which is per se incompatible with medical practice as it is generally conceived of today. It is that the mere removal of a symptom, without a corresponding gain in the subject's insight, is unacceptable to psychoanalysis. Since the goal of psychoanalysis can be well summarized in that pithy statement that had such significance in ancient Greece: "Know thyself,"[16] it would be surprising indeed if a discipline that was exclusively or even primarily concerned with the restitution of disturbed functions were to live up to its demands. (This gives us the opportunity to consider more fully the implications of one of the many definitions of psychoanalysis. If psychoanalysis is a method through which the maximum verbalization of psychic phenomena is to be achieved, and thereupon the conveyance of maximum knowledge and insight to both observer and subject, then the name psychoanalysis should be withheld from any procedure which is not structured in such way as to reflect and advance those aims.)

It is, of course, a fact that, in the practical context of everyday life, we tend to regard the psychoanalytic situation primarily as a therapeutic one. When the patient asks for help, we start his psychoanalysis with the tacit understanding that there is a significant chance of his being cured. This therapeutic coloring that pervades the psychoanalytic situation is the outcome of tradition and practice, however, and does not reflect the essentials of the psychoanalytic process. The pain caused by the neurotic symptom and the patient's desire to be freed from that pain are only the sparks that set the psychoanalytic process in motion. In my experience, optimal results are obtained when, after the clinical disappearance of symptoms, the patient continues the analysis—no longer for the immediate purpose of eliminating pain, but for the far more comprehensive purpose of obtaining maximal knowledge of his personality: that is, when it is no longer the pleasure principle that is the dominant force in the psychoanalytic process, but the reality principle,[17] so that the psycho-

---

[16] Hartmann (1959) recently defined analysis as "a systematic study of self-deception and its motivations" (p. 20).

[17] Cf. Freud (1940a): "The ideal conduct for our purpose would be that he [the patient] should behave as normally as possible outside the treatment and express his abnormal reactions only in the transference" (p. 70).

analytic process has acquired that degree of autonomy in the patient's life which makes it independent of the comparative fortuitousness of the neurotic symptomatology.

I have tried to show that the fundamental character of the psychoanalytic situation is that of a scientific investigation and—in line with this—that the subject's interests are most effectively advanced when psychoanalytic practice is in fact structured as a scientific investigation. In all this, I had in mind the ideal type of psychoanalytic situation; in reality, of course, ideals are never attained but only approximated. However, I want to touch briefly on a situation in which research that is seemingly in the service of psychoanalysis may become detrimental to the subject. This occurs when research concerns itself with a partial aspect of the personality, disregarding its structure as a whole. If a researcher, in the course of investigating dream psychology, asked a subject to continue all his free associations to his current dreams, and then interpreted these associations in order to obtain more pertinent material, he would do damage to the subject by not considering the total structure within which these dreams occur.

It is a curious fact that nowhere is there any objection expressed to a scientific investigation of this or similar kinds. Even the fiercest opponent of lay analysis would probably not object to the psychoanalytic investigation, by someone medically untrained, of single functions, or of a partial aspect of the personality, in spite of the fact that he would undoubtedly object strongly to such an investigation of the whole personality. This limitation of interpretation, or of the psychoanalytic investigation, to a partial aspect of the subject is comparable to so-called "wild analysis" (Freud, 1910a), in which the injudicious or faulty overemphasis on a partial aspect, along with a corresponding negligence of the whole ensemble of psychic conditions, may lead to transitory infringement upon a patient's state.

In Freud's own scientific career, there is an example that may illustrate the point in question. I have in mind the case history written in 1901 and published four years later. It was the first of the five great case histories, the pillars on which Freud's clinical work rests. Comparing it with Freud's four case histories published in the *Studies in Hysteria* only six years earlier, one can see the great step forward that Freud has taken in his clinical approach, his growth in stature as a clinician. The technique of free association has already started to show evidence of the rich harvest that it is to yield. Thus my comments at this point are not meant to detract from this case history's great value, but rather to show the pitfalls that Freud managed to avoid.

The paper was intended for publication under the title "Dreams and Hysteria" (Freud, 1905e, p. 10). Indeed, the two dreams that Freud analyzes at the close of the patient's treatment are the center of the presentation. Although, from the perusal of this paper, a good deal can be learned about the neuroses proper, the chief intent is clearly to demonstrate the validity of the psychoanalytic theory of dreams, the indispensability of dream interpretation for opening the sluices of the unconscious. This particular case history is usually discussed in connection with the problem of transference. In spite of several references to transference, and although a full theory of transference is set forth in the last section, it is still astonishing to observe the striking clarity with which Freud was able, from the timing of a highly concealing dream context, to gather the patient's intention of leaving the treatment (Freud, 1905e, p. 70, n. 2), a few weeks in advance of her actually doing so.

Yet the practice, or rather the technique, of transference interpretation was still in its earliest stages. Thus, when the patient announced, near the beginning of one hour—shortly after she had reported the dream which contained the key to the etiology of her neurosis—that she would make this the final hour of her treatment, Freud replied in essence that for the remainder of that hour they would go on with their work—that is, he did not make her announced decision the center of transference interpretation. My guess is that it was Freud's intense research interest in dream psychology that interfered with his consideration of the situation as a whole. At that time, the synthesis of psychoanalytic practice and research had not yet been fully achieved.

I should add that Freud later dealt with this very danger in a special paper on the way in which dream interpretation should be used in the course of a psychoanalysis. There he stated: "It is of the greatest importance for the treatment that the analyst should always be aware of the surface of the patient's mind at any given moment, that he should know what complexes and resistances are active in him at the time, and what conscious reaction to them will govern his behavior. It is scarcely ever right to sacrifice this therapeutic aim to an interest in dream-interpretation" (Freud, 1911c, p. 92).[18] This passage sounds like an epicrisis

---

[18] Yet, cf. two pages later: "Occasionally, of course, one can act otherwise and allow a little free play to one's theoretical interest; but one should always be aware of what one is doing" (p. 94).

to the premature ending of Dora's analysis. Yet it was at the same time an act of renunciation in the service of science, for it is reasonable to assume that Freud's own intense interest in dream psychology did not grow less with the passage of time.

Not only was his book on dreams the work which he knew would secure his place on the Olympus of Western science; dreams were the psychological area in which, in times of doubt, he could find reassurance that the scientific edifice he was building was correct and solid (Freud, 1914a, p. 20; 1933a, p. 16). A fixation on dream interpretation, an over-valuation of its function, an insistence that the psychoanalytic procedure requires concentration on the full explanation of each dream, would thus have been an understandable foible. In 1901, shortly after the publication of the book on dreams, we find Freud on the verge of evolving such a clinical approach; but apparently his overcathected interest in a part function was soon replaced with concern for the total psychological personality, which was the sole guarantee of that maximum harvest of insight that was contained potentially in the psychoanalytic situation.

It is consequently of no minor significance that: (1) increasingly the psychoanalytic techniques (if they can be called that) which are now being recommended, chiefly by the so-called neo-Freudian schools, tend to be restrictive rather than expansive, and do not aspire to attain even an asymptotic utilization of the maximum content contained in the psychoanalytic situation, but stop far short of it; (2) the bulk of current psychoanalytic literature seems to consist of segmental studies; (3) the investigation of part functions is considered to be not incompatible with an investigator's nonmedical status, while a clinical situation that seems to call for a total approach is regarded as reserved for the medically and psychiatrically trained alone.

I have left untouched a score of problems that would legitimately find their place in a full description of the psychoanalytic situation. Thus, for example, I have omitted any discussion of transference, which is an integral part of the psychoanalytic situation. There are, of course, many more such questions; merely to enumerate them would be cumbersome enough.[19] As to whether, in the analysis of syndromes other than the neuroses, such as the functional psychoses and the delinquencies, the psychoanalytic situation is structured in the same way as I have shown for the neuroses, this context does not permit the opportunity to discuss.

[19] For a profound discussion of the matter, in the full context of psychoanalysis, see Stone (1961).

In this section, I have limited myself to the one point which impresses me as decisive in any deliberation concerning the implications of the rejection or acceptance of lay analysis. By way of conclusion to this section, I point to the course that Freud himself steered from therapy to research. In 1909, Freud wrote: "For a psycho-analysis is not an impartial scientific investigation but a therapeutic measure. Its essence is not to prove anything, but merely to alter something" (Freud, 1909a, p. 104). But only eight years later, he wrote the proud sentence: "Even if psycho-analysis showed itself as unsuccessful with all other forms of nervous and mental diseases as with delusions, it would still remain justified as an irreplaceable instrument of scientific research" (Freud, 1917a, p. 217).

4

On the Scope of Applied Psychoanalysis

Many arguments may be raised against the account I have just offered of the psychoanalytic situation—among them the historical one. Psychoanalysis was born in a therapeutic situation, so this argument goes; it owes its existence to the therapeutic intent of its discoverers, Breuer and Freud. Both Breuer and Freud, during the early years when they were using the cathartic method, were motivated by that intent; both of them, prior to the beginnings of psychoanalysis, had been prominent practitioners and clinicians in other medical specialties. Persons suffering from painful symptoms sought medical help, and the merits of Breuer and Freud's new method were initially evaluated in terms of its clinical success. To be sure, from the beginning the heuristic value of this new method was apparent to both, and neither held back his beliefs concerning the formation of theory in their first joint publication (Breuer and Freud, 1893-1895). Nevertheless, the decisive question at that time was the way in which the symptom responded to the treatment, and a contemporary observer would have been correct in regarding catharsis as a therapeutic technique used in a medical specialty.

At this point, we might consider Freud's own opinion concerning the inception of psychoanalysis. He himself places the beginning of psychoanalysis proper either at the two dates, 1895 and 1900—that is, at the dates of publication of *Studies on Hysteria,* and *The Interpretation of Dreams* (Freud, 1926b, p. 269)—or at the latter date alone (Freud, 1924a, p. 191).[1]

It is important to compare these two publications. In the earlier work, the clinical viewpoint is the overriding one: it is the therapeutic intent that dominates procedure. In the later work, hardly anything is said about therapy, the clinical viewpoint has been well-nigh eliminated, and we are dealing with a book of pure psychology—systemic psychology, I hasten to add.[2] Indeed, it may come as a surprise to some that the majority of Freud's greatest and most important publications were not written within a clinical or therapeutic framework. Besides *The Interpretation of Dreams,* the book on apraxias (1901), on wit (1905b), *Totem and Taboo* (1913-1914), *Beyond the Pleasure Principle* (1920a), *Group Psychology* (1921), *The Ego and the Id* (1923a), *Civilization and its Discontents* (1930a), and *Moses and Monotheism* (1939) are not medical publications, whether the term 'medical' is taken in the narrower or the broader sense.

Nevertheless, a fuller consideration of the matter will force us to recognize that system psychology could have been founded in nineteenth- or twentieth-century Western culture *only* by a physician, for system psychology could start only with a study of man in conflict, and it was to a physician that such a man would go, for solace and, if possible, treatment.[3] The historical truth of this proposition is clarified in an article by Sir Francis Galton (1879-1880).[4] It is impressive to observe how close

[1] Cf. also Freud (1914a): "The history of psychoanalysis proper . . . only begins with the new technique that dispenses with hypnosis" (p. 16). Later Freud made an observation which suggests that, for him, analysis started to be what it is only after it had become a psychology: "With the theory of dreams, analysis passed from being a psycho-therapeutic method to being a psychology of the depths of human nature" (Freud, 1933a, p. 15). Consider also Freud's letter to Fliess in 1898: "If the ascertaining of the few points required for the explanation of neuroses involves so much work, time and error, how can I ever hope to gain an insight into the whole of mental activity, which was once something I proudly looked forward to?" (Freud, 1887-1902, p. 269).

[2] Cf. Freud (1924a): "From the date of *The Interpretation of Dreams* psycho-analysis had a twofold significance. It was not only a new method of treating the neuroses but it was also a new psychology; it claimed the attention not only of nerve specialists but also of all those who were students of a mental science" (p. 200). Cf. also Freud (1925d): "From the time of the writing of *The Interpretation of Dreams* psycho-analysis ceased to be a purely medical subject" (p. 62).

[3] For obvious reasons, the 'man of God' to whom a man in conflict might also have turned was not prepared for discoveries which only the empirically oriented scientist was equipped to make.

[4] Zilboorg (1952) was the first to show this historically important link between Freud's technique of free association and Galton's experiment.

Galton's observations came to those made by Freud, not so many years later, concerning free association—the most astounding being Galton's report that this technique led to the recollection of events long past that seemed until then to have been forgotten. A good many other passages could be cited to prove that Galton's experiments may legitimately be regarded as antecedents of Freud's technique. Now Sir Francis had obtained a medical degree, but he never became a physician and, although he held the birth of psychoanalysis in his grasp, so to speak, he made no further contribution to either its birth or its growth.[5]

Of course, psychoanalysis had many antecedents. Most often, they are to be found in the writings of literary figures—Freud (1930b, p. 210) himself found such an instance in a letter written by Goethe—and for that very reason these anticipations were not followed up by systematic elaboration. Yet Galton's paper was a strictly scientific one, not an outgrowth of literary fancy or intuition, and even that very impressive advance did not lead, with Galton himself, to systematization. Thus, one is justified in assuming that if, at about 1900, the dynamics of human conflict were to be discovered at all, that discovery would apparently have to be made by the mind of an inquiring physician. Because of this historical and, in terms of analysis, external constellation, it was in fact an inquiring physician who did develop system psychology.

It quickly became clear to Freud that, in this technique, he held in his grasp the beginnings of a new science, a scientific psychology such as man had been in need of for an exceedingly long time. Yet whatever the historical constellation may be that determines the origins of a science, these need not be the decisive elements in determining the logic of development of that same science.

Freud's conception of psychoanalysis in its earlier phases laid stress on the therapeutic aspect. In 1913 he defined psychoanalysis as "a medical procedure which aims at the cure of certain forms of nervous disease (the neuroses) by a psychological technique" (1913a, p. 165). In this earlier definition, psychology plays the role only of the means by which psychoanalytic cures are brought about. In 1923—ten years later—Freud assigned a triad of meanings to the term psychoanalysis: (1) "a procedure

[5] In an article by Galton (1879) written somewhat earlier than the one just referred to, this astounding statement is to be found: "The more I have examined the workings of my own mind . . . the less respect I feel for the part played by consciousness. I begin with others to doubt its use altogether as supervisor, and I think that my best brain work is wholly independent of it" (p. 433). In this article Galton also describes a self-experiment that anticipates some of Jung's later association experiments.

for the investigation of mental processes"; (2) "a method . . . for the treatment of neurotic disorders"; (3) "a collection of psychological information" leading toward a new scientific discipline (Freud, 1923b, p. 235).[6]

The question may be raised, in the light of Freud's own definition, what advantage or necessity I find for the elimination of one of these meanings (to wit, the therapeutic one), or for denying what is an undeniable fact—that psychoanalysis is in fact carried on (and taught) for the purpose of curing patients suffering from certain forms of neuroses.

I do not, of course, deny social reality, nor am I ignoring the fact that many neurotic symptoms do disappear in the course of a psychoanalysis, never to return. I have merely raised the question of whether one is making an accurate logical analysis when one describes as primarily therapeutic a process which is patently engaged in for the purpose of establishing a knowledge of facts, and in order to discover the explanation for them. Moreover, I think that we might profitably apply the method of field study to the problem at hand. The history of science does not confine itself merely to recording the sequence of scientific discoveries and theories; it also investigates the specific historical circumstances and processes within which scientific progress has taken place.

The processes of professional practice and scientific inquiry have their own particular sociological loci. Medicine, for example, includes both medical practice and medical research. Sometimes these are pursued by different people, sometimes by the same person. Often, the medical practitioner will spend his entire working day examining patients, and then ordering or carrying out what their recovery calls for. By contrast, the medical scientist may spend his whole day in the laboratory—examining body fluids, or analyzing the chemical composition of organic substances, or carrying out animal experiments—never once during his entire medical career writing out a single prescription, or examining a single patient. There may sometimes be observed a combination in the same person of medical practice with research. Yet, with rare exceptions, we are able to define and describe the different sociological loci at which medical practice is performed on the one hand, and research on the other.[7]

[6] I believe that this triad has now become the most widely accepted conception. It was made the basis of Alexander's (1932) evaluation of the medical role of psychoanalysis.

[7] The fact may be adduced here that medical research is also performed at the patient's bedside. (Indeed, this kind of research comes closest to the structure of the psychoanalytic situation.) Yet, even here, the physician is generally in a position to assert rather readily which action is serving the uses of therapy and which is fulfilling the

It is my contention that there is unclarity regarding this whole question in the field of psychoanalysis. There is now general agreement, as I have noted above, that psychoanalysis is at once a method of psychological investigation, a method of treatment, and a scientific discipline. But one may then ask: who is it that carries out the psychological investigation, and what are the circumstances under which this is done? Further, who treats disease with psychoanalysis, and under what circumstances is this carried out? As we shall see, Freud answered these questions in his concluding remarks to his book on lay analysis, and thus introduced a far-reaching viewpoint into the whole logical scheme of psychoanalysis. Yet, curious though it may seem, even though his book was widely discussed in its time, no one, as far as I know, seems to have become aware of the new conception that Freud had introduced.

Prior to that time, the term "application of psychoanalysis" covered two different areas: (a) investigations employing the concepts and theories of psychoanalysis for explanatory purposes in the "mental sciences" (*Geisteswissenschaften*) (Freud, 1923b, p. 252),[8] and (b) practical activities organized in correlation with psychoanalytic theories (cf. also Freud, 1907a, 1924a). The best example of the latter is psychoanalytic pedagogy and infant-raising, structured in accordance with psychoanalytic principles and theories. An early and well-known example of the former, in the field of biography, is Freud's *Leonardo* study (1910b), in which he endeavored to reconstruct such of Leonardo's unconscious processes as would explain some aspects of his work and some details of his life history. A more recent example would be Freud's book on *Moses and Monotheism* (1939), in which he tried to explain certain details of Jewish history and some features of the Jewish national character.[9]

Psychoanalysis proper was at that time the name given only to the situation in which the psychoanalyst analyzed the patient. The discussion of lay analysis, which necessitated renewed inquiry into the scientific and practical aspects of psychoanalysis, apparently led Freud (1927a)

demands of scientific experimentation. The actual coincidence of experiment and therapy occurs only rarely—for example, when a new drug is being tried out.

[8] This definition is certainly too narrow, since there is also an application of psychoanalysis to biology. Notwithstanding its use of definition by enumeration, Freud's paper on the "Claims of Psycho-Analysis to Scientific Interest" (1913a), with its outline of a variety of applications, is still the best summary of what the early view included in applied psychoanalysis.

[9] For a systematized presentation of the application of psychoanalysis to the special field of art, see Kris (1952).

to differentiate along new lines between psychoanalysis and its application: he spoke then, as he had not before, of "the application of analysis to the treatment of patients" (p. 254). He had not done that previously, when it had been the treatment of patients that was regarded as psychoanalysis. His new view was expressed even more clearly in the following: "For practical reasons we have been in the habit—and this is true, incidentally, of our publications as well—of distinguishing between medical and applied analysis. But that is not a logical distinction. The true line of division is between *scientific* analysis and its *applications,* alike in medical and in non-medical fields" (Freud, 1927a, p. 257, italics by Freud). Freud, however, never elaborated upon this new line of division, and we are forced to speculate as to what situation Freud had in mind with regard specifically to the "logical distinction" between scientific and medically applied psychoanalysis. Apparently, by 'scientific' psychoanalysis Freud meant the psychoanalytic situation, in which the attainment of insight is the guiding principle, and from which anything that may impede the gaining of knowledge—even if it might lead to an immediate abatement of symptoms—is excluded.

It may be countered that, in most instances, the subject loses his symptoms during the course of such a psychoanalysis, so that no sooner has treatment been sent out of the door by research, than it comes in again through the window. In most scientific inquiries, to be sure, the object of examination is changed by the very act of examination itself. In putting a thermometer into a liquid in order to measure its temperature, we change that temperature, even if only to a minimal and short-lived extent; if this were not so, the thermometer could not in fact record it. (The histological examination of tissues involves even more serious changes in the object of inquiry.)

The gradual recession of symptoms in the process of psychoanalysis is the equivalent of temperature change in the course of temperature measurement. The symptom per se is equivalent to a resistance; it blocks the way to full understanding. When symptoms fall aside in the course of an analysis, this may be correlated with the removal of resistances and the subsequent emergence of understanding of what lay concealed behind and in the symptom.[10] The change in temperature induced by the in-

---

[10] While this general statement is essentially correct, nevertheless—as always in psychoanalysis with general statements—it needs qualification. It is well known, for example, that symptoms may also disappear when the patient is determined to escape further analysis. A rapid or sudden disappearance of symptoms may sometimes be the sign of a bad prognosis with regard to carrying the analysis to a satisfactory ending (cf. Freud, 1923d, p. 112f.; 1933a, p. 213).

strument of measurement is negligible for practical purposes, and it is therefore usually not considered; modifications of symptoms, however, are visible and significant, and they demand the attention of the analyst, and of both the patient and his environment. From the social or common-sense point of view, the relationship between symptom and treatment may seem to be the same, whether we are dealing with pneumonia and antibiotics or neurosis and psychoanalysis. Yet a logical analysis has shown that the two relationships are essentially different and that Freud was correct when he put the psychoanalytic situation into the category of scientific analysis. Two passages may be quoted here from a paper by Freud antedating the book on *Lay Analysis;* historically, they are stepping stones toward Freud's final formulation in the *Question of Lay Analysis.*

In the first of two articles for the *Handwörterbuch der Sexualwissenschaft,* Freud (1923b) compared the nonmedical application of psychoanalysis to the application of psychoanalysis in psychiatry: "It [psychoanalysis] is in a position to play a part of the same importance in the studies of religious and cultural history . . . as it is in psychiatry" (p. 252). Since psychiatry is unquestionably a medical specialty, Freud is clearly here referring to the area of the medical application of psychoanalysis.

A far more telling passage in this respect occurs earlier in the same article. Comparing psychoanalysis with hypnotic and suggestive treatment procedures, Freud writes as follows about psychoanalysis: "The removal of the symptoms of the illness is not specifically aimed at, but achieved as a by-product [*Nebengewinn*] if the analysis is properly carried through" (p. 251).

This sentence undoubtedly was not meant the way it may sound, when quoted out of context. Freud wrote it in illustration of a specific aspect of psychoanalysis as a treatment method, whereas I am referring to it in a context in which, according to my understanding of the logic of this science, treatment is the secondary or subordinate aspect of the psychoanalytic situation. Nevertheless, Freud's formulation here approaches the general conclusion which he drew in 1927, and it may therefore be regarded as a historical antecedent.

In support of my assertion that, logically, the psychoanalytic situation is not primarily a medical or treatment situation, more quotations from Freud's own writings could be referred to. Yet the significance of any such quotations is thrown into question by the fact that most experts in the field, despite their acknowledgement of Freud's contributions, believe that mental science has outgrown his theories.

A short digression may be permitted at this point concerning the orthodoxy or dogmatism of which that group of psychoanalysts is accused who by and large adhere to Freud's basic theories. The scientist's ambition and function are, we may agree, to make far-reaching discoveries. It is not surprising therefore that many talented people have tended to grow tired of "standing in the shadow of" Freud's genius (cf. Freud, 1914a, p. 51). Thus, new theories and techniques that are at bottom irreconcilable with Freud's psychoanalysis have been put forward by a considerable number of psychoanalysts Furthermore, there is a public which is always eager to hear something new, and will gratefully acclaim the innovator. There are also the students, who have observed in the course of their studies that a medical theory, more frequently than not, remains true for not much longer than two decades, and are inclined therefore to regard the latest published text as 'truer' than its predecessor. (This aside from the fact that, during a student's formative years, the transference potential is satisfied only through his belief that his own teacher is the best, and practically infallible.) All this makes it seem desirable— if prestige, success, and career are to be considered—to produce something that may impress the reader as 'going beyond Freud.'[11]

In view of these tendencies, which are quite pervasive in contemporary

---

[11] On the other hand, the desire not to go so far beyond as to lose one's claim to the title of analyst is also noticeable. I have recently come across a document which quite clearly illustrates both these trends. I refer to the program of the *Internationaler Kongress für Psychoanalyse und ihre Weiterentwicklung* (1961), arranged by the German Psychoanalytic Society (not to be confused with the German Psychoanalytic Association, which is a component Society of the International Psycho-Analytic Association). In it, all schools (Horney, Fromm, Sullivan, Alexander, Rado, Schultz-Hencke, Stekel) are called psychoanalytic "further developments" (*Weiterentwicklungen*). Empty phrases, such as that Freud's work is best appreciated when it "does not dogmatically congeal, but further develops vitally through new empirical results and insights [*nicht dogmatisch erstarrt, sondern sich durch neue empirische Ergebnisse und Erkenntnisse lebendig weiterentwickelt*]" thinly disguise an eclecticism that is lethal to any real advance of the science. How far this eclecticism goes can be seen from the fact that even existential analysis was not omitted from this hodgepodge. Are such expressions indications of a mental impotence or inner exhaustion that have arisen in our time in the psychological field?

The extent to which the poison of eclecticism and traditional sham arguments has spread, can be deduced from the stir which was evoked by Dr. Gitelson's (1962) timely and sober warning. I refer, for example, to an editorial signed by Drs. Rado, Grinker, and Alexander (1963), and Dr. Masserman's letter to the *International Journal of Psycho-Analysis* (Zetzel, 1963, pp. 384-386). The former is a mere repetition of hackneyed arguments, such as might impress those who are ignorant of the history of psychoanalysis in particular and of science in general; the latter is certainly original in its incivility, and at the same time remarkable for its exhortation to follow one of the principles adopted by the recent Ecumenical Council. Dr. Gitelson brilliantly discussed this whole range of problems in his presidential address to the Twenty-third Congress of the International Psycho-Analytic Association in Stockholm.

psychoanalytic research, there is little likelihood that an exposition of Freud's concept of the psychoanalytic situation along the lines presented here will change the reader's mind. I could introduce the argument that, in view of Freud's genius (which is not denied even by those analysts who disagree with many of his basic theories), and the fact that it was he who discovered analysis and established its basic structure and directions, he is likely to have known what would best ensure its further growth. This argument may—perhaps justifiably—be called specious.

I recognize that my argument may be further weakened when one considers the posthumous publication, the *Outline* (1940a), in which Freud presents psychoanalysis once again as a therapeutic discipline and does not at all speak of treatment as an application of psychoanalysis. It will be of interest, however, to examine the structure of that book.

It consists of three parts. The first was called by James Strachey "The Mind and its Working,"[12] the second, "The Practical Task," and the third, "The Theoretical Yield."

Parts one and three are pure psychology, and it is difficult to see how they could be brought either directly or indirectly into a meaningful medical context. One can see the possibility of such connection only in the middle part, which consists of two sections: "The Technique of Psychoanalysis" and "An Example of Psychoanalytic Work" (the larger part of which is also pure psychology). Our problem seems to hinge on the section on technique, which is written in terms of medical psychology, as when Freud (1940a, p. 62) sets forth his "plan of cure."

In my view, however, the first paragraph of this section greatly reduces the medical implications: "A dream . . . is a psychosis, with all the absurdities, delusions and illusions of a psychosis. No doubt it is a psychosis which has a short duration," etc. (p. 61).[13] This is a very radical statement (with which, by the way, many analysts do not agree[14]), and if it is true, then it tears down any wall that may exist between

[12] The actual title of this section in the German edition is "The Nature of the Psychic" (*Die Natur des Psychischen*), although this title was itself derived from another of Freud's manuscripts (cf. Freud, 1940b, p. 64).

[13] Freud's formulation in 1932, which is slightly different, is even more revealing. He wrote then that psychoanalysis reveals the dream, "as it were, as the normal psychosis of mankind" (Freud, 1932, p. 297). The original reads even more strongly: *die normale Psychose des Menschen* ("the normal human psychosis").

[14] When Freud (1924a) writes: "Now a dream is not a morbid symptom but a product of the normal mind" (p. 200), this should not be understood to be in contradiction with the above quotation. Cf. also Freud (1924e): "The close affinity of this psychosis [Meynert's amentia] to normal dreams is unmistakable" (p. 151). For a metapsychological differentiation, see Freud, 1917b, p. 229f.

psychopathology and normal system psychology. It demonstrates once more that the only road to normal psychology is through the study of the pathological. Freud expressed this concretely when, inquiring into the difference between neurosis and psychosis, he wrote: "We call behavior 'normal' or 'healthy,' if it combines certain features of both [neurotic and psychotic] reactions—if it disavows the reality as little as does neurosis, but if it then exerts itself, as does a psychosis, to effect an alteration of that reality" (Freud, 1924d, p. 185).[15]

In medicine, I believe, there would probably be general agreement that pathology and pathophysiology are the main portals to the understanding of normal physiology,[16] but I am not certain how many analysts would agree that the study of psychopathology is necessary to an understanding of psychological normalcy. (It is possible, of course, that the concept of 'normalcy' has no legitimate place in the science of man.[17]) Apparently human psychology cannot be investigated without involvement with what in present-day terminology is called 'sickness,' for the purely psychological facts with regard to the structure of the psychic apparatus that are contained in the major part of Freud's *Outline* were obtained, and can principally be obtained, only through the observation of diseased subjects.[18] To be sure, the section on technique in the *Outline* can for the most part be translated into terms that are free of medical implications, for the technique Freud proposes in the *Outline* is, as in the rest of his technical papers, one in which everything designed for the

[15] August Aichhorn looked upon 'normal' behavior as a mixture of neurosis and delinquency. I believe that a combination of these two propositions is in order, and that normal behavior will one day be understood as a composite of neurosis, psychosis, and delinquency.

[16] Deviations in general have two effects: (1) the abnormal, the deviated, the unusual, arouse man's thinking, while the normal, the accustomed, is merely taken for granted; (2) the inquiry into the disturbed and the deviated usually reveals the prerequisites for undisturbed functioning. The analysis of dreams—that is, of a disturbance of the state of sleep—has led to an understanding of the psychological prerequisites for sleep (Cf., e.g., Freud, 1925d, p. 44).

[17] The matter becomes immeasurably more complicated when we consider Freud's view of how the ego may become capable of avoiding illness (neuroses and psychosis). Freud (1924e) suggests that, among other ways, the ego may accomplish this "by deforming itself, by submitting to encroachments on its own unity, and even perhaps by effecting a cleavage or division of itself" (p. 152). Since Freud speaks here *expressis verbis* of "a new field of research," this would strongly suggest that, in addition to viewing normal behavior as a combination of types of pathological processes, he also favored an approach that could be called in its own right the 'psychopathology of normalcy.'

[18] And yet there is a passage in Freud's (1921) work that contains this reservation: "Equal care must be taken in this connection to avoid two sources of error—the Scylla of underestimating the importance of the repressed unconscious, and the Charybdis of judging the normal entirely by the standards of the pathological" (p. 138).

cure of patients is identical with what is designed for the purpose of increasing both the investigator's and the subject's knowledge. It is clear that the new viewpoint that Freud introduced in his defense of lay analysis, if carried to its logical end, would call for rather lengthy explanations and refined conceptual analyses. Yet the possibility of setting forth the psychoanalytic technique in psychological terms without medical implications does not negate the fact that Freud himself did not proceed in this way, but without compunction presented psychoanalytic technique in terms of medical psychology or therapy. Thus Freud appears not to have drawn any further consequences from his new systematization of 1927, and instead continued to write in his former vein, in which the psychoanalytic situation was a therapeutic one. Should one conclude from this that Freud changed his mind, that he purposely did not abide by the new viewpoint he had himself introduced? I do not believe so.

For expository purposes, the old procedure is, of course, the more suitable. Yet when conclusions are drawn which relate specifically to the alleged therapeutic implication, it is necessary to insist on an exact conceptual analysis.

To return to Freud's *Outline*, we should not forget that the middle part ("The Practical Task"), which seems to belong with medicine or therapy, is sandwiched between two other rather broad parts which are, in the main, psychology. Of the many citations that could be offered from the *Outline* in favor of equating psychoanalysis with psychology, I shall briefly discuss only two. The third part, in which Freud (1940a) returns to theory, begins: "All of the general views and assumptions which were brought forward in our first chapter were, of course, arrived at by laborious and patient detailed work of the sort of which we have given an example in the previous technical section. We may now feel tempted to make a survey of the increases in knowledge that we have achieved by work of this kind . . ." (p. 103). Here therapy would seem to be presented as an unavoidable detour on the road toward the single goal of investigating the structure of the psychic apparatus. And further: "We have found that it is not scientifically feasible to draw a line of demarcation between what is psychologically normal and abnormal; so that that distinction, in spite of its practical importance, possesses only a conventional value. We have thus established our right to arrive at an understanding of the normal life of the mind by studying its disorders—which would not be admissible if these pathological states, neuroses and psychoses, had specific causes, operating like foreign bodies" (p. 104).

Indeed, not only do we find expressed here the claim of psychoanalysis to share the field of psychology with normal psychology; psychoanalysis seems to be put forward as the only road to normal psychology. I do not think that Freud changed his mind about the new systematization of psychoanalysis which he had briefly suggested in 1927.[19]

At this point, the reader will wish to know more about medically applied psychoanalysis. By scientific psychoanalysis, Freud meant the psychoanalytic situation of classical analysis; that can scarcely be doubted. But what is the social locus of medically applied psychoanalysis? Who practices it, and what form does it take?

To avoid any misunderstanding it must be stated at once that medically applied psychoanalysis may, of course, also have scientific value; the two concepts are not opposed. If a physician prescribes an aspirin for a patient suffering from a cold and makes sure that the patient feels better after a few hours (the whole procedure is a mere triviality in medical practice), that may be described as a crude scientific experiment: the physician has confirmed the beneficial effect of aspirin on upper respiratory infections. In this instance the scientific gain is negligible: a crude observation of everyday life has been confirmed, but it still remains unknown whether the symptom would have subsided without the aspirin, or whether other factors, such as the suggestive power of pharmaca, have played a role in bringing about the improvement. Whatever the area of medically applied psychoanalysis may be, the scientific gain in terms of insight into the structure of the personality will be smaller when compared with the results of psychoanalysis proper, as may be expected, in the light of the fact that one situation is totally structured toward establishing true-false values and toward extending the range of insight, while the primary aim of the other is the patient's recovery.

---

[19] On the other hand, if they are taken literally, Freud's remarks about psychoanalytic therapy in his *New Lectures* may also be adduced against my position. Of course, in a series of lectures intended for students at a medical school, he would have had to discuss the therapeutic concept of psychoanalysis, which persists at the societal level whatever the result of logical analysis may be. But what does Freud really say about therapy, at least in the introductory paragraph? Psychoanalysis *"originated* as a therapeutic procedure"; "it has gone far *beyond* that"; "it has never given up its native soil [*Mutterboden*]"; "it *still* relies upon contact with *clinical* material"; "empirical data upon which we base our theories can be obtained in no *other* way"; therapeutic *failures* set new tasks; clinical reality protects against *excesses of speculation* (see Freud 1933a, p. 207, italics mine). It seems to me no exaggeration to say that Freud almost apologizes here for referring to psychoanalysis as a therapy, as if he felt obliged to explain why psychoanalysis, despite the maturity it has gained, still appears to be clinging, as it were, to its origins.

Before we proceed, however, a point of terminology must be introduced here. For the sake of brevity, in the next section I shall call an analyst who is primarily interested in and motivated by the therapeutic intent, and who therefore looks at the psychoanalytic situation as belonging to a medical specialty, a "medical analyst."[20] This means something quite different from a medically trained analyst, who may or may not become a medical analyst. Although it may sound paradoxical, in accordance with this terminology, a lay analyst also becomes a medical analyst, when he accepts the view of psychoanalysis which this term denotes. In the following section, I shall be dealing with the problems of 'medical analysis,' in the sense just indicated.

[20] Freud (1926a, p. 232) uses the term "medical analyst" occasionally.

5

Polemics

Polemics are likely to prove somewhat unpleasant, even under optimal conditions. They express opposition, and they arouse opposition; they cannot be carried on effectively without hurting someone's feelings. Often they convey the impression that the person conducting them is prejudiced, or has an ax to grind, or is acting in response to some purely personal motive. I shall spend little time here examining the degree to which such factors are involved in what I have to say, nor shall I defend myself in that respect. I wish merely to make a general apology in advance for whatever unpleasantness I may cause.

As will be seen, I believe that serious consequences have already followed from the way in which psychoanalysis is organized in this country. Although I am aware that I may be attaching too great an importance to this situation—in the sense that perhaps matters would not be greatly different even if Freud's fundamental position had been adopted with regard to lay analysis—I shall go ahead nevertheless, since I believe that the restrictions upon psychoanalysis which now obtain in this country are harmful in several respects, and I regard the situation as sufficiently grave to override any questions of personal comfort.

I might have called this chapter (tongue in cheek, perhaps) "The

Application of Psychoanalysis to Medicine." It seems wiser to identify it from the start as what it is: a polemic against the organization of psychoanalysis as a medical specialty—or worse still, as a subdivision of psychiatry. In no other country has the representative psychoanalytic association committed itself so solidly and irrevocably as in the United States in favor of medically applied psychoanalysis. While the mode of organization of a science never completely determines the mode of its future development, it does favor one or another trend. In what follows, my purpose is to bring to light and to characterize certain trends that, I believe, are undeniably at work in psychoanalysis in the United States and will manifest themselves even more conspicuously in the future.

In order to make such a prediction, it may be necessary to cast a glance back to the past. Fortunately, the history of psychoanalysis in this country has been written by a writer-psychoanalyst who knows every nook and cranny of it, since he has been one of its principal participants, and is thus not only a writer of that history, but in part also its maker.

There is no doubt, according to Oberndorf, that psychoanalysis has now become a branch of psychiatry in this country. Proud of that fact, he writes in praise of the process by which it occurred, although occasionally a note of reservation creeps in:

> Psychoanalysis had finally become legitimate and respectable, perhaps paying the price in becoming sluggish and snug, hence attractive to an increasing number of minds which find security in conformity [Oberndorf, 1953, p. 207].

Yet, only forty pages later, the question of becoming "legitimate" and "respectable" is forgotten, and it is the 'victory' over Freudian dogmatism that is regarded as responsible for the good fortune of psychoanalysis in this country. Then Oberndorf (1953) writes:

> American psychiatrists refused to be stifled by theoretical dogma or prescribed rules of technique, but instead boldly adapted the powerful implement of psychoanalysis in the advancement of social and medical ideals. They did not feel at all uncomfortable in their neglect of scholarly considerations when as pragmatists they favored that which endures because it is serviceable [p. 247].

One must indeed be grateful to the author for setting forth, of his own volition and without any inhibition, such self-revealing comments as the two just quoted. Their spirit is in direct contradiction to the spirit of science.

It is precisely in becoming "sluggish and snug" that science *throws away* its claim to being a "legitimate and respectable" area of human endeavor. Oberndorf's view of the matter—which proceeds in the opposite direction and produces the opposite conclusion—is not merely false, it is altogether topsy-turvy. And after such reasoning, to speak of "boldly adapting" psychoanalysis—and of doing so in the teeth of "theoretical dogma" and "prescribed rules of technique"—that is boldness indeed, but not on the side of reason!

One reads with a similar sense of uneasiness Oberndorf's paeans to "security in conformity," or the apparently needless words of comfort he holds out to those who, by his own account, "did not feel at all uncomfortable in their neglect of scholarly considerations." When the "pragmatists" lie down in the "attractive security" of the "serviceable," science lies down with them—on its death-bed.[1] This inversion of values is made complete when Oberndorf calls this attitude "liberalism," and asserts that it is because of it that "the American Psychoanalytic Association has grown to be a strong and powerful and even formidable force in American psychiatric education . . ." (p. 247).

I have put these trenchant statements by Oberndorf right at the beginning of my polemics, since they confirm the fears which Freud harbored as to what would happen when psychoanalysis became the handmaiden of psychiatry. Further, they free me of the need to prove what the approach toward psychoanalysis has been among some of those leading analysts who have been the most active spokesmen for medical analysis.

One cannot help raising similar criticism upon reading Hendrick's Presidential Address of 1955. One regrets his not having heeded Charles Dickens' advice—quoted by Oberndorf (1953, p. 247), when he was praising American pragmatism—to love "the Real less, and the Ideal somewhat more." There is a tone of pride, almost of boastfulness in Hendrick, even stronger than that which we have already met in Oberndorf's eulogy. Indeed, if the plight of European analysis and the low esteem it has won from medicine and community alike are compared with the fabulous rise of psychoanalysis in this country, one is inescapably reminded of those tales of the last century in which the ne'er-do-

[1] Cf. Hendrick (1955), speaking against those few members of the American Psychoanalytic Association who trained lay analysts: "Expediency is always a poor excuse, and in important affairs it works only temporarily." (p. 583f.)

well scion is shipped to this country, where, so the fable went, he becomes a millionaire.

As a matter of fact, there is probably no other country in which psychoanalysis could have become to the same degree 'the brand that (ostensibly, at least) dominates the market.' Under present conditions, a physician who wants to be a successful psychotherapist will have to claim, in most instances—whatever method of psychotherapy he may actually employ—that he 'psychoanalyzes' his patients. Hence it is not surprising that Dr. Hendrick's Presidential Address sounds at times—if I may continue the market metaphor—like the Board of Directors' report on some sprawling industrial combine. The flourishing of the Association is demonstrated quantitatively by the large number of Institutes, and the ever-increasing number of members. We are not even deprived of the customary encouraging forecast of growth, which in this instance looks to membership "growing by geometrical rather than arithmetical progression" (Hendrick, 1955, p. 562).

At this point, however, it becomes necessary to raise the question of whether the term psychoanalysis always signifies the same thing when it is used by different persons. What is Oberndorf's concept of psychoanalysis, for example? Let us take as a paradigm his first private patient, of whom he says that she was "treated strictly by psychoanalysis." The patient was a woman of thirty-five, who suffered from visual hallucinations. "She was treated in sessions of an hour twice a week from July 1909 to June 1910 and continued to consult me about once a month from 1912 to 1915." Oberndorf considered the result of the treatment "a transference cure which, however, has persisted for over forty years" (Oberndorf, 1953, p. 106). If the seriousness of the patient's symptoms is taken into account, this must be regarded as an impressive success, especially in view of the fact that the analysis was conducted by a beginner.

I was curious about the technique used, however, particularly because of the small number of interviews. The case was used by Oberndorf (1948) in his book, *Which Way Out*, as a basis for one of the fictional stories ("Christmas Card"); and from that account, I got the impression that Oberndorf's technique was not that used in psychoanalysis, but was comparable instead to the quasi cathartic method which Freud had used in the case of Katharina (Breuer and Freud, 1895, pp. 125-134). However, I was even more surprised when I went back to the original case report (Oberndorf, 1912), where, to my amazement, I was informed by Oberndorf himself that he had used a technique which must be described as both *anti*cathartic and *anti*psychoanalytic.

The patient had had a lover; while their relationship had by that time been discontinued, her longing for him persisted. Oberndorf considered it "a duty, if possible, to restore her interests to her home and family, which was attempted through long conferences in which the entire situation was minutely discussed, and later through suggestions in the hypnoidal state. Thus I was able to gradually produce a marked aversion for her lover" (Oberndorf, 1912, p. 445).

From this account it is evident that, by suggestion, feelings of aversion were artificially created in the patient with the intention of reducing the intensity with which the patient's conflict would manifest itself in a certain social area. "Complete aversion for her [the patient's] lover has been engendered notwithstanding his continued proximity," wrote Oberndorf (1912, p. 447) in another passage. It is quite understandable that the patient herself summarized the outcome by saying that her " 'troubles have been replaced by a cold, clear sadness' " (p. 448).

It is puzzling, to say the least, why Oberndorf, forty-three years after he had performed this mutilating operation, should still insist that the patient had been treated "strictly by psychoanalysis." Certainly no common denominator can be found between this and the work of Freud, and one cannot protest sufficiently strongly against connecting such regrettable incidents with psychoanalysis in any other way than by contrast. Instead, the ethics and rationale of this procedure must be uncompromisingly rejected.

I have gone into the details of this case report—which, in fact, holds only a subordinate place in Oberndorf's *History*—because it is indicative of what a physician may turn psychoanalysis into when he is motivated solely by the therapeutic intent. There is another publication about which a similar comment can be made, although its position is not quite as aberrant as Oberndorf's. I am referring to *Psychoanalytic Therapy: Principles and Application* by Alexander and French (1946).

Here we are no longer dealing with a single incident of which one may say, perhaps, that it was exceptional. This is the product the staff of a whole institute of national stature—the Chicago Institute for Psychoanalysis—published under the names of leading medical analysts, and the outcome of a process of planning, deliberation and discussion that must have spanned several years. Furthermore, the technique devised was not designed as an emergency measure, to be employed in a difficult clinical situation on otherwise intractable symptoms; it is put forward as a "standard" technique, to be replaced only under special circumstances with the technique worked out by Freud.[2]

The authors propagate a technique in which insight is assigned a secondary role and its utilization reduced to a minimum. Treatment is constructed in such a way that the therapeutic process is reduced to "correctional emotional experiences." The reorganization of the personality—if that can be achieved by this method at all—is entrusted to experiences created within the patient's relationship to the physician, of a sort that had been missing in the patient's upbringing or past. Apparently a formula well known from magic procedures furnished the foundation of this approach: since it was emotions that made the patient sick, emotions shall cure him.

Thus, for example, if the patient had a harsh father who always berated him, the therapist was to be very friendly and express admiration for him. Or, if the patient becomes, in the therapist's estimation, too dependent, the therapist will not do what the "orthodox" psychoanalyst would try to do: get to the bottom of this dependency by demonstrating to the patient the repetitive elements, the preceding infantile pattern, the function it serves in the present situation, and many such aspects; instead, he will decrease the number of therapeutic meetings in the hope that, through this restriction of support, the patient will, so to speak, be forced to 'come to his senses.' To point to one outgrowth of this technique, I may cite briefly the instance of an "intensely depressed" patient, a refugee physician, whose "successful" treatment consisted of one meeting with the therapist, in the course of which some repressed unfriendly feelings against his wife and son were brought to light, the whole treatment culminating in the advice to have an office outside his home (Grotjahn, in Alexander and French, 1946, pp. 155-157).[3]

[2] It should be recorded that a strange silence has developed in Chicago about the principles for which this book stands; some even claim that the clinical use of this technique was so short-lived that it is no longer existent. Still it is reasonable to ask how psychoanalysis could ever have fallen victim to such bizarre aberrations as can be found in this publication.

[3] This single instance makes one wonder how Alexander could, a decade later, claim that "no reader of the case reports published in *Psychoanalytic Therapy* can justly maintain that the significance and role of interpretations were overlooked, or minimized by the authors" (Alexander, 1956, p. 142). Furthermore, Alexander writes occasionally as if he believed that the majority of analysts think that the emotional experiences related to the psychoanalytic process are of no concern or relevance. It is significant, however, that he cannot agree with Bibring when the latter asserts that the various tools employed in psychoanalysis form "a hierarchical structure, in that insight through interpretation

It is not my intention here to speak either for or against the clinical value of such therapeutic procedures; but when the authors assert that this technique will be the legitimate successor to the classical psychoanalytic technique as developed by Freud, when with enviable modesty it is proclaimed that, with the formulation of this technique, the next phase of psychoanalytic treatment, logically evolved out of the previous stages, is already opening, then one must object and say bluntly that, whatever the merits of the technique may be, such statements merely testify to a basic misunderstanding of what psychoanalysis is.

In all mental output, one can find a reflection of "the spirit of the times," such as will either favor or obstruct research (Boring, 1955), and in the publication of the Chicago Institute, such an impeding spirit can be seen clearly. The deprecation of insight in favor of emotional factors; the belief in the adage, "Nothing succeeds like success" (Alexander, French, et al., 1946, p. 40)—such characteristics warrant our making an assured connection with what is happening on a broader scale. The fact that such distasteful features of our era are made basic to the new technique is sufficient ground for a rather skeptical attitude, even when the question of standards of psychoanalytic technique is left out of consideration.

It is quite significant that, for however short a time, the originators of this technique were able to regard it as legitimate psychoanalysis. It can be properly classified, in my opinion, only as an attempt at the *application of psychoanalysis to medicine*. Without Freud's discoveries, to be sure, the text could never have been written; but that is the only tie to psychoanalysis that I can discover. Otherwise, the authors appear to be trying (quite in conformity with the principles of medical practice)

---

is the principal agent and all others are—theoretically and practically—subordinate to it" (Bibring, 1954, p. 762).

In his later writings, Alexander has become a little more sophisticated than he was in 1946, but by and large he still follows his initial trend. A new argument which strikes me as particularly odd, but most revealing of the medical analyst, is Alexander's assertion that he sees in the insistence of some analysts that the psychoanalytic method is essentially and significantly different from other psychotherapeutic techniques, an expression of their practical fight to retain their identity (Alexander, 1956, p. 153). Yet he seems to be quite certain that "in their actual practice, however, all psychiatrists [I assume that Alexander means their techniques] become more and more similar, even though one may practice pure psychoanalysis and the other psychoanalytically oriented psychotherapy" (Alexander, 1954, p. 725).

This is an error, I believe, even with regard to those analysts who have been trained according to the principles of "corrective emotional experiences." For a critical observation on the consequences of this technique, see Greenacre (1956, p. 440). For further comments, see Appendix I.

to eliminate everything that stands in the way of performing treatment *cito, tuto, jucunde*—an aim which, because of the structure of the mind, can never be legitimately attained within the framework of psychoanalytic therapy (Freud 1926b, p. 264).

Advances in psychoanalytic technique per se can be measured only in terms of deepening insight into the structure of the mental processes. Anna Freud's book, *The Ego and the Mechanisms of Defense* (1936), brought about just such an advance in psychoanalytic technique, and it would be altogether wrong therefore to call it an application of psychoanalysis. The proposed technique, rather than having the effect of cutting off further pathways of exploration, *enlarges* our insight into the processes taking place within the personality. Through the deepened analysis of the defenses, classical psychoanalysis has been organically advanced, the operational area of psychoanalysis has been extended, the ego can be subjected to a more thorough scrutiny than before. In short, a depth of structural change is now made possible by this research, such as previously lay beyond the range of the psychoanalytic orbit.

The two examples I have chosen must be called applications of psychoanalysis to medicine, even though the authors themselves presented them as *bona fide* analysis. They were not the work of 'outsiders'; they come from leading analysts with a national and even an international reputation. Since they involve such outstanding figures in American psychoanalysis, one may well ask how many of their disciples have also been imbued with that same false spirit, and have also evolved ideas which, if accepted, can only lead to the degeneration of psychoanalytic technique.[4]

---

[4] Recently, the Chicago tradition gave birth to a document in which we see what is probably the acme of distorted psychoanalytic technique (Grotjahn, 1960). It takes hold of a clinically correct observation—namely, that individual psychopathology is, in many (perhaps even in most) instances, deeply embedded in the unconscious of the members of the group among whom the subject has been growing up and/or living; but it uses this truth to produce a basic distortion of *bona fide* psychoanalytic technique. If one wished to study the correct technique for handling the "family neurosis," one would do well to turn to some papers by August Aichhorn (whose work, by the way, is not even mentioned by Grotjahn). There one would find the thinking of a great clinician who, even though he had not been trained in medicine, was so well endowed with clinical experience and insight that he was able to decide where the psychoanalytic technique could properly be used as such, and where it had to be modified—that is, he was able, as the occasion demanded, to distinguish between *psychoanalysis* and *its application*. In Aichhorn's writings one can see also how much can be achieved by way of clinical tact and acumen, without the analyst's having to fall into the wildest sort of acting out, or the use of needless (and dangerous) histrionics (see Aichhorn, 1936, 1947).

We shall have more to say later about the aversion that we have already noted to a technique based on interpretation, insight, and reconstruction. At this point, we wish to lay stress on the not infrequent practice of equating the *disappearance* of a symptom, as the result of whatever psychotherapeutic means, with a *cure* brought about by psychoanalysis.[5]

It now becomes necessary to examine the relationship between psychoanalysis and psychiatry prevailing in this country. It is sometimes described as symbiotic. Hendrick (1955, p. 581), for example, reminds us that the older generation of psychiatrists had a sympathetic view toward psychoanalysis and even assisted in cementing the beginnings of the organization. In turn, they became "our teachers, who developed during the first quarter of this century in a few Eastern clinics a new approach to psychotics in particular and to psychiatry in general." The future historian may discover in this so-called "new approach" the effects of Freud's early work, or of that of Burghoelzli, (Jung, 1907). Yet, be that as it may, the schism between psychiatry and psychoanalysis has been less deep-going in this country than in Europe.

The relationship between the two was not quite as smooth as one may gather from Hendrick's (1955) brief remark, and a great deal of resistance had to be battered down before psychoanalysis could become "*a basic science of psychiatry*" (p. 568, italics by Hendrick). I assume that most psychiatrists and psychoanalysts would agree that "psychoanalytic theory provides the conceptual core of dynamic psychiatry," or that it is "the heart of contemporary dynamic psychiatry" (Bandler, 1960, p. 91f.). Yet upon closer scrutiny, one discovers that this is a bloodless heart, without septum, sinuses, or valve—no more than a crude muscular tube.

Before hailing modern dynamic psychiatry and its psychoanalytic 'core' and 'heart,' therefore, one has to make up his mind about the value of half-truths. To be sure, one can find conspicuous traces of psychoanalysis in dynamic psychiatry, but the absences or omissions are equally conspicuous. Dynamic psychiatry is psychoanalysis trimmed to order, to fit crude clinical requirements. If a long view is taken, it is of question-

[5] One of the most revealing statements in this regard can be found among the answers to a questionnaire that Alexander sent out to leading psychiatrists and psychoanalysts: "I think that the only difference between psychoanalysis and what is done in all clinics, is that in the clinics patients are seen sitting up and rarely over twice a week. There is no longer any substantive difference between analysis and 'psychotherapy'—there is only good and bad analysis, and analysis practiced by graduates of institutes and by those who are not" (Leon J. Saul, in Alexander, 1956, p. 255). This, if further proof were necessary, would demonstrate the profoundly distorted conception of psychoanalysis held by the medical analyst.

able value, and, if its teachings are measured against what is actually known about the human personality, it is incomplete and, by virtue of this very incompleteness, wrong (cf. Gitelson, 1951).

Just as psychoanalysis has not fared very well with its new host, dynamic psychiatry, living as it does a starved and stunted existence there, so psychiatry in turn has not fared so well in the domain of the medical analyst. It was certainly never Freud's intention that psychoanalysis should replace psychiatry. "Psycho-analysis," he wrote "is related to psychiatry approximately as histology is to anatomy" (Freud, 1916-1917, p. 254f.); since, in Central Europe, anatomy played the largest role among the preclinical subjects, he was obviously attributing to classical psychiatry no minor position.

The absence of the teaching of classical psychiatry in this country is quite regrettable. Students are immediately introduced into highly debatable intricacies of depth psychology without having had any preparatory courses in psychopathology. What a delusion or a hallucination is—in fact, the whole of descriptive psychiatry—is all but eliminated. The consequent low level of diagnostic standards, which permits a diagnosis of schizophrenia for any patient who shows even mildly bizarre symptoms; the vanishing ability to conduct an adequate psychiatric interview, or to write a sensible psychiatric case report—such things cannot be discussed here, but they must be mentioned, if only in passing.

Thus the present 'union' between psychiatry and psychoanalysis is not necessarily as advantageous in both directions, no matter how it may seem to the analyst who is interested primarily in the application of psychoanalysis to medicine.

One immediate consequence of the union is a shift in the direction of responsibility. At least some of the leading psychoanalysts seem to feel a degree of responsibility to psychiatry that almost goes beyond their sense of responsibility to psychoanalysis proper. At any rate, that is the impression one might easily get from the study of another Presidential Address, in which Bandler (1960) stresses the lack of leadership of the American Psychoanalytic Association, "in respect to research, to advanced studies, and to the development of psychoanalysis as a science" (p. 390). In the educational field, however, matters appear to be quite different, for in this area the Association *has* taken leadership. Thus, Bandler speaks emphatically of the "obligation to psychiatry, to residents in psychiatric training" (p. 400)—obligations which, in his opinion, the Association is now shouldering. He warns against a predominant interest in education, however, and takes note of "the burning ambition of our students . . . to become training analysts *rather than contributors to the science of psychoanalysis*" (p. 390; italics mine.)

In a recent article by Jack A. Chambers (1964) on "Creative Scientists of Today," we read:

> . . . the less creative scientists are predominantly concerned with opportunities to combine teaching and administrative duties with research, while the overwhelming choice for the creative scientist is the opportunity to do really creative research. . . ."

Hendrick (1955) speaks even more clearly:

> What was so recently a small profession, the very special interest of a few individuals in the deepest possible exploration of unconscious fantasies and memory traces, has become in the last ten years a large profession, composed predominantly of younger psychoanalysts who devote an important fraction of their time to the applications of analysis to psychotherapy, psychosomatic medicine, and even to fields so far from depth exploration, at least as usually practiced, as group therapy, "community psychiatry" and "preventive psychiatry.". . . Our earlier responsibility was for ensuring adequate preparation of candidates for the treatment of patients by analysis, and for the scientific exploration of the unconscious. . . . We have now also responsibility to other professional groups . . . (p. 588f.).

As with Oberndorf earlier, here we find an explicit statement of the spirit that truly moves the leadership. When the predominant type of psychoanalyst is knowingly devoting an important part of his work to nonanalytic activities, the growth of psychoanalysis as a science is in danger. I am in agreement with Hendrick's (1955) enthusiasm when he refers in his address to "this tropical proliferation of the psychoanalytic jungle" (p. 588); but a 'jungle,' I must remind him, is wild and impenetrable vegetation that, for human ends, must be cleared and replaced with orderly cultivation.

The psychoanalytic profession does not, I believe, bear up well under a plurality of loyalties. If penetration into the unknown territories of the human mind by the psychoanalytic method cannot absorb the whole interest of the explorer, that in itself is a bad sign with regard to his contribution to psychoanalysis. It is hardly likely that such an analyst has ever truly felt the delight—one must even say transport—that is concomitant with the practice of Freud's psychoanalysis; nor has he probably ever experienced the thrill of discovery that comes with seeing the most characteristic facets of a human personality arise out of the debris of the subject's initial and restricted self-knowledge. If, having actually had such opportunities to satisfy (in the most ingenious way that man has ever devised) the profound curiosity that man has about man, he is then ready to turn over an important part of his time consistently to group therapy, counseling, or other diversions, then one can only conclude that, in his own practice, he has not truly integrated the techniques of psychoanalysis, which still remain, as it were, foreign bodies within his intellectual and professional metabolism.

Not that the activities I have mentioned are of no *social* relevance. From the community viewpoint, it may be a wholly praiseworthy undertaking to evolve new techniques of therapy along psychoanalytic lines, even if these should be of only questionable value when measured in psychoanalytic terms; nevertheless, it is a loss to psychoanalysis when the analyst concerns himself with other techniques and other areas, for then his own psychoanalytic technique is more than likely to degenerate. I gladly take note of exceptions to this rule; yet I have found, too, that those who are well known for their proficiency in true psychoanalysis usually turn out to be rather poor psychotherapists, and are really not proficient in any professional activity outside of the classical psychoanalytic situation. Here is a paragraph from one of Freud's lectures, which the analyst might well put up on his office wall, as some physicians do with the Hippocratic Oath:

> The practice of psychoanalysis is difficult and exacting! It cannot well be dealt with like a pair of spectacles, which can be put on for reading and taken off when one wants to go for a walk. As a rule, psycho-analysis either possesses the doctor entirely or not at all. The psychotherapists who occasionally make use of analysis, do not, as far as my experience goes, stand on a firm analytical basis. They have not accepted analysis as a whole, but have watered it down, and perhaps removed its 'sting'; they cannot be counted as analysts [Freud, 1933a, p. 209].

The ease with which some analysts forsake part of their analytic practice in favor of applications stems in part from the demands that the community puts upon them; but it also stems from the burden of the psychoanalytic situation itself. It is my belief that to conduct analysis in such a way as to conform with the spirit pervading Freud's work, is one of the most difficult of tasks, and that most of the techniques with which innovators try to replace Freud's, offer as their chief advantage the fact that they are very much easier to handle. If the disagreements about technique between the 'orthodox' school and other groups are examined closely, one will find that each of the latter takes issue with—advises against—some part of the classical technique. All of them, therefore, as far as I can see, are advising against the full reconstruction that Freud made the goal of psychoanalysis, and which is undeniably the most difficult aspect of the technique that Freud evolved.[6]

Since the pleasure principle is active in all of us not only after our working hours, but also during them, it is not surprising that the intensive and prolonged labor required in order to penetrate to the archaic matrix out of which the adult personality arose, is too great for most. However, if that type of analyst should prevail in the psychoanalytic organization, for whom the psychoanalytic situation is a secondary aspect of his daily schedule, or who believes that "a genetic reconstruction of the past is less important for the patient than for the physician" (Alexander and French, 1946, p. 22)—under such circumstances, the whole level of the organization would, inevitably, decline gradually and, by imperceptible but relentlessly accumulating changes, the logical development of psychoanalytic science would be diverted into false and dangerous directions.

There is an important lesson to be learned from the present situation of psychoanalysis in this country. The psychoanalytic organization has flourished under the leadership of men who have been primarily interested in the therapeutic aspect of psychoanalysis, and have concentrated their efforts on accomplishing a task which by rights should have been assigned to psychiatry. In order to carry out its functions as a part of psychiatry, the new science had to be organized from the beginning as a medical specialty. In fact, as we have seen, that was also the shortest road to respectability.

One of the consequences of this reduction of psychoanalysis has actually been a conspicuous accumulation of power in the national association. Hendrick (1955) states, for example: "Our success . . . , hugely magnified by our growth in numbers and by the esteem of other medical groups, has given us unsought and unexpected powers, the equivalent of powers of faculty appointment, selection of students, and the curricu-

[6] More will be said about this point later (Chapter 8), when I discuss the relationship between psychoanalysis and the universities.

lum policies of universities, and the powers of accreditation of specialty groups by Boards recognized by the A.M.A." (p. 589). After reading this declaration, one is reminded of those bitter words of a great British historian about the consequences of power and of absolute power, for it is clearly of absolute power that Hendrick is speaking.

Yet the reader may assert that the turn from research to education, the preoccupation with serviceability and therapy, and the corresponding neglect of psychoanalysis as a research instrument in systemic psychology, all sprang from far deeper sources than seem to be suggested here, and are therefore essentially unconnected with the question of lay analysis. Is it not true that an undetermined number of medically trained psychoanalysts, perhaps even the majority of the Association's membership, did not go along with this development, but stuck to their guns and focused their endeavors—in many instances brilliantly—upon the furtherance of science?

No doubt such an objection is correct. I have already drawn a strict distinction between medically trained analysts and medical analysts. After completing his medical training, an analyst may, of course, develop—and many do—into a strict scientist of systemic psychology, with a proper balance between his scientific and therapeutic attitudes. On the other hand, he may become a medical analyst, interested solely in the therapy of symptoms, and therefore without any concern for the maintenance and development of psychoanalytic standards. There is no strict correlation between the kind of preanalytic training that he has had and his later position with regard to psychoanalysis. It is in that same sense, as I have noted above, that even a lay analyst may develop into a medical analyst. I could cite, for example, the extreme biologism of the English school, whose founder was a lay analyst, yet whose theories were such as one might perhaps have expected from a mind that had suffered the strait-jacket training of a medical school with a rigid biological orientation.

The individual mind may, of course, be able to curb the immediate effects of anything so fortuitous in its own development as four years of training; what I am referring to here is a *statistical* effect, which may ultimately impose on American psychoanalysis an even more specifically medical character than it has now. Merely because the effect of preanalytic training in medicine may, in some individual instances, be neutral with regard to determining the character of the analyst's later orientation, the consequences of the *enforcement* of medical training should not be underestimated, as far as the final trends within a whole group are concerned.

On the other hand, if four years of medical training do not necessarily have a decisive bearing per se upon the psychoanalytic potentialities of the analyst, neither does their absence necessarily curtail them. This is well known to even as stern an opponent of lay analysis as Hendrick. He freely admits that few would deny "the proven competence, even greatness, of individual laymen, not only to understand and embrace our science, but to serve patients and students preeminently as their therapeutic or training analysts" (Hendrick, 1955, p. 580). I do not know upon how many of his medical colleagues Hendrick could bestow similar unqualified praise; therefore we do not need to add a single word about the suitability and propriety and justification of lay analysis. But when he limits this praise to "gifted laymen in Freud's days," is he in all seriousness affirming that such a vintage could grow only on the soil of Europe, and only in bygone days? Is there any shadow of a doubt that this country can, at present, produce an equal competence and greatness in the realm of lay analysis?

Yet Hendrick would deny membership and equivalent rights in the Association to any lay analyst, whatever his skills and talents, merely on the ground that he does not possess a medical diploma. And this, even though Hendrick is apparently not so certain of the merits of the American development of psychoanalysis, as he shows, for example, when he states: "Possibly psychoanalysis would have evolved more significantly, have been a greater scientific contribution of more value to our civilization, if from its inception in this country it had, as in England, not been preeminently a profession of doctors." To be sure, he adds: "It is conceivable; I do not think so, but I do not know" (Hendrick, 1955, p. 580).

I respect this admission of uncertainty; but I cannot help wondering how those who now unhesitatingly oppose and seek to curtail lay analysis will feel, should it turn out that they were wrong. Science is the cornerstone of our society, and whoever impedes its growth in any way whatsoever commits an unpardonable offense both against it and against human society. On this, we shall have more to say later.

Yet I wonder why, despite his own admission of the possibility of error, Hendrick was able—and content—to find "no suitable occasion for re-arguing the tattered dialectics of the *lay analysis problem*" (Hendrick, 1955, p. 580, italics Hendrick's). Was it not unbecoming, to say the least, to use pejorative language on a matter that Freud considered decisive for the future of his life work? And why so deprecatory an attitude toward a problem which may, as he himself says, have found the wrong solution in this country? Certainly, there is no doubt that American psychoanalysis will continue along the course that it has taken, and it may be that the President was tired of the prospect of having to turn once again to lay analysis in his address. Yet this should not call for contempt.

When Hendrick discussed "the principle of unauthorized training" (an ominous misnomer), which forbids members to do any training in psychoanalysis outside of the accredited institutes, he used harsh words for those who were 'guilty' of having trained lay analysts.[7] He called them "over-individualized individualists" and spoke of them as being "without shame." This is strong language, indeed, and in my opinion wholly out of proportion to the actual situation. I am certain that Hendrick did not really suspect base motives in those members who thought the plight of lay analysts grievous enough to warrant overriding the statute. Such action has perhaps had its precedents in the past, as the speaker himself may have inadvertently admitted when he recalled the events of 1930 in which he and three others, "recently returned from the Berlin and Vienna Institutes, set up a seminar . . . and pursued control analyses and didactic discussion" (Hendrick, 1955, p. 565f.). I very seriously doubt that the constitution of the Boston Psychoanalytic Society, which was in force at that time, gave him or his colleagues the power to do so.[8]

It is instructive to note that Hendrick did not feel contrite about such overstepping of bounds a quarter of a century later—perhaps because, as it turned out, he was extremely successful in his willfulness, and "by the fall of 1931 older members of the Boston Society had accepted our new idea of standards for training and membership" (Hendrick, 1955, p. 566). Such success is now out of the question for those who are idealis-

[7] Fromm-Reichmann (1956) has suggested that, in view of the impossibility of suppressing lay analysis, steps should be undertaken to select lay analysts more carefully and to provide adequate training for them, "instead of fighting their existence" (p. 257).

[8] The detailed history of the Boston Psychoanalytic Institute was recently published. However, it does not become clear from that publication to what extent "the Freud Seminar" (Hendrick, 1961, pp. 2-4) violated the constitution of the Society. No doubt the principles of the four members who initiated the seminar were sound and their actions did prove highly productive in the course of time. Thus the history of this "seminar" may show how necessary and beneficial bold action can be, even at those times when such action does not remain within the bounds set by a Society's statutes.

tic enough to bear the odium of fighting for lay analysis through practical action. Yet, I fear that Hendrick has become the victim of a belief which he did not regard so highly thirty years ago, and against the pernicious effects of which a good many sociologists and historians have long warned, but in vain—namely, that a majority vote, simply because it is a majority vote, is always on the side of what is right. What does surprise me is the intensity of the President's emotion about a 'dead' issue which, as he said himself, has no practical relevance, since there is only a negligible minority interested in it.

6

The Relation of the Biological and Anthropic
Sciences to Psychoanalysis

In this chapter I shall discuss the interrelationships between psycho-analysis and some selected sciences. This will give me the opportunity to elaborate on a key problem, the bearing of medical knowledge on the practice of psychoanalysis. I shall introduce this section with a comment on psychosomatic medicine, which has contributed so greatly to the medical aspect of psychoanalysis.

PSYCHOANALYSIS AND THE BIOLOGICAL SCIENCES

No doubt, among the many factors that together militate against the acceptance of lay analysis, the growth and flourishing of psychosomatic medicine is not the least. Although I do not regard myself by any means as an expert in that field, I may be permitted to offer a few thoughts about it.

The body-mind relationship has occupied man's thinking for thousands of years, so that we already find statements dealing with that problem in the writings of the ancient Greeks. Freud's interest in the relationship between body and mind, however, did not grow out of a metaphysical interest in the problem; it was the product of clinical circumstances.[1] There were three problem areas relevant to this question that Freud found himself compelled to take into consideration: (1) patients suffering from neurasthenia and anxiety neurosis complained about a variety of unpleasant bodily sensations; (2) in hysteria, the leading symptoms were disturbances of well defined physical functions; (3) some dreams were apparently to be explained by the dreamer's physical condition, for example, by a state of hunger or by any other intense physical urge.

An attempt to explain a variety of clinical data led Freud to views which can best be epitomized by three different models of the body-mind interrelationship. (1) The effect of soma on the psychic apparatus: in neurasthenia and anxiety neurosis, the psychic apparatus is not strong enough or not well enough prepared to tolerate the amount of undischarged somatic excitation. (2) The effect of the psychic apparatus upon somatic function: in hysteria, it is the psychic apparatus which imposes its will upon the somatic function. (3) Co-operation between soma and psychic apparatus: in the dream produced by somatic stimuli, the psychic apparatus uses somatic excitation for the fulfillment of its own design.

Thus, with Freud, psychopathology developed three different models, each of which represented a different type of relationship between mind and body.[2] It is important to note that none of these models is employed to explain physical disease nor do they contain any implication of that sort of explanation.

The situation is quite different in an early paper by Freud (1905c), which may be regarded historically as the introduction of psychosomatic medicine into psychoanalysis. I stress the historical viewpoint here since, for all practical purposes, the paper had no effect on the actual evolution of psychosomatic medicine. Freud's "Psychical (or Mental) Treatment" was put out in 1905 in a semipopular two-volume publication; it remained unnoticed by psychoanalysts. It was not included in Freud's first edition of his collected papers,[3] but was republished in 1942 in the

[1] I omit here Freud's (1887-1902) early theoretical deliberations (see also Freud, 1888-1889, p. 23f.).

[2] Organ neurosis, the dysfunction of an organ as the result of a supposed toxic factor produced by an increase of its erotogenic role, was discussed by Freud upon the occasion of his paper on visual disturbances (1910c, p. 218). This did not require a fourth model, however, since it is in fact only a particular subdivision of the first model.

[3] I am grateful to Miss Anna Freud for informing me that she is almost certain that the reason for the exclusion of the paper was that Professor Freud did not consider it good enough to be included in the *Gesammelte Schriften*. [I owe thanks to Professor Saul Rosenzweig for his kind permission to report here his recent important discovery that the paper by Freud under discussion was actually published in 1890. This, of course, explains some of the puzzling elements that are encountered in this paper.]

German London edition. Ever since then, it has been rarely cited. Some of its points may be regarded by many as having been surpassed by research done since then.

This paper by Freud is unique in so far as the strongest *psychosomatic* claims are put forward, with a boldness for which one would search in vain in others among Freud's publications. In this paper, Freud wanted to correct a prejudice that obtained in contemporary medicine—namely, that in the reciprocal relation between body and mind, mental events were represented "as determined by physical ones and dependent on them," but "the effect of the mind upon body found little favor in the eyes of physicians" (p. 284). Pathological influences of the mind upon the body, Freud asserted, are achieved through affects. Depressive affects, "such as sorrow, worry or grief, reduce the state of nourishment of the whole body, cause the hair to turn white, the fat to disappear and the walls of the blood-vessels to undergo morbid changes" (p. 287). What is surprising is Freud's belief, almost taken for granted here, that persistent emotions of a certain kind may cause pathological changes in the walls of blood vessels (he was probably referring to arteriosclerosis). Likewise Freud claims "a large bearing" of affects on the resistance against infection. The instance he cites is noteworthy: "A good example of this is to be seen in the medical observation that there is far greater liability to contract such diseases as typhus and dysentery in defeated armies than in victorious ones" (p. 287).

It is even more surprising when depressive affects are considered to be "often sufficient in themselves to bring about both the diseases of the nervous system accompanied by manifest anatomical changes and also diseases of other organs" (p. 287). Although Freud qualified this statement by saying that "it must be assumed that the patient already had a predisposition" to the disease, one can deduce the significance he attributed to the affects from his adding that this predisposition had hitherto been "an inoperative one" (p. 287). In the light of such an extreme opinion, it is no wonder that violent affects are regarded as capable of having adverse effects upon the course of organic illness. Yet here again Freud surprises us by saying that "there is no lack of instances in which a severe shock or a sudden bereavement brings about a peculiar alteration in the tone of the organism which may have a favourable influence on some well-established pathological condition or may even bring it to an end" (p. 287). By "well-established," I assume Freud meant "based on cellular pathology."

Furthermore, there are two references in the paper to psychic death.

"Finally," he says, "there can be no doubt that the duration of life can be appreciably shortened by depressive affects and that a violent shock, or a deep humiliation or disgrace, may put a sudden end to life. Strange to say, this same result may be found to follow too from the unexpected impact of a great joy" (p. 287f.) And further: "It is not so easy to produce evidence of the influence of *volition* on pathological somatic processes; but it is quite possible that a determination to recover or a will to die may have an effect on the outcome even of severe and precarious illnesses" (p. 289, italics by Freud). When Freud raised the question of the effects of fearful expectation, and inquired whether it is true (as he seemed inclined to believe) that the *fear* of infection may endanger a subject at times of epidemic, he again turned indirectly to the problem of psychic death.

He was also convinced that, despite the "pious fraud and inaccurate observation" operative in many instances among "miraculous" cures, patients have been cured not only of illnesses of mental origin, but also of "illnesses with an 'organic' basis which had previously resisted all the efforts of physicians" (p. 290). It may be quite significant that Freud spoke, in connection with so-called miraculous cures, of the repression of illness.[4] Did Freud betray here a preoccupation with the formation of a psychological theory of the origin and therapy of organic illness? Anyone who was more ambitious therapeutically than Freud was in 1905, or who knew as much about the affects as he did at that time— and had the tools to deal with them—might easily have felt tempted to extend psychotherapy to the treatment of organic illnesses, most of which were in any case being treated at that time only symptomatically. There is no indication, however, that Freud wavered in his drive toward a comprehensive theory of the personality, a drive which would have been endangered by a deviation toward what was later to be known as psychosomatic medicine. He never returned explicitly to this area.[5] Subsequent psychosomatic research nevertheless sounds like a logical development or continuation of the perspective Freud put forward in 1905.

It is impossible to make a simple characterization of psychosomatic medicine since, in that body of knowledge, one encounters a wide spec-

---

[4] Strachey, in translating this passage, used the term "to suppress," etc. (Freud, 1905c, p. 289). But the German original does not say *zu unterdrücken* but *zu verdrängen* (Freud, 1905d, p. 298), which might better be translated as "to repress."

[5] At best, only a remote connection can be seen in Freud's later designing of a hypothetical model of psychobiological processes in the growth of malignant neoplasms (Freud, 1920, p. 50).

trum of theories, from the quite primitive to the quite refined; all of them, I believe, share the assumption that the repressed has such an effect on body tissues as, under certain circumstances, may lead to pathological cellular changes. This effect is at times direct; at other times, it is achieved by a detour through vegetative, hormonal, or other functions which then become the causes of cellular pathology. Indeed, although disease is experienced by man as something that need not occur, as an irregular interlude in his habitual mode of life, it is, on the contrary, so regular and unavoidable that it should truly be called a part of life, at least of man's life (and perhaps of that of domesticated animals). It is freedom from disease throughout a person's life that would be altogether exceptional and therefore not to be expected, and it is precisely this inexorable regularity that makes disease such an important subject for psychological research.

This same regularity is also true with regard to psychopathology; we know now that no person has ever been utterly free of it. Freud gave much thought to the question of what it is in the *condition humaine* that makes psychopathology a permanent and regular part of the human inventory. One may feel tempted to say, for example, that a mental organization that dreams is prone to evolve symptoms of a psychogenic order (cf. Freud, 1916-1917, p. 456f.). But that would be a simplification, for animals—which are definitely far more resistant, and perhaps even altogether immune, to neuroses[6]—do dream, and so do infants, in a developmental phase in which neurotic pathology is certainly not the rule. It is safe to say that a mental organization that forms dreams beyond the scope of simple wish fulfillment is structured in such a way as to make the evolvement of psychopathology highly probable.

In the light of the now recognized ubiquity of psychopathology, and of the further recognition that the structure of the human personality is such as to make psychopathology inescapable, the idea is also emerging that the inescapability of man's physical pathology is linked to those same circumstances that make him so highly susceptible to psychopathology. During the prescientific era, the greatest minds, at least in the Occident, regularly looked upon physical disease as psychogenic. From the Old and New Testaments, in which physical disease was the outcome of disobedience to the word of God or of a lack of faith, to Dostoyevsky, for whom 'nerve fever' was the consequence of intolerable

[6] About the problem of neuroses in animals, see section on "Extreme Biologism and Sociologism," in Chapter 9.

conflict tension; from primitive medicine, in which all diseases without visible causation were regarded as the effects of demonic powers (Neuburger, 1906, p. 7), to Schopenhauer (1819), who believed that the bite of a dog in greatest rage was fatal to a man, even if the dog was not suffering from rabies (p. 1005), disease has been conceived as of something more than a series of organic processes, or a single physical event.

Scientific medicine dehumanized disease by viewing man the way Descartes had taught it to view him, as a machine. The rewards were great: man acquired an astounding power of control over the majority of diseases. Yet, despite this fabulous increment in man's power, the role played by disease in any individual life was not diminished; only the tragic general consequences of most diseases were eliminated, so that it became 'unfashionable' to die before one's sixth decade. In short, medical progress, for all its triumphs, has not helped a bit toward eliminating that worst of all diseases—death; it has served only to postpone it. In that sense, disease may impress some as a sort of rehearsal, a death in miniature to keep man from forgetting his earthly limitations; it may even be inferred that an organic structure that has to die must also get sick. Such reasoning may be refuted in many ways.

Freud (1940a) once made a far-reaching observation that may be interpreted as favorable to psychosomatics: "It may in general be suspected," he wrote, "that the *individual* dies of his internal conflicts but that the *species* dies of its unsuccessful struggle against the external world . . ." (p. 23, italics by Freud). Proceeding from that premise, one may attempt to evolve a pathology which centers in the concept of inner conflict, and to establish a correlation between the structure of the inner conflict and the structure of the disturbed organ function. Actually, that is what has been tried very often in the field of psychosomatic medicine. Yet, as so often occurs, we find another statement in Freud's (1924c) work that, if anything, points in the opposite direction: "At birth the whole individual is destined to die, and perhaps his organic disposition may already contain the indication of what he is to die from" (p. 174).

If we now turn to the clinical data derived from the psychoanalytic situation per se, we appear to obtain a full confirmation of the theory of psychosomatic medicine. Quite often, we accumulate an abundance of material that can be brought into meaningful context with symptoms of physical disorder; this occurs quite independently of the nature or severity of the disease. Whether it is a simple cold and a virus infection, a migraine and a backache, obesity and emaciation, intestinal ulcer and asthma, tuberculosis and hyperthyroidism, or coronary disease and even malignant growth, in short whatever we touch of the whole spectrum of organic diseases, at each point we arrive by investigation at a multiplicity of psychic processes which together force upon us the conclusion that this particular organization *had to* suffer from this particular illness at this particular time because of an inner unresolved conflict. Furthermore, there is hardly a single analyst, psychotherapist, or psychiatrist who has not observed how, in the course of treatment, some of these diseases have disappeared, allegedly because of the resolution of conflict. There are even a few who profess to have obtained favorable results in instances of cancer; this is, no doubt, an unwarranted claim.

The claims with regard to the cure of organic disease by psychotherapeutic means are in their diversity reminiscent of similar claims that have been made with regard to schizophrenia. Indeed, almost every expert in the field has on record cases of schizophrenia that he has 'cured' —which is surprising, in the light of the fact that this is the most malignant of the mental disorders. It was only Freud who, so far as we can judge from his writings, never found the occasion to send forth such happy tidings, perhaps because he never succeeded in curing any physical disease by his psychotherapeutic technique. It is important to take note here of how Freud later epitomized his clinical psychosomatic experience. Concerning the bearing of organic disease upon the formation of neurotic symptoms, he said: ". . . a pathological somatic change (through inflammation or injury perhaps) sets the activity of symptom-formation going; so that this activity hastily turns the symptom which has been presented to it by reality into the representative of all the unconscious phantasies . . ." (Freud, 1916-1917, p. 391).

On the effect of physical disease, he made the following observation: "It is instructive . . . to find, contrary to all theory and expectation, that a neurosis which has defied every therapeutic effort may vanish if the subject . . . develops a dangerous organic disease" (Freud, 1924b, p. 166). Fifteen years later, Freud repeated this same observation, but in greater detail, when discussing a form of resistance that is contributed by the superego (the unconscious sense of guilt): "This resistance," writes Freud, "does not actually interfere with our intellectual work [of therapy], but it makes it ineffective, indeed, it often allows us to remove one form of neurotic suffering but is ready to replace it at once by another one, or perhaps by an organic illness" (Freud, 1940a, p. 75).

Psychic conditions that may have the effect of preventing disease are suggested in a technical observation that Freud made much earlier: "When the arrangement [of the analyst's leasing a definite hour to the patient] is adhered to, it turns out that accidental hindrances do not occur at all and intercurrent illnesses only very seldom" (Freud, 1913b, p. 127).

There may be additional remarks scattered through Freud's works that are relevant to the psychosomatic problem (of course, I am omitting here his observations on the psychoneurotic disturbance of physical functions), but all of them, I believe, will be found to be characterized by a similar discretion and cautiousness, so much in contrast with his bold statements in 1905 (Freud, 1905c). It is most noteworthy, indeed, that a scientist who, for a short while, took a position so strongly foreshadowing modern psychosomatic medicine, rather abruptly and quickly withdrew to a quite conservative attitude in that same area.

Historically, it is of interest that, at least once in his lifetime, Freud *considered* what has since become the cornerstone of psychosomatic medicine, but then dropped it, even though it may at first have looked to him like a well documented and reliable insight. What made Freud change his mind so profoundly in a matter of such great concern? I do not pretend to know the answer, of course, since apparently no material relevant to this question has been published. The sympathetic attitude that Freud had towards Groddeck suggests that he felt no objection to the psychosomatic research of others, but kept himself conspicuously out of it.[7]

And, indeed, very serious objections can be raised against the use of psychoanalysis for psychosomatic research. Some analysts have tried to establish correlations between specific physical disorders and specific elements of mental structure. Despite the seemingly convincing evidence that they have published, clinical experience does not confirm these correlations.[8] To be sure, instances of this sort can be observed, but so can an ensemble of factors that do not at all follow the asserted correlation. That there is some sort of correlation between biological type, personality type, and disease type, all of which probably stem from a common matrix, is highly probable; in fact, it has been proven to a certain

---

[7] See Freud's letter of 1917 to Groddeck (S. Freud, 1873-1939, pp. 316-318), where a general remark about the body-mind problem can also be found.

[8] Cf. Gitelson (1959, p. 170f.) for an elaborate comment on this question of specificity and its history.

extent, by a branch of medicine called *Konstitutionspathologie* (Brugsch and Lewy, 1926-1931). This, however, has nothing to do with correlations between specific diseases and specific psychological factors.[9]

The following hypothetical situation might also be considered. If the members of a group were suddenly brought to the point of fainting by inhalation of an otherwise harmless gas whose presence could not be detected, and if they were subsequently subjected to careful psychological inquiry, in all probability we would find in each single individual a number of psychic elements that could be brought into meaningful connection with the physical event. Therefore, we might be inclined to establish causative links between those elements and the fainting spells (cf. Schur, 1955). In other words, there is in every human being a store of repressed material, feelings of guilt or masochistic tendencies that would be activated by something like sudden fainting. It would be impossible to suffer from organic disease, particularly over long periods of time, without that disease having an activating effect on the proper psychic elements (Schur, 1955, p. 148).[10]

I had a noteworthy experience in the Army that should be mentioned here. Trainees suffering from gastrointestinal disturbances were sent to the psychiatric consultation service when the physical examination did not reveal organic pathology, although the vast majority of them reported a history and a symptomatology that easily fell within the scope of one or another of the well-known physical syndromes. One soldier came to my attention, however, who was different from the majority of those whom I had seen up to then. He too presented gastrointestinal complaints of the sort I had listened to so often, but on questioning he also revealed a psychogenic history that fitted his symptoms perfectly. He had frequently seen his mother step with the heel of her shoe on his father's

[9] It seems as though psychosomatic research is in a dilemma. Correlations established by statistics, questionnaires, life histories, etc., are to be accepted only with great reservations, for obvious reasons. On the other hand, there are objections to psychosomatic research via psychoanalysis, which I shall presently discuss. One also wonders occasionally, when reading a psychosomatic case history based on regular psychoanalytic investigation, whether the analyst was so strongly preoccupied with and motivated by his interest in the psychobiological nexus that he neglected those minimum safeguards without which an operational field of technique based on interpretation becomes contaminated.

[10] Here the citation of Freud's model of the dream provoked by somatic stimulation is very much in place (Freud, 1900, pp. 220-240). It also serves as a warning against the assertion made by so many that, from the examination of a detailed history, a decision can be made as to whether the patient is suffering from a neurotic or an organic disorder (cf. Stone, 1954, p. 569). In Freud's writings, there is an interesting instance of his basing a diagnosis of organic disease upon formal aspects of the history, despite the presence of many factors strongly indicative of a neurosis (Freud, 1905e, p. 16, fn. 2).

abdomen, since this brought relief from the pain the father felt in his stomach. It was at this same anatomical locus that the patient now felt his own pain.

This was my first instance in the Army of what impressed me as a *prima facie* psychogenic history of gastric trouble, and I scheduled him for psychotherapeutic interviews. However, I lost the patient shortly thereafter because a diagnosis of duodenal ulcer had been made in the meantime, based upon X-ray examination, and this entitled him to a discharge. It struck me as ironic that it should be this one instance, so convincingly suggestive of psychogenesis, that turned out to be an organic case.

It is often said that the response of physical symptoms to suggestion has diagnostic value. This, too, is erroneous. A young woman close to death was transferred to the psychiatric ward. Among her symptoms were tetanoid cramps—which subsided shortly after a few soothing suggestions were made, of the sort one makes when one wishes to hypnotize a patient. Another example I owe to a colleague: a patient was sent to the psychiatric ward because of uncontrollable vomiting, for which no physical cause could be established. After a hypnotic session, the symptom subsided; yet a few days later an ileus was diagnosed, which had been overlooked in a previous X-ray.[11] The speed and ease with which psychic elements can be connected in a seemingly meaningful way with symptoms of organic disease should serve as a warning. In my experience, it is often easier to establish such links than to discover the causative elements of *bona fide* psychoneurotic symptoms.

The reason is not too difficult to find. The formation of a psychoneurotic symptom has served, basically, to conceal a secret. It is quite consistent with its history that any danger of having to reveal that secret should arouse strong resistances. In the case of physical disease, the ego's defense apparatus is usually weakened, and repressed con-

---

[11] However, as Freud correctly pointed out, there are some special symptoms which cannot be produced on a psychogenic basis (1893a); it is conceivable that, in some instances, the reverse is also true. In that case, however, it is not the history, but the structure of the symptom itself that is pathognomic.

Already in 1891, Freud (1891b) stated that "some symptoms of organic disease are accessible to hypnosis, and that the organic change can persist without the disturbance of function which it has produced" [manche Symptome organischer Krankheiten der Hypnose zugänglich sind und dass die organische Veränderung ohne die von ihr ausgehende functionelle Störung bestehen kann (col. 725)]. I owe thanks to Dr. Paul F. Cranefield for having called my attention to Freud's paper of 1891 which he recently discovered.

tents, regardless of the original depth of their repression or of the intensity of countercathexis, are carried by physical symptoms like riders into the fabric of the ego. Because of the ever-active buoyancy of the repressed, physical symptoms become the container of the repressed and the contents of the two may become fused.[12]

Again I must refer to Freud's model of the dream provoked by somatic stimulation. Repressed contents that are ordinarily inaccessible, under such conditions find free access into the dream, since the force of the physical irritation cannot be warded off by the ego in the same way as repressed contents unsupported by somatic upsurge. Consequently, every physical symptom must be regarded as meaningful—that is, as the potential occasion for an interpretation in the psychoanalytic situation; the physical symptom may even become the carrier of the most deeply repressed, which, without physical irritation, might never have come to light.

It is altogether legitimate within the psychoanalytic situation to interpret the repressed contents that have become fused with the physical symptom, but it does not behoove the analyst to decide upon questions of causation.[13] Nevertheless, the analyst has to analyze all phenomena that become psychologically relevant—that is to say, within the psychoanalytic field, he must regard every physical symptom as psychosomatic.[14]

Yet there are well-known instances in which patients who had labored under frequent and long-lasting diseases were able to live a life unmolested by disease after a psychoanalysis was carried to success, and there are other instances in which a physical disease that had defied

[12] I omit from consideration here the general libidinization that is often provoked by physical disease, and the reduction in guilt feelings vis-à-vis the repressed which reaches consciousness in this way.

[13] The theoretical implications of psychogenic vs. somatogenic causations have been discussed by Schilder (1921). Schilder introduces the concepts of the "somatogenic intrusion" (Einbruch des Körperlichen), which is correlated with a change in the operative level of the psyche (psychische Niveauänderung). By way of the "principle of the double pathway" (Prinzip des doppelten Weges), he points to the formation of identical or almost identical psychic phenomena which are either somatogenic or psychogenic in origin. Schilder's article shows the epistemological justification for the interpretation of somatic symptoms. Freud's remarks about the 'epileptic reaction,' which may occur either on an organic or on an affective basis (Freud, 1928, p. 181), permit us to speak of a 'principle of the common pathway.' The fact is that the two principles refer to the same state of affairs.

[14] The literature that could be cited in connection with the psychosomatic problem is enormous. I shall restrict myself to the following: Fenichel (1945), Schur (1955a), Greenacre (1958), Rangell (1959), F. Deutsch (1959). For the philosophical implications, see the splendid article by Feigl, 1958.

physical therapy subsided under the influence of psychoanalysis. There are two remarks which I wish to make regarding this. First, there is in many diseases a tendency toward recovery. About this self-limiting predisposition on the part of most diseases, which is rarely discussed (cf. Ehrenberg, 1923), little is known. I assume that psychic factors play an important role in its realization. Thus it comes about—probably with some frequency—that a disease will last longer than would appear to be biologically 'necessary,' chiefly because of interference or intensification by the psychic apparatus. With regard to recovery, the psychic factor may thus be of direct relevance.

Furthermore (one rarely sees this discussed; but cf. Bonaparte, 1960, p. 441; Schur, 1955a), a successful analysis will not only affect the leading symptoms but usually has its impact also on the vegetative nervous system. A patient's gait, the tonus of his muscles, his posture and breathing rhythm will change; his whole mode of life may undergo modification. Much of this may occur subliminally, or for other reasons may not come to direct observation. Thus a successful analysis may have direct effects on bodily spheres that are per se outside of the pathological area, but nevertheless have a significant effect upon health or disease.

This excursion into psychosomatics seemed appropriate to me because it has a bearing, even though a remote one, on our subject. There are a significant number of analysts who find in the psychosomatic area the very hub of psychoanalysis, and who therefore regard the analyst who did not go through medical school as hopelessly out of place. Yet I do not see what else can be done in the psychoanalytic situation than to trace along associative lines every phenomenon that makes its appearance in the operational field, and to gather as many links as possible.

I remember well the appearance of jaundice in a young man whose analysis had been proceeding satisfactorily, although slowly. The patient and I were both well aware that what we were discussing was a physical disease, yet both of us approached it in the very same way as we had previously—and for a long time—been approaching his spermatorrhea, of whose psychogenic origin (utterly unrelated to any physical condition) both of us were convinced. The psychoanalytic profit was immeasurable, an outcome which I could reaffirm for many other instances of this kind.

I do not see how medical knowledge had any bearing at all on the psychoanalytic working through of all the psychic material that was attached to the physical symptom. Such knowledge is, of course, indispensable when one sets out to establish the hierarchy of physical and mental functions or emotions,[15] or their circular causation. But that, as I have already stated, seems to me to transcend the bounds of the psychoanalytic situation.[16]

The following verses by Goethe may be quoted in this context:

> *noch niemand konnt es fassen,*
> *Wie Seel' und Leib so schön zusammenpassen,*
> *So fest sich halten, als um nie zu scheiden,*
> *Und doch den Tag sich immerfort verleiden.*[17]
> (*Faust*, Part II, verses 6893-96)

Not only do these verses underscore the limitations of our knowledge in that area, which are as stringent as they were of yore; they also present the gist of the psychosomatic problem more succinctly than most of the literature of the day: the constant discord between psyche and soma within a perfect harmony. It is precisely this discord or antinomy that seems to me to contain the key to the problem, as well as being the impassable bar that it is.

Yet, even if it should turn out that I underestimate the heuristic value of the psychoanalytic situation vis-à-vis the etiology of organic disease, the frequent assertion that lay analysts should not practice psychoanalysis or psychotherapy because, with their lack of medical background, they might easily fail to recognize the existence of an organic disease, is scarcely tenable. It is interesting that no specific instance of this has yet been published, for we may be certain that there are observers enough who would not mind doing so, if there were any to publish. What one usually finds cited are examples of patients who were sent to a specialist by their medically trained analyst, upon the appearance of

[15] Cf. Freud (1927a): "I also share the view that all those problems which relate to the connection between psychical phenomena and their organic, anatomical and chemical foundations can be approached only by those who have studied both, that is, by medical analysts" (p. 257).

[16] A statement by Schilder may illustrate further the disparity between the psychoanalytic situation and psychosomatic research in the narrower sense of the word: "The possibility of understanding a symptom," writes Schilder (1940), "as the expression of psychological tendencies does not prove that this symptom is psychogenic in character" (p. 219).

[17] No one has yet comprehended
How soul and body fit so beautifully together
And hold each other so firmly, as if never to separate,
And yet continuously make the day miserable for each other.

physical symptoms that would supposedly have been regarded by the lay analyst as psychoneurotic.

Ernest Jones (1927a) reported such an instance during the discussion of lay analysis (p. 193). It concerned a patient who, in the course of analysis, complained of "pain in the neighborhood of the anus when going to sleep." Although the patient himself regarded the new symptom as "probably aroused by our current discussion of his anal-erotic complex," Jones urged him to consult a surgeon; the diagnosis was carcinoma of the rectum. Yet, when Jones reported this incident as having generally unfavorable implications for lay analysis, he did not at the same time make any attempt to estimate the number of medically trained psychoanalysts who might just as easily have overlooked the possibility of physical etiology in this situation.

I am reasonably certain that a well-trained lay analyst would have wished this patient to be physically examined because, in general, he would not be laboring under the misconception that the history of a symptom by itself either confirms or refutes the existence of any one type of etiology. I myself have had the opportunity of becoming familiar with the work of two lay analysts, and I have been astonished how often they were right in suspecting physical factors to be relevant (in one instance, in disagreement with the referring physician) in a patient's symptomatology.

A closer examination of this question will reveal that the decisive factor for the psychotherapist is not his knowledge of all the physical syndromes there are, for nobody can remember them anyhow, and furthermore the identical symptom may be physically caused in one instance and in another psychoneurotically. The truly decisive factor is the *formal* difference between the psychoneurotically and the physically ill patient; this difference, which may be called phenomenological, cannot be described adequately, but it is recognized by the talented psychologist. That question is too complex to be discussed here; but I do wish to deal with the hypocrisy that surrounds it.

No reports are published which would tell us the ratio of medical errors—namely, how often a medically trained analyst has requested a medical examination which proved to have negative results, or how often one has failed to recognize the physical nature of the symptoms in question. Curiously enough, the instances of misdiagnosis that have come to my attention have always occurred with physicians. I wish to cite two of these instances, involving excellently trained, experienced physicians, for they seem to highlight the pitfalls of everyday practice far more than to lend support to the constant and unsubstantiated prattle about the inadequacy of lay analysis.

A female patient, a highly masochistic person who, aside from sporadic physical disease, had a lifelong history of a large number of psychogenic physical symptoms, had been treated by me with psychotherapy. After an interruption of many months, she sought my advice because of a cough and insomnia. In the first interview after her return, I was able to call her attention to a relevant factor which, I felt, strongly implied a psychogenic origin for her cough: a hated relative of hers had recently died, after suffering from a disease that had caused a strong cough. Nevertheless, forewarned by observations that I had gathered during her previous treatment, I insisted that she be treated by a former internist who was now a psychotherapist. She assured me that two specialists of unquestionable competence had found no physical causation for her symptom; I still insisted. The colleague to whom I had her transferred reported a few days later that he found extensive pulmonary metastases in her chest X-rays.

The other instance is perhaps more instructive; it was observed by a colleague. A young neurotic woman was sent by a gynecologist for analysis because of psychogenic amenorrhea. The analysis took a satisfactory course, yet the main symptom did not subside, even though the (medically trained) analyst had the definite impression that the analytic progress was such as to warrant expectation of change. Renewed physical examination now brought to light a tumor, after whose removal menstruation once again took place. In this instance, one can observe with particular poignancy how the "behavior" of a symptom during treatment may suggest to the analyst an etiological clue.

Here we come face to face with a question of technique which I do not find discussed in the literature, and which the medical analyst would very likely not even regard as a serious question. Is it compatible with classical analysis to advise a patient to be physically examined, once the analyst's suspicion of physical involvement has been aroused? I once raised this question in a seminar; the chairman held that the proper procedure would be to analyze the motives for the patient's failure of his own accord to seek a physical examination.[18] If we take Ernest

---

[18] Cf., however, Stone (1961): "There are occasions when, for example, it is insufficient to interpret why a patient does not go for physical examination" (p. 32).

Jones's patient as our example, this would mean that the analyst, when the new symptoms appeared and the patient jumped to the conclusion that this was the effect of the new phase of the treatment, should have focused the patient's attention upon his belief in what may be called the 'omnipotence of the mind' (a belief all too frequently encountered), and then should have limited himself to drawing into the psychoanalytic process the patient's reluctance to be physically examined. The tendency toward thinking in extremes is well known; after a period of theory formation, dominated by the viewpoint of rigorously strictly physical causation, a swing to the other extreme has been growing (and not only in the lay world).

The question in general terms is how far the psychoanalyst is directly responsible for his patient's safety. In our society, there is a general belief that the responsibility of the psychotherapist includes—perhaps even *especially* includes—the patient's physical health. Nevertheless, in view of the recommendation, accepted by psychoanalysts of the classical school, not to disturb the course of the patient's analysis by giving advice, it is reasonable to ask whether we have here a legitimate exception to the rule. However, one is forced to consider whether what we are dealing with here is a cultural bias, and to ask why psychotherapy should have a greater responsibility in this area of the patient's life than in others.

There are people to whom wealth is more important than health; they might well wish the analyst to protect them against acting out in the realm of finances, perhaps even to advise them on the management of their wealth and property. Or what would be the degree of responsibility toward those who say: "Good name in man and woman is the immediate jewel of their souls. Who steals my purse steals trash"? Finally, the patient for whom his children's future is immeasurably more important than his own health or wealth or honor may by the same reasoning conclude that the analyst has a responsibility to him for advice on the mental health of his progeny.

I am aware that these brief remarks may lend themselves to critical comment, but it still seems to me to be justified to state that, while there are innumerable situations in which the analyst's specialized knowledge might well preserve the patient from harm, the analyst is not a 'counselor.' His sole responsibility is to center the analysis as best he can in those areas where the patient acts out instead of acting in a reality-adequate way, where he shows resistances and defenses and reveals the repressed. After such a properly conducted analysis *has been completed*, the patient should be capable of handling his financial affairs efficiently, and of raising his children to be healthy.

The question nevertheless remains: since in most analyses the symptomatology reverberates (at least temporarily) in the physical area, how is the patient to distinguish between such reverberation and the manifestation of genuine physical pathology? As far as I can see, there is, in terms of the ideal type of classical analysis, no other answer to be given than that which applies in the case of those other areas in which psychoanalysis will reverberate—namely, to explore the patient's motives. However, a general reservation is to be added.

As is well known, some patients are prone to respond with physical disease to the initial anxiety at the start of a treatment, or to the first signs of recovery from neurosis after a lengthy analytic treatment. In my opinion, however, upon the appearance of a new set of physical complaints, no matter when this takes place, a physical examination is indicated. Jones said that his medical knowledge was evoked as soon as he was confronted with the patient's complaint; did he mean to imply also that, if the particular syndrome had not yet become known at the time he attended medical school, or if he had forgotten it, then the patient would have been doomed? I believe that, even when the analyst is already convinced that the patient shows psychogenic symptoms, it still remains his responsibility to keep in mind the necessity of a physical checkup.

The only instance, I think, in which the choice of a medically trained analyst may be preferable is one involving the type of patient I have briefly referred to earlier, whose masochism leads to manifestations of physical disease under the guise of neurosis. Unfortunately, here the greatest caution on the part of the analyst may prove of little avail, since such patients trick even experienced specialists, as indeed happened in the recorded instance. One has to make the best of a bad deal here and, because of the bad prognosis, to send the patient to a medically trained analyst, although even this precaution may often be of little use.[19] Such patients are few in number, however; they are very uncharacteristic and, from the way in which they in particular need to be dealt with, one

[19] Freud (1940a, p. 76) introduced in his *Outline* a group of patients among whom I believe the patients just mentioned belong. According to his account, a defusion of instincts had taken place in them, and the consequently freed excessive destruction was directed inward.

cannot validly deduce whether or not medical education is justly required as a general prerequisite for the practice of psychoanalysis. If it really were, every analyst would have to spend considerable time in hospitals periodically, not only to refresh his memory, but also to acquaint himself with a large number of new discoveries. Furthermore, to which field of medicine should this be limited? Would internal medicine be sufficient? Would it not be necessary to include almost all other specialties?

A medically trained analyst who relied on his own knowledge of medicine, in deciding whether he was facing physical or psychoneurotic symptomatology, would greatly endanger his patient's health. I do not see how he could proceed at all differently from the way in which the lay analyst would have to—namely, to take note of that earlier-mentioned formal difference of appearance between the physically healthy and the physically sick patient, and to rely on the results of examination by the medical specialist.

There may be an objection that only the medically trained person is able to integrate this formal difference of appearance because of his extensive opportunities for observation. Practice does not confirm this.[20] For the ability to detect the appearance of a sick person, one does not need to study medicine; such an ability can be observed in mothers. An adequate, that is to say, an unambivalent mother knows that the child is sick before the pediatrician does.

To sense physical disease requires a kind of percipience like that needed to sense hidden affects. Every analyst knows situations in which he has felt the presence of depression, rage, hatred, love, or some other emotion in his patient, although nothing pointing to such a conclusion had yet been verbalized by the patient. Although reconstruction may sometimes bring to light the signals to which the analyst responded, more often than not one has to conclude that subliminal data are apparently able to convey the patient's true emotional state, in so far as the unconscious is the main relay in the grasping of another person's unconscious (Freud, 1912a, p. 115f.).

Thus it would seem that the contribution of medical knowledge to the

[20] One of the consequences of psychosomatic medicine is that physical diagnoses tend to be overlooked. It is my own policy, and particularly in instances where I have to designate a specialist for a checkup before starting the analysis of a patient, to recommend an internist who is far from psychosomatic medicine. A "clean bill of health" from him is, in my experience, more reliable.

qualification and competence of the psychoanalyst is overrated,[21] at least with regard to protection against overlooking the signs of physical disease.

An experience that I had in August Aichhorn's child guidance clinic lives indelibly in my memory. After studying a case history, turned over to him by the social worker, he advised that the child be sent to the hospital clinic for what he thought to be an organic illness. I inquired why he thought so, for I could not recall a previous instance of the kind. He then briefly discussed with me the family constellation and the child's symptoms—which, in his opinion, did not fit together. This episode exemplifies the area from which an etiologic impression may be gained by the lay analyst; in this instance, the impression was, in fact, confirmed later.

It may properly be objected that Aichhorn was an exceptionally intuitive analyst, who cannot be taken as a yardstick; yet an equal objection can be raised against Jones's experience with the patient suffering from carcinoma. The comparison between these two examples may show, in the last analysis, the greater effectiveness of the psychologist who does not depend on the symptoms per se, which are too often misleading, but on the evaluation of impressions, total situations, or dynamic constellations.[22]

In view of my earlier comments, I trust that the reader knows by now that I did not think that a *final decision* as to whether a disease is organic or psychogenic can be made on this last score, either, and that I am merely considering whence and by what means clues suggestive of one or the other may be derived in the psychoanalytic situation.

Still another group of objections against lay analysis rests on the belief that a neurosis cannot be understood by anyone who is unfamiliar with man's biological organic substructure, for the basis of psychoanalysis is, after all, biology. An extreme formulation of that position has been made by Kaufman (1951, p. 1), according to whom "psychoanalysis is biologically based and body bound." With due apology for taking advantage

[21] Primary dependence upon medical knowledge may even have a detrimental effect, although a discussion of that danger would lead us too far afield. It is, however, worthwhile to reflect briefly on this paradox: that the physical safety of a patient may be more fully safeguarded in the hands of the lay analyst than of the medical one if the latter really believes that he can make the decision between physical disease and neurosis on the grounds of the patient's history or kind of symptom—an approach which is far less satisfactory than that of the lay analyst, who under all circumstances leaves the decision to the specialist when new physical symptoms appear.

[22] For an example of this kind, see Gitelson, 1959, p. 167. In this instance, the medically trained analyst met with a clinical situation that was seemingly identical with a well-known physical syndrome, yet he derived the psychogenic etiology from the dynamics of the patient's life situation at that time.

of this latter linguistic extravaganza, one might equally well say: "Psychoanalysis is sociologically based and culture-bound."

It is one of the most noteworthy aspects of Freud's work that the biological and environmental aspects are represented in his work in a perfect balance, for both aspects harbor per se the danger that the individual may tend to be viewed as a medium of either or of both. Indeed, in terms of forensic psychology, it is quite adequate for a defense attorney to present a defendant as the 'product' of his inheritance and/or environment.

No system psychology could ever result from such approaches. The center of Freud's work is the psychic apparatus, and its structuring under the influence of inheritance and the biological substructure on the one hand, and of the environment and culture on the other. Of course, one indispensable prerequisite for this psychic apparatus is the physical substructure, but the environment is another; any emphasis on the one, without balancing it by an emphasis on the other, is certain to lead to faulty conclusions.

The relevant question here is what knowledge of the physical substructure is necessary in order to understand the structure and structurizing of the psychic apparatus. Here, we are leaving the clinical field, and therefore cannot avoid speculations about general principles. Many a passage from Freud's works could be profitably cited here, but none seems to me to be as comprehensive and succinct as the following: "The mental is based on the organic" (Freud, 1910c, p. 217), a passage that is particularly valuable, for Freud then went on to show what the consequences are for the analysts, whose "work can only carry them as far as this basis and not beyond it."

The interrelationship between psychoanalysis and biology has been frequently discussed. Here I wish to refer only to Schilder's paper in 1933, and Bernfeld's in 1937. Schilder presents a series of biological facts, which he links with basic concepts of psychoanalysis. The recessiveness of a factor, for example, as postulated by Mendel's law, is connected by analogy with the mechanism of repression. I have selected the simplest model here, but it is surprising to how great an extent most of the biological writings by analysts can be reduced to the setting up of analogies. Bernfeld turns forcefully against such a procedure, on grounds of principle and method, and quite rightly rejects the idea of the anal-erotic bee, as put forward by Broughton (1927, p. 144).

Bernfeld, however, does not limit himself to criticism, mainly of Ferenczi's bioanalysis, but outlines his own program. According to him, psychoanalytic biology would have to proceed in terms of vectors and topological models (Bernfeld, 1937, pp. 224-234),[23] if the pitfalls of thinking in analogies were to be avoided. Bernfeld's conceptual analysis and his methodological program are impressive; as far as I can judge, they make sense. The point is that Bernfeld's models would lead to the establishment of a mathematical formula whose general scientific value would be immeasurable, but whose value for the analyst, in terms of a better understanding of analysis and its biological foundations, would be highly questionable.

It is, to say the least, quite uncertain which part of what is offered today as the biological foundation of psychoanalysis will survive precise scientific analysis. There is no doubt in my mind that a scientifically valid link will at some point be established between biology and psychoanalysis, but that will probably take place at a level so far distant from the contents with which the analyst deals in his actual studies that, notwithstanding the scientific value of these abstract formulae, psychoanalysis per se will not be significantly enriched. In other words, the more biology grows as a science—that is to say, the more it becomes abstract—the less assistance it will have to offer to psychoanalysis, which has profited from biology mainly by way of its concrete evidential findings. For example, the neurophysiological tension between cortex and subcortex (which illustrates so vividly the conflict between ego and the drive, perhaps even between self and drive), is of no primary use to the analyst, aside from its confirmatory value. The psychological state of conflict could never be derived from the biological fact, and the analyst's understanding of man in the state of conflict would remain the same, even if the neurophysiological findings were quite different.[24]

In evaluating the relationship between biology and psychoanalysis, two apparently contradictory aspects of that relationship must be considered: biology as an ancillary science, indispensable to psychoanalysis, and biology a danger to psychoanalysis. Freud was aware of this double aspect, and it is thanks to his masterly handling of this question that psychoanalysis has been able to enjoy all the benefits that can be derived from biology, without becoming trapped in any fundamental pitfalls.

The danger from biology lies in the temptation to deny the relative

[23] Alexander had in 1935 applied the vector concept to psychoanalysis. For a criticism of his vector analysis, see Bernfeld (1937, pp. 224-227).
[24] I shall presently take up briefly an area in which psychoanalysis does depend directly on the findings of physiology and pathophysiology.

autonomy which the psyche has vis-à-vis the body. At the beginning of life, psyche and physical function coincide: a sick infant is always physically as well as emotionally sick. Every emotional disturbance leads to physical dysfunctions, and every physical disease inescapably upsets the working of the psychic apparatus (cf. Schur, 1955a, p. 122). The other extreme is best exemplified by Pasteur who, although afflicted with semi-paralysis at the age of forty-six, a few days after his apoplectic attack, dictated—unbelievable as it may seem—a note on an intricate scientific problem, with such precision and excellence that it could be presented to the Academy only one week after the attack (Descour, 1922, p. 155f.). So great can the victory be of mind over body.[25]

Yet innumerable observations proving that the mind does not float in a biological vacuum, but is rooted in an organic structure, may easily lead to a 'biologizing' (*sit venia verbo*) psychology which no doubt has heuristic value, but is not the science of man's mind.

As is well known, the port of entry of biology into psychoanalysis is the study of what Freud called the Id.[26] Inextricably connected with the Id and its elements, the instinctual drives, is the concept of a task or demand imposed on the psychic apparatus.[27] This task can be objectively described in physiological terms. The dynamic relationship between the psychic apparatus and an instinctual drive; the pleasure-pain and constancy principles which characterize the ways in which this relationship is consummated—these are cornerstones of psychoanalytic psychology, belonging to the biological sphere.

The organic part of man is often placed in contrast to the ego; but Hartmann (1952, p. 19) has reminded us that the ego is, of course, also based on an organic structure. Yet, when the body functions adequately, the relationship between the ego and the organic structures that support

[25] This example of the relative autonomy of mind with regard to body in the adult may easily be disputed. For example, if the hemorrhage had occurred at a different location of the central nervous system, his mind might even have fallen into a permanent stupor. Yet Jellinek (1947) has presented clinical material that superbly demonstrates this central thesis of the relative autonomy of the mind. According to his observations, it sometimes depended on the state of attention whether or not certain physical traumata had a lethal effect. Also, in patients exhausted by hours of agony, he observed behavior patterns shortly before death that seemed incompatible with their physical condition.

[26] Cf. Freud (1933a) when he states, "However jealously we may in other connections have defended the independence of psychology from all other sciences," in the investigation of the drives "we are really discussing biological psychology, we are studying the psychological concomitants of biological processes" (p. 131f.).

[27] Hartmann points out that the drives were at times regarded by Freud (1948) "not only as factors acting on the mental apparatus from without, but also in a sense as working in the mental apparatus itself" (p. 371).

it is essentially different from the relationship between the ego and the drives. The latter put tasks upon the ego, whereas the central nervous system, for example, supports the ego. Under normal circumstances, there is no conflict between the ego and the organic substructure in which it is rooted.

It thus becomes evident that only certain biological facts are relevant to psychoanalysis in the narrower sense. Yet I have the impression that it has never been clearly stated what determines whether or not a biological fact becomes endowed with psychological relevance, not to speak of the absence of any clear statement as to the hierarchy and types of relevance. Although I am aware of the possibility that, with further advances in insight, every biological datum will come to be recognized as psychoanalytically relevant, I nevertheless doubt that this is likely to happen.

Even with regard to generally accepted connections, it is difficult to state exactly what their relevance is (Hartmann, 1952, p. 17f.). Freud, for example, in discussing repression, frequently refers to flight. Apparently he was thinking of an evolutionary nexus between flight and repression, and regarded the latter as a form of internalized flight. Is the conclusion warranted that if, in the course of evolution, flight had not been developed in animals as a technique for escaping danger, man would therefore not have evolved the mechanism of repression? It is not likely that there would be agreement among analysts on how that question is to be answered, and I raise it here only to illuminate the lack of precision which still obtains in many areas that psychoanalysis shares with biology.[28]

Another general aspect of the relationship of psychoanalysis to biology —one that may be called antinomic—can best be discussed in connection with "imprinting" (Lorenz, 1935). It is hardly likely that another biological observation will be found to confirm the psychoanalytic theory of infantile experiences (memories and traumata) as satisfactorily as does

---

[28] Freud used evolutionary schemata quite frequently. Although their didactic value is unquestionable, it is uncertain which of them, if any, will stand the test of time. Some of them may have to be enlarged in order to survive. If flight, for example, is defined so broadly as to be capable of including Schneirla's (1959) "withdrawal response," which is apparently ubiquitous in the animal world, repression may rightly be viewed, in its evolutionary aspect, as the internalization of a biological mechanism that has made survival possible ever since the dawn of organismic life. As a matter of fact, in Freud's evolutionary schema of repression as presented in *Inhibition, Symptoms and Anxiety* (1926c, p. 92), a difference is made between stages which Schneirla would call withdrawal and avoidance.

the occurrence of imprinting in the early phases of the development of some animals. Nevertheless, it must be acknowledged that nothing of the psychoanalytic theory would have to be changed if imprinting did not occur at all in animal life. This part of psychoanalytic theory is so well founded on empirical observation that no new findings in animal psychology could eliminate its implications. Yet it is legitimate to refer to the corroborating significance of imprinting when the psychoanalytic theory of infantile life is discussed. Indeed, the discovery of imprinting has made it possible to place the psychoanalytic theory of infantile life within a broad evolutionary context; thus this part of the theory has become more firmly anchored in a general outlook with regard to organismic life. Although imprinting and the effects of infantile experiences are, to be sure, not identical, they are sufficiently closely related to be viewed as two stages of a single evolutionary process. Nevertheless, while we know that every psychological observation requires a corresponding physiological one, it still remains a matter of intellectual tact, and not, by any means, dependence on rule, to decide upon the correctness and the necessity of interrelating specific psychological processes with data obtained through biological research.

It would be of the greatest interest to ascertain the contribution of biology to ego psychology (cf. Hartmann et al., 1951, p. 6f.). Problems such as the neutralization of energy, or more generally the transformation of drive energy, will probably find their solution in physiological research, but that takes us out of the realm of the psychoanalytic situation. While biology's place in a psychology of the drives is, though far from being precisely stated, somewhat clarified, even that has not yet been accomplished with regard to ego psychology.

Upon perusal of the literature, it becomes rather clear that the psychoanalytic situation, and all the knowledge that can be obtained by its proper use, will not permit a final decision about Freud's last contribution to the psychology of drives, his theory of the death instinct. Here, as in the case of neutralization and the sublimation of drive energy, biology—that is to say, physiology and pathophysiology—must be called in, and must be accepted as the final arbiters.

Yet I am not aware of any focal problem of ego psychology whose solution would depend as completely upon one of the biological sciences. I do not take into account here one aspect of the genetic problem. It is quite possible that the origin of the ego can be determined only by the study of physical processes. Yet this is mainly due to the fact that the subject is inaccessible to study by psychological methods. I want to add a word on the position I am taking here.

There is no doubt that the processes within the ego are also based on biological factors and that there is therefore no reason to limit the relevance of the biological factor to processes in the id (Hartmann, 1952, p. 19). Everything we can observe in the psyche implies the existence of processes which can, in a general sense, be called biologic. Yet there are *degrees* of relevance. When we study thinking processes in an intoxicated person, we are still doing psychological research; the observations thus obtained require a psychological explanation, just as do the thinking processes of the unintoxicated. However, the biological factors are not identical with regard to the two subjects, even though they overlap.

It is a legitimate responsibility of psychology to define differences in biological relevance. To do this, knowledge of the biological process is not always necessary, as can be seen from the clinical fact that, in some instances, brain pathology that has produced no physical signs can be diagnosed nevertheless by psychological examination. In contrast with my thesis, Hebb (1949, p. 8f.) has demonstrated the great bearing upon "the theoretical problem of behavior" of the finding that the central nervous system is constantly active, even when it is free of external stimulation, as has been proved by electroencephalographic studies. Notwithstanding the importance of this finding, I think that in such constellations an exact conceptual analysis will also demonstrate that the "leap" from brain to mind is illusionary, even though it may serve constructively to stimulate new psychological research.

The constancy per se of CNS activity does not warrant any one psychological conclusion, for the activity of all parts may lead to their mutual neutralization, or it may reduce mental life by overstimulation, in a manner comparable to the epileptic seizure. The finding of constancy was meaningful to Hebb because, prior to the electroencephalographic findings, he was already dissatisfied with the S-R formula. He was able to use the new finding to make the existing theory more sophisticated.

With all this, I do not wish to dispute the necessity and productivity of the psychologist's study of brain physiology, pathophysiology, and pathology, and their effects upon mental life. Nevertheless, the specifics of the psychological event as yet cannot be derived from the specifics of the organic event; *bona fide* psychological theory can at this stage lead only as far as those fringe areas where the psyche's orbit ends. But when psychoanalysis steps outside the limits of its proper field and resorts to the use of biological models, then biology once again becomes the arbiter. At one point, Freud (1920a, p. 25) attributes the specific character of the system Cs. to the surface position of the cortical grey matter and the consequent ceaseless impact of external stimuli. This tentative biological model would be shown to be invalid, however, if Penfield (1937) should be right in his finding that the seat of consciousness lies instead in the diencephalon.

To be sure, if understanding of a mechanism—or of any mental phe-nomenon, for that matter—must include the knowledge of all preceding causal links, then of course an infinite mass of details drawn from anat-omy, physiology, biochemistry, embryology, etc., would have to be known. Experience shows that somebody who is an expert in all these causative links, as far as they are known, may still feel rather helpless vis-à-vis some data of the mind, for reasons which Kety has recently set forth.[29] Freud was well aware of that situation, which he epitomized in his com-ment about the many years he had spent on the study of the medulla oblongata without learning anything about anxiety (Freud, 1916-1917, p. 393).

Despite this apparent rejection of physiology and anatomy as a source of enlightenment for the analyst, Freud's theories are saturated with biology. There are, for example, the many biological models he uses for propaedeutic purposes, or with the intention of coming closer to an understanding of psychological data: the reflex as a model of the drive (Freud, 1915, p. 118); collateral circulation as a model of the effect of an impediment to genital gratification upon libidinal pathways (Freud, 1905a, pp. 151, 170, 193); or the comparison of fixation with unde-scended testes (Freud, 1916-1917, p. 339).

It is true that Freud likewise took models from other fields, which he used abundantly for identical purposes. When we take note of the fact that the constancy principle and the concept of defense are cornerstones of psychoanalytic theory, however, we must recognize that we are deal-ing with patterns that today hold a central position in modern physiology and pathophysiology. The curious circumstance that nevertheless reduces the importance of the study of medicine for the psychoanalyst is that

[29] He wrote: "there remains one biological phenomenon . . . , for which there is no valid physiochemical model . . . ; this is the phenomenon of consciousness" (Kety, 1960, p. 1861).

these concepts were not, historically, taken over from biology,[30] but were put by Freud into the center of his psychology on the basis of his psychoanalytic observations (Hartmann, 1956, p. 436).[31]

Furthermore, about half of psychoanalysis deals with the structural changes that the psychic apparatus undergoes under the impact of instinctual demands. Yet how much needs to be known about the physiology of the drives, in order to understand this part of psychoanalysis?[32] That is a difficult question to answer. One would think offhand that the phenomenology and the clinical data of the sexual drives and their disturbances are of greater importance than the intricacies of endrocrinology (cf. Hartmann, 1948). Yet, curiously enough, relatively little instruction along those lines is given at psychoanalytic institutes, and the science of sexology has made less progress than might have been expected in view of the new vistas that Freud opened up.[33]

It still remains a moot question, therefore, whether knowledge of the forms in which the sexual drives put their task upon the psychic apparatus is more relevant for the analyst than endocrinology, or less so. Depending on the direction research will take, one will receive more emphasis than the other; yet it is safe to say that, more than any mass of details regarding the organic substructure, what psychoanalysis generally requires may be called biological thinking. It has always seemed to me that it is in embryology that this type of thinking finds its most clear-cut embodiment. Here the idea of organic development crystallizes into a superb demonstration. Nevertheless, it cannot be said that the acquisition of biological thinking is to be looked for only in the study of any one fact or group of facts. There is one example of how biological thinking may be integrated in truly impressive fashion by a nonmedical person.

The following quotation from Nietzsche shows with striking clarity

[30] Freud's constancy principle goes back historically to Claude Bernard. For the psychoanalytic literature on homeostasis, see Orr (1942), Kubie (1948), K. Menninger (1954). For one example of the confirmation of a theory of Freud's by biology, see Kety (1960, p. 1864).

[31] Cf. Freud (1925d): "It . . . became possible . . . to use its [psychoanalysis] data as a means of discovering a new piece of biological knowledge" (p. 35). Where the translation talks of "discovering," the original text uses the word *erraten*, which literally means 'to guess at,' 'to divine,' or 'to conjecture.'

[32] Cf. Freud (1926a): "To find one's way about in it [the topic of sexuality] one of course needs anatomical and physiological knowledge, all of which is unfortunately not to be acquired in medical schools. But a familiarity with the history of civilization and with mythology is equally indispensable" (p. 210).

[33] Kinsey's splendid collections of data, though often adversely criticized by psychoanalysts, should be mentioned here (Kinsey et al., 1948, 1953).

that biological thinking can be acquired even by someone trained in philology. Nietzsche wrote:

The state of consciousness is the last and latest development of the organic, and hence its most unsettled and weakest [part]. Out of consciousness originate innumerable bad choices which cause the unnecessary and premature ruin of animal and man. . . . Were not the [self-] preserving association of the instincts so much more powerful, and did it not serve as a regulator of the whole, mankind would have to perish through its distorted judgments, its indulgence in spinning dreams with its eyes open, its superficiality and credulity, in short, through its state of consciousness; or rather, without the former, the latter would have gone out of existence long ago. Before a function is fully developed and mature, it is a danger to the organism; it is a good thing that it is effectively tyrannized—and not least by the pride therein! One thinks: here is the *core* of man, the persistent, eternal, last, and most original part of him! One considers consciousness to be a fixed, given magnitude! One denies its growth, its discontinuities! takes it as a "unit of the organism"!—This ridiculous overestimation and misunderstanding has the extremely useful consequence of *preventing* its all-too-hurried shaping. Because mankind believed that it possessed consciousness already, it did not strive to acquire it—and even now this has not changed! *To absorb knowledge* and to make it instinctive is still an entirely new task —a just dawning, scarcely visible task perceived only by those who understand that up to now only our *errors* have been absorbed and that our entire consciousness rests on errors.[34]

[34] "Die Bewusstheit ist die letzte und späteste Entwicklung des Organischen und folglich auch das Unfertigste und Unkräftigste daran. Aus dem Bewusstheit stammen unzählige Fehlgriffe, welche machen, dass ein Thier, ein Mensch zu Grunde geht, früher als es nöthig wäre . . . . Wäre nicht der erhaltende Verband der Instincte so überaus viel mächtiger, diente er nicht im Ganzen als Regulator: an ihren verkehrten Urtheilen und Phantasiren mit offnen Augen, an ihrer Ungründlichkeit und Leichtgläubigkeit, kurz eben an ihrer Bewusstheit müsste die Menschheit zu Grunde gehen: oder vielmehr, ohne Jenes gäbe es Diese längst nicht mehr: Bevor eine Function ausgebildet and reif ist, ist sie eine Gefahr des Organismus: gut, wenn sie so lange tüchtig tyrannisirt wird! So wird die Bewusstheit tüchtig tyrannisirt—und nicht am wenigsten von dem Stolze darauf! Man denkt, hier sei *der Kern* des Menschen; sein Bleibendes, Ewiges, Letztes, Ursprünglichstes! Man hält die Bewusstheit für eine fest gegebne Grösse! Leugnet ihr Wachstum, ihre Intermittenzen! Nimmt sie als "Einheit des Organismus"!—Diese lächerliche Überschätzung und Verkennung des Bewusstseins hat die grosse Nützlichkeit zur Folge, dass damit eine allzuschnelle Ausbildung desselben *verhindert* worden ist. Weil die Menschen die Bewusstheit schon zu haben glaubten, haben sie sich wenig Mühe darum gegeben, sie zu erwerben—und auch jetzt noch steht es nicht anders! Es ist immer noch eine ganz neue und eben erst dem menschlichen Auge aufdämmernde, kaum noch deutlich erkennbare *Aufgabe, das Wissen sich einzuverleiben* und instinctiv zu machen,—eine Aufgabe, welche nur von Denen gesehen wird, die

These lines were written in 1881, at a time when mechanical thinking was flourishing in science and the humanities, by a man who preferred the study of history to that of the living organism, and who, had he studiously read all the textbooks of his own time, would probably never have been inspired to develop such ideas, almost unsurpassed by anything written on the subject since then. Such is the power of the human mind that, in spite of a lack of curricula and certificates, it may develop ideas which even the brain of the most erudite psychosomaticist would probably never have produced.

But Nietzsche was a genius, it may be objected, the exception from which a generalization can by no means be derived. Yet one can still learn from his example that there are a great many sources from which biological thinking can be acquired, not the least of them being the study of his works, which might well prove to be a better preparation for the analyst-to-be than a study of Boyd's excellent text on pathology.

Is it not strange that there are psychoanalysts who seriously believe that the understanding of man depends upon the knowledge of a certain body of nonpsychological data? Yet the argument goes further: in order to understand the neurotic subject studied by psychoanalysis—that is, a sick person—the sick body, its diseases, the problems that beset the organically sick patient ought to be, even *have* to be known. I am forced to regard this argument as the result of ignoring rather plain facts. An impressively large number of persons in whose life organic sickness has played a significant role will report that it is the exception to be treated by a physician who recognizes the patient as a *suffering* being. I could detail a long list of experiences to illustrate this; my claim is that it is in psychoanalysis that the understanding of suffering is acquired.

During the course of all too many psychoanalyses, one has the painful opportunity to observe the emotional injuries that the patient has had to suffer at the hands of his physician. I know specialists of the highest reputation, in whose waiting rooms a nurse or secretary will take the patient's history with other patients listening; the crowded waiting rooms themselves bear witness to what I speak of; and I do not raise here the question of what a clinic patient has to endure, although the latter abuse may perhaps be unalterable under present conditions.

Yet, what if we should turn to psychosomatic practice, where the emo-

---

begriffen haben, dass bisher nur unsere *Irrthümer* uns einverleibt waren und dass all unsere Bewusstheit sich auf Irrthümer bezieht!" Translated by the author from Nietzsche's (1882) *Die fröhliche Wissenschaft* (p. 47f.). Italics Nietzsche's.

tional factor is, after all, the center of attention? As far as I was able to observe in my clinical experience, the patient does not fare too well there, either. Over and over again what happens is that he acquires a deep feeling of guilt upon finding out that his obstreperous unconscious is the purported source of his painful symptoms. He feels particularly helpless, since the organic traces that his unconscious conflicts presumably leave are far beyond his control; this is significantly different from his help-lessness vis-à-vis the repressed, where the course of defense against it leads to the formation of psychoneurotic symptoms. Thus burdened both by guilt and by helplessness, he does not, in many instances, find any relief there either.

These critical remarks should not be taken as a general statement. There are, of course, those extraordinary physicians—still definitely a small minority—who combine human greatness with outstanding pro-fessional skills. The vast majority of physicians, however, are harassed by a load of responsibilities, shortage of time and constant hurry—and humaneness needs time: the hurried man cannot be humane.

The epitome of suffering is surely to be found in the mentally dis-eased. It is significant to discover in the history of medicine how little the knowledge of the diseased body and the organically diseased patient has helped the medical profession to understand and deal with suffering of the mind. Every so often, a layman has appeared on the stage of med-ical history to bring solace and relief. (Perhaps he should have been forbidden to do so, since he was without a medical diploma!)

These are by no means matters of the past alone. Statistically, I am certain that it could be proved that in present-day society the vast major-ity of patients suffering from major psychoses are treated in a medically quite acceptable, yet humanly altogether unacceptable way. The neurol-ogist and general psychiatrist who subjects schizophrenic and depressed patients one after another to electroshock treatment is by now a well-known type of specialist. He does not "believe in" psychotherapy—and the truth is he does not practice it. Shock treatment comes to be dis-placed by drug treatment, and it becomes quite acceptable in general practice to subject schizophrenic patients to a therapy that is limited to one of the tranquilizers.

One should compare these therapeutic techniques with those described by Schwing (1940) or Sèchehaye (1947, 1950), two lay analysts. It is not a question at this point of taking a stand for one or the other mode of treatment, but of demonstrating that the layman without medical

training may find approaches that bear witness to a profounder understanding of the sick person's plight than the average physician who has
gone through medical school.

I am tempted to present incidents that I myself have had the occasion
to observe, in order to demonstrate the shortcomings of medical analysts,
although they will be—perhaps rightly so—regarded as exceptions, and
thus explained as individual failures that do not warrant general conclusions of any kind. The advantage of such examples, however, would
be to show that what is quite inacceptable in the light of systemic psychology becomes acceptable, perhaps even advisable, from the medical
point of view. This becomes quite clear as soon as the basic situation of
medical practice, the patient's physical examination, is considered. As
is well known, such physical examination makes it impossible to proceed
further in the psychoanalytic exploration. Yet I do not find the consequences of this impossibility discussed in terms of the medical value of
psychoanalysis. What are the real consequences of the fact that the very
core situation of medical practice is incompatible with the practice of
psychoanalysis?

It may be said that a similar situation is met with in other medical
specialties. The ophthalmologist limits his examination to the visual system, leaving the patient's general physical condition to the internist.
That is true enough, but it describes an essentially different situation.
When, as the result of medical specialization, it turns out for practical
reasons to be better that the treatment of special organ systems should
be assigned to specially trained physicians, there is no objection in principle to any specialist examining whatever organ system he considers
relevant. If need be, the ophthalmologist will not hesitate to take a
patient's blood pressure or to determine his neurological status. With
regard to psychoanalysis, however, it is not a question of convenience,
but a matter of principle. This fact alone—since it concerns the basic
situation from which all medicine takes its start, and without which the
whole edifice of medicine is unthinkable—takes psychoanalysis out of
the medical orbit. Yet I wish to go a step further, and to demonstrate
that psychoanalytic tact is essentially different from medical tact.

Alexander (1946, pp. 98-101) introduced a new test to decide the
question of a patient's treatability. He demonstrated how, in one instance,
he had reached the conclusion that a sixty-year-old businessman, who
was suffering from a phobia (in my own opinion, the patient showed

early signs of either a degenerative disease or a malignant psychiatric disorder) was not suitable for treatment. He quickly made what appears to be an adequate appraisal of the rather desperate situation in which the patient, for whom the necessity of retirement was unacceptable, found himself; but he then subjected him to questions and explorations of a sort that consistently brought him back to this most acute issue, which the patient had succeeded fairly well in denying as an issue up to then.

It is worthwhile rereading this report, so striking in its revelation of the therapist's insistence on irritating the patient by repeated attempts at deprecating his precarious defenses. It becomes understandable therefore that the patient (apparently losing his patience) should have "called for his wife and departed." Unfortunately, the author, who was later informed of the cessation of the patient's phobia ("he no longer mentioned going to the office but was *content* to stay at home," italics mine), did not seek to find out whether the patient may have fallen victim to a paralyzing depression.[35] Here is an example of how the medical analyst, for the sake of a sham exactness, can lose his sense of tact[36] (and, concomitantly, his humaneness). Consider merely the idea of a test (did Alexander actually mean a psychoanalytic test?) in the first interview of a severely sick patient who finds himself in a desperate reality situation!

The other example concerns the handling of a fifty-year-old married woman who suffered from schizophrenia, centering in the well-known delusion of an influencing machine, which she asserted was moving her clitoris. After the customary course of electroshock treatment (which was followed by clinical improvement), the analyst told the patient that "she was suffering from an emotional upset based on difficulties involving masturbation; that if her clitoris was moving and affording her sexual pleasure it was because she was herself moving it. I told her that if she would assume responsibility for her own thoughts and feelings, it would be easier to help her. She responded to this explanation by lapsing into a state of psychomotor retardation . . ." (Linn, 1958, p. 307). The author seems to base his belief in the wholesome effect of this procedure on the patient's later clinical improvement. Yet, while this way of dealing with

---

[35] The reader may recall that Oberndorf's (1912) treatment, to which I referred earlier, resulted in the patient's "cold, clear sadness" (p. 448).

[36] I am quite convinced that Ferenczi (1926) was wrong in reproaching Alexander in particular with a relative lack of "susceptibility to shades of difference" (p. 225); any analyst who becomes a medical analyst is more than likely to lose that susceptibility. (Concerning analytic tact, cf. Freud, 1926a, p. 220.)

a patient may be quite compatible with medical ethics, it is altogether incompatible with what psychoanalysis stands for.

Despite the great progress that the teaching of medicine has made in the last thirty years, despite the enormous good will that so many persons of influence have shown in setting up a training program that will result in the medical student's becoming competent in matters of tact, empathy, and understanding, I believe that Freud's distrust of the effect per se of the study of medicine is still valid.[37] To be sure, the study of medicine does not seem to have the same adverse effect on every student, or else one could not explain why there are and have been so many excellent medically trained psychoanalysts. Yet it is quite possible that these latter, because of their particular endowments and personal interests, and perhaps even because of accident, escaped the detrimental effect that the study of medicine may have in matters of the mind—an effect which can be seen all too clearly when the medically trained analyst turns into a medical analyst. One wonders how many students of medicine, well endowed by their disposition for a productive psychoanalytic career, completed their studies deprived of the chance ever to realize these assets.

On closer inspection, this assertion concerning the unfavorable effect that the study of medicine may or will have on a person's psychological sensibility loses its perplexing aspects. In almost all medical schools, the student's earliest studies have to do with the morphology, structure, and physiology of normal organs; from there he ascends to pathology. Even where pathology is introduced at an earlier stage, the student must occupy himself extensively with diseased organs and their dysfunctions—which, however, do not make up a suffering human being. Indeed, one may even say that physical pathology and subjective suffering are incommensurable, for while someone may know everything there is to be known about the pathology of the body, he may still be ignorant about the psychology of suffering.

When I stress the fact that the same physical involvement, even if it is life-threatening, may cause great suffering in one instance and remain almost unnoticed in another, I am only trying to show how little actual correlation there may be between involvement and suffering. Yet even a total correlation would not disprove my previous assertion about their

[37] Cf. also Freud (1919a) about the advisability of teaching psychoanalysis at universities, and his correspondence with the President of the Hebrew University in Jerusalem (Rosenbaum, 1954).

incommensurability. When I further recall to the reader the fact that knowledge of all the physical prerequisites for color sensation would not make the blind man know what red or blue is, or even help him to imagine them, the application of this truism to our problem is obvious. Thus the well-trained physician, most eager to help his patient as speedily and effectively as possible, thinks first of organs and functions; the mind is, in the last analysis, of interest to him only in so far as it may interfere with the effectiveness of his treatment.

The physician knows that overtaxing the patient's morale may result in a serious depression or worse; he therefore has to humor him in order not to lose an important partner in an adventure-laden enterprise that involves at best a calculated risk. Beyond this, any interest becomes a diversion and an interference with the physician's concentration upon the one great enemy he faces—the diseased organ. As a noteworthy exception, and an admirable example of its kind, I refer to a modern technique evolved by Coleman to protect children against the trauma so often produced by tonsillectomy (Coleman, 1950; Goldman and Crain, 1957). Here the physician succeeded in converting into play an event so frequently traumatic to the child.

Although this welcome progress should not be questioned, nevertheless one may foretell its limitations. The technique of making a surgical intervention seem almost pleasurable does harbor the seed of masochistic attitudes and of denial. I can already imagine how, after many years, when Coleman's technique has become generally accepted, a countermovement may set in that is oriented toward the child's acquiring insight and learning to differentiate between play and reality—after which a selective, individually adjusted procedure may be evolved, the very small or sick child being protected by play, and the more mature child being burdened by the pain of reality, although in such a way as not to let the experience grow into a trauma.

However, I will now cite an opinion that is diametrically opposed to mine. In 1943, Zilboorg wrote:

> Is it necessary to be a physician, if you know well how the human mind works? It is more than necessary; it is imperative. Any attempt on the part of a psychologist to treat and to cure any sick person is charlatanism, no matter what cloak of respectability he may wear . . . . There is no magic in the fact of being a doctor of medicine, but there is one special aspect of being a physician which cannot be acquired anywhere but in medical training. The medical student, whatever specialty he may

choose after his medical training is completed, is thrown into close contact with patients—with people who are ill, who suffer a great deal, and who frequently die under his own eyes. At the bedside he learns many things which one can never learn from any book or in any spontaneous way. He learns to work in an atmosphere of illness and death without the average man's anxiety. He learns to walk among wrecks of people—stuporous, comatose, writhing, quietly receding from life or gradually rising back to it. He learns to walk in this atmosphere without disgust and without horror, with equanimity and with serenity. He learns to do all this without becoming hard and indifferent. Serene, seemingly impervious to the anxiety of death or disintegration, he still preserves the ever present concern for those occupying the sickbed . . . . He learns to know man as no one else knows him. Through the years of training a peculiar sense of responsibility for the sick man is inculcated into the doctor [Zilboorg, 1943, pp. 19-21].

This viewpoint, I have already previously tried to refute. What Zilboorg is delineating here is an idealized scheme of what a physician is, which may in fact be true of the very few who are the chosen. The grim reality of the conflicts, anxieties, and denials, particularly regarding death, which are found with fair regularity in the analyses of physicians, is left out of consideration. Zilboorg almost seems to assert that, at the end of medical training, we have a physician free of neurosis. It may be advisable to read Simmel's (1926) paper on the psychopathology inherent in professional medicine (cf. Nunberg, 1938).

To be sure, a person with his own bent and interest in this direction will have a splendid opportunity, while going through medical training, to learn about pain and suffering. Indeed, he may even become a master in transforming for a patient an experience that might otherwise threaten dread, despair, and permanent injury to the mind, into one from which the patient will emerge wiser than he was before, closer to a full grasp of life, and imbued with a new and vigorous understanding of the value of life. But to think that the study of medicine is a prerequisite for this, or that going through it creates a special disposition toward that mastery, would indeed falsify the clinical record.

The mere perusal of Tolstoy's (1884) *The Death of Ivan Ilyich* proves that, without medical knowledge, one can penetrate to deeper levels of the understanding of anguish than most physicians have ever succeeded in doing. To be sure, Tolstoy's understanding is not a scientific one, while scientific insight is precisely what is aspired to by the psychoanalyst. Yet, if a man unequipped with medical knowledge is able to penetrate to such depths in his observations, the conclusion is clear that medical knowledge is not necessarily the royal road to the understanding of pain and of the psychology of disease.

PSYCHOANALYSIS AND THE SCIENCE OF MAN

It now behooves me to turn to that other great group of sciences, those which investigate everything that is directly or indirectly connected with man's mind, or which reflect the element of human nature. In searching for a comprehensive term to designate this group of sciences, one is tempted to consider such terms as 'mental sciences,' 'humanities,' or 'anthropology'; but they have already been pre-empted by areas with a special meaning, and their usage in this context might create misunderstandings. For brevity's sake, I shall therefore use the as yet unencumbered term "anthropic sciences" and "anthropic scientist."

To show what I mean here, I can call upon the well-known example of the explorer who finds in the desert a previously unobserved petrified pattern. After its measurement, reproduction, and exact description have been completed, he will have to make a decision as to whether the pattern has been produced solely by the interaction of matter with physical forces, such as wind, storm, rain, oxidation, etc., or is the product of human activity, such as that of a craftsman, an artist, a priest, or a playing child. A complete account of all the possibilities would, of course, reveal even more complex situations, not so easily classified. The pattern could have been left by footprints, for example, or by the traces of an object that had been moved by human hands. What is significant is that the approach and interpretation will be basically different, depending on whether one assumes that the causative links that led to the pattern consisted solely of physicochemical forces, or included one relevant link reflecting human activity (in its broader meaning).[38]

In the first case, the scientist may succeed in reducing all the causative links to physicochemical events; in the latter case, he will not be able to, for in addition to purely physicochemical processes, we will have to consider processes that have human origins and human meanings. If it was the activity of a priest that was involved in producing the pattern, the

[38] An exact analysis of this example would overtax the reader's patience unnecessarily. How should we classify the pattern, if it is the result of a human biological function? If the pattern is the result of a scatological funeral rite, for example, we find both groups of sciences involved in the explanation of the pattern.

explorer may have to consider the possibility that the pattern was connected with, or was the result of a magic rite, the full meaning of which cannot be reduced to merely physicochemical processes.

The natural scientist will, in most instances, seek to explain all events that he is investigating in terms of physicochemical processes. As long as there is still a gap in the links preceding the event that needs to be explained, and he has to assume for it processes or forces of another kind, such as an *élan vital,* he does not consider his task accomplished. Physics and chemistry thus occupy a central position in the natural sciences, although the natural sciences are, as a matter of fact, more than physics and chemistry.[39] If a skeleton is found, it has to be classified; the appearance and habitat of the live animal have to be reconstructed, etc. All this mentation is not directly connected with physics or chemistry, even though it leads to the description of facts which, in other special fields, have been or will be reduced to chemical and physical events.

Thus we observe in the natural sciences the application in practice of a large variety of methods, each of which is subtly adapted to the particular requirements of the respective field; yet each of these fields in turn requires physics and chemistry in order to complete the explanatory *sine qua non.* The role of physics and chemistry is twofold in this concerted effort: progress in physics and chemistry improves methods of observation and fact-finding (the modern electron microscope, for example); on the other hand, new discoveries in physics and chemistry are bound to enlarge the explanatory vistas of natural sciences, since each step forward in physics and chemistry increases the probabilty of being able to reduce as yet unreduced data to the fundamental physicochemical processes.

The equivalent position is held by psychology in the anthropic sciences (cf. Hartmann, 1927, pp. 24-36; Freud, 1933a, p. 198; Alexander, 1932, p. 252; Simmel, 1940, p. 165). Nevertheless, while the key position of physics and chemistry is acknowledged by the majority of natural scientists, such a position is denied by most anthropic scientists with regard to psychology. One meets with the effort quite frequently—and with the intention, set forth *expressis verbis*—to explain cultural phenomena *without any reference to psychological data.*

A number of branches of the anthropic sciences are able to produce

---

[39] Whether all biological processes are essentially reducible to physicochemical events has, of course, been discussed from many different angles. For an interesting objection, see Le Corbeiller (1946, p. 81).

significant work without drawing on psychological data, forming their basic concepts and theoretical system in such a way as to exclude the inroads of psychology. A history of any given cultural element or object may be written in such fashion that all existing objects, or all representative samples thereof, can be correctly described, dated, and analyzed in terms of techniques, aesthetic values, style, and other such properties, and then grouped according to their similarities, differences, or contrasts with regard to each element or the patterns of such elements.

As is well known, the next steps involve the establishment of developmental lines within the same class of objects, or within a related class of objects. Nevertheless, the anthropic sciences do not stop at establishing such correlations. Once a class of objects has been adequately ordered, correlations are also established with elements alien to that class. Thus, the development of a certain ornamental form may be correlated with a change from the nomadic to the agricultural mode of living. However, some—perhaps most—investigators try to limit class-disparate correlations to a minimum, stopping instead with an analysis of samples of the class under investigation, along developmental lines established according to time sequences, in which they describe carefully the changes that occur as the class of objects increases through additions made by subsequent generations. On the other hand, there are schools of thought that explain changes within a class of objects systematically by way of the effects of a different class. Thus, historical materialism tries to explain art, religion, and other cultural elements through economic facts and their effects on political organization. Others correlate cultural data with biological factors, such as race; still others see in art manifestations of man's religious attitudes, etc.

Thus a large variety of correlations is to be found in the anthropic sciences, which still lack any general agreement as to the contents of their ultimate reductions, such an agreement as now obtains in the natural sciences with regard to physics and chemistry. Yet, just as we know that all the contents of what is investigated by the natural sciences are, in the final analysis, physicochemical events, so it can be stated with equal certitude that all the contents of the anthropic sciences are, in the final analysis, caused by human activity. Where the subjects of investigation in the natural sciences are physicochemical processes, the subjects of anthropic research are manifestations, deposits, traces of human activity. The only element that unfailingly appears throughout the anthropic sciences belongs to psychology—which is precisely the reason why the overwhelming majority of statements found in the anthropic sciences can be converted into psychological ones.

When it is said that a certain form of vessel is found in the neolithic era, this can be converted without changing the statement's correctness into the following: "There were people, or a person, who in the neolithic era produced this form of vessel"; likewise, the statement "Prices fell in the eighteenth century" can be converted into "People offered and bought merchandise in the eighteenth century at a gradually falling price."[40] It is irrelevant in this context whether or not every single finding in the anthropic sciences is convertible in this way; yet one argument that is likely to be raised may be refuted briefly.

It will be said that only a small part of the anthropic scientist's work can be converted into the type of statement I have set forth, since most of the anthropic sciences investigate group-related contents. While the psychology of groups may differ significantly from the psychology of the personality at specific points, it remains psychology, and these differences do not affect any claim that psychology is basic to the anthropic sciences.[41]

Since the contents of the anthropic sciences are all related to man, scientists have derived many psychological insights from the study of culture. Of course, man's cultural achievements necessarily embody something of his psychology;[42] yet it is risky to build psychology solely on the results of the investigation of cultural achievements. A more reliable method is first to establish psychology by the direct observation of man, and then to complement these insights by the study of culture. This was the path that psychoanalysis took.

A general tendency can be observed in the anthropic sciences to hide psychological statements behind the description of cultural facts; or casually to contrive a new brand of psychology to suit some immediate needs; or to select as the 'current' psychology the one which may have some appeal to the anthropic scientist. This disorder and arbitrariness in psychological matters is the result of several factors. Since 'everyone knows something' about psychology, through self-observation and the

[40] Cf. Freud (1933a, p. 198): ". . . nothing that man makes or does can be understood without the aid of psychology . . . ."

[41] See Freud (1933a): "Strictly speaking, indeed, there are only two sciences—psychology, pure and applied, and natural science" (p. 245). For the relationship between individual and social psychology, see Freud (1921), de Saussure (1950, pp. 9-12), and Hartmann et al. (1957, p. 7f.).

[42] It is not historically unusual that highly complex processes have been used initially to examine a simple one; Lavoisier's experiment with the metabolism of animals, in order to prove the nature of oxidation, is one example.

observation of others, most people feel free to make psychological statements without regard to the safeguards of science, apparently unaware that a common-sense judgment in psychology harbors as great a chance of error as common-sense judgments in the natural sciences. Also, of course, it is far easier to use psychological explanations according to one's personal bent than to expose them to the rigorous scrutiny of science.

An important historical fact must also be considered here. The pre-Freudian anthropic scientist did not have a scientific system psychology which would have been suitable for his purpose. In most instances, the reason why academic psychology did not prove itself usable was that it was predominantly medial whereas, for the explanation of man as a creative agent, it is a system psychology that is required. Were man a medium, he could never have created culture.

After Freud had established the foundations of psychoanalysis, anthropic scientists were no longer justified in continuing their looseness and arbitrariness in matters of psychology. Yet, since the findings of psychoanalysis infringed upon common sense and aroused discomfort, it is understandable that psychoanalysis came to be shunned by most anthropic scientists. There were only a few, like the keen-minded Alfred von Berger, author, professor of literature, and Director of the Viennese Burgtheater, who immediately acknowledged the value of Breuer and Freud's *Studies on Hysteria,* and recognized that here was a key to the scientific understanding of cultural products.[43] It did not take Freud long to demonstrate the heuristic value of psychoanalysis for anthropic sciences.

It was the *Leonardo* study (Freud, 1910b) that introduced the new era of the application of psychoanalysis to the anthropic sciences.[44] To what extent Freud's new method had a bearing on them outside the narrow orbit of the psychoanalytic movement, I do not wish to discuss. The two most remarkable anthropic essays that Freud wrote, the *Leonardo* and the *Moses* essays, were generally not well received. Of the many reasons for the disbelief with which most of the specialists in the an-

[43] Significantly he gave his feuilleton the title *Surgery of the Soul* and wrote: "We do not know how science judges Breuer and Freud's theories. The poets are altogether on their side and that is no small thing. For until now the poets were those who knew and asserted the most and the best about the secrets of man's soul" (von Berger, 1896; my own translation).

[44] The date of Freud's *Leonardo* study should, for the sake of accuracy, be advanced to 1907, when Freud (1907b) published *Gradiva,* but that paper did not acquire as much prominence as the *Leonardo* study. With some degree of correctness, one may call Freud's book on *Jokes* (1905b) his first anthropic contribution.

thropic sciences met Freud's deductions, I shall deal with one, which is rarely considered, probably because of its abstract character.

Freud's genius consisted of an extraordinary ability to unfold a seemingly simple phenomenon as the end product of a large number of (synergistic and antagonistic) forces, from whose dynamic interplay he was able to derive a chain of processes that finally led to the phenomenon under investigation. Thus he succeeded with compelling logic in deriving the complex structure of the psychic apparatus from a psychological element as seemingly simple as the dream.

It is precisely this disproportion between the initial terms and the richness of the final inferences that aroused the suspicion of the expert, just as we tend to distrust the honesty of a man who, from only a small initial investment, harvests a fortune. To turn to another example: the reader may recall Sherlock Holmes's remarkable ability to deduce a huge array of facts from the observation of a small, seemingly trivial element, which others might not even consider it worth their while to take note of. What was accomplished by Conan Doyle for the entertainment of the reader, by the employment of his flourishing imaginative powers, Freud realized in a rigorously scientific way. Indeed, the disproportion between the huge volume of deduced facts and the very small amount of initially known elements is very striking in Freud's anthropic work. In the *Leonardo* study, we encounter just such a disproportion, large enough at any rate to make the anthropic scientist[45] reject the far-reaching conclusions that Freud drew from a brief childhood recollection which Leonardo had jotted down on one of his many manuscript pages.

The greatest achievement of analytic mentation that Freud brought forth, in my opinion, can be found in his *Moses and Monotheism*—a book that I shall return to later in a more significant context—in which he deduced the past history of a whole nation from an unusual characteristic in one of its traditive legends. Here the area from which the deduction started was really microscopically small, while the scope of the deductions was enormous. Such disproportion alone, without the consideration of any other factors at play, prompts rejection by the academic anthropic scientist. Whether their criticisms have been right or wrong, it must be admitted that, to judge the results of Freud's anthropic research, one must understand psychoanalysis. Yet psychoanalysis cannot, on the whole, be learned from books, and I shall soon have to turn to an

---

[45] Cf. Schapiro's (1956) criticism of Freud's *Leonardo* essay.

examination of what conditions must be fulfilled to make possible its application to anthropic research.

Among the natural sciences, as I have shown above, physics and chemistry have a *public standing* that is vastly different from that which psychoanalysis has among the anthropic sciences. If the botanist or the zoologist sets out to account for an observation that he has made, and finds that he needs an understanding of the chemical processes involved, he will study the chapter of organic chemistry that is applicable to the problem in question. He has probably taken courses in chemistry and is familiar with its basic methods, vocabulary, concepts, and theories; yet he may never have reached the particular complexities involved in the observation in question. In spite of this, he will accept as correct what he finds in a reputable textbook, and will not necessarily insist on its validation by a repetition of the experiments recorded in the textbook. Chemistry is a respected branch of natural science: the bulk of its findings have become part of a scientist's 'common-sense' thinking, while the areas in which chemists have not yet achieved agreement are well defined.

This is not the case with regard to psychoanalysis. No expository and comprehensive text has yet been written whose correctness is accepted even by the majority of analysts. Thus, when the anthropic scientist wishes to inform himself about scientific system psychology, he faces a serious problem. Even should he decide in favor of the views of the founder of psychoanalysis, and therefore ignore the critical claims of analysts or of those psychoanalytic schools that have since formed theories significantly deviating from Freud's—not to speak of the claims of that vast majority of experts who reject psychoanalysis outright—it will be very hard for him to ascertain or to understand what Freud's final theories were.

For he changed many of his initial views: some he developed further, some he refuted, and some he brought into harmony with later discoveries; others, however, he left in the shape of their original formulation. Thus, it is not always easy to determine which may need reformulation, and which can still stand on their own merits. Consequently, the anthropic scientist would have to start with Freud's earliest publications and, repeating in miniature Freud's own path of development, work his way through to the final *Outline*. This is a unique situation in present-day science, for the study of modern science does not generally require the perusal of the works of the founders.[46] Furthermore, if psychoanalysis is to be used constructively in the anthropic sciences, more is required than just the understanding of psychoanalysis itself[47] (cf. de Saussure, 1950, p. 61f.).

The bulk of psychoanalytic writing has been done by professional psychoanalysts, whose main (almost exclusive) source has been the psychoanalytic situation—that is to say, the direct observation of a subject striving toward the expression of his free associations. To be sure, psychoanalysts have also applied the knowledge thus acquired to some branches of anthropic science, and especially to anthropology, literature, the pictorial arts, and biography. Nevertheless, the majority of those who have applied psychoanalysis in this way were not necessarily experts in the field to which the application was made. Yet it almost goes without saying that the reliability of conclusions is guaranteed only when the anthropic scientist achieves a mastery both in psychoanalysis and in the subject to which he applies it.[48] As a matter of fact, some of the criticism that Freud's own anthropic work met with was based precisely on the assertion that he was not an expert in the specific anthropic science. Whether this criticism was well taken or not is of no consequence here, for even if we were certain that Freud did not err in his applications of psychoanalysis, that would not be grounds for abandoning the insistence that mastery in two fields is necessary today, if psychoanalysis is to be applied reliably to the anthropic sciences.[49]

What contribution to psychoanalysis can be expected from psychoanalytic anthropic research? The answer to this can be given with particular succinctness with regard to language, which holds a unique position in the psychoanalytic situation. Language is not only the chief medium through which the subject communicates with the observer in

[46] Cf. Hartmann (1956) and Gillispie's (1960) remark about the study of Copernicus's famous treatise, *De revolutionibus orbium celestium libri sex* (p. 19). It is quite possible that only an insignificant number of our contemporaries have ever seen the text, much less read it. The necessity of studying original scientific works in great detail and with great exactness is characteristic of the initial stages of development of a new science.

[47] See chapter 7, on the training of the anthropic scientist.

[48] Cf. Freud (1933a): "Such an application [of psychoanalysis to fields of knowledge] presupposes a technical knowledge which the analyst does not possess; while those who do possess the knowledge . . . do not know anything of analysis" (p. 199).

[49] Geniuses usually have 'good luck,' it is true; yet research, as badly as it needs geniuses, cannot rely on them alone. The flourishing of a science requires the average scientist just as urgently as it does the genius. If the author of a recent paper is correct in his assertions, Freud had, even in his most daring anthropic venture, the *Moses*, more 'luck' than most of his critics seem to have been aware of (see Chandler, 1962).

the psychoanalytic situation; it is also the *only* operative tool at the observer's disposal, his *only* therapeutic medium, a situation not to be found in any other area of medicine. The analyst takes language for granted, using it without deliberation about its structure and innate form. He uses it the way the X-ray machine is used by the internist, who may know very little indeed about the physics of X rays, but is nevertheless expert in handling the machine and in interpreting the film produced by it.[50]

Starting with his study of aphasia (Freud, 1891a), Freud made a few contributions to the psychology of language, the most notable of which in my estimation is the article on "Negation" (Freud, 1925b). Far-reaching as the other linguistic implications may be in his *Interpretations of Dreams,* in this context it is only necessary to mention his finding that the dream cannot directly represent a 'no.' Thus, when he turned toward ego psychology, the ability to negate a content became a matter of focal interest. In his paper on "Negation," Freud showed that a sentence, in addition to containing an objective reference (a matter of fact), may also contain a structural relation that is an outgrowth of the psychic apparatus.

Negation is a syntactic form in which a repressed content can be verbalized, without arousing mental pain or discomfort, and without actuating resistance. The self admits indirectly the existence of a repressed content by means of a configuration whose structure equips the ego to believe in its nonexistence. That is to say, the syntactic structure is correlated here with personality structure or, speaking more modestly, with a limited area of personality structure. Language becomes relevant here, not as a tool with which to convey contents, but as the direct carrier, in its structure, of personality structure.

This is a quite remarkable characteristic, going beyond the triad of functions: representation, expression, appeal (Bühler, 1934; Loewenstein, 1956), attributed to language. Is this true of other linguistic forms, too? Is it possible that all existing linguistic forms are the husks of structural personality elements? What psychological structure is, for example, reflected when discourse takes the form of a question? How can man pose a question at all? (See Olinick, 1954, 1957.) From the psychological point of view, one may say *cum grano salis* that a question

---

[50] Yet there is a score of medical and nonmedical specialists who are constantly working toward the improvement of the machine. There is no obstacle placed in the way of their performing further experiments to improve the accuracy of X-ray diagnosis.

can be asked only when, in one sense, the questioner already knows the answer.

When I arrive in a town with the layout of which I am unfamiliar and ask for directions, I have a certain schema in mind, such as relational pattern of right and left, whose actual structure I do not know but expect to find out from the person I ask. Every so often it happens that patients ask questions without having any possible answer in mind; when they are asked what answer they think *might* be given to their question, it turns out that they themselves do not know of any. In this situation new possibilities of linguistic research of importance to the psychoanalyst are opened up—all the more so since the analyst does not limit his linguistic activity to interpretation, but asks questions himself, an ill-founded procedure as long as so little is known about the structural aspect of questions.

If we could be certain that Freud's paper on "Negation" is paradigmatic, and that all syntactic forms are correlated with (or perhaps even manifestations of) definable structural constellations, there would be some likelihood that the translation into metapsychological terms of such highly structured linguistic patterns as hypothetical statements or hypothetical questions would lead to the discovery of structural personality patterns not yet known. How far psychoanalytic linguistics may go can already be foreseen in dim outline when patients are observed who prefer direct to indirect speech in reporting on past conversations. The sense of time is apparently disturbed in this clinical type, in so far as there is a fixation on the present; from this prevalence of the present, one can deduce a disturbance or rather a narrowing down of value systems.

Furthermore, psychoanalysis was evolved in the countries of the West, all of which use languages that, in spite of the great variations among them, share a common structural foundation. There are, however, linguistic areas whose languages are structured differently, and we do not know whether, to a person speaking such a language, psychoanalysis in its present form could be applied at all.[51] In other words, what is the actual influence of the structure of occidental languages upon psychoanalysis? Since their basic structure is an invariable factor within the geographical area in which psychoanalysis has been principally cultivated, this question can hardly be resolved within the occidental world alone.

[51] I owe to Mr. Ernst Federn the suggestion that psychoanalytic experiences in Japan or India may, by now, permit an answer to this question.

Concomitantly with solving the problem of the metapsychology of negation, Freud laid the cornerstone of a metapsychology of grammar, or more precisely, of syntax. Without a metapsychology of syntax, the psychoanalytic technique is deprived of an invaluable steering instrument. Yet it seems that, with Freud's essay on "Negation," the metapsychology of language came to a standstill once more, even though the essay made a beginning which should really have served as the prelude to an 'interpretation of language.'

In order to bring my view on this matter to the fore as succinctly as possible, let me state the following hypothetical situation: If a choice had to be made between complete knowledge of the structure and physiology of the brain and knowledge of the metapsychology of grammar and syntax, there could not be a moment's hesitation in choosing the latter as more important to psychoanalysis, in spite of the former's incomparably greater importance to medicine. To do otherwise would be to forget that psychoanalysis is above all, and exclusively, system psychology.

Is it to be expected that—in view of the present character of the organization of psychoanalysis in this country—such a metapsychology of syntax will ever be written? It would require an eminently gifted linguist with particularly broad analytic experience. Assuming that there is such a linguist, and that he discovers the problem and is attracted by it, is it likely that he will abandon his linguistic interests and study medicine? Or are we to rely on the chance that some eighteen-year-old, eminently gifted linguistically, will discover the problem at that age, and will therefore turn to the study of medicine in order to accomplish this work later?

Anyone who, in his early formative years, arrives at the intention of becoming an analyst, will have to wait for seven years—assuming that he *has* been accepted by a medical school—to find out whether his application to a psychoanalytic institute will also be accepted, that is, whether he will be permitted to go through psychoanalytic training. For seven years he will have to devote his efforts to topics which are almost totally unrelated to the subject he is interested in before he can find out whether that effort has been worthwhile.

On the other hand, someone who is extremely gifted psychologically will probably not go into medicine at all, but will study instead anthropology, psychology, the history of art—all subjects which will bring him into far closer contact with the human personality than the study of medicine ever could. After having integrated any one of these fields, he may discover that psychoanalysis, as a road to the understanding of man, is superior to any other. Under prevailing conditions, however, he will then have to sacrifice seven more years—medical school, one year of rotating internship, and two years of psychiatric residency—before he can even start his psychological training; and that, in turn, may take him from three to five years longer, before he can return to the field of his primary interest.

No creative mind—and most creative minds are impatient—will tolerate such a delay. If impatience makes him seek out a shortcut, he will—assuming, of course, that he has enough money to do so—undergo a personal analysis and study the psychoanalytic literature. Yet there is the chance that—unless he has truly unusual talent—this training alone will not suffice to make him a first-rate researcher in any field of anthropic psychoanalysis. It was Freud's genius that enabled him to make the first thrust into the field of linguistic metapsychology: he posed the question in a particular instance, and found the answer. Yet it is folly to rely on the appearance of similarly lucky coincidences rather than to create opportunities for the linguist to go on from where Freud stopped.

I could go right down the line of the anthropic sciences and show that, from almost every one of them, psychoanalysis has something to gain. What, for example, was the psychology of the man of the Renaissance, or of ancient Greece, or Rome? When we study the anatomy and physiology of the human organism, we are probably correct in assuming that the physiology of the ancient Greek's body was the same as that of twentieth-century man, and that Socrates' pulse rate lay within the same limits as those we now find in a group of people living under similar environmental conditions. Even within this area surprises may occur: do we know whether the body of the Hindu Fakir follows the physiological laws that hold true for us? Be that as it may, there is no doubt at all that the personality variance from one historical period to another, indeed from one geographical area to another within the same historical period, is considerable.

To be sure, the identical functioning of such basic laws as the pleasure and reality principles must be assumed; further, the identity of primary instinctual needs, and the approximate identity of some defense mechanisms—such as repression, regression, and projection (at least in their more archaic forms)—seems certain enough. Nevertheless, as to the structure of the superego, the individual defense mechanisms, the extent of identification, the distance or closeness of the superego, the sense of identity, and a long list of other factors—with regard to all these, there is no reason to assume an identity through all historical periods.

System psychology, after all, should not seek to ascertain the psychology of only a limited range of personality types; it should outline the whole gamut of forms in which it has been possible for man to make his appearance. For the realization of such a goal, all the anthropic sciences have to work together. That is why the prohibition of lay analysis not only profoundly injures the anthropic sciences, it also injures psychoanalysis itself.

7

On the Training of the Psychoanalytic Anthropic Scientist

The effect of stimuli upon the psychic apparatus is one of the problems of psychoanalytic research, and therefore knowledge of the nature of these stimuli is of no small import to the psychoanalyst. The relationship between psychoanalysis, as the science of the psychic apparatus, and the sciences of specific classes of stimuli can perhaps best be exemplified with reference to biology.

Initially, Freud's interest had been in the unorganized part of the personality, the Id, which comprises the instinctual drives. Here, it is bodily stimuli in the form of instinctual demands that impinge upon the psychic apparatus; consequently, a significant part of the *Three Essays* (1905a) is devoted to endocrinology.

In order to explore man's drives, however, Freud did not first have to study biology. He gained an understanding of man's instinctual development and of the structure of the drives through psychoanalytic exploration. His turn toward physiology was motivated primarily by the desire to test and to validate the body of knowledge he had gained in the psychoanalytic situation. As I have already mentioned, he was in fact able to predict what future biological research would bring to light in this regard. Here the relevance of system psychology, as compared with medial psychology, becomes particularly clear.[1]

Aside from generally fertilizing and being fertilized by psychoanalysis, biology possesses a specific relevance to the formation of psychoanalytic theories, of the sort that I have mentioned earlier. As is well known, Freud's theory of the death instinct has been rejected by the majority of psychoanalysts (Brun, 1953); and, indeed, the frame of reference within which this theory was formulated is so far distant from psychological data that it is biology that will have to decide whether Freud's genius arrived at the truth in this instance also.

Freud's early division of drives into those based on love and those based on hunger (object drives and ego drives) was derived from a poem by Friedrich von Schiller (1795a), the German poet. Although this derivation was only incidental, it is still noteworthy that Freud resorted, in a matter of biology, to drawing upon *belles-lettres*. Freud must have been particularly happy to cite from this poem, for in it Schiller derides philosophy on the grounds that it "always appears ridiculous when it wants to enlarge knowledge and to give laws to the world, out of its own resources, and without admitting its dependency on experience" (Schiller, 1795b, my translation).

There is strong evidence, it seems to me, to indicate that the concept of the death instinct goes back to Freud's paper on "The Three Caskets" (1913c)—which would seem to suggest that it was through the study of Shakespeare's tragedies that this concept came into being. It is quite conceivable that a great psychologist-dramatist should have the ability to set forth in his tragedies an aspect of human existence so deeply buried in the objects of clinical investigation as to defy direct observation. Verification of this hypothesis regarding the roots of Freud's theory of the death instinct would add a pointed illustration of the absurdity of the present division between medically trained and nonmedical analysts.

It was only recently that I became aware of the following passage in Freud's writings. In introducing the concept of the death instinct, he said: "It is indeed a strange instinct that is occupied with the destruction of its own organic home! It is true that the poets speak of things

---

[1] The equivalent process in medial psychology would be the drawing of inferences about the physical structure of the universe from the results of a psychological exploration of perceptions. Wolfgang Köhler actually tried to achieve this; the error in his approach has been convincingly demonstrated by Straus (1935, pp. 214-219).

of this sort; but poets are irresponsible beings, they enjoy the privilege of poetic licence" (Freud, 1933a, p. 145). Although I may be laying too much stress on the fact that Freud's next succeeding association, following the remark about the strangeness of this drive, leads him first to the poets and only thereafter to pathophysiology, I am inclined to take this sequence as an indirect confirmation of my hypothesis that Freud did derive the idea of a death instinct from Shakespeare's tragedies.

There are, I repeat, other genuinely psychoanalytic problems awaiting solution by biology and physiology. I do not think that psychoanalytic observation can itself decide whether, in sublimation, an actual transformation of energy takes place, or only a change of the object toward which the drive is directed, or whether any neutralization of drive energy takes place at all.

In psychoanalytic anthropic research, a two-way path is to be observed, similar to the one just set forth. When Freud inquires into Leonardo da Vinci's life history or the origin of religion, he is carrying system psychology into an anthropic field, delimiting an area left unexplained by other disciplines, or proving the ineffectuality of an existing set of theories by applying psychoanalytic insight in their place. Yet the anthropic sciences, in turn, deal with areas that have a bearing on the psychoanalytic situation per se. A satisfactory study of the relevant stimuli impinging upon the psychic apparatus from without would certainly require the utilization of more than one of the anthropic sciences.

Conscience is the residue of a long historical development. The contents of the superego vary with variations in national, religious, and class membership. Actions that may be identical in content nevertheless have to be evaluated differently from one another, depending on the social background of the subject. To understand fully the moral precepts that the child must integrate, the history of the group in which the child has been raised needs to be known. In analyzing a subject, to be sure, this factor does not usually present itself as directly relevant: the analyst deals with the proximal stimuli impinging upon the psychic apparatus, without pursuing those stimuli to their distant historical sources. In some instances, however, if I can trust my own experience, this factor may become clinically relevant.[2]

When I had the occasion once to analyze some persons who had grown up in Russia, I developed the definite impression that the subject

2 Alexander (1932, p. 37) has stressed this point, which is usually neglected in psychoanalytic literature.

was a character out of a Russian novel, particularly one by Dostoyevsky, and I began to wonder to what extent I was confusing what may be called a national trait with a neurotic symptom. I have presented the problem in a rather simplified form. I would like to refer, for a more complex instance, to Freud's (1939) book, *Moses and Monotheism*, in which he made the attempt to isolate a psychological pattern occurring with statistical frequency in a certain ethnic group, and to pursue it to its historical origin.

Further, a psychological theory of the higher functions—such as creativity, or aesthetic or ethical sensibility—presupposes knowledge about what man creates, and what he regards as beautiful and ethical, and this again requires reference to the findings of the anthropic sciences.

I spoke earlier of a metapsychology of language; this concept can be fruitfully extended to other anthropic sciences. I should like to demonstrate this, using Freud's (1900) *Interpretation of Dreams* as my example. In the seventh chapter, after inquiring into the meaning and sources of dreams, and discussing the method of ascertaining that meaning and the mechanisms involved in dream work—that is to say, after reaching the point at which another author might well have considered his task fulfilled—Freud set out to prove instead that all the findings he had set forth so far did not explain the dream, and then proceeded to explicate, in universally valid psychological terms, the processes leading to the dream. This path of psychoanalysis leads to metapsychology—which I believe to be necessary for the subjects of anthropic science.

Since the dream, neurosis, and psychosis are purely subjective autoplastic phenomena, it is obvious that they fall within the orbit of metapsychology. Yet Freud's inquiry into jokes similarly led to his writing a metapsychology of jokes, and thus extending metapsychology into that area of anthropic research, since the joke is not a purely psychological configuration but part of the cultural inventory. The metapsychology of a historical process, of social institutions, of art—in short, of all the subjects of anthropic research—thus becomes conceivable. The basic general goal of psychoanalytic anthropic research would consequently be a *metapsychology of culture*.[3]

It is quite apparent that the medical profession does not have the resources even to consider, no less to venture upon such an undertaking. If a metapsychology of culture is ever to be written, it is the anthropic

[3] Cf., for example, Bychowski (1951) for such an attempt in the area of artistic creation; and, to a certain extent, also Kubie (1958b).

scientist who will have to do the bulk of the work. Yet, even should such a program prove to be too ambitious, or based on wrong premises and therefore unworkable for theoretical reasons, the anthropic scientist is indispensable if psychoanalysis is ever to evolve a complete theory of personality, and if psychology is to make its requisite, or even its minimal contribution to anthropic research. In turn, as will be shown later, if anthropic research is to reach the maximal concretization of its potential, this can come about only through the efforts of analytically fully trained anthropic scientists.

What should be the psychoanalytic training of an anthropic scientist, to enable him to make his contribution to any of the problems I have mentioned, which lie outside of the psychoanalytic situation proper?

That anyone who wants to grasp fully and evaluate psychoanalysis must be analyzed himself is accepted almost as a truism in some quarters (Lewin and Ross, 1960, pp. 39, 45). Yet, as will be seen, it is not altogether unnecessary to say a few words on the subject. In his early writings on technique, Freud described the channels of communication between analyst and patient as follows: "Just as the receiver converts back into sound waves the electric oscillations in the telephone line which were set up by sound waves, so the doctor's unconscious is able, from the derivatives of the unconscious which are communicated to him, to reconstruct that unconscious, which has determined the patient's free associations" (Freud, 1912a, p. 116).[4]

Since the analyst's own unconscious is the source from which what will ultimately become the interpretation takes its start, his communication with his own unconscious must not be hindered. If he himself harbors resistances, he will select only those unconscious messages that are ready to reach the level of conscious ideation in him—and he may distort them as well.

Freud called the area of bluntness that may impede the analyst's perceptiveness "the blind spot," a term which was coined by Stekel (1911, p. 532), and has since acquired wide usage. Important and valid as the theory of the blind spot still is, one wonders whether it is really the blind spot that is nowadays the greatest threat to the analytic process. Times have changed: patients now seek treatment on the grounds that, as they themselves start by saying, they are suffering from an Oedipus

---

[4] Regarding Freud's specific reference to physicians in this quotation, cf. Strachey's (1958, p. 88) introduction to Freud's "Papers on Technique." (If Freud had written this paper later, he would probably have written, 'the analyst's unconscious.')

complex; and pregenital sexuality is discussed on the stage with greater candor than in the analyst's office. The distortion seems to make its appearance rather in the form of a projection, in so far as the analyst perceives in the subject nothing but his own defects.[5] The result is a lopsided, distorted picture, leading to theories that must be characterized in those same terms.

The blind spot and the projection both threaten anthropic research. Freud's original advice with regard to the analyst's own analysis has not lost any of its importance since it was first given, although opinions are still encountered occasionally that seem to attribute only a secondary importance to the personal analysis.

Kubie has published a detailed program for the establishment of a new profession, Doctor of Medical Psychology (cf. also Brody and Grey, 1948). In it, he has presented a training curriculum for the new profession: one part of it consists of weekly sessions of group therapy for three years, "until finally, and as a part of their own further training, the students were ready to undergo individual preparatory psychoanalysis" (Kubie, 1954, p. 152). Notwithstanding the general soundness and excellence of Kubie's views, one has to take exception to this particular suggestion. Why should the future Doctor of Medical Psychology start with group therapy, which will only make his personal analysis more difficult, if not impossible? Will not his personal analysis in the long run determine whether he is eligible at all for the profession he has chosen? Yet personal analysis would definitely seem to be moved to a secondary place in Kubie's setup.

The problem involved in the training analysis goes far back in the history of human thought. To a certain extent, I am reminded of Socrates's opinion that "the most skillful physicians are those who, from their youth upwards, have combined with the knowledge of their art the greatest experience of disease. They had better not be robust in health, and should have had all manner of diseases in their own persons" (Plato, *Republic* III, 408, p. 673). Indeed, if perfect mental health were possible, possession of it would rule out any such person as a capable psychoanalytic observer (for many reasons, not to be discussed here). On the other hand, general experience shows that neurotic ingredients in

---

[5] Cf. Freud (1937a): "It looks as if a number of analysts learn to make use of defensive mechanisms which enable them to evade the conclusions and requirements of analysis themselves, probably by applying them to others" (p. 353). Cf. also Alexander (1956, pp. 182, 192f.).

the observer's personality may impede and falsify the whole psycho-analytic process.

It is not least for reasons of this kind that schools of systemic psychology differ in their opinions concerning the structure of personality to a much greater extent and in a far more essential way than is encountered in other fields of research. Chiefly because of historical factors, psychoanalysis is still suffering from the childhood diseases experienced by a science when the results of its research, erroneous because they have been gained through the employment of faulty techniques, are nevertheless taken as valid.

Disagreements obtain in all fields of flourishing research. In sciences of long standing, such disagreements are unavoidable, precisely because the accumulated facts on hand permit various interpretations. But the disagreements that separate the various schools of psychoanalysis are of a different nature; here many an artefact produced by the analyst's own ineptitude is set forth as a property of the subject under investigation.[6]

The situation can be compared aptly with that which for a short time confused astronomical research. As is well known to the historian of psychology, individual differences in recording the times of stellar transits had considerable import for the development of experimental and physiological psychology (Boring, 1929, pp. 134-153). It was observed that there was "a personal equation" (cf. Freud, 1926a, p. 220) that accounted for the individual differences. Experimental psychology succeeded in obtaining reliable data from which it was able to measure the extent of the individual deviation. Here was an instance in which man did not function as a perfect medium. In order to use him as such, the observer had to be "calibrated" (Boring, 1929, p. 137).

"Calibration of the observer"[7] is an excellent term for the goal of the training analysis, even though we are not dealing with quantifiable differences. Here, too, a person should be capable of making himself a

[6] Cf. Freud (1926a): "An abnormal person can become an accurate physicist; as an analyst he will be hampered by his own abnormality from seeing the picture of mental life undistorted. Since it is impossible to demonstrate to any one his own abnormality, general agreement in matters of depth-psychology will be particularly hard to reach" (p. 220). And yet among those who have made great contributions to psychology, there is also considerable psychopathology. Alexander (1956, p. 190f.) has made an attempt to determine the characteristics of psychological endowment. I am not certain that his findings go very much beyond surface characteristics, since they fail to deal with the structural properties of the psychologically endowed personality.

[7] I am grateful to Professor Boring for informing me that the expression "to calibrate the observer" probably originated with him.

perfect medium—in this instance, however, for the purpose of recon-structing a subject's personality. The curious complication has to do with the extent and the depth to which the prospective observer is to be "reconstructed"; for, by contrast with the recording of stellar transits, which required only medial functions, the work of the psychoanalytic observer demands systemic functions.

It is precisely this circumstance that makes the training analysis so important and so difficult: the observer's entire personality is engaged in the psychoanalytic situation, whereas the recorder at the telescope had merely to connect a visual stimulus with an auditory one. And yet even this latter task—so simple when compared with the psychoanalytic as-signment—required psychological safeguards for its fulfillment.

Furthermore, once the peculiarities of an astronomical observer's per-ceptive and reacting functions were determined, that knowledge made possible the derivation of correct data from his recordings, falsified as they had been by those same peculiarities. If the 'personal distortion rate' of a researcher in systemic psychology were known, the results of his investigations could perhaps also be transformed into correct ones. How-ever, in the psychoanalytic situation, the technique of investigation has a continuous bearing on the very course that the investigation itself is taking.

An interpretation may be overlooked; a resistance may be provoked by a premature interpretation; a patient's critical remark may arouse a hid-den anger in the investigator, and give the analysis an artificial direction —all of which may lead to conclusions that, had the proper technique been used, would have been essentially different. Thus, what to an observer may appear to be a *bona fide* finding, which he assigns to the subject as an objective trait, may be the result of an inept technique of investigation, so that it is only under exceptional circumstances that even knowledge of the researcher's blind spots and projective tendencies would permit a transformation of his findings into correct ones.

No better method has yet been devised than the researcher's personal analysis in order to shut off these sources of error.[8] In psychoanalytic

---

[8] The extent and depth of the training analysis that are minimal and optimal for the future analyst have been widely discussed. In Freud's work, contradictory statements are found. In 1926 he wrote of "the analyst's obligation to make himself capable, by a *deep-going* analysis of his own, of the unprejudiced reception of the analytic material" (Freud, 1926a, p. 220, italics mine); and in 1937, he even suggested that the analyst should submit every quinquennium to an analysis (Freud, 1937a, p. 353), attributing the greatest significance to the effect of the analyst's own analysis. In the same paper,

anthropic research, the question of blind spots and projections is no less acute than in the psychoanalytic situation per se. On many subjects that the anthropic researcher investigates, he has by no means neutral feelings. When he examines the life history of an author or artist, he may like or dislike, admire, or detest his works; when he looks into a historical event, he may sympathize with one of the contending groupings, because it is a proponent or an antecedent of an ideology that he shares. Here subjectivity of reaction may succeed in remaining concealed with particular ease, being at least ostensibly absorbed in seemingly objective judgment.

In the natural sciences, biases can be reliably ruled out, for mathematics and experimentation are the best checks so far devised against subjective distortions. It is well known that even these excellent checks do not always provide foolproof protection against personal bias, but a mistake made here is quickly detected, and usually does not outlast a generation of researchers.[9] In view of the negligible function assigned to mathematics in anthropic sciences, and the ambiguous results of experimental research in this area, the danger of falsification by value statements that range outside of a true-false scale is enormous (Cassirer, 1944, p. 21). Insight into the history and function of the researcher's personal value system still seems to be the best available protection against distortions in anthropic research; and it is certain that such insight requires a deep thrust into the unconscious, and can be obtained only through prolonged analysis.

Although the search for objectivity has come to be taken for granted, it is still true, nevertheless, that the deepest insights are gained by minds that are profoundly entangled on the emotional level with the subject of their researches. Indeed, it is not only within the area of discoveries

however, he greatly cut down its importance by asserting that "for practical reasons this analysis can be only short and incomplete," its main object being an opportunity for "the instructor to form an opinion whether the candidate should be accepted for further training." Also, when Freud states that the training analysis "has accomplished its purpose if it imparts to the learner a sincere conviction of the existence of the unconscious" (p. 352), that view militates against a deep-going analysis. Freud's expectation that the analytic process initiated by a short training analysis will go on of its own accord, I cannot discuss here. About the difficulty inherent in didactic analysis, see A. Freud (1950).

[9] Rostand (1960) reports on one of the outstanding incidents of self-deception in science, when for two years a large number of scientists (physicists, biologists, physicians) described the existence and effect of N rays (discovered by René Blondlot, a leading French scientist), until it was proven that such rays do not exist at all.

in the natural sciences that the emotional factor is of relevant importance, but also within psychology and the anthropic sciences generally.

Jones (1956), in his study on "The Nature of Genius," has made a noteworthy contribution to this subject (pp. 3-34). Hanns Sachs (1944), in his recollections of Freud, has frankly set forth the libidinal factor that tied him to the subject of his biographical essay, and yet—probably quite rightly—has denied that any disadvantage necessarily arose therefrom with regard to the correctness of the outcome. "On the whole," he wrote, "idolizing, if it is perfectly genuine, will add to the truthfulness rather than stand in its way . . . . He [the biographer] is so sure of the greatness . . . of his hero that he does not mind giving away his sins or even his weaknesses" (p. 9).

Although many of Sachs's readers have not shared his assurance (cf. Bailey, 1956, p. 391), it must be admitted that, with his fine psychological sensitivity, he was aware of—and candidly explicit about—a problem to which, I believe, no adequate answer has been found yet. Notwithstanding the indisputable necessity of training analysis for the purpose of calibrating the observer, there are certain emotional involvements necessary, in order to turn an analyst into a good analyst. I doubt that we know very much about the nature of these involvements. This problem is probably outside the scope of discussion of the training analysis, and I shall therefore leave it at that.

When it is said that personal analysis is the core of training in system psychology, this should not be interpreted as minimizing theoretical instruction. Personal analysis is the first step toward a profound understanding of psychoanalysis: it removes the emotional obstacles; once that has been done, there remains only the intellectual difficulty that is commonly present whenever a new body of knowledge is to be integrated. For as wide as may be the array of psychological insights acquired in the personal analysis, they are not of a general theoretical nature, and do not cover the body of psychoanalytic knowledge. That is why extensive theoretical instruction is no less necessary.

A third area of psychoanalytic training warrants extensive discussion. It is my contention that the psychoanalytic anthropic researcher not only needs full clinical training—such as the two or three supervised analyses that students customarily carry out, in fulfillment of present training programs, before graduation from an institute—but also that he has to have the opportunity for continuous clinical work, if he is to live up to the requirements of his task.

The difficulties of psychoanalytic anthropic research are considerable, and the demands put upon such a researcher are much greater than those facing anyone who limits his research to the psychoanalytic situation. The latter investigates the living material that the analysand pours forth during the long series of psychoanalytic sessions. Any conclusions that the analyst draws can be checked and rechecked; most of them he keeps in abeyance, since they are tentative and therefore must be expected to be replaced by others, or improved by further insights.

The anthropic researcher, however, is dealing with a petrified record. The material at his disposal is in final form. New finds may confirm or disprove his theories, or they may stimulate the development of more refined ones. But in his actual work he cannot usually expect to tap new wells upon which to draw for the revision of his theories.

It is certain that, in the investigation of the life of a historical person, the immediate material has a background of innumerable unconscious processes, whose direction must be known if any real understanding of that life history is to be attained. Since the known details incorporate the unconscious in one way or another, the unconscious is in principle obtainable, once the researcher has found the key to it.

In general, in this kind of work, one cannot apply acquired knowledge in the way in which a theoretical science is usually applied in practice. The interpretive work of the anthropic researcher is not purely intellectual; it is also intuitive, and to an even greater extent than in the psychoanalytic situation.[10] This should not be misunderstood. The anthropic researcher does not *rely on* his intuition; he *needs* it and he *uses* it—but by careful check with the known details of his subject matter, and by drawing on general knowledge, he makes his decisions as between probable alternatives.

The danger of falling into intellectualization, or the mechanical application of psychoanalytic tenets or knowledge makes constant contact with the live clinical material indispensable. It is from the clinical situation that the researcher draws both stimulation and the clues that he must pursue in his research. Freud reported that the stimulation to write his essay on Leonardo's childhood recollection came directly from his clinical contact with a patient of his (Jones, 1953-1957, vol. 2, p. 346).

[10] The various mechanisms and psychological prerequisites of the analyst in the psychoanalytic situation have been described and investigated by Reik (1935). The corresponding work in the area of psychoanalytic anthropic research has not yet been undertaken.

If the analyst's anthropic research does not grow out of the live psycho-analytic situation, it may easily become stale and routine, and degenerate into a bookish application of bloodless generalizations.

The epistemology of psychoanalytic anthropic research cannot be discussed here, but I want to refer briefly to an experience of my own. Years ago, I was engaged in a piece of psychoanalytic biographical research. At times, my preoccupation with the research overshadowed my clinical interests, and I would have welcomed a fellowship so as to be able to devote myself entirely to work on my manuscript.

Looking back, however, I have no doubt that the impossibility of my withdrawing from clinical work proved to be an advantage that could not have been matched by any advantage I might have gained out of freedom therefrom. It turned out that, whenever I got stymied in my understanding of the details of my theoretical subject, and felt quite helpless because of the absence of any further clues, I would arrive at the solution—with a degree of regularity that sometimes seemed uncanny —through listening to analysands. At times, the solution would suddenly come to my mind while I was listening to a patient, without any clearly visible connection between my own idea and the patient's associations.

I assume that there always was one, and that my own association was not unrelated to what the patient was telling me. Yet, more frequently than is compatible with the mere assumption of coincidence, patients would furnish material directly related to the problem in question. The most impressive incident took place at a time when I was puzzling over the question of the double, in the form of a lifeless puppetlike statue. A patient brought a dream whose principal element was exactly this theme, and her associations presented me with the solution I was striving for, right on a platter, as it were.[11]

Such episodes offer much food for thought, and may prove important for an as yet unwritten theory and methodology of psychoanalytic an-

[11] It is significant that my preoccupation with this research problem did not interfere with the contact between analyst and analysand. Yet, at another time, when I was rather intensely preoccupied with the study of Pavlov's theory of conditioned reflexes, and with a critical comparison between it and psychoanalysis, three patients who had been referred to me for psychoanalysis declared—one after the other—either immediately or after a short while, that they wanted to discontinue the analysis, or else to be transferred to another analyst. That was unusual; and I now believe that it was my preoccupation that was unconsciously felt by the patient. What struck me was the difference in effect between research, on the one hand, at whose center stands interpretation, and which therefore probably makes the analyst's unconscious 'object hungry'; and, on the other hand, research that is purely theoretical, and can easily dispense with the live clinical material of the present.

thropic research. Here is still another challenging problem. Theoretically, any single mind is as infinite as the external world, so that the complete study of one mind alone should familiarize one with almost all possible complications. Yet this is obviously not the case in practice.[12] Even extensive clinical experience leaves wide gaps in one's acquaintance with basic human issues. This alone demonstrates how urgent it is that the anthropic scientist maintain what may be called his clinical fitness.

As a final point, clinical experience should be noted as the testing ground for new theories, such as the anthropic researcher is certain to evolve. His work cannot remain limited to the mere confirmation of known psychoanalytic theories; he is bound to *enlarge* our knowledge of man. We know well how easily errors may occur, even when theoretical formulations are based on observations made in the psychoanalytic situation, well protected as that is by many safeguards. Yet the possibility of error is far greater in the comparatively unprotected situation of anthropic research; and thus the psychoanalytic situation becomes a laboratory from which the anthropic researcher can derive controls similar to those that the natural scientist obtains in his laboratory.

Although Haeckel's theory, "ontogeny recapitulates philogeny," no longer holds true, it is still valuable as a working hypothesis; so, too, Nietzsche's (1876-1878) statement, "In sleep and dream we go once more through the syllabus of earlier humanity" (p. 26, translation mine), may still harbor an important point. It seems to me that occasionally, in the analysis of a neurotic patient or of one belonging to the borderline group, an aspect appears that is very close to some past culture or civilization, so that one almost has the impression that one is getting a direct glimpse into ancient or medieval culture.[13]

To return to present social realities, it can be stated with some degree of certainty that the existing psychoanalytic organizations, in whose

[12] Although the probability exists that the repressed part of a richly endowed personality may run almost the entire gamut of the principal fantasies, or types of fantasy that mankind has produced, the great variety of techniques by which the ego deals with them cannot be represented in one individual. Yet, if we knew more about personalities like Shakespeare, who gave artistic form to the whole universe of personality declension, we might find that the artistic genius actually lives out creatively almost all dimensions, in miniature, of human behavior.

[13] The resemblance between the psychology of the psychotic patient and the earliest stages of mankind's development has been noted more than once. See also Freud (1913a, pp. 184-187; 1913g; 1926a, p. 212). For a presentation of the methodology and extent of the application of psychoanalysis to the *Geisteswissenschaften*, see particularly Hartmann (1927, pp. 24-36).

hands psychoanalytic education now lies, would not refuse to extend their co-operation in the personal analyses of anthropic scientists. An adequate theoretical training program might also be set up, upon the request of the Universities. In some instances, a selected few might even be permitted to carry out a small number of supervised analyses. But it is equally certain that all such co-operation would cease at once, if there were the slightest indication that the trained anthropic scientist intended to become a practicing analyst. It must be repeated therefore that a reform of anthropic science is not at all likely to occur, at least in our own time.[14]

In view of the present dilemma, one may suggest recourse to co-operative undertakings. Would it not be a sound solution to this problem for a psychoanalyst who was interested in anthropic research to combine his efforts with those of an anthropic scientist who had been trained in psychoanalysis as far as present social reality permits?[15]

Such partnerships have been established occasionally, and no doubt some valuable work might be accomplished that way. If, by accident, two congenial minds thus met, it might even lead to the production of results of high caliber. As a basic solution, however, I would not rest too much hope on that idea. In my opinion, psychoanalysis has not yet reached the stage at which that sort of joint effort would be of guaranteed promise with regard to research.

The research team proves productive, it seems to me, in those phases of research in which agreement has already been reached about a large body of data and about basic methodology, and at times when the effort required is greater than the individual potential. Psychoanalytic anthropic research cannot yet be divided up into single areas or aspects,

[14] Jones records in a critical vein the fact that lay analysts become full-time therapeutic analysts. He believes that there would be no objection if students from other fields learned psychoanalysis, practiced it for two years to deepen their knowledge, and then returned to their original research, to apply there the psychoanalytic knowledge that they had acquired (Jones, 1927a, p. 181). My contention is that, under such conditions, no adequate psychoanalytic research in the anthropic sciences could mature. In reply to Jones's critical observation, it may be countered that the full-time therapeutic work of lay analysts did not interfere, for most of them, with their accomplishing remarkable research work in their original fields—accomplishments of which they would not have been capable if psychoanalytic practice had been only their short-time bride.

[15] Wohl and Trosman (1955), insensible to the basic laws of creativity, have suggested in all seriousness, with regard to the essay on *Leonardo*, that Freud should have "allowed his manuscript to be scrutinized" by an expert in history (p. 39).

assignable to different persons. My prediction is that such planned research affiliations (I leave aside the accidental meeting of congenial minds) would lead to interesting results—but of a low level of originality. To be sure, that may prove to be the best that can be done at present.

Here it becomes necessary once again to return to Freud's statement concerning the detrimental effect that the study of medicine may have on a subject, in terms of his future analytic possibilities. The principal and, as I see it, the only relevant tool of the analyst is interpretation. Now in every science, except those still limited to description, interpretation occurs. When the biologist studies a slide, he interprets shapes and colors. When the internist examines a patient by auscultation and percussion, he interprets sounds. But the interpretive expertise that the student of medicine acquires is different from that which the analyst needs to have.

Although I do not subscribe to the distinction between explaining and understanding that acquired such importance since Dilthey,[16] it must be admitted that interpretation in the natural sciences and interpretation in the anthropic sciences presuppose the activation of different functions. If nothing else, practice proves this. There is, for example, the well-known phenomenon of the highly capable natural scientist, who is keenly observant with regard to physical or organic data, who is eminently ingenious in setting up the proper experimental conditions, whose mind is ready to evolve theories—and yet who remains utterly blind when it comes to psychological matters. There is even a great likelihood that, to the majority of such unusually creative natural scientists, psychoanalysis seems to be little more than a heap of nonsense.

The opposite phenomenon, of course, is also well known: the talented intuitive psychologist, endowed with the finest empathic sensibility, to whom natural science remains something of an enigma. At least, very little comes to his mind when he studies it. Yet, if someone is proficient in the anthropic sciences, there is a chance (although by no means a necessity) that he will also possess a fine talent for psychoanalytic interpretation. Because of resistances, he may not be able to apply that talent in the psychoanalytic orbit, but nevertheless he does possess it; whereas the talented natural scientist is likely, in most instances, to have

[16] See, for example, Jaspers (1923, p. 19). For the best discussion of the problem from the psychoanalytic point of view, see Hartmann (1927).

not only his resistances, but also his lack of psychological sensibility.[17] In other words, the probability that an eminently talented anthropic scientist also has what is needed to make a good psychoanalyst is greater than would be true of his equivalent in the field of the natural sciences.

Freud's intellectual gifts manifested themselves not least in his ability to 'play both registers' with equal originality. It is, I believe, unique that a man who, as a beginner, wrote an outstanding biological paper (Freud, 1877), which far outdistanced contemporary biology in the boldness of its ratiocination (Gicklhorn, 1955), and who followed this achievement with similarly oriented research of equal quality almost to the end of his fourth decade, should have become the founder of a branch of psychology, which he then combined with the most fertile research in anthropic science.

This double endowment cannot be expected of the average scientist, and I have observed some embarrassing consequences when someone who was of more than average proficiency in some branch of natural science switched to psychoanalysis. *Cum grano salis*, of course, I would even venture to guess that, in many instances, high endowment in a natural science will tend to reduce the probability of proficiency in psychoanalysis.[18] What, then would be the best intellectual preparation for the study of psychoanalysis? Which complementary science or sciences would increase the likelihood of the student's developing the best disposition toward psychoanalytic proficiency?[19]

The answer to this question has certainly become more complex with the progress of psychoanalytic insight. There was a time when a talent for reconstructing the repressed might have been considered the best psychoanalytic disposition. Although this function has not lost any of its importance, more emphasis may be put at present on the perception of the ego in its struggle with the id, superego, and reality. In what complementary science can one study such processes in the open, with-

[17] The difference I am delineating here is a psychological and practical one, and does not warrant any conclusion concerning the theoretical foundations of either group of sciences.

[18] A notable example to illustrate this state of affairs would be Robert Bárány (1876-1936), Nobel Prize winner (1914), whom Freud "refused to take as a pupil some years ago because he seemed to be too abnormal" (Jones, 1953-1957, vol. 2, p. 189).

[19] Freud (1927a) enumerated some of the branches of learning in which the analyst should acquire some proficiency: "elements from the mental sciences, from psychology, the history of civilization and sociology, as well as from anatomy, biology and the study of evolution" (p. 252; see also Kubie, 1954). I am not approaching the problem from the scholastic point of view; I am trying to reduce it to a functional problem.

out the cover that must be pierced in the study of the human personality before these processes become recognizable? It is in the study of anthropoid behavior, I believe, that some of the impulses roaming through the human id can be observed unconcealedly, although even there the observer may acquire too optimistic a view, since the desires in man's repressed really aim at worse things than the anthropoids are capable of performing during most of their lifetime.

Anthropoid group life (cf. Zuckermann, 1932) is still, in my opinion, the best introduction to an understanding of what Freud (1913g) meant in *Totem and Taboo*. In studying animal life in general, one would learn the 'state of nature' from which man wrested civilization and culture and would thereby, by contrast, better understand the latter. The history of mankind offers, in turn, a superb opportunity to study the dynamics of human action—its incentives, successes, and failures. Each subject has its own aspect, which means, in effect, its own specific way of aiding in the preparation of the future student of psychoanalysis.

The study of history, for example, would demonstrate the great role that aggression has played in man's life. The study of man's customs— his superstitions, mythologies, and religious systems—would be, in turn, an excellent preparation for the study of the compulsive-obsessional neuroses and the group of schizophrenias. The value of child psychology is obvious. Integration of the genetic principle in psychoanalysis would be excellently prepared for by the study of embryology. The section on inflammation in the study of pathology would serve the same function with regard to the question of defense. The importance of direct acquaintance with the physically sick and mentally deranged patient is unquestionable.

It will very likely turn out that there is almost no single scientific field concerned with organic life or human activities from which a profitable introduction to psychoanalytic thinking could not be devised. But the student might very well become acquainted with all these fields, and still not come any closer to an understanding of psychoanalysis. It is really a question of how the topics are taught. In principle, the urge to fathom the unconscious, the habit of viewing man as in a state of conflict, and as a product of the past, may be kindled by penetration into any of these fields; but one could just as easily recommend a study of Shakespeare's tragedies and comedies as the most royal of all the royal roads that hold the promise of an introduction to psychoanalysis.

I cannot forego recounting here an experience I had during my contact with August Aichhorn. As is well known, he was the only psycho-analyst to develop what became a literally inimitable psychoanalytic technique of the therapy of delinquency, with which he greatly enriched the field. In view of his having been such an eminently successful lay analyst, it may be worth while to consider his preanalytic training. He had studied engineering for a few semesters, later became a teacher, and only later still became engaged in dealing with delinquents. As the superintendent of a municipal institution for delinquents, he had ample opportunity to gain clinical experience. In psychoanalysis, he found a theory that made possible at least an approximate explanation of the bewildering observations that he had made (cf. Freud, 1925c, p. 273; A. Freud, 1951). Here, then, was a person with extensive clinical ex-perience, who had already experimented with therapeutic techniques on his own, and who therefore entered upon his psychoanalytic career with a well defined problem in mind.

It was fascinating to observe Aichhorn at work, because his faculty for making correct guesses was extraordinary. From clues that, in general psychoanalytic work, would be regarded as irrelevant, he was able to reconstruct with uncanny rapidity that which was psychologically rele-vant in the delinquent's present, and he was thus capable of eliciting *in a first interview* a reliable transference—which is, as anyone who has ever tried it will confirm, quite an outstanding achievement. Of course, I was greatly interested in the way in which Aichhorn had acquired this stupendous psychological capacity. What he told me was (aside from its being considerably less momentous than I had expected), I am sure, not the whole story; but he used to refer more than once to the fact that, during his early years, he had trained himself for a long time in making guesses about people in rather commonplace situations.

Thus, while sitting in a trolley car and observing how one of the other passengers was seated, and how he held his newspaper, he would try to imagine (and consequently to predict), in the greatest detail, how that same person would rise from his seat, and how he would behave while leaving the car. He asserted that it took him a long time to learn to make correct predictions of this sort, but that he had greatly profited from the training. The pursuit itself was time-consuming, of course, for he often had to wait a long while until the person he was observing reached his destination. But the aim of his unusual practice is quite clear: he wanted to train himself—and he did so successfully—to achieve empathy with the whole person through the use of a single detail.

Because of the delinquent's obduracy and callousness, and his firm determination not to form a transference, the analyst is forced to reconstruct the subject's personality from mere details of surface data. Although such self-training as Aichhorn undertook bore wonderful fruits in his own case, it would be folly simply to recommend it to others, or to include it in a training program. What happened in his case was that an eminently gifted psychologist was able to devise methods of study that stood him personally in good stead. As a matter of fact, however, no one else has yet proven capable of following him, and of practicing the technique whose theory he worked out, with a proficiency that even comes close to his, not to speak of equaling it.[20]

Here one must add, of course, that psychoanalysis does not aim at a 'practical' knowledge of psychology—what is called in German *Menschenkenntnis*. Any successful salesman is probably better equipped than the analyst to make a snap judgment about a person on first contact, and to manipulate customers in a way that will induce them to make a purchase.

From Freud's frequent misjudgment of his followers, which is well known from Jones's biography, it seems apparent that he was no *Menschenkenner*.[21] I would compare this situation with that of Einstein who, despite (or perhaps because of) his very deep insight into the physical structure of the universe, seems to have been quite helpless in the use of a gadget. Yet, in order to treat delinquents, *Menschenkenntnis* is an indispensable prerequisite. What made Aichhorn so remarkable was the combination, so rarely found, of superb *Menschenkenntnis* with equally developed psychoanalytic capabilities, in the primary sense of the word.

[20] Ernst Federn (1960) seems to believe that Aichhorn's technique is teachable. Right as he may be about the teachability of a therapeutic technique for schizophrenia (as a matter of fact, there is a large number of psychiatrists and psychoanalysts who report treating schizophrenics successfully—even though without necessarily curing them), I fear that he is wrong concerning the psychoanalytic treatment of delinquents. At least, I do not know of anyone who has acquired the skills requisite for the employment of that technique. It has always puzzled me why the psychotherapy of schizophrenics (which is difficult in its own right) should be still so much easier than that of delinquents.

[21] Cf. Jones (1953-1957): "We all agreed, that he [Freud] was also a poor *Menschenkenner*—a poor judge of men." Jones defines the term as meaning "one who has the intuitive capacity of correctly appraising the character and personality of other human beings" (vol. 2, p. 412). Sachs (1944) reports that Freud "himself always insisted that he was not a *Menschenkenner*." Sachs unfortunately gives the English meaning as "mind-reader" (p. 58). In his preanalytic years, however, Freud seemed to have aspired to be a *Menschenkenner*, and derived considerable satisfaction from any proof thereof. (See his letter to Martha Bernays of February 10, 1886 [Freud, 1873-1939, p. 207].)

I have set forth Aichhorn's example in such detail in order to show that, in the present phase of psychoanalytic development, it is probably quite wrong to insist on any kind of curriculum as preparatory for the training in psychoanalysis. There are some (perhaps the majority) for whom the study of medicine is the best psychoanalytic preparation; there are, however, undoubtedly a significant number of people who could be excellent analysts, but who would either fail in the study of medicine, or would not profit from it in any way, in terms of a disposition toward psychoanalytic proficiency—or worse still, might even be less equipped for that career after graduation from medical school than they were when they started in medical school. The wisest thing would be to evaluate an individual's prospects as an analyst solely on the grounds of what his present endowments are, independently of the particular intellectual area in which his interest in psychoanalysis was kindled, or in which those present endowments have proven productive.[22]

[22] If Alexander (1956) should turn out to be really correct in his assertion that a "well-developed introspective faculty" (p. 190f.) is a decisive index of psychoanalytic endowment, that would indeed be one of the most consequential arguments in favor of lay analysis; it would also speak strongly against looking for analysts among graduates from medical schools, institutions in which nothing at all is done for the exercise, growth, or cultivation of introspection (cf. Chapter VIII, "On the Restricted Selection of Psychoanalytic Candidates").

8

Some Specific Topics

I shall deal in this chapter with several separate aspects of lay analysis.

On the Restricted Selection of Psychoanalytic Candidates

One immediately harmful effect of the insistence that psychoanalyses are to be carried out solely by medically and psychiatrically trained persons is *prima facie* evident: it leads to a frightening reduction of the pool from which psychoanalysis can obtain new life blood. The paradoxical situation now exists in this country that psychoanalytic training institutes can select their students only from a pool that was itself carefully preselected, and for quite different purposes.

College graduates applying to medical school are certainly not selected for admission on the basis of their psychological endowments. The obligatory premedical courses, which are utterly unrelated to anything even smacking of psychology, would prove this, if further proof were necessary. If one were to restrict graduate training in physics only to those who completed their undergraduate work in a school of fine arts, even that would not be quite as bad as the present situation in psychoanalysis, where the prevailing selection requirements are more far-fetched than even such absurd conditions.[1]

Further, one rarely hears discussed the special affinity between womanhood and the practice of psychoanalysis. A comparison of psychoanalysis with other professions will show that there are not many in which—proportionally speaking—so many women have participated, and attained a status far above average by the excellence of their skills and their writings. Indeed, if the percentage of outstanding women to be found among outstanding psychoanalysts is considered in general, there can be no doubt that women seem to be particularly well suited for this profession. It is also interesting to note that more women analysts seem to be concerned with the technique of psychoanalysis than men: the number of women among those considered to be the best practitioners is quite surprising.

By contrast with the situation in other professions, proficiency in psychoanalysis does not seem to be detrimental to the evolvement of those qualities that in our society and in our time are regarded as womanly. To be sure, there may perhaps be very few professions or occupations that are inherently incompatible with the evolvement of psychological womanhood; but it is probably correct to say that the successful woman in most professions and occupations is quite often a masculine type. Upon closer consideration, it becomes evident why this is not as true of the psychoanalytic profession, which requires passivity rather than activity in the professionally relevant situation.

The emphasis here is on listening; the interpretation to be given is obtained, not by research or by active scrutiny, but rather by contemplation and the free play of one's ideation. Listening and meditation may contain a danger of regression. There may be among many men a silent rebellion against the passivity that seems to be required so clearly in psychoanalytic technique,[2] whereas a woman may find the realization of her best qualities in it.[3] The intrapersonal tendency toward conflict inherent in the psychoanalytic situation may be far less pronounced among women than among men.

[1] Cf. the opinions of Drs. Alexander and Knight, cited later, about the psychological endowment of students in other fields than medicine.

[2] I am convinced that, in essence, the psychoanalytic situation does *not* impose a true passivity on the analyst. An adequate discussion of this problem would lead too far; suffice it to say, however, that many analysts do feel this kind of participation to be passive.

[3] Cf. Freud (1901): "Women, with their subtler understanding of unconscious mental processes . . ." (p. 156, n. 1).

Yet, with all this, it seems that the participation in and contribution of women to American psychoanalysis are waning. This is understandable, if one keeps in mind the relatively small percentage of women accepted by American medical schools. In Europe, everyone who graduated from that high school-college hybrid called the *Gymnasium* was qualified to study medicine. Most medical schools, at least in Central Europe, were so organized that their 'imposition' on the student was rather meager. Attendance in classes was not obligatory, except for a few practical exercises. The bulk of what a student had to do was to take his three *rigorosa* (obligatory series of examinations), and no one really cared how far his training went. A very large number of students spent significant portions of their time in extracurricular studies, such as attending classes in the humanities; and thus it came about that many who were not endowed for medicine per se could go through the study of medicine without becoming seriously involved in it.

In this country, it is quite different. A halfhearted study of medicine is impossible, for the selection of medical students is quite rigorous. Certainly the medical schools will not favor in their selection of students the type of woman whose predominant assets lie in empathy and the art of listening; and it is questionable whether this type of woman would expose herself at all to the rigors of medical study, the way it is organized in this country. Therefore, it is highly probable that the contribution of women to psychoanalysis will become increasingly smaller in the future.

According to recent statistics, the percentage of gifted college graduates applying to medical schools is growing steadily smaller. The student material from which medical schools will be able to select will be —unless this trend changes—of a lower caliber than before (Ceithaml, 1955; Editorial, 1960; Hutchins and Gee, 1961; Rusk, 1961). How will this affect the future of psychoanalysis? The renaissance of physics nowadays attracts the gifted college student interested in the natural sciences, who in an earlier period might have gone into medicine, and thus perhaps eventually reached a psychoanalytic institute. Therefore it is reasonable to raise the question whether that loss could not be made up through lay analysis. After all, there is a good chance that this curtailment of sources of talent, which sooner or later must make itself felt in the psychoanalytic institutes, could be compensated for by winning some of the gifted students who would otherwise have gone into the anthropic sciences because of their lack of interest in the natural sciences.

I can quote here two leading analysts whose views will reveal how easily institutes might find a substitute for the threatening loss—a substitute that, if their own opinion is to be trusted, might well turn out to be even better than what it would be replacing.

Alexander (1932) wrote of "the experience that candidates who have some acquaintance with the humanities are far superior in their psychological understanding of the mentally sick to candidates trained only in medical and natural sciences . . . . Furthermore, sympathy with the emotional life of others is more characteristic of the man of philosophical and literary culture than one who, though medically trained, knows nothing of the emotional life of the sick or of psychology in general" (p. 262).[4]

Knight, in his Presidential Address of 1952, made an important statement with reference to the problem under discussion: "Since relatively few physicians are interested in or trained for research, and since many psychologists *are* interested in and trained for research, our regulations may have the effect of drying up the supply of research psychoanalysts" (Knight, 1953, p. 215, italics by Knight). And further, in comparing the type of analyst trained in the third decade with those in the fifth, he had this to say: "They [the majority of students of the past decade or so] are not so introspective, are inclined to read only the literature that is assigned in institute courses, and wish to get through with the training requirements as rapidly as possible. Their interests are primarily clinical rather than research and theoretical" (Knight, 1953, p. 219).

Knight's last comment refers mainly to specific difficulties created by postwar conditions, which may have been, at least partly, remedied since then. But the cited comments are sufficient to create some doubts as to the value of Bandler's (1960) suggested remedy—namely, that if our psychoanalytic institutes will not, without some change, be able to produce sufficient analysts to cover the needs of the community, we should merely increase the number of training analysts, and lower the age of candidates for acceptance at institutes (p. 399). Somehow this sounds as if analysts could be produced in conveyor-belt fashion, so that the solution of the problem would require nothing more than administrative measures. No answer is offered to the question of where candidates should be obtained under present conditions. Is the crux of the matter the fact that there are not enough training analysts available? Or

---

[4] The same holds true with regard to the evolvement of introspection (see earlier).

is it not rather the fact that a sufficient number of candidates *suitable for analytic training* are not available?

Furthermore, is the community really better served, the larger the number of analysts (that is, is the *number* of analysts actually the matter of greatest interest of the community?) or is not the decisive question one of *talent?* Bandler, in considering how to stimulate advanced studies and research, suggests the formation of new committees (Bandler, 1960, p. 401) to fulfill this aim. Once more, we observe the trust in administration—which, once it is properly organized, 'has to' lead to the desired results.

Yet I wonder whether the formation of new committees and new study groups will prove to be enough of an administrative innovation. The psychoanalytic situation per se is comparable to an experimental situation, and psychoanalytic research grows directly out of it. If psychoanalytic research is falling off, this is not due to any lack of administrative measures; it is a definite sign that the psychoanalytic institutes are no longer being supplied with adequate student material.[5]

I would like to go even one step further—but with the caution that this next step is based on an as yet untested hypothesis. Observations that I cannot set forth in detail here have left the impression that the inner treasury out of which a person's later creativity is formed goes back to his puberty and the early years of his adulthood. I cannot yet set the upper time limit one must reckon with in this respect, but my inclination is to set it at somewhere between the ages of twenty-five and thirty. My hypothesis, expressed in a simplified form, would therefore be that, after that age, man becomes generally incapable of forming original thoughts, ideas, or outlooks.[6]

In this crude form, this conception is, of course, untenable, for there are a good many instances in which men have made their most original discoveries, or have been creative, in a most highly individualized fashion, after that age. I omit from consideration those instances in which these advances were brought about primarily by accident. If we leave such instances aside (they form no more than a minority), there are still many left that appear to contradict my hypothesis. Yet, when one has

---

[5] It is also possible that the techniques of training analysts have deteriorated under the influence of medical analysis. If the modification of training analysis in the Chicago Psychoanalytic Institute, about which Alexander (1956, p. 184) reports, is truly indicative of what is happening on the national level, one can only be pessimistic. (For further comments, see Appendix I).

[6] This theory does not, of course, rule out the importance of the first quinquennium.

the opportunity to learn more fully the history of such original work, one is surprised to discover how much of it was performed during the early years. The preformed state is often a fantastic one, and therefore not realizable as such; what the later years do is to mature, purify, and rationalize the early original seed. One gets the impression that, if the adolescent or the young man had not formed those ideas or fantasies, the mature person would never have been able to obtain the stuff out of which the original contributions grew.

Freud is an example of this. He himself discovered a childhood root of the method of free association (1914a), which is so impressive as a piece of creativity belonging to his mature years. Indeed, when one reads the letters that he wrote to his bride, only some of which have been published (Freud, 1873-1939), and which were written when psychological research was still quite distant from his mind, one is surprised to find many later discoveries already dimly outlined, although they were almost casually thrown in.[7]

If my hypothesis is correct, we have found an additional relevant reason why psychoanalytic research has not made "a greater scientific contribution of more value to our civilization" in this country, as Hendrick (1955, p. 580) has so rightly said. Since, by and large, analysts are physicians, it is only reasonable to assume that the vast majority of them were interested in biological imagery during those adolescent, early formative years to which I have attributed decisive importance with regard to the emergence of later original creativity. It may seem ridiculous to speak of biological imagery during adolescence. Of course, we know that all daydreams, at whatever age, have at their core an instinctual drive, or the defense against it, and usually both; but it makes a great difference for the subject's cultural potential whether the bulk of his daydreams is bound directly to the instinctual core itself—that is to say, contains more or less crude sexual fantasies—or whether the instinctual impulse leads to a wealth of 'sublimated' fantasies. In these latter, the analyst can, of course, still find the adumbration of instinctual impulses,

---

[7] I am fully aware of the difficulty involved in validating my hypothesis. I want to cite here only that extraordinary incident of Loewi's decisive experiment on the chemical transmission of nervous impulses, for which he was honored with the Nobel prize. It was the content of a dream, although "consciously I never before had dealt with the problem" (Loewi, 1953, p. 33). This makes the incident different from similar examples, which usually involve dreams by those who had previously been intensely preoccupied with a problem that ultimately found its solution in their dream. Loewi's experience may, I think, be interpreted in such a way as to favor my proposition.

but they also contain a broad stream of culturally valuable wish fulfillments, which lay the foundation for the subject's later well-organized, culturally creative work.

My thesis, in short, is that, in his later creative work, the adult falls back over and over again on his store of adolescent daydreams, most of which may become repressed. According to this thesis, the potential and the duration of a person's creativity are therefore established at a far earlier stage than would seem to be likely from the actual record.[8] My present clinical impression is that it is *adolescence* which is relevant to the formation of the cultural potential, and that the content, direction, and the duration of later creativity are in effect already determined during this period.[9]

According to this view, one would expect to predict that the majority of medical freshmen will show in their daydreams—in so far as they form any of a sublimated character at all—far fewer propensities toward dealing with the conflicts or the destiny of man than do their confrères in the anthropic field. It is, as far as I know, something of an exception when a candidate for a psychoanalytic institute turns out to have formed his intention of becoming an analyst during his college years, and to have studied medicine for just that purpose. It seems to be rather the rule that he formed the intention only during the course of his medical studies, or after he graduated, or after his rotating internship (when he had to choose a specialty), or, worse still, after he had failed or become disappointed in his first-choice specialty.[10]

I do not regard this as a situation that favors later original research in psychoanalysis; and I think that it would be far more promising to select analysts from among those who, during their adolescence or early manhood, were preoccupied with fantasies or other forms of intense ideation related in a general way to man and his problems. Such persons are to be found, for example, among students in various departments of

---

[8] Refined investigation, however, may demonstrate that this *alea iacta* already occurs in the first quinquennium. For the early development of cultural interests in Freud himself, see Freud (1925d, p. 8). There the genetic groundwork of his endowment with regard to natural objects and human relations is briefly mentioned.

[9] It would lead far afield if I ventured, at this point, a hypothesis as to the character of the childhood development that will lead to an adolescence such as holds promise of later creativity, during the years of adulthood.

[10] In the light of Lewin and Ross's (1960, p. 80) recent publication, this assertion may be unjustified, unless one is to assume that the questionnaire on "Pathways to Psychoanalysis" touched on an unpleasant point which necessitated rationalization on the part of those answering.

the nonmedical university faculties, who will probably later go on to obtain Ph. D.'s.[11]

When a science is fully established, as medicine and physics are, and has become an integrated part of a cultural tradition, its basic concepts are already taught during the early stages of education. It is well known that the best preparation for the study of physics is the high school physics course, and for the study of medicine, the elementary courses in physics and chemistry plus an extended study of biology. Here, then, is another basic situation that shows how untenable the present trend against lay analysis is. For, if an adolescent were to ask today for advice about the best means by which to ensure later proficiency as a physician, there would be no long debate about how to answer him; yet if he were to ask the same question about psychoanalytic proficiency, what analyst would venture to tell him to study chemistry, physics, and biology?

The uncertainty about what is the best preparation for psychoanalysis —a doubt that is well justified, despite the present certainty that psychoanalysis is a medical specialty—is evidence of the fact that psychoanalysis has not yet become integrated into contemporary civilization. It still holds an esoteric place. No society desiring to attain a place in modern civilization would try to do so without physics or medicine; but psychoanalysis is far from being regarded as a *sine qua non* in the same way. It is the ambiguous societal standing of psychoanalysis that is reflected in the problem of preparatory studies.

It is thus still because of accidental occurrences, for the most part, that a person's interest becomes aroused in analysis. While the preliminary disciplines of physics and medicine become readily familiar to all who possess an interest in and endowment for each respective field, the same cannot be said of psychoanalysis. Thus the present situation makes it advisable to select analysts from among *all* those who are interested in psychoanalysis and seem to be talented in the field. Psychoanalysis, if it is to continue the progress it has made, cannot be 'choosy' with regard to the preanalytic training that candidates went through; it must draw upon available talent, wherever it is to be obtained.

Medicine, which is an awe-inspiring and highly respectable science, is not, after all, that choosy. Chemists, physicists, biologists—in short, all

[11] It is also noteworthy that candidates start their analyses at an age when—if my thesis is correct—their creative potential has already been fixed. Analysis may cure a neurosis at that age level, or it may free creativity from inhibition; but it does not seem to be capable of having any relevant bearing upon the potential itself. (For the age distribution of candidates, see Lewin and Ross, 1960, pp. 59-71.)

those interested in the natural sciences—are invited to add their share to its progress; and they do so, and richly. It is all too often forgotten that a surprisingly large number of outstanding medical discoveries were made by men who never acquired a medical degree, the great Pasteur being not the least among them.[12]

To be sure, the large number of Ph.D.'s who today put their talents at the service of medicine, and without whose collaboration medical progress would be severely retarded, do so without infringing upon the area of 'medical tradition' that is put to such a severe test by lay analysis. Yet this absence of infringement has not been the result of any particular awe or respect on their part for medical tradition or for any particular policy. The structure of medical research does not make for any such infringement: it is altogether irrelevant to the diagnosis of a specimen who took it out of a patient's body. Furthermore, it is often forgotten how many areas of medical responsibility have been surrendered more or less completely to the lay person. There were times when the application of an intravenous injection required a fully trained physician, and an assistant who usually was also a licensed physician; today it is done often by a nurse. And yet here is a situation in which a mistake may cause harm to a patient of a sort that is immeasurably more grievous than that which can be caused by even an incompetent lay analyst.

I suppose that the objective to this argument will be that the nurse does not decide upon the choice and timing of the injection. If damage is done, it is caused by negligence, and not by any lack of the knowledge necessitated by the circumstances. Yet this is applicable equally to lay analysis: the kind and timing of treatment can be suitably determined by a physician; if, in the course of treatment, harm is done to the patient, such damage will have been caused by negligence, and by no means as the result of unavoidable ignorance.

The injury done to psychoanalysis by artificially limiting the area from which to obtain new lifeblood is enormous, and in sharp contrast with the parallel situation with regard to medicine.

A Medical Analyst Looks at Society

In an expository article for the thirteenth edition of the *Encyclopaedia Britannica*, Freud (1926b) wrote, as the concluding sentence of the

12 It may be of interest to note that, as far as I can determine, at least nine scientists who were not physicians received the Nobel prize between 1901 and 1950 for eminence in medicine or physiology.

section on "Subject-Matter of Psycho-Analysis": "It is enough to say that psycho-analysis, in its character of the psychology of the deepest, unconscious mental acts, promises to become the link between psychiatry and all these other branches [social anthropology, the study of religion, literature, history, and education] of mental science"[13] (p. 269).

What is significant is that psychoanalysis is defined here as a link between psychiatry and the anthropic sciences, not as a subspecialty of psychiatry. Those who vigorously oppose lay analysis may object—to some degree, perhaps, correctly—that to regard psychoanalysis as a subspecialty does not mean to eliminate its role as a link. They may point to the many papers written by medically trained analysts, pertaining to the humanities or the anthropic sciences, by way of proving that the medical profession is quite capable of meeting the requirements of both of the functions just mentioned. Indeed, I am well aware that some remarkable anthropic papers have come from the pen of medically trained analysts; what is more, I have never made the claim that all medically trained analysts must of necessity develop into what I have called medical analysts.

Medical education, of course, does not of itself prevent an analyst from becoming an analyst of the character that Freud had in mind. I have only asserted that, if analysis were to be entrusted exclusively to physicians, the tendency to develop psychoanalysis as a psychiatric subspecialty would be greatly strengthened, and that function would probably become its sole and final end. I also raise the question whether one can already anticipate what would be the caliber of the anthropic contributions made by psychoanalysis, once it had established itself fully as a medical subspecialty.

I am inclined to believe that one can so anticipate, in the light of some of the contributions already made by medical analysts; in this connection, I shall discuss some of the anthropic work done by Alexander,[14] who is a notable representative of medical analysis. Originally, while in Europe, he was in favor of lay analysis (although with the expectation

[13] The term Freud used was *Geisteswissenschaften*.

[14] I often take Alexander's works as paradigmatic, even though the field abounds in examples that one could use to demonstrate the inadequacies of medical analysis. Alexander's writings, however, are more suitable for a critical discussion than those of many others, who often use unclear language and complicated ratiocinations, which would take up considerable space to unravel. Alexander is almost always simple and direct; he rarely leaves the reader in doubt as to where he stands. Consequently, it is much easier for one to show the fallacies of which he has made himself guilty than in other instances.

that the distinction between the lay and the medical analyst was bound to disappear); since his move to this country, he has adapted his views to those prevailing here. There are optimal prerequisites for outstanding psychoanalytic anthropic achievement present in his case, since his formative years, according to an autobiographical sketch, were spent in the shadow of the greatest anthropic works.[15]

I shall consider at this point mainly two papers by Alexander: "The Psychiatric Aspects of War and Peace" (1941a), and "Defeatism Concerning Democracy" (1941b). These were produced shortly before the United States entered World War II, and form part of Alexander's (1942) more comprehensive book, *Our Age of Unreason*, published in the midst of the war.

The subjects were most timely since, during those years, this country was going through one of its gravest crises, and good advice was needed indeed from an enlightened anthropic researcher, who was armed, to boot, with the sharpest and most advanced anthropic methodology. I regret that space does not permit me to go into detail here as much as I should like to, for one really has an opportunity here to demonstrate the sort of disasters that the anthropic sciences must expect to arrive at when medical psychoanalysis is applied to history or sociology.

It is not easy to summarize Alexander's paper on war and peace: at some points he is divided in his own thinking, yet at the same time, he tries to cover up the paper's inner contradictoriness. One aspect, however, stands forth clearly: the author's belief and trust in the efficacy of the unification of smaller groups. His principal thesis is that larger national units are in fact formed only when one constituent group subjugates weaker groups by force. This process he regards as rational, and *per contra* the decay of larger units into constituents as irrational. War is the rule between national groups where there is a difference of interests; within the group, on the other hand, conflicts arising from differences of interests are solved, not by force but peacefully. If abstention from violence is possible, when there are conflicting interests *within* the group, then, the author reasons, it must also be possible in similar situations *between* national groups. It is only necessary to enlarge the individual conscience beyond the national boundaries, so that it encompasses a still larger group—namely, the whole of mankind; then no one will

---

[15] See Alexander (1940b). However, a disparaging remark that he made about archaeology to his father, after his graduation from high school (p. 308), may have foreshadowed the fact that the humanities would not fare well with him.

have resort to violence for the solution of conflicting interests. Yet the individual conscience somehow always seems to limp behind the social reality.

First, therefore, an all-encompassing social organization is to be created; then the enlarged individual conscience will follow, and conflicts of interests will be resolved peacefully at every level. The establishment of larger units is so important in the author's thinking that it appears to be a matter of secondary importance to him which group turns out to be the constituent one, so long as conquest at its hands leads to the final integration of the weaker.

Thus, at a time when the European democracies were fighting for their lives against the German onslaught, the author predicted that the future historian would evaluate that war as having the same character as the intra-Italian war of independent cities, although at that time it was, "of course, still an open question whether England or Germany will be the crystallization point of this future Pan-Europe" (p. 513). And two and a half pages later he added: "The future history of Europe will be entirely different if the coming Pan-Europe is organized under British or German predominance. From a distant historical point of view the end effect might be the same. The road to it, however, would certainly be smoother and less tortuous in the first than in the second case" (p. 516).

The author is aware of the essential difficulties to be encountered in the creation of such a superorganization. Having asserted that the prerequisite must be the subjugation of all weaker groups by the strongest, he merely goes on to regret that the democracies do not resort to force in order to create such a state, but instead leave the application of violence to the totalitarian states. How to subjugate half the world by force, while still maintaining any claim to being a democracy, strikes me as being perhaps the prize question of our century; to answer it would, I fear, take more than even Alexander's acumen.[16]

Furthermore, I think that Alexander may very well have overstepped

---

[16] In his main thesis of the elimination of violence through the formation of larger units by the subjugation of smaller ones, the author—very likely inadvertently—repeated Freud's reasoning. Unfortunately, he omitted one important qualification. Cf. Freud (1933b): "It is impossible to make any sweeping judgment upon wars of conquest. Some, such as those waged by the Mongols and Turks, have brought nothing but evil. Others, on the contrary, have contributed to the transformation of violence into law by establishing larger units within which the use of violence was made impossible and in which a fresh system of law led to the solution of conflicts" (p. 278).

the bounds of his competence as a psychiatrist and psychoanalyst, when he took to advising the League of Nations as to which wars to conduct, and which not. That sort of problem is usually left to editorial writers. And besides, in what area did he contribute anything new? In his opinion, Freud did not make "a fully satisfactory analysis of the problem" (p. 511), in his letter to Einstein (Freud, 1933b). Notwithstanding Freud's own dissatisfaction with his answer, in the light of the immensity and the urgency of the problem, I have not been able to perceive where Alexander, as long as he speaks as an analyst, introduces any new theoretical opening. If anything, Alexander's paper amounts to little more than an obfuscation of some of the points that Freud set forth clearly.

When he reasons, for example, that Freud's general statement about human conflicts being in principle settled by force (Freud, 1933b, p. 274) is of dubious value, in the light of the peaceful settlements of conflicts occurring within a community, he simply disregards the two printed pages (Freud, 1933b, pp. 275-277) in which Freud is dealing with the dynamics of precisely those peaceful settlements. Perhaps he just did not like Freud's analysis, for Freud, in delineating his impressive evolutionary scheme, does not lose track of the remnants of aggression still visible even in those very conflict-solving techniques. In putting the settlement of conflicts by war into stark contrast with the prevailing ways of solving intracommunity conflicts, Alexander follows a rather static mode of reasoning.

One may say the same thing about the antinomy he tries to create between communities fighting each other, on the one hand, and, on the other hand, dominant groups forming new and larger units out of hitherto independent communities. Freud was aware, of course, of the process of large units falling apart (Freud, 1933b, p. 278), a process which makes it impossible to expect any lasting solution from unification. Alexander also discusses this trend, but it remains a negligible factor in the scheme that he finally devises, and he reaches the (by the way, wrong) conclusion that "only if the constituent groups voluntarily give up their independent existence . . . will the larger social organism become a stable institution" (p. 515).[17] Freud, on the other hand, was well aware of the inherent danger in the tendency toward unification; he put it into a classical statement: "Thus the result of all these warlike efforts has only been that the human race has exchanged numerous, and

[17] However, this did not prevent Alexander from quickly resorting once more to his original thesis of forceful subjugation.

indeed unending, minor wars for wars on a grand scale that are rare but all the more destructive" (Freud, 1933b, p. 278).

Although no appraisal of this sort is to be found in Alexander's paper, I may perhaps have overstated the case when I questioned its originality altogether. In 1941 it had not yet become the fashion to describe the mentality of those whose political opinions differ from one's own in terms of psychopathology. Alexander is against pacifism; thus the pacifists are rather badly battered by him. In his mind, they are all a bad lot: the pacifist may be considered as "neurotic," "dreamer," "subject to wishful thinking," not daring "to face reality," escaping "into fantasy"; pacifism must similarly be considered as a "morbid phenomenon," the "rationalization of self-destructive wishes" (p. 504f.). This is all the more striking since Freud (1933b) discussed his own pacifism at length (pp. 285-287), and even asserted, "We are pacifists because we are obliged to be for organic reasons, and we then find no difficulty in producing arguments to justify our attitude" (p. 286).[18]

I must assume that Alexander did not have Freud's and Einstein's abhorrence of war in mind when he lashed out at pacifism, nor, for that matter, those parts of the New Testament that forbid participation in aggressive acts for whatever reason—although a more precise statement concerning the area he wished to cover with the term "pacifism" might have been desirable. Be that as it may, I am in agreement with Alexander in one respect. In the Army, I had to deal with conscientious objectors, who were motivated by pacifism for religious or political reasons; and I must admit that almost all of them struck me as suffering from a variety of psychopathological syndromes, most of which were of fairly severe nature. But this was a selected group; on principle, I must object vigorously to calling a person neurotic because of any sort of political or ethical conviction he may hold.

To be sure, Freud called religion a mass delusion, and there is much to be said in favor of his view; but he certainly did not say that the religious individual is delusional. Moreover, Freud called religion a mass delusion, not for any ethical precept that it recommended, but in so far as the religious systems have made—and continue to make—claims with regard to the facts that have been disproved by science; in turn, they have denied, and often still deny, some of the results of scientific research.

[18] See also Einstein (1934).

Even if it could be proven that certain forms of psychopathology occur with greater than average frequency in a group that is characterized by belief in a certain value system, it would still be methodologically wrong to link psychopathology with value systems in general, or with that particular belief. Yet, aside from this serious flaw in method, the author was apparently altogether unaware that his paper actually furnished a foolproof justification for extreme pacifism, and that such pacifism is in fact the only rational conclusion that one can draw from his own premises.

The following deductions will demonstrate this: If it is only after the elimination of smaller groups as groups, and their inclusion into larger ones, that progress can be made in human domestication; if, further, war is unavoidable between independent groups in cases of conflicting interests, while violence is absent on such occasions within the larger group; and finally if, whichever group serves as the crystallization point of the larger entity, the end effect "from a distant historical point of view" is the same, the only difference being with regard to the degree of smoothness with which the unification is established—if all this is so, then it is the apodosis of the pacifistic conscientious objector's creed that is truly rational, and the horrors of war become ludicrous.[19]

I have gone into detail on Alexander's views on peace and war, not because that formidable subject per se demanded our interest at this point, but because I wanted to set forth a paradigmatic illustration of how a medical analyst deals with a problem of anthropic research. Do we not observe in this instance an approach that can be meaningfully connected with the general pitfalls of medical analysis? In my opinion, we do. We also observe here that same emphasis on 'serviceability' (Oberndorf, 1953, p. 247) and practicality, along with the subsequent reliance on 'common-sense judgments,' arrived at without consideration of all the aspects of personality structure. To call the pacifist a neurotic is to manifest a crude sort of biologism, such as one is compelled to see in the voluntary and intentional abnegation of simple self-preservation nothing but a disease.

Frames of reference that lie outside and beyond the true-false value system of the scientist are applied, and certain historical processes are described as 'rational.' Unless we are willing to apply a crude kind of

[19] I am certain that the author did not intend his thesis to be understood in quite that way; but it is highly significant that inadvertently, by the very process of simplifying Freud's more complicated reasoning, he produced suitable tools for the defense of extreme pacifism.

Hegelianism, neither the formation nor the decay of large groups can be called either rational or irrational per se. As a matter of fact, a stream of the greatest cultural values has been created by civilizations that split up into small units. The author's *ultima ratio*—that the democracies should form a new 'league of nations" by the use of force (coalition by coercion) —strikes me as one of those 'common-sense' schemes that one runs into every now and then, which are chiefly distinguished by their utter disregard of both human nature and history.

Was there not one Charles Lomax Delbridge (1916) who thought that he knew *How To Make War Impossible?* According to him—and I do not see any flaw in his reasoning—the United States should annually put aside a large amount of money, so that in case of war a sum of $1,000 (and citizenship) could be given as a reward to "every enemy soldier deserting, surrendering or being taken prisoner." Was he wrong when he concluded: "I know human nature and the mathematical laws of percentages and averages well enough to enable me to say, beyond any possibility of even the shadow of a doubt, that there is not an army nor a navy on earth today that could be held together in the face of that award"? I must say that I am more inclined to believe Delbridge than Alexander.

If we pursue Alexander's views still further, however, we shall observe the following. Before Pearl Harbor, we still find the praise of man, who "only under the influence of propaganda and often even of alcohol can . . . be persuaded to kill" (Alexander, 1941a, p. 512), in time of war. After Pearl Harbor, when this same article is reprinted in *Our Age of Unreason,* this passage disappears. Similarly, before Pearl Harbor, it was merely an 'open' question whether England or Germany would be the victor (Alexander, 1941a, p. 512); after Pearl Harbor it became a 'crucial' question (Alexander, 1942, p. 331).[20] I quoted earlier the ominous passage on the identity of the end results, whether democracy or fascism won in Europe (Alexander, 1941a, p. 516); this passage also disappeared in the version printed after Pearl Harbor, in which we read instead that "much will depend on whether the British, Germans, or Russians control the situation" (Alexander, 1942, p. 334).[21]

[20] Although *Our Age of Unreason* was published after Pearl Harbor, the final manuscript may have been finished a short time before. The time difference would not disprove my subsequent conclusions.

[21] The absence of bibliographical accuracy might also be mentioned in passing. In the Preface to *Our Age of Unreason,* there is no indication whatsoever that the reprinted articles differ in important points from the originals.

When these different versions are carefully weighed, the conclusion must be drawn that—perhaps unknowingly to Alexander—an opportunistic element was at work: the subtle adaptation of views to the requirements of the day. This same opportunism is also visible, however, in Alexander's presentation of American history, which he paints, in contrast with his image of European history, in the most peaceful terms. He reduces the Mexican and Spanish Wars to "mere incidental military operations" (Alexander, 1942, p. 324), an opinion that is not shared by every historian.[22]

He further omits the Indian Wars, which for many decades were conducted with so much cruelty, and which therefore militate strongly against the concept of a peaceful history of the United States. He omits as well the terrible depredations committed against the Negroes, amounting in toto to an undeclared war against a race. An unprejudiced evaluation of American history will show that in this part of the world, too, each generation has had its war.

In trying to determine the source of this opportunistic element, one is forced to reflect anew on the therapeutic techniques that the physician who adheres to medical psychoanalysis is prone to apply. More often than not, one can note a tendency toward eclecticism. Since it is the *shortest* route to clinical recovery that is the cherished goal, the desire to supplement analytic therapy with drugs, intravenous injections, shock treatment and what not can scarcely be denied. Here, too, no opportunity will be overlooked to seize hold of the fashion of the day, in order to keep abreast of the therapeutic fads. The actual harm that can be caused to individuals in this way may be open to question; but the harm done to anthropic research cannot be denied, and constitutes a grave danger.

This danger lies particularly in the tendency toward a relative optimism that creeps insidiously into this kind of research. Whether or not Freud's concept of a death instinct is confirmed by later physiological and pathophysiological research, it would show better judgment to assume the existence of such a drive so long as its nonexistence has not been proved. In times of crisis, preparation for the graver eventualities is much to be preferred to a trust in more favorable conditions.

In *Civilization and Its Discontents*, Freud (1930a) outlined in broad strokes a series of problems that must be solved on the road toward a

[22] See Millis (1931) for a highly instructive history of the Spanish-American War, and the deep effect it had on a whole generation, and probably on the entire further course of American history.

balanced state of man's cultural world. The perspective he describes is not very attractive, for the issues that mankind has yet to face are of truly awesome proportions. When Freud's book was written, European history had not yet taken its turn toward the worst. The twelve years or more that elapsed before Alexander's *Our Age of Unreason* was published were to produce a saddening confirmation of some of Freud's worst anticipations.

What did Alexander offer in 1942 as a remedy for this new situation? Economic competition should be replaced by economic co-operation, through the mechanisms of government mediation and reconciliation (Alexander, 1942, p. 313). Foreseeing some trouble in this area, he quickly added that only "some industries might profit from central control and planning, others from private initiative and freedom from interference and regulation" (p. 321). What is to decide between the alternatives? Scientific inquiry, rather than the prejudiced generalizations of theorists, we are told. Unfortunately, the author forgets to tell us how one is to distinguish between these two. Yet, even if Alexander's economic idyll should prove to be feasible, was Freud in error in his assumption that the problem of human aggressiveness goes far beyond any particular form that the distribution of wealth may take (Freud, 1930a, p. 113)? And does anyone really think that human aggressiveness can be bought off at so cheap a price? Alexander's sublime trust in the effects of institutional changes may not be commendable, but it is enviable.

He writes further: "Neurosis, criminality, snobbishness, and social tension between dissenting groups manifest the discontent arising from the cultural lag" (Alexander, 1942, p. 314). By which he means, I take it, "the lag of emotional attitudes behind changes in social structure" (Ogburn and Nimkoff, 1940)—surely a strange explanation to hear from the author of *The Criminal, the Judge and the Public!*

Alexander (1942) further advises the American people to make strides in trends which seem to him to "show their tender beginnings": "an appreciation for the creative use of leisure, a sense for the amenities of life (apart from mere comfort!)" (p. 316); "the dream of comfortable slow-moving automobiles which . . . are not designed to swallow the miles . . . but to glide in a leisurely fashion," etc. In short, he recommends as a cure of the ills of our times: waste of time (p. 317).

On the other hand, "if our ambitions for self-expression remain on the economic level alone . . . the rapid disintegration of our whole system" (p. 319) will inevitably result. People should devote themselves more to writing poems and teaching school children (p. 320); and he adduces, as a further argument in favor of his recommendation, that "nothing is more fallacious than to consider intellectual and artistic accomplishments as economically unproductive. . . . Pictures or poems have long been exchanged for shoes and butter," (p. 319f.)—but here, I fear that the author is showing himself to be guilty of a cultural lag.[23]

Two more instances should be cited of the many I could set forth to demonstrate the inadequacy of anthropic research when it is entrusted to the medical analyst. Alexander (1942) expects much of value for the solution of the crisis of our times to come from education: "an educational development of psychological attitudes which are not yet universal" (p. 340). His advice is that people should be educated to develop a broader conscience, emotional maturity, and a sense of responsibility (Alexander, 1941b, p. 649). Indeed, we need no ghost to come from the grave to tell us that; but worse: the belief in such illusory certainties is an impediment to research on, and prevents the understanding of, the present; and if anyone were to organize his actions around such recommendations, he would be condemned to failure.

Notwithstanding the great importance of education, a study of Bernfeld's (1925) basic text on the limitations of education should convince the reader that hope in education as the solution to fundamental issues is a time-honored illusion, and should by this time be laid to rest. Freud weighed educational possibilities on various occasions. In his *The Future of an Illusion,* he expressed the hope that a grandiose experiment in rearing children without the inculcation of illusions would demonstrate that the primacy of intellect in human life is more than an illusion; he suggested an *"education to reality"*[24] (italics by Freud, 1927b, p. 49). In

[23] It gives one a rather strange feeling to read Alexander's recommendation of the leisurely life when more and more our times seem to require an extraordinary effort on the part of all members of the community, if we are to safeguard the mere survival of our civilization. It is deplorable that, although Alexander ostensibly made use of psychoanalysis, he did not succeed in grasping the elements that basically characterize our century.

I shall quote one sentence from Spengler that is relevant in the context of the advice Alexander gives to the American nation: "And I can only hope that men of the new generation may be moved by this book to devote themselves to technics instead of lyrics, the sea instead of the paint-brush, and politics instead of epistemology. Better they could not do" (Spengler, 1917-1922, p. 41).

I am afraid that the new generation will have no free choice in the matter, and that hard necessities will force them to stick to technics, to the sea, and to politics.

[24] However, Freud was well aware that his own trust might prove illusory; cf.: "Education freed from the burden of religious doctrines will not, it may be, effect much change in man's psychological nature" (Freud, 1927b, p. 54).

his letter to Einstein, he also brought up the issue of education, limiting it this time to "an upper stratum of men with independent minds, not open to intimidation and eager in the pursuit of truth"; but he reached the conclusion, nevertheless, that he was dealing with "a Utopian expectation" (Freud, 1933b, p. 284). Education is a factor of considerable social importance and consequence; but to expect salvation from this quarter reflects nothing but ignorance of the reality of the historical process.

We are further offered by Alexander (1942), as a conclusion, "the fact that the development of the social sciences is at present more urgent than further technical advice" (p. 341)—a statement that it is curious to read now, at a time when mere physical survival depends, to begin with, on technical progress. Indeed, if our culture did come to possess an adequate social science, much would be gained thereby. But I fear that the author implies merely that more people should study sociology, and more money should be invested in sociological research.

That would, however, definitely make for a cultural lag. Sciences cannot be created in that way: millions of dollars could be poured into various departments of sociology, which would certainly lead to an increase in the number of publications, and yet the creation of a true sociology would still remain in doubt. Any serious student of the history of science knows that the development of a science depends on far more serious and complex factors than the presence or absence of good will— or the number of dollars or number of people that one can mobilize for this purpose.[25]

No, we cannot find here any satisfactory orientation about the future; and Alexander's book belongs to the type of work that Freud (1930a) so tellingly characterized: "And it is this battle of the giants that our nursemaids try to appease with their lullaby about Heaven" (p. 122).

The reader may have come to feel impatient because of the length of my critique—it is really only a small part of what ought to have been said —but I do not think that it is a waste of time to go into such detail. By prolonged use of measures which amount in effect to indoctrination, hopes in psychiatry and in psychoanalysis have been raised high. A book such as *Our Age of Unreason* must lead to grave disappointment, and to justified doubts about psychiatry and psychoanalysis, if one attempts to take it seriously as a guide-rope to, and perspective for, the future. One

25 See Le Corbeiller (1946).

must therefore stress the fact that it has almost nothing to do with psychoanalysis as such, but is probably the best that a mind oriented along the lines of dynamic psychiatry and the medical application of psychoanalysis can produce on the topic.

I share Alexander's concern about mankind's ignorance on the question of how to deal with the crisis of our times, and it is for that reason that I have tried to demonstrate the consequences of one—seemingly unimportant—detail in our present organization of anthropic research, a demonstration that I could not have carried out better than by this critical analysis of some of Alexander's sociological work.

"Psychoanalysis Comes of Age" and the Lure of the University

The development of psychoanalysis in this country is often contrasted with that in Europe before 1938, in so far as there psychoanalysis lived what many people have chosen to regard as an ivory-tower existence (Alexander, 1938;[26] Oberndorf, 1953, among others). It is true that psychoanalysis in Vienna existed, so to speak, in isolation: it was not taught at the University, and the Psychoanalytic Society maintained hardly any contacts with other groups. In this country, on the contrary, such isolation has come to an end, and psychoanalysis maintains a close contact with psychiatry and medicine, as well as with the humanities. This has been heralded as a step of great progress, beyond the supposedly deplorable situation that existed in Europe (at least in Vienna), from the birth of psychoanalysis, at the turn of the century, until 1938, when psychoanalysis was officially stamped out.

As long as a historian is capable of being distracted by the trimmings, he is bound to overlook the essentials. True, the universities did protect themselves against the new science; true, whoever wanted to be respectable did dissociate himself academically from the taint of having accepted the new psychology, which was referred to, more often than not, only in critical and disparaging remarks. But these conditions reflect only on the universities, state hospitals, and psychiatric clinics; they are without any relevance to the question of the organization of psychoanalysis per se.

In the Viennese Psychoanalytic Society itself, after all, almost all areas of human knowledge were represented, so long as they were concerned

26 However, in 1932, Alexander had written that, in Europe, " a considerable part of the rising generation of psychiatrists regard the study in one of the Psychoanalytic Institutes as a necessary complement to their training" (p. 254).

with the study of man. To be sure, there may often have been only one person representing a large area of knowledge. Yet, as a matter of fact, the Society did include the historian, the physicist, the internist, the psychiatrist, the educator, the historian of art, etc.—all of them equally well trained, and with equal access to the psychoanalytic material. The only requirement for membership was proficiency and scientific reliability as a psychoanalyst.

In this society, there was, then, the nucleus of a miniature academy of sciences, including both the natural and the anthropic sciences, the institution being held together by the primary interest of each member in the systemic psychology of man, and thereby living up to the demand placed upon modern science at its inception: "La vraie science et la vraie étude de l'homme, c'est l'homme" (Charron, 1601).

The same situation held for other European societies that did not exclude lay analysts. The outcome was a series of discussions of a liveliness and breadth hardly to be matched elsewhere, and an impressive output of papers bearing on all phases of anthropic knowledge. These appeared in the twenty-three volumes of the European periodical *Imago*, which was started in 1912 precisely for the purpose of providing an outlet for the application of psychoanalysis to the cultural sciences.

Does the fact that this intimate co-operation and cross-fertilization between the various disciplines took place outside of the universities warrant speaking of an 'ivory tower' position of European analysis? Of course, the *prestige* of psychoanalysis and of psychoanalysts would have been greater if the professor of history had announced from his chair that Freud was making invaluable contributions to the understanding of the history of man; but what would have been the real advantage to psychoanalysis itself?

Those who deprecate the purportedly 'ivory-tower' position of psychoanalysis should, in my opinion, consider this question: whether the American situation, which is characterized by the contact between medically trained analysts and a relatively large number of unanalyzed and analytically untrained medical specialists, along with representatives of the humanities, *outside the psychoanalytic societies,* is to be preferred to the Viennese situation, which was characterized instead by a regular and intensive cross-fertilization, *within the psychoanalytic society,* between medically trained analysts and lay analysts representing the humanities. The 'ivory tower' thesis that one hears so often loses much of its meaning as soon as one analyzes carefully what is actually involved; then one recognizes that the phrase is merely a catchword.

Moreover, one should consider the fact that, had psychoanalysis been permitted to continue its development in Europe, this trend would probably have borne even more distinguished fruits than it did up to 1938. Although a trend against lay analysis had become noticeable, it is almost certain that Freud's authority—and later his memory—would have kept the doors open to worthy nonmedical analysts, who would thus have been guaranteed adequate training and practice. The interest in psychoanalysis was on the upswing, and whoever examines the periodicals of the pre-Hitler years will discover that psychoanalysis, either openly or in disguise, had started to make its appearance in even the venerable and conservative pages of traditional psychiatric periodicals.[27]

All that, of course, was wiped out by merciless persecution; and it will be many decades, if ever, before psychoanalysis in Central Europe recovers from the injuries it suffered twenty-five years ago. As in so many other matters, the center of gravity of psychoanalysis has shifted to the United States; and it is probable that its development, from here on, will principally depend on how it fares in this country.

The naïve attitude of "favoring that which endures because it is serviceable" (Oberndorf, 1953, p. 247) might, perhaps, have been justifiable as long as the "Pope in Vienna," as William A. White called Freud in 1919 (Oberndorf 1953, p. 136), was carrying on basic research. So long as the genius's mind kept up the evolvement of new theories in accordance with new insights and discoveries, the pragmatist could scoff at metapsychology, or laugh at such theories as the death instinct. Times have changed, however. No one else will carry the burden of basic research, if the analysts in this country do not; and the best thing that could be done for psychoanalysis, science, and the community would be to forget, for a while at least, such questions as how many appointments members have in hospitals and universities, and whether or not the American Psychiatric Association regards psychoanalytic societies as *bona fide* parts of their organization, and instead to make the growth of psychoanalysis the sole question.

The break with the European tradition, so to speak, was announced by Alexander in his Presidential Address of June 1938. We know how apt

---

[27] Cf. Freud (1925d): "At the present time German psychiatry is undergoing a kind of 'peaceful penetration' by analytic views" (p. 61).

he was to scent new phases; on that occasion, he did not hesitate to declare that, herewith, "Psychoanalysis Comes of Age."

Two references in particular strike me as noteworthy in that important document:

1. In his advocacy of a "more precise, more quantitative knowledge, for more exact experimental evidence," Alexander (1938) felt compelled to issue a warning against psychoanalysis's deteriorating "into a one-sided emphasis upon sterile, thoughtless description as a contrast to theory," and even went so far as to warn against "misjudging and defaming every deduction as speculation" (p. 305).

How did it happen that a gathering of scientists needed such a warning in 1938? Is it really possible that any practitioner would ever come to feel so strongly against the Aristotelian syllogism that he could defame any deduction as a conjecture? Either Alexander was misjudging the intellectual level of his audience, or else things had grown far worse than even an imaginative pessimist could have guessed. Whichever alternative may be correct, we can see once again the at least potential danger that pragmatism holds for psychoanalysis.

2. More important is what Alexander had to say about the psychoanalytic movement. *Die psychoanalytische Bewegung* was the name of a journal, five volumes of which were published from 1929 to 1933, under the leadership of A. J. Storfer (the last volume under Hitschmann), by the *Internationaler Psychoanalytischer Verlag*. It was a delightful magazine, hovering charmingly in the psychoanalytic borderland of history, literature, philosophy, and other fields.

I do not think that Alexander had this innocent journal in mind when he spoke of the psychoanalytic movement, but rather Freud's (1914a) paper "On the History of the Psycho-Analytic Movement," the chief intent of which was to come to grips with Adler and Jung, setting forth that which makes psychoanalysis different from their views. Thus the existence of a psychoanalytic movement highlights the idea of difference, of what separates psychoanalysis from other areas of science. Such an idea must be offensive to a person like Alexander (1938), who equates "the stubborn martyr attitude of the fanatic" with "the insistence upon the specific nature of the psychoanalyst as distinct from all other scientists" (p. 303).[28]

[28] That is how he characterized the attitude that he thought he had observed in some older analysts. He considered the "antagonistic attitude toward medicine" as "a historical remnant of the initial feud between Freud and the Viennese medical group."

That psychoanalysis is, in its essential features, different from any other science could be doubted only by someone who was trying to win approval from the medical profession—as also becomes evident in the conclusion he draws that "the sooner psychoanalysis as a 'movement' disappears, the better." When he expressed the hope "that the expression 'psychoanalytic movement' will soon sound to us as strange as would 'ophthalmological movement' " (*ibid.*, p. 303f.) (a goal which Bandler declared to have been reached in 1960, [p. 389]), he may not have been aware that there *is* a vigorous ophthalmological movement, at least in this country, where the public is aroused to give its share to the blind, and is alerted to take full measures against diseases that may result in blindness. Even physics, that oldest and most exact of sciences, has generated a 'movement' all over the world; and no nuclear physicist would, I believe, be unaware of the movement that he has the honor to participate in, nor would he shun the responsibility that he is carrying in being a nuclear physicist.[29]

Alexander writes: "The cultural mission of psychoanalysis to force man to face his own nature objectively has been accomplished" (*ibid.*, p. 303).[30] To which the answer is brief: not so! There is not the slightest evidence to justify such a statement. We observe here once more the narrowed horizon of the physician who has his heart set on the application of psychoanalysis to medicine, and who therefore thinks that a real victory is to be celebrated because psychoanalysis has become acceptable to the medical profession.

In spite of that fact, psychoanalysis remains at bottom a foreign body in medicine. Whether this is necessarily so, or only a temporary phase, is not the question here. Yet there is no doubt much lip service in this respect. Psychoanalysis has become fashionable; and I am afraid that Alexander has let himself be seduced by the gentle words one occasionally reads in nonanalytic publications.

Does he not know, for instance, that a substantial part of our population is still taught and still believes that masturbation is a mortal sin, and would therefore—even now—be incapable of viewing it as a developmental phenomenon, whose absence during childhood or adolescence

29 The aversion toward regarding psychoanalysis as a movement has not been limited to those who have been distant from Freud; it was also expressed by an analyst who was as close to Freud as Ernest Jones was throughout his psychoanalytic career (cf. Jones, 1959, pp. 201-236, particularly p. 205).

30 Cf., however, Freud (1933a): "There are so many more people who believe in the miracles of the Blessed Virgin than in the existence of the unconscious" (p. 208).

would in most instances be a sign of bad prognosis? Indeed, it would be correct to say that, as long as man believes in the existence of God, he reveals—and maintains—his inability to face his own nature.

The full introduction of psychoanalysis among the anthropic sciences would necessarily lead to a change that could only be compared with a revolution, in that all our textbooks of history, as well as of its allied subjects, would have to be rewritten in time. Now that psychoanalysis has been denatured by having made the handmaid of psychiatry, and its maximum effect upon anthropic research has been blocked off by the practical squeezing out of lay analysis, the psychoanalytic movement has been artificially stunted. Whenever a society is led to block off the maximum utilization of a science, it is necessary to uncover and combat the hindering forces, in order to facilitate the free development of that science, and to carry its application to its potential maximum.

Alexander is right: the times of a psychoanalytic movement are gone; but that is an artificial result, a manufactured 'cultural lag.' It is also a defeat for psychoanalysis, as well as a grave loss to society.

The present phase of the denaturalization of psychoanalysis is not the last. The next step will probably be the official and final submergence of psychoanalysis in psychiatry, by making the practice of psychoanalysis dependent on certification by a board of psychoanalysis, which would function as a subspecialty board of the American Board of Psychiatry and Neurology. One attempt to organize psychoanalysis in this way has recently been thwarted; but it is probable that if the present trend continues, it will come to pass after all, and in the foreseeable future. It will be paralleled by the gradual absorption of psychoanalysis by the medical schools, where it will be safely lodged and rest for a long time, a Sleeping Beauty that does not disturb the sleep of humanity.

At this point, a general comment must be made about the universities. They are the mainstays of present-day research: eliminate them from that area, and scientific progress would be brought almost to a complete standstill. This eminent position in cultural life has been held by the universities not only during the new era; the institution can look back on a history covering a millennium. If I now express serious doubt about the wisdom of having psychoanalytic training and research incorporated by the universities, this should not be construed as implying any criticism of those institutions as such.

History seems to indicate that, during times of transition, the universities lag. I have only to cite two sentences from Merton's discussion of Hall's excellent paper on science in the seventeenth century to show this.

> It may not be too much to say that it was in the coffee-house rather than the classroom . . . that the mutual education of scientists took place; [and,] . . . that no one thought of basing research laboratories in a university; an institutional invention which seems simple enough, once the idea of a laboratory occurred at all, and yet one which . . . was remote from the prevailing conception of a university [Merton, 1959, p. 25].

In times of transition, when systematized knowledge is being shaken to its foundation by new discoveries, and the introduction of new systems of thought requires fundamental changes in administration and organization, the reason why the universities tend to lag is precisely the usual excellence of their achievements. They cannot, it seems, at the same time achieve such excellence and maintain a readiness for essential changes. Once the new trend has been integrated, however, they once again move into the forefront of advance.

It is a fact of extraordinary significance that Lavoisier's work was not carried out within the confines of a university (Gillispie, 1960, p. 215). Darwin was likewise not connected with a university. Even the discoveries of Gregor Mendel, which laid the foundation of modern genetics, occurred outside of university confines.[31] Freud's psychoanalytic work was done outside the academic orbit, despite his closeness to the university during his neurological years. It also should be mentioned that Oswald Spengler, one of the most original thinkers of the twentieth century, had no academic connections. To put it in a nutshell: genius and the universities do not go well together.[32] Yet, even though it is clear that as yet no other genius has made his appearance in the American Psychoanalytic Association, and therefore the particular prob-

---

[31] One of the few contacts that Mendel established with the university proved most deleterious to his experiments. The advice that Carl Nägeli, Professor at Munich, gave him to carry on his experiments with hawkweed was the worst possible suggestion he could have received (Iltis, 1924; see also Gillispie, 1960, p. 329).

[32] This broad statement needs qualification, of course, inasmuch as a genius whose work takes place within an area established by tradition does not in fact arouse as much opposition as one whose creativity starts a new tradition. It would be instructive to draw up a history of achievements brought about outside the academic orbit (see Gicklhorn and Gicklhorn [1960], for important documentary material regarding Freud's relationship to the University. The book, aside from the documentary material it contains, cannot be recommended, however, because of its many errors, distortions, and misinterpretations [cf. Appendix 4]).

lem of genius would not be likely (at least directly) to impede the integration of psychoanalysis by universities, nevertheless the analyst is in the difficult situation of carrying forward the work of a genius. For psychoanalysis is still Freud, even though many an attempt has been made to change this very 'difficulty.'

Here one can make a curious observation—how many of the psychoanalytic innovations suggested in the last two or three decades actually have the effect of making psychoanalysis absorbable by universities or hospitals. Dynamic psychiatry, or psychosomatic research as it is being carried on at present, and even Alexander and French's therapy by 'corrective emotional experiences'—all these fit well into existing research institutions at the university level. Yet, psychoanalysis as Freud saw it is still as refractory to academic absorption as it was in Freud's time. Indirectly, by means of this historical argument, it may be shown that these later branches are regressions rather than progressions, since any advancement beyond Freud should—one might logically expect—make the new achievement even more refractory to integration by universities than Freud's psychoanalysis.

Particularly in the case of dynamic psychiatry, one can show that it makes psychotherapy so much easier than the rigorous stringency of what Freud required even a half-complete psychoanalysis to be. I think one has the right to be distrustful of new techniques when their chief significance lies in the ease and comfort they bring to those who practice them. As a matter of fact, one can state specifically against which part of Freud's psychoanalysis the so-called Neo-Freudians turn most readily. It is the reconstruction of the infantile period that arouses their objections.

In reading Freud's case histories, one gains the impression that such reconstruction can be accomplished easily enough; but I suppose that almost everyone who has tried himself to reconstruct a running developmental history of a patient's infantile neurosis will agree that unusually great demands are put on the analyst's synthetic functions, memory, acumen, attention, and understanding. I can well imagine that many feel relieved upon hearing that this aspect of Freud's teachings is not as valid as the analysis of the patient's resistances and transference, both of which are so often quite readily visible, and fall like ripe apples into the therapist's lap.

The point is of such major importance that the following passage should be quoted at full length, since its truth has not lessened, I am certain, during the forty odd years since it was written:

Strictly considered—and why should this question not be considered with all possible strictness?—analytic work deserves to be recognized as genuine psycho-analysis only when it has succeeded in removing the amnesia which conceals from the adult his knowledge of his childhood from the beginning (that is, from about the second to the fifth year). This cannot be said among analysts too emphatically or repeated too often. The motives for disregarding this reminder are, indeed, intelligible. It would be desirable to obtain practical results in a shorter period and with less trouble. But at the present time theoretical knowledge is still far more important to all of us than therapeutic success, and anyone who neglects childhood analysis is bound to fall into the most disastrous error [Freud, 1919b, p. 183].

And, as if he foresaw the temptation of analysts to abridge the analytic process, Freud raised his voice once again later to make sure that only a technique which aims at the full reconstruction of the infantile period would be regarded as psychoanalysis. Thus he wrote in 1925(e): ". . . the analyses of neurotics shall deal thoroughly with the remotest period of their childhood. . . . This requirement is not only of theoretical but also of practical importance, for it distinguishes our efforts from the work of those physicians whose interests are focused exclusively on therapeutic results and who employ analytic methods, but only up to a certain point" (p. 248).

Many, indeed, are the ways in which this necessity of removing the childhood amnesia is combatted, and almost the whole history of the psychoanalytic schools dissenting from Freud can be focused around this one issue. Be that as it may, if Freud's psychoanalysis were to be integrated by an academic institution, the latter would have to make adaptations and to carry out reorganizations that might be comparable in their extensiveness to those that the medieval university had to perform in order to adjust to the changes brought about by the scientific revolution.

Since neither the value of psychoanalysis nor its importance has yet been acknowledged by society to the extent that psychoanalysis—at least in the analyst's estimation—dèserves, it is clear that no academic institution would be likely to agree to deviate from tradition and present usage to the necessary extent; it is rather psychoanalysis that would have to adjust to academic requirements. Yet since the true analyst should be primarily and solely an analyst, it would be unfair to expect that any one of them should willingly assist in the foreclosure of psychoanalysis even to the highest bidder—in this instance, whoever would demand from psychoanalysis the fewest basic changes as the price of academic standing. Could the psychoanalyst be "possessed entirely" by psychoanalysis, as seems to be necessary, according to Freud (1933a, p. 209), if analysis were to be absorbed by a university or hospital under such conditions as obtain at present?

I think that only the analyzed can truly decide on matters of psychoanalytic training and practice. Thus the dean of the medical school would have to subject himself to a training analysis, yes, even to a full training.

"Psychoanalysis can never be merged into medicine as a special subject, as a branch of therapeutics: it can only enter it in its entirety as a *half* of equal importance" (italics by Alexander). That was written by Alexander in 1927 (p. 229). Yet there is no institution in the United States today that could grant psychoanalysis even that half, since training in organic medicine requires more time, expense, and effort than fits in with the capacities of the individual. At present, psychoanalytic standards can be maintained, as in the psychoanalytic institutes, only when the institution preserves its independence from any nonanalytic agency.[33]

Even under such favorable circumstances, the training does not fulfill its entire purpose, in so far as psychoanalytic anthropic science is omitted from the training programs. Alexander solves this problem, too, in a simplified way:

"Our institutes," he writes, "should be small but high grade universities of psychoanalysis in which candidates receive instruction both in practical clinical and theoretical subjects with a well-balanced biological and sociological orientation, and not merely professional schools . . ." (Alexander, 1938, p. 305). Yet one may ask where are the psychoanalytic historians, sociologists, and biologists who could fill the instructorships on the staffs of such psychoanalytic universities? Or did Alexander have in mind the taking of measures that would achieve no more than this: to release the psychoanalytic candidate for graduation better educated in human affairs and in cultural matters than the average physician is? What would be done then would be nothing more than to call in a sociologist, a historian, etc., and have them teach the same courses as are offered at the average academic institution.

From the point of view of psychoanalysis, however, this would be misleading. If psychoanalysis is in actuality what it has said that it is, then the conclusion is inescapable that under its aegis a *new* history,

[33] For a discussion of this problem, cf. Kubie (1952).

sociology, etc., must arise, and that these new subjects must be taught at a university of psychoanalysis. Since these disciplines are not yet in existence, however, it behooves the existing institutes, in my opinion, to lay the foundations for the psychoanalytic university of the future. For this purpose, lay analysis would have to be released from its present bonds and anthropic scholars trained alongside medical men.

It is always hazardous to predict; but, assuming that psychoanalysis will still be regarded as a scientific systemic psychology, the future historian of science will not wonder why the academic universities of our time did not integrate psychoanalysis, so much as he will be forced to grope for an explanation as to why the *bona fide* psychoanalytic institutes did not undertake to make psychoanalytic anthropic research possible. He will feel puzzled, in the same way as we are when we study the history of the seventeenth-century universities.

Thus, psychoanalysis may have come of age legally; but this promising youth who was full of new ideas, restless, inquiring, filled with surprising observations, and vigorously striving for insight into all areas of the human cosmos, has been transformed by starvation and neglect into a pale and lethargic organism with an appalling complacency about its lack of interest in its own future scientific growth.

History, I am certain, will see in the early group that gathered around Freud the first realization of the idea of an academy of unified science, an academy of the science of man which, even though it functioned socially 'in an ivory tower,' made the first great step toward the realization of the inherent potential in psychoanalysis. Perhaps that step forward was too great for our time, after all, being made possible only through the presence of that towering mind whose shadow was cast upon it. And perhaps it is in accordance with the laws of history and man's inertia (Alexander, 1942, pp. 198-200), therefore, that psychoanalysis must regress to what it was at the hour of its birth—a specialized technique of a treatment procedure—before it can grow once again into what it was destined for by its creator[34] and by its own intrinsic character.

This seems to be the proper place to ask, concerning those who have not resisted "the temptation to flirt with endocrinology and the autonomic nervous system" (Freud, 1927a, p. 257)—that is to say, those who have

[34] Cf. Freud (1925f): "Its [psychoanalysis's] original significance was purely therapeutic . . . . But connections which could not be foreseen in the beginning caused psycho-analysis to reach out far beyond its original aim" (p. 214). For a further discussion of the subject, see Appendix 1.

earnestly tried to turn psychoanalysis into a medical specialty—how far they have succeeded in the eyes of their medical colleagues. I shall give two answers, one almost two decades old,[35] the other of recent vintage. In 1943, the *Journal of the American Medical Association* published an editorial on "Psychoanalysis and the Scientific Method." Of its critical remarks, the following deserve especial attention:

> Psychoanalysis has a nomenclature and diction that have been characterized as an unintelligible jargon. True, mathematics, physics and chemistry employ special symbols. It should be possible to make the language of any science understandable, at least with the help of a dictionary. A sentence such as the following, however, from a recent article in the field of psychoanalysis is without value to the uninitiated and its real significance even to those actively working in the field may be questioned: "This ego-feeling cathexis in turn depends on the compatibility of the single element with the whole ego unity."[36]

The scientific validity of that sentence, when it is placed in its proper context, and of course its sheer intelligibility, would be doubted, I presume, by very few analysts. Yet the writer of the editorial was quite correctly pointing out—and for that purpose, he could have selected an even simpler sentence—that psychoanalytic terminology is, in effect, a foreign body in the medical curriculum. To understand correctly the bulk of psychoanalytic literature, and not to remain content with a mere smattering of concepts and terms, takes years of hard work, perhaps the almost exclusive devotion to this aim for a few years.

This is quite different from the situation encountered in other medical specialties.[36a] True, recent advances in physics, chemistry, and biology also require learning and hard work on the part of the physician who received his professional training between the two World Wars, and who must as a result integrate new terms during the course of his practice. Nevertheless, the new generation of students learns about these same advances in their premedical courses, so that the difficulty arises for them only to the extent that these sciences make new and essential discoveries *after* they have finished their training. Furthermore, when the physician is dealing with new concepts in physics and chemistry, he is

[35] I trust that its age will not detract in any way from its relevance. It might just as well have been made recently.

[36] For the offensive sentence, see Weiss (1942, p. 483).

[36a] For the particular difficulty encountered in integrating psychoanalytic terminology, see Hartmann (1958, pp. 133, 138).

facing a situation essentially different from that which he meets up with in psychoanalysis. In the former, he has to fit something new into a frame of reference with which he must surely be familiar by that time; in the latter, he has to make a new beginning.

There is a logical continuity from the atom and the molecule to the cell and its behavior under normal and pathological conditions, and medicine will never give up its implicit goal of understanding the processes in the diseased body in terms of chemical and physical processes at the molecular level. With the introduction of the first psychological term, however, the frame of reference is cracked, and a discontinuity in the logical scheme is established, which many philosophers and scientists are still trying to bridge, but which necessarily, as matters stand now, continues to remain a chasm.

In my opinion, it is altogether correct for the editorial writer to point to the special place that psychoanalysis has to occupy in the medical scheme of things. That is to say, it can be accepted formally, but not actually integrated; and in spite of the official welcome it may receive, in view of the prestige that it has acquired since its birth, it is still condemned to second-class citizenship among the medical sciences, like a resident alien.

The A.M.A. Journal's editorial quoted above closes with an appeal that is probably intended to bring analysts to their senses: "By abandoning unscientific procedures and by adapting itself to the rapid evolution of the psychosomatic medicine as a specialty, freudianism will achieve greater scientific stature and fulfill more promptly its early promise of extending the borderlines of medical knowledge." The problem could hardly be put more succinctly. "Unscientific procedures" undoubtedly covers precisely those elements that make psychoanalysis different from all other sciences, so that abandoning these in order to become a branch of psychosomatic medicine would be merely trying to make itself palatable as a sort of sub-subspecialty. Since the mind has a bearing on the symptom—whether that bearing be organic or functional—the science of the mind must find a rightful place somewhere in medical education. It is my contention, however, that if the physician wants to deal adequately with those effects of the mind, he must become a psychoanalyst.

This will be disputed. There are a large number of physicians who, without having gone through the complex psychoanalytic training, nevertheless combine psychotherapeutic techniques with physical treatment, to the benefit of their patients. I do not contest this, and yet I feel that these techniques are in most instances inadequate, if they are measured by the knowledge accumulated since 1900. They are, to be sure, socially sufficient: the physician, the patient, and the patient's family ask for no more, and are therefore content with what they are offered. But to operate properly with the use of psychoanalytic knowledge requires prolonged and deep-going studies; no compromise can be made.

The functioning of the natural tact, sympathy, and common sense which a humane and sensitive mind may possess can easily be disturbed by an insufficiently digested theory whose full understanding would require years of study. I have been told that in the Army a situation arose which necessitated the issuance of a circular requesting that the young neuropsychiatrists abstain from asking soldiers whether or not they had ever had intercourse with their mothers. The events which made such a circular necessary revealed the existence of some extraordinary misunderstandings of psychoanalysis; they still serve as a clear warning against the dangers which lurk in the possession of a mere smattering of psychoanalysis.

The relative advantages which the introduction of psychoanalysis into the medical schools may seem to offer, in terms of prestige, respect, and research possibilities, are far outweighed by the almost certain dilution of psychoanalysis as a science, and the debasement of its technique—both of which are practically unavoidable when viewpoints alien to psychoanalysis per se are converted into essentials.

The other quotation to which I wish to call attention comes from a journalist who was clearly biased against psychoanalysis, but from whose articles about psychoanalysis in the United States (Browning, 1961a, 1961b) something of importance can be learned—namely, that a significant section of the psychiatrists and physicians representative of American medicine regard psychoanalysis as the wrong path toward the understanding of mental disorders. As a nationally known psychiatrist has said, about the unusual upswing that psychoanalysis took in the United States around the middle of this century: "The reaction has set in against psychoanalysis and the pendulum is swinging the other way" (Browning, 1961b, p. 29).

Notwithstanding the distortions customarily met with in most newspaper reporting, a perusal of Browning's articles will leave the reader with the impression that, after all, perhaps not so much would be lost if psychoanalysis stopped courting medicine and returned to its own fold, giving anthropic research an equal standing with medicine. Yet, I believe that psychoanalysis would legitimately earn greater respect than it does now, if it concentrated on its own business, and occupied itself with the discovery of all the facts that legitimately fall within its scope, and with the evolvement of related theories, instead of trying to dress itself up as a medical specialty.[37]

How little psychoanalysis belongs as part of present-day medicine, and in the university medical departments, can be seen from a fact that may seem somewhat unrelated at first. It is safe to say that no contemporary psychoanalyst has the slightest chance of becoming a Nobel Prize laureate by virtue of a psychoanalytic discovery that he has made or may yet make, and that this is not due to any particular or *ad hoc* prejudice of the Caroline Medical Institute in Stockholm. It is just not conceivable that any analyst could observe in the psychoanalytic situation a fact or a combination of facts, or could derive from such facts a theory, that would be—as fully as one has the right to expect of a discovery honored by the Nobel Prize—a contribution to the progress of medicine.

REIK'S THEOREM AND CHILD PSYCHOANALYSIS

In his discussion of lay analysis, Theodor Reik (1927, p. 241f.) put forward the following hypothetical situation and its implication. Let us assume, he suggested, that it has been proven, beyond doubt and unassailably, that Freud's researches on neurosis and psychosis were conducted from false premises, and that therefore his findings have been shown to be in error, his conclusions being valid only in so far as they pertain to a personality unaffected by psychopathology—that is to say, to a normal mind. The implication would be that all the psychic processes that Freud described, in order to explain the genesis and structure of various forms of psychopathology, were in fact correlated with dysfunctions of the endocrine system (or, from the point of view of biochemistry today, of any biochemical system).

As a result, a new therapeutic approach, quite different from the psychoanalytic, and supposedly far more reliable and precise in its indications and effects, would become necessary and practical. No patient, of course, would any longer submit, in the light of such new therapeutic possibilities, to the discomfort of a prolonged psychoanalysis—with its

[37] The crowning blow that medical psychoanalysis has thus far received occurred, of course, in Bailey's Academic Lecture of 1956, which clearly demonstrated how terribly isolated psychoanalysis remains, even in the realm of psychiatry, despite all claims to the contrary.

uncertain outcome, to boot—nor could he be advised to do so. Moreover, with this discovery it would also have become clear that psychopathology could no longer be used as a source of insight into man's mind, as is the case in the psychoanalytic laboratory.[38]

In such a state of affairs, the analyst for whom psychoanalysis had been all along nothing more than a medical specialty would now feel free to limit his therapeutic activity to finding out which of the various drugs should be prescribed for the particular symptom presented by the patient. That is to say, his interest in the neuroses and psychoses would not have changed; but, instead of subjecting the patient to psychoanalysis, he would now subject him to a physical treatment. According to Reik's theorem, an analyst acting thus "may be an excellent physician and neurologist, but his interest in psychoanalysis does not seem genuine" (1927, p. 242). The psychologist, on the other hand, would turn to the investigation of the normal mind, and find other ways in which to continue his research into man's personality structure. As for him, his psychological interest would not have changed; but his interest in the neuroses and psychoses would have vanished.

Reik's theorem, curiously enough, has come close to becoming a clinical truth: at least the biochemists themselves assert that they are approaching the realization of therapeutic possibilities of this sort. Indeed, such a therapeutic blessing might well turn out to be a blessing not only for the suffering patients, but likewise for psychoanalysis itself. At last true psychological research, unencumbered by the therapeutic burden, could be carried out without restriction, and the vast fund of skills now slumbering in many of those who are engaged in anthropic research could become contributory to psychoanalytic research.[39]

[38] This conclusion would be not altogether a necessary one, if it were to be applied to actual clinical reality; but it is admissible within the framework of Reik's theorem.

[39] Recently, Turkel (1962) published an article in which "mental therapy" is declared to be valueless, since 50 per cent of our hospital beds are occupied by mental patients. The author asserts that science now has methods "which make Freud as obsolete as the Wright Brothers' airplane or the treatment of syphilis with 606." Within the framework of the enlargement of therapeutic possibilities, Turkel's firm assertion of scientific advance may well be correct, and for reasons which I have given above, I would welcome such advance. But I must admit that his reference to 50 per cent of the hospital beds, etc., worries me. On one point, however, he is wrong, I am sure; that is when he says: "If he were still alive today, Freud would have turned to these new methods of treating mental illness, rather than use psychoanalysis." If the medical analysts are consistent, they may soon find themselves having to go along with Turkel's views. But since Freud, at least, was principally interested in the structure of personality, it testifies to a basic misunderstanding when Turkel offers the opinion that Freud would have turned into a pharmacologist.

I should like to make two additions to Reik's theorem, in order to avoid misunderstandings. In the first place, it was meant as a theorem, and nothing more. Secondly, with regard to his observation that, theoretically speaking, Freud might just as well have made his discoveries through the exploration of the normal mind, I would go a step further and assert that, in all probability, Freud would have made his discoveries even if he had continued his neurological research.

Actually, it was in his work on aphasia, published in 1891, that he took the first step toward the exploration of the personality, in this instance damaged by diseases of the central nervous system. Disturbances of ego mechanisms, of instinctual life, and of superego functions occur in this form, as well as in the functional disorders. It seems to me likely that, in the former area, there is even a greater breadth and a wider variety of disturbed functions than in the latter. There are other advantages to conducting psychological research on organic cases—for example, the relative constancy of the disturbance. In short, the brain-damaged personality is indubitably an excellent subject for psychological research.

Reik, furthermore, did not imply that, if his theorem was ever realized, it would prove that Freud's conclusions were wrong. A subject may suffer from a severe headache developed as a consequence of a posthypnotic command, and yet this same headache may subside as soon as he takes aspirin. It is even likely that Freud's own concept of psychopathology rests on the existence of biochemical processes of the kind now being discovered. The evidence of disturbed biochemical processes in neurotic or schizophrenic patients would not yet per se prove psychoanalysis to be erroneous, and Reik did not mean his theorem in that sense. But in its clear-cut distinction between analysis and medically applied analysis, Reik's theorem is excellent; and the fact is that the progress of biochemical research may in the long run free psychoanalysis of those who are not genuinely interested in psychology as a science, but in therapeutics alone.

I am forced to draw such a conclusion, if only for the following reason. If anyone were to attempt to deny the losses that psychoanalysis has suffered so far from the prohibition of lay analysis, or even to assert that such losses are far outweighed by the advantages obtained through having turned psychoanalysis into a subspecialty of psychiatry, I do not see how he could ever justify the present state of child analysis in this country.

If adult analysis is evaluated purely from the human, or the humane, point of view, there is enough to be praised. After all, it is a really comforting thought that our civilization provides a setup, almost an institution by now, which enables the individual to reveal his innermost mental recesses without the dread of punishment, reprimand, loss of prestige, or exhortation for moral betterment. But this matter of humaneness is even more telling in the area of child analysis.

The sufferings that children have been exposed to during the course of human history constitute one of the most revolting chapters of human cruelty. Yet, even when they have been spared such atrocities as befell Saturn's or Chronos's children; or those of Medusa; or some children in English society, even as late as the nineteenth century, when they were caught in the act of stealing; or, finally, in our century, Jewish children caught by the Nazis—I say, even if we eliminate such unspeakable atrocities, childhood is an unhappy period under the very best of external conditions, a fact movingly described by scores of authors and poets.

There is a basic misunderstanding between the adult and the child, which Ferenczi (1933) characterized in the very appropriate phrase: "Confusion of tongues between adults and the child." The anguish inherent in childhood does not, of course, gainsay the occurrence of exquisite childhood joys and delights, possibly unmatched by any adult pleasures. Yet these joys and delights are, in the average childhood, only exceptions; and adults often remember from their childhood incidents or even periods of sadness, frustration, and grief, which no adult unhappiness can match. In the course of analysis, it very often turns out that these incidents of suffering actually occurred more frequently than had been originally recalled, and that childhood took place under a general sign of sadness, only occasionally interrupted by episodes of incomparable joy. That is why almost every adult harbors (manifestly or latently) excessive reproaches against his parents or their substitutes.

Yet, with all this, nothing is more frustrating than the efforts of a loving adult to relieve the child of his grief. Since he does not know the actual source of the grief, he will more often than not achieve nothing more than a temporary cheering up. At the very beginning of child analysis, at a time when the technique of dealing with children did not yet quite deserve that name, a most propitious incident took place. It was on April 25, 1908, that—as far as is known, for the first time in the history of mankind—a boy, aged five, admitted to his father in all seriousness his oedipal wishes, without thereby arousing anger, enmity, or revengefulness in the father, who had been apprised of the imminence of the child's confession beforehand by Freud (Freud, 1909a, p. 92). Viewed in the context of history, the event is unique and may well be regarded as a turning point.

One may recall that, over two thousand years earlier, at a time when civilization had already made great strides, a Macedonian king was praised for letting his son rest at his side armed with a javelin. As Plutarch, who records this feat, writes: ". . . he was not so afraid of his son as to forbid his standing beside him with a weapon in his hand." And he refers to "fathers who brought their children, husbands their wives, children their mothers, to untimely ends" (Plutarch, p. 1074).[40]

I consider the episode in the child's analysis to be worthy of extended comment at this point, because it shows some of the potentialities inherent particularly in child analysis, which may lead to a degree of liberation for the child far beyond that which reformers and legislators sought in the nineteenth century for the protection of children. It is the most individualized process conceivable. When the adult reaches the analyst, his emotional life has generally suffered deep injury. His emotions no longer have direct access to the volitional sphere: a break between action and fantasy has occurred; he has submitted to the frustration imposed on him, and has given up the claim of the dream to realization. The child, inhibited as he may be, still harbors such claims; his emotions, however distorted they may be, still may find direct access to action. This quality of being still unbroken by reality imposes unique demands on the skills of the therapist, but it also makes the analytic process far more individualized than with the adult.

Classical child analysis—that is to say, a procedure that explores the roots of the child's mental and emotional life—is on the decline. There are few who practice it or learn its technique. A large number of substitute techniques have been evolved, such as play therapy or simple interviews. Often the therapeutic measures are limited to a change of environment, or to simple counseling of the parents.

---

[40] Plutarch reports this story about Demetrius, son of Antigonus and Stratonice. Curiously enough, in the same life of Demetrius, the history of Antiochus, stepson of another Stratonice, is also told (pp. 1015ff.). He fell in love with her, but decided to kill himself by starvation because of the hopelessness of the situation. The family physician, guessing the true reason for his decision, induced the king by a clever trick to give Stratonice in marriage to his son. I believe that this story does not disprove the point I have made in the main text with regard to the historical importance of the analysis of Little Hans. (The identity of names of the two Stratonices in the same chapter of Plutarch's Lives may warrant further psychoanalytic speculations.)

It is enlightening to hear, for example, what the medical analyst has to say about child analysis. "Not too many analysts," writes Oberndorf (1953), "retain sufficiently childlike traits to become at home in psycho- analytic psychotherapy with children from the ages of two to ten or twelve" (p. 242). Should this astonishing passage be understood as an expression of disdain, directed by the 'mature' analyst who treats adult patients towards the person who wastes his time with children? Why should the presence of "childlike traits" be the *sine qua non* for the per- sonality equipped for the analytic therapy of children? Can it be that the medical man had an uneasy feeling about so many children going psycho- logically unattended, and eased his conscience by affirming that there are just not enough childish people on hand to fill the quota of child analysts?

As a matter of fact, the medical profession is not in any position to fill the need for child analysis; the majority of child analysts have been up to now lay analysts. Furthermore, it has been frequently observed that child analysts, after years of practice, give up their specialty to devote their full time to the analysis of adults. Oberndorf (*ibid.*) says: "As the therapist grows older he or she is apt to lose patience with the dif- ficulties of psychotherapy with children and is likely gradually to change to psychotherapy with adults." I doubt that it is a matter of patience; the demands put upon the child analyst, the mental strain that he is subjected to, are enormous. Is it possible that the doctor of medicine just does not have enough idealism for such exigencies?[41]

Child analysis (*cum grano salis*) occupies a position and function in psychoanalysis equivalent to that of embryology in medicine. When one is studying medicine, one does not hear very much about embryology, for the curiosity of the physician will not, in general, go beyond the area of the given data; and that area stops far short of that with which the embryologist deals. Yet, if a complete and satisfactory history of the patient's pathology were to be written, in almost every instance of dis- ease relevant references to embryology would become necessary.

The corresponding relationship is much clearer in analysis. In child analysis, genetic reconstructions gained from the psychoanalysis of adults can be tested; furthermore, the analyst may obtain, through child analysis, knowledge of many factors such as mechanisms, genetic phases, pre-

[41] Berta Bornstein (1948) has made a study of the unconscious barriers that impede the adult's understanding of the child.

stages of functions, and so forth, which it might be impossible to obtain through the analysis of adults.[42]

One would imagine that at least the analyst's own personal curiosity would force him to return over and over again to direct observation of the area that he has to keep constantly in mind when analyzing adults. Otherwise, he would be in a situation comparable to that of the philologist who has to correct and interpret Latin texts, but without ever having studied the history of Roman society.

Without the removal of the shackles that, for all practical purposes, now make lay analysis impossible, nothing will spark the long overdue renaissance of child analysis. The equanimity with which the gradual disappearance of child analysis has been viewed gives me the feeling that the spirit of dynamic psychiatry has spread much further than is officially acknowledged. Since dynamic psychiatry omits exact genetic reconstructions, the medical analyst can endure the impending disappearance of child analysis without regret. Some medical analysts who are satisfied with an incomplete version of the human mind even warn against letting the psychoanalytic process go as far as is needed in the reconstructions of early episodes.

The demand that the practice of child analysis should also be reserved for physicians leads to an interesting implication that brings out with particular clarity the ridiculousness of the opposition to lay analysis.

If the basic pattern of the parent-child relationship or of the teacher-child relationship is studied, it will easily be recognized that the potential of injury to the child's mind is greater in these relationships than in child analysis. A father or mother must act upon a child without any knowledge of that child's unconscious background. *In nuce*, the child analyst often has to undo the damage that parental care has caused in the child. Furthermore, the damage done to children in the schools is often immeasurably great.

If the analysts were consistent, they would have to demand that not only all parents and teachers, but also all priests and ministers, study

---

[42] It is my experience that analysts who have had extensive experience in child analysis generally have a clinical approach in adult analysis superior to that revealed by those who are inexperienced in the other area. Of course, this is not a rule: there are, to be sure, many analysts who would not improve their techniques of adult analysis by experience gained in child analysis, not to speak of those who are lacking in any aptitude at all for conducting such analysis. Yet, if the psychoanalytic profession were practiced in accordance with ideal standards, every analyst would have at least one child in treatment.

medicine before they are permitted to take care of their wards. To be sure, mothers do take adequate physical care of their children without any previous medical training: they can do this because their physical care does not generally lead to an action of medical relevance. But, in raising children, parents unfortunately indulge constantly in actions of psychoanalytic relevance, and therefore they should not be permitted to 'practice the raising of children' without previous medical training.

Freud indirectly shed some light on the problem when, after having set forth the advisability of the personal analysis of educators, he wrote: "The analysis of teachers and educators seems to be a more practicable prophylactic measure than the analysis of children themselves . . . . Parents who have experienced an analysis themselves . . . will treat their children with better understanding" (Freud, 1933a, p. 205).

Without knowledge of the structure of the child's personality, the educator is forced to make decisions that may be most far-reaching and consequential to the child's future mental health; intimate knowledge of the child would surely seem to be necessary here, unless such decisions are to be based on almost arbitrary guesses.

In the instance of the parent and the teacher, the medical analyst will agree that a personal analysis, particularly when it is combined with theoretical instruction, is sufficient preparation for them to be able to fulfill their functions adequately, and he will by no means advise the study of medicine. But if the medical analyst were consistent, he would have to maintain that no parent and no teacher can truly understand the child unless he possesses an adequate knowledge of the organic substructure of the child's personality.

Psychoanalysis and History

When one believes strongly in a cause, one may easily overestimate its area of effectiveness, its historical function and meaning, its importance to mankind, and its future.

In my early years, I was involved in such a situation. Viennese skiers were then divided into two camps: one, which was rather small, was convinced that true skiing called for the use of one rather long ski-pole;

The title of this section is, perhaps, somewhat presumptuous. I shall discuss one aspect of the problem only, and that rather superficially. For the role of trauma in history, see particularly Langer (1958). Two special studies (Feldman and Bronson, 1959; Brown, 1959) on the topic have been published more recently; I was unable to work them into this volume.

the other, comprising a comfortable majority, stuck to two short poles. The interesting thing about the minority group was that, under the leadership of its president, what amounted to almost a philosophy of life gradually took shape around the advantages and the superiority of one-pole skiing. It is a pity that there was not a man of the stature of Jonathan Swift among us, to write in his mature years a satire on the 'cause' of one-pole skiing.

I would not quite know what to answer if, after reading the following, someone accused me of still putting my faith in one-pole skiing.

The crisis of our times has been described by so many authors, and from so many viewpoints, that it has become a rather hackneyed subject. I have no reason to flatter myself into believing that I can add any basic new insights on the question. Since we have a fair record of the past, it is not impossible to orient oneself by way of comparison with it, even though essential features do make the present different from the past. About the following, however, there should be little doubt: this is a crisis that should not be regarded as similar to that of the eighteenth or sixteenth century. One has to go further back to find its like; and a truly compelling comparison can be made with the end of antiquity, when the value system of the Graeco-Roman orbit was breaking down, and Christianity was gradually rising.

What it was precisely that caused the breakdown of the Roman Empire is not yet known; while various reasons have been put forward, no agreement has yet been reached on the question. Indeed, it seems that among the many riddles that man's intellect has not yet succeeded in solving, foremost among them looms that of the decline of empires and of great civilizations (Mueller, 1958).[43] Similarly, there is a disagreement that approaches the character of sheer ignorance with regard to the roots of the present crisis. One could easily fill a whole book with suggestions that have already been made concerning that question; and it would be folly for me to enter the discussion. Yet I cannot forego making one comment, at least, since it strikes close to the heart of the matter I am discussing.

Among the many explanations that have been put forward for the demise of the Roman Empire, I was struck by one that came from a psychoanalyst's pen and, by and large, went unnoticed. It was the thesis in Hanns Sachs's "The Delay of the Machine Age" (1933), which con-

[43] See, however, a recent article that seems to differ (Eisenstadt, 1961).

tains an important clue to the problem in question. Sachs's basic proposition is developed as follows:

The Roman economy was fundamentally a slave economy; yet, with the *Pax Romana*, the supply of slaves dwindled. In the absence of new sources, the slaves on hand became valuable, and were no longer regarded as expendable. Their social position, and their protection by law and by custom, improved. The natural supply of new slaves by propagation was not sufficient to satisfy the needs of an economy that had developed into an economy of trade, of the far-flung exchange of a great variety and quantity of goods. Thus, the needs of the empire and the structure of the economy would both have warranted the use of machines.

Furthermore, the level of Roman mathematics and physics was sufficiently high to have made a machine age possible. As a matter of fact, Roman civilization was already familiar with such machines as the hydraulic press; yet there is no indication of any plan or even intent to put those machines to a useful economic purpose. Instead, they were used in circuses, during stage performances, or for direct entertainment.

Sachs proposes as an explanation of this puzzling attitude the bodily narcissism of Graeco-Roman man—the overruling narcissistic importance that the perfect body had for the man of classical antiquity, which made it impossible for him to allow a machine to do what the human body could accomplish. The man of antiquity would have responded to productive machines with the same sense of weirdness and 'unnaturalness' that we would feel nowadays in the presence of a machine that could think, act spontaneously, or have feelings. We have granted to our machines physical—that is, bodily—actions, but not what may be regarded as psychic functions, in the narrower sense of the word.[44]

The technology of Graeco-Roman civilization had at its disposal, for the fulfillment of its utilitarian goals, only such tools as *enhanced* single bodily functions, and were designed to *increase their efficiency;* it was not their function to *replace* them. With the development of Christian teaching, however, the body was downgraded, and the narcissistic cathexis so far reduced, that the projection of the body into a physical object, and the surrender of bodily functions to an inanimate thing, were no longer regarded as unthinkable.

Indeed, the psychologist may look at the Christian era as a grand if unavoidable detour, whose achievement was to lay the psychological

---

[44] Consider the sense of eeriness that the idea of a lie detector seems to produce in most people.

foundations for the creation and acceptance of machines. Christianity accomplished this goal to perfection: no area outside the Christian orbit could have shown a comparable ingenuity in devising, producing, and using machines.

A challenging perspective opens up here. There is the possibility— which may at this point seem quite faint, and yet is of the highest importance to anyone who is groping for an orientation—that, had the ancient Roman reached a higher level of ego organization, or had his self defeated or grown beyond the level of body narcissism characteristic of that historical period, he might have been capable of evolving a machine age that would have preserved his empire, and thereby saved the whole Occident from the necessity of first going through the bleakness of the Dark Ages.

It is gratifying to be able to quote the following passage from a recent publication (White, 1962, p. 28), since it contains a theoretical frame of reference that justifies Hanns Sachs's construction:

> The historical record is replete with inventions which have remained dormant in a society until at last—usually for reasons which remain mysterious—they 'awaken' and become active elements in the shaping of a culture to which they are not entirely novel . . . . As our understanding of the history of technology increases, it becomes clear that *a new device merely opens a door; it does not compel one to enter.* The acceptance or rejection of an invention, or the extent to which its implications are realized, if it is accepted, depends quite as much upon the condition of a society, and upon the imagination of its leaders, as upon the nature of the technological item itself[45] [my own italics].

It should be clear why I have set forth Hanns Sachs's bold hypothesis. In our times, we have achieved extraordinary levels of research and application in the physical sciences, and have thereby begun to approach the

---

[45] The reader will have observed the far-reaching consequences of this splendid statement. In all simplicity, a single frame of reference is created in which historical, technological, economic, and psychological research are integrated; within it, all possible variations of specific constellations can be deduced. White, too, comments on the delay of the machine age. It is especially important to note that sources of power were known even in the Hellenistic period. (Cf., p. 89: "The expansive force of heated vapour had been noted in Hellenistic times, but for more than a thousand years little effort was made to use it.") He speaks of the "millennium between the first appearance of the water-mill and its wider application," which seems almost "incomprehensible" to the modern mind (p. 84). Very correctly, he calls the technological progress of the eleventh century "the symptom of a new attitude which was to alter the whole pattern of human life" (p. 85).

mastery of the physical sphere of our planet—that is to say, we have continued from where the development of Roman civilization broke off, and have realized what could be only an unrealizable potentiality within the Roman orbit, precisely because of the limitation placed upon the self in its relationship to external reality. During a process of repression and sublimation that lasted for almost a millennium, however, in the course of which man had to give up part of his body narcissism, the body was placed in a new scheme of values.[46]

Thus the limitation in man's relationship to the external world which obtained in antiquity has been replaced by a limitation in man's relationship to his body: certain physical pleasures have become no longer accessible at all, or only in modified form, or only at the price of strong feelings of guilt or of character deformation. I mean, particularly, male homosexuality, whose essential connection with the ancient feeling about the body, and with the consequent inability to evolve a machine civilization, Sachs has already pointed out.

But where is the limitation on modern man to be sought? Is there also in our civilization a potential solution, latently present, but unrealizable because of a limitation in the self? Is it possible that in our era these two factors of potential solution and simultaneous limitation have taken the form of psychoanalysis and modern man's reaction to it?

The development of Occidental culture after the decline of the Roman Empire was ill-fated. At the beginning of the Christian era stands a great psychologist, who went far beyond what ancient psychology had been capable of producing: St. Augustine. So far as I know, he was the first to give infantile amnesia its due importance—a conclusion which may be regarded as the historical, if not the actual, hour of birth of modern psychology. His great psychological discoveries were, of course, made under the aegis of the Catholic Church; otherwise, this enormous stride into the field of psychology might have led to a flowering of the science of psychology. As it was, such a science did not evolve; instead, the science of man, as developed under the tutelage of the Church, had to be brought into, and kept in accordance with theological dogma.

[46] The details of this complex historical process have never been set forth. It is striking to observe what acceleration the development toward the machine age gained when, during the Rennaissance, after having been so severely mauled by Christian indoctrination, body narcissism grew in strength—without, of course, ever reaching the form and intensity that had obtained in antiquity. One is inclined to compare the creation of machines under the impetus of the resurgence of body narcissism with the return of the repressed, as it takes place in neurotic symptom formation, or with the restitutive processes in schizophrenic disorders, after the withdrawal of cathexis from reality.

Thus, when at last man's feeling about the body had been sufficiently dehydrated and the natural sciences did burst forth, there was no psychology at hand whose application would have rendered a much needed service. The natural sciences have given Western man mastery over the physical world; psychology would also have given him mastery over man's mind, and rendered him capable of offering constructive direction to the unimaginable growth of his own physical power, by aiming it consistently toward the goal of human welfare.

It may be unfair to reproach the Church for the lack of such a psychology, for the evolvement of a scientific psychology was fundamentally incompatible with that dogma which was mainly responsible for the process of enforced body depreciation. Nevertheless, by the irony of history, in imposing this frustrating depreciation of the body, the Church itself was establishing the prerequisite for the flowering of the natural sciences. This may sound somewhat strange, for Church and science are usually viewed as being constantly at loggerheads.

Here an antinomic factor is to be observed in the development of science. It is true that Church and science are in essence irreconcilably opposed; yet without the preceding dominance of the Church, science might have never developed—or perhaps not in the seventeenth century, but much later. Similarly, while Victorianism and psychoanalysis are irreconcilable, one cannot ignore the fact that, without the preceding blotting out or denial of manifestations of passionate life, as happened toward the end of the nineteenth century and at the beginning of the twentieth, it might never have occurred to Freud even to attempt to realize the psychoanalytic situation.

We often forget what a high degree of repression (or of sublimation, as the case may be) is necessary, before it is possible for two people of different sex to discuss objectively, and in solitude, matters that are per se of such potentially stimulating character as those customarily discussed in the course of a psychoanalysis. Had Freud's findings been known one hundred, or even fifty years earlier, the psychoanalytic situation would have led to the sort of scandals that the Church avoids by having confessionals constructed in such a way that priest and penitent are separated, while it is the penitent that remains publicly visible.

Thus one may also have to take into account the fact that, in St. Augustine's times, that degree of repression and sublimation had not yet been achieved that makes the development of a systemic psychology possible; and one may therefore have to acknowledge that the present and future tribulations caused by the fateful delay in the development of system psychology could not, after all, have been spared mankind.

With Freud, at any rate, the Occident was given, at last—perhaps even too late!—the great gift of systemic psychology. The degree of bitterness with which this gift was received, Freud himself has described; yet mankind does finally hold the tool—one might even say, I suppose, 'machine'—with which man may yet learn to master his own mind.

Nevertheless, a surprising turn has taken place, the reasons for which I cannot decipher, and which therefore strikes me as a curious sort of puzzle. If one reads the current psychiatric and psychoanalytic literature, one may easily obtain the impression that human civilization is threatened by hysteria, obsessional neurosis, schizophrenia, stomach ulcers, asthma, colitis, dermatitis, or any other form or kind of disease.

True, neurosis and disease cause damage in a great many different ways: neurotic parents breed their own neuroses in their children; neurotic teachers injure their wards; neurotic husbands mar their wives' happiness and vice versa; and absenteeism from work caused by neuroticism causes huge losses to the economy. The damage becomes graver when we consider those disturbances that are close to the neuroses. Delinquency and criminality in the form of stealing, burglary, or murder cause untold unhappiness; nicotine and alcohol addiction deprive our economy of huge amounts of money that, constructively invested, could greatly reduce this country's many ills. Yet all these disorders, terrible as they may be, and grievous as may be their effects, merely *burden* our civilization. They are a drag on the potential maximum that our civilization can achieve; they are a great embarrassment in times of emergency; but they do not per se destroy our civilization.

It becomes a somewhat different matter when we consider those disorders that, because they are socially disguised and insidious, do not prevent anyone from achieving status or filling a key societal position. Such disorders may include a more or less latent neurosis, or psychopathy, or even psychosis. In a training camp in which I worked as a military neuropsychiatrist, the general in command was obviously suffering from a psychosis, probably belonging to the schizophrenic group. The damage he caused was, of course, not as great as it might have been, had he held an overseas command; but, even in the zone of the interior, his mismanagement was deplorable and was detrimental to the war effort. If we imagine a judge who uses his position to ward off his own delinquent impulses, or who is corrupted himself, we can easily imagine what detriment he will cause to the community. (I do not need to adduce other examples; many will be found in Lasswell's [1930] text.) Such persons may actually, perhaps greatly, endanger civilization; but I doubt that even they are capable of destroying it.

My thesis is that, even if all members of the cultural community were devoid of serious psychopathology, our civilization would, notwithstanding its better chance of survival, still be in great danger. It may even turn out that such a happy state of affairs as freedom from psychopathology would not appreciably reduce the objective historical precariousness and vulnerability of the present epoch.

The degenerative factor so widespread in the mental life of the Roman élite, I presume, accelerated the decline of the Empire; but even the perseverance of the renowned virtue of the early Rome, along with a relative freedom from psychopathology, would not have preserved the Empire. There may very well have been only one solution, after all, to the crisis of the Roman Empire—a solution of the character that Sachs has suggested. That the Romans did not introduce machines into their economy was by no means due to any kind or form of emotional disorder, but to a limitation of the development of the self.

Thus, there seems to be a historical factor that—outside of and beyond the mental health level of a community, its adjustment to reality, its willingness to sacrifice and even its maximal integration of the reality principle—determines what may be called the destiny, fate, or simply the future of a civilization. The point of Sachs's construction was that all the economic and intellectual prerequisites for survival were at hand at the end of antiquity; what the factor of ego development did was to prevent the realization of what lay within the grasp of ancient Rome.

The very thing that ancient Rome was lacking, we hold quite tightly in our hands: we have made maximum use of machines. And yet, despite all our technical ingenuity, once more the prospect threatens of a possible decline and fall. Obviously, this time it is something quite different from what the Roman Empire was lacking in that needs to be integrated and used profitably; for our age is well protected against almost any disease; food and merchandise can be produced and distributed in prodigious quantities; and unsurpassable weapons, defensive as well as aggressive, are in ample supply. Nevertheless, no one seems at all certain in what condition the world, or any part of the world, will be a decade from now.

It has been said so often that it has become a truism, that man, despite his mastery over the physical world, and to a large extent also over organic life, has not acquired mastery over his own history. Is this then the area of ignorance that threatens his survival?

One is reminded at this point of a poem by Goethe (1827) dedicated to the United States:

> America, thou hast it better
> Than our continent—the old one:
> Thou hast no ruined castles
> And no basalts.[47]
> You are not disturbed within,
> In the fullness of life,
> By useless remembrance
> And fruitless discord.
>
> Make use of the present with good luck!
> And when your children write stories
> May good fortune protect them
> From stories of knights and robbers and ghosts [translation mine].

Thus wrote Goethe, who envied this country's freedom from the ballast of the past. Yet plenty of ballast has accumulated since, even though no decayed castles dot the American landscape: fate has spared her children stories of knights, robbers, and ghosts, and instead has ordained for them the far worse fate of mystery, detective, and murder stories. Yet Goethe was essentially right: the beginning of America's independence had the character of a free choice, unencumbered by any burden of medieval feudalism, whose vestiges were still keeping Goethe's Europe under their yoke during his formative years.

What Goethe did not express in this short poem is the fact that the seemingly free choice at the start of America's history as a nation was in reality the end product of a long development, which had got under way to a certain extent within the ancient Graeco-Roman orbit, but had never previously evolved the momentum that it demonstrated when the Founding Fathers were faced with the choice of either defeating tyranny or being suppressed by superior strength. In short, the upsurge of a new political system in the New World was historically as strictly determined as was the persistence of the old system in the Old World.

[47] Goethe assumed erroneously that there were no basalts (a rock of ancient age) in America. Among his notes the following was found:

> North Americans, happy to have no basalts,
> No forefathers and no classical soil [Goethe, 1819].

The movement of history, supported by the physical geography, led in the one instance to growth, expansion, and wealth, in the other to atrophy, shrinkage, and poverty. Expansion of the new system took its course with breath-taking rapidity:

1776	To the Allegheny
1783	Mississippi
1819	Florida
1848	Texas and California
1854	Commodore Perry in Japan
1897	Hawaii
1898	Puerto Rico, Philippines
1909	Panama
1917	in Europe
1945	Europe's and Japan's dependence

This is just a sketch of the highlights of the most rapid expansion that an empire has ever taken. The truly remarkable fact is that this nation, one hundred and seventy years after its foundation, was, for a span of five years (1945-1950), the virtual ruler over the entire surface of the planet: it was the owner of the only universally accepted currency, and it held in its hand such economic power that almost every other country was directly or indirectly dependent on it. And the accumulation of all this vast power had been bought at a lesser sacrifice of life on the part of its own people than was involved in one year of medieval plague. Yet when the extension and the duration of the Egyptian, Roman, Spanish, and British Empires are compared, one discovers that the increase in their spatial extension is in inverse proportion to their endurance in time.

Will Spengler's prophecy concerning the end of empires also be fulfilled, along with so many of his other predictions? He foresaw the foundation in our time of giant empires, which in the end would decay into small units, emerging in the midst of a world-wide cultural decline. Toynbee (1949), however, says no to this prediction; there is no necessity for such a tragedy, he asserts.

Toynbee's reasoning is remarkable. True, he says, the twenty or thirty cultures that have existed before this have all declined; most of them have disappeared, and those that have not yet disappeared show definite signs of decline—all, perhaps, except ours. Yet, he continues, it would be a mistake to draw the conclusion that decline and ensuing death are the course that a culture necessarily has to take.[48] "Any statistician will tell you that when you are dealing with such small quantities as twenty or thirty the margin of error in your inferences from the statistics is bound to be very high" (Toynbee, 1949, p. 108). I wonder whether he is really right about that statistical deliberation. Of course, twenty or thirty is a small sample, compared with the numbers that the statistician is accustomed to dealing with. But is there not also a difference in statistics as to whether a rare or a frequent event is being investigated?

If I wanted to establish the age frequency of New York subway riders, a sample of thirty would be very small, indeed, and any conclusion drawn therefrom would be almost folly. If, however, I find out that, in a sample of twenty geniuses (by definition, a rare occurrence), all were first-born sons, the area to which I may properly extend my conclusion will be far larger than in the previous instance of the age frequency of subway riders—unless, of course, I drew my samples exclusively from a certain historical period or a certain limited group. What Toynbee did not state explicitly is the fact that he had not done any sampling at all, but dealt with *all* events of the type under consideration.

Statistically, we happen to be in a very favorable position. First, it is highly improbable that any culture has existed of which we do not know; and secondly, if we should still discover one—such as the Minoan civilization—of which we were ignorant for such a long time, we can be certain that it is one that has already perished, or else it would have been known to us by now along with the rest, for the entire surface of the earth has now been scanned by the human eye. Thus we must regard the historian's statement that all the cultures of the past have perished, not as a conclusion based upon sampling, but as the complete and correct description of all the instances of the class that have occurred up to the present.

[48] When Toynbee explains the death of civilization mainly by way of "war between local states and another kind of warfare" (p. 108), I am certain that he is unduly simplifying an extremely complex problem. He cites an exceedingly profound remark of General George Marshall, to the effect that the collapse of the Roman Empire was foreshadowed, a millennium before it occurred, by the Peloponnesian War.

Indeed, the Peloponnesian War was the first great Occidental tragedy, from the consequences of which we are still suffering—not so much because of the war itself, but because of the spirit that it manifested. I do not know whether Alexander the Great's hankering for the East can be linked with the turn taken by Greek politics. If his genius had taken him westward and Europe had been hellenized directly, without the Roman 'mediation,' how many fatal crises might Occidental civilization have been spared!

Therefore it still seems to me that Spengler's theory of the 'biological' necessity of the death of a civilization is worth while considering. All organisms must die, it seems, as soon as they cannot grow any more. Tissue cells kept under conditions that make possible continuous cell division can go on growing for ever, as far as one can tell. The ancient trees on the West coast of the North American continent can still go on growing, which is why they have not yet died.

We know that natural death in the human species is either a heart death or a brain death. Significantly, the cells specific to the heart and to the brain, by contrast with those of almost all other organs, do not divide; and therefore the natural death of man originates in the dysfunction of either of these two organs—unless 'accidental' death occurs earlier, and from other sources. Applying this biological law to civilization, one may conclude that a civilization that has reached its growth maximum must die. However, it must be admitted that transfers of conclusions from one area, within which they are valid, to an essentially different area, are not binding.

Aside from objections of this type, I must also turn against Toynbee's qualified optimism. For millennia, mankind had dreamed of being able to fly, and then, in the seventeenth century, the force of gravity was discovered. Now the knowledge that there is a force keeping us drawn to the surface of the earth would seem to provide a very pessimistic outlook, indeed, for someone with his heart set on flying. Yet it was precisely with the birth of this new and saddening thought that the seed to its overthrowal was born.

By and large, I would say that the recognition of the inevitable is—in 'important' matters—the first step toward its conquest. Psychologically, this means that as long as there is hope, mankind does not move; it is only under the lashes of fatal certainty that a ray of chance emerges that man will show his best, and solve the unsolvable. The planes that course through the sky are the best illustration of how a 'pessimistic' view is undone.

The 'statistical' evidence speaks against the survival of our civilization. If a sickness has been observed in thirty patients, all of whom were felled, a sane physician will shudder when he observes the first signs in the thirty-first, particularly when he is cognizant of the fact that those thirty instances are all that are known to have ever occurred. Thus, it is not wanton pessimism to state bluntly that the future of the West is hopeless, and that our civilization is marked with the signs of impending annihilation. The only hope we have is that, if every soldier in the last battalion knows that he is lost, he will generate that superhuman effort that may result at least in the survival of a platoon. Such a survival would be a victory, and the beginning of a new era. Yet victory will not depend exclusively on morale.

I recommend here—as I did earlier with regard to the alternative theories of human aggressiveness—that in order to avoid bitter disappointment, one should assume the more pessimistic (that is to say, more provocative) alternative—namely, that our present civilization will die, just as its ancestors, siblings, or cousins did.

Yet, to return to the former point, if our civilization should die at the developmental point it has now reached, this will happen either because it will be facing a reality situation that cannot be conquered objectively—such as the Indians were facing, when the West took hold of this continent—or because of our ignorance and impotence in the matter of history. As far as the physical tools of survival are concerned, we own them aplenty.

There are goals which many a man would like to attain and which we know he will never reach. For example, at best man will be able to extend the average life span, perhaps even to double it; but he will never be able to do away with death.

In other instances, man ascribes failure to attain his goals not to his ignorance, but to external forces. Thus, I suppose that, when Rome fell, the trickery and mischievousness of the barbarians were held responsible by some, just as the typical occidental person is ready to see in communism the true sources of our present unrest. Such thoughts are usually formulated in the following way: If the Russians had our political institutions, so far superior to those that obtain in their country, no serious conflicts or dangers would exist.

Yet, far-sighted historians were predicting the tension between the West and Russia at a time when no one even dreamed of a communist power, and it is still highly questionable whether it is the difference of political institutions in the two power centers that is really the principal point keeping the world in its present unbearable state of tension.

It is futile to go into a discussion here of the means that are so extensively used today to safeguard national survival. They are in essence of the same category as those that were at the disposal of the old Romans: maximum physical power for defense or attack, and alliances. We should not let ourselves be blinded by the vastness of the technical difference between that time and this. The Occident has not learned anything essentially new as to how to master its own history—which is all the more surprising in view of the fact that historical research has, since antiquity, made progress of a truly extraordinary character, even though it does not bear comparison with the advances made in physics.

The historical knowledge of ancient Rome was really surprisingly poor; and I feel justified in saying that we know more even about Rome than the Romans did, not to speak of the history of their neighbors, or of the Greeks, and so forth. Furthermore, the intervening fifteen hundred odd years have, through the mere advance of time, added so much by way of historical events and processes that one might well have expected such vast accretions of knowledge at least to provide the materials for insight of such a kind as would make possible the mastery of what still apparently takes its own course quite independently of the intent of man's strivings.

This unknown factor that we are in search of, whose absence deprives man of mastery over his own history, may to a certain extent be a psychological one. The advance of history is, after all, a question of making decisions—of deciding about the future in such a way as to safeguard the group's existence. The fate of nations may be compared with that of individuals whose strivings for self-preservation are often profoundly reversed, as in the case of a person who repeatedly gets into serious car accidents, and finally falls victim to one.

I am referring here to incidents that may seem to the naked eye to be attributable solely to the force of circumstances. Unquestionably, man is exposed to forces outside of his influence. Yet it is reasonable to assume that a significant role in accidental deaths is played by unconscious masochism. When a fatal car accident occurs, objectively (in terms of physical and social reality) the guilt may lie completely on the side of the survivor; yet the victim might have survived, had his reflexes worked faster. That is to say, an examination of the objective factors that lead to an event may not reveal those unconscious forces, knowledge of which would make the same event appear in an entirely different light.

Therefore, the principal questions to be answered here are: can psychoanalysis make a relevant contribution to the science of history? Is this contribution of such a kind as to endow mankind with the power to master its own historical processes?

There is no country today, except one—as I shall presently show—that has at its disposal an adequate insight into its history. In every country, there are masses of records, collections of data, descriptions of the past, and theories about causal factors; yet all this apparently does not provide, in almost any instance, sufficient insight to make for mastery over the country's historical destiny.

In our own time, there has occurred a coincidence—or, better still, a near-coincidence—which should have aroused more attention than it actually has. As is well known, the Jewish people longed for over two millennia to find a haven in their old homeland. The word 'longing' does not, indeed, do justice to that passionate desire, that pining for the Holy Land—so strong that no evidence to the contrary could discourage the hope, the conviction that God's promise would be fulfilled.

Yet it seemed that all the prayers, all the sacrifices and acts of obedience, were of no avail before 1948, when at last the Lord's word came true. But (and this was noted only by a few intellectuals among the Jewish people), a decade or so before this came to pass, one of Israel's greatest sons had written the psychological history of his own people, with whom he had previously appeared to be only superficially involved.

Whether my view of a direct connection between Freud's book on *Moses* and the creation of a Jewish State is confirmed, or turns out to be an illusion, the publication of the book is itself an eminently moving event. Freud, who had never visited Palestine, who was a dyed-in-the-wool atheist if ever there was one, who had almost never participated in a religious act—at least during his adult years—discovered in a legend about the founder of the Jewish nation one element that did not 'fit.' This trifling discrepancy from what was to have been expected, if the legend had followed its own type, led Freud to make a comparison with the historical documents and with the traditional history of the people; and, starting from this discrepancy, he constructed a bold hypothesis as to what the true events must have been that, out of an aggregate of people, formed a group so firmly riveted together that it was never thereafter to be destroyed, neither by great powers vigorously aiming at its annihilation, nor by intensely centrifugal forces at work within itself. In spite of all the blandishments designed to encourage 'passing,' and in spite of the repeated physical destruction of substantial numbers, there always remained a sufficient number of Jews to ensure unbroken continuity.

This extraordinary 'staying power' demanded an explanation. Following his customary approach, a psychoanalyst would be inclined to think that something extraordinary must have happened in the dark days of the nation's childhood, for such singular consequences to come into being. From his patients' extraordinary vicissitudes, Freud had grown accustomed to reaching back into the dark days of their childhood, so as to unearth there the extraordinary events that laid the foundation for the later extraordinary consequences.

Thus, he read the history of his people almost like a patient's history, reconstructing from the evidence at hand the events that actually (so at least he thought) had taken place, which had escaped preservation in tradition because of the all-inclusive mechanism of repression, only to hit the dawning consciousness of the people like a trauma. Just as in a therapeutic analysis, he thus reconstructed an early childhood trauma. The patient was suddenly capable of achieving what for two-and-a-half thousand years he had wanted to do, but had been incapable of doing!

If this causal connection really exists, one may say that the Jewish people were the first to achieve mastery of their own destiny through insight, after the first psychological history of any nation was written— by a man who (for historical reasons) was one of their own. I am fully aware of the many arguments that will come to one's mind against the drawing of such conclusions, as well as of the possibility that Freud's hypothetical construction was wrong and simply led to a new myth. At least, historians whose voices deserve to be listened to have so asserted. In our own lifetime, we may not ever find out whether or not Freud discovered the truth when he wrote *Moses and Monotheism,* nor are we likely to know for sure whether or not his mental achievement contributed to the deliverance of his people.[49]

I am merely pleading against disapproval or dismissal of such views as may sound fantastic at first hearing, before it has been demonstrated beyond doubt that they are wrong. It would be necessary, for example, to ascertain whether or not those whose wisdom and action brought liberty to the Jewish people had read Freud's treatise, and whether a

[49] One engaging possibility we shall not discuss here—namely that, even if Freud's reconstruction was a myth, it may have been just the sort of myth that a nation fighting for its independence needed, and therefore did make its contribution toward the ending of the diaspora. Whatever may be the extent of the truth in Freud's construction, in no other book did he accomplish an intellectual deed of such magnitude. As he himself says, his treatise seemed to him "like a dancer balancing on one toe" (Freud, 1939, p. 95)—an appropriately chosen metaphor, for in essence Freud's whole construction hung on the one disharmonious element he had discovered in a legend. The deductive faculty revealed here, the ability to view a complex as the end product of a plurality of forces—that is to say, the capacity for dissolving a unit by analysis into its genetic components—all these surpassed in this instance, I believe, even the achievement of his book on dreams.

significant change in their procedure, or in their very determination on action, took place thereafter.

As long as there is a shred of possible truth in the belief that the psychoanalysis of a people, by unearthing the unconscious factors at work in their history, may bring mastery to them, and lead to the sort of action that guarantees preservation, that possible truth ought to be pursued by means of intensive research. Furthermore, even if the best reconstruction on hand—Freud's theory about the origin of the Jewish people—should one day be established as erroneous, that would not prove that the psychological history of a people *cannot* be written, or that the principle underlying Freud's historical study is wrong.

Little as we may know about the background of the mental life of the Roman at the end of antiquity, it may be assumed that he would not have been able even to imagine an economy built on machines. If a towering mind had been capable of such exact prediction, or of a theoretical construction of that sort, the Romans would surely have called it an utopia or the product of a bizarre mind. Their power of imagination may have had room for a King Midas-like fantasy, of a God coming upon the world, or giving power to a man, to make things grow faster, or to assemble the disparate into usable objects (the idea of the *deus artifex*); but the idea of a machine constructed by man achieving useful ends was, I am certain, beyond the limits of the Roman's mental equipment. Curiously, a similar state of affairs exists at present in the matter of psychoanalysis. The idea of changing the personality by genetic and resistance interpretations is not conceivable by the average person, unless he has himself gone through such an analytic process.

There is no difficulty for modern man in conceiving of neurotic symptoms being healed by drugs or by surgery, by encouragement, or by the preaching of a new philosophy; yet the analytic process per se remains alien to the thinking of the twentieth century.[50]

---

[50] That is the reason why, in the last analysis, Alfred Adler defeated Freud. What is put forward as psychoanalysis in a good many publications is a type of psychotherapy much closer to Adler than to Freud. When Alexander bases his therapy on the adage, "Nothing succeeds like success," he takes a position fundamentally different from Freud's, and almost identical with the technique of individual psychology. Ansbacher and Ansbacher (1956) try to demonstrate on what are, in my opinion, solid grounds, that the so-called Neo-Freudians are essentially and actually Neo-Adlerians. It is not an accident that Alexander became the best known analyst in the United States: he made analysis a common-sense science; he adapted it to the horizon of the medical man; and, with his sensitivity to the present, he made analysis fit those limits which are imposed by the temper and climate of our century.

For the decline of psychology in our century has become evident. It may be observed not only in the increasing prestige of those schools that are in disagreement with Freud, but also in art and literature and philosophy. One might take a look at the art of impressionism—for example, by studying a portrait by Degas and examining its psychological content —and then look at paintings of Picasso during the last three decades. Such a comparison will reveal the decline of psychological insight in art.

Even more impressive would be a comparison of nineteenth-century novels with the literature produced as this century has progressed. With Proust, the era of giant psychologist-romanciers came to an end, so that Freud projects like an intruder into a twentieth century that knows a lot about man, but has lost its sense of what man really is.

I need only mention Nietzsche to demonstrate the psychological poverty of present-day philosophy. If further proof were needed, I would refer to the well-nigh universal use of drugs or of other physical means in the treatment of the functional psychoses—a very impressive sign, indeed, of the present break with psychology, and of the belief that there will never be a true science of man's mind.

Thus the present hostility of the average psychoanalyst toward lay analysis fits well with our times. Just as the Romans relegated machines to circuses and to theaters (instead of building a new world on them, and thus a new culture and their means of survival as an empire), so our society relegates psychoanalysis to the medical offices for the sake of treating psychopathology.

Huge as may be the benefits that psychoanalysis as a treatment method has bestowed upon a huge number of suffering patients; productively as it may have fertilized other treatment methods; humanely as it may have influenced the Western attitude toward homosexuality, the perversions and crime; stimulating as its effect may have been on many arts—still the essence of psychoanalysis has remained esoteric. It has been integrated only by a negligible number of experts who, for obvious reasons, have stood aside from the contemporary historical process. Yet even if these experts held societal key positions, their effectiveness could not be appreciably greater than that of those who have actually put their hands on the wheel of history, since psychoanalytic knowledge has not yet been extended to those processes that are significant and relevant to the historical process. In order to take that step, it is necessary that thinking in terms of psychoanalysis be integrated by a large number of cultural scientists, in the same sense as a knowledge of physics and chemistry is expected to be at the fingertips of anyone who wants to work in any of the various departments of natural science.

What can be observed is that, instead, a romantic version of psychoanalysis, a distortion of it that equates psychoanalysis with a kind of sexology, is now socially effective. Science very often becomes popular in the form of a myth; we can observe the same thing to be true of the ideas of Karl Marx. What has become socially effective is a mythological version of his writings, for they themselves are very hard to understand, and require a keen mind, well trained in many fields. Indeed, one may even surmise that outside the narrow group of experts it is only the mythological equivalent of any science that becomes socially relevant in collective thinking. My emphasis on the fact that psychoanalysis has not yet been integrated is not based on the observation that a distorted version of it is popular, so much as on the repeated observation that experts well-trained in science and whom one may therefore expect to be adequately equipped to understand it, nevertheless misunderstand it.

My guess is that, aside from the subjective personal factor of resistance, there is also a historical factor that may, in part, be effective among many analysts. They see mainly the therapeutic aspect inherent in psychoanalysis, and not its potential value as the builder of a new civilization, which would, if my theorem is correct, differ from the present civilization as greatly as one in which natural sciences are put to their maximal use differs from one in which such use is socially not effective, because it is merely dormant. Here the necessity does arise of finding an answer to the question of what the factor is that now blinds us with regard to the proper integration and use of psychoanalysis—the equivalent, so to speak, of the Roman's blindness with regard to the proper use of the machines that he potentially held in his hands.

To find an answer to that question would require one's being able to carry out the well-nigh impossible task of totally projecting oneself outside of one's own historical period, by way of complete abstraction from one's most cherished ideals, illusions, and prejudices. But man's relationship to his illusions makes such abstraction impossible. As I suggest at another point, he would rather renounce the gratification of his physical needs, even his life, than admit the impermanence, even the evanescence of those same illusions. Here he is deeply incapacitated with regard to learning from history. For not only is the physical substance of a civilization tainted by the seed of its extinction; the same is true of its values.

History deals with mankind's illusions with terrible cruelty. What is left of the bias of Graeco-Roman man? What of that of the early Christians? The historical process—at least on the cultural level—proceeds with a terrifying radicalism; there is little synthesis to be seen growing out of thesis and antithesis. No shred of ancient civilization and art has been truly preserved in our own, despite all our admiration of them; if the early Christians had been able to foresee the record of the contemporary West, they would have turned away with a broken heart from the Gospels. Even if we go back only fifty years, it must be admitted that the honor of the self-reliant and proud Victorian man would feel deeply humiliated by the present, what with the end of colonialism, the emancipation of women, the breakdown of sexual restraint and propriety, and the dominance of unionism.

But apparently man cannot integrate the idea of the shortlivedness of the values in which he believes. He will humble himself before his gods, because indirectly they are the projective creations of his own mind, so that his religious adulations are in fact self-adulations; but he cannot visualize the future of his society humbly: either he believes in its indefinite conservation, or else he anticipates a new one, the character of which will depend on the particular set of illusionary values that he holds.

This lack of objectivity *vis-à-vis* culture and value systems impedes the necessary projection of the self outside the realm of contemporary values. Thus the task on hand might be compared to a person's lifting himself by his own bootstraps. Yet the task remains—to put into metapsychological terms that barrier which the self would have to overcome in order to reach a higher structural level. Some speculation upon the matter is therefore not out of place. It is in all probability once more a narcissistic rigidity that has delayed the evolvement of a superior personality state. Whatever assertion can be made with any certainty is possible—as often happens—only in negative terms: namely, that this time it is not a matter of bodily narcissism, but predominantly of a narcissism of the mind.

In examining those attitudes and beliefs prevalent in the contemporary West that can be regarded as narcissistic crusts, responsible for spots of obtuseness in the self, the following quickly come to mind: nationalism, racism, religion, and property. It is pretty clear that these institutions are narcissistically overcathected: one's own nation or country is generally regarded as superior to others; it is also fair to say that racial prejudices are ubiquitous in the West despite frequent denials; one's own god is always better than the other man's; even one's own property absorbs important proportions of one's narcissism. In comparing the man of antiquity with modern man, one may feel inclined to speculate that both have the same amount of narcissism, and that Christian teaching has not succeeded in appreciably reducing narcissism per se, but has effected only a shift away from the body to substrata less material than the body, yet without achieving that conversion of narcissism into object love which was, after all, one of its original principal aims.

It may not be superfluous to mention that some of these institutions were actually charged with less of a narcissistic cathexis in antiquity. Surely, the Roman was more tolerant in matters of religion than we are; and I believe that such concepts as sovereignty and nationalism were unknown as we conceive of them now. Should his relationship to property also have been more tenuous than ours? In racial prejudice the West regressed even beyond pagan bodily narcissism, almost to the point of caricature of the latter. Indeed, it is impressive to observe how vast a personality area Christian ideology and ethics has left untouched.

It almost seems as if the world would become a better place to live in, if narcissism—once the abandonment of its bodily form had served its purpose, and machines had been created—again took the form that it had in antiquity. Indeed, such trends as freer sexual customs, the upsurge of homosexuality, and the emphasis on sports may appear to be attempts to return to antiquity.

Yet these are but surface changes; a true return to antiquity would be impossible despite the disappearance of everything reflecting the Christian spirit from modern society. If such a return ever occurred, science would probably come to a standstill, just as it would if our society became a *civitas Dei*. The effects on science of these two cultural poles can be better understood if one considers the status of the senses in the different civilizations. Socrates, shortly before his death, had the following to say: "He who has got rid, as far as he can, of eyes and ears and, so to speak, of the whole body, these being in his opinion distracting elements which when they infect the soul hinder her from acquiring truth and knowledge—who, if not he, is likely to attain to the knowledge of true being?" (Jowett, 1937, vol. 1, p. 449); and St. Anselm warned against sitting in a garden, because "things were harmful in proportion to the number of senses they delighted" (Clark, 1950, p. 2). When the senses overreact to stimulation—that is to say, when the whole psychic apparatus reverberates under the impact of the messages they have to convey—or when, by contrast, all interest is withdrawn from those messages—in either instance, science as it has developed since the Renaissance is rendered impossible.

Furthermore, the basic trend that a civilization is taking can hardly be changed by decision and planning. Despite a rising aversion for science, in view of the terrible weapons that it has produced, science cannot and will not be eradicated. Yet, a return to the true spirit of antiquity, or to the true spirit of Christianity, is out of the question; one of the few possibilities left would be an extension of science beyond the physical and organic. Is it possible that the full integration of the concept of the unconscious, with all its implications and ramifications in Freud's sense (which does not need an explication at this point), would have the effect of reducing man's narcissistic rigidities?

Such an integration might, after all, change essentially the order-of-value schemes so deeply ingrained in contemporary man. It would mean a process in which the blows that man's narcissism has suffered at the hands of science, and which Freud has succinctly described (1925f), would be converted into a true reduction of man's narcissism.[51] The focus on the unconscious, indeed, reduces the rank attributed now in the scheme of values to a person's name, prestige, and social position. Strangely enough, in psychoanalysis, one may discover the seed of a synthesis of the Graeco-Roman and the Christian feelings about man. The body is reinstated to its previous dignified position, and the personality is denuded of its luminous paraphernalia by a focus upon what it 'really' is, and not on what it appears to be. In a lighter vein, I would say that, if grievous injustices are not to occur, the Lord ought to study Freud's psychological writings before the Last Judgment.

Whether psychoanalysis actually contains the seed that may lead to the growth of a new civilization and culture is, of course, highly debatable; but it is certain that no societal forces are observable that are ready to use it for such purposes. Therefore, I am certainly indulging in an optimistic illusion when I assert that, by the proper use of psychoanalysis, a new world, a new culture, and the means for the survival of the Occident could be built. However, the reader who has followed me thus far will not be astonished to hear this opinion.[52]

---

[51] I deliberately omit in this context the formidable problem of aggression, limiting myself merely to some factors which customarily give rise to aggressive outbreaks.

[52] For an attempt to apply psychoanalysis to a problem of recent history, see Appendix 2.

ONCE MORE: MEDICAL ANALYSIS VERSUS LAY ANALYSIS

I have (1) compared the relationship of anthropic research to system psychology with that of the natural sciences to physics and chemistry. (2) Following Sachs, I have suggested that the Roman Empire fell because it was incapable of replacing slaves with machines, and that this inability was not enforced by ignorance but by a limitation in the development of the self—that is to say, in the last analysis, by a psychogenic reason. (3) I have further suggested that the contemporary inability to solve the relevant problems of our present historical period is caused in part by the lag in anthropic research, and that this lag is due in part to the neglect of psychoanalysis in anthropic research. (4) I have tried to prove that psychoanalytic anthropic research has been made well-nigh impossible by the prohibitive measures on the question of training taken against lay analysis by the official organizations; and I have expressed the hope that freedom of research—in this instance, the willingness of the American Psychoanalytic Association and its component societies (which administer the only adequate psychoanalytic training facilities in this country) to train lay analysts—would lead to the evolvement of an anthropic research that would provide the tools with which to solve the problems faced by the Occident.

As the reader can well imagine, I am fully convinced of the correctness of my reasoning; but, in view of the formidable character of the problems involved, and the futile attempts that have so far been made by the most illustrious minds to solve some of them, it would be folly for me to assert that I *know* I am right. The laws of biology and history may be immutable; and, fight as we may, our civilization may be destined to perish. Nevertheless, we should at least put up the strongest fight we are capable of, and not perish ingloriously.

Yet, although I must admit that I am only *convinced* of the correctness of my conclusions, and do not *know* whether I am right, I can say that I *know* that our society is not flexible enough to guarantee the fullest development of anthropic research in the way in which research in physics is now ensured, and that lay analysis and psychoanalytic anthropic research will not, in our time, become an integral part of the American scene. Again, whether this incapacity will have all the dire consequences that I have set forth, I do not know, although I have strong *convictions* on the question. But I do *know* that medical analysis is not equal to fulfilling the requirements of anthropic research; and I shall now prove this, by a final example.

In a paper on "Psychology and the Interpretation of Historical Events," Alexander (1940a) singled out "one important psychological fact which has a decisive bearing upon the correct interpretation of historical events" (p. 50). This fact, which Alexander made the center of a presentation to the American Historical Association (December 1939),[53] was the misapplication of the psychoanalytic concept of rationalization.

Now rationalization is an interesting subject for psychoanalytic research. It stems from Freud's observation of Bernheim's experiment in Nancy.[54] In it, a subject was hypnotized and ordered to carry out a posthypnotic command. When he obeyed and was then asked the reasons for his action, he did not say that he did not know, but instead invented an ostensibly rational reason. This primary meaning of rationalization—namely, the invention of a (nonexistent) motive—has been replaced with one that is rather less rigorous—namely, the pretence of a motive which, though present, was of only secondary importance. The idea is that the action would not have occurred if the unconscious motive had been absent, whereas the secondary motive was at best merely auxiliary; or the secondary motive may be said to provide the reality situation in which the primary wish can find gratification.

Now Alexander turns against those who try to reduce the relevant motivations of social actions to selfish motives—by asserting, for example, "that the surgeon by amputating a patient's leg only gives vent to his cruel sadistic tendency, that he is really a latent sadist"—and who, in this way, "overlook the surgeon's wish to help the sufferer" (p. 51). To be sure, even the inclusion of the "wish to help" would not change the diagnosis of latent sadism; but Alexander was right in stressing the fact that individual actions cannot be accurately explained by reducing motives to "nothing but" statements (cf. Hartmann, 1960).

Yet, I am not certain that Alexander himself has not contributed greatly to this fallacy. When he writes (Alexander and Staub, 1929): "The flight of the judge into the worlds of pseudo-exact paragraphs of the law, this puzzling horror with which the learned jurist tries to avoid

---

[53] This was by no means an ordinary meeting. It was convened for the express purpose of presenting an analysis and application of the cultural approach to history, and Alexander was expected to set forth the psychoanalytic view regarding the techniques of cultural analysis.

[54] It was Jones (1908) who introduced the technical term into the psychoanalytic vocabulary.

the understanding of the human motive . . . ." (p. 19); or when he calls the colonizer who says he has to civilize aborigines by means of a strict discipline a *Kolonialsadist;* or when he describes pacifism as "a morbid phenomenon," a "manifestation of self-destructiveness," etc. (1941a, p. 505), then I wonder whether he himself has really lived up to the standards he preached in that speech.

Secondly, Alexander (1940a) said on that occasion: "Nothing is more discouraging to me than to see how even the scientific mind regularly becomes a victim of this primitive pattern of dialecticism [i.e., first to deny the repressed and now to see nothing but the repressed]" (p. 51). Are we to believe that at the time of that meeting Alexander truly felt that there was nothing more discouraging than an occasional faulty application of the concept of rationalization? Hitler had spread his terror over Europe, the war had broken out, and a German victory was a horrifying possibility. Roosevelt faced a strong isolationist opposition, and there was doubt all over the world whether or not this country would make its contribution to the defeat of fascism; news of atrocities committed against political prisoners and Jews in the name of German 'destiny' and 'purity of race' had already been received by that time—and with all this, was it still a fear lest atrocities be explained solely by human aggression, or lest consideration of the conscious social motive be omitted, that was the *epitome* of Alexander's discouragement?

The Crusades, for example, were, as far as I know, replete with unspeakable atrocities against the nonbelievers. Still Alexander turns against the belief that they were motivated by "nothing but *ad hoc* invented motives . . . and are merely hypocritical pretenses to hide the only drawing force, the thirst for power" (p. 53). He later adds: "It might be true that Pope Urban initiated his Crusade basically not for the liberation of the Holy Sepulchre, but in order to acquire more prestige and power for the church . . . . He could, however, win for such an imperialistic maneuver the cooperation of a man like Godfrey of Bouillon and the support of the masses only by appealing to their pure and sincere religious fervor" (p. 56).

From what source does Alexander derive such knowledge? Where is the historical documentation for the "pure and sincere religious fervor"? He himself concedes on the very next page that "historians may become discouraged and disillusioned in facing these self-deceptions which hide the *real* motive forces behind all great and small events of history" (italics mine); this, by the way, would seem to indicate that the self-deceptions are, after all, not quite so real. Yet for the clinician, he continues, "the same phenomena are a source of hope . . . . The psychiatrist senses in these phenomena of self-deception the low but permanent and inescapable voice of human conscience. All these pretensions of higher aims are nothing but desperate efforts to win the approval of the conscience"; and he feels satisfied that, "instead of cynical admission and acceptance of the solely predatory aims, at least one part of the personality upholds social ideals" (p. 56).

Here the clinician has been apparently deserted by his good sense. A cynical gangster who even goes so far as to boast of his disregard for human values and life, may still be moved by the pleas and tears of the victim he is on the verge of killing, for admittedly selfish reasons and without any reference to a rationalized self-deception of an idealistic flavor. However, there was not the slightest chance that a Jewish child or a Jewish adult would have been able to arouse the pity of a convinced national-socialist, or a heretic that of an inquisitor.

Historical experience and historical observation show the very opposite of Alexander's claim—that the stronger and the more consistent are the rationalizations, the greater is the inhumanity. How could the inquisitor give in to pity, if the torture of the heretic was ordered *ad majorem gloriam Dei?* A national-socialist would have risked, in sparing a Jewish life, the self-reproach of having betrayed the *Führer.* Rationalizations are by far the best safeguards for the gratification of the destructive drives.[55]

But not only was Alexander's contribution wrong in its content, it is even more deplorable for its omissions. It was published seven years after Sachs's fundamental paper on *The Delay of the Machine Age;* Freud had already published two parts of his *Moses* in 1937, and the whole text was published in 1939.[56] Waelder had written his basic text about

---

[55] If Alexander had only read Freud's works with greater care! In his letter to Einstein, Freud (1933b) outlined the problem: "It is very rarely that an action is the work of a *single* instinctual impulse . . . . A lust for aggression and destruction is certainly among them [motives for assenting when human beings are incited to war] . . . . The gratification of these destructive impulses is of course facilitated by their admixture with others of an erotic and idealistic kind. When we read of the atrocities of the past, it sometimes seems as though the idealistic motives served only as an excuse for the destructive appetites; and sometimes—in the case, for instance, of the cruelties of the Inquisition—it seems as though the idealistic motives had pushed themselves forward in consciousness, while the destructive ones lent them an unconscious reinforcement" (p. 281f., italics by Freud).

[56] Many contributors to this meeting cited literature that had been published in 1939, but it cannot be asserted with certainty whether or not Alexander had had access to the book before writing his address.

mass psychoses six years earlier, and had given clinical evidence there of how it was possible for regressions to a level lower than that of the ego's habitual performance to be brought about in the course of historical events, adding an appendix to his book about the contemporaneous historical situation (1934); last but not least, Freud had published *Civilization and Its Discontents* ten years earlier, his book on *Group Psychology* nineteen years earlier, *Totem and Taboo* twenty-six years earlier. Not one of these contributions is even mentioned by Alexander; it is quite apparent that history lies beyond the ken of the medical analyst.

Thus, even if one assumed that lay analysis would not bring forth all the blessings that I anticipate, at least I have shown what a failure anthropic research can be when it is carried on by a medical analyst. His efforts are incapable of filling the gap brought about by the lack of a sizable number of psychoanalytic anthropic scientists.

If I now look back at the road I have traversed thus far, I fear that, in my attack against the medical and in favor of lay analysis, I may have given the impression that I believe the training of the future psychoanalyst in an *anthropic* science to be a guarantee against a possible decline of psychoanalysis. The fact is that, if the practice of psychoanalysis were made impossible for medically trained psychoanalysts, and a doctorate in an anthropic science were made obligatory, I would turn as vigorously against such a state of affairs as I have done against the present setup.

It is, however, a challenging task to speculate as to what course psychoanalytic research would now be taking, if psychoanalysis were exclusively in the hands of lay analysts. It is difficult to approach this question empirically, since there are so few adequately trained lay analysts. Moreover, it is not likely that the distortions of psychoanalysis found among the anthropic researches of lay analysts would be uniform, since the area of anthropic research is differentiated and variegated to a greater extent than medicine. It is not even likely that the tendentious proclivity to be anticipated would be the same, regardless of whether a lay analyst had studied law or history before he became a psychoanalyst.

To be sure, variegated as the picture might be, it would still be a challenging task to examine some of the claims and conclusions found in the psychoanalytic publications of lay analysts. Psychoanalysis has not fared better with some of them than with the medical analysts, even though the injury may be of a slightly different kind. Despite Jung, the messianic idea may be more apt to arise in the anthropic scientist[57] than in the physician, hardened as he is by his familiarity with the realism of biological processes.

There is no kind of preanalytic training that will guarantee the adequacy of the future analyst. Everything depends on innate talents, personal analysis, and the theoretical as well as practical training of the candidate in psychoanalysis proper. Yet I still insist that a realistic appraisal must lead to the conclusion that, if the preanalytic training of later candidates is uniform—that is to say, if only physicians or lawyers or historians or social workers became psychoanalysts—then psychoanalysis must take a lopsided course of development. Psychoanalysis would be best served, would in fact become a kind of academy of the science of man, only if the widest possible spectrum of experts were represented among the fully trained and practicing psychoanalysts.

Any speculation is vain regarding the optimal proportion between medically trained analysts and those trained in the anthropic sciences. One is reminded here of Freud's praise of Ferenczi, at a time when he was the only Hungarian analyst, "but one that indeed outweighs a whole society" (Freud, 1914a, p. 33). I knew a group in which lay analysts constituted an infinitesimal fraction of the total membership, yet one of them was able to give the whole group color and perspective, and to set the main course of their research direction. In that instance, even a large number of average lay analysts would not have produced a significant change, for the atmosphere was already saturated with the spirit of anthropic research, because of the great talents of that one lay member.

[57] That the messianic idea may incite a lay analyst for a moment even to repudiate psychoanalysis as a science can be observed in a review of Jones's Freud biography by Bettelheim, who quotes the following sentence from a letter Freud wrote to Jung in 1906: "It [psychoanalytic therapy] is in essence a cure through love." This sentence the reviewer rather eccentrically calls an "authoritative statement about the nature of psychoanalytic therapy . . . with its utter refutation of the technicians of the deep interpretations and of the artisans of the dynamic dissection of the human psyche" (Bettelheim, 1957, p. 420). This truly sounds as if Freud had recommended love as the therapeutic agent instead of interpretation, a conclusion which can only be the outcome of the reviewer's own dissatisfaction with the emotionally ungratifying, dry, and rational deliberations of scientific thinking. Indeed Freud himself, just before writing to Jung, had moved by way of his case history of Dora (Freud, 1905e) into the ranks of "the technicians of deep interpretation." If, however, one should read the whole letter that Freud wrote (Jones, 1953-1957, vol. 2, p. 435), one would find that the reviewer had permitted himself to be guilty of misrepresentation, for all that Freud conveyed was that a patient can be cured only in so far as he can form a transference. (Prophetically, he had written to Jung, in the same communication: "One cannot explain things to unfriendly people.")

Either the future of psychoanalysis will depend on the contributions of a large number, whose cumulative effect will maintain the rate of growth that is indispensable if a science is to make progress at all; or else system psychology will again have the good luck to be fertilized by one of those great minds that leap across generations.

Is the present organizational setup of psychoanalysis of such a character as to make it probable that that sort of mind will be used to the best advantage of system psychology, if it appears outside the medical field? I have heard sometimes that, if a person is really well endowed as a psychoanalyst, and eager to become one, he will gladly make the detour of medical training; I have also heard it said that he *should* do it—even if it be proved that such a detour has no bearing on his later proficiency —if for no other reason than to contribute his share to the maintenance of the present high professional standards of psychoanalysis in this country. Thus it may seem that my futile plea in favor of lay analysis favors a kind of intellectual pleasure principle, combined with a denial of what is due the reality principle.

To be sure, enlargement of knowledge is always commendable, whatever area may be included. But I fear that it will be rather the average mind that bows to what society declares to be reasonable. It is often the truly gifted one who is unable to study that which the situation demands, independently of whether or not he is personally interested in it. Giftedness is often allied with one-sidedness; the very active mind is often a very stubborn one. The creative mind will consider such detours as no more than a waste of time; and, unfortunately, it might be just the unusual person with the greatest potential in terms of future service to psychoanalysis who would regard the study of medicine as not fitting into his scheme of values.

9

Extraneous Dangers to Psychoanalysis

CHURCH AND STATE

Science has become such an integral and significant part of society that its existence and function are taken for granted these days. Its history shows, however, that its present status was arrived at in a struggle against powerful forces.

It sounds almost incredible to us when we read in Humboldt's *Kosmos* (written only little more than a century ago) a justification for the scientific description of the physical world—the sort of description which at that time must have been regarded in many circles as conducive to the spread of disenchantment with nature (Humboldt, 1845-1850, vol. I, p. 19). An equivalent situation occurred once again when Freud, in publishing the case history of a female patient who was suffering from hysteria, felt compelled to apologize for his inquiry into sexual topics, and for his discussion of them with a young woman (Freud, 1905e, p. 9).

The areas protected by taboos against scientific inquiry have become greatly diminished, but they still exist—and many a writer must feel un-

---

The reader should turn to Robert Waelder's (1963) study, in which some of the topics dealt with in this section are handled at a greater depth than here.

comfortable even today when investigating the religion or the social structure of his time. Furthermore, while some sciences have achieved a comparative autonomy, others—and psychology is one of them—still depend *in toto* on societal forces, as would become evident if a map were drawn of the distribution of scientific endeavors all over the world. We could then plainly observe the striking unevenness of that distribution.

Physics, chemistry, and medicine are accepted in all centers in which research of any kind is being undertaken. Where no research is being carried on in any or all of those fields, that in itself is a definite sign that the prevailing economic system does not provide sufficient funds for it, or that the cultural level does not contain the prerequisites for natural science. Furthermore, it is more than likely that the physics, chemistry, or medicine in all those different research centers are approximately the same. They are by and large internationally interchangeable—a situation altogether different from how matters stand with regard to scientific psychology.

Even within a single cultural and geographical area, one finds different kinds of psychologies being taught and developed. It is especially noteworthy that psychoanalysis is almost totally missing in whole continents, and in some places is even forbidden. Its highest concentration is to be found in England and the United States. Highly industrialized Protestant democracies seem best able to furnish the societal prerequisites for its flourishing. The explanation for this unusual historical fact will not be sought here; the conclusion must be drawn, however, that the existence or nonexistence of psychoanalysis in any given area depends upon the societal forces in a manner different from that which holds true for some of the other natural sciences.

As long as a science has not yet been fully integrated—and that, I believe, happens only when the society recognizes that it depends on that science for its survival—the possibility exists of its suppression or disappearance. This potentiality for negation cannot be measured, however, solely in terms of the openness of the resistance, or the vociferousness of the opposition. The voices raised against vivisection and animal experimentation are, in this country at least, far louder than those raised against psychoanalysis; yet we can be fairly certain that vivisection and animal experimentation will never be prohibited at the national level. I would not dare to be as certain about the future of psychoanalysis, even though the contemporary national climate seems extremely favorable to its growth and development. One of the most powerful of the societal forces opposing psychoanalysis is the Catholic Church, which would not hesitate to forbid psychoanalysis, or to make its existence impossible in any other way, if the power situation permitted.

In a letter to Arnold Zweig (September 30, 1934), Freud (Freud, 1878-1939) reported the rumor that Father Schmidt, an Austrian priest who was close to the Vatican, was responsible for the prohibition of the *Rivista Italiana di Psicoanalisi*.[1] Freud even refrained from publishing his *Moses* book while in Vienna, fearing that he would thereby rekindle the Church's ire, which he had already aroused with *Totem and Taboo*.

A convincing document, revealing the extent to which Catholic hostility against psychoanalysis may go, is an article by Allers (1934), an eminent representative of Catholicism. When, in 1934, the Austrian parliamentary system was abolished, and the Catholic Party arrogated to itself absolute power, Allers requested that suppressive measures be taken against institutions connected with psychoanalysis, such as child guidance clinics. For years, he wrote, he had stressed the fact that psychoanalysis is founded upon a materialistic philosophy; such institutions, he had insisted, are not to be merely supervised, but have to "disappear"—unless "an absolutely unchristian, indeed, anti-Christ spirit" was to be allowed to make headway (p. 17, translation mine).[2]

That the spirit of psychoanalysis is unchristian, I myself doubt.[3] That it is hostile to Christ may perhaps be correct—if Christ is defined in terms of deity. But that much is true of science in general. If it is properly used, science may become the source of the greatest blessings, making permanent some of the miracles that Christ was able to perform only

[1] The *Rivista* was founded in 1932 and published for two years. When it was prohibited, someone who was close to Mussolini intervened, and the prohibition was lifted. Yet, because of the intervention of the Vatican (probably through Padre Gemelli), the ban was reintroduced (I gratefully acknowledge receipt of this information from Dr. Edoardo Weiss). I myself recall the rumor that the prohibition of the Italian review was a compromise, since what Father Schmidt really wanted was the prohibition of psychoanalysis in Austria. But, as in other instances, the tragic and the trivial met, the Austrian government being allegedly loath to accede to such a move, in view of the influx of hard currency brought in by the American students of psychoanalysis.

[2] Although somewhat less strongly opposed to Adler's individual psychology, Allers made the same demand with regard to the educational institutions of that school, because of their alliance with socialism. I consider it quite remarkable that a scientist and scholar should appeal to the political executive of the country on metaphysical grounds for the suppression of the work of his colleagues! The reader may be interested to hear that the psychoanalytic child guidance clinic in Vienna handled an annual case load of about eighty to one hundred children. Apparently, even this modicum of psychoanalytic activity was felt to be insufferable.

[3] Pfister has devoted many of his writings to proving the closeness of the spirit of Christianity to psychoanalysis (see Pfister, 1927, 1944).

sporadically. Yet, at the same time, and by the same means, it unremittingly destroys the image of Christ. A great Christian like Thomas à Kempis (1441) foresaw this, anxiously warning against too high an esteem of learning: "The more complete and excellent your knowledge, the more severe will be God's judgment on you, unless your life be more holy" (p. 29).

Man's curiosity has extended the reach of science to the smallest particles of substance, and to the remotest parts of the universe, and nowhere has God been discovered. As a matter of fact, in most Christian countries, textbooks of the anatomy and physiology of the human body are published without any reference to a divine power—which, I imagine, would have been unthinkable in mediaeval times. Nevertheless, the historical fact that an incredible amount of knowledge has accumulated that has not necessitated any reference to God has had the effect of making the images of God and of Christ wane until they have become pale figments of the mind, mere abstractions.[4] Initially, the Church opposed science; but when science became indispensable to human welfare, and thereby proved its strength, the Church condoned or even integrated those parts of it that were not in glaring contradiction with the revealed texts.[5]

A chunk like Darwin's theory of evolution has proven, however, to be permanently unpalatable and indigestible; and this, I fear, will also be true of psychoanalysis. Physical matter and man's body have been regarded as closer to the 'devil,' so to speak, than to God; but the soul is God's, and thus the Church's direct domain—and in that area, therefore, the possibility of the sort of compromise that has been made in the basic physical sciences, and in wide areas of the biological sciences, is ruled out. As is well known, it is Zilboorg especially, in this country, who has tried to prove that psychoanalysis and religion—and the Catholic Church in particular—are not at loggerheads in principle (see later); but it is plain, at least from the two publications (Sheen, 1949; Gemelli, 1955) about which I shall have a few words to say below, that psychoanalysis

---

[4] I am referring here only to the social effect that science has had; theology has meanwhile been busily removing the spiritual barriers between science and faith.

[5] A quotation from Goethe's *Faust* can be applied to this process of digestion:

> The Church has a strong stomach:
> It has devoured entire kingdoms,
> And yet has never overeaten.
>
> [verses 2836-2838, translation mine].

and Catholicism are separated, and in fact so far apart, that even a discussion between them appears to be senseless.[6]

Sheen's (1949) book, *Peace of Soul,* should be read by every analyst, if only for the purpose of knowing how Freud and psychoanalysis have been introduced to a group which is numerically the largest on the national level. The book is highly regrettable, not only for the instances of bad taste of which the author makes himself guilty during the course of his attack against psychoanalysis (including two gross errors of quotation from Freud[7]), but also for the author's many errors regarding psychoanalytic theory, practice, and aims.

Gemelli is a scholar; yet the following is adduced as an argument *against* Freud's theory of dreams: "Further investigations . . . have shown that dreams contain the residuum of waking hours; but representations which have exhausted their interest do not return in dreams . . . ." (Gemelli, 1955, p. 28). This almost proves that Gemelli had not studied *The Interpretation of Dreams* which, after all, is a minimal requirement for someone who wants to judge Freud's work. I hasten to add that even a complete knowledge of psychoanalysis would almost certainly not have reconciled Gemelli to his opponent, in this instance. Yet these misinterpretations of psychoanalysis make it easier for him (and others) to depreciate the value of Freud and his work in the eyes of neutral readers, only few of whom may become suspicious when Gemelli brushes aside Freud's entire structural theory in one sweep, by writing that he refuses "to accept Freud's hypotheses about *id, ego* and *superego.* These concepts

---

[6] Gemelli even goes so far as to say "that any *conversation* on this subject [the world of religion and especially the Catholic world] with him [Freud] or with one of his faithful followers is out of the question" (p. 11, my italics). If Gemelli did not actually think that it would contravene Catholic moral theology even to talk to a Freudian psychoanalyst, one would have to regard this as simply a translator's mistake (there are other occasional unclarities in the text).

[7] Fromm (1950, p. 8) called Sheen's attention to one misquotation, which did not keep Sheen from letting his book be published without correction. Sheen quotes as *Freud's* opinion what Freud *expressis verbis* says his *opponents* will assert (cf. Sheen, 1949, p. 81 and Freud 1927b, p. 36). Fromm calls this manner of quotation a "distortion"; that, I think, is an understatement. In the other instance, Sheen writes: "But once psychoanalysis asserts that 'man is not a being different from the animals, or superior to them'. . ." (p. 81). For a while, I thought that this quotation was merely erroneous, for the source that Sheen gives, the *Introductory Lectures* (Freud, 1916-1917), simply does not contain it anywhere. However, the sentence does occur in one of Freud's papers (1917c, p. 141), in which he deals with "the researches of Charles Darwin and his collaborators and forerunners." Thus it is clear that Sheen is here too pursuing his objectionable method of quotation. It is, of course, obvious that Freud could not possibly have equated man and beast, if only because the Oedipus complex, the principal vehicle of cultural achievement, is absent from the animal kingdom.

are completely lacking in any basis, to such an extent that not a few among more recent psychoanalysts . . . have been unwilling to accept this tripartite division" (p. 36f., italics by Gemelli).

If psychoanalysis really stood for what Sheen and Gemelli assert that it stands for, it would deserve rejection as a theory unworthy of consideration. One of the central issues raised is that of sin and moral value. Here the Catholic critics make themselves guilty in part of an abuse of linguistic ambiguity, for sin generally is taken to denote the transgression either of divine law or of a moral principle. Psychoanalysis does not recognize the former, and that fact has been falsely used by the critics as their basis for pretending so often that Freud did not acknowledge the latter, and had declared any form of guilt feelings to be a neurotic symptom.[8] To be sure, more can be found in Freud's writings on neurotic than on reality-adequate guilt feeling. Two things are mainly responsible for this: first, the fact that Freud seems to have objected to analyzing those who rightly felt, or ought to have felt, guilty—i.e., delinquents, criminals, or dishonest people.[9]

[8] Cf. Zilboorg (1951) about this claim: "This is not even a caricature of Freud's thought; it is rather a hostile misinterpretation of something by people who failed to understand" (p. 101). However, it may be that Zilboorg later changed his mind, to judge from a paper published posthumously (1962b).

[9] One instance of this is to be found in Freud's writings, where he describes dealing with a patient who, during the course of treatment, had turned out to be an unconscionable character, in such a way that the patient preferred to discontinue treatment (Freud, 1909b, p. 197). Patients who are in our society regarded as morally reprehensible—those, for example, who suffer from perversions—were taken into treatment by Freud without any censure. What his own feelings were on the matter is irrelevant: if he truly desired to understand such disorders, he could do no other than put aside his own moral feelings.

That these were strongly developed should go without saying. References to Freud's personal feelings, his character, or his personality, so frequently set forth in discussions of his findings and theories, are often used as a way of supplying credibility for the critic's objections, under circumstances in which arguments based on enquiry are lacking. The reader who is interested in passages to be found in Freud's writings which intimate how he might have felt personally about perversions, is referred, for example, to Freud, 1905e, p. 49f. or 1905a, p. 161. Jones (1953-1957, 2, p. 422) speaks of Freud's "unusually great sexual repression."

In this context, it is also worthwhile to remind the reader that Freud requested from the patient, as the condition of his being analyzed, "a certain measure of ethical development," and warned against dealing with "a worthless character," since in such an instance the physician "soon loses the interest" necessary for the conduct of an analysis (Freud, 1904, p. 254). Cf. also Freud's (1905f) statement that "neuropathic degeneracy" cannot be treated by psychoanalysis (p. 263).

Of course, these are references from the early years of psychoanalysis, but they are of importance in determining the 'climate' surrounding the beginnings of psychoanalysis. For a document of Freud's later years, revealing the tolerance and human understanding of perversion, see his letter of 1935 to the mother of a homosexual man (Freud, 1873-1939, p. 423f.).

Further, a reality-adequate feeling of guilt is no psychological problem, once the origin of moral sentiments, ethical convictions, and the
working of conscience have been explained.[10] However, the schism between psychoanalysis and Catholic ethics centers on the very concept of
the normally functioning superego. According to Sheen, human existence fulfills its function only when it leads to conversion (of course, to
Catholicism). If Freud had stated *this* to be the function assigned to the
superego, there might still have been some room left for disagreement,
although it would have been reduced to a minimum.

As might well be expected, any psychology that takes a view of the
nature of religious dogma less intransigent than Freud's is more acceptable to the Catholic Church; as a matter of fact, we find Karen Horney
and C. G. Jung occasionally quoted favorably, although the acceptance
of Jung by many Catholics seems to alarm Gemelli at times even more
than do the theories of Freud, which have much less likelihood of finding a favorably disposed Catholic ear.

Psychoanalysis is an empirical psychology, and as such does not include among its primary functions that of deciding ethical questions,
even though it can contribute much to ethics secondarily (Hartmann,
1960). Directly, it can do little more than register the moral, ethical,
and religious values that it comes to observe in the subjects of its investigation, trace their history, and ascertain their effects.[11] However,
in this pursuit it enters unavoidably into areas in which the Church
demands full power of decision.

The Catholic Church, for example, considers masturbation to be a
sin under whatever conditions it occurs, and the eventually ensuing
feeling of guilt to be an adequate reaction. Notwithstanding the possibility that masturbation may turn out to be not as harmless as has been
generally thought among analysts, the damage caused by abstemiousness
—at least during the formative years—is certainly greater. At least, that
is the clinical experience; and it is therefore by no means licentiousness,
or neglect of morality, when an analyst tries to free a subject from the

[10] I will quote only one passage from Freud to show how wrong and superficial those
critics of Freud are who assert that he regarded all feelings of guilt as neurotic. "An
interpretation," he wrote, "of the *normal*, conscious sense of guilt (conscience) presents
no difficulties" (Freud, 1923a, p. 50f.; italics mine).

[11] In its function as an applied science, it also has a voice on the history of religion,
and is thus entitled to set forth a theory of its origin. However, Sheen seems to have
been less concerned with this aspect of psychoanalysis.

pangs of conscience attached to masturbation.[12] Sheen demands, in effect that, whenever a person infringes upon Divine Law, he *should* be exposed to a feeling of guilt, since that is his first step toward conversion (cf. also Pius XII, 1953). But psychoanalysis, as an empirical science, has no choice but to apply in this instance the same frame of reference that is fundamental to science in general—that is, to build its theories and constructs upon observational data.

I am writing here upon an issue which impresses me as being central to our times, and which will certainly loom large in the history of ideas of our century: the question of the foundation and vindication of religion, and the foundation and vindication of moral values.[13] Atheism has a long history in the Occident (Mauthner, 1924), and its current spread is not a new danger to the Catholic Church. The new elements that have been added, however, seem to have placed the Church in a position immeasurably more precarious than it has ever before experienced.

I once observed an instance that may illustrate what is 'new' in the Church's situation. In 1948, two events occurring at the same time aroused public attention in New York: one was the outbreak of a smallpox epidemic; the other was General Marshall's departure to Moscow for negotiations with the Russian government, in order to alleviate the international crisis, which was in its initial stages at that time. Newspapers which reported the medical measures initiated by the New York City Council to prevent a further spread of the epidemic, also encouraged their readers to pray for the success of Marshall's mission.

Here we can observe an important—and, from the practical and sociological point of view, perhaps the most important—source of man's religious desires and aspirations: dangers uncontrolled by man's insight and practical ingenuity. Had science not yet found the means to control smallpox, the appeal for prayer would, I am certain, have also been extended to the danger of disease; under the prevailing conditions, however, it is likely that only a very few went to church for the sake of curbing the epidemic, as compared with the substantial number that went to ward off the political danger. Such a conclusion would, of course, be anathema to Catholic doctrine, which has vigorously rejected Freud's stress on the child's prolonged helplessness as an important

[12] It is also a clinical observation that there is a greater chance of a subject's acquiring mastery over the sexual urge when he is freed from feelings of guilt than otherwise.

[13] Hartmann (1960) has recently laid down the theoretical foundations for the psychoanalytic approach toward values.

source of religious sentiment. My contention is, however, that it can be proven that man's religious desires and needs tend to spread under the impact of serious dangers that lie beyond his control; and with the reduction of such danger areas, the relevance of religion would in turn be reduced, if my hypothesis is correct.

As a matter of fact, notwithstanding the contemporary strength of the churches, and particularly of the Catholic Church, and notwithstanding the many religious resurgences that we may still expect in the future, the churches are gradually losing ground, and have already been driven to the defensive; the ecclesiastical offensive, so characteristic of the first millennium and a half of the Christian era, has become a fact of past history in our era, and it amounts to a 'victory' when the churches are able to hold their own over a decade.

This, of course, is brought about by man's 'irrationality,' so to speak. The belief in a deity should be independent of the question of mastery over dangers; much has been said by religionists, in fact, in favor of the claim that man's success in banishing the scourge of smallpox should make him feel more humble and grateful to God than he was when he was so easily victimized by it. However, the skeptic may request evidence, and even suggest an experiment. Let the baptized babies of one hundred pious couples grow up without vaccination, and let those of an equally large number of atheists grow up under its protection; and then let us compare the statistics.

Yet we know that even this modest experiment is a 'sin,' since it sets out to tempt God; we shall therefore have to continue to discuss God on purely metaphysical grounds. The fact nevertheless remains that man's irrationality will tend to undermine the religious impulse as science progresses, while in all probability atheism would suffer a crashing setback if the experiment just described should lead to two hundred childless atheists and two hundred pious parents.[14]

Yet, it may be objected, is not modern man still exposed to dangers despite all the progress that science has made? To be sure, he is, but these dangers have a psychological texture basically different from that which characterized the dangers that mediaeval man faced. While the

---

[14] It has often been asserted—and Zilboorg (1962a *et passim*), in his defense of theology, follows suit—that theology and science can never truly disagree. Nevertheless, it is significant that this laudable attitude does not lead to an abandonment by the apologist of dogmatic and theological claims that are in definite disagreement with the findings of science, but rather to the declaration that the latter findings are erroneous.

latter was forced to see, in all the evils that befell him, God's hand lifted against him in retribution, modern man has become convinced that most of the dangers that he is facing—unemployment, crime, atomic warfare —are man-made, and could therefore be banished, if only man were to behave in conformity with the progress that science has made—that is to say, if he utilized that progress in a manner more in keeping with the inherent blessings it has to offer.

Of course, there would still remain a good many dangers for man created by nature; but history has already shown that such dangers become controllable, once research has lifted the veil from their secrets, and man's strongest impulses have tended to become drawn toward scientific inquiries into the hitherto unknown, rather than toward prayer. Modern man has turned away from God, not because of depravity or arrogance, but because a significant emotion that filled the being of mediaeval man has become far less intense for him. Even this last statement needs qualification, perhaps, for modern man is shaken by anxiety. Yet what was experienced earlier as reality anxiety is now acknowledged to be neurotic anxiety.[15]

Whether my thesis is correct or not, the historical fact remains that religion has started and is continuing on a downward path, while the further development of science cannot be halted now, regardless of whether its application is leading to a new golden age or to the extinction of mankind. As a result, we no longer hear the Church objecting to research in the physical sciences, or in the greater part of the biological sciences. Yet the entrance of science into psychology by way of psychoanalysis has apparently threatened the loss of the last—and, for the Church, its most important—bastion.

Some passages in the writings of Sheen and Gemelli convey the impression that a pathophysiological theory of neurosis would meet the requirements of Christian metaphysics better than would a psychogenic theory. The idea of a physical poison penetrating into the brain and affecting the mind seems less offensive to Catholic religionists than the idea of a mind that falls sick in itself and by itself. I would suppose that

[15] An adequate discussion of the subject would have to start with a psychiatric evaluation of Freud's (1923c) "Demonological Neurosis," in which it was noted that phenomena of an unquestionably autoplastic nature were treated both by the patient *and* by his environment as if they existed as a part of objective reality. It is therefore questionable whether this type of psychopathology can truly be called a neurosis, even though the disturbance analyzed by Freud had the same function as that which the neurosis would fulfill in an equivalent conflict of modern man.

an evil effect of the body upon the mind is not, in this framework of belief, inherently offensive, since nothing good is to be expected, after all, from corrupted flesh; but a disease of the mind whose source lay in the mind would imply—even though remotely—a dysfunction of the soul. It is with the concept of the soul that the first barrier is reached, insurmountably separating system psychology from Catholic doctrine.

The concept of the soul has had its own long and complex history, and space does not permit us to become involved in its intricacies. One of its most fundamental properties, however, as postulated by the Church, is that of detachability from its physical shell. It is not clear to me whether this Christian dogma about the soul includes the possibility of data accessible to observation, prior to the actual detachment of the soul; in any case, the main stumbling block is the Christian's absolute knowledge that something exists in man which survives his death, and then continues to exist in separation from him. It is a strange thing to see Zilboorg, who took such a strong 'scientific' stand in favor of the exclusion of nonmedical people from psychoanalysis, taking a stand in favor of the existence of the soul.[16] If it exists, then the analysts should certainly know about it. Since the soul will have to appear before its creator, the patient entrusted to the analyst's care ought to be prepared by the analyst for being taken in charge by the priest.

Stern (1955) has approached this problem from its practical side: he strongly recommends first straightening out with the patient the immediate acute problem, without getting involved in theological discussions, such as might only serve to engender or strengthen resistances; only thereafter would he proceed to the problems of spiritual reconstruction. However, he does not say just where the borderline is between what he calls following Husserl "psychologism" and following Maritain "angelism"[17]: in the first, all of the patient's anxieties are reduced "to the level of purely psychological mechanics"; in the other, the patient's

[16] Zilboorg's comments are not without their (unintentionally) humorous aspects, as when he is discussing Pope Pius XII's allocution of April 10, 1958 to the members of the thirteenth International Congress of Applied Psychology. To the embarrassment of the opponents of lay analysis, "the Pope speaks of psychologists and physicians as if they are, or mostly are, the same persons." It sounds a bit lame when Zilboorg finds himself forced to explain to the reader that "the Pope is not discussing the licensing of psychologists, for which conditions and rules vary from country to country" (Zilboorg, 1958, p. 191).

[17] When Stern (1955) says, "It is obvious that the non-moralizing attitude of the Christian therapist creates a psychological atmosphere that is dynamically quite different from the non-moralizing attitude of an unbelieving therapist" (p. 131), he is in effect evading the question. (Perhaps he has elaborated on the point in another article.)

problems are treated "as though the carnal substrate did not exist" (p. 132). The *summum bonum* he finds in the physician's assistance by the *vis medicatrix Dei* (p. 140)—which has, indeed, made astonishing progress during the last hundred years, through the good services of a substantial number of unbelievers, while, throughout the pious Middle Ages, this same *vis* proved to be ominously weak.

Stern raises an interesting point. He asserts that, "if a Pascal or a Kierkegaard or a St. Augustine were to consult a dyed-in-the-wool, Freudian analyst, all of his tortures, his anxieties, his dark nights might gradually be removed," and as a result "the anxiety would be completely dissolved, even down to that precious residuum of creativeness" (p. 132). It is indeed a fearsome prospect that, if such a towering mind as that of some present or future St. Augustine should through grave error find its way into a psychoanalyst's office, the Occident might thereby become deprived of one of its possibly most fecund minds. Yet, the question Stern raises is misleading; for, if there is any such problem, it is not a matter of what psychoanalysis would do to the religious genius alone, but to genius in general. The dark nights are not the privilege of the religious man; they are often found in the histories of the scientist, the poet, the composer—when these are similarly driven by extraordinary endowments. Seeking psychotherapy does not bespeak a St. Augustine. In any case, I am certain that he would not have profited greatly from Stern's therapy either.

Stern may have observed that the genius is almost absent from the list of Freud's patients. There was, we know, a brief encounter with Gustav Mahler; the matter was settled in a day (Jones, 1953-1957, vol. II, p. 79f.). We still have little concrete knowledge about the psychology of genius; Stern's reasoning is purely arbitrary. Before assuming that psychoanalysis must necessarily destroy the creativity of genius—for if Stern's hypothetical example were correct, the conclusion he draws would have to be extended to take in every genius who suffers anxiety— it may be appropriate to consider some possible alternatives: (1) the genius does not need psychoanalytic treatment, because his psychopathology, while resembling that of the neurotic, is of an entirely different structure, which leads to alloplastic creations of value, rather than merely exhausting itself in autoplasticity; (2) whatever autoplastic admixtures may be blocking the afflorescence of his genius are removed by the psychoanalytic process (if the analyst cannot distinguish between the autoplastic dross and the creative endowment, his genius patient will soon enough break off the treatment); (3) knowledge of the genius's infantile history, and insight into the mechanics of the creative process, do not reduce the artistic potential.[18]

Stern seems to be quite certain that the attainment of psychoanalytic insights must inevitably stop the flow of what would have been productive emotions, thoughts, desires, ambitions, and realizations of self. Clinical experience does not confirm this conclusion. Yet, particularly in view of Zilboorg's thesis, presently to be cited, I would rather assume that it should be hard, if not almost impossible, to differentiate between disease and neurotic conflict, on the one hand, and a healthy conflict about grace and faith, on the other; for Zilboorg (1943) says: "No wonder . . . that Freud found the unconscious, irrational language in which man couches his religious faith and the performance of his religious service to be the language of primitive, irrational, infantile imagery. He could not have found anything else, for the psychic apparatus cannot express itself in any other way" (p. 325).[19]

I take it that this is meant to be a reversible equation: the absolute can manifest itself only through the infantile; and it is only through the study of the archaic in man that inquiry into the representation of the absolute can be conducted.[20] This conclusion is not a cogent one. Furthermore, in the analysis of the scientist, the connection between scientific activity and infantile neurosis and history can be observed over and over again; in general, there is no difficulty distinguishing between the subject's scientific statements and his subjective imagery. To be sure, they may at times become entangled; but it is usually quite easy to detect the specific point of fusion between the scientifically correct context and infantile imagery.

One might well imagine that the closer the subject comes to an experience of revelation, the greater grows the distance from infantile conflict. The convergence upon the numinous could, to be sure, precipitate progressive (in contrast to what is usually called regressive) tendencies, essentially different in character from the infantile. That does not seem to be the case; but then no one can set up rules in accordance with which faith ought to manifest itself. I only want to suggest that Zilboorg's

[18] To my way of thinking, the real danger in our times is that a mind such as Hoelderlin's may be mistakenly subjected to shock treatment, at a time when he is still capable of creating values.

[19] Stern (1962, p. 6) attributes a different meaning to this passage than I do.

[20] Loewenstein (1951, p. 38n) reports hearing the same opinion expressed by a patient who was a believing Christian.

assertion, appealing and convincing as it may sound at first hearing, is not useful, and certainly not binding.

Yet, if there is a soul in addition to the psychic apparatus; further, if that soul—or the mind—by means of faith is capable of grasping supernatural truths through revelation; and finally, if the soul's salvation depends on the subject's conversion—then it would surely be the psychotherapist's chief duty to lay the foundation in the subject for his future conversion. There may, of course, still be some question as to the right technique. Stern, for example, may be correct in saying that "the carnal substrate" must first be set right; to me, such a position seems somewhat inconsistent: if faith can move mountains, it should all the more easily be able to move the "carnal substrate" (aside from the fact that it is not altogether clear why *only* the healthy or the nonneurotic should be capable of true faith). Be that as it may, it is obvious that a principal issue hinges upon the question of whether revelation is possible—that is, whether faith can lead to recognition of or insight into the supernatural, and in particular to absolute, supernaturally given values.

I surely cannot be expected to make an original contribution to this problem, which has engaged the most illustrious minds in the Occident for many centuries. In any case, the difficulties that stand in the way of fruitful deliberation arise primarily out of several considerations that are usually put forward against a 'scientific' discussion of the subject.

It is said that (1) decisions on such matters can be made only by the theologian; someone who believes only in science—that is to say, a scientist—does not have the training and the knowledge required for such a discussion; (2) the absolute cannot be grasped by empirical measures; its recognition is also a matter of grace, and therefore any conclusions derived from rational deliberation—*a fortiori,* from the realm of experimentation —are irrelevant to this universe of discourse; (3) the axioms of science are antithetical to any understanding of the supernatural.

These arguments are valid per se. It is quite permissible to assert that something exists beyond the empirical, and that this extraempirical realm can be penetrated only by such noncognitive functions as faith. Yet those who put forward such propositions—which, taken by themselves, are unassailable—must also take cognizance of two postulates from the realm of science: (1) The supernatural may be exempted from scientific enquiry, but only so long as it stays in its own domain. When it intrudes into the physical world, it must submit to the tests and standards of observation, just as does that part of the world that is by definition accessible to the empirical method. (2) The absolute must be free of contradiction, and essentially different from the relative and the finite as they meet the senses, or else the absolute would be contradictory to itself—which is excluded by its very definition.

Now the faith of Occidental man in revealed truth rests on the Old and New Testaments. The absolute revealed itself in empirical processes, such as the incarnation of God in Christ, and Christ's resurrection. These two events, being historical, should not require acceptance on faith, but —like any other historical process—should be accessible to proof. Yet the documentation for these two crucial events is in no better shape than is the Trojan War in the Homeric epos. A war of some kind probably took place; but I seriously doubt that Zeus, Apollo, and all the other Greek gods actually interfered with human affairs in the way we are led to believe by the epos.

The New Testament—unless I am required to accept on faith the historical events described therein, which would surely be going beyond the area properly assigned to faith—contains a very large number of inconsistencies, and does not embody any wisdom so sublime that the assumption of a supernatural force is required. The figure of Christ has historical precedents (Jensen, 1906); the ethics laid down by and large conform with the spirit of the time, as has been further proven by recent discoveries. Finally, other cultures have produced documents that bear favorable comparison with it.

Consistency has been woefully lacking in what we are supposed to believe in as given by revelation. Two properties above all others are attributed to God in Occidental theology: omnipotence and infinite love. It is a striking feature of the two Testaments that neither of them really documents either omnipotence or infinite love. Atheists have gathered all the necessary material to demonstrate the fundamental lack of consistency that pervades the Bible (see, e.g., Lewis, 1946). Quite aside from such incidents as God's first making Pharaoh stiff-necked and then punishing him so horribly for an action for which He himself was directly responsible, the idea that Christ had to be crucified in order to redeem mankind from original sin, beautiful and elevating as it may be, nevertheless carries all the earmarks of the talion principle; it is altogether inconceivable that a being of infinite love should not have forgiven Adam at once, and given him another chance. It is noteworthy how, in the Testaments, God behaves, after all, in accordance with man's own self-imagery.

If the probabilities are to be weighed, it seems more in keeping with our observational data to recognize that certain inborn propensities of the psychic structure compel man to conceive of God, and to attribute to God an appearance and a mode of behavior that vary historically and individually, rather than to affirm that God can reveal himself to man only in accordance with the laws of the psychic apparatus, and to talk as if man could really enter into God's channels of communication. Zilboorg's proposition concerning the relevance of the psychic apparatus does not explain at all why the contents of revelation always seem to show all the earmarks of a projection. Nicolas Cusanus came far closer to the truth when he said—and he was not the first to do so—that every being has to see itself in God; it can see only its own truth in Him (*De visione Dei*, cap. VI, fol. 185f., after Cassirer, 1927, p. 34). The remarkable thing is that Cusanus, who contributed so much to laying the foundations of modern science, also took a long step toward psychologism. Abstract knowledge and concrete faith may, after all, function in inverse proportion.

However, the actual situation is far more complex. When Occidental man discovered that, by his own researches, he could unearth more reliable truth about reality than he could ever derive from any of the traditional texts, that discovery of itself caused a tremendous stir: so many became distrustful of the reliability of the texts, that the Church felt threatened in her very existence (cf. White, 1895). Yet, with the further progress of science, the understandable hopes evoked by the discovery of the hitherto undreamed-of intellectual potency inherent in man's mind suffered great disappointment. It turned out that, as soon as man went beyond description, he could arrive at only approximate truth, and that his knowledge was therefore not absolute but relative.

Even the best-founded theory can be true without qualifications for only a limited time. To be sure, some illustrious minds have formed theories which it has taken many generations to improve on; but the truly scientific mind faces a seeming dilemma: on the one hand, it aspires to enlarge the present state of knowledge to the maximum; on the other, it hopes that the newly established theory will be improved soon by an even better one. Interestingly enough, it is only about some negative statements that one can reach absolute certainty. The relativity of knowledge is a burdensome thing, and has discouraged many.

In this quandary, theology steps in. What at first looked like defeat is turned into victory once again; the theologian, casting aspersions on relative knowledge, promises to make out of the bricks of natural experience an edifice of the science of God which is everlasting and absolute. Thus Smith (1955), who berates modern man because he "has come to trust the scientific method as the only test of truth and hence to overestimate its yield" (p. 146), finds that "science enriches theology." He writes: "Strictly speaking, theology has no need of ancillary instruments including philosophy itself, but the *theologian* has such a need because of the weakness of human reason. When other knowledges contribute to the work of the theologian . . . lowly sciences actually become theological. . . . The more we know about biology, the more insights become possible into the nature of spiritual life" (p. 177; italics by Smith). Whether this attempt at absorbing science into theology will be as successful as Thomas Aquinas's absorption of Aristotle remains to be seen. At present, it is more commonly the ethical content of revealed religion that is held up, as against 'unethical' science.

Yet whether Freud was right or wrong in his conclusions about religion, it is surprising to hear from Zilboorg that Freud did not 'understand' religion.[21] It often happens that a patient's first response to an interpretation (which later on he will accept as correct) is to say to the analyst: "You don't understand me." The word 'understand' may mean 'to obtain insight into' or 'to be sympathetically inclined toward.' Because Freud was not sympathetically inclined toward religion, he was said not to understand it, to underestimate its value, etc.[22]

In view of *Totem and Taboo* (Freud, 1913g) and the book on *Moses* (Freud, 1939), I think that such a claim is preposterous. I say this even though it is precisely the former that is cited as proof that Freud fell short of the mark; I do not deny that one day data may be amassed to prove that Freud did err. Whatever the historical steps may have been that brought into existence religion and its prototypes, it is highly probable—I feel inclined even to say certain—that one or several generations went through terrible traumata at its dawn. For historical times, we have the example of Christianity, whose birth pangs coincided with the disruption of the Roman Empire, one of the greatest catastrophes that the Occident had to go through.

Yet, whether he turns out to have been right or wrong, Freud, in order to even make a sensible guess at what specific sufferings and conflicts

[21] That Sheen and Gemelli make the same assertion is not, of course, surprising.
[22] I suppose that the Catholics must similarly assert that Protestants do not 'understand' Catholic doctrines—and vice versa.

might have led to certain religious or protoreligious formations, had truly to immerse himself in the spirit of religion. It is understandable that those who have integrated religion in order to escape those very conflicts to whose abatement, according to Freud, religion owes its origin, should cry out upon hearing a recital of the conflicts averted by faith. A constellation of forces is met with here that is comparable to that obtaining in the psychoanalytic situation.

A history of religion which is in accord with historical truth has, necessarily, to be rejected by those who believe in religion—or else psychoanalysis would be wrong in one of its primary assumptions. (According to the psychoanalytic theory, this rejection would *have* to occur in case of a correct reconstruction, yet unfortunately rejection alone will not suffice as a test of truth.)

Furthermore, in establishing a parallel between compulsive neurosis and religious ritual and ceremony, Freud apparently made himself guilty, in the eyes of many, of a basic misunderstanding (cf. Zilboorg, 1943, p. 309). Yet here one can refer to the results of a large body of investigations. Without exception, it has been found that religious ritual and ceremony are connected with ambivalence in the group or in the believer, no matter how deeply that ambivalence may be repressed or camouflaged. And, finally, they are the inevitable product of psychological constellations similar to that which leads to compulsive neurosis.[23] Here one can also invoke the rule of consistency. An omnipotent being of infinite love and wisdom would hardly be likely to care whether or not a ritual is performed; such a being would have regard only for human feeling, thought, and action. If the Church were indeed right, and God actually took offense at the omission of a ritual, then the human mind would be capable of a level of abstraction and insight superior to that of God's— which would be contrary to the very definition of God.

What I have in mind can best be demonstrated by a quotation from Sheen. Not being a student of Catholic theology, I have no way of knowing how far he is repeating doctrine, and to what extent he is being original and personally responsible; but the passage in question, I believe, corresponds to medieval custom, and seems to fit well into the Catholic

[23] Ceremonies and rituals, to be sure, may also be followed for purely social reasons, or as the consequence of identification and habit. Whenever they acquire an intensely personal meaning, however, one can discover the root of ambivalence that is so successfully overcome in most instances by religious institutions. Fromm (1950) makes an exception for certain rituals (p. 108), calling them "rational" rituals. I very much doubt that this differentiation has any bearing on the psychoanalytic thesis.

metaphysics. Sheen (1949) sets forth the notion that "the Church has a tremendous spiritual capital, gained through centuries of penance, persecution, and martyrdom," that has already gone beyond the need of individual salvation. Therefore, "the Church took these superabundant merits and put them into the spiritual treasury, out of which repentant sinners can draw in times of spiritual depression" (p. 189). (Marx, by the way, would have enjoyed this incursion of economics into theology; here the revelation of the extent of archaic compulsiveness is quite striking.)

Are we to believe the theologian when he says that prayers can be collected like anything else—he aptly compares the "spiritual capital" to a blood bank on which the Church draws, in order to give a member "suffering from spiritual anemia" a blood transfusion—and can even be transferred from one account to another? This is an instance of concretization, understandable in terms of certain properties of the psychic apparatus, but by no means compatible with the presupposition of a divinity. It is even a particularly impressive example of the archaic concretization of an unconscious content.

His new insights, however, brought upon Freud—and upon psychoanalysis—the reputation of being 'unethical.' Even Stern (1955), who takes a rather sympathetic view toward psychoanalysis, presents it as considering marital fidelity to be per se no better than adultery (p. 130); Sheen, of course, persistently asserts that psychoanalysis deprives man of any sense of responsibility. If Stern had said that the psychoanalytic evaluation of behavior depends on the nature of motivations discovered, he would have been right. When marital fidelity is enforced primarily by anxiety, all the time harboring aggression against the object to which the subject feels inseparably bound, then psychoanalytically it will not be regarded as valuable per se, but rather as the background to the defense against anxiety and to the discharge of aggression.

Stern, along with other such critics of psychoanalysis, has overlooked the fact that the new microscopic method, which permits the tracing of pregenital and aggressive minutiae, may in the future come to be recognized as having created the prerequisites for a true ethics; that faith may be misled (Crusades and religious wars being among the outstanding historical examples of this); and that insights derived from the use of psychoanalytic theory are of superior effectiveness precisely because of the enlargement of responsibility that they necessitate.

Quite generally there seems to be a basic misunderstanding about

Freud's opinion regarding responsibility. How extensive he considered the orbit of man's responsibility to be can be learned from a little-known paper, in which he said that man is responsible even for his dreams (Freud, 1925g). How is this to be reconciled with the psychoanalytic claim that the repressed has the power, in given circumstances, to impose itself, although usually in a disguised form, upon the ego and that the ego possesses only limited means to influence the repressed? The question of implicit responsibility often causes practical difficulties in the carrying out of a psychoanalysis. As a matter of fact, man does bear the responsibility for all his actions, thoughts, feelings, and, as I said before, also his dreams. But in most instances he is prevented from carrying out that responsibility. The goal of a psychoanalysis is to convert implicit responsibility into potentiality for its actual fulfillment.

The element of relativism that science has introduced and validated is sometimes played down as an escapist technique—the fact being, on the contrary, that it is the insistence upon a supernatural absoluteness of values, the insatiable longing for certainty, that is a direct expression of the pleasure principle. For centuries, belief in the absolute truth of the written tradition had satisfied this need, providing Occidental man with a haven which had freed him from the disquieting feelings of responsibility of choice and doubt. It is one of the great pages in the history of the development of man's mind that he has learned to be strong enough to endure the burden of relativism.

As I have stated previously, the scientist knows well that the theory of which he is so proud, because it so splendidly fits the data that he has accumulated by means of complicated experiments, will one day be proved to be wrong or inadequate, and will be superseded by others. Indeed, if he is a true scientist, he will wish for that day to come—for the greater his theory, the greater will be the advance that will build on it and replace it (Weber, 1919, p. 138). Whatever he holds to be the truth is qualified by this addition: *in the light of our present knowledge.* The incredible self-discipline, the fundamental renunciation of the longing for absolute truth,[24] that is imposed on man by the pursuit of science is also a step forward in ethics.

[24] Zilboorg ignores the profound abnegation of narcissism that lies at the bottom of every scientific discovery, no matter what the degree of the individual scientist's own narcissism, when he speaks of the "megalomania" of the person for whom science is the maximal approach to truth, as contrasted with the humility of the truly religious— a humility which, of course, actually rests on a confirmed belief in the possession of absolute truth (Zilboorg, 1962a, pp. 104-116).

Interestingly enough, the germ of the concept of ethical relativity is to be found in the New Testament itself. "Let him cast the first stone" was an important step toward an ethics not based on an absolute good and an absolute bad—an ethics to which the analyst would add the suggestion that even he "who is without sin among you" does not *have to cast* any stones. By extending the area of objective research to include that which had hitherto struck man as disgusting and reprehensible—and therefore best left undiscussed—Freud not only did the science of man a great service, he also laid the cornerstone for a new and all-embracing system of ethics, in which much that has heretofore been condemned will be accepted, and much that has been accepted, recommended, and even praised as virtuous, will be rejected.

Deepened insight into the manifestations and the development of aggression, ambivalence, pregenitality, narcissism makes truly ethical behavior possible; for a behavior whose code is fashioned in accordance with precepts issuing 'from the outside'—even if this outside source is hallowed by the traditions of millennia—is only an approximation of ethical behavior, it is not yet fully integrated, internalized, self-reliant behavior in fulfillment of the ethical ideal.

In the hierarchy of values, that ethical action which is carried out without any expectation of reward is the highest; religion cannot provide such a framework. Sheen was apparently nettled by Freud's persistent demonstration that religion functioned in the service of the pleasure principle; his book against psychoanalysis is therefore a mere *tu quoque*. Over and over, he asserts that psychoanalysis is an easy way out, a superficial way of condoning sinful conduct. He compares the relief expressed in his paraphrase of the "Pharisee's prayer": "I thank Thee, O Lord, that my Freudian adviser has told me that there is no such thing as guilt" to the: "O God, be merciful to me, a sinner"[25] (p. 63).

Stern, who seems to understand a great deal more about the sufferings of man than Sheen does, knows that a good many patients actually crave condemnation and blame (Stern, 1955, p. 131), which means that the

---

[25] One further passage from Freud's writings may be quoted to show the absurdity of one of Sheen's most persistent charges against psychoanalysis. "If a patient of ours," writes Freud (1926a), "is suffering from a sense of guilt, as though he had committed a serious crime, we do not recommend him to disregard his qualms of conscience and do not emphasize his undoubted innocence . . . . What we do is to remind him that such a strong and persistent feeling must after all be based on something real, which it may perhaps be possible to discover" (p. 190).

analyst's categorical statement of the patient's guilt would, in effect, reduce his feeling of guilt. The fact that the analyst does not evaluate the patient's actions, but instead prepares him to recognize the true meaning and function of those actions himself—that fact enlarges the subject's *responsibility* to a degree that seems to me to be unattainable within the religious framework.

Although in the minds of a good many people psychoanalysis is conceived of as Sheen views it—as a process providing the patient with a crutch, or with the opportunity to be dependent, that is to say, to gratify his infantile needs—it should be remembered that the pathway of an analysis, if it is to lead to a cure, must be expected to be paved with frustration, mental pain, and at times even anguish. This may even be regarded as one of the drawbacks inherent in the therapy, limiting the number of subjects to whom it can be applied.

I wish now to deal briefly with the problem of conversion—one of the religious phenomena that occurs with some regularity, and is frequently put forward as evidence of the truth contained in religion. Indeed, it does sound convincing when well-informed men, at the peak of their mental powers and in the full bloom of life, declare without a shred of doubt that they have discovered God; that the world and their lives have suddenly appeared in a new light; that their hearts are filled with joy or contentment or bliss, as the case may be; and that all the conflicts which had loomed so large are ended, now that their existence has found a new direction. It is especially embarrassing to science that, among such converts, there have also been prominent scientists who, by no means at a time when they had reason to feel afraid of or threatened by the approach of death, have nevertheless declared that their previous scientific outlook on life was quite wrong, and that, furthermore, such a conversion as they have undergone could have occurred only with the assistance of Divine Grace.

Conversion is, indeed, a highly interesting phenomenon. Of the vast literature on it, I shall draw upon only the classic text by De Sanctis (1924), who conducted his inquiry in a strictly scientific way. Being an agnostic, he did not want his work to be understood as either confirming or disproving religious claims. "Psychology is unable to arrive at any conclusions, except in regard to its own objective" (p. 4).

Of paramount interest in our context is the construction of a typical history of conversion with which the book ends.

X, in his infancy and boyhood, knew and practised the Catholic religion, without having . . . the slightest tendency to question the articles of faith taught him by his mother and by the catechism . . . . At twelve X felt the first torments of eroticism . . . . At the age of fourteen X was at the height of the crisis of puberty . . . . Doubts regarding religious matters were suggested by his secondary studies, doubts which . . . led . . . to complete religious indifference . . . . X . . . , throughout the period between his twenty-second and thirtieth years, was a radical in politics and a freethinker in philosophy; and, . . . a fanatical evolutionist . . . . On various occasions domestic misfortune, illness, isolation, and certain shattered illusions of love turned his mind towards unwonted reflections . . . . Somewhere between the ages of forty and forty-two, and by a pure coincidence, X was present at some religious ceremony . . . [pp. 245-284].

The reader can easily imagine how this story goes on, and how it ends. It is, of course, not typical of the conversions of adolescence, nor of mass conversions, but it is the most striking, and psychologically the most interesting, type of conversion. For the analyst, the infantile and childhood experiences, the disappointments in life, and the partial regression at forty-two—all these constitute the important cornerstones of this history.

The age is significant; for many, especially among the males, it is truly an age of crisis. With their arrival at what is apparently the psychobiological peak of male life, the self is shaken by worry about the future and regret about the past. The recognition of failure thus far to fulfill one's potentialities, and a dawning sense of despair about the likely permanence of such lack of fulfillment, impel the self to have bold recourse to the past. That earlier period of bliss, when it was part of the mother—brief, and perhaps until then regarded as irrevocably lost—it projects into the future, which comes to be viewed as a steady, if ever so gradual, approach toward a state of eternal felicity.

The psychoanalyst can imagine the range of mechanisms that conjoin to produce this sense of harmony, based on the feeling of possessing absolute truth. De Sanctis makes a distinction between 'normal' and pathological conversions, yet fails to provide us with any reliable differentiating indices. Just as the output of good poetry requires poetic endowment, so the end result of a conversion also depends on the subject's religious endowment, and in turn on the basic structure of his personality. It is important to remember that mutations almost identical in form with religious conversion also occur outside of religious life, in the political or the philosophical field. They are all endowed with the same formal qualities; they "are to be found, not only in paganism, but in all times and among all peoples, no matter what their religion" (De Sanctis, 1924, p. 34).[26]

Every true conversion is psychologically an 'act of grace,' since it provides the subject with a wish fulfillment, the extent and intensity of which is without any parallel. I would imagine that not only the Catholic Church but the other churches as well regard as 'true conversions' only those that bring the subjects into their particular fold. If refined analysis should confirm the fact that conversions, in the general sense, occur with formal regularity at certain points of emergency—in widely different areas of human intellectuality and spirituality, and yet with psychologically identical end results—then the use which the theologians make of conversions would become highly questionable, indeed. For if the separate churches were each correct, then one would hardly be likely to find identical psychological mechanisms in all the different types of conversion.

Be that as it may, one observation of De Sanctis's should at least put an end to the belief that, in conversion, faith leads to contact with the supernatural. He says, probably quite rightly, that conversions fall within the area of predictability—an assertion which, in my opinion, at once takes it out of the range of the supernatural. In order for a true conversion to take place, certain psychobiological conditions must, to begin with, be fulfilled. Not that these conditions alone suffice to foreshadow the event; a personal factor must also be added, the nature of which is fairly well described by De Sanctis: a certain kind of disappointment in life, and the desire to possess absolute truth. The desire for absolute truth is, incidentally, probably universal; but the fortitude and the endurance to bear relative truth is a variable to be considered in the prediction of conversion.

The frequently heard objection will likely now be repeated—namely,

[26] In Indian life and philosophy, so much more aware than ours of man's psychobiological needs, there is a 'last stage' (*āśrama*): that of the wandering holy beggar (*bhiksu*) (Zimmer, 1951, pp. 155, 157-160). *Bhiksu* fulfills special functions, which are, of course, different from those of Occidental conversion, in line with the differences between the value systems obtaining in the East and the West; nevertheless, *bhiksu* does seem to provide an institutionalized way of living during the final period of life (the postretirement phase, so to speak), while retirement is merely wished for or dreaded by Western man, who is left to his own resources at that occasion. At any rate, conversion does seem to solve quite satisfactorily the otherwise unsolved problem of the postretirement phase, for which the Western tradition offers no institutionalized solution.

that the analyst reduces religion to weakness, helplessness, and similar elements with a negative, deficitlike character. Monsignore Sturzo's statement that "conversion consists in an active unification of the personality, determined by the unexpected outbreak of disturbances of the emotional life,"[27] comes close to the viewpoint presented here; in fact, it reminds me to add that conversion is also in the service of the synthetic function (Sturzo's "active unification") (cf. Nunberg, 1930): where a break had been observed earlier, harmony reigns now. Yet at this point the age-old dichotomy between science and religion, knowledge and faith, cognition and belief, faces us once again: the convert has obtained a new synthesis, perhaps; but it is probably at the price of the denial of some aspect of reality.

I cannot determine the exact historical point at which this dichotomy arose. At a time when science was still dormant, Occidental man had no choice but to accept the revelatory dictum. Quite aside from the risk he might run to his physical security by not doing so, the average person actually had no alternative.

Whether faith amounts to a true synthesis or to denial depends on two variables. One is the extent of the knowledge available: so long as the actual knowledge of reality does not substantially transcend practice, and is not founded on either experiment or mathematics—with the result that man is in effect forced to rely either on authority or on tradition—then the probability of conflict is less. Moreover, the closer the image of God remains to human proportions, the less difficult is the task of reason. It is when omniscience and infinite love are attributed to a supreme

[27] Quoted after De Sanctis (1924, p. 270 n. 31). De Sanctis has convincingly demonstrated, at least to my satisfaction, that conversions do not occur suddenly, but are announced in advance by typical psychological phenomena. A psychoanalyst's investigation of the subject would show, I am sure, that this "unification" of Monsignore Sturzo's does not occur as unexpectedly as he seems to assume. And yet there is a point of *essential* disagreement between Sturzo and psychoanalysis; it would revolve around his assertion that the believer's assent is voluntary. Father Thomas Mainage (1915, p. 372f.) supports the doctrine of grace: he affirms that it is the supernatural that draws the convert irresistibly, and in that respect differs from Sturzo.

Undoubtedly, many of those who have undergone conversion do describe the process in these very terms; but if we are to assign to their self-observation any reality beyond that of the merely subjective, then we must also accept as objectively correct the statement of many artists that *their* inspirations come from supernatural forces (cf. Kris, 1939). Nietzsche maintained that the poet forgets where he got his wisdom—from his father, his mother, from teachers, from books, and particularly "from the priests," believing instead that a god speaks through him. He further described the effect that the poet's creative originality has on his hearers, who also believe that he is "the mouthpiece of the Gods" (*Das Mundstück der Götter*) (Nietzche, 1886). Here we have the same factors conjoined that can be properly applied to the convert and his environment.

being, that excessive demands are put on mechanisms such as denial and reversal into the opposite.

A closer acquaintance with nature reveals the terrible pain and suffering that most animals are subjected to; nature is then seen to be a cosmos of merciless killing—and with no euthanasia. More sensitive minds may even be perturbed by the revolting sufferings to which infants and children have been exposed, both before and after the birth of Christ. Events that are incompatible with the existence of an omniscient and omnipotent being filled with infinite love are almost without number, so that theology has truly had to strain all its resources in order to rationalize the embarrassing ubiquity of suffering and destruction. A rational synthesis of observable data is greatly facilitated, once this construct of a supreme being is dropped; but the maintenance of such a construct is preferred, so long as the mind insists on obtaining answers to such questions as the beginnings of space and time, the answers to which cannot be based on observable data.

Thus, whatever contradictions religion may provoke in the modern mind, its indispensability in the past to the evolvement of civilization and culture is undeniable. It is conceivable that a mind such as Freud's would have turned, in St. Augustine's times, toward theology and metaphysics, and for obvious reasons.[28] Likewise it may be speculated that St. Augustine, had he lived in the nineteenth century, would have turned toward science,[29] since by then the center of gravity of intellectual fascination had shifted far from theology. Indeed, the world no longer holds its breath when Rome pronounces a new dogma, and an encyclical in most

[28] From various sides Freud has been reproached for the speculative side of his writings. It is almost certain that Freud's work will go down in the history of science as one of those rare examples of a unification of the keenest observational power with the boldest theoretical potency. It is of interest to observe that this twofold character had already appeared in Freud's first publication, at the age of twenty-one, in which he was the first to describe correctly the histology of an organ that had been examined previously by others, and also the first to consider the possibility of intersexuality—a theory that later became so important (Gicklhorn, 1955, pp. 10-19). A mind with such an indomitable theoretical bent would have had, in a different period, the endowment for forming a bold and comprehensive metaphysical construction.

[29] Cf. Sarton (1927): "He [St. Augustine] developed the idea of potential creation, thus reconciling (more than 1,400 years before there was a theological need for it) the Christian idea of creation and the scientific idea of evolution" (Vol. I, p. 378). According to Sarton, the idea of potential creation implies a theory of evolution. The ability to make a synthesis of the seemingly disparate, which is quite noticeable in Freud, is also to be seen in St. Augustine; Sarton writes, for example, of St. Augustine's "unique combination of ancient thought, Christian faith, and modern psychology" (Vol. I, p. 383). Indeed, many a disturbing claim of psychoanalysis finds its precedent in St. Augustine's writings.

instances causes a stir in only a limited area of the cultural orbit; but the world does hold its breath when a man floats in space around the world, or when the discovery of a drug to combat tuberculosis is announced.

Thus Freud's role in the dethronement of religion should not be overrated; he was probably quite right when he asserted that his treatise on religion would not change the mind of a single believer. The existence of God had been disproven by a good many, to their own satisfaction, before Freud; he did not initiate a tradition, he joined one. His particular contribution was that he produced a consistent and comprehensive psychological theory—without considering at this point its correctness or incorrectness—of the origin of the idea of God, and of the subjective prerequisites for religion. In Freud, the necessity and inescapability of religion was demonstrated in terms of the psyche itself, and without any resort to the supernatural.

Be that as it may, the caution with which Freud proceeds in suggesting a change with regard to religious upbringing, his awareness that this suggestion may prove impracticable, and therefore possibly dangerous to the preservation of culture (Freud, 1927b, pp. 51-54)—these are answer enough to those who persistently clamor that Freud underestimated religion. The motivating force behind his proposals on indoctrination was not his own personal aversion toward religion, but rather his concern lest religion prove incapable of protecting culture.[30]

When Sheen tries to prove that religion has a therapeutic effect, he is only repeating what Freud (1921) himself thought when he wrote that "so long as they [religious illusions] were in force they offered those who were bound by them the most powerful protection against the danger of neurosis" (p. 142).[31] If anything, Freud may well have been overestimating religion: one might have expected a far more scathing criticism

[30] It is a little strange to hear over and over again the advice to resort to religion as a remedy for the evils of our times when, at the end of one and a half millennia of Christianity as a social and political force, we find the world in so terrible a condition as it is. If science, after so long a period, has not yet bettered la condition humaine, then it will surely be discarded. Fromm (1950) distinguishes between authoritarian and humanistic religions (p. 34); Ostow and Scharfstein (1954) apparently follow Fromm in distinguishing between bad and good religions (p. 154). Such a differentiation, of course, implies the possibility of forming an ideal religion—an undertaking which would be of great value, but only if there were really in man "a need to believe," as Fromm, and Ostow and Scharfstein (p. 159) (apparently again following Fromm), seem to assume. Yet it is questionable whether such a need really obtains in the adult with regard to religion, and, if it does exist, whether culture would not be better served by its finding gratification through other channels.

[31] Cf. Freud's (1910d) earlier statement about "the extraordinary increase in neuroses since the power of religions has waned" (p. 146).

from a man who was great and secure enough to assert that his own convictions might one day be revealed to be illusions (Freud, 1927b, pp. 53-55), and who did not feel the trepidation that assails many a 'believer' upon the mere consideration of such an eventuality.

Yet I cannot agree with Zilboorg (1943), if he really meant what he seems to imply, in his statement that psychoanalysis "brings a biological, observational, scientific proof of the revelatory intuition which has inspired religious teachers since the time of St. Augustine" (p. 319). Nor do I think that Freud would have agreed with that statement, for any attempt by Zilboorg to prove that there is no dichotomy between science and faith (Zilboorg, 1955; see also Dempsey, 1956, p. X) would have struck Freud as an illusion.

In this debate about science and religion, the relative impotence of religious institutions in taming human aggressiveness and destructiveness is of paramount significance. There have been quite a few primitive religions that have even ordered human sacrifices; yet when we turn to the more advanced monotheistic religions, we discover a surprising array of cruelties, not only in the laws of the Old Testament, but also in those of the New Testament. If we go one step further, to examine the actual conduct of the churches and of the believers, the record becomes appalling; it would be difficult to decide whether there have been more acts of love, or of cruelty and destruction, resulting from even the New Testament and its adherents, in concrete social practice.

As Gibbon (1776) so impressively says: "Even admitting without hesitation or inquiry all that history has recorded, or devotion has feigned, on the subject of martyrdoms, it must still be acknowledged that the Christians, in the course of their intestine dissensions, have inflicted far greater severities on each other than they had experienced from the zeal of the infidels" (Vol. 1, p. 299). This statement contains a great historical truth; at the same time, it is one of the most discouraging conclusions to be drawn from Occidental history, underscoring the fact that religion has not in practice fulfilled its professed function.

Man's innate destructiveness has not been subdued by the Christian Churches to such an extent that the continuation and preservation of civilization can even now be regarded as assured—and this in spite of the fact that there are not very many instances in which a civilization has been subordinated to ecclesiastical tutelage so profoundly, and for so long, as the Occident has been to the Catholic Church. Hence Freud's distrust of religion was fully supported by the lessons of history; and since no one is yet in a position to decide whether or not man's hope in science is also an illusion, he rightly recommended that mankind make a fresh attempt, this time under the guidance of science. When Zilboorg (1955, p. 99f.) speaks of "egocentric" science, however, largely because scientific discoveries have so often been abused, he is wrong; for natural science does not offer counsel or advice, nor does it set forth demands; it only gives answers—and only to questions that have been properly asked.

Yet there are no limits to such questions, within the ever-increasing area that can be penetrated by human intelligence and reason. Freud was one of those who constantly asked questions of nature, and without inhibition; but, as of yore, the Church is already raising its objections to such questions, and warning against too deep an advance into the unknown. The straitjacket that the Church wants to put on systemic psychology and psychotherapy is, at this point in human history, rather frightening. Belief in "the autonomy of free will" is persistently adhered to (Pius XII, 1953, p. 429)—and that alone, it seems to me, would at once take psychology out of the realm of science. The ethical evaluation of man's conduct is squeezed into the existing dogmatic categories; "personalistic ethics" is rejected, and man is denied the right to make his own ethical decisions. The therapist's task, if anything, is to make himself a tool of the Catholic dogma (Pius XII, 1953, p. 430).

Ten years ago, the Pope turned *expressis verbis* against "certain forms of psychoanalysis," warning against them as "the only means of relieving or curing psychical sexual trouble." The principle of making the repressed conscious was called "trite," and its therapeutic validity declared to be false, "if it is generalized without distinction" (Pius XII, 1953, p. 431f.).[32] For therapeutic purposes, "the indirect treatment" is recommended. It is not "licit" to bring to consciousness "all the representations, emotions and sexual experiences which lie dormant in the memory and the unconscious" (Pius XII, 1953, p. 43). Here—and for *moral* reasons! —man's greatest virtue, his desire to know everything, is denied the right to fulfillment.[33]

[32] For a far more conciliatory attitude, and an attempt to bring theology and psychoanalysis into a mutually beneficial relationship, see Plé (1952).

[33] Cf. also Pius XII (1952): "Where instincts are concerned it would be better to pay more attention to indirect treatment and to the action of the conscious psyche on the whole of imaginative and affective activity. For a man and a Christian there is a law of integrity and personal purity, of self-respect, forbidding him to plunge so deeply into the world of sexual suggestions and tendencies" (p. 308). Gemelli (1955) maintains that Freud's doctrine is "one-sided since it places the genesis of neuroses exclusively in the dynamic of the unconscious" (p. 118). This argument, so often heard, in this instance makes no sense at all, particularly since the author himself disproves it, in his

A still further delimitation is put upon psychoanalysis when it is asserted that there are secrets that should "on no account be divulged, even to a doctor" (Pius XII, 1953, p. 432). These are the secrets of Confession, those of a professional nature, and "other secrets." Although some French Catholic analysts seem to have tried to adjust the psycho-analytic technique to this demand (Gemelli [1955, p. 139] extends the area of "other secrets" to include those "which, if revealed, would do injury to the reputation of the other person or persons"), one must recall here what Freud (1916-1917) reported about the failure of treatment of a patient who "was bound by his oath as a civil servant not to communi-cate certain matters" (p. 288f.). As one might have expected, the patient's whole resistance gathered behind that one content that had been exempted from the analytic rule.

It is of the greatest importance to take note of the fact that such an ecclesiastical demand, which would be binding upon the believer, would make the development of system psychology impossible; for almost every one harbors secrets of the kind referred to in the Pope's warning. There are probably a number of reasons why the Church is so opposed to psy-choanalysis as it was understood by Freud[34]; one of them may be the complete rejection of compromise inherent in his method, which relent-lessly strives toward encompassing all available data, as contrasted with the deviationist theories, all of which, as far as I can survey them, limit themselves to specific areas of the personality.

No doubt, psychoanalysis in the form created by Freud is, in its prac-tical effects, the psychological theory that is most dangerous to institu-tionalized religion.[35] But here a reservation must nevertheless be inter-

---

own opening chapter, where he writes: "Psychoanalysis is concerned not only with the unconscious conceived of as something by itself, but with the whole personality and its dynamic endeavors. This personality has a structure of its own," etc. (p. 15). (Alas, that the left hand should not know what the right is doing!)

[34] Sheen, in the New York Herald-Tribune of July 21, 1947, made it a special point to affirm that he was not critical of psychiatry, or of the psychoanalytic method in general, but only of Freudianism. See also Monsignore Pericle Felici (quoted in Ford, 1953), according to whom the practice of psychoanalysis and being subjected to it amounts to a mortal sin. Ford also objects to the method of free association as un-Christian!

[35] Gemelli presents Caruso's (1952) and Daim's (1951) work in Vienna as if these were revisions of psychoanalysis. It would be a grave mistake to view the present Vienna school of religiously and metaphysically oriented psychotherapy as a phase of psycho-analytic development. Of course, if one takes away from these schools what they have taken over from Freud's psychoanalysis, not much of any scientific value is left; but to regard them as 'further developments' of Freud's psychoanalysis simply because they make use of some of his discoveries would be like asserting that Hörbiger's world ice theory was a further development of Copernicus, because it too was heliocentric.

posed. It has been maintained by many that religion cannot be equated with the teachings and the rituals of the churches (cf. Fromm, 1950). In a certain sense, one might even say that true religion and an official church are incompatible. It is more than likely that, in the enlightened future—in which, I hope, man will at last have decided the irksome question of whether God has existence or is an illusion—it will be acknowledged that those who have need of a church for their religiosity have developed only a prestage, or perhaps a pathological form, of a truly religious attitude.

For even if there should one day be agreement among civilized people that no God exists, that decision will by no means eliminate what may be called religious feelings. This last term, to be sure, may be misleading, for it has to do with a broader area, about which I do not want to say any more at this point than that this group of sentiments might with better justification be called 'cosmic experiences,' of which only a subgroup includes the religious feelings as such. Another subgroup takes in the aesthetic feelings, or experiences in relation to art. In a moving passage, Sarton (1952, p. 451) describes the appearance of such sentiments among scientists. Just as the cognitive process may deal with any observable element, so the cosmic experience may likewise grasp any perceptive content. Freud adumbrated the problem in his discussion of the "oceanic" feeling (1930a, pp. 64-73), which is probably the fountainhead of the wide variety of experiences I am alluding to here.

It is my own feeling that Freud did not sufficiently stress the importance and the meaning of cosmic experiences. My tentative explanation would be that he may have felt an aversion to this type of experience because of one of its peculiarities: although it belongs with psychopathology, in the broadest sense of that term, it is not symptomatic of a disease. The self is quite alert when undergoing it, and yet it submits to something essentially irrational, an illusionary falsification of reality. This is one of those instances, however, in which the self may surrender without punishment to the irrational, indeed must accept the irrational as a valid part of its existence, and without thereby necessarily infringing upon the reality principle.

Perhaps the subject has already carried me too far afield. My point is that, if psychoanalysis is incompatible with religion, it is so only in terms of the churches: to an even greater degree than any other science, psychoanalysis *is* a threat to the established churches and to dogma. That is why the Catholic Church is fundamentally opposed to psychoanalysis in the form in which Freud wanted his discoveries and his theories to be understood and practiced. The Church has already shown in the past, and elsewhere, its relentless determination to put a stop to psychoanalysis; and it may be expected that in this country, and in our time, it will also do its very best to cut down to the absolute minimum the practice and the social effects of true psychoanalysis. In view of the great authority and influence that the Church wields, it is more than likely that psychoanalysis will eventually be pushed onto the defensive.[36]

I believe that, in general, analysts are prone to underestimate the dangers from this quarter. But I want to add a few more words, beyond the practical aspect. To be sure, some outstanding scientists have been believers. Newton—who was, in the estimation of many, the greatest scientist that ever lived—took the Bible literally, as is well known, and yet his religious beliefs did not interfere in any way with his research. There was no awareness on his part of any dichotomy between his science and his faith; on the contrary, his faith seems to have stimulated his science (cf. Koyré, 1957). Indeed, it is quite possible for a physicist to study the elementary particles of the atom, and at the same time to maintain the belief that God created the atom. But the scientific outlook in general tends strongly to look at God as a product of cultural evolution rather than as a metaphysical entity.

It is quite impressive to read through a volume such as *The Evolution of Life* (Tax, 1960), in which a sort of grand review is held of views on the evolutionary principle, and its contributions to the understanding of life. The establishment and development of this principle was accomplished side by side with the most radical casting off of any idea of a divine power. Mehlberg's (1958) terse statement: "Scientifically unsolvable problems have no solution and are therefore unsolvable by any other non-scientific method as well" (p. 105) could well serve as the cornerstone of the structure of science.[37]

The nonreligious scientific approach does not provoke too great a stir any longer, so long as it is limited to physics or biology; but it can still

---

[36] Cf. Zilboorg (1951): "For despite the extraordinary influence of psychoanalysis particularly in the United States . . . a true understanding of psychoanalysis is still wanting . . . . The accusations . . . are still quite strong in many a religious and freethinking circle respectively" (p. 63).

[37] How hesitant the anthropic scientist still is about radically casting off the notion of a divine power seemed to me to be strikingly illustrated by Kroeber's text on the statistical distribution of genius: in it, Jesus found no place (Kroeber, 1944).

create quite a stir if it is extended to the study of man and to religion itself.

One question, perhaps distinct from the subject at hand, is whether the weakening or the strengthening of religious organizations would be more desirable for Western civilization. Freud thought that there was a danger in basing ethical behavior on the belief in the existence of God; many historical observations can be adduced in support of his assertion.[38]

I have not yet broached the question of the effect that religious beliefs may have on the scientist who does research in the field of system psychology. It is rather obvious that an orthodox religious belief will narrow his field of vision; and it is highly probable that, even if the image of the godship takes on a highly diluted form, it will still have an adverse effect upon his psychological sensibilities. How difficult it is to view the world without what the analyst would call 'magic admixtures,' Freud (1924b) took note of, when he spoke of "the dark power of Destiny which only the fewest of us are able to look upon as impersonal" (p. 168).

No doubt, the average person cannot, without difficulty, outgrow his infantile experiences to the extent that research in system psychology sometimes demands of him. This problem is also of interest in so far as it touches on certain internal dangers to psychoanalysis—a topic that lies outside the subject matters of this chapter, but which I shall discuss briefly. I have in mind one part of Erich Fromm's contribution to psychoanalysis—particularly the exposition of his views in the Terry Lectures (Fromm, 1950). By expanding the concept of religion so as to take in "any system of thought and action shared by a group which gives the individual a frame of orientation and an object of devotion," he succeeded in discovering the psychoanalytic movement to be a "quasi-religious" one (Fromm, 1959, p. 87). He then went on to assert that "the psychoanalytic cure of the soul aims at helping the patient to achieve an attitude which can be called religious in the humanistic . . . sense of the word" (Fromm, 1950, p. 93).

Fromm's line of thought proceeds in a remarkable way. He first establishes a (more or less arbitrary) definition of religion that would embrace everything between—and including—the P.T.A. and the Nazi Party;

---

[38] Tillich speaks of the inability of all contemporary cultural agencies—including the churches—to reduce anxiety. He suggests that all these agencies should admit their powerlessness; further, that they should recognize the anxiety-producing effect which they create, precisely by their measures to reduce it; "then the third step is not far away: the rediscovery of the right word which is able to ban chaos and anxiety" (Tillich, 1950, p. 26).

then he selects within this wide spectrum that which suits his need, assigning to 'religion'—as he now understands it—properties that are not contained in his primary definition, but which are derived from the more conventional usage—namely, "the quest for the values of the ideal life." After which, he ends up transforming psychoanalysis into what amounts to an ethical system, which seems to me to be no less dogmatic than the authoritarian religions that he—by his own account—abhors from the bottom of his heart.

Contrary to all clinical evidence, he maintains that "anyone who has failed to achieve maturity and integration develops a neurosis of one kind or another" (Fromm, 1959, p. 28). This erroneous statement is a necessary part of Fromm's edifice, for he denies that anyone can feel satisfied when his life is restricted to the gratification of physical needs and the pursuit of work, and seems to believe that the patient can be cured of his psychopathology "only if he is capable of adopting a higher form of religion" (Fromm, 1950, p. 31). When he postulates that the aim of analytic therapy "is essentially . . . to help the patient gain or regain his capacity to love" (p. 87), he seems to be describing one goal of psychoanalytic therapy that is probably shared by most analysts; but when he asserts that "whatever symptoms he [the patient] may present are rooted in his inability to love"—that is to say, in his lack of "capacity for the experience of concern, responsibility, respect, and understanding of another person and the intense desire for that other person's growth" (*ibid.*)—he is once again disregarding clinical realities, and adding a definition of love which may very well be the expression of his own high idealism, but is utterly divorced from any scientifically defensible position.

Thus he derives the goals of analysis from the religious experience, and in all sincerity sets up Tillich's "ultimate concern" (Tillich 1951, *passim*)—which he defines as a concern "with the meaning of life, with the self-realization of man, with the fulfillment of the task which life sets us" (Fromm, 1950, p. 94f.)—as an integral objective of the psychoanalytic process. All this then winds up in a demand for the development of "an attitude of oneness not only in oneself, not only with one's fellow men, but with all life and, beyond that, with the universe" (p. 95).[39] We see here the epitome of dogmatism in a pseudo-scientific

---

[39] I do not think that I am misinterpreting the author here, although he does not come back to this point when he is applying concepts drawn from religious experience to the psychoanalytic process (Fromm, 1950, pp. 96-98).

garb. In reading some of Fromm's work, one becomes painfully aware that, if the leading psychoanalytic groups were to adopt his views, a new kind of religious dogma would actually be spread by an organization that should be devoted primarily to scientific research and training.

There is no doubt that some sections of Fromm's writings can have an elevating effect on readers who are in search of an ideal, while others may be useful in the evolvement of a psychoanalytically oriented ethics; but as a contribution to system psychology, his writings as a whole are more or less worthless. It is noteworthy that Fromm strikes at the foundations of individuality, when he tries to impose upon man a particular form of superego, which may be quite suitable for a specific personality type, but has no general validity.

Fromm's work is an instructive example of how easily system psychology can become corrupted under the impact of a strong religious impulse. One can learn from it that the danger for systemic psychology, greater even than that which comes from the official or established churches, arises from the analyst's own repressed. An analyst should, of course, know as much as he can about the value systems predominant in his society and about their history (and Fromm does seem to be an expert on the history of religion); at the same time he should be aware of what his own unconscious imagery of religion is. Otherwise, he may write a book like Fromm's *Sigmund Freud's Mission,* a book replete with sins of commission and omission,[40] its worst aspect being the fact that Fromm apparently has no knowledge of Freud's charity, his spontaneous and immediate empathy, and his subsequent charitable actions. One of the most touching instances of this has been reported by Goetz (1952),[41] and it clearly disproves the existence of an assortment of vices and unsavory character traits such as are attributed to Freud by Fromm, and are fundamentally incompatible with charity.

Thus Fromm's book is a lasting document to the author's possibly unconscious jealousy and hatred. It may be a confession of his gnawing feeling of inferiority to the genius on whose shoulders he stands, when he thus tries to erect into an edifice (which turns out after all to be a mere house of cards) this malicious attack, which he needs solely in order

[40] For a detailed critical review of Fromm's book, see Waelder (1963).
[41] The details of this episode will be found in Appendix 4; here I wish to add Ruth Mack Brunswick's (1928) report of Freud's charitable measures in support of a former patient who had become destitute (p. 441), and Peters's (1962) recent account of Lou Andreas-Salomé's life, in which we can read of Freud's "sending her generous sums" (p. 288), when she was in an acute predicament.

to substantiate his *tu quoque*. This latter he sets forth in the form of an accusation that Freud suffered from "messianic impulses" (Fromm, 1959, p. 108), and created "a quasi-religious movement" (p. 87).[42] However, I do not doubt that psychoanalysis contains the seeds of an ethical system better suited to our times than that contained in the old religious texts.

The supposed ethical superiority of the revelatory scriptures may have been true at the time of their origin. Since that time, man's ethical ingenuity has gone far beyond what the Judeo-Christian world was able to create at the onset of the decline of the Roman Empire. I am referring here, of course, to thought systems, and not to actions. If proof were necessary of this development of ethics, one would have only to compare, for example, the terrible punishments with which homosexuality is threatened in Leviticus and the modern concept of homosexuality as a disease. Dostoyevsky, in *The Brothers Karamazov*, defined the area of responsibility that modern man faces in stating that everyone is responsible for whatever happens at any time.[43] It does not make a demand for any specific feeling, such as "Love thy neighbor as thyself"—which, on the one hand, is an impossible demand anyhow, and, on the other hand, is no longer adequate to meet the exigencies of the present.[44]

It is altogether remarkable to observe how a historical process in our own century—from Hoover's welfare program for the hungry in Central Europe after World War I, through Roosevelt's lend-lease, to the current support of the underdeveloped countries—even though much of it was born out of selfishness, and has been deficient in many respects (as practical undertakings usually are), still approximates Dostoyevsky's grand ideal. Furthermore, in the great philosophies that came into being in the

[42] Through the inscrutable whims of providence, the unpleasant and reprehensible character deviation and the psychopathology attributed to Freud by Fromm somehow manage to lead, in Freud's discoveries (according to Fromm), to just those theoretical results that Fromm disagrees with. The analysis of Freud's personality was apparently written by Fromm with the intention of indirectly proving thereby the correctness of his own theories. To complete the work that he had started, Fromm would therefore have had to add an analysis of his own personality, in order to let the world see (at last!) the psychological prerequisites that are necessary for the cognition of psychological truths.

[43] This formulation has also the distinction of expressing a matter of necessity. More and more, it becomes evident that a rejection of this 'inflated' superego would lead to the destruction of civilization and culture.

[44] It would be a worthwhile undertaking to examine the Bible's ethical precepts in the light of the new psychology. In view of the rather widespread occurrence of masochism, the demand to love the object "as thyself" is somewhat dangerous. On the other hand, the appeal to narcissism as the foundation for altruism is altogether insufficient. A great deal of unhappiness is caused by the fact that many people do not love others *more than* themselves, but instead destroy those whom they love just as cruelly as they destroy themselves.

nineteenth century—such as Nietzsche's, which has been so terribly misunderstood—and likewise in psychoanalysis, the germs of new ethical systems that promise to go far beyond the Christian system are already contained. In order to be ethical, one must know man, and he who knows most about man has thereby the securest foundation for being ethical; he may not use his knowledge of man for that purpose, but the potential is there. Only on the basis of psychoanalytic insight can an ethics adequate to our times be written.[45]

The dimensions of the current ethics of civilized nations are clear at least to this extent: they move within the basic categories of sublimation and object love, and are directed against archaic pregenitality, ambivalence, aggression, and narcissism. Freud's unpardonable sin was his proof that Christian ethics itself is not without pregenitality, ambivalence, aggression, and narcissism. This revealed a terrible mistake in the arithmetic of Christian metaphysics, for which revelation alone it became necessary for the Church to 'turn the tables' and to raise against Freud's psychoanalysis the reproach of 'immorality'—even though Luther might never have been moved, as the popular account has it, to nail his ninety-five theses to the church door at Wittenberg, if the Popes had lived out their lives as morally as Freud did.

I can imagine that, many decades from now, when the full meaning of the historical process of our times is better understood than it is now, an effect of Freud's work will be observable, and that it will be compared with Luther's, as a 'second reformation,' which may lead to the total replacement of religion as it is known and practiced today (cf. Mitscherlich, 1963). This new way of satisfying man's metaphysical urges will have been purified of archaic concretizations and magic, and will culminate in experiences of the sort that Freud described as 'oceanic'—not primarily of an infantile nature, but highly refined sublimations, in which the self becomes absorbed in the cosmos, and loses itself in the infinity of time and space.[46] In one of his *Xenien*, Goethe suggested a way to replace religion:

45 Cf. Thomas Mann (1936): "I hold that we shall one day recognize in Freud's life work the cornerstone for the building of a new anthropology and therewith a new structure . . . , which shall be the future dwelling of a wiser and freer humanity. This physicianly psychologist will . . . be honored as the pathfinder toward a humanism of the future . . . ." (p. 115).

46 Some of these ideas may seem like nothing but derivations from some of Fromm's tenets. Yet I think my outline does not contain a suggestion of values to be imposed upon the human mind. (It seems to me that the term 'second reformation' was used by Fromm, but I have been unable to locate it.)

> He who possesses science and art
> Also has religion;
> He who is without those two
> Should have religion.[47]

Freud (1930a, p. 74f.) thought that in the latter half of the stanza Goethe expressed an idea different from his own. Nevertheless, the idea that religion is replaceable and should be replaced, and the intimation that what will replace it will be of a higher order than the original and therefore to be preferred (even though religion is adequate for whoever cannot do better)—all this adds up to a statement that is fundamentally in keeping with Freud's basic views. Therefore, it may be taken as a prophecy of things to come, to which psychoanalysis, I trust, will contribute its proper share.

Yet psychoanalysis does contain an additional thought which makes religion appear to be preferable for the majority for a long time to come. As Freud indicated, the psychoanalytic inquiry into vital phenomena does not lead to the conclusion that life has any meaning. Formulations such as "the aim of all life is death" (Freud, 1920a, p. 38)[48] do not bear happy tidings to man; and Freud's conclusion that the question of the purpose or aim of human life has "never yet received a satisfactory answer and perhaps does not admit of one" (Freud, 1930a, p. 75), even should it be proven to be correct, will not for some time yet keep man from insisting that life *must* have a meaning, since otherwise it would be unendurable (*ibid.*).[49]

No doubt, admitting to one's conviction that life has no meaning or purpose, or—what may amount to the same thing, at least in the estimation of most people—that life's meaning is death, is evidence of very poor salesmanship, as if a salesman were to stress only the unpleasant qualities of his merchandise. The Churches and Marxism are, in that respect,

---

[47] Wer Wissenschaft und Kunst besitzt,
  Hat auch Religion;
  Wer jene beiden nicht besitzt
  Der habe Religion [Goethe, 1826; translation mine].

[48] Yet for an important qualification, see Freud 1933a, p. 147.

[49] When Freud wrote Romain Rolland that he did not rejoice, console, or edify man (Freud, 1873-1939, p. 370) and therefore could not count on being loved by many, one feels that one can detect a note of regret between the lines. It is therefore interesting to hear Dilthey (1905, p. 135) say about Shakespeare (whose concept of man is not so far from Freud's) that his "tragedies are the mirror of life itself. They do not console us, but they instruct us about human existence like no other product of European literature" (translation mine).

in a more favorable position. The meaninglessness of life is for most people a terrifying idea and heartache, and a burden almost too heavy to bear. Yet, if the meaningfulness of life is questioned at the emotional level, that fact is, in most instances, taken to be evidence of a neurotic symptom.[50] If a person is healthy, he may question and even negate life's meaning and purpose, within intellectual or philosophical contexts, and with great intensity; but it will not become an emotional problem involving his own life.[51] The process of life per se, so long as it is undisturbed, provides the sense of meaningfulness directly and unquestionably.

One's evaluation of life in its broad and objective contexts must not be confused with one's subjective feeling about one's own life; and although the classical theory of psychoanalysis maintains the view that life has no meaning or purpose, the cured patient does leave analysis with the feeling that his life is meaningful and purposeful. Perhaps the goal of psychoanalysis will some day be defined in terms of the self's strength to be capable of the full integration of the meaninglessness of life, without the avowal of appreciable intra- and intersystemic conflicts. For the present, such a definition would be out of place.

I cannot conclude this section without two general considerations, which may demonstrate the extent to which the Occident has become alienated from religion. There seems to be agreement in the Catholic camp that the psychiatrist does have his proper place in society, and that it is his rightful function to treat all forms of psychopathology. From the Pope to Karl Stern, priests are even warned against becoming involved in the practice of psychotherapy.[52] Yet Jesus did not distinguish between the healthy conflict about faith, and neuroticism; He knew only man in anguish. As to the source of that anguish—whether it was physical dis-

50 In a letter in 1937, Freud remarked: "The moment a man questions the meaning and value of life, he is sick, since objectively neither have any existence; by asking this question one is merely admitting to a store of unsatisfied libido to which something else must have happened, a kind of fermentation leading to sadness and depression" (Freud, 1873-1939, p. 436).

I believe that the first sentence can be understood as saying either that whoever raises the question of life's meaning and value *feels* sick, that is to say, depressed; or that, when the problem of life's meaning has become a personal issue rather than an intellectual problem, that fact in itself suggests psychopathology. It seems that an unquestioned feeling of rootedness in the world is the prerequisite for an undisturbed object relationship.

51 As with almost all general statements about psychopathology, here too the creative mind is the big exception. What for the majority may be a sign of disease or disturbance is often, in the case of the creative person, a signpost pointing toward achievement.

52 Cf. Gemelli (1955): "Priests and religions should abstain from engaging in psychotherapy. Leave this responsibility to doctors" (p. 52).

ease, neurosis or psychosis, or a mother's grief about her child's impending death—all this was secondary: the *whole of human suffering* was in all its forms of equal concern to Him. In that, He followed the ancient tradition, according to which the priest and the philosopher were, both of them, also physicians of the soul. That "carnal substrate" of which Karl Stern speaks, and which the man with the medical degree must take care of, was accepted by Christ as His responsibility, too.

Thus the mere fact that the Church itself now rejects primary responsibility for dealing with neurotic or psychotic anguish is an index of the theoretical shipwreck that it has suffered since the days of the Renaissance. For whoever does not understand dreams, neuroses, and psychoses does not understand the healthy mind, either. It may be that, in spite of any knowledge of psychopathology he might obtain, the working of the sound mind would still remain a riddle to him; but he should know that the understanding of psychopathology is the prerequisite to any understanding of man. Consequently, the development of modern psychiatry, and the fact that its application is now recommended by the Church, when viewed in the light of the history of ideas, add up to a defeat for the Church even greater than her curtailment in matters of secular power.

Many among the faithful once had the hope that all that there is to be known about the world can be learned from the revealed texts; hardly anyone would now attempt to maintain this claim. Yet it might at least, perhaps, have been expected that *all that is relevant to man's psyche* is to be found in the Scriptures. The acknowledgment by the Church of the validity of psychiatry was—if all the consequences of that historical act are candidly considered—a step of far-reaching self-limitation, amounting in effect to self-mutilation.

The other consideration I draw from an episode in Western philosophy. Kierkegaard (1843) made the Abraham-Isaac episode, in which a father is ordered by God to sacrifice his son, the center of a tract that goes right to the heart of Christian faith. Perhaps in that episode man came to be as closely involved with God as he ever can; and thus, indeed, it becomes a crucial incident, a focal situation with regard to the believer's relationship to his God. Yet there can be no doubt that, under no matter what contemporary conditions, if a man were to assert that God's voice had commanded that he sacrifice his beloved son, he would be committed to an institution. Whatever might be the theologian's rationalization for this, that social fact alone shows the extent to which the revealed texts have lost their roots in Western society, and have become foreign to the mainstream of European civilization.[53]

I said earlier that psychoanalysis will probably be pushed onto the defensive; that, in my opinion, has already occurred, in view of the recent publication of a book with the title *The Freudian Ethic: An Analysis of the Subversion of American Character* (La Piere, 1959).[54] The book contains a sociological analysis of contemporary society and of psychoanalysis, the latter for the most part appearing under the name of "the Freudian ethic" or "Freudianism." 'Ethic' is understood here as "a people's character or ideals of character, rather than a code of morality" (p. 11).

Following Max Weber (1904-1905), the author puts forth the idea that Protestantism created a new ideal of man in contrast to that of the Middle Ages. This new idea of man was that he is "by nature independent and individually self-reliant"; possesses "great capacity for moral courage," by contrast with his previous passive endurance of socially imposed physical hardship; has "the capacity to be lord and master of all that he surveys" (p. 15). "The ideal man in the Protestant ethic is, thus, a man of action rather than of passive acceptance, he is a man who is strongly motivated and has both the courage and the confidence to seek the satisfaction of his needs." His worth as a human being is measured solely in terms of his accomplishments. The stress upon individual enterprise implies man's personal responsibility for his own welfare (p. 16).

I do not think that I need to continue with the description of this ideal of man. It is plain that such a conception cannot but have ramifications in man's outlook on life, his habits, and his philosophy. Such a man, to choose just one facet, will not marry early—that is, not before he can fulfill his responsibility toward a family; in Freud's terms, he will punctiliously adhere to the reality principle, and forego the pleasures

---

[53] I am aware that I have approached the problem of religion, as it appears in Freud's work, in a somewhat one-sided way, emphasizing Freud's atheistic content, and the practical issues of psychological and cultural relevance. Freud's writings can, however, also be evaluated in terms of the place they have in a history of occidental religion—as, for example, Taubes (1957) does in a very impressive paper. I have left this aspect aside.

[54] The ominous subtitle is found only on the book jacket; it is missing from the title page.

of the present in his concern for the future.[55] He is anything but an escapist, and grapples vigorously with tasks. La Piere believes—and probably rightly so—that adherence to this ideal and its realization have made this country the great country that it is; or, to be more precise, that it *was*, for the whole Protestant ethic has disappeared, according to La Piere, and has been replaced by the Freudian ethic, which is in every single respect its opposite.

It may come as something of a surprise to some analysts to learn that Freudianism is "a doctrine of social irresponsibility and personal despair" (p. 53); that the Freudian ethic does not "grant to the individual the ability or right to *do* anything . . . . If literally applied [it] would keep him from attempting anything positive, to say nothing of attempting to devise anything new . . . . It reduces man to a passive state . . . . It is contemptuous of the world of external realities" (p. 63; italics by La Piere).[56]

'Freudians,' even though they do not dispute the notion that man may possess the positive attributes that the Protestant ethic assigns to him, believe, according to La Piere, that such attributes "are inimical to the individual's psychic welfare . . . should be exorcised by psychoanalysis; and to prevent their development, society should be remodeled to accord with the Freudian idea of man." The "Freudian ethic" is itself characterized as follows: "absence of strong social motivations . . . , lack of constraining or inhibiting social principles, lack of supernaturalistic or other fixed faiths . . . , lack of set goals, lack of any rigorous system of personal-social values and sentiments, and complete absence of any sense of obligation toward others" (p. 64). I think I may be permitted to stop there.

La Piere presents the theory and practice of analysis, as he understands

[55] The ideal man of the Protestant ethic is almost identical with the narcissistic type as described by Freud (1931): "There is no tension between ego and superego . . . and there is no preponderance of erotic needs. The subject's main interest is directed to self-preservation; he is independent and not open to intimidation. His ego has a large amount of aggressiveness at its disposal, which also manifests itself in readiness for activity. . . . People belonging to this type impress others as being 'personalities'; they are especially suited to act as a support for others, to take on the role of leaders and to give a fresh stimulus to cultural development or to damage the established state of affairs" (p. 218).

[56] It is high time that someone composed an anthology of Freud criticism. One would then be able to observe that people whom one might expect to be well informed make their criticisms of Freud in altogether contradictory and ultimately quite ill-founded terms. Thus La Piere attacks Freud on the grounds that "his concept was not a synthesis of pre-existing elements" (p. 39); whereas Bailey in his Academic Lecture of 1956 tries to prove that Freud's work did not contain anything original, but consisted *only* of pre-existing ideas, so to speak. (Cf. Freedman's [1957] reply to Bailey's attack on Freud's originality.)

it, in a condescending and mocking way. Nevertheless, he does not tell us how he came into possession of all that intimate and detailed knowledge of 'Freudianism.' Monsignor Sheen at least went through the motions of quoting Freud (even though with errors); Professor La Piere does not quote Freud even once. In his 'brief analysis of Freudianism,' he apparently depended for the most part on an article by Horace M. Kallen (1937) in the *Encyclopedia of the Social Sciences*, about which he says that it "is undoubtedly the most objective, unbiased treatment of the subject available" (p. 34n.). It is altogether probable, therefore, that what we have here is an academic person accusing, condemning, and even ridiculing an entire theory, without any first-hand acquaintance with it at all.[57]

La Piere, however, takes an important step beyond even the galimatias with which he tries to impress a gullible reader in his version of Freud's theories. He connects 'the Freudian ethic' directly with most of what he considers to be the evils of our time; and many a psychoanalyst will be even further surprised than he was at first, upon hearing that *he* directly or indirectly contributed to turning the United States into 'a nation of weaklings'; to making it possible for many children to leave their progressive schools with the belief "that they can get away with anything —anything short of murder, and perhaps even that" (p. 128); to "the current tendency . . . to use probation and parole as a means of evading in whole or in major part the punishments prescribed by law" (p. 173); to the current widespread custom of Americans to marry early, and then irresponsibly to bring one child after another into the world; to the violation by the new bourgeoisie of "all the principles of prudence that were evolved through empirical experience by the old *bourgeoisie*" (p. 204); to the formation of bureaucratic organizations that enable an office-holder to avoid strain through feeling provided with security ("that, the Freudians hold, is necessary to his mental stability") (p. 222); to the

---

[57] In *Social Psychology*, by La Piere and Farnsworth (1936), some of Freud's works are cited. Since Farnsworth is a professor of psychology, it is likely that it was he who was responsible for the handling of the psychological sections. The level of the discussion of psychoanalysis in *Social Psychology* is not quite as low as it is in *The Freudian Ethic*; nevertheless, it still betrays a mind that has not looked into Freud's works with even that minimum of attention that is indispensable for the grasp of complex subject matters. For example, the authors apparently relied so much on hearsay that they did not even take cognizance of Freud's own definition of *Trieb*, which is generally translated as 'instinct,' and which they therefore thought to mean, in Freud's writings, "complicated systems of inherited behavior patterns" (p. 39). While that definition is true, of course, when the term is used in animal psychology, it is altogether different from what Freud meant when he used the term *Trieb* (cf. Hartmann, 1948, p. 378).

reduction of the rights of the individual through increasing control by the government ("based upon the implicit assumption that man is fully as weak and inherently incompetent as the Freudians profess him to be") (p. 241); to the degradation of the American farmer; to the spread of trade-unionism, etc.

La Piere's thesis, couched in psychoanalytic terms, would read as follows: a nation integrated by and dedicated to the exercise of the reality principle and to the service of the superego, in terms of enterprise, foresight, courage, self-reliance and responsibility, has been corrupted and debased into an 'anxious crowd,' dominated by the pleasure principle and surrendering to cravings for security; the avoidance of pain through the symbolic return to the womb has become the chief aim of the American nation. And it is the Freudian ethic that has been mainly instrumental in setting into motion this malignant process.[58]

The assertions that La Piere makes with regard to psychoanalysis, its theory and its practice, are so preposterous and bizarre that they do not even deserve serious rebuttal.[59] The only way to refute them is to quote them. However, I do have to add one qualification: although the reader will probably lay aside the book with the conviction that it was Freud who caused the corruption of the worthy and stalwart American tradition, it would be wrong to assert that La Piere says this, when he writes in the abstract. After all, he *is* a sociologist, and he knows that ideologies do not invade countries from out of the blue sky—or from Europe, for that matter, and then proceed to degenerate a robust nation.

Thus he writes in the Preface: "There is a concordance between the emergence of this [Freudian] new ethic and a number of educational and organizational changes . . . . But concordance and cause are not synonymous, and nowhere in the pages that follow is there any intent to imply that Freud, Freudianism, or the Freudian ethic is the cause of concordant changes in our family life, in education, in judicial practices . . . ." Rightly enough, he says that this would mean the employment of "the pre-scientific idea of simple cause and effect." To be sure, he reminds the reader only very occasionally of this highly commendable reservation; perhaps inadvertently, however, he writes so profusely and convincingly in this same prescientific vein that even the writer of the

---

[58] It is interesting to compare La Piere's imaginative pictures with Fromm's sociological analysis of the psychoanalytic movement (Fromm, 1959, pp. 105f., 111-114).

[59] To give one more example, how should one go about answering an author who writes: "To Freud . . . men of enterprise . . . are neurotics" (p. 34)?

book-jacket overlooked this reservation altogether, and affirmed that "the author shows how the Freudian ethic . . . has so captivated the average American that there may be a dangerously large reduction in initiative," etc.

Indeed, I shall now quote a passage in which all reservations are cast aside, and we have what amounts to the accusation of a Freudian conspiracy against socially productive values. Thus La Piere considers the following possibility: "Freud and his disciples might turn out to be unconscious *agents provocateurs,* hastening the revolution by intensifying the corruption of the capitalist masters of contemporary society—or at least that of their bourgeois henchmen" (p. 156). This, perhaps, is brought about by the fact that the Freudian ethic is taught mainly to children of the wealthy or middle classes. "A less doctrinaire interpretation of the class-linked aspect of the Freudian ethic," says La Piere, may regard this fact as occurring in the services of social mobility.

Yet the reader would be grossly mistaken if he thought that *anything* socially valuable could come from the Freudians. La Piere writes: "But the Freudians have not entirely ignored the masses. And while their efforts on behalf of the masses are both limited and segmented, they are doing what they can to discourage the emergence of effective competitors for the social positions that are held, or will in time he held, by those who have been systematically inducted into the Freudian ethic" (p. 156). Here the author throws away those prefatory reservations of his altogether, and indulges freely in a schematization that is only comparable with the phantasmagorias of *The Wise Men of Zion.*

The background of the book can be reconstructed with relative ease. I suppose it is meant as a sequel to Max Weber's eminent work: *The Protestant Ethic and the Spirit of Capitalism* (1904-1905). Even the most mediocre editorialist on some provincial weekly must have noticed that this country has changed profoundly—and very alarmingly, at that. Thousands of people in all walks of life are ardently searching for those causes that may have brought about ominous changes that can be epitomized under the caption: a frightening decline of the West, and a frightening rise of the East. Many a man will look back with longing to the older days, which were so different in spirit, in outlook—and in actuality. Now, if the background of this so productive past was the Protestant ethic, then one has to do no more than to find what new ethic has corrupted the present. And what image would be more likely to captivate the reader, in that context, than that of the 'Freudian ethic'?[60]

La Piere is, undoubtedly, cognizant of Tawney's (1926) work, which adds to Max Weber's thesis an analysis of the historical causes that led to the birth and flowering of the Protestant ethic. Occasionally, La Piere cannot help tracing the history of some of the present social phenomena that so nauseate him, back to a time when Freudianism was obviously as innocent as a lamb of any power to corrupt, for the simple reason that it did not exist at all, or else was in its infancy. I am not a historian or a sociologist, but it seems to me that the Protestant ethic had long ago run its full course. It had defeated itself; it had disappointed its own adherents so thoroughly that it had lost its hold on the nation, quite apart from the fact that its economic foundation was no longer present.

Its last representative in power seems to me to have been Herbert Hoover. There was an enterprising man, courageous, self-reliant, responsible, and full of forethought. He and his predecessor, likewise a paragon of the Protestant ethic, inspired the nation; and it followed them faithfully, pouring all its money savings as investments into the whirlpool of enterprises created by still other self-reliant and courageous men of forethought. The demise of this faithful trust of the nation in those who represented it in the leading areas of enterprise is so well known to most surviving adults that no further word is necessary.

La Piere owes us some explanation, at least, for the strange coincidence that what he misleadingly calls the Freudian ethic should have been realized in administrative forms at the very time when the total bankruptcy of the Protestant ethic took place, at the end of the boom years. Moreover, he passes over, in total silence, the previous crisis of the Protestant ethic. If anyone were to read a history of America from 1896 to 1946, such as is set forth by Morris (1947), he would see at once that La Piere has fabricated a spectre.

Already old Mark Twain had known that the American dream had not been realized, it had been betrayed (Morris, 1947, p. 101). And Howells had decried the fact that—long before the time when Freud supposedly 'coerced' Americans into early irresponsible marriages—the

---

[60] In truth, the author would have had to call his book *The Freudian Ethic and the Decline of Capitalism* to make the parallel with Max Weber complete. But the word 'decline' in a book title would bring it into competition with a classic of this century, which does not sit well with the American public, primarily because of its deep pessimism. I regret the necessity of putting Max Weber's and Oswald Spengler's names side by side with La Piere's.

new morality was being founded on the creed that "you pay, or you don't pay, just as it happens" (p. 104). And again, still referring to a period of pre-Freudian ethic, Willa Cather had concluded that the free play of individuality had become reprehensible, since the only incentive that society recognized as meritorious was the making of money (p. 132). And here is Sherwood Anderson, writing in the 1920's about an America with whose character Freud had nothing to do: "Everywhere lives are lived without purpose. Men and women either spend their lives going in and out of the doors of houses and factories or they own houses and factories . . . and find themselves at . . . the end of life without having lived at all" (p. 147).

I could fill page after page with quotations from serious American writers, proving that the crisis traced by La Piere to the doorstep of analysis has existed in America at the time when psychoanalysis had at most no more than a tiny foothold in one or two metropolitan areas, and was elsewhere practically unknown. Yet it is most significant that psychoanalysis lends itself so beautifully to serving as the scapegoat. In less sophisticated circles, it is the Jew, the Negro, or the Catholic; but to use *them* as scapegoats in academic circles has a bad flavor. Psychoanalysis serves the purpose perfectly: it is wrong, unscientific, lecherous, irrational—almost everyone knows all that so well, that it does not need any proof.

It is this adverse picture of psychoanalysis that so many have, so strongly that a man in a responsible position can pass a devastating judgment on it without even troubling to inform himself what it is all about. It provides 'convincing proof' so readily that many a publicity seeker in the political field may be tempted to choose it as the bogey in the name of which he can provide the credulous with an easily grasped explanation of all that is wrong with this country.

I am afraid that La Piere's unwarranted attack on analysis, however, is only the beginning of an onslaught. He gives a very poor picture of the American soldier of World War II (forgetting that identical criticisms were made in World War I), and has no doubt that this bad record is the outcome of a malignant psychology. The notion that a certain group of scientists (whether unintentionally or deliberately) would weaken our military preparedness and contribute to the undermining of the morale of our soldiers is a grave accusation, whether it is raised in peace or war; it must be understood by many as calling for the taking of practical steps against the evildoing of that unscrupulous group.

Psychoanalysis is here put on the defensive. Attacks by scientists may be ignored, as Freud preferred to do. But here an ostensible proof is presented, of considerable mass appeal, that psychoanalysis is a public danger, and has already in fact corrupted the foundations on which this country's survival depends.

La Piere indulges freely in inconsistencies. He acknowledges the fact that Freudianism (not psychoanalysis) has "received the sanction of the medical profession, and many recognized scientists have been converted to Freudianism" (p. 50). However, he warns that "the weight of authority is the kind of evidence that makes up the data of opinion polls," and sagely adds that belief in the flatness of the world does not make the world flat. Yet, in a footnote four pages earlier, he had cited Gengerelli's article of 1957 as "one of the few recent attacks by a professional and academically recognized psychologist" (p. 46), and added his own note of commendation. Evidently what made the article worthy of this was its criticism of psychoanalysis. (I doubt very much that Gengerelli would be, in La Piere's eyes, "a professional and academically recognized psychologist" if he had been in favor of Freudianism.) Thus, *agreement* with psychoanalysis carries no more weight than an opinion poll; that is to say, it is only revealing of what people *believe*; an *attack* on psychoanalysis, however, is a statement of "proof."[61]

An outsider cannot easily check on the arguments set forth by the author at crucial turns of his argumentation for he gives no references or explanations. Here is no struggle between faith and science, such as we discussed earlier; here science faces science. On principle, therefore, the uninitiated reader may, in view of the high academic positions held by the author, regard him as endowed with superior judgment. To be sure, if the reader is of liberal or progressive thought, he may feel some-

[61] Bailey uses the same technique. He quotes many statements adverse to Freud and psychoanalysis as proof of their incorrectness. Yet when he comes to talk about authors who try to prove the truth of psychoanalysis by referring to "its triumph over opposition," he continues: "This is the proof theologians sometimes use to prove the truth of Christianity which the analysts disdain" (Bailey, 1956, p. 396). It is also inadvisable to claim that psychoanalysis is a science. For, Bailey writes: "So have I read books on the science of metaphysics. There is also a Christian Science" (*ibid.*). When Oberndorf (1953, p. 248) refers to the large number of books based upon psychoanalysis which are published, Bailey (*ibid.*) replies: "Swedenborgian and Rosicrucian books are still written." If psychoanalysis were widely accepted without contradiction, I assume that the argument would run that only the trivial and the self-evident, after all, meet with general agreement; but if it were to be ignored or rejected by everyone, then that would no doubt be taken to be a *sure* sign of its intrinsic worthlessness.

what repelled by the author's persistent adherence to what are, to say the least, traditional and conservative views.

In the course of his explanation as to why sex played such a considerable role in Freud's theory of neuroses, he adduces an argument that is really quite entertaining. The reader may recall Janet's argument that psychoanalysis could have originated only in a city as immoral as Vienna; to which Freud replied that a more reasonable proposition might have been that frequency of neuroses is to be observed in a community whose members impose on themselves exceptionally strict prohibitions (Freud, 1914a, p. 37f.). La Piere (1959) sets forth a variant of Janet's argument, but—unintentionally, I am certain—fashions it in such a way that it comes close to Freud's argument. According to him, Vienna in the time of Freud was a once-great city in reduced circumstances: "in sociological terms it was a highly disorganized and demoralized community; in lay terms, it was a city of sin." Further (still according to the author), men and women of means engaged "in elaborate, perhaps even highly ritualized, extramarital play." This "ran counter to the strict and rigid moral code of bourgeois Jews." Thus, "Freud's patients were atypical neurotics, i.e., their mental distress was commonly occasioned by the opposition between their training in sexual morality and the social pressures that demanded violation of that morality" (p. 62).[62]

In listening to this jumble one is tempted to recall Schiller's words in *Piccolomini*:

> *Wär' der Gedank' nicht so verwünscht gescheit,*
> *Man wär' versucht, ihn herzlich dumm zu nennen.*
> [Were not the thought so deucedly smart,
> One would be tempted to call it heartily stupid].

When a sociologist turns psychoanalyst, he may easily go astray. The situation that La Piere speaks of is not 'atypical'; it is daily fare to the clinician. A substantial number of neuroses are precipitated by temptations to which the subject is exposed upon entering into a new environment, or by external factors.[63] In the army, for example, such cases were legion. For obvious reasons, the largely unconscious urge for homosexual

---

[62] Cf., however, Plé (1952): "When he [Freud] brought his observation to bear on the healthy, he seems to have met with only a very impoverished moral life—that of the conservative bourgeoisie of the Imperial Vienna of 1900, or of Kant's Categorical Imperative" (p. 4).

[63] Cf. Freud 1912b, pp. 233-235; 1926c, pp. 94, 158; 1937a, p. 328; 1940a, p. 83.

gratification was intensified during military service; in many, this led to the outbreak of neuroses.[64]

Thus, even if La Piere had been right in his initial assumptions, it would still remain puzzling why he should have thought that Freud must therefore have become a victim of the observation of something 'atypical.' But the real heart of the matter is this: were La Piere's assumptions correct at all? When Freud elaborated upon sexuality as one of the etiological factors of neurosis, Vienna was the flourishing capital of a still respectable empire. On the other hand, after the collapse of the monarchy—a period with regard to which La Piere's description of 'disorganization' might have had some semblance, at least, of truth—Freud was working predominantly on the psychology of ego and superego.

Further, when La Piere asserts that Freud derived his theories mainly from the observation of neurotic Viennese Jews, he is once more pontificating in direct contradiction to the facts. In the *Studies* (Breuer and Freud, 1893-1895), four case histories were written by Freud. Frau Emmy von N. was, as a soon-to-be-published study by Dr. Anderson will prove, a German-speaking Christian woman of noble birth;[65] Miss Lucy R. was an Englishwoman and, in all probability, a Christian; Katharina was the daughter of an innkeeper in the Austrian Alps, and Alpine innkeepers were Jews only under the rarest of circumstances; the descent of Fräulein Elizabeth von R. is unknown.

Furthermore, of the five major case histories published by Freud separately, one involved a young Jewish woman (Freud, 1905e), to whom La Piere's remark might have had the greatest likelihood of being applied, were it not for the fact that she had already, at the age of eight, begun to develop symptoms (Freud, 1905e, p. 21); another involved a Russian Christian (Freud, 1918); another, the memoirs of a German Christian (Freud, 1911b); still another, a five-year-old Jewish boy (Freud, 1909a), who could not possibly have reached the developmental stage referred to by La Piere. The descent of one patient is unknown, yet he had already suffered in his sixth or seventh year from "a complete obsessional neurosis" (Freud, 1909b, p. 162). All in all, once more a striking disproof of one of La Piere's many arbitrary and unfounded pronouncements.

[64] Of course, the stimulation by external excitation ought not to be overestimated as the cause of neurosis, for the occurrence of neuroses also depends upon the integration of the prohibition, the degree of sublimation, the intensity of the repressed drives, etc.

[65] I am thankful to Dr. Ola Anderson for permission to refer here to the results of his research into the life history of Emmy von N.

Yet, despite all the grave errors that La Piere commits, and notwithstanding his total ignorance of psychoanalysis, he does point to something that may warrant our attention. The problem that La Piere has touched on, even though poorly and confusedly, may perhaps be more adequately formulated as follows: Did Freud, in explicitly opening up wide areas of the personality that had been left uninvestigated before, and which contain forces that may be inimical to society, thereby directly or indirectly engender fears, since he did not at the same time provide society with the means for solving these problems on a group scale?[66]

One aspect of Freud's work was the scientific delineation of those areas in which culture and civilization do not promote individualism, but rather tend to hamper and destroy it. He went far beyond the usual complaints about the effect of the machine age; instead, he touched upon that essential point that is probably true of all higher civilizations. The poets have known about it: the following verses by Goethe, addressed to the Heavenly Powers, best convey what is meant here:

> You lead us into life.
> You let the wretched man become guilty,
> Then you abandon him to his anguish;
> For every guilt finds vengeance in this world.[67]

Man now expects and demands—quite aside from physical comforts and possessions—more than he did in the pre-Freudian era, in terms of inner freedom and harmony, and knowledge about himself. Man has become more self-observing, more aware of the inner cosmos, vast areas of which he had known of previously only in the form of projections into works of art and religion.[68]

[66] Zilboorg (1951, p. 89f.) has made some incisive remarks about why some people feel that Freud failed them.

[67] "Ihr führt in's Leben uns hinein.
Ihr lasst den Armen schuldig werden,
Dann überlasst Ihr ihn der Pein,
Denn jede Schuld rächt sich auf Erden."
Cf. Freud (1930a, p. 133).

[68] Cf. Freud (1923c). Although Freud speaks of a demonological neurosis within the specific context of the painter Christoph Haizman's (d. 1700) disturbance, I must repeat here that this disturbance had a structure entirely different from those now met with in our century. The belief in the concreteness of God and of the Devil in those days offered the opportunity for re-encountering internal forces and conflicts in the shape of projected external events.

The problem is an extremely complex one and no more than a few aspects of it can be raised here. Is true individualism possible on a large scale, in the midst of a huge community whose economic mode of existence is founded on industrialization? If true individualism is not possible except among the few, then do not half-measures breed more needless conflict and harm than outright authoritarian measures would? Sheen has rightly pointed out how little psychoanalysis can do in terms of reducing mental disease on a national scale. Recalling Freud's (1919c) well-known statement that "the large-scale application of our therapy will compel us to alloy the pure gold of analysis freely with the copper of direct suggestion" (p. 158), I myself doubt that even the creation of this alloy would produce a satisfactory solution.

Science in general not only contributes to the solution of problems, it also creates problems. It may be true that modern man is actually more ignorant, in a sense, than the man of Aristotle's time, since the contemporary scientist poses more questions that are as yet unanswerable than did his colleague of antiquity. In the same sense, man since Freud knows a great deal more about his ignorance of his own self than he did before; and Freud has greatly extended man's responsibility toward himself and toward others. La Piere has perhaps reacted only to the inquietude that Freud indirectly set loose in the world, an inquietude wholly absent from the Protestant ethic, in which achievement is both a resting point and a reassuring pole.

The fact is that psychoanalysis tends to find itself in a somewhat ambiguous position, when it comes face to face with group problems. I was able to observe this during my service in the U.S. Army. When an epidemic of some sort broke out, there were for the most part no alternative decisions to be considered. In one of the training camps that I was assigned to, meningitis was endemic. A plan of treatment—almost one hundred per cent successful, by the way—was worked out by a member of the staff (Dr. Hyman Katz, formerly Major M.C.), and it can truthfully be said that that was the only procedure that could have kept the death rate down to a minimum.

In contrast to that state of affairs, consider the following situation: During the course of my service, I was transferred from a training camp that had the lowest AWOL rate among all the IRT Centers within the zone of the interior, to one that had the second highest, if not the highest of all. Shortly before my arrival, my predecessor, Dr. Oscar B. Markey (formerly Lt. Col. M.C.), had instituted a remedial program, so effective that later experiences showed the necessity for very few additional measures. Within eight months, the AWOL rate at this Center dropped to the national minimum.

Now the interesting aspect of the matter is the fact that Dr. Markey's program contained no disciplinary actions at all, but only psychiatric procedures, a program of lectures, and other morale-building measures, whereas discipline at the camp from which I had been transferred had been built basically on the severest possible court-martial sentences. Thus one can see that measures directly opposite in form, spirit, and structure may lead to identical statistical results. To be sure, the court-martial technique was inexpensive, and required a minimum of effort; Dr. Markey's program, on the other hand, was expensive, and depended on the effort, the good will, and the ingenuity of the training personnel.

In wide areas, behavior patterns desirable from the point of view of community welfare can be induced by either technique, authoritarian as well as democratic.[69] It is precisely this that makes psychiatry and psychoanalysis (by contrast with physics, chemistry, and biology), replaceable when problems of community significance are to be solved. The threat of capital punishment in the Army might even have a significant effect on the rate of venereal disease—seemingly, a predominantly biological problem. One may even say that, to a certain extent, the authoritarian techniques are more secure. Democratic procedures are always somewhat risky, so long as they have not yet been carefully tested and adjusted, or have not yet become traditional.

Furthermore, democratic techniques—or democracy in general—may turn out to be a stupendous luxury: they permit dissent and deviation. There is no doubt that in those civilizations that do not permit children alternatives of identification, but force even the young to integrate convictions about the general and the specific, and about the roles that they will have to assume—which generally happens in those societies in which a monolithic government or a church authority is in power—the frequency of neurosis is reduced. Psychoanalysis, an instrument in the service of the most highly developed individualism so far known, must necessarily be a thorn in the flesh of the Catholic Church, or of authoritarian government. Psychoanalysis attempts to get the subject into a state in which he is capable to exercise freedom of choice; yet freedom of choice may prove to be a luxury and an unnecessary complication in terms of the total history of a group, even though the democratic way of life sets it up as a desirable goal.

[69] In my opinion the experiments performed by K. Lewin and his collaborators (1938, 1939), which seem to prove the opposite, are unreliable.

La Piere fights against the idea that there is a basic conflict between individual and society. He believes that it is the Freudian concept of social life that inevitably results in "the setting up of a fatal opposition between the individual and society" (La Piere and Farnsworth, 1936, p. 24, n. 23). This is an exaggeration. In the case of the tragic hero this sort of fatal opposition does occur, as Sophocles's and Shakespeare's tragedies seem to suggest; but the majority of mankind is conformist, and the sociologist, more often than not, deals with the conformist part of the community. Freud demonstrated how the road of conflicts develops from the lack of conformity in the new-born to the conformity of the adult, and he revealed the conflicts that are to be found behind the surface conformity. La Piere ignores or denies most of this, of course. Yet his own book, taken as a *document humain,* is the expression of an individual who suddenly sees himself surrounded by a society of which he cannot approve, and to which he is therefore in opposition.

In the last analysis, one may surmise that his anger is the consequence of a bad conscience, in so far as the ideal in which he has ardently believed has failed him, and he is not enterprising enough to form a new one. In this conflict, a scapegoat must be looked for—the villain that upset the harmony of the past. Since the happy future can be envisaged only as the return of a past that has in reality been—probably irretrievably —lost, at least this past can thereby appear without blemish, the innocent victim of the forces of darkness.

There are a huge number of similarly disappointed men who hanker for the restoration of the past. La Piere has set up a precedent that could easily be followed by others. Since the results of psychoanalytic inquiry still tend to offend common-sense thinking, system psychology is eminently suited to serve as a scapegoat. The chances are that, in the future, it will be made the object of accusations ever increasing both in intensity and in extension—and that these accusations will, by that time, be made also by the secular authority.

Extreme Biologism and Sociologism[70]

In what follows little mention will be made of the brain and none whatever of molecules. Psychical processes will be dealt with in the language

---

[70] Only after I had completed my discussion of objective psychology did I peruse Kardos's (1962) precisely written text. My discussion would probably have been differently organized, and also centered on slightly different problems, if I had had an earlier opportunity to acquaint myself with that book.

of psychology; and, indeed, it cannot possibly be otherwise. If instead of 'idea' we chose to speak of 'excitation of the cortex,' the latter term would only have any meaning for us in so far as we recognize an old friend under that cloak and tacitly reinstated the 'idea.' For while ideas are constant objects of our experience and are familiar to us in all their shades of meaning, 'cortical excitations' are on the contrary rather in the nature of a postulate, objects which we hope to be able to identify in the future. The substitution of one term for another would seem to be no more than a pointless disguise. Accordingly, I may perhaps be forgiven if I make almost exclusive use of psychological terms [Josef Breuer, in 1895; cf. Breuer and Freud, 1893-1895.]

I turn now to another danger that psychoanalysis will have to meet. How great this danger is I shall demonstrate by way of a striking example, which I derive unfortunately from the intellectual vicissitudes of a former psychoanalyst. I refer to the effect that the ideology of communism—warrantedly or not—may have on some intellectuals.

Nothing is more difficult than to reach an objective judgment with regard to an ideology on which men's minds continue to be divided as intensely as they are on communism in our century. The extremes of such judgments are well known: on the one hand, complete rejection of Marxism for moral, scientific, and practical reasons, as the potential destroyer of everything for which the Occident has stood; on the other hand, its complete acceptance for moral, scientific, and practical reasons, as the potential guarantee of peace to all mankind, and of the gratification of all the sound and healthy needs of every individual. As in most matters whose discussion is not strictly regulated by scientific canons, it is probable that neither extreme is right. As of now, it is anybody's guess what history's ultimate judgment will be on the major questions in this great crisis, under whose spell mankind stands at present.

One implication of that ideology, which is relevant in this context, seems rather clear, however: it is in essence antipsychological.[71] Why communism in Russia, for example, finds it necessary to be antipsychological, I do not want to consider here. It may well have been that aspect of it, among others, that made Freud averse to this ideology, in spite of the many bitterly critical remarks that one can find throughout his work concerning the basic institutions of our own society. Furthermore, in

[71] As an introduction to the history of the fight of Marxism against psychoanalysis, see Bernfeld (1932). For the initially friendly acceptance of psychoanalysis in post-revolutionary Russia, see Luria (1923, 1925).

view of Freud's strong stand against religion in general and against the churches in particular, and in the light of his early belief in the efficacy of reforms, one might have expected to find him welcoming Marxism as an ally. Yet the way in which Freud expresses himself when writing on Marxism seems to me to convey a mood of apprehension, which may have appeared uncalled-for or exaggerated at the time he offered his comments, and yet, leaving the political implications aside, may have been all too justified.

Dr. Walter Hollitscher was born in Vienna in 1911. According to the biography on the jacket of his last book (Hollitscher, 1960a): "He studied philosophy, medicine and psychology in Austria, in Switzerland and in England. Eminent scientists were among his teachers. Hollitscher regards the Austrian Labor movement, with which he has been connected for decades, as the source of his societal insight and convictions. He has been a full professor of philosophy at the Humboldt University (Berlin), and has published numerous papers on the philosophy of nature and on epistemology."[72]

Since no word is said here about his previous psychoanalytic affiliations, it should be added that he received his psychoanalytic training in Vienna. In 1939, he published a paper which he had read in 1938 in the seminar "On Science and Method" at the Vienna Psychoanalytic Institute (1939a, p. 398n.). However, as far as I have been able to determine, his name does not appear in an official membership list before 1944, when he is referred to as an associate member of the British Psycho-Analytical Society. Further reference is made to him as an Assistant Scientific Secretary of the *Wiener Psychoanalytische Vereinigung* (A. Freud, 1946, p. 170), and as a member of the same Society in 1948 (A. Freud, 1948, p. 273). After that, his name seems to disappear from the psychoanalytic records.

Thus he was engaged for at least a decade in the psychoanalytic movement. The extent and intensity of his activity can be seen from the four papers (1938, 1939a, 1939b, 1943) and a book (1947a) that he pub-

[72] A paper of his (Hollitscher, 1938, p. ʾ21) contains these additional biographical notes: "He studied under Schlick and Waismann, Ph.D. in 1934; the title of his doctoral thesis was: *On the Reasons and Causes of the Controversy about the Principle of Causality in Contemporary Physics* [Über Gründe und Ursachen des Streites um das Kausalprinzip in der gegenwärtigen Physik]; was instructor [Demonstrant] at the Institute of Anatomy (University of Vienna); did preparatory scientific work at the International Institute for the Unity of Science; is candidate at the London Psychoanalytic Institute and scientific collaborator of the International Central Office [Zentralstelle] for Psychoanalytic Bibliography."

lished during that time.[73] I have been told that Dr. Hollitscher practiced psychoanalysis in London. He apparently did not graduate in medicine, but is listed as a Ph.D.[74]

Hollitscher's writings have been well received. Fenichel (1946) introduced his abstract of Hollitscher's (1943) paper with the following comment: "This is a very stimulating logical analysis of the concepts of psychological health and illness undertaken with thoroughness and many digressions into various problems of the logic of science."[75] Hollitscher's main interest, so far as one can gather from his psychoanalytic writings, was the logical clarification of psychoanalytic concepts and methods. What moved him was the question of whether or not psychoanalysis has the standing of a true science, in the sense of the natural sciences. Can subjective findings be translated into an objective language? And can psychological assertions be tested by intersensual and interpersonal methods of validation? (Hollitscher, 1939a, p. 401).

Hollitscher was eminently well prepared to carry out this arduous and thankless task of the logical analysis of psychoanalytic concepts and propositions. Not only did he have an enviably clear grasp of psychoanalytic theory, as can be seen from his exposition (1947a), but he had also received optimal training in modern logical analysis, having come from the Schlick-Carnap *Wiener Kreis* ("Vienna Circle") of Logical Behaviorism (Bernfeld, 1941). What he tried to prove was that the psychoanalytic concepts stand up under the rigorous tests that logical behaviorism had established as the touchstone for scientific propositions. His work was, of course, only a beginning; but it was a very promising one.

There can be no doubt that he regarded psychoanalytic theory as valid, not only in so far as he had subjected it to logical analysis, but also as he presented it in his Introduction, in which he, for the most part, let Freud speak for himself. It is clear that the Introduction was not meant to serve solely as an exposition of Freud's findings and theories, with the author functioning merely as a sort of inquiring reporter, while with-

[73] To his psychoanalytic writings must also be added the review of an article (Hollitscher, 1942). His 1940 paper is a German version of the 1943 one. The 1947(b) booklet is an enlarged version of the 1943 and 1940 writings, respectively.

[74] Thus, in accordance with my definition, he is to be called a lay analyst, although I am sure no analyst has ever known as much anatomy, in view of his having been a *Demonstrant* at the Institute of Anatomy. It is quite likely that he finished his medical studies, but—for reasons unknown to me—he did not graduate.

[75] Feldmann (1949), too, expressed himself favorably on Hollitscher's book.

holding his own views; instead, there were reservations and critical remarks interspersed in which the author expressed his disagreement with Freud's work in applied psychoanalysis.[76]

Thus we would be entitled to say that Hollitscher was fundamentally convinced of the scientific correctness and validity of Freud's basic theories, for at least a decade during his years of maturity. Psychoanalysis had not in this instance been accepted in a rush of youthful enthusiasm; it had not been accepted under the impact that an awe-inspiring genius may have on an ambitious but impoverished mind, which hungers for transference. Hollitscher did not make it his own because it was fashionable or profit-making—for in Vienna it was neither; and he did not give it his approval and support just because he was ignorant of other schools of psychology, for in his 1943 paper he cites the literature on reflexology from Bechterev to Pavlov, which, I am sure, he had studied profoundly even before his first psychoanalytic paper in 1939.

Nor can one say that he had accepted analysis under the overwhelming effect that its 'romantic' aspect, its seemingly paradoxical nature (when measured against 'common-sense thinking' in psychological matters) so often has on the *turba novarum rerum avida;* it is with admirable coolness and mental distance, with a complete absence of any element that could serve as a stimulant for fantasy or imagination, that he uses the sharp edges of his logical tools.

One may perhaps be inclined to suspect from his writings that he knew psychoanalysis only from theoretical study, and one may therefore wonder whether his convictions would have been able to stand the test of practical experience. But he had undergone a personal analysis, a fact which eliminates the possibility that his psychoanalytic knowledge consisted solely of a rigid and bookish conglomerate of theories. The extent of his clinical experience cannot be learned from his own writings; but his stay in London must have afforded him ample opportunity, and after his return to Vienna we find him acting as the scientific secretary of a psychoanalytic institute—which, one would expect, should prove that he was still in basic agreement with psychoanalytic theory.

This makes it all the more difficult to understand Hollitscher's (1960b) book review of Wells's (1960) Pavlovian critique of Freud. In it, the *whole* of psychoanalysis is uncompromisingly rejected, while Pavlov's

---

[76] Hollitscher (1947a) writes: "The latter [Freud's contributions to cultural psychology] were highly speculative and controversial in quite a different manner from the real 'clinical' discipline of psychoanalysis" (p. 99).

doctrine is elevated to "a genuine psychological science regarding man's central psychic achievements." When he deals with Freud, Hollitscher is reluctant to grant him even the standing of a 'misguided genius': Freud possessed some traits that one customarily encounters in genius, but the measure of genius is "the objective achievement which *has to be verified* vis-à-vis the matter-of-fact, acknowledged criteria of science and *has to prove true in practice*" (translation mine; italics by the author).

The Lord gave, and the Lord has taken away. Gone are all those finely chiseled arguments for the truly scientific nature of psychoanalysis, those proofs that psychology as evolved by Freud deserves to rank among the natural sciences. Now, "the invention of an ever so original mythological world of concepts—within whose speculative realm there are 'psychic energies' and 'psychic apparatuses' and 'psychic systems' of many kinds"—can lead to nothing but "a pseudoscientific fallacy." In his latest book, Hollitscher (1960a) pursues the same line of criticism of Freud. Thus, there can be no doubt that psychoanalysis has lost one of its truly promising epistemologists, a man who, with his enormous knowledge and analytic keenness, might have rendered an essential and indispensable service to the formation of psychoanalytic theory. I do not think, in fact, that the damage he can now do to psychoanalysis will be nearly as great as the advance that psychoanalysis might have made with his co-operation.

I do not know how this tale strikes other analysts. On its first impact, I found it incredible, bewildering, and confusing. One should not try to counter with the assertion that this is not the first time that an analyst has defected, for on closer examination this is revealed to be a unique event, without any comparable precedents. Jung and Adler, to begin with, had not been analyzed; further, they evolved theories which, for better or worse, still show many elements of their intellectual parentage, in spite of their own numerous deficiencies. All or some of these factors are also present among defectors of more recent date. Each of them undoubtedly gained great narcissistic gratification from the act of deserting the camp; yet many of them, if not all, have admitted, in one way or another, their debt to Freud, acknowledging his contribution to the advancement of psychology, despite their often harsh criticisms of his theories.

One must also consider how prone to personal conflict and unconscious involvements he is, who is close to the burning bush. The younger generation of psychoanalysts has it easier in this respect. Fascinating as it must have been to work close to Freud, the situation must, I presume, have been fraught with psychological dangers.[77] Unless one was endowed with an unusual degree of inner confidence, security, and devotion, the probability was great that he would end either in rebellion or in surrender. As soon as a genius has become a historical personage, the intensity of this type of conflict is greatly lessened, even though it is never completely eliminated (cf. Freud, 1930b, p. 211f.).[78]

When Rank defected from psychoanalysis, his new theory provided the semblance of a justifiable motive (Rank, 1924). This theory of the birth trauma is in all probability wrong—that is, empirically wrong; yet the structure of the theory is not per se in contradiction with the general framework of psychoanalytic theory formation.[79] In other words, in order to decide whether Rank was right or wrong, I have to go through the case histories of patients who have been psychoanalytically investigated: I must turn to the empirical evidence in order to make a decision. This, I think, is quite different from the way in which the analyst should reach a decision as to the substance of Pavlov's theories.

Furthermore, with regard to my assertion of uniqueness in Dr. Hollitscher's instance, there is substantial historical evidence of analysts giving way to ideological pressures. Indeed, if the incident had taken place in the Soviet Union, or in one of the countries in her orbit, I would not waste another word on it. Of course, there have been analysts who have foresworn their psychoanalytic allegiance; but the instances that I know of occurred under most distressing circumstances. It is not within everyone's capacity to thrive under the hardships of martyrdom, or to face with equanimity the gradual starvation of one's wife and children. Therefore I think analysts have been criticized unjustly for having turned away from analysis while they were living in countries whose political organization did not permit the practice of psychoanalysis.

But Dr. Hollitscher was in England and left that country for Vienna,

[77] For documents dealing with the early days of the psychoanalytic movement, in which this atmosphere of tension can be felt, see Andreas-Salomé (1912-1913), Nunberg and Federn (1962).

[78] I am aware of the objection to this general statement. Clinically, a continuation of the oedipus conflict can be observed in the realm of ideas, ideologies, and philosophies. The intensity of this conflict is by no means weakened by the abstract nature of the object. But my position on conflict reduction (not conflict elimination) is, I think, fairly correct so long as it is limited to the generation of psychoanalysts that grew up without personal contact with Freud.

[79] That Rank's new theory was not out of keeping with the psychoanalytic framework can be clearly seen from Freud's initial reaction to it. Cf. Jones (1953-1957, vol. III, p. 61f.) See also Freud (1873-1939, p. 352f.).

where there was no dictatorship at the time of his return. To be sure, the practice of psychoanalysis did not become a lucrative business in Vienna after World War II; but there is not the slightest indication that it was a mercenary purpose that could have served as the conscious or unconscious motive when Hollitscher changed camps.

These facts therefore, whether taken singly or collectively, indicate that what psychoanalysis confronts here is a wholly novel situation, to unravel which would take a special psychoanalytic inquiry.

Let us now turn instead to what it was that Hollitscher replaced psychoanalysis with, for what 'intellectual price' he gave up that theory about whose correctness he had been convinced, after all, at least for a decade.

When I now proceed to challenge Pavlov's explanation of psychopathology and of man's mental life, I do so with the understanding that I may one day be proven to be wrong.[80] Science and God have this much in common: they are both quite unpredictable. Who would have thought, in the modern era, that old Aristotle was right, after all, and that space is not infinite but finite, endowed with a measurable, even though constantly changing border? What can a scientist do but depend on the probable, in the light of the sort of knowledge that he is able to gain from observation?

Yet Freud, with the profoundest sagacity, has reminded us that "the probable need not necessarily be the truth and the truth not always probable" (Freud, 1939, p. 30); and, most disconcertingly, the historians now tell us that Copernicus and Kepler would not have adopted the heliocentric theory, if their conclusions had been patterned in accordance with what *appeared* to be most probable, as measured in terms of their actual knowledge of the universe (Kline, 1953, p. 116f.). Thus their theories were formed 'against all the evidence' (to put it in a perhaps exaggerated form)—and still they were right. In spite of the relativism that weighs so heavily on the work of the scientist, there is no place in his world for mere arbitrariness, and changes of theory take a lot of explaining.

The basic idea of Pavlov's theory revolves around the conditioned reflex. The core situation which underlies all of his work is that in which

---

[80] Pavlov's experiments and theories have been most ably discussed and criticized in many quarters. The criticism of Pavlov's work that follows does not offer anything essentially new. It is only a sort of summary of the way in which Pavlov's work may appear to some psychoanalysts.

a dog is tied to his stall, in an environment devoid of all stimulation except for one intermittently given stimulus, his salivary glands then being studied with regard to the number of drops of saliva produced in given time units. The crux of the matter is the indubitable fact that the saliva is produced not only in response to direct stimulation of the oral mucosa through the application of food (unconditioned reflex), but also in response to any other stimulus, applied to any other sense organ, so long as it has preceded the unconditioned reflex a number of times (conditioned reflex).

There are many contradictory statements in Pavlov's work, and one gets the impression that he was a rather impetuous thinker. I suppose that one can cite from his works statements that will disprove my contention; nevertheless, by and large I believe that I am right in saying that the structure of Pavlov's core situation is presumably meant to be paradigmatic of *all* those phenomena included under the broad term 'psychic'—that is to say, thinking, speech, love, despair, and so forth. All these, I take it, can ultimately be explained, according to Pavlov, as reflexes. This in turn assumes the stimulation of a receptor, from which excitatory processes take their start, ultimately leading to the stimulation of effector organs.

To be sure, this simple scheme does not suffice, according to Pavlov, to explain the whole gamut of phenomena observed; and therefore a variety of processes has to be introduced, all of which occur in the cerebrum. Bridger properly objects to the claim that, for Pavlov, the basic law of higher nervous activity is the conditioned reflex. He used it, says Bridger, only "to ascertain objectively the molar physiological processes of higher nervous activity," such as "excitation and inhibition, and the laws governing those processes he described as irradiation and concentration, and their reciprocal relation, i.e., negative and positive induction" (Bridger, 1958, p. 96f.). Still the basic model in Pavlovian psychology of what is ambiguously called 'psychic life' is the conditioned reflex; and, in order to explain its presence or absence, various processes are assumed to take place in the cortex and the subcortex.

The core schema, as described above, remain essentially unchanged by the assumption of ever so many additional cerebral processes, however, for nothing but reflexes can be produced in the whole wide world of organismic life. The assertion, to continue, is that scientifically—that is to say, objectively—nothing further need be said about the psychic life of beast or man, since mind is, after all, nothing but the function of the central nervous system. Pavlov seems to have been convinced that the psychologist, in studying the activity of the central nervous system, was thereby examining objectively the whole realm of psychic life.[81] The cerebral function is the causative mechanism of psychic life—if there is any such thing; and a purely psychic causation is regarded as impossible, its assumption being, according to Wells (1960, *passim*), the product of an anthropomorphic, religious, and reactionary philosophy.

It is noteworthy that in Pavlov's research Descartes found his ultimate fulfillment (Straus,[82] 1935, pp. 1-25). Descartes put the reflex at the center of his theory of the body, which he regarded as a machine; the soul followed quite different laws. Pavlov took the fateful step of extending Descartes' theory of the body by trying to prove that psychic phenomena are also nothing but manifestations of the body machine, following exactly its laws of reflex. Thus Descartes, like a second Columbus, seems to have discovered far more than he ever intended or knew.

It is worthwhile noting the comments that Pavlov's work has evoked among the psychoanalysts. It seems that Luria (1926) was the first to compare in detail the work of Pavlov and other Russian physiologists with psychoanalysis, asserting their compatibility.[83] Yet it was above all French who, while aware of the differences between Freud and Pavlov, nevertheless tried to prove that Pavlov's findings are compatible with, perhaps even confirmatory of, the basic psychoanalytic findings; or, to use French's words: "The results of these two very extensive investigations must be fundamentally very closely related to each other in spite of differences in emphasis" (French, 1933, p. 1166).

Kubie (1934) correlated the psychoanalytic therapeutic situation with

[81] Wells (1960, p. 177) objects to the equating of psychology with the physiology of the higher nervous system. He says that the latter is rather the prerequisite for the former. But on the preceding page, he speaks of the "confrontation of the two *psychologies*" (italics mine), evidently meaning those of Pavlov and Freud. Wells enumerates still other 'prerequisites' for psychology; but I do not see what then remains of psychology itself but description and classification (Wells, 1960, p. 176), once Pavlov's doctrine is accepted. It seems to me that Pavlov's opinion was that psychology *is* the physiology of the highest nervous activity. In 1903, Pavlov still seems to be distinguishing between the psychic and the physiological (Pavlov, 1903, p. 59f.); but by 1906 the two appear to be identical (Pavlov, 1906, p. 87; see particularly the translator's footnote).

[82] Straus's book contains the most penetrating refutation of Pavlov's psychology. It is regrettable that his book is not available in English.

[83] See, for the same opinion, Drabovitch (1935). Of particular interest is his quotation from a paper by Frolov in 1926, apparently using one of Freud's findings in his experimental work (p. 31).

Pavlov's core situation,[84] while Schilder (1935) was critical of large sections of Pavlov's theories. The discussion that followed French's paper had, in fact, already demonstrated that opinions were (almost evenly) divided, Myerson (1933, p. 1202) among others considering Pavlov and Freud as diametric opposites. Indeed, how could it be otherwise?[85] Pavlov's psychology is insuperably medial, just as Freud's is insuperably systemic.

The psyche in Pavlov's scheme is a pure medium of cerebral process. Why consciousness is necessary at all, or what its function may be, does not become clear from Pavlov's writings. The cortical cells could just as well affect each other directly, and finally find discharge along different pathways, without their having to squander energy on useless psychic phenomena. Choices have no place in Pavlov's world.[86] What happens are reflexes, and reflexes are rigidly determined (Pavlov, 1926, p. 32). And—at least in 1903—Pavlov did not find any essential differences between plant tropisms and man's eternal search for truth. "The movement of plants toward the light," he asked rhetorically, "and the seeking of truth through a mathematical analysis—are these not phenomena belonging to the same order?" Pavlov's answer was in the affirmative; they are each the last link in a chain of adaptabilities.

It is striking that the two core situations—that of Pavlov's objective psychology and that of psychoanalysis—should be so completely mutually exclusive. Pavlov's initial situation is structured in such a way that only medial processes can reach the level of observation; Freud's initial situation, on the other hand, is structured in such a way that only system processes can come to observation: whether the subject is silent or babbles or talks reasonably, he is forced to reveal system properties.

Nevertheless, Freud did not deny the existence of medial processes, while in Pavlov's system there seems to be no place left for systemic functions or processes. Because of this essential difference between Pav-

[84] More recently, Kubie (1958a) once more asserted that Pavlov and Freud represent "mutually supplementary techniques which are in no way opposed to one another, either in technical procedure or in theoretical implications."

[85] It is highly improbable—not to say preposterous—to expect that, in recording the number of salivary drops produced by dogs tied to a stall and exposed to a minimum of stimulation, Pavlov could learn anything significant about mankind, which built the Pyramids and Chartres. It would be just as improbable—and no less preposterous—to expect that Freud should be able to derive from the psychoanalytic core situation, while listening to his patients' free associations in relation to their dreams, conclusions about the number of salivary drops produced by Pavlov's dogs.

[86] The concept of choice is, of course, not contradictory to the law of determination (Freud), since the choices themselves are determined.

lov and Freud, the one studying medial processes and the other systemic, it is basically correct to say that they are diametrical opposites. Yet there are points at which they could meet. Should Pavlov's experimental situation take a turn that made the observation of systemic phenomena inescapable, then agreement might occur; and similarly, if the followers of Freud were to be forced to investigate medial processes.

Pavlov's theories can be criticized from two standpoints. One can set forth observations and theories gained from other areas, and point out the contradiction between them and objective psychology; or one can examine objective psychology on its own grounds, so to speak, to see whether it is internally consistent and fulfills what it promises.

Even if one leaves aside for the time being the more complex psychological configurations, and limits oneself to the simplest situation, Pavlov's core situation—to which he returns innumerable times, and upon which he built objective psychology—one meets with a combination of factors that gives rise to doubt and puzzlement.

The first thing that strikes one is a peculiar antinomy—namely that, if Pavlov is correct in his analysis and interpretation of the core situation, conditioned reflexes cannot be formed under conditions outside the laboratory, and therefore cannot have the relevance to the animal's learning process that Pavlov himself sought to attribute to them.[87] In order to demonstrate the formation of conditioned reflexes, Pavlov puts the experimental animal into an environment devoid of external stimuli. This, to begin with, never occurs in nature. Thereupon, he introduces one single stimulus, or a pattern of stimuli, that is to be conditioned, and this is followed by the unconditioned stimulus. The same situation is then repeated several times, without the slightest variation, until the erstwhile neutral stimulus evokes a conditioned reflex.

The establishment of conditioned reflexes is an extremely sensitive affair. When the dog is put on a table, instead of in the usual experimental situation (Pavlov, 1903, p. 55), or is moved from one room to another,[88] or when the experimenter is changed (Pavlov, 1926, p. 45), then the reflexes disappear—at least, temporarily. On the other hand, it may be sufficient to have a piece of clothing belonging to the experi-

---

[87] Hebb (1949, p. 174f.) has made the astute observation—which overthrows the very foundation of Pavlov's theory—that the conditioned response is by no means a duplicate of the unconditioned. If Pavlov's theory were correct, once the dog heard the bell ring, he would have "to make eating movements, with his nose in the food dish, until the food itself appears."

[88] See, however, Boguslavsky (1958, p. 269) for a different opinion.

menter brought back into the room, to have the reflex reappear, after it has disappeared (Pavlov, 1925, p. 366).

As to the influence of traumatic events, there are contradictory claims. Pavlov repeatedly asserted that the flood in Leningrad in 1924 made conditioned reflexes disappear. Leake (Brazier, 1959, p. 173f.), however, maintained that, even after the 300 days of the Leningrad siege, during which the animals had not been under study, all their conditioned reflexes were found intact. The present opinion of Soviet physiologists seems to be that "once a conditioned reflex was established, it could never be removed."[89] According to Pavlov, the effect of the trauma of the flood had been so great that, subsequently, even the sound of bubbling water had the same effect as the original trauma.

I emphasize here the necessity for exact repetition, which is postulated as a prerequisite for the formation of a conditioned reflex (see, however, Hull, 1939, p. 9). What is the likelihood that such coincidences will occur outside of the laboratory, particularly if we take into consideration all the other factors that are apparently necessary for the establishment of reliable conditioned reflexes? Furthermore, Pavlov has also demonstrated that if the conditioned stimulus occurs a few times without being followed by the unconditioned one, the former quickly becomes neutral. Are there many situations in nature in which events are as regularly coupled as Pavlov deems necessary for the formation of conditioned reflexes, so that the animal could ever acquire those reliable patterns so urgently needed for survival?[90]

If Pavlov's interpretation of the core situation were correct—that is, if animals could learn only by way of conditioned reflexes—then it would be a miracle, indeed, for animals to survive at all. Hull has offered an illuminating example of a situation basic to survival in which conditioned-reflex learning makes no sense. It concerns defense reflexes. For obvious reasons, it is necessary for survival that the animal not come

[89] The discussion that followed Leake's statement, on the semantics of the word "remove," indicates some of the problems connected with the finding. To what extent, in case this new theory is confirmed, it would destroy Pavlov's classic theory, I do not know. At any rate, it will be interpreted by many as a confirmation of one of Freud's basic findings on the human psyche—namely, the indestructibleness of memories.

[90] This objection to Pavlov's core experiments may perhaps sound as if I were ignorant of the essentials of experimental technique. How often does it happen in nature that a ray of light goes through a prism in an otherwise dark environment? Yet Newton was right in his conclusion that white light is a composite of the colors of the spectrum. If it can be proved under any particular set of conditions that white light is a composite, however, then it is thereby proved that it is always a composite. Pavlov's experimental situation is differently structured.

into direct contact with dangerous agents, but instead take flight upon its first perception of a danger signal. Now, if the conditioned defense reflex is successful and the animal escapes, the unconditioned stimulus will not follow, and there will be no reinforcement. The consequences would therefore be that, after a few successful escapes, the conditioned reflex would weaken and even disappear; the animal would then no longer respond immediately to danger signals, but rather wait until the actual stimulus reached it—a situation which would expose it over and over again to contact with the dangerous agent. If, however, the experimentally demonstrated extinction of conditioned reflexes is not operative with regard to defense reflexes, the animal would have to continue to react—but to irrelevant stimuli; and thus a disorganized pattern of behavior would set in (Hull, 1929, pp. 509-511).

There is a study, whose merits have not yet been sufficiently recognized, in which Gustav and Wolf (1937) have demonstrated with particular clarity the untenability of Pavlov's theory. Their essential point is that the concept of the conditioned reflex is not adequate to explain human development. Even observations made during the course of the conditioning of newborn infants will lead to wrong conclusions, if they are not checked against observations made under natural conditions.[91] Further, Albanian children who, because of their environmental conditions, had shown developmental deficits, caught up in their development, once they were brought under proper conditions, with a rapidity contrary to what was to be expected, if conditioned reflexes were the leading mechanism of development (Danziger and Frankl, 1934).

The introduction of object constancies is also left unexplained by a theory of conditioned reflexes. One of the most basic steps in human development is to draw out of the infinite flow of sensations and perceptions certain patterns, which show a specific structure, and thus gradually acquire the character of objects. In order to achieve this, a multiplicity of stimuli must be neutralized (Gustav and Wolf, p. 329), a process that is not to be confused with Pavlov's inhibition or differentiation. (Piaget's [1936, 1937] work may be cited in this context, to

[91] The authors demonstrate this by utilizing the study by Marquis (1931) who tried to prove that, contrary to Pavlov, even the newborn can acquire conditioned reflexes. In general one obtains the impression that observation of the dogs under laboratory conditions prevented Pavlov from the observation of many phenomena that would now be described as *imprinting*. (See Scott [1962] for a survey of animal experimentation far closer to natural conditions than that of Pavlov.)

demonstrate the whole complexity of development in the infant, from reflex dependency to thought, insight and action.) I found the argument particularly convincing when Gustav and Wolf described two possible outcomes, if man were compelled to cope with his environment solely by means of conditioned reflexes and their extinction. This could lead, they asserted, either to a form of existence in which almost every stimulus produces reflexes, since an enormous number of stimuli would become accidentally conditioned (the world being, in effect, overloaded with meanings);[92] or, if the extinction of conditioned reflexes does occur, then the upshot would be the return to a condition of rigid limitation to such reflexes, such as obtained in the initial stage.

In the following, I want to add to the observations that have been adduced to contravene Pavlovian psychology two observations of my own, which I have made in a Welsh terrier: As a puppy he learned, after a few futile attempts, to abstain from chasing birds, but never from chasing squirrels, although he was equally unsuccessful in ever catching one. (As I learned later, this seems to be a specific characteristic. Cf. Lorenz, n. d., p. 126.) Furthermore, every evening his dish with food is put into a corner of the kitchen and almost every night he waits until his master picks it up and carries it into the bathroom adjoining the master's bedroom. Then the dog starts prancing excitedly ahead and, depending on the intensity of his appetite, he starts to eat either immediately or after a while. It is rather exceptional for him to eat his food in the kitchen; when this does happen, he leaves a portion in the dish, waiting as usual until it is carried into the bathroom. This ritual developed gradually. Since the dog was a poor eater as a puppy, his master carried the dish, that had been left untouched by the dog in the kitchen, into the bathroom, in order to give the puppy an opportunity to satisfy his hunger during the night. This resulted in the dog's habit of eating his main meal around midnight, almost exclusively in the bathroom. He is, however, quite ready to eat tidbits at any time of the day or at any place. It is also noteworthy that the ritual subsides whenever another dog is present, who, following natural inclinations, eats his food in the kitchen as soon as it is offered. Furthermore, when the dog was taken to the country during the summer months, he developed a new ritual which was quite different from that which he maintained during his city life.

[92] Cf. Hull (1929, p. 509f.) for the defense reflex.

I do not see how either of these observations could have been explained with even the full panoply of Pavlovian psychology.

To learn about the present status of Pavlovian psychology, one should study the report of the first Conference on the Central Nervous System and Behavior (Brazier, 1959). After perusal of that document, one wonders how much is really left of the classical theory, as Pavlov developed it. The crux of the matter is expressed by Teuber when he stresses the fact that the "relation [of the Pavlovian concepts] to actual events in the brain is so entirely hypothetical," and wonders why those concepts have assumed such a crucial role in theory construction. "Perhaps," he continues, "the reason is that Pavlov's constructs had been enunciated in such a forceful way by a distinguished physiologist, as if they were physiological entities" (Brazier, 1959, p. 180f.).

Indeed, it would be quite surprising if a valid conclusion could be drawn regarding the structure of processes involving the central nervous system, merely from the observation of stimuli and responsive behavior. After all, the bulk of Freud's conclusions has to do with psychic processes, and he reached those conclusions from the observation of psychic phenomena. Pavlov, on the other hand, observed behavior under the impact of stimulated sense organs and reconstructed physiological processes.[93]

The leap from stimulus-response behavior to physiological process is a dangerous one, and scientifically not warranted. Lashley's experiment with the brain itself makes Pavlov's basic construct highly questionable (Brazier, 1959, p. 228f. See, however, Zangwill, 1961, for the limitations of Lashley's views.).

Let us take Pavlov's core situation. In principle, if one begins by not seeking any observation arrived at by other methods, then the processes in the central nervous system intervening between receptor and efferent organ may be constructed at will. I am therefore at liberty to assume that the conditioned stimulus excites the whole cortex, while the neutral stimulus excites only certain groups of cells. According to this construct, the subcortical center would respond only when the whole cortex was excited. But in this context I would have been at equal liberty to assume that the conditioned stimulus excites only special cell groups, etc.

What I am saying is that the central nervous system has its own structure, and that this does not follow some logic derived from other areas

[93] Cf. Vowles (1961): ". . . the dangers of equating behavioural complexity—which may itself be only apparent—with complexity of neural mechanism" (p. 28f.).

of observation, and then imposed on it. It is my impression that Pavlov, in spite of his efforts to free his research from any possible anthropomorphizing construct or imagery, actually indulged in such imagery quite unrestrainedly when talking about processes in the central nervous system.

When the dog falls asleep, the cells of his brain are inhibited. Perhaps so. I could just as well have assumed that a sleep center has been over-stimulated—but for the fact that sleep is certainly *experienced* as an inhibition. I could show a similar anthropomorphizing tendency in most of the concepts proposed by Pavlov. As a matter of fact, even now, after the stupendous progress that neurophysiology has made since Pavlov, it is still unclear "what goes on in the brain during conditioning, whatever conditioning may be," and whether conditioning is not a very special case (Teuber, in Brazier, 1959, p. 228).

Freud warned against drawing conclusions from the psyche with regard to the cerebrum. It would have been an easy enough matter to have postulated a 'conflict' between subcortex and cortex, in view of the universal 'conflict' between passion and reason; but observations made within the psyche are neutral in this respect, and the findings of psychoanalysis are not changed by whether or not the neurophysiologist discovers a disequilibrium between cortex and subcortex, or between different areas of the cortex. One would not be entitled to derive from either finding a contradiction to the psychoanalytic observation.

I agree with Schilder when he says: "When animal experimentation invades the field of higher nervous activity and behavior of animals, it should not be forgotten that its results cannot be valid when contradicting acknowledged results of psychological research" (Schilder, 1935, p. 170).[94] Schilder speaks of Pavlov's physiology as "pseudophysiology, popular mosaic psychology expressed in physiological terms" (*ibid.*). It can also be called, as some have called it, a "brain mythology." I shall give examples later of assertions that Pavlov made concerning brain processes—assertions which are so improbable that it hardly seems necessary even to discuss them. Yet Pavlov describes these processes with the sort of conviction and certainty that one usually expresses when referring to sensory data.

Now one may say that the cerebral processes, as they are described by

[94] These words were, apparently, aimed at Pavlov's theory of the mosaic character of the cortex (Pavlov, 1926, pp. 219-233), a theory which hardly any neurophysiologist will defend at present.

Pavlov, are equivalent to Freud's metapsychology. Yet that would be quite without justification. When Freud speaks of a 'psychic apparatus,' and describes a variety of processes involved in its structuralization (as he does in his metapsychological papers), he is always aware that he is dealing with auxiliary constructions, and therefore repeatedly expresses his readiness to replace them with more suitable ones, as soon as clinical evidence should have showed up any or all of them as inappropriate. Furthermore, in his metapsychology, Freud was not attempting to transcend psychology; instead, on the basis of a very large number of psychological observations, he was trying to reconstruct in abstract terms the underlying processes involved.[95] The leap from observations made of specific events to a general description is a quite legitimate and necessary step in science. Pavlov, however, observed only stimuli and behavior, and his attempt to leap from that series of observations to a generalization of the physiological processes is not legitimate. It is amazing that physiologists should still continue to think in Pavlovian terms, as if they were unaware that these terms involve constructs, most of which have not been validated by observation. The certainty, however, with which Pavlov himself employed terms that denoted constructs and not perceptive contents warrants the use of the characterization, 'brain mythology.'

By contrast, it is of interest to observe the bearing of experimentation upon psychoanalytic findings, in a field that has been so extremely controversial as that of Freud's dream symbols. The way in which Freud was able to find translations for certain dream elements, for which patients frequently did not produce any associations—or none, at least, that contributed anything relevant to their interpretation—need not be discussed here (cf. Freud, 1900, pp. 350-353). Suffice it to say that the source of Freud's insight did not lie outside the field of psychology (or of its application to culture).

The symbols suggested by Freud were confirmed by experiments conducted by Hartmann and Betlheim (1924), with patients suffering from Korsakoff's psychosis.[96] Here a certain form of organic pathology results in a change of memory functioning of such a nature that, when the patient tries to recall the contents of the past, it is a subjective imagery that comes to his mind instead. The medial aspect of the memory func-

---

[95] I am not discussing here Freud's (1937b) clinical reconstructions, which fall into a different category of inductive methodology.

[96] Freud's symbols were also confirmed by Schroetter (1912), through dreams experimentally induced in hypnotized subjects.

tion has been gravely disturbed; memory now serves for the expression of contents significant of the subject-system.[97] To regard these experiments as confirmatory of Freud's findings is legitimate, since Freud's theory of symbols is not rooted in matters of physiology. It is, in fact, altogether irrelevant to the psychological theory of symbols which part of the cerebrum may be diseased, or with what kind of disease it may be affected, so long as contents of one character are spontaneously replaced with others, in accordance with the rule of correlations asserted by Freud.

The factual part of Pavlov's discoveries neither confirms nor contradicts Freud's findings, since it contains references only to medial processes. If, however, it had been proven that (1) Pavlov's assumption is correct that psychogenic causation is nonexistent, and (2) all of human or animal behavior is reflex reaction to external and internal stimuli, then psychoanalytic theory would have had to be essentially changed. Galambos states: "Imagine an organism . . . not capable of acting 'hungry,' 'thirsty,' 'sexually motivated,' and the rest. Conditioning studies on it would certainly turn out differently, and perhaps learning would be impossible" (Brazier, p. 287).

Furthermore, observations made of an animal in an environment devoid of stimuli except one—interesting and important as they may be— are, in my opinion, a poor foundation for a theory designed to encompass the psychic life of animal and man. Yet Pavlov was never able to detach himself from this basic situation, and in 1932 he reasserted most emphatically: "The central physiological phenomenon in the normal work of the cerebral hemispheres is what we have called the conditioned reflex" (Pavlov, 1932a, p. 87). Several auxiliary processes had to be assumed in order to explain the colossal variety of behavior patterns actually observed, even under the simplified laboratory conditions. Yet it must not be forgotten that 'hypnotization,' which gravely interferes with the 'normal' functioning of the cerebrum, "begins when the dog enters the experimental room, sometimes even before he gets on the stand, increasing as the experiment progresses" (Pavlov, 1932b, p. 77).

The processes or mechanisms in the brain which are necessary, according to Pavlov, for the explanation of behavior are: excitation, inhibition, extinction, irradiation, concentration, positive and negative induction

[97] The experiments by Hartmann and Betlheim are also significant, in this context, in that the aspect of memory disturbance that is demonstrated cannot be explained in any way by the conditioning of reflexes.

and disinhibition. None of these processes was studied by direct physio-logical observation; they were all constructs, based on the observations of reflexes under changing laboratory conditions. All the concepts involved are anthropomorphic in nature, the result of the way in which a mind trained in physiology would feel inclined to assume that a brain cell, or the cortex or a part of the cortex must behave, if it is to produce the observed reflex.

The following quotation about negativism in dogs may serve as a sample of 'brain-mythological' thinking:

> The conditioned stimulation from the area of the cortex is more or less uninhibited, producing innervated excitation in the correspondingly positive innervated part of the motor area, which on account of its hypnotized state is in the paradoxical phase. Therefore the stimulation does not lead to excitation of this part but to a deeper inhibition. Then this unusual and localized inhibition evokes, by the law of reciprocal induction, excitation of the negative phase of negativism. On removal of the stimulus the unusually inhibited positive part passes, by virtue of internal reciprocal induction, into the excitatory state, and the in-duced excitation of the negative part becomes inhibitory and of itself positively induces the positive part. Thus the positive part after the first of its unusual inhibitions becomes doubly excited. Consequently, if the hypnotization does not go further after giving and removing the food one or several times, the positive phase predominates and the dog begins to eat [Pavlov, 1932b, p. 80f.].

By juggling the concepts employed above, *any* observation made in the laboratory can be explained. Pavlov's theory cannot be disproved with-in the framework of his research setup, because it is structured in such a way that no possible behavior pattern could fall outside it. We find some-thing similar in religious thinking: when an earthquake destroys all the houses, but leaves the church standing, that is taken to be a sure sign of God's will; but if it is the church alone that is destroyed (as happened once in Spain), then that is interpreted as God's benevolent warning.

To be sure, Pavlov's statement, quoted above, may be correct. But in order to prove that this is so, neurophysiologists will have to make great progress in their experimental work. There is reason enough to doubt even Pavlov's fundamental conception of the reflex and, as far as I know, Lashley's tentative conclusions have not yet been disproved.[98] It seems

[98] Or at least have not become obsolete. (For arguments against the theory of equi-potentiality, see Hebb, 1949, pp. 39-43.)

almost incredible that, after the experimental evidence that Lashley brought to light, objective psychologists have nevertheless continued to use a terminology that may actually have no objective referents.

More incredible still is the fact that Pavlov himself brushed aside a study which so completely fulfilled the highest standards of experimentation as did Lashley's, with the simple statement that the latter (and W. Koehler, and R. M. Yerkes) "evidently have the desire that their subject remain unexplained" (Wells, 1956, p. 61). Lashley, aside from his factual evidence, has the merit of putting his finger on the two danger points of Pavlov's way of forming theories. In discussing Pavlov's positing of inhibitors and inhibitors of inhibitors, he asserts that the necessity for the formation of new hypotheses can be resolved "by making enough gratuitous assumptions concerning elementary neurophysiology,"[99] and he adds: "But the truth is that our hypotheses have so far exceeded our facts as to be beyond any experimental test, and the piling on of a few more speculations is likely to make the whole structure collapse of its own weight" (1929, p. 126). Furthermore, in discussing the lucidity of explanations achieved by means of the reflex hypothesis, he adds: "But this lucidity has been achieved at the sacrifice of truth and it seems better to admit ignorance and to be guilty of vagueness rather than blind ourselves to significant problems" (p. 172).[100]

Lashley was not the only neurophysiologist to demonstrate the shortcomings of Pavlov's mosaic theory, but his experiments do so with particular effectiveness. The relative equipotentiality of cortical areas, if confirmed by further investigations (and the theory does not seem to have been disproved as yet; cf. Brazier, 1959, pp. 228f., 242, 259; cf. Zangwill, 1961), is incompatible with Pavlov's classical theory. Not only in neurophysiology, but—as we presently shall see—also in psychiatry, Pavlov thought he could demonstrate "correspondences between ever more restricted anatomical divisions and smaller units of behavior until some ultimate anatomical and behavioristic elements are reached"; "but this is clearly not the principle of neural organization" (Lashley, 1929, p. 162).

The crux of the matter is "that the unit of neural organization is not

[99] As a matter of fact, even today one does not know for certain whether the inhibitory process hypothesized by Pavlov really exists at all (cf. Brazier, 1959, p. 324).

[100] Cf. also: "The [reflex] theory has the advantage of simplicity which makes for its popularity as a slogan; but when one is confronted with the necessity of accounting for a particular group of activities, above the level of the spinal reflexes, . . . the inadequacies of the theory become evident" (p. 163).

the reflex arc" (p. 161), and Lashley's findings point to "a functional organization independent of differentiated structure and to some more general energy relations within the central nervous system" (p. 167). In other words, "functional differentiation must be largely independent of both the macroscopic and microscopic structural differentiation" (p. 125).[101]

Be that as it may, Pavlov's general theories are of lesser relevance here than are those that he held about the neuroses, a subject that is central to psychoanalytic research. As is well known, Pavlov derived his own theory of neuroses from the observation of dogs. He succeeded—or so he and his school assert—in producing experimental neuroses in dogs. Yet the assertion—if correct—that neuroses do occur in dogs would in effect destroy one of Pavlov's own chief tenets—that of the precise "machine-like" responsiveness of organisms (Pavlov, 1926, p. 14f.). Machines cannot have neuroses; they can only break down or suffer from dysfunction. A neurosis presupposes that something happens that ought not to happen, or that something does not happen that ought to.

For example: A man wants to cross a street in order to shake hands with a friend, but at that very moment he is seized by an attack of anxiety and must stop; or a man wants to insert his erected penis, and at that same moment loses the erection. These are two typically neurotic symptoms.[102] Yet the neurosis does not consist per se, in the man's momentary inability to cross the street, nor in his losing the erection.

If, upon starting to cross the street, he observed that a car was approaching, at great speed; or if, upon setting out to insert his penis, he observed his mistress's husband enter the room—under such circumstances, the very same behavioristic outcomes would have taken place, but without any neurotic implication. On the contrary, if under those conditions, he

[101] The untenability of Pavlov's classical theory is also revealed in some passages from the writings of his own school. See, for example, Bykov (1942): "We must acknowledge that any newly formed temporary connection is of a complex nature, for it includes the concealed stimulation from the *milieu intérieur*. Thus, a temporary connection is not a reflex in the generally accepted meaning of the term, but a complex reaction of a higher order, though resembling in some of its features a usual reflex. Therefore, a temporary connection is an intermediary link between reflex processes and psychic phenomena. The mechanism of the formation and development of this complex reaction enables us to approach more closely that which we subjectively recognize as a sensation" (p. 392f.). A vast retrenchment of Pavlovian claims is likewise implied when Bykov writes of "Pavlov, the founder of the physiological theory on the activity of the *substratum* of psychic phenomena" (p. 403; italics mine). See Adrian (1946) for a discussion of the relationship of certain neurophysiological hypotheses to psychoanalysis.

[102] These examples do not, of course, cover the entire area of neurosis, since neuroses may occur in man without the disturbance of overt and observable functions.

had crossed the street, or *had* started intercourse, then that might well have been taken as indicative of a far more serious disturbance than a neurosis. The attack of anxiety and the cessation of the erection were neurotic symptoms, not simply because they interfered with the subject's goal attainment, but because the failure of goal attainment was brought about by an inner conflict.[103]

For a change in behavior to be neurotic, therefore, certain preliminary conditions must be present: (a) the subject's complaint; (b) the failure of achievement because of internal reasons; (c) the evaluation of the subject's behavior in relation to a normative base line (that of goal attainment under a different set of internal conditions). Yet these alone are merely the surface elements of the neurosis. In terms of system characteristics, a neurosis also requires the existence of (d) a conflict, in which at least one of the conflicting forces is not conscious, or—and this is so more often than not—both conflicting forces lie outside the realm of consciousness.[104]

As far as I can see, only one of these conditions is fulfilled in the so-called animal neuroses.[105] In those states in the dog which the objective psychologist calls neuroses, the animal does show signs of displeasure, it does want to escape from the situation—which, I suppose, may be taken as the equivalent of the 'complaint' of a human being. In other words, it is highly probable that, if the dog did possess the faculty of speech, it would say, under such conditions: "I am suffering."

The failure of achievement, however, is demonstrated by the objective psychologist in terms of the dog's failure to form new conditioned reflexes, or to maintain those already acquired. Yet those situations are assigned arbitrarily by the experimenter as the base line of normal behavior in the dog. If Pavlov's basic theory is accepted, then the so-called 'neurotic behavior' of dogs can be nothing else than the manifestation of unconditioned reflexes (for example, defense reflexes), or of conditioned reflexes, since there are no other categories of possible behavior. 'Neurotic

[103] Not every failure of goal attainment because of inner conflict is neurotic; but an exact differentiation would, at this point, lead us too far afield.

[104] Unusual clinical examples of neuroses can also be cited, which do not live up to all conditions I have enumerated. It is not to be expected that, in a formulation of principle, all the fringe occurrences can be included. There are, for example, many instances known in which no complaints occur. Such instances do not negate the scheme, however, for the conditions are well known under which the neurotic who has repressed the displeasure caused by the symptoms would nevertheless become conscious of them.

[105] I limit myself here to the writings of Pavlov at present in English translation, and to Gantt (1944).

behavior' in dogs would then mean nothing more than the fact that some conditioned or unconditioned reflexes have occurred which ought not to have occurred, or that some conditioned or unconditioned reflexes have not occurred which ought to have occurred.

With regard to the human being, the 'ought' or 'ought not' can be determined by reference to the subject's *intention* and to his (objectively determinable) *functional potential;* with regard to the dog, it is the *experimenter alone* who does the determining. Even the situation on the basis of which he establishes the base line of the dog's normal behavior (Pavlov's core situation) is an artificial one; and there would be nothing to prevent the experimenter from positing that any dog which—upon being tied to its stall—formed conditioned reflexes, in conformity with the experimenter's prediction, was a neurotic one.

On what rational grounds can it be asserted that it is more normal for a dog to form conditioned reflexes while in the *camera,* than to bark and to make all sorts of attempts to run away? For, after all, we do know that the dog has freedom reflexes, too (Pavlov, 1917).[106] I do not see on what grounds the activation of one type of reflex as against that of some other type can justly be made a yardstick of normalcy, of neurosis, or of any other behavioral category of that order. Here would be an opportunity to demonstrate the fallacy inherent in the concept of 'adjustment,' as it is understood in most psychologies. In the case of Pavlov's doctrine, this becomes particularly evident, since no attempt was apparently made to determine whether the type of dog most suitable for the experiments in conditioning is also the type that possesses the best chances for survival under natural conditions.

Yet, whatever the specific nature of an animal's behavior may be, it is always, according to Pavlov, the product of two variables: stimulus and

---

106 As a matter of fact, the bulk of Gantt's experimental dogs were highly selected, unruly dogs usually being discarded (Gantt, 1944, p. 37). The whole idea of taking the disturbance of conditioned reflexes as the yardstick for neurotic behavior is, in my opinion, an unwarranted transfer of certain concepts of human behavior to animals. I assume that the argument runs somewhat as follows: When a person undresses, goes to bed and turns off the light, he has created a *milieu* of stimuli that conditions him for sleep; if this conditioned reflex does not occur, however, then he must be suffering from neurotic insomnia. This, however, would be an unwarranted conclusion. The conditioned stimulus may fail to evoke the conditioned reflex, for example, only because the subject is preoccupied with important work that demands continued thought, or because he has just been told that a close relative is suffering from a fatal disease. If the conditioned reflex did still occur unfailingly under such conditions, then *that* fact might well be taken as a sign of disturbance.

brain process.[107] The stimulus is a chance factor, dependent on changes in the environment. The brain process consists of a shuffling and re-shuffling of excitations and inhibitions that irradiate or concentrate. No matter how wide the variety of the events in the cerebrum may be, they are rigidly determined and therefore apersonal. At this point, to be sure, Pavlov and his school introduce another variable—the dog's 'tempera-ment' (a highly anthropomorphic concept). It is this temperament that will decide whether a brain cell is stable, excitable or lethargic. In any case, however, it too is physiologically given, so that the principle of rigid determination is not endangered by that variable.

How is the occurrence of a neurosis possible under such conditions? The very concept of deviation makes no sense, unless we introduce a value system. As a matter of fact, Gantt, the principal American spokes-man for Pavlov's school, writes, in conjunction with experimental neu-roses: "The animal must decide between right and wrong, i.e., what corresponds to reality and what does not." Here he not only falls into the worst kind of anthropomorphic projection, but he also offends a basic Pavlovian precept: for choice definitely lies outside of the realm of reflexes (Gustav and Wolf, 1937, p. 315). What is more, he asserts something for which there is no trace of experimental evidence. The making of a decision always presupposes the ability to weigh alternative possibilities; but nothing has been set forth that even suggests that an animal is endowed with that ability.[108]

In his discussion of experimentally induced neuroses, another factor is introduced by Pavlov, "*a difficult collision, an unusual confronting of the two opposing processes of excitation and inhibition*" (Pavlov, 1925b, p. 361, italics by Pavlov). This state Gantt (1944) called "conflict," writing: "The term conflict is based upon the concept for which there is some evidence that excitation and inhibition are mutually exclusive processes" (p. 42). As I have pointed out before, it is still quite debatable whether a process of inhibition exists at all in the cerebrum, and caution is all the more in order, therefore, with regard to any supposed conflict between excitation and inhibition. Gantt is apparently aware of this, for

[107] The state of the effector organ can be omitted in this context; the state of the brain cell belongs, as I shall presently indicate, to the brain process.

[108] This will be disputed by some animal psychologists. See, for example, Lorenz (1952). But even if my formulation should be proven to be too extreme, there may be agreement that the dog's sudden *decision "between right and wrong"* is an unwar-ranted assumption, which would not be able to hold a legitimate place in Pavlov's own construction of what a dog is.

he writes: "Pavlov's concept of the collision of excitatory and inhibitory processes is an hypothetical one with little direct factual evidence."

So far so good; it is surprising, however, that he adds: "Such a state of affairs, however, is common in the physical sciences." By way of examples, he refers to atoms, molecules, the electronic theory, etc., remarking that they "are fully as theoretical as are Pavlov's theories of brain dynamics" (1944, p. 179). I am certain that the physicists would object strenuously to such assertions, and would point to considerable 'factual evidence'[109] at their command, of a sort that is missing in Pavlov's experimental neuroses. Be that as it may, it is interesting to examine the history of the concept of collision or conflict in Pavlov's theory of neurosis.

It seems certain that it was while he was reading one of Freud's case histories that this idea struck his mind.[110] A female patient of Freud's had had to nurse her father, who she knew would soon die. She suffered terribly from this knowledge, yet "had to take pains to appear cheerful vis-à-vis her father in order to conceal the danger from him" (Pavlov, 1956, vol. 1, p. 467). Freud—or so Pavlov asserts—had found out by psychoanalysis that this was the basic trauma leading later to the neurosis. Pavlov evidently refers here to the case history of Elizabeth von R. (Breuer and Freud, 1893-1895, pp. 135-181).

Yet Pavlov did not reproduce Freud's observation correctly. What Freud wrote was that the patient "forced herself to appear cheerful, while he [the father] reconciled himself to his hopeless state with uncomplaining resignation" (ibid., p. 140). The patient was exposed to such conflict for many months without any neurotic effect. Freud rightly remarked that "it was a case history made up of commonplace emotional upheavals, and there was *nothing about it* to explain why it was particularly from hysteria that she fell ill, or why her hysteria took the particular form of a painful abasia" (Italics mine; Breuer and Freud, 1893-1895, p. 144).

[109] When the degree of certainty and exactness that is characteristic of physical theories is claimed for a theoretical edifice as vague and questionable as Pavlov's neurotic brain processes—which are almost wholly derived from observations of the relationship between stimuli and behavior—then we are face to face with basic problems of thought or, more precisely, of the psychology of scientific thought. I pointed earlier to a similar state of affairs in Pavlov's work, when he set forth what could at best be a hypothesis, as if it were the content of sense data.

[110] In his Wednesday seminar of January 14, 1931 (Pavlov, 1956, vol. 1, p. 102), he reported this, later expressing to Ralph Gerard his indebtedness to Freud (Kubie, 1959, p. 33). It is, therefore, all the more surprising to hear that Pavlov apparently felt an aversion to Freud. At least one of the participants in the seminar of February 27, 1935, when Pavlov propounded a theory that coincided with one of Freud's, referred to Freud as one "whom you do not particularly like" (Pavlov, 1956, vol. 3, p. 105).

As a matter of fact, the first incident that laid the seed of the later neurosis was quite different. At the urging of her father, the patient had once, during her father's illness, gone to a party where she met a man with whom she had been in love. Returning home "in a blissful frame of mind, she found that her father was worse, and reproached herself most bitterly" (*ibid.*, p. 146). Freud thought it was the contrast between these blissful feelings and the worsening of her father's state that constituted "a conflict, a situation of incompatibility." The outcome of this conflict was that the erotic idea was repressed from association.

In the light of later discoveries, we have to add, of course, the unconscious feeling of guilt aroused by this accidental coincidence. This type of conflict is far more complicated than the one that Pavlov seemed to remember, and which he regarded as a "collision of the excitatory and inhibitory processes" (Pavlov, *ibid.*). Furthermore, it is historically important that Pavlov had apparently read the *Studies on Hysteria*, for Chapter III ("Theoretical") by Breuer, as I will presently show, should take a prominent place in any historical review of objective psychology.

Though it is difficult to see how Freud's case histories in the *Studies on Hysteria* might have given rise to a theory that explains neuroses in animals through the collision between excitation and inhibition in the form of an unresolvable problem, one detects in Josef Breuer's third chapter, views that come surprisingly close to Pavlov's basic theory of neuroses. Indeed, one may call them almost identical. In discussing circumstances that bring about "an abnormal somatic phenomenon in which the excitation is discharged" (Breuer and Freud, 1893-1895, p. 210), Breuer refers to observations Mach (1875) had made when studying *Bewegungsempfindungen* ("sensations of movement"). Mach had observed the onset of a feeling of nausea when sensations of movement were in discordance with the optical impression. The same sensation occurred when he attempted to force stereoscopic images which were widely separated. Mach's theory was a physiological one: stimuli were prevented from proceeding on the proper tract and had to enter others. Breuer added: "Here we have nothing less than the physiological pattern for the generation of pathologically hysterical phenomena as a result of the coexistence of vivid ideas which are irreconcilable with one another" (*ibid.*, p. 2). It will not be without piquancy when the historian of science takes notice of the fact that in the writings of one and the same scholar two sciences as different as psychoanalysis and objective psychology were foreshadowed.

Pavlov's pathophysiology of neuroses thus appears to be a simplified version of what Breuer had already expressed much earlier about the physiological substratum of hysteria in humans, in a less anthropomorphic imagery than is implied in the picture of a battle going on in the cerebrum between excitation and inhibition. Yet here we might do well to retrace the steps that Pavlov took. A rather complex situation in human affairs was reduced to a simple one, in which two ego-syntonic impulses or feelings (according to Pavlov, "I have to pretend cheerfulness" vs. "I am grieved by the knowledge of impending death") come into conflict because of a reality situation.[111] Any person exposed to such circumstances would be likely to feel an impulse and its inhibition—which could, in general terms, be called a clash between excitation and inhibition. But, without hesitation, this frame of subjective human feelings was projected onto the dog's cerebrum by Pavlov, and from then on treated as if it had to do with events actually observed in space and time.

The situation of choice, however, by means of which Pavlov and his school attempt to prove the correctness of the theory of experimental neuroses in animals, is one in which the differentiation of stimuli is made impossible for the experimental animal. A dog is conditioned positively to a stimulus consisting of, let us say, one hundred metronome beats, and negatively to one of sixty beats. This difference of forty beats does not impose upon the animal any particularly difficult task of differentiation. The negative conditioned stimulus is now increased, with no observable change in the dog's behavior and achievement. When, however, the negative conditioned stimulus comes close to the positive stimulus—when it reaches, let us say, 96 or 98 beats—then reactions begin to be observed that are regarded as neurotic. The animal becomes, temporarily at least, incapable of differentiating between the stimuli it has easily distinguished up to then, and it may start whining, refuse food and even try to escape.

According to Pavlov and his school, the neurosogenic stimulus is now creating both excitation and inhibition, for 96 beats is close enough to 100 to elicit at the same time both the positive conditioned reflex of excitation and the negative conditioned reflex of inhibition. Since Pavlov believed that excitation and inhibition are processes that can be added

111 Under *such* conditions, no neurosis can ever arise, not only according to Freud's theories, but also in the light of repeated clinical observations. The precipitating conflict that Freud has described can under no circumstances be reduced to the opposition of two contradictory brain processes.

and subtracted, one would expect the result to be zero, in so far as the two processes keep each other balanced; as a matter of fact, however, all dogs seem to show, under such circumstances, unusual behavior of varying severity, from moderate restlessness and panting of short duration (Gantt, 1944, p. 50), to severe changes—such as the refusal to eat, the appearance of defense reflexes where positive conditioned reflexes should occur, disturbances of the genitourinary system, etc. (the latter even over many years, as happened to Gantt's experimental dog, Nick).

In my opinion, no satisfactory evidence has been advanced to prove that extraordinary and difficult tests of differentiation do arouse a conflict in the animal, even if we omit internal conflicts—such as are truly necessary, if we wish to speak of a neurosis—and speak only of such conflicts as may arise between the animal and its environment. The whole idea of a struggle between excitation and inhibition in the animal's cerebrum stems from the experimenter's knowledge that the *objective structure* of the physical stimulus is in effect a compromise between positive and negative stimuli, a sort of 'no man's land.' To assume that this aspect of the physical structure is also significant psychologically is purely arbitrary. One is justified only in saying that the physical 'no-man's-land' stimulus aroused pain or displeasure or anxiety or something of that sort in the animal.

When Pavlov writes that "All [animals] would declare that . . . they were put through a difficult test, a hard situation. Some would report that they felt frequently unable to refrain from doing that which was forbidden and then they felt punished for doing it . . . , while others would say they were . . . unable to do what they usually had to do" (Pavlov, 1932c, p. 84), there exist no observational data that would confirm such assumptions. The dog's equipment does not seem to contain equivalents to "test," "forbidden" or "have to do." Reference to displeasure is in this instance sufficient as an explanation of subsequent behavior. The question then becomes, "Why does the exposure to stimuli that objectively cannot be differentiated arouse in dogs displeasure of a particular kind?"

It must not be forgotten that the experimental chamber is not a neutral place for the animals; they enter it with certain anticipations.[112] These expectations are based on past experience: the objective psychologist would say that the environment is not neutral, but conditioned. Auditory

[112] For a reference to expectation and conditioning, see Brazier (1959, p. 370).

and visual conditioned stimuli to which the animal was exposed in the laboratory were either followed or not followed, in each instance, by an unconditioned stimulus. In some instances, the unconditioned stimulus occurred in accordance with the animal's expectations; in others, it did not occur. This was either due to some complication in the animal, or it happened because the experimenter was not following the rules that he himself had first made the animal integrate.

When, however, a stimulus is given that cannot be differentiated, the animal is exposed to what is in fact a new situation, which is *not* the composite of two previous, familiar ones—as a purely physical analysis may perhaps suggest. The animal finds itself in a situation in which it cannot correctly anticipate either food or the absence of food; it is at that moment, apparently, that anxiety or something of the sort sets in. This would be comparable to a situation in which we had been habituated to anticipate definiteness, but without warning were faced with something indefinite or unexpected; under such conditions, we too would respond with sensations of displeasure.

If I came home to find my room empty, or with all the furniture turned over, or in any shape that made it impossible for me to establish any connection with past experiences, I would feel startled. When an animal is exposed to stimuli that are beyond its ability to differentiate, it is thrown into a state not of conflict but of displeasure; it has met with something that is incompatible with its past experiences, different from what it was trained to expect. (In almost all the animal experiments supposedly producing neuroses, I find an unfortunate absence of perceptive analysis.)

The animal's perceptions are structured quite differently from those of the human adult. It is difficult for us to get a clear picture of this basic and very significant difference. Werner (1940) speaks of "the high degree of unity between subject and object" in animals (p. 67). The distance between perceptive content and the self, which man is capable of sustaining, is absent in the animal.[113] It seems that the allegedly neurotic dog was being exposed, in those situations of difficult differentiation, to something comparable to our perception of a *Gestalt* lying between two typical ones—for example, the 'almost circle,' about which we cannot decide whether it is a circle or an ellipse. Gestalt psychology has investigated this quality in configurations; it is called *Gestaltprägnanz*. Such configurations give us at times a feeling of displeasure or disquietude.

[113] The problem of sense- or stimulus-bound behavior is, of course, a general issue in animal psychology.

In view of the relative decrease in our dependence upon perception, such uneasiness ordinarily has no major consequences for us; but the degree of displeasure aroused in the animal may be comparable to that which many people feel when they are exposed to certain scratching sounds, to which they respond idiosyncratically with the well-known 'goose flesh' sensation, precipitating strong emotional reactions and 'defense reflexes.' Gantt (1944, p. 151) speaks on occasion of a 'pathological environment,' a concept which is extremely useful. In all the instances of alleged animal neurosis that I have come across in the literature, it has struck me that the experimenter first sets up an environment which, because of its perceptual structure, cannot but have a confusing effect on the subject, and then asserts the existence of a neurosis when the subject responds in a way that is really quite in accord with such a perceptual situation.[114]

Gantt's case history of Nick (1944, pp. 67-102) offers a splendid opportunity to demonstrate the weakness of animal experimentation in the field of neuroses. I want to mention only such things as the danger of describing as 'neurotic' what are basically peculiarities characteristic of the species (the equivalent danger in clinical neurosology would be to evaluate group specific peculiarities as neurotic); the reliance upon a highly deficient case history, in so far as the dog's experiences *outside the laboratory* were scarcely considered; the lack of adequate attention to the effects of a severe punishment to which the dog had been subjected in the laboratory, etc.

Curiously enough, the experimenter considered it to be particularly neurotic that the dog showed his 'symptoms' whenever some stimulus reminded him of the laboratory. This sensitiveness is, in my opinion, rather indicative of the dog's intelligence. Since he had been subjected to severe displeasure in the laboratory, he understandably anticipated

---

[114] For a critique by a biologist of neuroses in animals, see Penrose (1953). Cf. also Liddell (1950). In the latter, the material is presented and examined in such a way as to disclose the sensory framework and the perceptive roots that are relevant and necessary to the emergence of the so-called animal neuroses. It may seem to show inconsistency on my part that in one place I turn vigorously against a theory that maintains behavior to be sense- or stimulus-bound, and yet now, in the instance of the so-called animal neuroses, I seem to take the position of just that theory. However, I believe that this is not inconsistent. What I want to assert is no more nor less than that, in most recorded instances of animal neuroses, perceptual clues alone, as given in the seemingly neurosogenic situation, make the animals' habitual behavior impossible. This does not mean that the animal's behavior has now become stimulus-bound, but only that the effect of the perceptual clues is strong enough for us to reject the possibility of a *neurotic* reaction.

experiencing the same displeasure, whenever he perceived elements of the same environment. Such *pars pro toto*[115] reactions are not neurotic, but rather adequate conditioned reflexes, to use Pavlov's terminology, solely for the sake of brevity.

When an experimental animal acted in accordance with the experimenter's expectation, it was called well-adapted, stable, etc.; animals that were unruly and did not adapt well to the environment were—as has been mentioned earlier—usually discarded (Gantt, 1944, p. 37). Here is an instance of the value judgment that tacitly underlies such concepts as 'adaptation' or 'adjustment,' as they are used most frequently. If we look around the human world, we find similar situations. From the psychiatric point of view prevalent at present, pirates were poorly adjusted; yet they often survived the well-adjusted citizen whose valuables they seized. I am sure that Napoleon would have shown up in most modern tests as maladjusted. Finally, a group like the gypsies, who are typically deficient in adjustive capacities, nevertheless show an extraordinary capacity for survival.

If I were to employ Wells's vulgar sociologism, I could maintain that Gantt (and perhaps also Pavlov) were projecting the philosophy of the Western middle class into their evaluation of the dogs. As long as the dog is obedient, minds his own business, works for his living and is motivated above all by alimentary needs, he is a healthy, good, intelligent dog, and earns for himself all sorts of fine epithets. When he refuses to act as a medium of his environment, however, when he attacks, rebels, and wants to take off for a more pleasant environment, then he is 'unstable' and 'neurotic.' And so on. But my biases are different from those of Wells, and I therefore abstain from such constructs.[116]

What can be observed in the dog's behavior are displeasure reactions of the kind that can also be observed in infants. Some psychoanalysts and psychiatrists, it is true, may have a tendency to fall into the error of

115 They are different from those observed in human neuroses. There the *totum* is repressed, so that the patient responds in a way that contradicts his insight into the reality situation, when he is provoked by the *pars*. The 'neurotic' dog has no insight into the reality situation, and the perception of a part factor is therefore taken as the harbinger of the traumatic situation—quite rightly so, when viewed from the dog's limited perspective.

116 Yet I cannot overlook the arbitrariness inherent in Pavlov's and Gantt's decision as to what is 'disturbed' and what is 'undisturbed' behavior. In the section on "Disturbance in Behavior by Natural Emotional Shocks," Gantt (1944, p. 21) reports that the presence of a female in estrus has "a marked disturbing effect" upon the conditioned reflexes. In my opinion, it will greatly impede our understanding of animal behavior if such responses are to be regarded as 'nervous' or 'abnormal.'

Pavlov and Gantt, and to designate as 'neurotic' some reactions occurring in early infancy that cannot legitimately be called neurotic. When a mother is depressed, and the two-month-old infant stops eating, that is surely not a neurotic symptom. We are prone to call it such, chiefly because we know that infants who demonstrate a high degree of vulnerability to unusual stimuli will later develop neuroses. In human life, such early reactions do become, of course, crystallization points in the formation of *bona fide* neurotic symptoms. The animal apparently cannot get beyond displeasure reactions comparable to, or possibly identical with, those observed in infants, because other dimensions of mental functioning are absent from its equipment.

This is perhaps the right moment to mention in passing another basic deficiency in Pavlov's theories: the lack of differentiation among the mechanisms of learning. For Pavlov and his school, there is only one kind of learning: learning by means of conditioned reflexes—that is to say, mechanical learning. Yet there is also learning by insight, which definitely falls outside the area of any reflex. The theoretical implications of this variety have been clarified by Bühler (1918), who distinguished three "levels or stages": instinct, training and intellect (pp. 1-19).

'Training,' in this context, means exactly that type of learning which Pavlov regards as the only one. The German term is *Dressur*, which is a term used for the behavior of animals in a circus, who sometimes act as if they really had insight into the rather complex situations into which they are, in fact, forced to fit their actions. The more they create the impression of acting upon insight, the greater the awe they evoke; in reality, however, they show only what they have acquired after long and elaborate conditioning.[117]

How far one can go with this prepossession with the concept of the conditioned reflex, while simultaneously ignoring insight, can be seen in Gantt's discussion of some clinical tests that he devised. Patients were conditioned to press a rubber bulb upon the perception of certain stimuli, which was immediately followed by mild electric shock. Such an action as pressing cannot properly be called a reflex,[118] as Gantt himself indi-

---

[117] On types of learning, cf. also Lashley (1929, p. 14), Gustav and Wolf (1937, p. 335), Hilgard and Marquis (1940, p. 25). For Pavlov's fight against insight psychology, which he pejoratively called "idealistic," see Pavlov (1957, Section XII). The fact that learning can take place at a number of different levels has been generally accepted in animal psychology today (see Thorpe, 1956).

[118] Denny-Brown (1932) in his critical review of Pavlov's doctrine, suggested a more restrained and closer-to-fact use of the term 'reflex.'

rectly admits, when he speaks of the "voluntary motor component" of the conditioned reflex. It is surprising to find scientists indulging in obvious contradictions, such as can quite easily be avoided. The effects of insight can be very plainly demonstrated in the conditioning of those subjects to whom the experimental procedure has been thoroughly explained, and in whom insight thereafter has a significant bearing on the learning curve (Cole, 1953, pp. 281, 310-314).

The whole question of insight is important in this context, because one can talk of a neurotic symptom, in my opinion, only when the personality has been structured so far that at least a modicum of insight is present. When a child of three years becomes apprehensive at the sight of a person whose face is covered by a mask, that is not a neurotic symptom, but what Freud called "reality anxiety." When that same person takes off the mask, so that the child thereby gains insight into the structure of the reality situation, but then becomes apprehensive again upon the adult's covering his face, then we have an indication of a beginning neurotic symptom. So long as an organism is without the capacity for insight, and is steered only by perception (Pavlov's first system of signals), its behavior may be described in terms of *changes,* but never in terms of neurosis, for that always implies *behavior discordant to insight.*[119]

Before discussing Pavlov's explanations of psychiatric syndromes, it is necessary for me to deal with an important series of observations that has been afforded extensive elaboration in print. I am referring to changes in the vegetative functions—the cardiac and respiratory rates, and many such—as they have been investigated by Gantt in laboratory animals subject to conditioning experiments (Gantt and Hoffmann, 1940; Gantt, 1944; Dykman and Gantt, 1958). It is unnecessary here to go into details with regard to the excellent work done. Suffice it to say that cardiac and respiratory changes were found to take place in conjunction with the formation of conditioned reflexes, and that these were changes

[119] Once more, such a general statement needs elaboration. At this point, however, when neurosis is being discussed within the context of animal behavior, it should suffice as an approximate description of one aspect to be considered. Coming after a period of considerable overestimation of the *difference* between man and animal, present-day thinking is encumbered with the assumption of a near *identity.* (For an opposite view, see Beach, 1960.) Communication, for example, is often treated as largely the same in both, even though Karl Bühler (1918, 1934) has shown that animal language is totally lacking in the *Darstellungsfunktion* (representation function). (Cf. Luria's remark in Bridger [1960, p. 430] where there is no reference to Bühler.) One gets the impression that Freud may have been right, after all, in asserting that man alone has the privilege —as compared with other mammals—of possessing a special disposition to neurosis (Freud, 1926c, p. 152; 1926a, p. 211).

of varying magnitude, which persisted in one way or another, even after a conditioned reflex had been extinguished or inhibited. Unfortunately, these changes were also called conditioned reflexes, even though their structure—and apparently their meaning—was quite different from the sort that leads to behavior adjusted to the environment.

As is well known, Pavlov sought to keep psychology 'objective' by excluding any reference to such 'subjective' experiences as emotions, attitudes, volitions, etc. In this 'psychological' investigation, he observed the behavior of the salivary glands under varying environmental conditions. Physiologists and neurologists will agree that the referent of his observations with regard to the salivary glands was reflexes. He correctly assumed that the reflex is also indicative of something else in the animal —namely, a willingness to eat food. We would call this hunger; but in the language of objective psychology, it is the excitation of the food center, which causes "the stimulation of certain movements of the skeletal musculatures" (Pavlov, 1910-1911, pp. 147f.). These get the animal closer to the food, and are also regarded by Pavlov as reflexes.

As to man, we know that, in his walking, a number of reflexes are activated; but as Gustav and Wolf (1937, p. 313) correctly assert, a step is not only a movement of the legs, it also presupposes coordinations in the whole body, which are furthermore not the same for the first and the second step. Be that as it may, when a man takes a walk, that act cannot be reduced merely to a combination of reflexes. As for the dog, the Pavlovian school rightly maintains that we cannot in any way ascertain what subjective experiences go on inside it, and that it therefore cannot be decided whether the dog's locomotion toward a goal is anything more than a combination of reflexes, or is just that. Yet, in calling it a reflex, Pavlov has in fact arbitrarily decided the question, for reflexes, although they are necessary in the course of almost any psychic activity, are psychologically not relevant,[120] or are, at least, of a relevance different from that of wishes, impulses or actions. In terms of his own epistemology, therefore, Pavlov would have been entitled to speak only of changes in the skeletal musculatures that reduce the distance between food and animal, and not of reflexes.[121] This feature of Pavlov's theory, however, com-

[120] Cf. Freud (1920a) who says of the reflex that it occurs "without the intervention of the mental apparatus" (p. 30).

[121] For the two different ways in which the term "conditioned reflex" is used by Pavlov, see Gantt (1953, p. 55). At least at the beginning of his work on the conditioned reflex, Pavlov tried to differentiate between the physiological and the psychological experiment, in so far as experimentation in the area of unconditioned reflexes could be

pelled Gantt to use the term 'conditioned reflex' also for changes in the autonomic nervous system taking place elsewhere than in the effector organs, even though such reflexes have a function different from that originally assigned by Pavlov to the conditioned reflex. After all, the so-called cardiac and respiratory conditioned reflexes do not serve the organism's adjustment in the sense in which Pavlov thought that the salivary conditioned reflexes did.

It is highly probable that, in these vegetative reflexes, we have physiological indices of what in man is called 'emotion.' If someone were to insist that these changes in the animal *are* emotions, I would not argue that question at this point. The Pavlovian school seems—or seemed—to be of the same opinion, as the following paragraph will show:

> If the cardiac acceleration represents the inner emotional aspect, and the motor conditioned reflex the specific external component, we have the picture of an organism externally in adaptation to the environment but internally excited and reacting to the trace of a conditioned stimulus which long since ceased to have its former significance. The animal has achieved external adaptation but emotionally it is maladjusted. Thus there is a kind of cleavage between the outer specific muscular and the inner cardiac expression. There is this normal physiologic cleavage, adaptive inhibition in the specific response with persisting excitation in the general emotional reaction. The latter may even become more pronounced than it was originally. Thus, through this built-in principle of dysfunction, the organism tends to become a museum of archaic emotional responses, tied to the past internally while exhibiting freedom externally [Gantt, 1953, p. 81].

It seems to be regarded as bad taste among the Pavlovians to cite Freud, whose name was not even mentioned in this context,[122] even though objective psychology comes as close at this point to basic psychoanalytic views as can be expected under present conditions.[123] There is

---

regarded as belonging to physiology, whereas such experimentation as involved the conditioned reflex would be more properly regarded as an experiment in psychology (Pavlov, 1903, pp. 51-53). It seems that Pavlov did not maintain this viewpoint throughout, however; see, for example, Pavlov 1923, p. 329f.

[122] The same aversion toward citing Freud's name is apparent in the customary omission of his name in connection with homeostasis, although, in my opinion, Freud has priority in that respect over Cannon (see Orr, 1942; Kubie, 1948; Flugel, 1953, p. 47).

[123] Yet, five years later, there was ambiguity once more with regard to this problem— or so it seems to me. See Dykman and Gantt (1958, pp. 191f.), who make two possibly contradictory statements about the meaning of the vegetative reflexes.

still a great deal to which most psychoanalysts would object—for example, the use of "maladjustment" and "dysfunction" in this context. But one of the basic differences between Pavlov's and Freud's worlds seems to me to be greatly narrowed down, since here at last the animal is no longer conceived of as pure machine, pure medium; instead, the medial factor is heavily counterbalanced by system properties. When the vegetative nervous system becomes "a museum of archaic emotional responses," then one has the equivalent of the repressed part of the id, as postulated by Freud. Yet, to judge from the reports on laboratory observation, there are no indications of repression; the archaic is quite openly exhibited in that "museum"—which is, by the way, another reason for eliminating the concept of neurosis from animal psychology.

There are situations in which psychoanalytic theory can be profitably applied to findings made in the laboratory of the objective psychologist. Liddell (1950) replaced the animal's needs (or drives, in psychoanalytic parlance) which, in Pavlov's theory, function as the motors of conditioning, with the animal's 'vigilance.' He writes: "Contrary to Pavlov's conception, I know believe that the power for these anticipatory operations is not supplied by the instinctual energies of the animal's unconditioned reaction to food or to noxious stimulation, but rather by its alert and generalized suspiciousness or vigilance" (p. 184).

Vigilance is an ego function, by means of which the organism maintains relations with its environment. Its working depends on external stimuli and on the state of the drives. In a simplified sense, the unsatisfied drives may be said to have a bearing on the direction of vigilance. The hungry animal's vigilance, for example, will be quickly aroused by food. On the other hand, the id would be impotent in the quest for satisfaction, if the ego functions—one of which is vigilance—did not map out the pathway along which gratifications are available. From the psychoanalytic point of view, there is no "either-or" choice between Pavlov's and Liddell's theories, since the ego function should be considered within the context of id demands.

A passage from a letter comes to mind, written by Frederick the Great to Voltaire (September 27, 1737) about Cleopatra's monkey, "which had been trained to dance very well; someone had the idea of throwing nuts at it, whereupon the monkey forgot its dress, its dance and the role that it played, and pounced upon the nuts" (Kannengiesser, p. 54; my own translation). Frederick the Great used this episode for the purpose of satirizing priests and the Church; but it is well suited to illustrate the connection between vigilance and drive. It was vigilance that directed the dancing monkey's attention to the nuts; but the prerequisite for the monkey's shift in action was its hunger.

And now let us turn our attention toward Pavlov, the psychiatrist. After investigating the reactions of dogs with unending care, effort and devotion, he undertook to deal with man and his mental disorders. In 1935, he wrote: "In view of the fact that our data seemed to me sufficient for a physiological interpretation of the mechanisms of nervous diseases, I decided, two or three years ago, to visit the neurological and the psychiatric clinics (*of course devoting only a little time to the matter*)" (p. 469; italics mine). In 1930, in justifying his turn to psychiatry, he had written: "We have definite experimental neuroses in our animals (dogs), and in the same animals what is analogous to human psychoses, and we know their treatment. This was the raison d'être for my becoming *thoroughly* acquainted with psychiatry, of which practically no trace remained from my student medical days. Thanks to my medical colleagues I now have the opportunity to see different forms of mental disturbances" (p. 39; italics mine).

It seems that neuroses and psychoses were first created in animals; only then did Pavlov seek to become "thoroughly acquainted" with psychiatry. Furthermore, it seems almost certain that he did not spend more than a fraction of the time that he had devoted to dogs in the observation and study of emotionally and mentally disturbed patients, with whom he familiarized himself chiefly in a second-hand way, so to speak, under the guidance of his colleagues.

It is evident from his occasional remarks that he never spent any long periods of time studying the structure of a particular neurosis or psychosis, but evolved physiological theories which seemed to him to fit the symptoms that he had selected. Thus one of the first cases that he became interested in was that of a man who had been in a motionless state for many years. When the condition subsided, the patient reported that all that time he had grasped the significance of the events around him,[124] but had felt such a heaviness in his muscles that he could not move. Pavlov explained this syndrome by way of a strictly limited suppression of the motor area of the cortex (1919, p. 289).[125]

[124] Oddly enough, there is nothing to indicate that the patient's claim was checked by a test.

[125] This patient had apparently suffered from catatonia. What the underlying physical disorder, if any, is in such states, is not yet sufficiently understood. It is highly improbable, however, that an isolated area of the cortex has been affected; it may be that a

To learn how far brain mythology can really go, one has to listen to what Pavlov has to say about paranoia. Since he was certain that he was "able to make [render] pathological—and besides, in a functional way—an isolated point of the cerebral cortex, leaving all other points absolutely intact," he concluded that the paranoiac ("a mentally normal person . . . as soon as it comes to one definite subject, distinctly turns into a lunatic") "can be understood on the basis of our laboratory findings *relating to isolated disorders of separate points in the cerebral cortex*" (Pavlov, 1935a, p. 479; my italics). I could extend this to show Pavlov's inadequacy with regard to theory formation, in other instances.

As to schizophrenia, Pavlov's weakness can be shown experimentally. He thought, for example, that catatonia could be interpreted "as physiological protective inhibition, either restricting or completely excluding the work of the affected brain, which was threatened by the danger of serious disturbance or final destruction." He therefore warned against stimulating remedies, which would be "positively injurious" (1935b, p. 183). For years, schizophrenics have been subjected to the most stimulating treatments, in the form of metrazol and electric shock treatment; yet, skeptical as I am of the benefits of these treatments, it does not seem to me that Pavlov's theory has been confirmed in the least.

The incredible sorts of conclusion at which Pavlov was able to arrive, resting on the mosaic theory of the cortex, can be seen when, in all sincerity, he asserts that psychoanalysis can cure hysteria only when one isolated point of the cortex is diseased (Pavlov, 1956, vol. I, p. 194).

It is evident that Pavlov's psychiatry was the product of deduction, and required the abandonment of any adequate inductive methods. Pavlov's descriptions of the central processes in the brain were, to begin with, actually no more than constructs, derived deductively from stimulus-reaction observations in experiments on dogs, yet he dealt with them as though they were data derived from direct observations. Now he transferred these same constructs unhesitatingly to man, without even checking whether the input and output of a diseased patient had anything in common with the input and output he had observed in dogs.

It should not have been necessary for Pavlov to observe patients at all.

---

biochemical system is malfunctioning. Pavlov was certain that the patient's disorder had subsided because of aging. This explanation, I think, one can safely reject. Bleuler (1919) had already observed a long time previously that even a long-lasting catatonia may be discontinued, at least temporarily, by seemingly trivial events—which, however, must have been quite meaningful—that is, psychologically relevant—to the patient (pp. 126, 155).

Anyone armed with his terminology (excitation, inhibition, etc.) can figure out, just sitting behind his desk, what the corresponding brain processes *have to be,* if they are to lead to the variety of symptoms of functional disorders. I think it is unique in the history of science for a man who has been so scrupulous in the application of scientific methodology in one area (for which he was so deservedly awarded the highest honors that a man can attain in science) to 'run wild' when he enters a new field, and to fill pages and pages with what are for the most part untenable and unwarranted claims. It is perhaps even more striking how few people are aware that Pavlov received the Nobel prize for his work, not on the conditioned reflex, but on the glandular physiology of the alimentary system; the educated man who is not a specialist knows nothing of the latter part of his work, being wholly preoccupied with the first part.

Occasionally, one reads that Pavlov's theories are now considered to have been confirmed, and psychoanalysis to have been disproved, by recently discovered pharmacological therapeutics, which show beneficial effects for a substantial number of patients suffering from functional disorders (see Wells, 1956, pp. 11f.). That just is not so. As is well known, Freud anticipated the day of the pharmacological cure of neuroses and psychoses. If anything, he seems to have been far too optimistic in this respect.[126]

The difficulties still to be overcome are enormous, and the psychoanalyst would be grateful if pharmacology gave him at least a reliable adjunct, with which to reduce the formidable barriers to psychotherapeutic measures in such severe disorders as schizophrenia. But the psychoanalyst will not be inclined to accept bromides, caffein, and rest as curative agents for either neurosis or psychosis. It shows Pavlov's basic lack of psychological understanding, his tendency to ignore the difference between symptomatic and etiological therapy in the mental field, that he should even for a moment have thought that such therapeutic measures could

[126] See Freud, 1933a, p. 211, for an example of his positive attitude toward physical therapeutics. Freud's expectation that the neuroses would soon be cured by pharmacological means was expressed verbally to a number of people, as H. Hartmann and Waelder have confirmed. A highly interesting remark of Freud's on the biological theory of psychological processes is to be found in Kempf, 1958, p. 136, which reports Freud as saying that "it would be 'hundreds of years' before there would be sufficient evidence accumulated to explain" the psychophysiology of ego development. Cf. also Jones (1953-1957, Vol. 1, p. 259), for Freud's prediction that hysteria would be cured by the administering of a drug.

cure disorders of the mind.[127] Schilder's (1935, p. 167) statement: "They [neuroses in dogs, as described by Pavlov] can be cured by rest, bromides, and calcium, and if there is anything by which a neurosis in humans cannot be cured, it is by rest, bromides, and calcium" is just as correct today as when it was written.

This does not negate, however, the beneficial effect of sedation in functional disorders; I only wish to discuss briefly its limitations. It has always seemed to me that bromide—particularly (contrary to pharmacological claims) in the form of Elixir Triple Bromides—does have a beneficial effect on young men suffering from anxiety. Indeed, I have been so successful with this prescription that I was quite eager to prescribe it in the Army, where I could have cured with it a formidable number of young men suffering from anxiety states. I got into an argument about it with my chief, who objected to my prescribing bromides. He finally did give in; but my belief, derived from civilian successes, was deeply shaken. Nothing of that kind of success could be observed, and I had to admit that I had greatly overestimated the physical factor in evaluating the clinical observations.[128] When analysts quite frequently turn against physical therapeutic measures, it is not because of any objection based on principle, but rather because they are aware of the inherent shortcomings of such measures.[129]

Yet, in a discussion of Pavlov's work, there is a question of principle involved, centering around the problem of psychic causation. That higher functions do have a bearing on lower ones—can give them direction, activate them or inhibit them—is well known. Of course, this power is limited, and the lower function may thus assert its own right, so to speak, and may in fact be exercised with relative independence. It is conceivable that highly organized or structured matter, such as the cortex, creates a kind of field, in which shifts or shunts occur, which have their recoil or leave a track in the organic substratum.

I am searching for a model of psychogenic causation, although any

[127] Perhaps my criticism goes too far here, because in the twenties many psychiatrists also deceived themselves, just as Pavlov did, and thought that sodium bromide was a potent curative agent in psychiatric treatment (cf. Bailey, 1956-1957, p. 390).

[128] To be exact, of the many soldiers for whom I prescribed bromides for a few weeks without any success, there was one who reported an unquestionable improvement. Curiously enough, it turned out later that, in his case, the anxiety state had been prodromal to the outbreak of a schizophrenic disorder.

[129] Dr. Greenacre once (1950) pointed to the various fashions in physical treatment, particularly in the treatment of schizophrenia. A large number of remedies have been heralded as bringing permanent relief, but have not yet fulfilled what they promised.

such attempt is, of course, condemned to failure at present (cf., however, Strauss, 1955). Are we not still wholly ignorant even of why certain stimuli lead to the sensation of red, while others evoke blue; or why the stimulation of certain areas leads to color sensation at all, even though we do by now know a good deal about the physiology and psychology of the perception of colors? The question can be put in another, although perhaps quite crude, form: suppose we knew everything that there is to know about the brain; would our knowledge also contain everything that there is to be known about the mind?

No one would object to the statement that, even if we knew everything there is to know about the structure of atoms and molecules, that would not help us essentially in improving our undereshanding of a painting by Rembrandt. It might help us to understand better the physics of colors—which is one element, even though a subordinate one, of our understanding of the painting. It may be objected that my comparison is irrelevant to the question I have raised about the mind-body problem; yet I believe that we must at least face the possibility that even a complete knowledge of physical structures would not contain everything there is to be said about the mind. Since we are still far from being able to deal with such questions in an empirical way, it is best to leave the matter open, and not to block the vista by premature assumptions.

Yet I fear that it is precisely such blocking that occurs in the following remarks by Galambos:

> The concept of behavior as a neural organization problem—that behavior is merely the result of the actions and interactions of the neurons of the brain and spinal cord—was expressed in such phrases as 'integrative action of the nervous system' and 'objective study of nervous activity' by Sherrington and Pavlov, respectively. I suspect all of us would like to reject the mystical notions that contradict this view, the semantic ones that obfuscate it, and the obsolete ones that impede progress, and we would embrace, if we could, only rational ideas that further understanding [Brazier, 1959, pp. 303f.].

Even the magnificent progress that neurophysiology has made (as well as that made by psychoanalysis, if I may say so) will have to be more than trebled and quadrupled before the opportunity for a sensible discussion of this question becomes possible; it may even be correct to keep all speculations about the direction of the final answer in suspension until that day. On the other hand, it might, without intending to, have a hampering effect on the neurophysiologist's ingenuity, if he knew that his ambitious program would never be fulfilled, just as the psychoanalyst might permit his 'investigating reflexes' to slacken, if he knew that what he was investigating is in the long run 'merely' the product of molecular behavior.

Perhaps that is the reason why I had a penchant for Hollitscher's metaphor (dating from his pre-Pavlovian days), which struck me as very useful:

> Even today, when something is known about the way the central nervous system works, its function plays no greater role in the subject-matter of psychology than (shall we say?) the analysis of the electrodynamic processes of the telephone network would play in a description of a telephone conversation. The search for the seat of the soul need have no greater importance to the psychologist, it is true, than the search for the 'seat' of the telephone conversation has for the subscriber who is to react to what the man at the other end says to him. (The question "Where is a telephone conversation 'located'?" would generally be regarded as an ill-considered one. It seems to me that the quest for the 'seat of the soul' is just as unhappily formulated.) In short, as psychologists we are only interested in the way the central nervous system works because experience shows that it determines (or in part determines) the psychological processes. But the process which is being explained must obviously be defined independently of the *process by means of which* it is explained [Hollitscher, 1943, p. 131. Italics by Hollitscher].[130]

It may be that the sort of metaphor that Hollitscher put forward will one day be sustained as fact. To be sure, several types of telephone networks may be found; one can easily devise numerous models: each sound may produce a permanent change in a filament of the network, thus rendering it less usable for the conveyance of the next sound; or there may be filaments that are traversable only by certain sounds, and at that only intermittently, so that the speakers would have to make sure they had the right filaments at the right times if they wished to get through the sounds that they wanted to convey. Since this might be cumbersome, the operator might undertake to facilitate the conversation. Perhaps it would be known statistically what sounds were in demand, in what sequence and with what frequency, so that the operator could let par-

---

[130] Cf. also Hollitscher (1947b): "Physiology must not be confused with psychology" (p. 31).

ticular filaments light up in accordance with the statistical 'expectations'; the speakers would then have to fit their conversation as best they could into that statistical average. An observer, however, might then think that it was the filaments that made the speakers talk . . . . But it is time to break off, for I fear I have gone too far. Let us return to our starting point.

Dr. Hollitscher—who was, it should be recalled, a fully trained analyst, and who practiced psychoanalysis for many years—had written papers in which he had proven that psychoanalysis lives up to the requirements and standards of objective psychology—that is to say, is a branch of natural science. He professed such convictions, not out of youthful enthusiasm, but at a time when he had already gone through the fire of modern logic, and had sharpened his tools for the specific purpose of ascertaining scientific truths. Yet, more recently, he accepted Wells's book on Freud without a word of criticism (Hollitscher, 1960b), although Wells uses harsh words, indeed: he speaks of "Freud's unconscious, evil-wish, demon-theory of neurosis" (p. 218); he asserts that "Freud contravened every principle and every standard of procedure in the code of scientific investigation" (p. 299), and that his "dualistic subjective ideal-ism . . . posed little scientific danger to the semi-official ideology," and "enhanced that ideology by giving obscurantism a broader base in the mind and culture of the American people" (p. 235). *Ex pede Herculem.*

Wells's books on Pavlov and Freud do not add anything to our under-standing of either. The objections to psychoanalysis are perhaps some-what coarser and grosser than one generally encounters, while in his presentation of objective psychology he, for the most part, dogmatically repeats (without discussing any of the quite serious objections that have been raised against the classical theory of the conditioned reflex) what has been presented quite often, in textbooks and elsewhere. His worst shortcomings, however, are the infringements upon free science of which he makes himself guilty by his appeal to prejudice, in order to discredit a science that—as is well known—does rub 'common sense' the wrong way.

He rejects, for example, Freud's theory of the hereditary transmission of symbols, on the grounds that that would amount to the reinstatement of innate ideas, "long ago rejected by John Locke as theoretically and scientifically untenable and as politically reactionary" (Wells, 1960, p. 116). To call a theory "reactionary" (and the author operates with such value statements quite freely) is, of course, a *captatio benevolentiae,* when it is interjected into a scientific tract.

The problem of the origin of symbols has not yet been solved, and it should have been Hollitscher's task to let the reader know that the innateness of symbols is not the decisive question in psychoanalysis, since there are many analysts who affirm the acquisition of symbols by experience. It would be different if Wells had proven that symbols of the kind Freud referred to are nonexistent. I have myself always tended toward the assumption of the acquisition of symbols, rather than their hereditary transmission, but it is precisely one of the writings of the Pavlov school that indirectly confirms the possibility that Freud was right.

When Bykov (1942) maintains that the cerebral cortex is informed of the state of the organism at any given moment, and that it is an organ for the union of extero- and interoceptive impulses (p. 384), then one is entitled tentatively to assume that there is a cortical representation of inner organs—which, in turn, would amount to innate ideas. The evolvement of symbols from the cortical representations of inner organs would be a minor problem, once the existence of these cortical representations were assured.[131] In any case, a question such as that of the acquisition and/or the hereditary transmission of symbols is not a matter of belief or conviction, but of experience and observation.

Wells, as an outsider to psychoanalysis, cannot judge the relevance of a particular problem to the whole structure of psychoanalysis; but Hollitscher, at least, is very well informed, and he knows that Freud's theory of the origin of symbols rests on the impressions that one obtains most vividly during the course of a psychoanalytic investigation. To call the outcome of observation reactionary is puerile, just as it is to believe that any philosopher or scientist has ever said that last word on any issue of significance.[132]

It is similarly disheartening to find among Wells's reasons for rejecting Freud's theory of dream interpretation the threadbare statement that

[131] Not being a neurophysiologist, I perhaps have no right to set forth the following critical view quite so vigorously; but I doubt that Bykov's conviction with regard to the role of the cortex in the regulation of visceral processes is really as clearly proven as he thinks. See Hilgard and Marquis (1940) for literature regarding cortex and conditioned reflexes.

[132] It is also possible that Wells was simply unaware of the fact that the bulk of symbols, in the narrower sense in which Freud used the term, referred to physical organs and their functions. It does not seem that Freud was assuming the existence of innate ideas about external reality. The point in this context is, however, that *the whole* problem of the origin of symbols is not one of inherent significance; psychoanalysis will not stand or fall, according to the answer that future research comes up with in this area.

it is an "age-long but long-since discredited and discarded superstition that dreams have hidden meaning" (Wells, 1960, p. 226).

There is no doubt that Wells's presentation is a biased one. For example, one of the reasons why he considers the conception of unconditioned reflexes to be superior to that of instincts is that "it guides experimental work in the discovery of their precise number" (1960, p. 78). It would be important to know all the unconditioned reflexes, and one has the right to expect a definitive statement on that question in Pavlov's work. Yet he seems to have had an aversion toward committing himself in this respect, and a study of his work may show that, in this area, there is a reign of arbitrariness and disorganization, and practically of limitlessness.

In Pavlov's doctrine, unconditioned reflexes are, of course, attributed to the great biological urges, such as hunger, sex, and self-preservation, in the form of food, sexual, defense and orienting reflexes. But then we hear of the reflex of freedom, and of "an inborn reflex of slavish submission" (Pavlov, 1917, p. 285), which he also calls the "reflex of slavery." "How often and varied appears the reflex of slavery on Russian soil," he exclaims, and with his usual lack of hesitation he discovers in a story by Kuprin a character who "was made a victim of the reflex of slavery inherited from his mother," who was a higher servant in a rich Russian family. Here he came quite close to affirming the inheritance of acquired characteristics.[133] And then we hear that there is a "reflex of purpose" (Pavlov, 1916a) that is also unconditioned, and whose "most pure and typical" form is the passion for collecting (p. 277).

In this same paper, Pavlov postulates "a general instinct of life" that consists of "positive movement reflexes," the two strongest of which are "the food and the *focusing* (orienting and investigating) reflexes" (p. 277; italics by Pavlov). Yet all this leads "to a common, generalized grasping reflex." Later, it is the food reflex that is called the chief grasping reflex, and (to my surprise) one reads that "the reflex of purpose . . . is the fundamental form of the life energy of us all" (p. 279). Whether the guarding reflex, which Pavlov observed occasionally in dogs, was unconditioned or conditioned, Pavlov could not apparently decide with certainty, but he felt strongly inclined toward the former (Pavlov, 1916b, pp. 257f.).

[133] Pavlov suggests that, if the hero of the story had had insight into his own condition, he might, by systematic measures, have developed control over, and even the successful suppression of, this reflex.

Finally, to top this systematization of unconditioned reflexes, Pavlov speaks of a "therapeutic reflex" (Pavlov, 1932b, p. 77), which is "only one of the subcortical reflexes arising during hypnosis" (p. 81). Well, enough of confusion. It would seem to me that Freud's various phases of drive systematizations, unsatisfactory as they may seem to some, will stand up quite well in comparison.

One major shortcoming of Wells's (1956) work on Pavlov is the omission of an important general aspect. Pavlov (1932b) raised the question: "Do not we, normal people, constantly repress some of our movements and words, i.e., do not we send inhibitory impulses to definite points of the cerebral hemispheres?" (p. 532).[134] This seems to introduce an entirely new vista into objective psychology; it strikes me as putting conditioned reflexes into a highly subordinate place in the psychology of man. If man can send impulses to definite points of the cortex, why should he ever give up that freedom, and permit conditioned reflexes to master his life? I only wonder where this "we" is located. It can hardly be in the cortex. Freud's structural theory of the personality seems to me to be a more adequate operational tool, even though Dr. Hollitscher apparently does not think so any longer.

In his latest book (1960a), he summarizes his objections to Freud in a section headed "Man—an instinctual being?" (*Der Mensch—ein Triebwesen?*) I hope I am not simplifying the issue unduly when I say that the psychoanalytically relevant issue that he has raised is whether or not Freud was right in asserting that "An instinctual stimulus does not arise from the external world but from within the organism itself" (Freud, 1915, p. 118).

He seems to think that he has refuted Freud, when he places against this quotation from Freud the following from Pavlov: "The objects towards which instinctual actions are directed become known to the animal organism within ever enlarging areas of nature through signs or signals that constantly increase in variety, subtlety and complication. Thus it happens that instincts come to be more and more fully gratified, that is to say, the organism remains preserved in its environment with increasing correctness and security" (Pavlov, 1932a; translation mine).[135]

It is in this extension of the conditioned reflex to cover ever-widening

---

[134] If the translation is to be regarded as exact, then one must assume that the question is rhetorical.

[135] This paragraph has been deleted from Dr. Gantt's translation of Pavlov 1941. The German text can be found in the edition of Pavlov's works of the Akademie Verlag (Pavlov, 1956, Vol. 3, pp. 456f.).

environmental areas that Dr. Hollitscher (p. 466) sees the "true vicissitudes" of instincts (*die wahren Triebschicksale*). Pavlov's work on the unconditioned and conditioned reflexes seems to convince him of the nonexistence—or, at least, of the subordinate, and probably irrelevant role—of stimuli that "arise from within the organism itself." In view of his encyclopedic knowledge and the strictness of his thinking, I cannot believe that Dr. Hollitscher has overlooked one fact on which Pavlov and his school seem to agree—namely, that a state of satisfaction does render impossible the establishment of conditioned reflexes.

It is in keeping with Pavlov's thinking for one to say that the process of learning seems to presuppose a state of dissatisfaction. For the salivary reflexes, Pavlov has spelled this out,[136] naming hunger as one of the many prerequisites for the establishment of alimentary conditioned reflexes.[137] Yet hunger is altogether unquestionably a stimulus that "arises from within the organism"; for the sensation of hunger does not depend on the offer or the perception of food, but arises periodically, quite independently of the environment. One wonders what observations Hollitscher has since made that negate the assertions he made in 1947:

> When the mucous membrane of the oesophagus becomes parched or when a gnawing makes itself felt in the stomach, . . . the stimulus is of instinctual origin. Among stimuli which operate on our minds we have then to distinguish between those which are of instinctual origin and others which are physiological. We see . . . , that a stimulus of instinctual origin arises, *not in the outside world,* but from *within* the organism itself. Its mental effect and the actions necessary to discharge it differ accordingly [Hollitscher, 1947a, p. 23; italics mine].

Here the author is not interpreting, he is *describing* facts; but the existence of these very same facts is vigorously denied thirteen years later. However, the ever widening area covered by the conditioning process, as observed in Pavlov's classical experiment, is not in contradiction with Freud's views on instinctual drives, for Freud himself described the ever-widening range of objects cathected by drive energy. Indeed, one might correctly say that a major part of his investigation was directly and indirectly devoted to the explanation of that process through which the world becomes a field of cognition and action for an organism originally bound up in the gratification of needs.

[136] Cf. also Gantt (1957): "If we satiate an animal, we reduce the food-conditioned reflexes to almost zero, the cardiac component as well as the salivary" (p. 142).

[137] It is not out of context to mention here the limiting effect that castration has on conditioned reflexes in dogs, as that has been set forth by Pavlov repeatedly.

Dr. Hollitscher was not quite fair in his 1960 Freud quotations, which might easily leave the impression that Freud regarded man as nothing but a drive-ridden being. He should have added at least one more quotation: "The ego develops from perceiving instincts to controlling them, from obeying instincts to inhibiting them" (Freud, 1923a, pp. 55f.).

It seems that Hollitscher now prefers Pavlov's theory of neurosis, as a collision between excitation and inhibition, to Freud's. Now, it would be understandable if an analyst were to become dissatisfied with psychoanalysis as a therapeutic instrument. As a matter of fact, some (like Wells) think that the very fact that neuroses are still so frequent and widespread proves per se that psychoanalytic theories must be wrong; that argument, I am sure, would be unacceptable to Hollitscher, who must know that it becomes quite clear precisely from Freud's theories why the psychoanalytic procedure does not lead to success as often as the clinician would want it to. However, even though Pavlov (1932d) says that "the question of the relation between excitation and inhibition still baffles solution" (p. 529n.), still one wonders why objective psychology does not advise us more vigorously on matters of therapy.

After all, if a neurosis is really no more than a collision between excitation and inhibition, then indeed bromides, caffein, and rest ought to be expected to be of superior therapeutic efficiency. Objective psychology thus, in a sense, holds all the trump cards in its hands. It professes to know the relevant brain processes in neurosis; it can produce and eliminate the neuroses in animals at will; it has excellent drugs at its disposal to stimulate or to calm the cortical cells. What more is needed? Under these circumstances, a report on therapy from the Pavlovian school, which is almost devoid of clinical applications, shows a curious poverty. (I refer to Gantt's [1957] article in *Progress in Psychotherapy*.)

A clinical report frequently cited is that by Raymond (1956), which concerns the cure of a fetishist brought about by injections of apomorphine, along with the patient's exposure to the sight of the fetish (the patient had impulses to damage perambulators and handbags), just before nausea was produced.[138] Raymond's clinical report is not detailed

---

[138] On this occasion, Freud is cited, but it seems to me wrongly. The author says that "in spite of Freud's view that overt homosexuality might result if the fetish objects were removed, this has not happened in this patient." I assume he refers to Freud's (1927c) statement that fetishism "saves the fetishist from becoming a homosexual" (p. 154), which does not imply the conclusion drawn here.

enough to permit a psychoanalytic discussion,[139] but I wish to point out the disproportion between the theoretical knowledge of the Pavlovian school and the poverty of its clinical application and clinical implications.[140]

In any evaluation of Hollitscher's and Wells's views on psychoanalysis and objective psychology, it must be understood that there are two Pavlovian schools. The American school, for example, stays strictly within the framework of objective psychology.[141] Hollitscher's and Wells's views on psychoanalysis appear to be intimately interwoven with their political convictions; one may even doubt whether their unquestioning adherence to Pavlov's physiopsychology is not primarily dictated by those convictions. "A nasty song! Fie! A politic song! A vexing song!," says Goethe.[142]

Science has barely shaken off the tutelage of the churches and of religion, and already, in some parts of the world, we are able to observe the spectacle of some areas of science being put under new restrictions. To be sure, the political texture of a society does have a bearing, not only on the ideologies that obtain within it, but also on its sciences.

---

[139] A careful examination of Raymond's paper will readily reveal its shortcomings. There is the possibility, for example, that the patient suffered from a disorder of the schizophrenic group. Furthermore, no consideration is given to the effect on the patient of the possibility of his having to submit to a court trial if his symptoms did not subside. Therefore it is questionable whether the disappearance of the symptoms, as alleged by the patient and his wife, took place at all.

[140] As one example of the strange clinical fruits that Pavlov's theories may occasionally bear, the work of Salter (1941) may be cited. Gantt (1957), when facing the issue of "What of use has come out of fifty years' research in this area?" feels tempted to quote "What is the use of a new born baby?" (p. 140). That is all well and good; but the baby was fifty years old by then. I am altogether opposed to judging research in terms of its utility, and I am certain that I do not need to go into an analysis of the pernicious effects of such a philosophy. In this instance, however, I do raise that very question, because Pavlov has professed to have discovered the key to the understanding of almost every form of psychopathology; if that key were the right one, we should by this time have a specific, etiological therapy, since the causes he puts forward are quite accessible to pharmacological treatment.

[141] However, it may be remarked in passing that adherence to strict behavioristic, objective principles with rigid exclusion of the subjective, emotional, inner sphere occasionally leads, curiously enough, to purely anthropomorphic assumptions. Thus Richter (1958) writes: "Some of the observations indicate that the rats, as well as human beings, die from a reaction of hopelessness." Richter may be right; the experimental evidence is striking. On the other hand, Gantt (1944) reports observations that are impressionistic, deriving from such far-reaching conclusion as "the dog actually remembers with his heart" (p. 145, n. 17). He is even quite ready to give credence to Maeterlinck's beautiful but romantic interpretations (p. 166, n. 4). Such episodes, however, are rare and do not have any delimiting effect on the above statement. They are mentioned here only for their historical and psychological interest.

[142] *Ein garstig Lied! Pfui! Ein politisch Lied! Ein leidig Lied! Faust,* verses 2092f.

Leaving aside the descriptive sciences, one may say that the more that scientific propositions can be expressed in mathematical language, the more can we be certain that those propositions have been purified of any nonscientific admixture. Sciences such as psychoanalysis and objective psychology, which are still separated by enormous gulfs from the stage at which mathematics could play a relevant role (although Hull and Gantt have each tried to put certain laws into the form of mathematical equations), obviously cannot claim the same degree of objectivity as physics and chemistry.

I am sure that an aspect of the societal mood penetrated into Freud's psychoanalysis, although I do not think that I could demonstrate this. While it is more than likely, however, that later historians will be able to establish correlations between psychoanalysis and societal forces, we may feel quite certain that they will be able to do so as well, in large measure, with regard to behaviorism, objective psychology and Pavlov's classical theories. The *Zeitgeist*, societal forces, political texture were present in Galileo's work as well as in that of Sprenger and Kraemer. As Boring (1955) has so effectively shown, such factors have both stimulating and retarding, creative and destructive effects. The fact that a discovery was made under the impact of societal forces does not speak either for or against its correctness, any more than the absence or presence of neurosis decides it, as Hollitscher (1947a) so rightly set forth in his *Introduction* (p. 96).

The bearing of the political situation, however, can be shown directly by reference to Hollitscher's citations or footnotes. He has, as I have said before, an encyclopedic knowledge (the index of names of his last book shows more than 850 entries), and therefore one has the right to assume that he is familiar with the most representative works in each branch of knowledge that he takes up. The frequent quotations from Lenin's philosophical writings can perhaps be justified, yet they still make one wonder when they are set alongside the glaring paucity of references to the *Wiener Kreis*, to which the author formerly belonged. It is quite possible that those who say that Lenin was the greatest statesman of our century are right; whether he was a greater philosopher than Moritz Schlick, or superior as a logician to Rudolf Carnap, is, I think, extremely doubtful.

But I think there is no chance that any sane or well-balanced person, if he is free of ideological involvements, would consider Stalin to have been a great linguist or geometrician; yet Dr. Hollitscher cites him four times in those areas—with some degree of ambivalence, I think, for the quotations are of such utter triviality that they would serve to deter any intelligent reader from the examination of Stalin's scientific papers.[143] It is also a surprise to find Mao Tse-Tung cited twice—and as an epistemologist.

I should like to discuss both instances, but I shall deal only with one. There is really no dearth of documentation with regard to the relation between practice and reality on the one side, and thinking and abstraction on the other. Hollitscher affirms—and this, by the way, is highly debatable—that only by its corroboration (*Bewährung*) in practice is the correctness of a thought confirmed. To exemplify this, he lets Mao speak: "If one wants to acquire knowledge, he has to participate in practice that changes reality . . . . If one wants to learn to know theory and methods of revolution, then one has to participate in the revolution" (p. 13f.; my own translation from Hollitscher's German rendering). That thought is, of course, not primarily an epistemological one; it is fraught with political implications, and besides, at face value, it is wrong.

The selection of such authorities for quotation is obviously dictated by politics, certain names being plainly brought in for political purposes, while others are excluded or, if they are brought up, may be alluded to for critical purposes only. This is quite clear with regard to Freud; if further documentation were still necessary, I would refer to the author's concept of thinking as *"Probehandeln"* (experimental or trial action) (p. 23), which coincides with Freud's basic idea about the thinking process,[144] yet his name is not cited on this occasion. The idea that thinking is trial action is one of the concepts that psychoanalysis and objective psychology share.

As I mentioned earlier, in the investigation of medial aspects, there is a real likelihood that Pavlov and Freud will meet on common ground.

---

[143] How far the author lowers his standards on such occasions may be seen from the first sentence of his Stalin quotation about language: "Language is a means, a tool with whose help people communicate with each other, etc." Stalin's paper on *Marxism and Linguistics* seems to hold a particular fascination for this branch of the Pavlovian school, for Wells also quotes it (1956, p. 86) in a context in which the quotation is really out of place—namely, when discussing the very tricky and still undecided question of whether or not thought is possible without verbalization. The fact that Stalin asserted that it is "absolutely wrong" to say that thoughts arise without language really does not contribute anything to the substance of the problem.

[144] Cf. Freud (1911a, p. 221). It is quite probable, although I am not certain, that Freud was the first to use the term *Probehandeln* in connection with the psychology of thinking; in view of Hollitscher's excellent knowledge of Freud's work, it is quite likely that that was where he obtained the term.

As different as Pavlov's first and second signaling systems may be from Freud's unconscious and preconscious systems, nevertheless their similarities are significant and noteworthy; an undogmatic mind can permit itself to observe that and say so (cf. Bridger, 1960), but such a concession is taboo to Wells (cf. 1960, pp. 94-99), whose method is not that of critical analysis, but that of dogma, with its boundary lines derived from the nonscientific areas of vulgar sociologism, in which the question is decided in advance as to what is true and what is false.

I take this last instance as the final proof that Hollitscher let even minimal standards of objectivity dissolve, submitting himself instead to forces that ought not to have their say in matters of science. Those who hold political power may be expected to use it for their purposes in all the areas that are accessible to them, as can be observed from the rather quick succession of different versions of encyclopedia articles in the Soviet Union. But it is disheartening, to say the least, that a scientist living in a free country should voluntarily—since he is not threatened by the state power—negate his prerogative of service to truth, and instead permit his capabilities to be used distortedly in the service of political dogma.

Dr. Hollitscher can unquestionably claim the doubtful honor of being the first to follow up a career of having been an analyst himself by wholeheartedly welcoming a book in which it is proposed that psychoanalysis be "eliminated" (Wells, 1960, pp. 238, 240), thereby confirming his own earlier statement, in which he said:

> Psychoanalysts have not been the first or the only people to recommend that men should look inward and try to know themselves. But it appears to be their fate to recommend it most importunately and to support their plea with empirical evidence which affects everybody intimately. So strong are the feelings which their efforts arouse that the opponents of psychoanalysis regard themselves as absolved from the constraints alike of logic and of *academic courtesy* [Hollitscher, 1947a, p. 21; italics mine].[145]

[145] It is difficult to read without a profound sense of irony another statement of Hollitscher's, this time from his paper of 1938. Toward the end, he asserts that many of the psychoanalytic concepts and propositions are so clearly explicative (*klar aufweisbar*) that one could undertake the writing of a methodological paper with the title: "On Psychoanalysis. For the Educated among its Detractors" (Über Psychoanalyse. Für die Gebildeten unter ihren Verächtern [p. 20]). What a pity that he did not undertake it! With what profit both he and Wells could study it now! To be sure, he was not original in his use of the subtitle to Schleiermacher's book on religion; he was, in that regard, only imitating Hartmann (1927, p. 7).

It would be out of place to speculate about, or to try to reconstruct, the personal motives that may have been at work when Hollitscher replaced Freud's theories with Pavlov's theories of the human mind. Yet, in viewing Dr. Hollitscher's development as a scientist, one can hardly help thinking of one of the examples that Freud (1920) used in illustrating the compulsion to repeat: ". . . the man who time after time in the course of his life raises someone else into a position of great private or public authority and then, after a certain interval, himself upsets that authority and replaces him by a new one" (p. 22).

It would be quite understandable if Dr. Hollitscher had come to the conclusion that the prospects for neurophysiological research were more promising than those for psychoanalysis, or that he himself could make discoveries of greater importance to mankind as a neurophysiologist than as a psychoanalyst. He might even have been right in such an assumption; after all, we do not know which field for research a genius like Freud would select if he were starting out today as a student. But nothing of this sort can be read into Dr. Hollitscher's statements. What he is saying—manifestly or tacitly by his wholehearted, uncritical approval of Wells's book—is that psychoanalytic research is pseudo research, that its conclusions must therefore be wrong, and that all assertions made on the basis of Freud's methods must be discarded. Whatever the subjective personal background may be for his making this charge, it is unquestionably the consequence of his conception of the responsibility imposed upon him by an ideology.

That any ideology could have had such a deteriorating effect on an extremely keen and well-informed mind should be taken as a danger signal of extraordinary gravity. In a confrontation of Pavlov with Freud, one may perhaps think that it is a case of East facing West; yet a contrast of the very same character is encountered in a confrontation of Pavlov with Dostoyevsky, both of whom were Russians from top to bottom. They represented fundamentally opposing views of the nature of man: one reduced man to an absolute medium of his brain; in the novels by the other, man is wholly system and in constant conflict. In the Russian psychology of today, it is Pavlov's view and not Dostoyevsky's that is dominant.

If the imagery about present-day Russia that is officially propagated in the West is correct, then one may easily reach the conclusion that the ruling élite would like to give the community the structure of Pavlov's laboratory, and make the population respond to the primary and secondary signals in a predictable and predetermined way. Such a setup would require, however, an experimenter whose prototype, not being a medium of his brain, would be Dostoyevsky's type of man.

Whether this impressionistic remark is correct or not, it nevertheless can be asserted that, whenever empires have been built in the past, the majority usually has had to give up part of its individuality, and approach that sort of behavior which Pavlov assigned to his experimental animals. This is, indeed, the extraordinary thing about man—the ever-puzzling antinomy, the as yet unanswered problem—that under appropriate conditions man actually will behave as if he were one of Pavlov's dogs, while —given even a minimal change—he will reveal himself as a Dimitri, an Ivan or a Smerdyakov.

The two poles of man's position vis-à-vis the universe are sometimes represented in one and the same document. The Bible, after all, for the most part gives man autonomy and dignity, and yet at one point he is equated with the beast: "And the Lord said, I will destroy . . . both man, and beast . . . ; for it repenteth me that I have made them." (Genesis, 6, 7)

It must be remembered that the event I am discussing took place in a free country, and that the person in question had accomplished what looked like an integration of psychoanalysis. The situation is quite different with Wells in the latter respect. His book, symptomatic as it is, is no problem. Its aversion to psychoanalysis does not lie outside the range of well-known modes of explanation. His proposal to eliminate psychoanalysis has enough antecedents on both the right and the left not to cause any new or special perturbation. His mental biases with regard to the close correlation between political structure and science are frequent, and they are understandable in terms of his political leanings.[146]

How wrong both Wells and Hollitscher are can be demonstrated most

---

[146] His idealization of the Soviet Union is documented by his omissions, rather than by his positive statements, for he says nothing of the fact that, had Pavlov been born fifty years later than he was, he might not even have been permitted to study in what would by then be post-revolutionary Russia, because of his having been the son of a priest (Brazier, 1959, p. 185). The picture that Wells draws of Pavlov suffers greatly by its omission of Pavlov's brave protest against certain aspects of the Soviet system and against Stalin: when the members of the intelligentsia were being persecuted, Pavlov actually resigned from the Chair of Physiology in protest (Brazier, ibid.). One would almost think that Wells were ashamed to mention such evidence of fortitude and that he has also forgotten that the elimination or suppression of part of the intellectual élite happens almost regularly in the case of abrupt and deep-going changes. Of this, Lavoisier is the most tragic example.

simply by the fact that, in the United States, both branches of the science of psychology flourish side by side. Hilgard and Marquis give a beautiful account of how conscientiously the psychologists went about testing and retesting Pavlov's work and elaborating on it. I do not recall any instance of Church or State interference or threat in this regard, even though Pavlov's theories are profoundly atheistic and materialistic. In the same fashion, psychoanalysis has found an almost ideal haven in this country. Analysts are left to themselves to organize their research in the way they think it most suitable. Yet, even at the danger of repetition, I must say once more how highly probable it is that, in the freedom that these two sciences have enjoyed, within a capitalistic democratic republic based on a high degree of technology, and in the work that they have accomplished in this habitat, some fundamental societal forces are reflected.

Yet that does not imply any conclusion with regard to the truth or falseness of either science. Had Hollitscher not made his as yet inexplicable turn, he would have recognized that both Pavlov *and* Freud carried on investigations, each within his own rights. It is perfectly legitimate to record and order psychic phenomena, as they are observed longitudinally during the course of a psychoanalytic observation, and to deduce from those observations what are the underlying laws determining sequences, as well as the kind of structure that best fits the processes observed. Freud himself was quite aware that physiology might well be able to explain some of these observations, but felt that any decision on this was outside his legitimate competence. Epistemologically, he was correct in not going beyond the area of the psychic apparatus, except in seeking to determine the biological nature of some of the stimuli with which the apparatus had to cope.

Similarly, Pavlov legitimately extended the setup of his experimental work on the digestive system to a general inquiry into behavior under varying environmental conditions. There are two areas, however, in which criticism based on principle is called for. First, Pavlov had not studied brain processes, as he thought. The criticism that Pavlov has come in for on that score in this country is based on a serious effort to examine his views scientifically, and it is uncritical to seek to refute such criticism solely by reference to any supposed prior philosophical or political bias.

"Concepts of cortical physiology should be based upon more direct measures of cortical function," wrote Hilgard and Marquis (1940, p.

35); they are equally right when they assert that, without specific verification by means of direct investigation of the cortex, not much is gained
by the claim that inferential concepts denote cortical processes (*ibid.*).
The other area of valid criticism has to do with the premature extension
to humans of insight gained in experimentation with animals, and the
assumption of such highly structured processes as neuroses in organisms
that are not capable of them.

In principle, Freud and Pavlov examined quite separate processes, and
therefore should only rarely come into contradiction with each other.
The nexus between psyche and soma will be discovered, although perhaps in the distant future, by the direct observation of manifestations of
brain processes. To question the bulk of Freud's observations and theories on the ground of Pavlov's findings is unjustified. That Dr. Hollitscher did so must have been due to at least one extraneous factor. That
a fully trained psychoanalyst should fall victim, after his childhood, once
again, to a set of illusions, and thus lose the intellectual adequacy and
autonomy of reality testing, is a new phenomenon, thus far not explained by theory.

Can one really expect to weather the storm that will surely be unleashed against psychoanalysis, whichever way the chips of history fall,
without the good help of confrères in the other disciplines? When the
clouds gather, the good captain calls: all hands on board!

Addendum

At this point, I want to add a few thoughts about two other dangers
that may impede the optimal development of psychoanalysis, even
though these threats do not come from the outside. They can properly
be called: moderate biologism, and moderate sociologism.

Moderate Biologism. The first sentence of Freud's (1895) "Project"
reads as follows: "The intention of this project is to furnish us with a
psychology which shall be a natural science: its aim, that is, is to represent psychical processes as quantitatively determined states of specifiable
material particles and so to make them plain and void of contradictions"
(p. 355).

If one compares this impressive preamble of principle with the *Outline,* Freud's last work, one gets an inkling of the span that Freud traversed during the intervening forty-four years. The starting point was
strictly biologically oriented; yet from it there developed a psychology

which, although it paid its proper respects both to the organism and to society, nevertheless itself remained pure, untainted psychology.[147]

Thus Freud went through a phase of biologizing psychology—which was in keeping not only with the spirit of the times, but also with his own previous outstanding neurological work. The investment of energy that it must have taken him to recognize the futility of proceeding further along that path provided him with a permanent safeguard against becoming overimpressed with the structure of the central nervous system.

For a new generation of neuropsychiatrists, however, for whom the inventory of psychoanalytic mechanisms has become a matter of mere routine, while the new discoveries in the field of neurophysiology, neuropathology and biochemistry seem to be quite promising and even awe-inspiring, the temptation to dissolve the world of human conflicts into enzymes must be irresistibly attractive.

The fact is that biologism in a different form has tainted the work of some of Freud's followers. It predominates, for example, in the work of Melanie Klein, who had such a strong influence on the English school, which later spread to South America. Melanie Klein's work has been most ably criticized by Waelder (1936), Glover (1945), Bibring (1947); yet it seems that their criticisms were without any substantial effect on the thinking of the school, and further discussion with her would be probably useless. One argument against Melanie Klein's fundamental thesis has not escaped attention, and yet may not have been sufficiently stressed. As is well known, the effect of an archaic superego is a principal issue between the English school and classical psychoanalysis. From the point of view of the history of science, it is noteworthy that this disagreement should have been of a semantic character. Terms such as good and bad are employed in two different areas: the *physical* good and bad, mainly with regard to the sense of taste, and the *moral* good and bad, which are mental values. By equating these two sets, and using the terms in the latter sense where observation would warrant their use only in the former sense, Klein carries out a piece of legerdemain that makes it possible to ignore in theory the full impact of social reality on psychic

---

[147] On Freud's development from physiology to psychology, see Kris (1950, pp. 14-27). It is interesting to find some of Freud's basic psychological discoveries already foreshadowed in physiological and pathophysiological theories of the pre-analytic period. (See Hartmann, 1956, p. 427f., for Meynert's position in this respect.) Wernicke, for example, probably had no direct influence on Freud; yet, when the somatic processes as he postulated them (see Wernicke, 1900) are translated into psychology, the historical connection will become apparent.

development and structure. (We shall have to take up her psychology once again later—and at what may seem to be a somewhat surprising juncture.)

Of far greater significance are, in my opinion, the effects that modern drug therapy may have on the future of psychoanalysis. There can be no doubt that with the discovery of the modern pharmaca, which have such a potent effect on the human mind, psychiatry has entered a new phase. Although in the past the therapeutic effect of physical means of treating emotional and mental disorders has clearly been overestimated, and further experimentation has not confirmed what seemed to be initially promised, this time one gains the impression that chemistry has actually initiated a new therapeutic approach that will greatly and lastingly increase medical effectiveness in combatting psychopathology.

In this context, only a few words need be said about some of the specific relations between psychoanalysis and chemotherapy. Classical analysis cannot possibly have any effect on the frequency of mental disorders on a national scale, for Freud *expressis verbis* declared that his method is not applicable to the psychoses, but only to the neuroses.[148] If the extensive use of drug therapy were to induce at least a symptomatic cure of the major psychoses, on a national scale, one of the greatest of the present needs in this area would be resolved.

Some of the drugs, however, may also become an important adjunct to psychoanalytic treatment even of the classical type. This may occur in two situations:

(a) As is well known, there are patients who prove unanalyzable, even though their symptoms appear to fall within the accepted range of analyzability. They seem to suffer from a deficiency in their ability to form a verbalizable transference: they are incapable either of forming daydreams or of verbalizing them; perhaps they belong to the patients whom Freud described as the prematurely aged (Freud, 1918, p. 116; 1937a, p. 345). Because of their general mental rigidity, their analysis may come to naught. Some of the drugs may, under such circumstances, have a beneficial effect, in so far as, through their use, the transference suddenly takes a course leading to rich transference verbalizations.

---

[148] It is all the more surprising to hear Turkel (1962) adduce the fact that the number of patients in state hospitals has not been reduced, as a proof that " 'mental therapy' as practiced by psychoanalysts is virtually valueless"—as if neurotics were committed to hospitals. It seems also to have escaped his attention that the largest number of institutional beds are occupied by patients whose mental disorders have their origin in organic disorders.

In some instances, to be sure, this may be the only way out of an otherwise desperate therapeutic situation.[149] Yet it is to be feared that pharmacoanalysis will soon begin to flourish, with drugs being dispensed at the very first signs of the patient's resistance. The humanism that lies at the heart of Freud's psychoanalysis will then have suffered a fatal blow, for the method of choice will have become some drug or other—plus an interpretation. In this context, it is worth taking note of the reaction of a schizophrenic patient to the subjective relief of painful symptoms after he took some tranquilizers. He threw them away, saying: "They rob me of my symptom, and what should I do then?" Another patient flatly rejected the idea of taking pills, on the grounds that it would be cheating to take drugs, when—as she was convinced—a cure ought to be induced by understanding.

(b) During the course of an analysis, as we know, the treatment may take a malignant turn, in so far as the patient's defenses crumble under the impact of increased pressure from the unconscious, so that the patient develops acute symptoms of an intensity that is unmanageable with the tools at the analyst's disposal. In such situations, temporary drug therapy may save an analysis that would otherwise have to be interrupted or even discontinued.

With regard to both these types of situation, the actual occasions should be comparatively few. Yet the danger is great, as has already been mentioned, that analysts may take to resorting to drug therapy as an adjunct of analysis, in situations that would in fact be quite manageable, if the analytical technique itself were to be used judiciously. Impatience and the desire for a spurious sort of efficiency may overrule psychoanalytic acumen. In that way, drug therapy—instead of being a valuable adjunct to the psychoanalytic technique—may indirectly contribute to its deterioration.

There is another way, however, in which drug therapy may prove quite harmful to psychoanalysis. I shall demonstrate this by an example which, though it does not stem from psychiatric observation, may still be useful for our purpose. It has to do with certain events brought to light in a Swiss court (Justin, 1960).

A thirty-year-old married journeyman baker, a hard-working man, who had always led a life of honesty and probity, untainted by any manifest trait of delinquency, suddenly started to gamble in a city near his

---

[149] The above passage is the result of a discussion with Dr. Max Schur, whom I wish to thank for permission to include it here.

home town. From then on, he was doomed, relentlessly going on with his gambling. First he lost his and his wife's hard-earned savings; but he did not stop at that. Under various excuses, he borrowed eight thousand francs, which went the same way as their predecessors. Shortly after that, he started a series of embezzlements, and even though he was investigated by a court, nevertheless continued his gambling and embezzling. This was regarded as a very aggravating factor, so that, when he was at last sentenced, the court refused to grant a suspended sentence.

Yet it turned out that, during the interval, the culprit had changed back to his former mode of living. He had started to repay his debts; he had even refused to accept the help of his father, who was ready to undo the dire consequences of his son's financial escapades, and he was abstaining from any further visits to the gambling places. The reason for my recounting this incident lies in the explanation that the defendant allegedly gave for his sudden reform. On one occasion, when he was returning to his native town from one of his frequent gambling excursions, a detective who knew him said, without surprise or reproach, only casually: "So, so, Bruno, you've been over there again" (Justin, 1960). From that moment on, the spell was broken, and the man returned to his former exemplary modes of behavior.

For the analyst, this is, indeed, a rather perplexing situation. Here is a well-attested report of a single incident that brought an extremely severe gambling spell instantaneously to a halt. It may be objected that we are perhaps dealing here with a cyclic episode, which had run its course and would in any case have come to a halt shortly thereafter, its end being merely precipitated, so to speak, by this trivial and unspecific incident. Since the episode was neither observed nor reported by a psychiatrist, I would not feel free to argue the point; yet I would feel free to deduce that, by some strange coincidence, exactly those conditions conjoined which were requisite for the reinstitution of an operative superego that had been temporarily thrown out of gear.

In psychoanalytic parlance, I would reconstruct the relevant process approximately as follows: a fatherly authority, from which retribution was to have been expected, registered the misdemeanor objectively and without disapprobation, simply as having been observed; at that moment, apparently, the subject's own conscience, with its latent feelings of guilt, was enabled to become operative once more; a process of internalization that had been rendered temporarily inoperative was reinstituted.

All this is especially striking, in so far as many a gambler has been observed who was under exactly the same sort of spell as had apparently seized the unfortunate Bruno. I myself have never succeeded in breaking into such spells; yet the detective brought this one instantly to a halt. It all starts, generally, with the gambler's suddenly feeling compelled to bet —which he does about a half dozen times, with amazing success; then, carried away by the rapture of success, he goes on, only to end with considerable losses. The gambler's behavior during these spells is always the same. With each success, he sees a brighter and brighter future, and promises himself that he will test his luck only once more; with each loss, he is determined to stop—as soon as he has retrieved that part of his gain which he has so far lost. When his total gain has been finally exhausted, along with the savings which he had at the time when the spell set in, he swears that he will stop for ever—as soon as he has retrieved at least his savings; and for that purpose, he resorts to borrowing money. The striking thing is that there is apparently no power of persuasion that can stop him. No pleading, no report of previous experiences of the same kind, will make him give up further gambling as long as he is winning; the same is true as soon as the losses start. At least, I myself have not discovered any technique for providing successful interference once a man is possessed by the spell. Yet the "So-so-Bruno-been-over-there-again" incident shows that there do exist means for bringing such a spell to quiescence.

My proposition is that the Swiss incident is paradigmatic of all psychopathology whose etiology is not predominantly organic. In principle, I believe, any acute symptom can be brought to a temporary standstill— if the adequate psychological measure is instituted. Bleuler (1919) was puzzled by the same sort of problem when he observed that catatonic states may subside temporarily, under the impact of seemingly trivial events. If psychoanalysis had that key to all acute symptoms which the Swiss detective unintentionally stumbled upon, then practically all forms of psychopathology could be drawn into the psychoanalytic orbit, for the patient would probably form a positive transference to any person who had such power to deal with his symptoms. In order to understand man, all forms of psychopathology must be investigated with the same degree of precision as has been employed in understanding and dealing with the transference neuroses. Yet the psychoanalyst also follows the pleasure principle, and he too will probably pursue the path of least resistance.

Will anyone be willing to exercise the relentless effort that is required in order to carry through the difficult and usually ungratifying labor of scientific penetration into the unmapped area of the major psychoses (and criminality), when the dispensing of tablets can induce—and within a short time—a highly beneficial effect upon the symptoms? To dispense pills calls for infinitely less effort than to cut a pathway through the bewildering jungle of unpredictable, severe psychopathology. The ease with which the latter task can already be avoided in many instances— and there will be more and more instances in the future, with the further development of pharmacological progress—will sustain man's laziness. It will deter him from seeking to perfect the technical tool of psychoanalysis by forging it into an instrument adaptable to the broad spectrum of psychopathology.

It is small consolation that interesting and important conclusions may indeed be drawn from the variety of reactions that patients will show in response to the drugs. Dr. Bailey, in his unacademic *Academic Lecture* (1956, p. 403), states: "I shall give all the support I can muster to the biochemists and biophysicists." God is always on the side of the stronger battalions. Dr. Bailey has no love for the "psychogeneticists" who "continue to hurrah and haggle and recruit, and waste both valuable time and energy quarrelling with one another" (*ibid.*).

Well, perhaps Dr. Bailey has made himself the mouthpiece of the future here; perhaps biochemistry will yet wipe out the step ahead that psychology took in Freud's works. If only we could form some idea of the content of the Academic Lecture delivered a century after Dr. Bailey's! Will it be crammed with chemical formulas; or will it quote Dr. Bailey's choice with regret? No one now knows.

Yet *something* will have become clear—namely, that the long-sought chemical formula that eliminates schizophrenia will not have essentially improved the *condition humaine,* if viewed in subjective terms, any more than man's already established power over the bulk of the physical diseases has yet made him essentially happier. Biochemistry deserves the fullest support; yet when this is offered in a spirit of hostility to mental science, with an eye toward minimizing the effort to understand man's mind, then the destructive effects of chemical progress may prove to be greater than its benefits. Is not this great republic big enough to support *both* biochemists and psychoanalysts? It is indeed short-sighted to view the two as mutually exclusive.

If the clinical efficiency of drug therapy should (as indeed I fear it will—and automatically, too) weaken man's effort to understand all forms of psychopathology on the psychological level, then Western civilization may never find the solution to the two problems that most disquietingly beset our culture—namely, how to raise children without leaving them exposed to the dangers of becoming neurotic, delinquent or psychotic as adults; and how to organize group life so as to insure the peaceful solutions of those conflicts that unavoidably arise sporadically between groups. The pharmacologist may say that he is prepared to deal with psychopathology once it arises in the adult; but can he also ensure a mankind that is ready to digest its daily peace tablet?

This perhaps somewhat bizarre conception is directed toward counteracting the development of the exclusively medical approach to psychopathology. Psychopathology is *also* a medical problem, and I would be unhappy if anyone thought he could read between these lines some supposed objection on my part against the pharmacological treatment of it. Yet one must stress the fact, over and over again, that psychopathology harbors the secrets of most of those evils that have beset mankind since its dawn—evils that still make its survival as questionable, after two millennia of Christianization, as it probably was in those remote days when evolutionary changes stopped taking place on the organic plane, and instead the process of change shifted over to the areas of the evolution of civilization and culture—that is to say, when animal instinct was first reduced to man's drives, and then complemented by potentially rational action.

The danger to psychoanalysis that arises from the setting up of artificial dichotomies was already foreshadowed by Freud (1925f), when he wrote: "So it comes about that psycho-analysis derives nothing but disadvantages from its middle position between medicine and philosophy" (p. 217). Here he was referring to the dissatisfaction aroused in both the anthropic scientist and the physician by the synthesis that he had accomplished between the biological aspect of the human personality and its sociological or cultural aspect. Over and over again, one can observe how either one of these aspects is overemphasized to the detriment of the other, so that a lopsided theory of human development and pathogenesis arises.

Sociologism in moderate form raises its head right within the psychoanalytic movement itself, its foremost psychoanalytic representative being H. S. Sullivan. It centers its attention on man's actual relationship to others, in which it finds the key to psychopathology. The pitfalls and limitations of this approach can best be set forth, I think, in an examination of a representative clinical study. I have selected for this purpose

Cohen et al.'s (1954) study of cases of manic-depressive psychoses. To do full justice to the merits and demerits of this study, a long discussion would be necessary. But completeness is not the central question at this point, and I shall pinpoint only the area in which psychoanalysis forever parts ways with sociologism.

Of immediate concern to anyone endowed with some degree of clinical sensibility would be the fact that, although the title promises a study of manic-depressive psychosis, it turns out that the study is primarily concerned with the manic-depressive character (p. 136), or the cyclic personality (p. 119). Furthermore, the study seems to be the result of a survey of what is to be observed at the molar level.

Thus it was determined that the family background of most of the subjects was characterized by low prestige, or by some other kind of isolation within the community, etc. This observation, if it is correct— and a significant difference in sociological elements between the environments of those who later became schizophrenic and cyclic patients had been noted previously by others—would be, of course, of general psychiatric importance; it is without psychoanalytic relevance, however, so long as it remains untranslated into psychological terms. That is to say, there should have been an attempt to find out in what way the particular sociological constellation actually impinged on the development of the child's ego, what psychological stimuli needed to be correlated with the sociological structure and framework of the family.

It would be wrong to say that Cohen et al. made no attempt in this direction; by and large, however, they did not get very far beyond a molar sociological approach. On the other hand, when Cohen et al. had gained certain impressions about the character of the cyclic personality, they did not undertake the task of reconstructing, by the use of the analytic method, their patients' development from infancy to adulthood; instead, they constructed a picture—rather superficial in fact—of the social environment. Then they looked around for a model of childhood development that would best serve as a link between the two.

At this point, they took a rather surprising step: they found Melanie Klein's model of childhood development confirmed by their observations among patients of the cyclic group. I regard this as surprising inasmuch as, within the spectrum of the psychoanalytic schools, London and Washington are at opposite poles: in the former group, to simplify matters, man is the product of the struggle between life and death instincts; in the latter group, for whom no death instinct exists, he is the product of his environment. How is it possible then for East and West so peacefully to join hands when a configuration as controversial as cyclic psychosis or personality is being studied? In my opinion, it is because Melanie Klein's model of childhood development is at heart ahistorical, and almost independent of actual social reality. Since with her the childhood value systems arise in what amounts to independence of external reality, her model can be used without any consideration of the vicissitudes in any particular area.

One can use her model in almost the same way as that in which a historian can use anatomy. He is entitled to assume without any further inquiry that the same skeletal structure is to be found among all the people whose history he will present, so that he really does not need to *investigate* whether the leader of an army had a tibia and a femur. It was Cohen et al.'s task to investigate, with regard to their subjects, whether Melanie Klein's assertions about the infant's depressive position could really be confirmed in those instances. Yet they proceeded as one does in applied psychoanalysis, when insights that the clinician has gained from the living object of his investigation are applied to *natura morta*. This is wholly in keeping with the basic procedure of the sociologist, who is for the most part uninterested in the individual psychic process, and instead focuses on the problem: What do *people* do, under what *social* conditions?

Thus what Cohen et al. set forth is hardly ever the result of interpretations; usually, they are trying to prove a point merely by citing, for example, what a subject's mother had to report about his early upbringing. In the same fashion, their attention is mainly directed to the behavior of the subject in his direct contact with the therapist—that is to say, to the surface aspects of the subject's social terrain.

The basic process of melancholia—that structural change in the ego which Freud (1917d) described in the classical statement that "the shadow of the object fell on the ego" (p. 249)—finds no place in a sociologically oriented psychology. For Cohen et al., the manic-depressive patient is characterized by an "exploitative clinging dependency" (p. 127). No doubt, anyone who has tried to deal with severely depressed patients, or with certain types of melancholia, will have observed such clinging. Yet this clinging—as difficult as it may be to deal with clinically, and as intensely as it often occupies the main stage—is the consequence of something quite different in character. A process of almost catastrophic nature has taken place, leading, in Freud's words, to a *grossartige Ichverarmung* (full-scale ego impoverishment) (p. 246).

In Cohen's description of the journey to psychosis, she reaches lows characteristic of an Adler or an Alexander, as when she describes the motor that keeps the whole process going in the following words: "The patient incessantly hopes for and strives for a dependency relationship in which all his needs are met by the others . . . . After every depressive attack, he sets forth upon this quest anew. In the course of time, it becomes apparent to him that his object is not fulfilling his needs . . . . The patient redoubles his efforts and receives still less. Finally, he loses hope and enters into the psychotic state where the pattern of emptiness and need is repeated over and over again in the absence of any specific object" (p. 121f.).

Thus the melancholic spell is made comparable to the bankrupt ending of a blackmailing affair, or its like. In the light of the behavior of a patient suffering from *melancolia agitans,* this may seem quite convincing. Yet doubt must arise when one observes a melancholic patient who has turned away from the world, does not look at anybody, has fallen into complete silence, is incapable of eating or sleeping, and is filled with an anguish beyond tears. Then it may become clear that a psychological study of melancholia, built on a theory that will have nothing to do with the term "superego" (p. 124), is stillborn.

In this regard, there exist clinical proofs demonstrating the insufficiency of a sociologically oriented psychoanalytic theory. In 1939, I had to treat at the Billings Hospital of the University of Chicago, a forty-nine-year-old married man who was suffering from a depression of the clinging type, as described by Cohen et al. No interpretation was effective. He found himself in a constant state of painful dejection, and indulged in continuous complaining. The striking feature, however, was that the patient would respond to interpretations positively, alertly, and with considerable understanding, whenever he had first received one of his earlier injections of testosterone propionate intramuscularly. Then he would get up from the couch, greatly relieved, and remain cheerful for the rest of the day. An analytic session would then take a course such as can be expected in the case of a patient who suffers from a neurosis, and whose resistances are overcome by proper interpretation.

The analytic session took an entirely different course, however, when the patient was not first treated with the hormone. Interpretations had no effect, and the hour was uselessly spent with empty complaints; the patient would get up from the couch desperately complaining that "today the treatment did not help a bit." Repeatedly, the patient raised the question of what determined the fact that at times psychoanalysis had such a beneficial effect on him, while at other times it seemed to take no hold of him at all.

In order to exclude the effect of suggestion, Dr. Richard Sternheimer, who was supervising the patient's treatment as an internist, and who provided the hormone, agreed to introduce a double blind-check by replacing the hormone at times with ampules filled with oil. Thus nobody on the ward who came into contact with the patient—including myself, of course—knew, in any particular instance, whether the patient had received the hormone or a placebo. Nevertheless, I was regularly able to ascertain, from the course of the analytic hour, whether it was the hormone or the placebo that had been dispensed.[150]

I cite this clinical observation, because it seems to me to demonstrate the primacy of Freud's "full-scale ego-impoverishment,"[151] upon which the clinging of the depressed patient is built. It is easy to understand why an ego suffering from depleted libido clings to objects, and cannot be satisfied, no matter what they may do for him. Freud's outline of a theory of depressive disorders provides an adequate basis on which to explain the observations made by the sociologist-analyst. On the other hand, I do not see any way in which the theory of depression set forth by Cohen et al. could ever explain the observation reported.

It is not without interest, and probably significant of the present situation, that Myer Mendelson (1960), in his otherwise excellent survey of psychoanalytic thinking on depressions, puts Cohen et al.'s study on the same plane as *bona fide* psychoanalytic inquiries, without any regard for

[150] It seemed for a while as if the patient had become addicted to testosterone, but gradually he came to require smaller dosages in order to feel comfortable; by about nine months after the onset of the disease, he was able to stay well without any pharmacological treatment. Whether the observation reported here was a chance occurrence, based on the peculiarity of the particular patient, or has general validity, I do not know.

In a patient suffering from a rather severe depression and a hand tremor (initially diagnosed as psychogenic), testosterone had some, but by no means a striking, effect. However, it later became clear that the patient was actually suffering from Parkinsonism. In a sixty-year-old patient suffering from impotence and intermittent, short fits of depression, on the other hand, testosterone had no effect at all, while psychotherapy restored his potency with comparative speed.

[151] I do not think that my explanation of the patient's behavior sets me among those "who place psychoanalysis in opposition to endocrinology, as though psychic processes could be explained directly by glandular functions, or as though the understanding of psychic mechanisms could replace the knowledge of the underlying chemical process" (Freud to Alexander Lipschütz, August 1931; in Freud, 1873-1939, p. 406f.).

the differences in outcome between molar and microscopic investigations. Nevertheless, it would be wrong to conclude that I consider such studies as that done by Cohen et al. to be wrong or futile.

I think that they are necessary; I also think that they can serve a legitimate purpose—so long as the authors are aware of the theoretical framework within which they are moving. When they arrogate to themselves the decision as to which psychoanalytic theory of infantile development is right or wrong; when they believe that they are actually studying the psychodynamics of disease; or when they set out to uncover the reasons for the *quality* of experience (p. 104) of a child who is suffering from depressions—then it seems to me that they are aiming at goals that cannot be reached with their techniques.

Moderate biologism and moderate sociologism are both distortions or falsifications of two positions found in Freud's work. Since the newborn child is, psychologically, an instinctual being (*Triebwesen*), the axiom or working principle of pursuing the genesis of each phenomenon observed in the adult to its instinctual root seems appropriate.[152] On the other hand, Freud writes: "The ego was developed out of the id by the continual influence of the external world" (1940a, p. 43).[153] In that respect, impingement of the external stimuli upon the id may be regarded as the relevant psychic process, since what are to be observed in the adult are ego phenomena.

The method of the English school and that of the W. A. White group strike me as being vulgarizations of these two principles. What is particularly deplorable in the latter is the abandonment of basic technical principles, which were instituted by Freud precisely in order to safeguard minimal scientific standards.

As is well known, both Melanie Klein's and Harry Stack Sullivan's theories have had consequential effects, and the numerical strength of their adherents is, in each instance, considerable. What is especially striking is the geographical orbits of these two schools. I think it is almost certain that having been born in England or South America would make it impossible ever to become convinced of the superiority of Sullivan's theories; on the other hand, I wonder how many analysts in the United States have ever become adherents of the English school.

[152] A discussion that would do justice to all the problems involved in the application of this principle would lead us far afield.

[153] It has been questioned whether this is the sole principle of ego development; in Freud's writings, a start was made toward broadening the principles of ego formation. Cf. Hartmann (1950, pp. 79f.).

The effect of the cultural habitat upon the scientist generally is undeniable. After all, the same medicine is not taught either in the United States or in France or in Russia; therapeutic techniques vary from country to country; and trends of interest and tendencies within the area of theory formation differ in accordance with national ties. Yet I wonder whether there is any other field of scientific endeavor in which such vast differences obtain as do in psychoanalysis, even with regard to questions of fact. An inquiry into this state of affairs is not in order here; yet this much may be said—that even the very discrepancies or schisms that exist at present in psychoanalysis reflect the vastness and the profundity of Freud's total endeavor.

In Freud, one can observe a synthesis of the two working principles that I have set forth. Melanie Klein's model of childhood development, on the other hand, is steeped in Freud's original theories of the development of the libidinal and aggressive drives, while the W. A. White group is inconceivable without Freud's discoveries in the area of transference and of the development of the superego. Yet neither of these schools seems to be an extension, but rather a caricature or a falsification of Freud's original view.

The difficulty involved in advancing what Freud started arises out of the multidimensionality of his work—which is, in turn, nothing but a reflection of the infinite complexity of man's mind. The mistakes that these two schools commit on the grand scale are in essence the same as those that every theorizing analyst is bound to commit, in so far as he is incapable of drawing the whole panorama of the human personality into his deliberations, and is instead compelled by the narrow limits of the human mind to view only partial aspects. These two schools, however—and with an impressive consistency—develop views that are based on partial aspects, into theories that purport to include the whole personality.

Why such shrinking of the vast range that found representation in Freud's work should hold such fascination for so many, is not altogether clear to me. It would be wrong to assume that the investigator's intelligence is the sole decisive factor in his choice of theory. I feel certain that investigation would reveal that the I. Q.'s are distributed in about the same ratios among the various psychoanalytic schools.

Are we thus thrown back upon the theory of resistance? This might hold true for the W. A. White group, which attributes to the drives an astonishingly small bearing upon man's vicissitudes. Is it the comparatively small place assigned to the oedipus complex in Melanie Klein's edifice that makes that edifice so very attractive to her adherents? Is it, finally, the relief that comes with our thinking that our relationship to the world is not decided by the hazards of some wish we may have had at an age of some sort of responsibility, but rather by a drama occurring so early in our lives that we can almost equate it with 'heredity'—a concept which, even though it has been terribly feared at times, has nevertheless for a long period of time served to absolve mankind of responsibility for its own actions[154] (cf. Mitscherlich, 1963, p. 217).

[154] In view of the limitations of my own explanation for the surprising appeal that Mrs. Klein's psychoanalysis of infantile life has had for many analysts, I want to report on the remarks made by the late Dr. Kris many years ago in Vienna, and by Dr. Robert Waelder recently. Both of them emphasized the connection of Mrs. Klein's theories with religious doctrines—Dr. Kris with Calvin's doctrine of the inherent depravity of human nature, and Dr. Waelder with the struggle between good and evil that occupies the central position in Manichaeism. If Mrs. Klein's views gratify some traditional sentiments of religious provenance, that may be the key to the sociological significance of some of her views, as well as to their attractive power.

Appendix 1

The Desegregation of Psychoanalytic
Institutes and Medical Schools

One consequence of the development of medical analysis is the growing conviction that psychoanalytic training and research would best be served by being entrusted to the universities—that is to say, to the psychiatric departments of the medical schools. Psychoanalysis would then be officially stamped as a medical specialty. I have made some previous comments on this point, but I want to enlarge on them now, even at the risk of repetition, for there is no other administrative issue of practical significance with a greater bearing on the future of psychoanalysis in this country.

A substantial part of Dr. Alexander's (1956) book, *Psychoanalysis and Psychotherapy,* is taken up with the investigation of this problem; since his exposition is, I believe, the most extensive one written on this question by an analyst, it may be desirable to undertake a critical discussion of some of his arguments.[1] Alexander's qualified recommendation of the integration of psychoanalysis into university departments rests on his observation that "in the United States the medical schools are in the process of becoming ripe for the full acceptance of psychoanalysis" (p.

[1] Alexander's full presentation, along with the record that he includes of the opinions of leading psychiatrists and psychoanalysts on this matter, is too bulky to be discussed critically in all of its ramifications; nevertheless, at least the main trend of his thinking may profitably be discussed here.

185). In his opinion, the time has already come when psychiatric university departments are able to carry out both sorts of training—in psychiatry as well as in psychoanalysis (p. 197).

I shall set forth a few passages from the answers of three representative psychiatrists who were among those answering the questionnaire that Alexander sent out.[2]

Kenneth E. Appel, Chairman, Department of Psychiatry, University of Pennsylvania, member of the American Psychoanalytic Association, has the following to say about psychoanalytic institutes: "Rigidity, dogmatism, assertion, conviction, authority, indoctrination, so prevalent in many psychoanalytic institutes, are not education. Preoccupation with rituals, details, and money is frequent. They are indicative of obsessive-anal tendencies. The same applies to the hostilities, rancor, uncompromising spirit, and emphasis on authority" (p. 207). The analytic training, says Appel, leads to "delay in productivity and maturity. Creativity or efforts at creativity are often crushed. Curiosity is not encouraged, often stultified . . . . Somehow the training is too long" (p. 208).

About analysts, he also has some harsh words to say: "Unfortunately some who know the characteristics of maturity and *urge their patients to be mature and realistic* [italics mine] have not been distinguished for these qualities themselves. They are often very wishful and defensive." About the effect of training analyses: "Formerly friendly, warm, responsive, genial, cooperative persons become hard, defensive, hostile, distant, more self-considering, even suspicious at times, less contributing, more self-seeking financially. When this happens, they are more difficult to work with around hospitals and less collaborating in medical schools" (p. 210). It is a pity that the author does not let us know whether these conclusions are based upon local observations, or refer to the national level!

It would be out of place for me, of course, to examine the correctness of such claims. Perhaps Dr. Appel is right; I hope that he is not. But surely it must surprise the reader that an eminent psychiatrist who, according to Alexander, has become "ripe for the full acceptance of psychoanalysis," should hold the current training institutes in such low esteem, and would evidently reorganize them in a spirit alien to that which obtains now. The fact that he is a member of the American Psychoanalytic Association does not prejudice the case. At any rate, he

[2] The full record of their answers is published in the section on "Opinions of Contemporary Teachers in Psychiatry" (1956, pp. 202-265).

must be quite happy that Dr. Alexander's wish to attach the institutes to his department has not yet been realized.

Karl M. Bowman, Professor Emeritus (Psychiatry), University of California, made a statement that is both instructive and illustrative of what may be expected if the organization of psychoanalytic training does follow Alexander's proposed directions. He observed that, while among his residents who had not been analyzed some rejected Freudian doctrines rather strongly, "some of them swallow these teachings uncritically, . . . some accept part and reject part. This latter method seems to me evidence of a better balanced personality" (p. 212).

Since a balanced personality is undoubtedly one of the goals of a training analysis, the candidate, I presume, ought to be analyzed until he becomes mature enough to "accept part and reject part" of psychoanalysis. Here, at last, we have an objective index of success in training analysis! Yet the author's terse statement makes me conclude that it is immaterial *which part* is to be rejected and *which* accepted, just so long as something is rejected and something accepted. Unintentionally, perhaps, a certain pattern has been set up of what a modern psychiatrist should look like: he should be *eclectic*.

It is not a sign of *bon ton* these days to find Freudian doctrines in accord with observation, but the 'enlightened' person does not reject Freud, either: he shows his sophistication by 'appreciating' Freud, and yet demonstrating where Freud—quite understandably, I suppose—'erred.'[3] Bailey (1956) has described this kind of sophistication succinctly: "It has become a habit, in beginning a psychiatric lecture, to pay tribute to Freud's genius. Thus Montagu remarked: 'This general [pessimistic] viewpoint has received what is perhaps its most striking reenforcement from a source which undoubtedly represents the most insightful contribution to our understanding of human nature in the history of humanity. I refer to the psychoanalytic theories of Sigmund Freud.' He then proceeds to demolish the viewpoint. This is an old procedure" (p. 395). It could gain new life, I am sure, as a guideline for psychoanalytic university departments.[4]

[3] Cf. Freud (1933a): ". . . in the scientific world a kind of buffer state has been formed between analysis and its opponents, consisting of people who will allow that there is something in analysis (and even believe in it, subject to the most diverting reservations) but who . . . reject other parts of it, as they are eager to let every one know. What determines their choice is not easy to guess. It seems to be a matter of personal sympathies. Some take objections to sexuality," etc. (p. 189).

[4] Bailey's *Academic Lecture,* from which I have just quoted, should be carefully studied by those who are in favor of the desegregation of psychoanalytic training.

John C. Whitehorn, Psychiatrist-in-Chief (Johns Hopkins Hospital), is another leader in the field who sent in an answer to Alexander's questionnaire. One can get an inkling of the atmosphere in which psychoanalysis would be discussed in *his* training institute by taking cognizance of the following: "Freud, with bold imagination, tremendous personal ambition, and considerable dramatic talent, constructed the more attention-getting myths, and thereby patterned the new patter" (p. 261).[5] If anyone thought this to be a purely historical remark, he should take notice that Whitehorn himself "decided that instinct hypotheses were not very suitable for actual clinical use."

According to him, the idea of drive "fostered the illusion of scientific mastery," for it "lent itself to pseudo-quantitative quasi scientific formulation." "In a historical-speculative frame of mind," the author even thought that, if Freud had "not become tired and saddled with the leadership role for a dependent group, committed to his earlier overly mechanized formulations," he would have "in his more mature years" rejected his "early error."

It should be noted that Whitehorn registers with much gratification the fact that his own terminology is increasingly being used in the psychiatric literature, and professes to find "much similarity, if not identity, between Freud's observations and his stimulating speculations, and the phenomena for which in my teaching I have used the terms attitude, value, pattern of motivation, roles and personality" (p. 262). If there is, in fact, such identity as he speaks of, one wonders why he should have gone out of his way to evolve his own "patter." And how one can study 'attitude' without emphasis on the drives is puzzling, especially to anyone who has observed a hungry man before and after a meal.

Dr. Bailey—who disputes Freud's originality, whenever he is able to find a historical antecedent to a psychoanalytic discovery—would rightly say that all this is old stuff, for *post coitum omne animal triste* had already been observed by the ancients. Yet he should admit that there is merit in a finding that can so easily be overlooked by the so-called expert. Furthermore, Whitehorn's picture of a Freud who plays politics with his science and, out of regard for a dependent group, does not tell what he knows to be the truth is a baseless flight of imagination.

The pronouncements thus far cited reveal that ambivalence, at least,

[5] This last condescending remark is all the more out of place since the introduction of Freud's terminology is, in fact, comparable in its effect with Viet's introduction of symbols into mathematics.

and at the most hostility to psychoanalysis still seem rampant in academic psychiatry. Be that as it may, for the time being let us continue to celebrate the existence of the independent institute.

Alexander may be right in his assertion that "emotional resistance against psychoanalysis has become less and less evident" (p. 177) (but not necessarily less real!); he may also be right when he says that the prestige of psychoanalytic training has risen in the eyes of students and academic administrations (p. 185). Yet any analyst knows or ought to know that prestige is by no means a reliable index of how a thing is actually represented in a person's mind, and that prestige and feelings of abomination may live side by side.

The preceding group of citations, however, is of secondary importance, for any analyst who has integrated Freud's concept of resistance knows, once he has attended a psychiatric convention, that it is better for the growth of psychoanalysis that it should continue its present official status as an independent branch of science.

Once the question of 'ripeness' has been examined, we may turn to some of the other arguments that Alexander raises in favor of the desegregation of psychiatric institutes and universities. He believes that such a fusion would bring forth mutual blessings, one of which would be a significant accretion of knowledge and therapeutic potential. Alexander's dissatisfaction with the classical technique is known from his previous writings, and it is interesting that he expects to see emerge from a *rapprochement* between psychiatry and psychoanalysis a unified theory covering all psychotherapeutic techniques.

Therefore, in order to understand just what sort of progress it is that Alexander expects, it becomes necessary to consider what he means by psychoanalysis. For this, I recommend that the reader study his chapter on "Psychoanalysis and Psychotherapy" (Alexander, 1956, pp. 148-172), in which, by reading critically, he will find that I am quite justified in singling out a type of analyst to be known as the 'medical analyst.'

From the very beginning, it must be stated that Alexander's book is replete with contradictions; one may unhesitatingly anticipate that, should one of his statements be shown to be incorrect, he will be able to refer to another—in the same book—in which something quite different is stated. I want to deal with only one series of such contradictions.

1. One position that Alexander takes is that psychoanalytically oriented psychotherapy is more difficult than classical psychoanalysis (pp. 160, 166). 2. He agrees with those who maintain that personal analysis is not

necessary to the development of competent psychiatrists, including those who practice psychotherapy (p. 167). 3. Often "good, experienced psychiatrists, who are well acquainted with the basic concepts of psychodynamics," even though they have not received formal psychoanalytic training, will "recognize and interpret transference conflicts and resistances . . . as well as or better than many formally recognized psychoanalysts" (p. 167). 4. Psychoanalytic training will enhance the technical skill "of psychiatrists who do well without it" (p. 168). 5. Training analysis is an indispensable prerequisite of psychoanalytic training (p. 181).

Thus, one has to cut through a constant zigzag in order to reach the rock bottom of his error. I myself finally came to the conclusion that a technical example—which (for a change!) he did not contradict during the further course of his text—might be best suited to demonstrate that, while Alexander may be an excellent medical analyst, he really ignored, to say the least, the potential of the psychoanalytic situation as Freud understood it.

According to Alexander, the following situation obtains: The person who analyzes in accordance with the classical technique follows a "routine," which protects him "from making independent decisions, which have to be based not only on a general understanding of the case but also on a precise appreciation of the momentary psychodynamic situation" (p. 160). (I hope that Alexander does not think he is original in his emphasis on the latter.) But what are the independent decisions the medical analyst has to make?

> For example, the analyst who is not protected by routine may, at a given time, have to consider whether he should try to reduce the intensity of the patient's emotional involvement; he may decide that the patient's dependency can be counteracted by making it more [sic!] conscious, and therefore he may reduce the frequency of the interviews or interrupt the treatment temporarily so that the patient will be on his own for a while and will be made to feel that he need not rely continually on his therapist[6] . . . . Such considerations require evaluations which are not

[6] Whoever is acquainted with Dr. Alexander's clinical papers knows that he is a veritable crusader against "dependence." No one else, I think it is safe to say, has worked so hard to exorcise from the analytic couch this alleged poison. Yet I still believe that every patient is free, without any threat of suffering quasi punitive measures from the analyst, to show in his transference what are in fact his overriding attitudes and drives. Any analyst who permitted himself to interfere with that freedom would only be depriving himself thereby of the opportunity to determine what degree of structural change has taken place through increasing insight.

necessary if the psychoanalyst proceeds according to a standardized procedure [p. 160].

To set the record straight: The classical analyst would *never* consider a reduction of interviews or an interruption of treatment at such a point, because it would be in fact the *least promising* measure in terms of providing the patient with insight: it interferes with the working through process, and constitutes an acting out on the part of the therapist, who shows, in that respect, to a certain extent, dishonesty toward the patient. If the patient is pathologically dependent on the analyst and he should become 'more' conscious thereof, it is the analyst's duty to bring that fact to the patient's awareness, and to interpret it.

The choice of interpretation is, of course, not easy. It may be a genetic one, or it may refer to the function of defense; one may set forth the wish fulfillment that is contained in the behavior pattern, or refer to the drive to which it is related; one may focus the interpretation on the transference. In addition, it must be determined what imago the patient is following here; the analyst often includes in his interpretation a reference to the repetitiveness of a pattern; he may have to connect the dependence with a number of other elements, including a dream that the patient told him about many months earlier, or an apraxia that had occurred during the first interview. A gifted analyst could write a whole treatise on all the possibilities of interpretation that are possible, once it becomes a matter of 'counteracting' the patient's dependency.[7]

Each type of interpretation represents a different technique. For Alexander, however, it seems to be always the same, a routine technique, for in every instance nothing but words are used.[8] There can be no doubt that Alexander uses pejorative terms here under the guise of objectivity, without so much as presenting the ABC of the classical technique. The short paragraph I have quoted is of considerable importance, since it

[7] In connection with this technique of reducing interviews, Alexander writes: "Interpretation of the transference situation, of course, is imperative, but the effect of interpretation is greatly enhanced if at the same time the dependent gratifications of the transference are actually curtailed. In other words, facts are stronger than words alone" (p. 133). Which is exactly what the patient thinks. In bowing to the demands of the pleasure principle, he holds insight in low esteem, waiting patiently for the moment when the analyst will finally step out of his reserve. Since speed of cure is one of the cherished goals of the medical analyst, and the "timelessness of the unconscious" is not acknowledged by him, the whole psychoanalytic frame becomes distorted, and basic, clinically well-justified principles are hastily thrown overboard.

[8] It is almost like saying that artists are well protected from the necessity of making independent decisions, because they always use canvas, brush and pigments.

demonstrates once again that the stage of scientific psychology has not yet been reached. We are still living in times in which anybody is permitted to say anything about psychoanalysis, in any way that suits his purposes, without fear of making himself ridiculous. Only under such circumstances is it possible for Alexander to characterize the classical technique as 'routine,' or as a 'protection' against 'independent decisions.'

The classical analyst has to heed the momentary psychodynamic situation, of course, whenever he sets out to give an interpretation. The 'routine decisions' of the classical analyst are based on a huge number of factors.[9] In a clinical situation such as that described by Alexander, the classical analyst does not find himself in the enviable position of his colleague who may have had the good fortune to be trained by Alexander, and may therefore act like the rabbi who advised the woman who was suffering from the fear of a man lying under her bed: "Cut off the legs of the bed."

The classical analyst who follows the 'routine' aim of conveying the optimal insight to his patient may proceed in a variety of ways, each of which is reflective of a *different* technique. In Alexander's mind, the classical technique is apparently represented as a monotonous and therefore unendingly repetitive affair, in which no alternatives exist, but only one path can be traveled.[10] Great is the praise, however, that Alexander bestows on his own technique, which he already looked forward many years ago to seeing become the generally accepted psychoanalytic technique (Alexander and French, 1946)—a disaster that has not yet occurred.

By 1956, he has become more modest; he grants that training in classical analysis may have its own niche in a university department, side by side with psychoanalytically oriented psychotherapy and the organic treatment method—and in that way psychotherapy will become an instrument of insuperable excellence. He suggests that the psychoanalysts should step out of their reserve and forge from their instrument, which is at present applicable to a limited number of diseases only, one that is adjusted to all clinical syndromes. Intuitive psychotherapy will then grow into rational psychotherapy.

[9] Of course, a rule or a technical principle can always be called pejoratively a 'routine.' When Anna Freud (1936), for example, advises the psychoanalyst to take "his stand at a point equidistant from the id, the ego and the superego" (p. 30), this may appear to the outsider like a matter of routine, which is designed to relieve the analyst of independent decisions. Anna Freud herself of course took note of some of the great difficulties to be encountered in such a 'routine' position.

[10] Since there is a vast literature from which one can ascertain the multidimensionality of the classical technique, I refer only to one text (Fenichel, 1938-1939).

I for one have no objection to such a plan: the evolvement of a rational psychotherapy is surely a meritorious undertaking. It is not the *methodology* of this project that is of concern here. Since a large number of psychoanalysts have university appointments, the necessary psychoanalytic support is already available; and it is hard to see why for this purpose the psychoanalytic institutes should change the character of their present functional setup.

Alexander tries hard to create a community of academic daydreams. He writes: "Now, when psychiatry is not only ready but eager to assimilate in an undiluted form the teachings of Freud and the work of his followers, we feel that it becomes our responsibility to guide and facilitate this process of incorporation" (p. 151). Yet Alexander did not answer the question which some of the respondents to his questionnaire so embarrassingly asked him: "Which kind of psychoanalysis do you mean?" After all, in most cities there are *two* institutes, teaching theories and techniques that have little in common. When Alexander observes that the universities are eager to assimilate the undiluted teachings of Freud and of "his followers," one must ask which 'followers' he had in mind.

After all, if one attempts to assimilate undiluted Freud and undiluted Sullivan, or the former plus Frieda Fromm-Reichmann, or the former plus Rado, or the former plus Alexander, one cannot expect to do so without creating a dangerous toxic state, or allergy, that may overtax the idiosyncratic potential and destroy the organism before this process of assimilation has come to an end. This can be readily demonstrated through the examination of one of Alexander's clinical views, which is quite clearly incompatible with undiluted Freud. Alexander (1935b) declared the abbreviation of the psychoanalytic treatment to be the ultimate goal (p. 611), quite by contrast with Freud's views published two years later (1937a). Indeed, if the aim of symptomatic cure is replaced with the aim of achieving structural changes of the greatest possible solidity and extension, it is quite impossible to accept Alexander's ultimate goal. Of course, if an analyst is strongly motivated toward abbreviation of treatment, his clinical practice, as well as his views, may be adapted to conform with this goal. Consequently, we encounter the view already discussed (and rejected by Freud), that a patient takes refuge in regressions to preconflictual phases that are pathogenetically irrelevant, thus "retreating to the 'good old days' with their relatively minor conflicts" (p. 166). I doubt that such an *aurea aetas* really exists for patients that come for treatment; but even if it did, it could not have the significant effect on psychoanalytic technique that Alexander believes it to have.

He presents a case history, in brief outline, to prove his points. Despite the sparseness of the data provided, one gets the impression that Alexander inadvertently traumatized the patient by two remarks at the initial stage of the treatment. In the first, he called the patient's attention to a contradiction, in so far as the patient was sceptical of analysis, and yet seemed to put great trust in it—"otherwise he would not cooperate so conscientiously. This remark obviously called his bluff, and he left the interview with manifest embarrassment" (p. 108). The next day the therapist called the patient's attention to the fact that he had left, contrary to his usual practice, without shaking his hand. Subsequently, an intensive resistance developed (p. 108).

In spite of the little that Alexander has published about this patient, one nevertheless has enough to obtain the impression that the resistance was provoked artificially, by Alexander's therapeutic ineptness.[11] Here it would be necessary to discuss Alexander's concept of the dependence that appears in the transference relationship, his approach that, by and large, it is an irreducible entity, and his way of dealing with it. Without wishing to become involved in a technical discussion, I shall make two comments.

Freud discussed—most constructively, in his writing on the case history of the Wolf Man (1918)—the very question that Alexander raises about the technique of dealing with a patient's regressions. At that time, too,

[11] The example Alexander gives disproves his contention that the classical technique is routine. No reason is discernible why Alexander should have interrupted the unfolding of the patient's material at that point, and in a way so offensive to the patient, to boot. There is a strange contradiction between listening to Alexander's wholesome emphasis, on one hand, on "a precise appreciation of the momentary psychodynamic situation" (p. 160), and then, on the other hand, watching him produce artificially a type of transference reaction that "lasted for over two years" (p. 109). The choice of content and the timing of interpretation depends on such a huge number of variables that only with difficulty can all of them be surveyed simultaneously. Is it possible that Alexander is truly unaware of the extensive variability of the classical technique within its own seemingly narrow orbit, and that is why he is sure that the technique that he used before he became a reformer of technique was the classical one? Is it further possible that his apparent disappointment with the classical technique was caused by the faulty way in which he himself had used it?

For purposes of clarification of the present almost chaotic situation—in which almost anyone could justify his teaching his own brand of technique by the mere claim that use of the classical technique did not lead to the desired effect—it would be of great importance to obtain a detailed account of the technique that had actually been used. Yet this is no longer done. Small episodes referring to the course of treatment, and a long case history, are usually all that is obtainable.

voices were being raised about patients who try to evade responsibility and take refuge in the past, etc. Freud's answer was that, even if these explanations were right—which he seriously doubted—there was still nothing else to do but follow the patient, and bring to consciousness the path that infantile development had taken (Freud, 1918, p. 50).

The difference that Alexander raises, in terms of the technique to be used, between evasive regressions and such as are in the service of conflict resolution, is invalid. In one of the instances that he set forth, two premature resistance-provoking remarks, as mentioned before, had a patent bearing on the course the transference took (this was apparently never adequately analyzed). Another example, which Alexander has discussed a little more extensively, is even more instructive. Here, a clinically quite dangerous withdrawal in the patient (he stopped working and stayed at home, playing with his children) was persistently evaluated as "a regressive evasion from oedipal involvement," and the idea that it might "represent a return to an unsettled pregenital conflict" was rejected (p. 121). However, the patient's mother had died when he was six years old, and there was a complete amnesia regarding her. The clinical importance of such an extended amnesia should be clear. When it concerns a man's most significant love object, to boot, it would seem to be wiser to focus attention on this central problem, and rather superficial to overlook the fact that this patient was demonstrating quite markedly the "unsettled conflict" of early childhood.[12]

There are two statements by Alexander which indicate that the general atmosphere customarily pervading the classical analyst's office can be essentially changed by the techniques of the medical analyst. When Alexander comments on his technical device that he "called the patient's bluff" (p. 108), or when he writes that "both analytic treatment and chess are procedures of strategy in which two minds oppose each other" (p. 129),[13] he suggests that the focus of the psychoanalytic technique has shifted. It has become a means of outwitting the patient, instead of a royal road toward the gaining of insight. 'Calling the bluff' carries the implication of a prejudicial attitude toward a deceiver, a sly, cunning person. Defense, consequently, is reduced to sham, just as Alexander is

12 Alexander was aware that this patient had to protect himself "against the unbearable feeling of losing his mother" (p. 118), and yet he still insisted on the "evasive" nature of the regression.

13 This should be understood as signifying the opposition between the analyst and the patient's conscious ego on the one hand, and the patient's resistance on the other.

inclined to call transference reactions behavior "a kind of *one-sided shadowboxing*" (1956, p. 75; italics by Alexander).

It is also of interest to note that Alexander sees in the dependence of his patients (usually the problem is demonstrated in males) the great obstacle to the cure, whereas, by contrast, it was Freud's view that "an extraordinary amount of trouble" is caused in men by "the struggle against their passive or feminine attitude towards other men" (Freud, 1937a, p. 354).

Sapienti sat. Just as, in earlier years, everyone felt free to create his own psychology, to suit the needs at hand, it can now be observed that everyone creates his own psychoanalysis. Detailed case histories are no longer required. Techniques are approved merely on the basis of their effects upon the symptom. If the national picture of psychoanalysis is examined, it is to be concluded that the phase of scientific analysis—as created by Freud—has ended and wishful thinking has conquered reason. This is not true, of course, of all institutes; but it is no longer possible for the outsider to make up his mind which institute represents scientific analysis, and which one has suffered a regression.

Since these regressive forms of psychoanalysis have a far greater appeal to common sense, and some also try to adjust their concepts and technique to the requirements of other sciences, such as biology, medicine, or sociology, there is a great chance that Freud's scientific psychoanalysis, once absorbed by universities, would soon disappear altogether from the American scene. When Alexander writes that "it does not appear realistic to train psychotherapists on two different levels" (p. 167), he envisions a uniform training for both the psychiatrist who will engage in psychotherapy and the one who will become a psychoanalyst. Yet even this view is not held consistently, so that we read of special training programs for each group.

From Alexander's writings, it becomes apparent that psychoanalytic training would suffer no less than psychoanalytic theory and technique at the hands of the universities. Let us consider some of the training innovations that Alexander recommends. In Chicago, psychoanalytic candidates do not first receive theoretical instruction, which is then followed by practical application; instead, from the very beginning, they are exposed to a large number of patients in the form of clinical demonstrations, and case and diagnostic seminars.

Furthermore, they are presented with "both the traditional and the more recent theoretical views on the basis of their own first-hand observations" (p. 184).[14] Psychoanalytic theory is taught from the beginning "in a critical rather than dogmatic fashion. At the same time teachers are encouraged to expose without hesitation their own deviations from traditional formulations stating their reasons for their divergent views" (p. 179).[15] When he further emphasizes that, at Columbia University, "the learning was centered on the student's own experience with a great variety of cases" (p. 183), and expresses his approval of this technique, it becomes understandable on what grounds he writes that "the separation of psychoanalytic training from the residency training is becoming less marked as time goes on" (p. 195). Yet, in order to get the full meaning of this situation, one has to recall the tale of the clergyman who, instead of converting the salesman, buys life insurance from him.

I had always thought that a decision as to the correctness or incorrectness of psychoanalytic theories in part, or as a whole, can be arrived at only during the course of observing the psychoanalytic process. How a student of psychoanalysis can form any opinion solely on the basis of clinical demonstrations—and before he has received theoretical instruction—I do not understand, unless one is to assume that observations made during the psychoanalytic process itself are of merely secondary importance. It has always seemed to me that, particularly during the initial stages of psychoanalytic training, the student should learn to respect the psychoanalytic situation as the only psychoanalytic research setup at our disposal.

On what basis the student is to determine which criticism of the classical technique is valid, or which deviation from it is viable, until he has at least seen the classical technique itself in operation in a few instances, Alexander does not say. I do not know in what other field, or in what other institution, the tyro is given the impression that he can just go ahead and decide what is true and what is false. If the teachers at the Chicago Institute really air their disagreements among the students, the

[14] This sentence contains a rather ominous ambiguity, in so far as it is unclear as to what is meant by 'on the basis of.'

[15] I was rather surprised to find Alexander continuing: "Our emphasis was on teaching the student to think in dynamic motivational terms above everything else," since he had been asserting that the universities are training their candidates in dynamic psychiatry. His claim still remains unsubstantiated that this particular kind of training "does make for students who will learn how to learn from their own experience," and that it is "the only valuable approach in those fields which cannot rely on a routine repetition of well-established techniques" (p. 179). It is not quite understandable why "thinking in dynamic motivational terms" is less of a routine than thinking in genetic terms, and why the one aspect is superior to the other, since both are indispensable.

outcome can only be that the opinion of those who can form the best transference will be regarded as correct. Is it not significant how many analysts at the Chicago Institute accepted Alexander's new technique for a while? Did this really take place on the basis of experimentation and insight? Was it essentially a rational process? It is only if one denies the all-powerful effect of transference that these questions can be answered in the affirmative.[16]

If I am so far unable to detect the 'ripeness' of psychiatric university departments to take over psychoanalytic training, I have no difficulty detecting the ripeness of the Chicago Institute, if it were as Alexander describes it, to be taken over by any psychiatric department that accepts psychoanalysis as a trade name. Yet I am glad to learn that Alexander's description is not altogether valid anymore, for Grinker reports that "many of the teachers at the Chicago Institute teach orthodox psychoanalysis quoting line for line from Freud," and the Institute "has become stricter, less liberal!" (Alexander, 1956, p. 228f.). He laments this change, of course, but it is possible that practical results have already proven it to be preferable to make the beginner first learn the essentials of psychoanalysis, before he throws himself into experimentations that are in essence unconnected with psychoanalysis per se.

To what extent the essentials of the psychoanalytic situation can be misunderstood can be learned from considering another training innovation. It "consists in dividing the personal analysis of the candidate into two phases . . . . The interruption takes place when the training analyst feels that the candidate is ready to undertake his first supervised case. This interruption has been introduced on account of the frequent observation that the candidate's personal analysis often interferes with his supervised work. Under the influence of his own analysis, he is apt to project his own problems into the patient's material" (1956, p. 184).

To my conservative mind, it still seems absurd to say that a candidate is ready to start practice at a time when his personal analysis would hinder instead of support his supervised work. What kind of analysis is

[16] It is not without irony that one reads Eduardo Weiss (1933), stating emphatically: "Effective therapy results *only* from the lifting of the amnesic veil which envelops the infantile memories" (p. 309; italics mine), and observes his convincing clinical proof of the statement repeatedly made by others, only to hear him join thirteen years later the chorus of manipulative therapists, claiming: "The therapist may choose to refer to infantile neurosis in his interpretations . . . ; or he *may eschew all mention of the infantile conflict* and . . . base his interpretations *solely* upon the present situation" (see Alexander and French 1946, p. 52; italics mine).

it that *activates* in an analyzed candidate the projective mechanism—and to such an extent as to create a problem in his analytic work? Apparently the effect of those "corrective emotional experiences" is, after all, quite different from that of insight. (Lewin and Ross's book contains valuable material about training analyses in the United States; it also gives the literature.)[17]

I have mentioned more than once the tendency of the medical analyst to indulge in behaviorism, in so far as the disappearance of symptoms is made the measure of the psychoanalytic process. One can observe the equivalent for this in the belief (which is wrong) that a training analysis is to be evaluated in terms "of the student's actual achievements" (p. 182)—that is to say, that the supervisor can determine from the student's actual work whether or not he is freed of his 'blind spots,' or of any other impediment to his analytic work. Although my experience as a training analyst is rather limited, it does not confirm that belief. Surely the type of candidate who is quite proficient in sensing what is expected of him cannot have come only to my attention. Oddly enough, personalities appreciably ambivalent to psychoanalysis can do creditable work under supervision. In my opinion, Alexander would have done psychoanalysis a greater service if he had used his prestige to warn against this widespread (and mistaken) belief that the data obtained from supervision provide a reliable measure of the degree to which the candidate has matured as an analyst, although such data are, of course, to be considered in the candidate's evaluation.

Alexander seems to be rising above behaviorism, and raising the torch of true individualism, when he tries "to combat the growing trend to standardize the process of [training] analysis by quantitative regulations concerning the total number and frequency of interviews" (p. 182). Yet, when one hears that the present minimum requirements involves 300 sessions (which amounts, in practice, to an analysis of not quite 1½ years' duration), one may suspect other motives here than regard for the train-

[17] An unintentionally humorous passage in Alexander's book may be mentioned here. It concerns the suggestion by some analysts that the rather long-drawn-out training analyses for psychoanalytic candidates be replaced by shorter procedures, such as "psychodynamic sensitization" (Rado, in Alexander, 1956, p. 247) or "'psychotherapeutic' hours" (Branch, in Alexander, 1956, p. 265) for psychiatric residents. "There is a widespread apprehension," Alexander writes, "among psychoanalysts that this will dilute psychoanalysis by violating some of its basic principles. The opinion was expressed at the Ithaca Conference that these adverse effects could be overcome if the American Psychoanalytic Association would condone such modified procedures of personal analysis as legitimate and recommend them for psychiatrists in training" (p. 271).

ing analysis "as a highly individual process" (p. 182)—perhaps, instead, the desire to feel at liberty to experiment in this field as well, and to prove that 'psychodynamic sensitization' is sufficient for the psychoanalytic candidate, too.

The interesting point in this context is that if Alexander had been truly consistent, he would have had to become an advocate of lay analysis. He says that psychoanalysis is "one of the basic sciences in the study of man and belongs both to medicine and the social sciences. Its place is obviously in the universities" (p. 180). Therefore, he and his staff "decided to build a small model institution—a kind of small university . . . as a first step toward the unification of psychoanalysis with medicine" (p. 180).

By his own assertion, Alexander advocates thinking in terms of the logic of science. Would not this very logic require him to undertake an equivalent step toward the unification of psychoanalysis with the social sciences, before the actual integration of psychoanalysis by the universities takes place? Particularly since, in *Our Age of Unreason*, he propagates the development of the social sciences almost as a panacea for the ills of our times, one might have expected, if anything, an excess of concern on his part lest psychoanalysis become integrated with psychiatry *before* its indispensability to the social sciences has been proved *in practice*. How easy it would be for resistance to subvert the further growth of psychoanalysis, once it had been safely lodged in the psychiatric department!

Alexander rightly advises against making the organization of psychoanalysis dependent on its history; yet he invokes past history three times to prove that very point. According to him, psychoanalysts who believe that the "teaching and practice of psychoanalysis" should be kept under their control, have "lost sight of the fact that psychotherapy is older than psychoanalysis and is the traditional domain of the psychiatrist" (p. 151). If this were a valid reason for integration, then the Churches would have a greater claim upon psychoanalysis than do the universities.

Further, when he predicts that "psychoanalysis as a medical discipline will find its way back to its birthplace and natural homeland, the university, from which it has been separated for the last sixty years only because of the inertia of the human mind" (p. 185), he is definitely falsifying the record. Breuer's famous case "Anna O.," as well as the patients whose histories Freud wrote in the *Studies in Hysteria* and subsequently, were analyzed in private practice. The fact is that psycho-analysis evolved strictly outside of the university.[18]

Furthermore, Alexander sees in "our own outdated tradition" (p. 180) one of the obstacles to the integration of psychoanalysis by the univer-sities. One of these "outdated traditions," which Alexander felt it neces-sary to modify, was "the traditional insistence on uniformity of opinion" among analysts. He tries to apologize for these shortcomings by explain-ing that "the psychoanalyst quite naturally had to stress internal unity," since "internal dissension was thought to play into the hands of intellec-tual enemies" (p. 178); and he closes with the sage observation, "In-sistence upon complete uniformity of views is incompatible with science" (p. 179). Alexander takes the dogmatic, intolerant attitude of the analyst so much for granted that he does not even tell us where this knowledge of his comes from. Yet the accusation is a grave one. For what is being asserted is that psychoanalysis has been made an object of politics by the psychoanalysts themselves, which would be the same as if science were being manipulated for the sake of social advancement.

I find myself in a peculiar position in this respect, for Alexander, in speaking of "our" tradition, may be raising a self-accusation, and it may seem as if I were trying to console him by soothing his *pater, peccavi*. Yet, whom *did* he mean? himself? his colleagues? or Freud? The objec-tion of intolerance and authoritarianism has been raised repeatedly against Freud.[19] In some of his most beautiful passages, Freud has an-swered this reproach (cf. for example, Freud, 1933a, p. 197f.). I wish to add only that history shows how little Freud infringed upon the inde-pendence of his followers. How else is one to explain the fact that a

---

[18] I must repeat that this fact is not determinant in itself of how psychoanalysis should be organized now. It is, however, of interest to observe by what curious means Alexander tries to capture the reader for his academic daydream.

[19] The recent edition of Freud's letters contains one dating from 1924, which shows in a most touching way how movingly Freud pleaded with a collaborator not to attach any personal feeling to a theoretical disagreement between them. In this letter, there is not the slightest trace of authoritarianism, or of the demand that anyone change his opinion in order to keep in line with prevalent theories (Freud, 1873-1939, pp. 352-354).

Recently, another document has been made public which most impressively demon-strates how far off the mark those commentators are who attribute to Freud authori-tarian attitudes. In the volume of C. G. Jung's autobiographical reminiscences (1963, p. 361f.) a letter of Freud's to Jung was published, which dated from an early phase of their acquaintance. It will be difficult for the reader to find a historical precedent in which a man with a mind wholly devoted to science has spoken with equal softness, amicability, and tolerance to one who was apparently a professional *Geisterseher* ("ghost-seer").

substantial number of his collaborators, some of whom had been under his direct personal influence, were able to break away? The list is quite impressive: Adler, Jung, Stekel, Horney, Rank, Reich. The historian may one day come to deplore the fact that he was not more authoritarian, and instead left his followers free to indulge in errors of their own choice.

Did Alexander mean to say that the representatives of these various schools should all have been integrated into the psychoanalytic groups? I am sure he did not. At least, so far as I know, no Adlerian, no Jungian, and no orgone therapist has ever been invited to become a member of the Chicago Institute, in order to demonstrate his clinical methods. Or did Alexander mean that the psychoanalytic groups were not diversified enough? I do not know how it was in Berlin, but in Vienna the meetings were replete with the most passionate discussions, and in general I have never found discussions among analysts to be lacking in vitality and fire. A study of the psychoanalytic literature will confirm the fact that nothing would be more far-fetched than to decry any so-called "uniformity of opinion" among analysts.[20]

Science per se is the most rigid thing in the world. When Alexander says that "only a religion based on belief can insist on uniform tenets— science must not only tolerate but encourage criticism and diversity of ideas" (p. 179), I am sure that I know what he means. What I am not so sure of is that he is not abusing the meaning of that statement. In my father's house there are many mansions; in science, there is only one. Science rests on some tenets that are, in fact, uniform—and irreplaceable. Within its rigid framework, to be sure, one can observe a lot of movement. Yet at the heart of that movement, some points of relative stability exist—and are imperative.

It is not correct to say that the true scientist must discuss with the same degree of seriousness every theory or argument. Freud himself provides examples that disprove the belief that such is the scientist's duty. Since there is one, and only one truth, statements that contradict each other are likely to have only a limited lifetime in science. As a matter of fact, whenever Freud described the minimum requirements that must be fulfilled within the framework of psychoanalysis, he was quite liberal, formulating these requirements in such broad terms that the

[20] Since this was written, Dr. Nunberg and Mr. Federn (1962) have published the first volume of the Minutes of the Vienna Psychoanalytic Society, from which anyone interested in an objective account of the actual history of psychoanalysis can obtain first-hand evidence of the diversification of opinion among analysts, from the very inception of psychoanalysis on.

actual diversity of opinion among his followers was included without difficulty. Only when a system of thought fell altogether outside this wide frame did discussion become fruitless, just as there is hardly any sense to discussions between physicians and chiropractors. Yet there is not even a hint of truth in the assertions about the psychoanalyst's traditional insistence upon "uniformity of opinion," unless one means by that no more than his insistence upon adherence to a general methodology of investigation and verification—without which no science can exist at all.[21]

It is necessary now to take up another point, which has been quite ably and often discussed elsewhere.

The reader may have exclaimed impatiently, at some earlier point, that he is sick and tired of hearing the worn-out claim that Freud's writings are the *ultima ratio* of psychological understanding, so that we have to go back over and over again to check what Freud said, and to determine in what way our findings differ from his. As is well known, there is a group of analysts that proceeds by and large in this way, and the *vox populi* has not spared it such sharp criticism as that it is "dogmatic, orthodox, rigid, and uncreative," comparing its attitude toward Freud with that of the faithful toward the Bible. Alexander is, of course, more subtle than that; but his belief about the psychoanalyst's insistence on uniformity must have to do with the conviction of a still substantial number of psychoanalysts (even though that number is decreasing) that Freud's writings *are* a kind of *ultima ratio*. In order to explain or, in fact, to justify such a state of affairs, which is truly atypical in the history of science (cf. Waelder, 1956), I must make some comments on the psychoanalytic situation, as well as on Freud's writings.

From Alexander's writings, as well as from those of others, one gets the impression that what many object to is the way in which the classical analyst deals with the psychoanalytic situation, allegedly treating it as if it were a fixed or rigid entity, like an X-ray film, for example—an accumulation of grey spots, which can be interpreted in a point to point

21 In 1930 Freud spoke out against the ill-won popularity psychoanalysis seemed to enjoy in America, reproaching "American physicians and writers" for making "a hotchpotch out of psycho-analysis and other elements" and for quoting this procedure "as evidence of their *broad-mindedness*, whereas it only proves their *lack of judgement*" (Freud, 1930c, p. 254f.; *italics are in English in the original*). The United States has since become a haven for psychoanalysis, and if Freud were to write, today, another Introduction for *The Medical Review of Reviews*, he might use quite different language, but he would surely have repeated the essence of that statement in characterizing the direction that Dr. Alexander took in this country, after he left Europe.

fashion. The reader will recall Alexander's contrasting this delineation of the classical technique with the opportunity to make choices among modifications. Whoever has grasped the essence of the classical technique, however, knows that there is no such rigidity involved. The two variables, choice of content and sequence of interpretations—which in turn have to be correlated with a large number of variables—demonstrate that what the analyst faces is practically an infinity of choices whenever he makes a move—that is to say, when he undertakes to give an interpretation.

An outsider may perhaps not be aware how much depends on the choice of interpretation that the analyst makes. If an analyst says merely that he has analyzed a patient, that is almost a meaningless statement, so long as he does not state exactly what technique he has used. If he says that he has used the method of free association, he still has not conveyed much, either, because it all depends on the analyst's ability to give the right interpretation. Yet, on the problem of right interpretation, whole volumes could be written.

Furthermore, quite apart from the correct interpretation, whatever the analyst does in the psychoanalytic situation has significant consequences, which are themselves dependent on a multiplicity of variables. I have referred earlier to two remarks that Alexander made to a patient shortly after he started treatment. With these two remarks, particularly if their effect on the subject was not analyzed, the further course of that exploration was almost certainly thrown out of gear, so that the scientific outcome becomes highly questionable.

How many do use the psychoanalytic technique correctly is unknown, since reports detailed enough to permit their evaluation are practically never published any longer. We know that very many, or the majority, or possibly all, of the psychoanalysts today are using the technique in such a way that, in a fair number of patients, a fair number of symptoms subside. But only that technique can properly be called psychoanalytic which leads to the realization of the maximum potentially given when a particular individual is exposed to the psychoanalytic situation, or which constantly safeguards the pathway leading to such realization. To measure the psychoanalytic technique in terms of symptomatic changes is basically a corruption of the psychoanalytic situation, leading straightway to wild analysis, unless the deviation is rigorously justified, either clinically or theoretically.

In view of the subtlety of the psychoanalytic situation, the huge number of variables that determine the correct interpretation, the necessary integration of an incredible mass of details, it can safely be said that only very few are capable of handling the psychoanalytic situation correctly. From all this it becomes clear that the classical technique—if properly used—is an art, a great art, difficult to learn and requiring a lifetime to be perfected. Just as any artist worth his salt will never profess to have mastered his art to perfection, but will always see a new horizon still ahead, this is also true of the analyst.

All this leads me to believe that analysts should devote their primary attention to the elaboration of the psychoanalytic technique. There is a high degree of probability that, when an analyst's essential interests are diverted into other channels, his psychoanalytic technique will become perverted or will degenerate, or it will suffer a loss of that degree of reliability which is a chief prerequisite for correct scientific deductions. It is very difficult to become truly proficient in the mastery of two musical instruments, or to produce great poetry and great paintings; and in the same way analysts who are quite proficient in psychotherapy very often do not show anything like that same skill in using the classical technique. In turn, many who are well known for their masterly handling of the latter are rather clumsy in psychotherapy.

It will have become evident that, when an analyst reports his findings, they cannot be accepted on faith, as is usually done when a histologist makes a report of his findings, which may even include microphotographs to add weight to his proofs. When measurable contents, or contents reducible to direct sense perception, are under discussion, it is much easier to agree on their validation. The psychoanalytic situation inherently defies any attempt at such reduction, and it is therefore inescapable that an error should be able to survive for a longer time in this field than in other branches of science. Yet, despite the many doubts and uncertainties that surround contemporary research in systemic psychology, there is a yardstick that provides the basis for approximate certainty: that is the psychoanalytic case history. And with this I can turn to the psychological writings of Freud. My contention is that there are certain features in Freud's work which make it essentially different from the writings of other analysts, and further that the core structure of his work is as valid now as it was at the time when it was created.

Against this view, it will be said that Freud himself held different opinions about the same subject at different times during the course of his scientific career. Nevertheless, in studying his scientific development, it must be said that each time he realized the maximum obtainable in the particular research situation. Thus, investigation of the neurotic symptoms in hysteric patients in the state of hypnosis could not but lead to the views that he put down in the *Studies on Hysteria*. With the broadening of the observational area, and the improvement of the investigative tool, the results of Freud's research were concomitantly refined and improved.[22]

There are two factors above all that make Freud's work different from the writings of other analysts. His psychological work is *comprehensive*: it includes almost the whole of the human cosmos; nothing human escaped his scrutiny. In it, we find the fullness of human emotions—love, hate, grief, joy, rage, hope, despair, anxiety and terror; the spectrum of human action—from the abyss of perversion to the height of heroism, from crime to sainthood; the breadth of culture, from war to art. We observe man at the dawn of civilization and when great religions come to be born; and we see the unending vicissitudes of man's experience, from the anguish of birth to the final dissolution of death. I could be much briefer, if I were to mention the few things in the human setting about which he leaves us ignorant.

Only a few great minds have created a corpus so broad and so deep that a single life span is too short to fathom it. One can never have come to the end of reading Shakespeare's plays. The fool who believes he is 'through with' Shakespeare has not even started to catch a glimpse of him. There are not many others whose work contains such infinity. Freud is one of them; yet his was basically an ironic mind. His work is written in an easy form, fluid, sensual, appealing and palatable, so that the first few readings leave the student exhilarated by a sense of the wealth of knowledge that he has imbibed.

Only later does he discover the deception which Freud, like all great artists, has committed: he discovers the great scientist who is aware of his own ignorance and who therefore realizes that the answers he has found are *approximations*, that the best he can do is to give directions, viewing the goal from afar, without ever being able to reach it. The infinity inherent in Freud's work itself is only one of the many reasons why Freud's work cannot be fully integrated, and remains a cosmos reflecting

---

[22] To be sure, this view is not to be extended to include those theories that have to do with physiological processes, whose final evaluation requires confirmation or disproof from sources outside the psychoanalytic situation.

in some measure that to which it was devoted—human life in its infinite diversification and declensions.

I miss this absence of boundaries, this depth and breadth, in the writings of other analysts. To be sure, they have picked up here and there a few pebbles that Freud perhaps overlooked in his voyage into all corners of this world (for, although he did not visit every hamlet, he did keep on the move, and he saw every landscape that there was to see). I hope I am not overextending my metaphor when I say that a man who sits in a desert may, of course, easily come to think that the whole world is a desert. He may even evolve a theory about deserts that is fairly accurate—about deserts, but which will be quite unacceptable as a world geography to anyone who is aware of the variety of the surface structures adorning our planet.

Yet it is not only the comprehensiveness of Freud's work, nor its being the product of a far-reaching view, that makes it superior to others. I have spoken previously about the psychoanalytic situation and its difficulties, and have mentioned how easily it may give rise to error and deception. In order to make clear what quality is attributed here to Freud's writings, I shall have to use an example partly derived from history. Every reader of Paul de Kruif's *Microbe Hunters* will remember the delightful story of Antonj van Leeuwenhoek (1632-1723). For years he had supplied the Royal Society of England with reports on all the wonderful things that he could see, through the lenses which he had made, with a perfection unequaled in his time. Yet, despite his willingness to share his observations with the Royal Society, he stubbornly refused to allow Doctor Molyneux, whom the Royal Society had dispatched to Delft for that purpose, to buy one of his microscopes. He did let him—and whoever else wished to—peer through the lenses; but no one was permitted to own one of them. Let us suppose that no one else since then had been capable of making lenses of the same degree of perfection as Leeuwenhoek's. What would scientists be able to do during all this time but study the written records of Leeuwenhoek's work, and attempt to draw further conclusions from his observations—which, by the way, were incredibly accurate?

It is in just such, if not quite so bad, a situation that the contemporary analyst finds himself. It is my contention that Freud's genius rested not only on his superior powers of reasoning, or of abstract thought, but also on a perceptive endowment which made him capable of observing processes not accessible to sense perception under ordinary conditions.

In other words, Freud's perceptive capabilities have probably remained unequaled up to now. One of the few remarks that Freud left about the working of his own mind refers to perception. In one of his historical papers he wrote: "I learnt to restrain speculative tendencies, and to follow the unforgotten advice of my master, Charcot: to look at the same things again and again until they themselves begin to speak" (1914a, p. 22).[23] In an earlier paper wholly devoted to Charcot he had the following to say about the same technique: "He [Charcot] was not a reflective man, not a thinker: he had the nature of an artist; he was, as he himself said, a *visuel*, a man who sees. Here is what he himself told us about his method of working. He used to look again and again at the things he did not understand, to deepen his impression of them day by day, till suddenly an understanding of them dawned on him" (Freud, 1893b, p. 12).[24]

There can be little doubt that Freud in his explication of Charcot's particular faculties set forth qualities of his own, although he intimated once that he might not have been the *type visuel*.[25] The essential elements are: incessant looking until the object comes to life; before a solution can be found, the impression has to be daily strengthened or intensified (*verstärken*). To what end did Charcot use this extraordinary faculty of his? I find a faint flicker of irony in Freud's line of thought

[23] In 1924 Freud (1924f) expressed himself once more with regard to the deep impression that Charcot's "lesson" left on him.

[24] It may be necessary to give a literal translation of the first sentence: "He was not a ruminating person [*Grübler*], not a thinker, but an artistically endowed nature, as he himself called it, a *visuel*, a seer [*Seher*]." The German word *Seher* is more often than not used with the meaning of 'prophet'—which also happens in English, where the word 'seer' only secondarily (and rarely) has the meaning of someone who sees. As a matter of fact, if Freud's remark had not been preceded by his reference to the *type visuel*, a German-speaking person would have thought only of the former meaning. I must be very exact here and therefore explain that the German word *Seher* does not necessarily refer to a man who is capable of seeing the future, as is implied in the word 'prophet,' but also to that man who can see anything that exists but may not be accessible to ordinary sense perception. Thus Freud's way of putting it contains a particularly subtle implication. He says, in effect, that Charcot was not only a man who was extraordinarily perceptive, but also one who could perceive existing relations that are not given as sense data.

[25] At any rate, that is the conclusion, I believe, that has to be drawn from an early comment that Freud added to Charcot's division of types into *auditifs, moteurs* and *visuels*. "In dreams," Freud (1901) says, "these distinctions disappear: we all dream predominantly in visual images." With regard to child memories, we find something similar. They are visually represented in all types, "even in people whose later function of memory has to do without any visual element . . . . In my own case the earliest childhood memories are the only ones of a visual character" (p. 47). Yet in the course of his book on *The Psychopathology of Everyday Life* Freud gives a few personal examples that speak strongly against this claim.

when, upon describing the "practising of nosography" (p. 12), as Charcot himself called it, Freud compared the joy derived therefrom with that which Adam must have enjoyed "when God brought the creatures of Paradise before him to be distinguished and named" (p. 13). The unconscious or preconscious thought in Freud seems to have been that, while Charcot exhausted his perceptive keenness in the description of syndromes and thus brought order into chaos, he, Freud, would go further—he would use *his* perceptive abilities to solve the problems of the dynamics of the neuroses.[26]

I go into these details because Freud's obituary of Charcot contains between the lines a very important autobiographical contribution. In it Freud appears to me to be giving an outline of his own ego ideal (not to be confused with the superego) in terms of Charcot's personality and biography (and, indeed, a huge portion of the ideal he derived from Charcot was realized by him later), and yet simultaneously to be indicating in what respect he will go beyond his teacher. It would not be altogether correct to speak here of an 'identification,' even though that mechanism was at work. I would say rather that, through the contact with Charcot, Freud was enabled to develop an ideal that was latently slumbering within him.

What elements in this ideal really came from Charcot, and therefore might not have appeared in Freud if he had not gone to Paris, can probably never be determined any longer but we can be certain that what Freud wrote about the mechanism of looking, and its consequences, had been at least latently in him. I referred earlier to Gicklhorn's paper, which so forcefully impresses the reader with the eighteen-year-old Freud's visual and observational power. Yet, although the tyro came close to establishing a far-reaching biological theory, he did not push on hard enough to quite reach it. Still that observational power of his had grown since then, and it was now geared maximally to the human setting.

[26] There are two factors suggesting that Freud had made an identification with Charcot, even though perhaps on the surface only. For a while he too was driven, when investigating infantile cerebral palsies, towards "a clinical classification and differentiation of syndromes that have been highly confused and ambiguous" (Krafft-Ebing in 1897 about Freud's book [1897], in Gicklhorn and Gicklhorn, 1960, p. 97). Secondly, the appearance of Freud's study as it is known from photographs, when compared with that of Charcot's study as described by Freud (letter of January 20, 1896; Freud, 1873-1939, p. 194), indicates a possible resemblance which may suggest that Freud in furnishing his study was unconsciously guided by his Parisian recollections.

The switch from the microscopic slide to man was not only enforced by professional vicissitudes; it can already be observed in full bloom in Freud's letters to his bride (Freud, 1873-1939, pp. 7-218). What follows is a construction or, as many may call it, a phantasy. It has to do with Freud's perceptive apparatus. In some geniuses, the qualitative (or, as some believe, quantitative) difference that stamps them with genius, already begins at the periphery of the psychic apparatus. It is asserted that Mozart's ability to distinguish tonal qualities, for example, was unique. Goya made observations in nature whose correctness has been confirmed only by modern techniques of photography. In some of the great painters, this unique character of the visual apparatus can be observed with particular clarity. There are canvases which teach the beholder to look at the world in a new way.

Although the end-products of artistic and scientific endeavors are essentially different, they themselves share some of the psychic mechanisms that lead to their production. I find it relevant that Freud described Charcot as artistically endowed, yet did not say that he was an artist—which would have meant, coming from Freud, a scientist's criticism. I would guess also that Freud wrote here *pro domo*. Freud's artistic talent cannot be questioned, yet one way of depreciating the scientific content of psychoanalysis would be to call it a work of art. Although Freud never, as other scientists did, applied his artistic endowments to the production of any purely artistic work (the most he did was translations), it may be suggested that the structure of his perceptive apparatus resembled that which is to be found in artists.

I am thinking here of Goethe, great poet and writer and perhaps also great scientist, who once wrote about how he gained insight into the structure of nature. According to him, it was the *aperçu* that led to a truly relevant insight. By *aperçu*, he seems to have meant "the perceiving of what lies essentially at the bottom of the appearance" (Goethe, 1810, p. 247). About this way of working, Goethe told Eckermann:

> When, in the exploration of scientific objects, I reached an opinion, I did not demand that nature immediately acknowledge that I was right; rather I went after her, looking into her by means of experiments and observations, and I was quite content when she was obliging enough occasionally to confirm my opinion. If she did not, then she would probably bring me to another *aperçu*, which I went after, and which she

perhaps found herself more willing to confirm [Goethe, 1828, p. 222; translation mine[26a]].

Here we have something close to Freud's probing but imperturbable way of working. Whether or not it led Goethe, too, to relevant new insights is still debatable, and is, in fact, denied by some on convincing grounds (Kohlbrugge, 1913). Nevertheless, that is irrelevant in terms of Goethe's total work. The mechanism in the artist leads to the creation of esthetic values of the highest order; in the scientist, it leads to exciting discoveries within the structure of reality.

At any rate, it is my impression that Freud's faculty went far beyond the psychic *instrumentarium* of the average scientist who first gathers a series of observations, and then tries to construct his theories on the basis of them; or who first forms hypotheses, and then approaches his field of observation with a question in his mind. It seems to me that Freud had a distinctive talent for perceiving the forces that must have led to the phenomena under his observation. "To look at the same things again and again until they themselves begin to speak," as well as "perceiving of what lies essentially at the bottom of the appearance" would certainly be ingredients of that sort of perceptive act.

In Freud's case, I would guess that his specific perceptive ability was rooted in his knack for perceiving a complex phenomenon in its component parts, and as the product of an evolutionary process, as something that has become.[27] In reading his five case histories, the pillars on which psychoanalysis as an empirical science rests, one does not get the

---

[26a] Wenn ich bey Erforschung naturwissenschaftlicher Gegenstände zu einer Meinung gekommen war, so verlangte ich nicht, dass die Natur mir sogleich Recht geben sollte; vielmehr ging ich ihr in Beobachtungen und Versuchen prüfend nach, und war zufrieden, wenn sie sich so gefällig erweisen wollte, gelegentlich meine Meinung zu bestätigen. Tat sie es nicht, so brachte sie mich wohl auf ein anderes Aperçu, welchem ich nachging und welches zu bewahrheiten sie sich vielleicht williger fand.

[27] One may easily object that what is described here is a faculty characteristic of any original or creative observer. I doubt this, and would add a statement supposed to have been made by Flaubert. Despite its seeming similarity, it will reveal to an attentive ear a significant difference: "The thing to do is to examine everything you wish to express long enough and with enough attention to discover in it an aspect that no one else has ever seen or spoken of. There is something of the unexplored in everything, because we are accustomed to *employing our eyes only with the memory of what has been thought before about the object of our contemplation.* The very least object contains a little of the unknown. Let us look for it . . . . This method forces me to express, in a few sentences, a being or an object in a way that particularized it exactly, that distinguished it from all other objects or beings of the same race or species" (italics by the author; Josephson, 1928, p. 267).

impression that Freud is presenting explanations that have been constructed or deduced, or are chiefly the product of ratiocination; instead,
they sound like reports of an explorer who has visited unknown countries, and is now putting down the recollections of his journey, using
here and there a diary entry that he had scribbled down during the
course of his travelling. The deep impression that the study of Freud's
case histories leaves on the reader arises, among other things, from their
being descriptions of something *perceived,* not deduced. Freud leaves
the reader with the feeling that things happened exactly as they are
presented in the case reports, that Freud himself must have witnessed
them happening, even though objectively they are in fact *reconstructions,*
or composites sifted from the patient's reports. This effect upon the
reader cannot be explained only on the basis of Freud's literary mastery;
it is the result of the perceptive ability with which Freud encountered
man and which does not seem to have been duplicated in anyone else
as yet.[28]

This conclusion will become more probable when we consider that
what we call psychoanalytic theory must, indeed, have been represented
in Freud's mind in a way that can scarcely be compared with the representations in the minds of his followers, for everyone who has conducted
an analysis since Freud, has entered upon that undertaking with a set of
anticipatory ideas. Even if he tries to forget what he has learned in his
studies, so that he may approach the patient's productions in an 'unbiased' way, there still remains a latent group of concepts in his mind,
acquired from an area outside of his own immediate field of observation.

Freud had the great advantage of approaching the observational field
without a set of previously established ideas or conceptions. He had no
firm anticipations to be confirmed by observation. When he was listening
to his patients, he was "surrounded by question marks"—a situation

[28] The particular endowment which as it seems to me was so strongly developed in
Freud was the ability of rendering concrete something that is essentially abstract. This
is also one of the reasons why it will take a long time before Freud's findings have been
generally accepted. Yet it should not be forgotten that this concretization of the abstract
is quite generally the function of the scientific genius. A recent publication (Kuhn,
1962) may make it easier to formulate Freud's particular achievement in abstract terms,
and to understand better the present phase in the development of psychoanalysis as a
science. Kuhn introduces the concept of the 'paradigm' as the salient feature in the
history of science. Freud's contribution, then, would consist in the discovery of a large
number of paradigms; and an exact description of Freud's paradigms, as well as the
examination of which parts of Freud's work have acquired the status of paradigm, and
of the reasons why some have and others have not, would become one of the most
urgent tasks for a better understanding of the history of psychoanalysis.

which does not hold true for anyone who has conducted an analysis since then. Thus each item in the psychoanalytic vocabulary that he created was marked for him by a sense of newness and surprise, dating back to the moment when he first perceived the contents so designed. For all those who followed him, this same vocabulary was less 'new' or 'surprising,' and for some it has apparently already become tainted by 'routine.'

To perceive what is inaccessible to sense perception is, outside of the realm of art, a dangerous undertaking. Yet, whether we like it or not, it may be that, in certain developmental phases of science, this is the only way in which new discoveries can be made. As far as Freud is concerned, we know that the majority of experts in the field treat his work as if it were that of an artist, with some bearing on the science of psychology, but without that binding power that scientific treatises commonly have. Among psychoanalysts it is different: a large number of them regard his writings somewhat in the manner of my Leeuwenhoek simile. The uniqueness of his capabilities is recognized, and there is full awareness of the difficulties involved in arriving, through the use of the psychoanalytic situation, at truly new conclusions.

It may sound paradoxical, but I would say that, for the average mind, the psychoanalytic situation is extremely suitable, to check whether a certain set of propositions is true or false; but to discover anything new, or of far-reaching consequence, from the observational field as given in the psychoanalytic situation, seems to place unusually great demands upon the human mind. I doubt that, since Freud, much has been accomplished in this respect.

Psychology, I fear, will have to wait for the development of new methods of exploration, such as can be handled productively even by average minds—or else it will have to wait for a new genius. This new genius will be recognized immediately, not by his theories, but by his case histories. When a case history has been published of a quality superior to the 'five pillars' on which psychoanalysis now rests, then psychoanalysis will have entered a new phase.

Would it not therefore be one of the principal tasks of contemporary analysts to protect analysis against regrettable 'regressions,' to delineate carefully what part of Freud's work can be confirmed, and what part cannot, and finally to unearth the treasures that are still buried in his writings and, for whatever reasons, were never realized by Freud himself?

Such a program may prove to be offensive in the eyes of the majority. But I do not see clearly how else we should proceed.

It is admitted—at least by a great majority of analysts—that a full understanding of Freud's work is indispensable if one desires to undertake psychoanalytic research. Yet a full understanding requires the study of his total original writings (Waelder, 1956, p. 608f.). To study the writings of the originator is not necessary for the student of evolution or physics. A biologist can learn everything there is to learn about evolution from the textbooks; the number of physicists today who feel the need to read Newton's or Galileo's writings is minimal. The fact that analysis cannot be studied from textbooks, however, is of the greatest significance in the evaluation of 'where we are standing now.'[29] Yet the study of Freud's work is practically unending and, each reading, even for the experienced, opens up a new vista, just as with the reading of Shakespeare's plays.

The vast scope of Freud's work and the great variety inherent in the psychoanalytic situation leads, in my opinion, to the conclusion that only a towering mind will be able to push beyond the borders of Freud's writings.

From all this, it will have become clear that Alexander would have served the future of systemic psychology better than he did in suggesting an end to the separation between institute and university, if he had instead vigorously demanded the establishment of psychoanalytic universities. Only such institutions will be capable of preserving a level of psychological research worthy of Freud's tradition, and of making out of psychoanalysis the comprehensive science of man that its founder had enabled it to be.

It may be worth while summarizing at this point what makes psychoanalysis more vulnerable than other sciences.

1. Psychoanalysis is not societally rooted, as the natural sciences are. If the physicists or chemists were to go on strike, modern society—which is based on technology—would quickly collapse. If the psychoanalysts shut down their offices, that fact would cause a stir in only a small corner of modern society.

2. Large sections of the natural sciences are under the control of mathematics. It is one of the most impressive (and consequential) his-

---

[29] Waelder (1956) wrote the decisive paper on this question. However, he is not of the opinion that the present stagnation of psychoanalytic research is caused by a dearth of creative talents.

torical facts that man by his own thought acquired a tool which now, in effect, tethers his thinking, making it impossible for him to fall victim to his vagaries, dreams or illusions. Thus the evolution of thought has taken man, who is so prone in his thinking to sway to the side of his wishes and away from reality and the truth that it harbors, and has led him into a stage where, despite the persistence of such inclinations, he has lost the privilege (in some areas at least) of replacing truth with the products of what the psychologists would call 'wishful thinking.' No such powerful safeguard is afforded to the researcher in psychology.

3. Experiments, which are the next best damper upon man's natural inclination toward intellectual vagaries, have not yet reached in psychology the area that is relevant and significant in terms of the focal elements of man's personality. In the rare instances where this has happened, we may say that psychoanalysis has been 'confirmed' but not yet 'proved.'

4. The subject matter of psychology is not accessible to direct sense inspection. Thoughts, emotions, psychic functions are observable, but only when a dimension of interpretation has been added to direct perception (which, after all, also contains some, even though minimal, interpretative factor).[30] What is observable by means of direct sense perception is behavior; yet that is the result of a plurality of factors, many of which lie outside the realm of inspection by perception. Even when a psychologist sees and hears a subject weeping, he has to begin by determining whether the subject is malingering, is sincere or is acting upon a posthypnotic command, in order to orient himself about the 'reality' of the observed act.[31]

From all this it is evident that the integrity of the researcher's own personality is, in psychological research, and particularly in psychoanalysis, a matter of greater moment than it is in other areas of science. When psychopathology has affected the research functions of someone engaged in the natural sciences, that fact will be relatively quickly discovered. In psychology, particularly in depth psychology, it may on the contrary take a very long time. If one considers the attraction that certain types of psychopathology and particularly of psychopathy have for many people, and the tendency of the young person to direct his transference urges toward just that narcissistic person who needs and seeks

[30] Cf. Hebb, 1949, p. 17f.
[31] For the problem of validation in psychoanalysis, see Hartmann (1927 *passim*), Kris (1947), Waelder (1960, pp. 3-31).

self-aggrandizement, one can easily imagine what terrible damage undetected psychopathology may still cause to the progress of psychology.

5. There is still another circumstance that darkens the future of depth psychology. No other branch of science has as great a need as the field of psychopathology for the involvement of great talent. Yet great talent is usually undisciplined, impatient and, in many areas of conduct, eccentric. In psychoanalysis, by contrast with other fields of scientific endeavor, the process of data collecting requires a particularly high standard of integrity, patience and self-discipline. The life of a good analyst permits eccentricity at most in his dealings with his colleagues and his family, but not at all in his daily professional activities. Thus, the truly talented and unusually endowed applicant might well have to be rejected by the Institute, whose main concern for obvious reasons has to be the attainment of the highest professional standards (I have cited the Bárány episode earlier).

If all these factors are taken together, one may with justice be pessimistic regarding the future of psychoanalysis. It is even possible that, instead of progressing in a direction that would take it closer to the truth than Freud succeeded in reaching, it will decline to such an extent that nothing of truth will any longer be part of it. Yet it is not unreasonable to hope that, later still, it will be restored to the heights that it had reached by the time Freud departed and left the welfare of psychoanalysis to the responsibility of his followers.

Appendix 2

Further Notes on the Religious Controversy

Any attempt to make even an approximate estimate of the external dangers that actually or potentially threaten the development of psychoanalysis calls for further comments on those that are rooted in man's religious feelings.[1] In Sheen's book, one encountered a clear-cut situation: he did not understand psychoanalysis; he presented a distortion of it, so far-fetched that it cannot even be called a caricature; and he wound up rejecting the whole business *in toto*. Gemelli, who is somewhat better informed than Sheen, reached conclusions which are similar, if not quite so extreme. Thus, the very way in which both handled the question of psychoanalysis should make it relatively easy for any adequately informed reader to reach a correct conclusion.

However, within the Catholic movement, an entirely different sort of approach can also be observed—an approach which strikes me as being far more dangerous than that of the Sheens and Gemellis. If there were not so much written about God in Karl Stern's *The Third Revolution*, I would be tempted to call the book diabolical. Rarely, indeed, has anybody in my experience grasped so well the essence of Freud's work,

[1] For a splendid discussion of the main problems involved in the controversy between psychoanalysis and religion, see Ross (1958).

presented it with so high a degree of lucidity, and viewed it so correctly within the framework of the history of ideas—and yet, despite the high praise that one must accord parts of the book, its final outcome is a total subversion and negation of what Freud meant and did.

With an impressive display of ratiocination, Stern seeks to harness the forces that have been aimed against the social effects of religion, and to make them work for the Catholic Church. Indeed, in reading Stern, one is almost led to believe that Freud might have had a good chance of being one day beatified, and even of adorning the Catholic galaxy of saints—if only the scientist who made *agape* and *caritas* a living reality in the psychoanalytic situation, had not turned philosopher (which was really not his business at all, and only made him commit the most deadly of deadly sins).

Indeed—to follow the same logic further—if only Freud had not written *The Future of an Illusion, Totem and Taboo, Moses and Mono-theism,* and possibly *Civilization and Its Discontents,* there would have been a real likelihood that his works would now become recommended reading at Catholic colleges and universities (perhaps to the chagrin of Allers), and psychoanalysis would thus have attained the enviable opportunity of becoming firmly rooted in one of the most powerful cultural movements of the Occidental world.

Stern, who understands psychoanalysis, knows that the Church, by her total rejection of it, may once more expose herself to the commission of a grievous error, as she did so regrettably in the Galileo affair—which Stern somewhat apologetically calls "a theological intrusion" (p. 88), a very real understatement.[2] Indeed, this euphemism—together with the *Nihil obstat* and the *Imprimatur* that the author felt it necessary to obtain for his publication; does he not regard these as theological intrusions?—should make him suspect in the eyes of those who hold it to be the scientist's primary duty, as far as it is humanly possible, to reduce the effects of bias or prejudice on his work. These are all too apparent, however, when he puts Auguste Comte's dream of "a world in which revelation and faith would be entirely supplanted by science" in the same category as the Communist and the "racist" revolutions (p. 14).

Since Freud seems to have shared Comte's dream, Stern is moving

---

[2] I am reasonably certain that Stern would have found a more vivid image if, because of his having written *The Third Revolution,* he had had to undergo, at the hands of the secular power, the same anguish and humiliation that Galileo had to suffer at the hands of ecclesiastical power (cf. de Santillana, 1955).

dangerously close to Allers' appeal to the state authority for the suppression of psychoanalysis; for as much as he apparently admires psychoanalysis *plus* faith (as we shall see, his belief is that the majority of people are incapable of achieving faith without psychoanalysis), to the same degree he abominates psychoanalysis *without* faith.

How cunningly Stern tries to preserve Catholic dogma may be seen in his incredible assertion that "there is a direct line leading from Darwin to Hitler" (p. 88). He is once again making an understatement when he goes on: "It seems grotesque" (it *is* grotesque!) "to link up the innocent passenger of the good ship *Beagle* . . . with the concentration camps . . . ." Since he affirms that the theologian should not intrude upon science, he dares not take up the cudgels against the theory of evolution (which is still denied by the Church), but instead tries to denigrate it by an outrageous moral aspersion.

Yet, when the author plays dogmatic and metaphysical politics with science, he ought to be reminded that a good many fascist dictators of importance, from Pilsudski to Franco, have been Catholics; that Hitler grew up in a strict Catholic environment (a fact that should not obscure the contribution that a huge number of Catholics made to the defeat of fascism); that many of the Protestant countries in which the theory of evolution is taught without fear or hesitation have shown a commendable resistance to the poison of fascism; that fascism is not inherently based on racial discrimination, as can be seen from the fact that its first large-scale realization took place in a country as quintessentially Catholic as Italy; and that, lastly, serfdom and other terrible denials of the rights of the individual, during the periods of feudalism and absolutism, were supported by the Catholic Church. It is really quite distressing to have to deal with outright falsification dictated by ecclesiastical subterfuges in a tract that purports to be a critical analysis of the relationship between science and religion.

To prove some of his points, the author introduces a variety of arguments, a few of which I shall discuss.

He attacks the conclusions of sociology for their allegedly corrosive effect upon the morals of society. During the course of this attack, he also turns his attack upon the present-day methodology of sociology, for unwarrantedly excluding the insight into the truth that can be reached through non-scientific methods. The reasoning here pursues somewhat the following course:

1. If one sets out to prove the unprovable, or to make someone be-

lieve the unprovable, he is permitted to resort to the practice of reaching conclusions by analogy. Values such as good or bad, beautiful or ugly, "are not the object of science" (p. 55).[3] Although the author is quite correct in so far as mathematics does not deal with such values when it investigates the laws of numbers, he is in error with regard to the certainty of any such *general* statement, since the scientific approach at the present time by no means universally excludes values from among the objects of its investigation (cf. Hartmann, 1960). He modifies his statement to a certain extent by saying that science—that is, the social sciences—cannot either support or reject a hierarchy of values, such as the affirmation of the greater beauty of certain works of art, as compared with others. "Values are transcendental. They lie in an area which accumulative knowledge cannot reach" (p. 56).

Debatable as such assertions are, they surely do not justify his making the gratuitous statement that atheists "would have to burn all the great musical scores in a bonfire if they really lived what they preached" (p. 55). This is a *captatio benevolentiae*. It is not altogether clear why Stern calls beauty a transcendental value, apparently meaning by that something comparable to religious values.

The beauty of works of art is man-made, and we have some inkling of the psychological processes leading to their creation. What we know is terribly little, to be sure; but the creative process is certainly not one that threatens to be immune to scientific investigation. If anything, it is art (which the Catholic Church does not claim to have been given mankind by God, as knowledge of good and evil is, but which they acknowledge to be man-made), that may finally bring us round to discovering that values of good and bad have also been man-made. The 'discovery' by man that acts are good or bad does not strike me as calling for greater profundity on his part than the ability to create things of beauty.[4]

[3] Zilboorg holds the same opinion.

[4] In his review of Zilboorg's (1962a), book, Stern focuses again (in agreement with Zilboorg) on the irrational root of most phenomena of civilization. Correctly, he points to the similarity between the unconscious mechanisms of religion and those operating in the artist. When he continues that Freud "never came to deny the transcendental element in art," and adds: "This alone is sufficient proof that he was biased, and that his atheism was a personal and accidental element" (Stern, 1962, pp. 6, 18), I must state that such arguments are specious. Whatever observations, hypotheses and theories the psychological investigation of art or of any other cultural phenomenon may produce, I do not see what conclusions can be rightly drawn therefrom regarding the nature of certain historical events, such as the life of Jesus, or the origin of man's moral sentiments. It is not legitimate to allow assertions which purportedly refer to an ob-

Following an old tradition, Stern distinguishes "scientific method from poetic insight" (p. 56), "knowledge by connaturality as opposed to other forms of knowledge" (p. 102), "explaining as opposed to understanding" (p. 103). Truth can thus be reached by a variety of methods, none of which is superior to any other. The aim of this argument is obvious; it is one of the mainstays of the believer. Yet it draws an unwarranted conclusion from what may have been an exact observation. In studying the psychological processes that lead to insight, we are actually observing two groups of phenomena that have been fairly accurately described by the philosophers and the psychologists. The mistake that was made in the past was to underestimate the contribution of the so-called intuitive processes to scientific insight. It is now understood that 'poetic insight,' 'Einfühlung,' 'connaturality,' can also lead to scientific insight, and may even be indispensable to the scientist.

Consider Leonardo suddenly—so it seems—noting that the earth moves. It is highly improbable that this was the upshot altogether of experiment, observation, measurement or inductive thinking, taken singly or together. Yes, we can even feel quite certain that it was at bottom an intuition, like that of the early thinkers who postulated the atomic theory. Yet, if human knowledge had stopped at the level that Leonardo reached, the Catholic Church would still, I am sure, be putting books about the heliocentric theory on the Index,[5] and if the ancient Greek philosophy of nature had not been validated, the theory of atoms would still be in process of being debated.

So-called intuitive knowledge may be true or false. Its elaboration, testing, validation will decide its correctness (Ross, 1958, p. 523). Here I only want to say, in agreement with many others, that, while statements inaccessible to validation may be meaningless in terms of the reality about which they are supposedly predicating something, they nevertheless do have a crucial importance for the psychologists and the historians. What Stern predicates of religion is of the greatest significance in terms of his own personality, the tradition that he follows and the society he is living in. Thus a reality is correlated with knowledge gained by Einfühlung ("understanding," in the German sense of the

---

jective reality to rest on analogies, even though thinking by analogy may be an important tool in the formation of hypotheses, and may also be used productively for a variety of heuristic purposes.

[5] Galileo's *Dialogue*, as a matter of fact, was released from the Index only in 1822 (de Santillana, 1955, p. 305n.).

term) or "connaturality"; but this reality remains outside the area aimed at by such knowledge, so long as it is not validated. Of course, there is disagreement about the sufficient conditions for validation. Since Stern, however, belongs among those who regard validation and faith as disparate, a discussion of validation is unnecessary here.[6]

2. Another effort that must be classified as a *captatio benevolentiae* is the dismal picture that the author draws of what would happen, should the Western world continue to adhere to anything like the program that Auguste Comte outlined, and forget the mystery of the human person and of human values.

Indeed, one does not have to be a devout Catholic, in order to become alarmed about the trend that Western civilization has taken, for there is scarcely any significant group to the right, left or center, whether it is religious or atheistic, and no matter what its occupation or profession, that does not view the future more or less worriedly. One does not need to belabor the points of disagreement as to the significance of the different areas that are described as deserving concern, and the even more serious disagreements regarding the measures to be taken.

Stern's alarm is directed toward the decline of faith and the spread of the scientific spirit. He puts into the same pot all the cultural trends that get along without faith. Modern sociology, Pavlovian reflexology, and psychoanalysis (at least in its atheistic form, as it was presented by Freud)—all of these are considered to be equally involved in the destruction of a livable society. We have seen Stern threatening us with the mantle of Hitlerism, should we be brazen enough to accept evolution as a valid theory; now he predicts total dehumanization, if we should attempt to apply scientific principles to the world of human values and relations.

To be sure, modern sociology is not the most satisfactory of the disciplines, and I share the author's aversion to dealing with human problems by means of statistics. But I am not so certain as Stern is that this aversion of ours says very much about statistics itself. To criticize a science for its social effect is incongruous, for the true-or-false frame of reference is the only valid one to employ on such occasions.

If what Stern had in mind was merely to convince us that sociology is

---

[6] However, at one point, Stern (1951) could not resist the temptation to validate God when he cited the French biophysicist who figured out that the age of the earth would not be enough "for one protein molecule to occur as a chance combination of atoms" (p. 280).

unable to study the totality of the human mind, I do not think he would find many to gainsay him. As has been stated previously, any science that investigates man as if he were a medium investigates an abstraction. Yet there are, no doubt, some problems that can be tackled only by means of such approaches. When the author predicts that brain physiology "will obviously never bring about . . . knowledge of ourselves" (p. 49), he states as a fact what cannot be more than a belief (or a wish?). Many a historical example can be given to show how precarious such predictions are.[7]

As the reader may remember from previous pages, I am inclined to assume similar limits to knowledge; but I cannot see what harm would be caused by their being transcended. The knowledge thus gained might be more precise and reliable than that which is now obtained by rather cumbersome methods. What can be detected in Stern is a hesitation and an alarm about what science—misled science, he would say—will do to mankind. That there are fashions in science; that for given periods certain methods are overrated, or overstressed; that a program of research does not always fulfil what it first promised—all this happens, of course; but it does not justify alarm, for science misled by error has regularly found its way back to a new approach toward truth, provided it is left free of interference by forces outside of science. Stern does not propose to replace erroneous science by better science; what he aims to do is to draw a line beyond which science should not even attempt to go. Against such a demand for limitations upon science, one must set up the firmest opposition.

Stern puts up a firm barrier against any sociological examination of the Church. He says: "Either the Church is the Mystical body of Christ, or it is nothing"[8] (p. 54).

Apparently, the clean break between science and religion is much easier to handle in the physical sciences: the devout physicist may escape with greater ease than the anthropic scientist can, from the fear

[7] The most surprising is one I came across lately—a letter of Julius Robert von Mayer, one of the truly great physicists, to Josef Popper-Lynkeus, far less famous engineer and social reformer, in which he equates the problem of guided balloons with that of the *perpetuum mobile*, both of which he has put on his *index prohibitarum*, whereas Popper-Lynkeus "in all humbleness" dared to state a different opinion about the same problem (von Mayer, 1875; cf. also Barber, 1961).

[8] Here I think he is going too far. Even if it should finally come to be generally accepted one day that there is no such Mystical body, the outstanding cultural contribution of the Church remains a historical fact, so that she will never be regarded as 'nothing,' even by an atheistic historian.

that he is intruding upon God's realm. I do not myself see how anthropic science can ever fulfill its function, if it is to bow to an approach based on the imposition of different standards, depending on whether one is examining the magic rites of a primitive tribe, the priestly hierarchy and religion of the Aztecs, or the mystical body of the Church.

The conceptual frame would very likely have to be enlarged, as we proceeded from one to the next, but basically all three are to the scientist nothing more (nor less) than empirical configurations, testifying to mankind's inner need to form a religious imagery, 'religious' being taken here in its widest meaning. To postulate that one such configuration contains more of a transcendental reality than another is, in my opinion, a betrayal of science—the sort of betrayal which, to a certain extent, Galileo was expected during his trial to commit. Apparently he was able to withstand the pressure; his age protected him against the likelihood of torture. But what would have happened if he had had to submit to torture, we cannot ever know.

3. A general statement is necessary here. Often a devout psychoanalyst or psychiatrist will turn the psychoanalytic method on the unbelieving analyst, trying to demonstrate that it is the unbeliever's inner conflicts which have made him take issue with religion. I would have to take general exception to any such phraseology; but I want to state here only that Zilboorg's attempt to reconstruct Freud's (1933a) early conflicts about a beloved Catholic nursemaid who was imprisoned for theft (1953a) (cf. also Dempsey, 1956), does not measure up to its own promise.

To be sure, conflicts about religion (of an unconscious sort, I would guess) may have played a far greater role in Freud's life than Jones preferred to consider (Jones, 1953-1957, Vol. 3, pp. 349-351). I can hardly believe that any extraordinary achievement of Freud's—and what he had to say about religion will be appraised in years to come, I believe, as an extraordinary achievement, perhaps even as his greatest mental deed—could have been born out of a subjectively neutral background. He was too great for that; by and large, I assume that everything he wrote grew out of the lifeblood of conflicts over which he acquired, or sought to acquire, mastery.

Yet from this, so far as I can see, it would not necessarily follow that his disappointment over the Catholic nurse would lead to atheism. If Zilboorg had suggested that Freud's desire to discuss the topic publicly, or the interest he showed in the topic, may have had their roots in the infantile trauma, there I might be able to follow him with greater ease. If people were more given to stating their true convictions on religion honestly, I think that one would find the majority of scientists—or at least a statistically significant number among them—not believing in God at all, or at most believing in an abstract general principle (which is not too far from atheism), with only a few accepting the revealed origin of the two Testaments. In spite of the fact that, historically, the scientists whom we identify with the scientific revolution (Kepler, Newton) did maintain, quite explicitly, intense religious beliefs, we now find, in the words of a recent student, that "the highly creative men in their lives today . . . show either no preference for a particular religion or little or no interest in any religion . . ." (Chambers, 1964).

Where were the believing scientists among Freud's friends and colleagues? Did Breuer believe in God? How many professors of the Viennese medical school believed in God in 1890? They may have gone to church, but did they believe? In my opinion, the difference between Freud and the others was not his atheism, but his open profession thereof, and his interest in a scientific explanation of the phenomenon of 'religion.'

When the problem is raised of the bearing that Freud's personal conflicts or repressions may have had upon his theories of religion, we are faced with a particularly delicate question. The analyst is accustomed to expect dysfunctions of reality testing of some sort in most instances that come to his observation. Psychoanalytic theory does not require the assumption of disturbed reality testing in the case of heightened conflict, in the same way as the presence of a defense mechanism is assumed on such occasions. With regard to dysfunctions of reality testing, they have to be clinically demonstrated, and Dr. Zilboorg avoids the question when he 'deduces' from the fact (actual or alleged) of Freud's conflict about religion per se a dysfunction in his reality testing (cf. Ross, 1958, p. 525).

When Zilboorg introduces Freud's childhood history as a factor that enlarges the probability of error in Freud's investigations of religious phenomena, then one must ask: what are the indices, genetic or otherwise, that recommend a person as a *reliable* investigator in that area? If a person born on Christmas Day to orthodox Jewish parents first becomes a Quaker, and then is baptized in the Catholic Church, keeping this latter act as a matter which he preferred not to discuss with his friends —all of which the editor of Zilboorg's (1962a, p. x) religious writings tells us about him—are we to interpret these successive acts as signs of the gradual *resolution* of religious conflicts, or as indices of *continuing* conflict? When a writer who was born and raised as a Catholic tries to prove the truth of Catholic theology, are we to assume that he is responding to deepseated identifications—so that, had he been born and raised as a Mohammedan, he would now be trying to prove the truth of Muslim theology—or should we assume that his past has facilitated his insight into the truth?

All sorts of permutations occur: religious people become atheists, and vice versa. In short, it is very likely that, in almost every person, there are religious conflicts. As to their genesis and their bearing on reality testing, only a careful personal analysis could bring to light the relevant data.

Furthermore, many writers seem to believe that there was a particular resistance in Freud against believing in God. I do not know why it is necessary to assume such a resistance in Freud—or in any atheist, for that matter. I am almost certain that the vast majority of atheists have no personal reasons not to believe in God. The fear of punishment in the nether world that filled man's fantasy so intensely in earlier centuries would have no great effect on our contemporaries as a subjective deterrent to belief in a Divinity.

When Freud asserted so vigorously that belief in God is a wish-fulfilling illusion, he was contradicting his own childhood experience, during which, as he reported, he was an ardent reader of the Bible (Freud, 1925a, p. 8). Why should he not gladly have continued, or taken up once again, that childhood belief? The answer is simple. The atheist is unable to affirm the existence of a Divinity, for the reason that there is so little, well-nigh nothing, to support that thesis, except a personal feeling of the kind that does not prove to be a reliable compass in the search for truth. The assertion that faith should override intellect, the *credo quia absurdum*, the demand that one should rely on the emotional sphere alone in determining the existence of anything—all these are no longer acceptable. Stern's book is replete with infringements upon the integrity of the intellect that are altogether unworthy of a scientist.[9]

---

[9] Thus he implies, in all seriousness, that because Mozart was able to hear his works, with all their instrumentation, before he wrote them, Saint Theresa's voices were no hallucinations (p. 159). He also fails to make full use of his clinical experience, when he tries to disprove the existence of psychopathology in Saint Theresa on the grounds that "she was, apart from her supranatural experiences, a practical woman with a sense of humor, quite different from schizophrenia" (p. 159). It is well known that schizo-

Yes, if the intellect did confirm faith; if there were no sick children; if infantile mortality had been reduced, prior to the rise of science, or had by some miracle not occurred at all—to mention at random just a few 'if's'—then the atheist might have grounds for becoming convinced of the existence of a divinity. Indeed, if it were only sinners that fell sick, Stern would no doubt be happy to adduce such events as evidence of divine Providence. But the theologian, in all seriousness, demands the praise of God for giving Adam the freedom to sin, saying that, whatever turn empirical processes may take, they ought to enhance human faith in Divinity.[10] But this amounts to a further dethronement of the intellect, and an undoing of the little progress—if progress it can be called—that the Western world has achieved in the last three hundred years.

I know some of the counterobjections that the theologians make to such a charge. Faith that is made easy, they say, is no faith; faith that calls for evidence is not true faith. Well, that may or may not be true; if it is, then there is little kindness in this God, who seems to be playing a rather sadistic game with Western man. The devout person usually pictures the atheist as a person who seeks to escape responsibilities, and is amoral (Stern does not follow Sheen in this respect); yet he forgets that true belief in God itself functions in the service of the pleasure principle through the relief, comfort, and relative freedom from anxiety which it provides, while similar inclinations in the atheist would also find consolation and relief in the reverence of a deity—if he honestly could.

To summarize, there is no evidence of any particular resistance in the atheist against a conviction as to the existence of a divinity. His ethical and social values go in the same basic direction as those of the believer; yet he prefers to reduce the area of illusion. It is not against reason or the intellect to immerse oneself in artistic experiences; but it is an infringement upon the intellect when faith in God is derived from ecstasy. Quite generally, states of ecstasy or of intense feeling are not reliable channels through which to reach insights into objective struc-

---

phrenics can be practical and have a sense of humor; it is further known that there are monosymptomatic hysterias; finally, the wide area of psychopathies, as they are still incorrectly called, must be considered. In all this, I do not want to intimate that the Saint necessarily suffered from any of these disorders; I am merely pointing to Stern's weakness in argumentation—when it comes to a holy topic.

[10] For an attempt to brace faith by modern physics, see McLaughlin (1957).

tures. It is not clear why it is the religious experience specifically that should lead to such insights.

While the religious experience seems to indicate a direct link with the infantile, this cannot be asserted to the same degree with regard to scientific discoveries. Becoming a great scientist may perhaps have satisfied an intense infantile wish in Freud. His actual discoveries—particularly at the beginning of his career as a psychologist—were deeply offensive to the rational, humanistic outlook on life which he shared with the eminent scientists of the last half of the nineteenth century, such as Helmholtz and others.[11] Andreas-Salomé (1931) rightly takes this discrepancy between Freud's actual findings and the wishes and expectations that Freud harbored at that time as additional evidence of the reliability of his findings (p. 5f.). Whatever may be the link between the psychological processes that lead to scientific insight, and infantile experiences or wishes, the end result is free of the latter.

Einstein's mass-energy law ($E = m \times c^2$) was the highest abstraction that man's mind was capable of, at the moment when it was discovered —more reliable and more powerful than the trumpets of Jericho, and purified besides of all infantilism—a 'miraculous' event since it was unpredictable from the status of mankind's mind at the dawn of civilization. In other words, this was an improbable event. Later research may bring to light a certain measure of infantilism in the genius-physicist causally related to this final abstraction; from its discovery, mankind was —by means of this abstraction—potentially provided with such power as had been previously recorded only in myths and fairy tales, and attributed to heavenly forces.

Thus the formula also in a sense fulfilled a wish of mankind's; yet the equation per se is not magical, it is an abstraction, a crystal-clear *reflection of definable reality,* purified of all archaism, quite by contrast with any positive statement in the realm of religion. An assertion as simple as "God is almighty" is *prima facie* drenched in infantile ideologies, as can also be demonstrated with regard to almost every sentence in the existing religious tracts. To be sure, these are more than mere

[11] For Freud's beginnings as a scientist, see Bernfeld 1944. Problems concerning the history of ideas are of almost boundless complexity and subtleness (see the recent publication of Bry and Rifkind, 1962), and therefore any generalization in this area can scarcely do justice to historical truth. Thus Freud's research can be viewed, on the one hand as a defeat for nineteenth-century physiologism, on the other as a triumphant resurrection of the principles of nineteenth-century physiology within the psychological orbit.

infantilism; yet they are causally related to it. The scientific proposition, however, is per se divorced from it, despite the infantile background that the scientist may share with his religious counterpart.

4. One argument that Stern seems to delight in using is that Freud was a 'reductionist'—meaning that the results of his investigation of religion led to inferences of the following structure: x is "nothing but" y (p. 80). Stern is throwing together here two essentially different questions. He calls it a 'reductive' statement when "Freud reduces everything which, to the religious believer, is in the supernatural order, to something in the natural order" (p. 80f.).[12] This is not a reduction at all, unless one is to call any scientific statement that contradicts a theological claim a reduction.

If the scientist is expected to assert the supernatural character of religious phenomena as an axiom, then the scientific investigation of religion becomes impossible, for what Stern and many others are then demanding is conviction even prior to the examination of the facts. In disputing the supernatural character of religion, Freud was not very different from a large number of others, who may even form a majority among the contemporary contributors of culturally relevant values. Indeed, we do not know for certain how many among today's priests and ministers are not really true believers, but practice their profession for purely ethical reasons.[13]

We enter different territory when Stern begins to discuss Freud's actual inferences regarding the psychology of religion. When Stern asserts (as does Zilboorg) that Freud concluded "that religion is a compulsive-obsessive neurosis" (p. 82)—meaning, I suppose, that religion is 'nothing but a neurosis'—he not only has made a mistake in this summarizing of Freud, but he is also conveying the impression to the reader that Freud had no respect for religion, or that he underestimated its value or contribution. I have quoted earlier passages of Freud's work that disprove this assertion, and I shall quote Stern later, on an occasion when he himself is indirectly negating this objection.

If Freud ever asserted that religion is a neurosis, he would be obvi-

[12] For a splendid discussion of the pros and cons with regard to reductionism in psychology, see the section "Nothing But and Something More" in Boring (1942).

[13] Indeed, the scientific investigation of religion is severely hampered in so far as important facts—here, as in so many other socially relevant areas—are actually withheld. It is quite likely that important parts of Freud's theory about religion would be much more fully validated than is possible at present, if all the pertinent facts could be gathered without hindrance.

ously wrong. I shall quote first, from his earliest writing on the subject, a passage that perhaps comes closest to Stern's charge. Freud (1907c) wrote: "One might venture to regard obsessional neurosis as a *pathological counterpart* of the formation of a religion, and to describe that neurosis as an *individual religiosity* and religion as a *universal obsessional neurosis*" (p. 126f.; italics mine).

What Freud meant there, however, he set forth in unambiguous terms when he turned to the topic for the last time. At that time, he wrote: "I have never doubted that religious phenomena are to be understood only on *the model of the neurotic symptoms of the individual*" (Freud, 1939, p. 94; italics mine).[14] One must, I am sure, admit that this is something quite different from what the reader who relied on Stern would believe Freud's opinion to have been—particularly when we learn that "model of the neurotic symptoms" is here defined as "a return of long forgotten important happenings in the primaeval history of the human family" (*ibid.*), and that the obsessive character which unquestionably dominates large areas of Occidental religious life is regarded as a reflection of the historical truth that it contains.

There is no question here of 'debunking' religion. Freud had the greatest respect for the neuroses; he knew that they can destroy human life, being the expression of formidable, almost untamable forces. When he *compared* religion and neurosis, there was obviously no 'nothing but' in his mind. Stern, quite rightly, scents the flavor of an extraordinary drama in Freud's (1913g) reconstruction of the events that laid the foundations for human religiosity. He observes: "This is not quite the language and the thought of the typical 'debunking' scientist" (p. 83), and he admits that Freud has here added "something new" to the writings of the Enlightenment on religion.

When he remarks ironically that this is "somehow not the proper thing for a scientific atheist," that statement must have grown out of a certain discomfort. The Enlightenment was, after all, an indispensable historical process, and the fact that reason, after being chained unduly long by a certain monolithic institution, did misjudge the world in many respects, while dancing around in the joy of its first regained freedom,

---

[14] At another point, Freud (1927b) states *expressis verbis* that analogies from individual pathology cannot "exhaust the essential nature of religion" and further: "They [obsessional neurosis and amentia] are only analogies, by the help of which we endeavour to understand a social phenomenon; the pathology of the individual does not supply us with a valid counterpart" (p. 43).

is nothing for it—or us—to be ashamed of. Freud has, in this respect, surely, set a good many things right.

When at last an explanatory construction—right or wrong—has been found, which at least measures up to the greatness of the phenomenon to be explained, one would think that this would be heralded as a great step forward toward a rational explanation of the human world. For even if it should be disproved, nevertheless the construction per se has demonstrated for the first time the possibility that the phenomenon of religion can be made accessible to rational explanation. Yet Stern, curiously enough, draws the opposite conclusion—namely, that Freud came "just about as close to the world of revelation as he possibly could come" (p. 84), and calls Freud's antireligious writings "not quite rationalistic enough" and "odd." In short, he implies that Freud was a metaphysician who believed in the supernatural. Furthermore, since (as Stern claims) "scientific materialism denies tragedy," Freud apparently cannot be a scientific materialist.[15]

To prove his point, Stern has to go through extraordinary gyrations, of a sort not unfamiliar to a mind trained on Aristotle and Aquinas. He tries, for example, to prove that embryology without metaphysics is impossible. I shall not discuss these attempts to inject new lifeblood into a world which, despite its beauty and inner consistency and monumental grandeur, shows the symptoms of lethal sickness. Whether the concept of development can be satisfactorily defined in terms of scientific materialism, I do not know. I am fully convinced, however, that the answer has no bearing upon the question of the *prima causa,* or the supernatural essence of religion. That the concept of development has had a tremendous heuristic value, and that our insight into developmental processes has increased impressively as a result, are historical facts. There is a substantial likelihood that the mechanics of embryology will yet provide a picture of an unbroken series of physicochemical processes, wholly dispensing with vitalistic theories and assumptions.

Yet, to return to Freud's contribution to the psychology of religion, it will be asked whether Freud's own conflict about religion (if there was one) might not have had a distorting effect on his theorizing about it.

[15] When Stern tries to disprove psychoanalysis by correctly asserting that Freud's historical reconstruction of the beginnings of religion "is derived from somewhere beyond the biological diagrams" (p. 87), he has to recognize that, in those areas, he just has not understood the meaning of psychoanalysis, which would not be a scientific psychology in any sense at all, if its center were not, *in all of its assertions,* "beyond the biological diagrams."

A hidden or a conscious resentment—all too well justified, by the way, in the case of a man to whom mankind's future welfare was the major concern of his life—might very well have affected his objectivity.

There is one passage in Freud's work that has always impressed me as evidence of the fact that, in this unique person, the insistence upon truth always won out against what might have been preferable as a personal wish. "In the present case," Freud (1918) once wrote about a patient, "religion achieved all the aims for the sake of which it is included in the education of the individual. It put a restraint on his sexual impulsions by affording them a sublimation and a safe mooring; it lowered the importance of his family relationships; and thus protected him from the threat of isolation by giving him access to the great community of mankind. The untamed and fear-ridden child became social, well-behaved, and amenable to education" (p. 114f.); later, he wrote, with regard to the same patient, of "the pathological products of his struggle against religion" (p. 116).

Has ever a 'debunking' scientific atheist written with so much understanding and appreciation of the service that religion provides to the growing child, caught inextricably in the pitfalls of human existence?

5. A factual question, finally, is raised by Stern in his examination of Freud's theory of the origin of totemism. Sanders (1949) questioned Freud's theory of the origins of remorse and guilt in the sons after primal patricide (p. 53). Stern follows him (p. 84) in asserting that "there is actually nothing in Freud's analysis which would explain why the sons felt guilty at all after killing the father" (p. 84). To decide whether a psychological explanation is adequate or not is, in most instances, a difficult task, particularly when the question involves a prehistoric event that eludes direct validation. Yet it does make a difference whether an author *offers no explanation* at all, or offers one that is merely regarded as inadequate by some of his critics.

Freud, of course, was fully aware that his reconstruction required a special hypothesis, with regard to the arousal of remorse or guilt feelings after the crime, unless the existence of morality prior to the deed was to be postulated. Since, according to Freud's theory, primal patricide was itself the event that brought into being repentance, guilt, and later on religion, the assumption of a moral agency in man prior to the crime would have had no explanatory value. Freud, as the analyst well knows, derived the evolution of moral feelings from the original ambivalence of the sons toward the father of the primal horde. Once aggression was gratified, love remained, and that led to remorse (Freud, 1913g, p. 143; 1930a, p. 132). Freud later adduced still other factors; yet I wonder whether he ever felt fully satisfied by the explanation.

In his last book, Freud (1939) introduced what, in my opinion, may be regarded as an additional developmental principle. He discovered in mankind's progress from sexuality to spirituality—from concreteness to abstractness, so to speak—the effect of a pleasure derived from instinctual renunciation (pp. 182-193). To be sure, Freud assumed or observed the significance of this mechanism in a period following the establishment of the superego; but he did not find the exact reasons for the pleasure that occurs when an instinctual gratification is sacrificed without compensation.

My guess is that Freud may also have postulated the mechanism with an eye to the rise of morality—prior to the origin of superego and conscience—born out of endogenic involvements, and without imposition by external forces. This conjecture regarding what might have been in Freud's mind may very well be wrong.

The origin of morality, in the form of remorse and the renunciation of instinctual gratifications, becomes quite understandable, I feel, when the effect of women, particularly of the mother, upon the complex of forces is reconstructed. I must refer once again to the simpler life (even though it is complicated enough), of our cousins, the monkeys. Zuckermann (1932)[16] not only presented an approximation of the Darwin-Freud primal horde in describing his observations made while studying the group life of monkeys; he also found the most unexpected effect upon the favored female as a result of the decline in the overlord's dominance. The overlord is the only male that has access to the females of the group; the others are condemned to bachelorhood.

When the first signs of a weakening appear in the overlord, a real free-for-all breaks out, with such vehemence, that the prize female is killed in the scramble. The monkeys, however, who live in a sort of pre-fall-of-man existence, are not familiar with the concept of death, and are therefore not cognizant of that fact. What happens is approximately the following: the victor retires with his mistress, fornicating until she stinks so disgustingly that he has to leave her.

I therefore suppose that, after the prehistoric instances of human patricide, a terrible fight would arise among the sons, during the course

16 For a psychoanalytic study of the sex life of subhuman primates, see Hermann, 1926, 1933.

of which *the* female (or females) were gravely injured or killed. The remorse and mourning that necessarily ensued do not need further discussion. The anthropologists would know whether there is any evidence in favor of or against such a conjecture. The legend of the rape of the Sabine women may strike the inexpert as a remote reflection of such an event. As is well known, the Sabines wanted to revenge the rape of their women, who had become Roman matrons; but the women intervened and prevailed upon the combatants to cease fighting. An agreement was made, so that Rome was to be governed by a Roman and Sabine king alternately.

My main purpose has been to point out that, even if Freud's explanation should prove to be incomplete, not all avenues of natural explanation have thereby been necessarily exhausted. Stern was premature in his assertion that the origins of morality cannot be accounted for on the so-called natural plane. His readiness to resort to the supernatural—without any cogent reason—is a sign of an inner aversion to a rational explanation in this area.

I find this same impatience—along with the parallel feeling that the investigation of religious phenomena on the natural plane is a waste of time—also present in Stern's discussion of saints and of the religiously creative person in general. He very rightly castigates the error of looking at the artistic genius as a neurotic (cf. Lowenfeld, 1941). Of course, the genius is not wholly immune to neurosis, but much of his behavior that may look like flourishing neuroticism is the unavoidable concomitant of the creative act.

Stern may be right when he calls the genius "supranormal" (p. 159); this clinically correct viewpoint deserves to be extended to the religious genius. Much as I am convinced that genius and neurosis are different, I am just as strongly convinced of the difficulty involved in deciding which phenomena are to be correlated with the creative act, and which are *bona fide* psychopathology. I am certain that further research will deepen our insight into the basis for that differentiation.

In the religiously creative genius, one has to distinguish two extremes. One is best exemplified by St. Augustine. Whatever the final outcome of the dispute as to the essence of supernatural value, his place as a great philosopher and a metaphysician will probably remain undisputed. His thoughts found a lasting concretization in his works, which had such great influence on a wide range of disciplines in Western thought. His autobiography has to be examined psychologically in the same way as that of any other genius, with full consideration given to that psychopathology which is characteristic of the genius, and which does not find any place in the traditional categories of psychiatry.

The other extreme would be that of a young girl who reports the appearance of St. Mary close to a source of water. Once the rumor of the apparition has spread, the place becomes a famous point of pilgrimage, the water having acquired the reputation of achieving miraculous effects with ailing patients. Let us assume that this was the girl's only religiously productive act. Yet, her sole real contribution was her announcement that she had seen an apparition; the rest was taken out of her hands; what happened from then on was society's doing. From the psychiatric point of view, what took place was an autoplastic process, reconcilable in principle with the diagnosis of hysteria or schizophrenia. Thus, the psychological issue is here significantly different from that of St. Augustine, whose productions cannot on principle be reduced to any psychiatric disorder.[17]

Of course, just as the probable absence of bona fide psychopathology in St. Augustine is unlikely to convince the atheist of the supernatural nature of his experience, so will the autoplastic nature of the religious formation in the girl's case be unlikely to convince the believer of the hallucinatory nature of her apparition.

However, an interesting coincidence which I have brought up in connection with conversion becomes apparent. Stern (p. 166) seems to be in agreement with Helene Deutsch's (1944, pp. 28-30) psychoanalytic interpretation of the "Lady's" first apparition to Saint Bernadette Soubirous, as presented by Werfel. Despite this agreement on the psychoanalytic plane, he maintains that Deutsch's correct interpretation "says nothing about the question of the reality of the apparition." Since Helene Deutsch had shown the psychological preconditions, or rather the inner needs out of which the experience of the apparition grew, Stern raises the question: "Would she [the Blessed Virgin] not choose

---

[17] To clarify the issue, I should add that the neat differentiation between creativity and psychiatric disorder that I am suggesting here is far more complicated in practice. Creativity does not of itself preclude bona fide psychopathology; that is to say, St. Augustine may also have had a neurosis. But for certain reasons, not to be discussed here, it is no more than barely possible to establish a causative connection between the neurosis—if it was present—and Augustine's religio-philosophical creativity. Great creativity, however, may be combined—under specific and rare circumstances—with psychosis. It seems that this occurred in Strindberg (Jaspers, 1949). The most creative patient I had—without, however, falling into the class of genius—was a schizophrenic.

someone whose psychological constellation was such that it offered a natural response?" This is a frequently used argument against a psychological theory of the religious experience. The scientific theory is that, in all outstanding incidents of religious life—as, for example, in Bernadette —the existence of psychological factors can be discovered that make the religious incident predictable. Of course, this cannot be proved; but, by and large, it may be said to be highly probable that, in the majority of such instances, perhaps even in all of them, preconditions of this sort can be found. When Stern asks, "Why not?" it almost sounds as if he were asking why the Divinity should expend any greater effort than is necessary. Let the foundations for the apparitions and conversions be prepared on the natural plane; then, all the Divinity has to add is the final touch.

It would surely be a lazy Divinity that proceeded in that way. The human saints went to the *places of least chance,* in order to win unbelievers to Christianity. If one really agrees with the psychological explanations of apparitions on the natural plane, the additional assumption of a supernatural force becomes altogether superfluous. Grace that is limited to the accidental frustrations of a sensitive mind should be a contradiction in the minds of most theologians.[18]

Stern admits the difficulty there is in distinguishing between psychopathology and true religiousness (even the Church has to be careful before acknowledging supernatural events and grave mistakes occurred on that score; I regret that I cannot discuss here the tribulations that persons who later became saints were exposed to by the Church during their lifetime). To my amazement, he introduces, as the "only one perfectly reliable criterion," the following: "It is 'by their fruits you shall know them'" (p. 167) (a dangerous undertaking, to which I shall return later![19]). This is at heart a pragmatic index. An action or a psychic process is evaluated in terms of its consequences, a yardstick certainly not adequate either for psychology, or for orientation in history.

A few words should be said here about the autoplasticity of religiousness. This may be disputed in the light of the fact that charity stands at

[18] The unbeliever, of course, also takes note of the fact that the *Holy Father,* when ailing, rather rarely entrusts his health to the holy waters of Lourdes, but seems to prefer the more limited knowledge of a man trained on the natural plane.

[19] Apropos of Bernadette, I can only repeat at this point the observation that no miracles and faith and prayer had succeeded in reducing infantile mortality prior to the advent of a scientifically oriented medicine.

the pinnacle of Christian morality.[20] However, charity is not identical with religiousness. After all, there have been saints who lived lives of seclusion, in penitence and asceticism, without *their* lives being filled with charitable acts; we also know of outstanding instances of the greatest charity, performed without faith. The core of the religious experience is a certain kind of belief in God, which is a perfect example of an autoplastic experience. Art and religion are related, for example, but one of the essential differences between them is that art is bound to alloplasticity. As long as a work of art has not been *realized,* one cannot talk of 'art.' If Mozart's creativity had stopped with his *hearing* the beautiful music that he created, he would not have been accorded his standing as the greatest musical genius the world has known.

In spite of its essential autoplasticity, one must not nevertheless describe religiousness as a neurotic symptom, for while the two may be closely related in their autoplasticity, there are essential differences between them. Although it sometimes happens that neurotic symptoms cause a minimum of pain and functional disorder, this should properly be regarded as atypical, for the chief characteristics of the typical neurotic symptom are precisely the discomfort and disturbance of function that are created by it. If we disregarded the huge number of religious automata or uninspired followers, it can be said that true religion is ego-syntonic—something that can never be said of the neurotic symptom. Pain and defective functioning are certainly not the basic characteristics of religion, even though true religious feelings or beliefs may lead to either or both.

Thus, whatever may be the outcome of the ideational struggle over the concept of God, I am certain that one will not be warranted in calling religion a neurosis, in spite of whatever similarities of structure it may show—in terms of denial, repression, fixation—to the pleasure principle, etc. I leave aside the fact that, prior to the rise of science, there were historical periods during which religion offered the only available explanation of the world order, so that, merely by the fact of having

[20] The discussion of Freud's religious theories has often been confused by the failure to distinguish between religion and ethics (e.g., see Racker, 1956). Ethics has been part of religion, but the controversy between Freud and the Churches centers around *metaphysical assumptions* regarding the existence or non-existence of a Divinity, the revelation of Scriptures, and related problems not integrally connected with ethical or moral implications. The differences arising out of the ethical and moral issues have been splendidly discussed by Cole (1955), in his analysis of naturalism and dualism, and in his investigation of the position that the Scriptures take as against the historical development of Christian ethics and morals.

given an explanation at all, religion has been regarded as a kind of precursor of science.

6. Where I, without being a theologian, have to take Dr. Stern most seriously to task is in the fact that he omits from his discussion of psychopathology the Prince of Darkness. As far as I can see, he appears in Stern's discussion only as a *danger* of evil, in so far as, "if we are unduly preoccupied by evil, we become evil" (p. 184); yet neurosis is not merely a danger of evil, but an evil, if only by virtue of the fact that it stands in the way of faith, as Stern implies when he speaks of "the neurosis of unbelief" (p. 185).

When modern intellectuals address their peers, in order to win them over to revealed religion, they generally have much to say about the Divinity and almost nothing about the Devil, even though the latter is an integral part of Revelation, and man's fall might even have been averted, if God had not acceded to the snake's presence in the Garden of Eden. ("It was through the devil that man sinned and spoiled the nature God had given him," Leeming, p. 20.)

The almost consistent omission of Lucifer from such writings is quite understandable, since most enlightened intellectuals would regard an emphasis on Lucifer as a glaring proof of superstition. Nevertheless, Lucifer continues to hold his former place in Catholic theology, as the volume published under the editorship of Père Bruno de Jésus-Marie has demonstrated (Satan, 1952). In that collection of essays by well-versed and, I believe, renowned representatives of theology, we are warned over and over again not to be lacking in vigilance, if we are to catch the Old Adversary. The fact is that, as soon as we include him, the whole realm of psychopathology appears in a different light.

I do not find any way, once Catholic theology is accepted as valid, of refuting the assertion that neuroses and psychoses are the fruit of Lucifer's doing. The analyst finds himself in a peculiar situation here. The seeming paradox is this: While he would have great difficulty trying to find—no matter how hard he wished to—the hand of a just and benign divinity at work in the history of mankind, or of the human mind, it becomes all too easy for him to regard his observations of neurotics and their sufferings as evidences of Lucifer's efficacy. Thus, at the same time that he is forced to disagree quite basically with the theologian about the Divinity, he is also compelled to take exception to some of the modern theological views on the way in which the Devil manifests himself.

While, in earlier centuries, theologians were quite ready to perceive

Lucifer in a great variety of manifestations, the modern rules require the fulfillment of rather more stringent conditions before one may resort to exorcism. I do not think a Devil would be worth his salt (or his name, for that matter), if he still adhered to such medieval pranks as levitation or xenoglossolaly (cf. de Toquédec). I find myself, however, in agreement with Mgr. F. M. Catherinet, who has the following to say about the devil's action upon that "indivisible point" where "sensibility" and "the vital movement proper to the nervous system" meet:

It is precisely at this point of intersection and liaison between soul and body that theologians locate the action of the devil . . . . All that the devil can do is to influence the higher faculties indirectly by provoking tendentious representations in the imagination, and disordered movements in the sensitive appetite, with corresponding perturbations in the nervous system, synchronised as it is with the sensibility. Thereby he hopes to deceive the intelligence, especially in its practical judgements, and still more especially to weigh in on the will and induce its consent to bad acts . . . . The devil can profit from a disorder introduced into the human composite by a mental malady. He can even provoke and amplify the functional disequilibrium, and take advantage of it to insinuate and install himself at the point of least resistance. There he gets control of the mechanism of command, manipulates it at his pleasure, and so indirectly reduces to impotence both the intelligence and, above all, the will . . . . Such are the main lines of the theory of diabolic possession worked out by Catholic theology . . . . If all this is correct, we shall have to infer with the theologians that all true diabolic possession is accompanied, in fact and by a quasi-necessity, by mental and nervous troubles produced or amplified by the demon, and yet having manifestations and symptoms which are practically and medically identical with those produced by the neuroses. The psychiatrist, therefore, is free to study these symptoms, to describe these mental troubles, and to indicate their immediate causes. There he stands on his own ground. But if, in the name of his science, he pretends to exclude a priori, and in all cases, any transcendent cause of the anomalies in question, then he trespasses beyond the bounds of his special competence. Precisely by confining himself to his own methods he automatically foregoes any inquiry of this kind. Never will he find the devil at the term of his purely medical analysis, any more than the surgeon will find the soul at the point of his scalpel . . . . But the doctor who wants to remain a complete man, above all if he enjoys the light of his faith, will never exclude a priori, and in some cases may well suspect, the presence and action of some occult power behind the malady [Catherinet, 1952, pp. 175-177].

I was not quite able to follow Stern when he drew the picture of a Divinity who sought out the point of least resistance, for that would be strange behavior for a being endowed with divine omnipotence; but for a Devil to seek out the pathways of least resistance makes good sense. Mgr. Catherinet's theological views should convince a devout Catholic. It thus becomes clear, then, that the Catholic psychiatrist or psychoanalyst can never rely solely on scientific insight, but has a duty to consult the theologian, in order to make sure that a seemingly natural phenomenon is not of devilish essence. When de Toquédec (p. 190) writes: "There is no question of superposing a preternatural explanation on top of the natural one; it goes without saying that the principle of economy remains in full force," he is, I believe, contradicting Mgr. Catherinet's principle of least resistance; furthermore, he seems to misunderstand the nature of science.

Has science ever *fully* explained anything? A thing is fully explained only when *everything* that could possibly be ascertained about it scientifically has been ascertained. But this has never yet occurred in the history of science, let alone in the explanation of the neuroses. When the analyst says that Freud discovered the etiology of neuroses, he means that, along a certain span of the pathway taken by the development of the neuroses, Freud has set forth some of the necessary conditions.

I am not certain that, for any disease, scientific explanation has penetrated so far that the theologian can feel reassured that the Devil has not entered anywhere along its developmental lines. Therefore, "the principle of economy" is out of place here, and the full consequences of Revelation lead to the practical elimination of any trust in the conclusions derived from psychiatric investigation. Thus Stern has failed to give us the full evidence so clearly set forth in revealed Scripture; from a theological point of view, he may be called a 'metaphysical opportunist,' setting forth only those arguments that may capture the fancy of disappointed scientists, while at the same time withholding those that would, in all probability, offend their sensibilities.

7. Yet it is not only by his omitting the Fallen Angel from his metaphysical scheme that Dr. Stern has done an injustice to Catholic theology. At another point, he makes assertions (to be discussed below) that should offend Catholic sensibilities even more seriously—unless theology

has truly surrendered to science more than one imagined. I agree with Dr. Stern when he discovers in the psychoanalytic situation the blossoming of Christian virtues. The degree of understanding, and the absence of interference by condemnation, that are realized in the psychoanalytic situation, will perhaps induce the future historian to describe the latter as the fulfilment of a Christian ideal, through its concretization by secular ingenuity. To avoid any misunderstanding, however, it must be added that the analyst engaged in the psychoanalytic situation does not subjectively do anything particularly virtuous; he is merely following the basic principles of his craft, or better still, profession. Historically, however, the psychoanalytic situation requires ethical examination.[21]

At one point, Stern reaches conclusions which, if they are correct, would require the believer to adopt a new orientation toward the Church. He comes pretty close then to asserting that faith and neurosis exclude each other, and that psychopathology must first be removed by the medical expert, before true faith can blossom. "My purpose is . . . to show that often the vessel of reception is sick so that which is of the supernatural order is incapable of penetrating in a way we are used to when we think of the spiritual life. . . ." (p. 180). This said, he quickly takes a little step back, to say further: "This does not mean that the life of prayer loses its significance in that area" (p. 181). Yet, in Stern's own book, the life of prayer is of strikingly minor significance on the neurotic's road to faith.

Whether Freud was right or wrong in his views on religion, the conclusion becomes inescapable that, in the light of the ubiquity of the neuroses, a huge number of neurotic patients would be forever barred from finding faith, if that intractable *substratum carnale* were not first set right by a psychotherapist like Dr. Stern—who, after all, seems to put his faith in Freud's method, among the many being offered today on the psychiatric market. To be sure, Stern adds some un-Freudian techniques, once the *substratum carnale* has been cured; but that is not relevant at a moment when we are taking note of Stern's view of Freud's extraordinary contribution to religious life, in that at least half of Christendom (baptism, unfortunately, does not protect against neurosis) apparently must depend on psychoanalysis, if it wishes to arrive at the state prerequisite to faith.

---

[21] It is really Oskar Pfister, a Protestant minister, who has consistently pointed out the Christian elements concretized in the psychoanalytic situation and elaborated in psychoanalytic theory. I wonder why his writings were not cited by Dr. Stern.

If this is really so (and I am willing to accept, for the time being, Stern's premises), then I am forced to draw the conclusion that the historian must recognize an incalculable victory on the part of science, for it has now become clear that faith *needs* science, and apparently could not long survive if it were left unprotected by the discoveries of the materialistic empiricist. The admission that it is not prayer and the relentless search for faith that constitute the royal road toward faith, but that it is rather psychoanalytic treatment that will open up the sluices of faith, puts theology into a somewhat dependent position, and broadens the significance of science beyond anything that the Fathers of the Church or Aquinas would have dreamed possible.[22]

For scientists, however, it is necessary to distinguish, out of the confusing multiplicity of psychic manifestations, such entities as neuroses and psychoses and the allied categories. To what extent this procedure is adequate has become increasingly a matter of dispute. For historical and heuristic reasons, Freud had to start his inquiry into pathology with such concepts; there, this approach has been richly rewarded. But Freud's aim quickly became a *unified theory of the psychic apparatus*. In the New Testament, no difference is recognized between neurotic suffering and that caused by reality: Jesus meets human suffering on the same plane, from whatever source it comes.

I wonder whether the integration of such concepts as neurosis or functional psychosis into theology is compatible with revealed doctrine, notwithstanding the theological justifications offered. I had understood the Testaments to say that any human being is capable of evolving faith, Divine Grace being supposedly impartial. From Stern's reasoning, however, I would have to conclude that only a few are capable of doing their part by themselves on the way toward the true religious faith.

8. There are two quite potent arguments against Catholic theology: the historical viewpoint, and the law of determination of psychic processes.

Historical investigation has, indeed, revealed so many historical precursors to integral parts of the Christian ethics generally, that the *unique* position that Christianity claims for itself among religions must be seriously questioned. The historical method may also cast doubt on whether

---

[22] If Stern is right, and a well-ordered *substratum carnale* is the best road to salvation; and if the bulk of psychiatrists are right, and the new *pharmaca* are the best road to a well-ordered *substratum carnale*—then a time can perhaps be envisioned when thorazine and tophranyl will be distributed in Church before each sermon.

the Christian ethics are *superior* to those embodied in other religions; because of the difficulties involved in discussions about ethics, however, I leave that question aside. Stern is, of course, aware of the historical method and its consequences. He solves the questions it raises with the usual argument of prefiguration: Abraham prefigured the Divine Father (p. 171) and, further, "the prefiguration of the Incarnation can be traced in all people" (p. 175).

He is particularly averse to comparative religion, "which deprives matters of the spirit of their devouring fire" (p. 174)—as if it were man's emotional reaction to it that decided the truth of any assertion. The science of history, indeed, harbors the seeds of potent antitheological arguments (not as to theory, for theology is constructed in such a way that, by its own axioms, it makes itself unassailable). It is quite interesting to examine the documentation for the large number of miraculous cures that occurred in ancient Greece (Herzog, 1931; Edelstein and Edelstein, 1945), which are in fact more reliably documented than is Christ's resurrection. We would then have to draw the conclusion, I suppose, that Aesculapius prefigured the healing Christ.

Such auxiliary hypotheses will not, of course, have the effect of strengthening our confidence: what omnipotent Divinity would wish to mislead man so profoundly as to appear before him under a concealed identity? And why should we not take the dreams of the ancient Greeks and Romans as evidence that the gods of antiquity really existed? These dreams are accessible to psychoanalytic explanation on the natural plane, yet Zeus and Apollo may also have gone the way of least resistance. And if the healing Aesculapius is to be regarded as the precursor of the healing Christ, why should not the latter be regarded, in turn, as the precursor of the modern psychiatrist?

In viewing the panorama of religious and protoreligious phenomena—and, in particular, man's endlessly repeated assurance (each time, let us remember, with regard to a different divinity), that his God and only his God is the true one, and that only He is capable of performing miracles and only He has done so, each successive assertion being accompanied by seemingly irrefutable documentation—one cannot but recognize in man a deep-seated need to produce religion, comparable to the similar necessity of producing art. Whether such needs arise only when man lives in groups, or whether these necessities are as fundamental to his inventory as drives, which are per se independent of the environment, I for one do not know. Yet one question becomes worth looking into—

namely, is it easier for man to acquire mastery over his illusions or over his drives?

Nevertheless, even that does not seem to be an adequate formulation of the problem. The record strongly suggests that, in the construction of his religion, man does not act with the degree of autonomy that the Church attributes to the step. Thus, another conflict enters here: the free-will theory, as defended by the Catholic Church, and the law of multiple determination, as set forth by psychoanalysis. According to psychoanalysis, the believer does not act as a free agent: in the religious experience, the religious person is gratifying, unknowingly, an infantile wish as well as a drive. When Stern objects to psychoanalysis on the grounds that it supposedly asserts that certain religious acts are nothing but instinctual gratifications—"Holy Communion is *nothing but* canni- balistic oral introjection" (p. 81, italics by Stern)—his criticism does not do justice to psychoanalysis. Psychoanalysis would maintain only that such instinctual gratifications *do take place* during the course of the religious act (over and over again, this has been denied by theologians), and are its indispensable prerequisites. They are not in any sense viewed as the whole of the religious experience. Since psychoanalysis asserts that even relatively simple configurations, such as dreams, fulfil at least two functions, if not more, how could it possibly maintain that a configura- tion as complex as a religion, a religious act, a religious experience, can be correlated with one simple function?

There is no doubt that Stern at times tries to do with psychoanalysis what he insists that psychoanalysis does with religion: he tries to debunk it. The central issue is spirituality. In his argumentation, the "appalling idea" occurs to Stern that somebody reading his book might think that he was "attempting to 'explain scientifically' something which is of the supernatural order" (p. 155).

It seems that, once the facts and theories of psychoanalysis are known, and perhaps even integrated to the same extent as with Stern, it becomes increasingly difficult to maintain that strict barrier between the natural and supernatural order on which theology rests. Otherwise, why does Stern suddenly have to go on the defensive? At times, his book sounds as if he had written it for the sake of assuring himself that he is still a believer.

Yet anyone to whom the scientific investigation of spirituality is an "appalling" idea is likely to prove an untrustworthy captain on the voyage into the mysteries of spirituality. One might perhaps feel more confidence in this respect if the explorer at least had enough courage to face the possibility that the psychology of spirituality can also be charted on the normal plane. In the last analysis, Stern does little more than evade the issue. The supernatural essence of values is for him a matter of self-evident fact, and not a question he must first investigate and then decide.

Why does the historical method deprive the spirit of its devouring fire? Does not Stern reveal a weakness here, a fear that he may lose faith? Intellectual processes sometimes do delimit the intensity and freshness of an emotional experience. I have never understood how those listeners who follow the music of *Tristan* while reading the score can really obtain the adequate inner transport. On the other hand, I have not observed that any amount of scientific knowledge about the visual arts has reduced in any way the "spirit of fire" inherent in their enjoyment. Quite the contrary; with every intellectual advance, the aesthetic enjoyment has deepened. Nevertheless, I have never expected to discover the Divine in Rembrandt's paintings, even though the numinous is represented there in an unparalleled way.

No doubt, metaphysics can be saved—provided a halt is called to the historical method, and to modern psychology. But then a tract like *The Third Revolution* turns out to be not so much a landmark on the path toward truth, but rather the outcry of a deeply frightened mind, in danger of losing that precious shelter without which existence might become unbearable. At any rate, clinical observations to that effect were among the reasons why Freud discovered an infantile factor in religion, which is without any equivalent in science. We are facing here, once again, the issue of the legitimacy of conclusions based on psychological observations regarding nonpsychological entities. Or, in other words, are there stimuli whose nature can be determined by a scrutiny of the psychological reactions they have elicited?

If it were permissible to proceed in this way, then it might seem that certain psychological aspects of science are in no way different from their counterparts in religion. First of all, it is well known that psychopathology is at least as rampant, if not more so, among scientists as among deeply religious persons. There is no clinical evidence that the former are less infantile than the latter. What can be observed clinically —and has not yet been adequately explained—is that, in spite of the fact that many functions of a personality may have been affected even by malignant psychopathology, the capacity for testing reality within certain limited areas has been preserved.

This can be objectively ascertained by way of the verification to which all scientific discoveries have to be submitted when they are checked and rechecked by experts. It may be suitable to step out of the psychological frame of reference for a moment, and to look at religion and science from the point of view of what affects them as 'going concerns.'

Let us hypothesize that, in the course of his scientific inquiry, a scientist should discover the existence of God. It is at least conceivable that such a discovery would affect many scientists in the same way as many deeply religious persons might be affected by the discovery that God does not exist, and that their previous beliefs have therefore been illusions. Under the impact of such new insights, those in either category might develop considerable psychopathology.

Yet, with the passage of time, one would be able to observe the scientists going on with their work as before. All that had happened to them was that phenomena had been discovered for the existence of which they had not been prepared. Scientific reality testing would, however, continue as soon as the effects of the initial shock had settled. The ideal scientist, undoubtedly, would not have felt perturbed at all by such a discovery, but rather challenged to deepen his newly won insights. Indeed, it may be said that the scientific discovery of the existence of God would be the most extraordinary discovery that man has ever made, and would assure the fortunate discoverer the Nobel prize and mankind's eternal gratitude.

Yet, if the scientific disproof of God's existence should take place, that would, by contrast, be the deathblow to what is regarded today as church religion. It seems to me that, while science can only go on as before in either eventuality, that cannot be said of religion. The ideal scientist would not be 'derailed' at all, upon the discovery of the existence of God; whereas the truly devout person would lose the very foundations of his own existence if the existence of God were to be disproved. Thus, what is meant by science's relative freedom from infantile admixture is its inherent endowment for adjusting its method of inquiry to any set of phenomena encountered. Religion does not, apparently, harbor an equal 'adjustive potential.' (This, of course, will be denied by the believer.)

In the course of history, one can observe a repeated pattern. New discoveries of science are generally first met with ecclesiastical rejection.

After a while, when the new discovery has become part of common-sense thinking—that is, when it has become routinized or integrated; or has proven its practical efficiency, and cannot therefore be refuted—then a theological mind comes forward to prove (usually with some reservations) that the newly gained knowledge is valid, after all, and does not infringe upon theology or upon revealed truth.

This, then is the Church's 'adjustive potential.' However, the rules of this game should be established once and for all. If, as theology asserts, scientific discoveries cannot truly come into contradiction with revealed truth, a set of hypothetical findings should be established such that, if they were ever proven to be correct, they would, after all, disprove the correctness of Revelation. But this, I fear, may amount once again to tempting God.

Would not a person who, in the Middle Ages, asserted all or even some of the findings of modern science have been declared a heretic? Even Stern admits the existence of psychic processes whose structure is definitely incompatible with the doctrine of free will. He accepts the psychoanalytic observation of early, archaic identification, the 'osmosis' of values lodged in the parental unconscious by the child's own unconscious. No amount of free will could counteract such subtle influences. If one reads between the lines, one may be surprised by the shadow that Freud's work is on the verge of casting over Catholic metaphysics: it seems that to uphold the doctrine of free will is becoming an increasingly difficult task.

And here we touch upon a point that deserves serious examination. No religious text that could have had a substantial effect upon mankind has so far been produced (or 'revealed') that is not replete with contradictions. A body of literature exists in which these contradictions have been discussed at length, and there are also huge volumes in which reason and unreason have bravely fought to synthesize that which is irreconcilable. To be sure, scientists have also reached, separately, conclusions that are irreconcilable, and such irreconcilabilities are found even in the writings of one and the same scientist.

Yet there is a fundamental difference between religious and scientific contradictions. The latter are acknowledged, so that the bulk of them are eliminated in the course of scientific development, of course only to be replaced by new ones, most of which are resolved in turn by new discoveries, constructs, and theories. Religious contradictions are, by and large, static, as can be seen from the unchanging opposition of the various Churches and world religions to each other, and also from the permanence of Scriptures, once they have been sanctioned by ecclesiastical edict.

But more! As Day (1944, p. 89) has intimated in his splendid discussion with Zilboorg, religious texts that are devoid of contradictions do not gain any hold on mankind. This is a perplexing observation that speaks very much in favor of Freud's theories on religion, for thinking in contradictions, accepting contradictions and deriving pleasure from them, is encountered in the child and in the archaic products of collective imagination. There will probably be agreement that part of the fascination that emanates from the Evangels lies in the parables, so that whoever has discovered their beauty will not want to miss a single one of them; yet each of them contains the seed of a century of religious wars, so inaccessible are they to rational understanding.

I hasten to add that the previous statement is not reversible. Not all religious writings containing contradictions fasten themselves to the minds of large groups. Yet it is one of the most challenging tasks of the psychology of religion, which I think has not yet been tackled, to ascertain the structure of contradictions which will set man's religious imagination aflame.

Thus it can be said that contradictions are the eternal movers of science, in so far as their challenge is the motor that keeps scientific endeavors alive; the resolution of those that exist, and the emergence of new ones, is the history of science. The permanence of unchanging contradictions is, on the contrary, the basis of texts destined to function as the foundation of a successful religion. A text that in its content lives up to the requirements of logic, and is written in unambiguous language, will impress only an insignificant number of minds; it will either bore, or not be understood by, the majority of those who find their ultimate wisdom in religious texts.

9. There is one episode in the Scriptures that seems to trouble Stern —as it has others, too—and he treats it in a highly unsatisfactory manner. In my opinion, acceptance of this episode makes it impossible for a devout person ever to take upon himself the responsibilities of a psychiatrist. I am referring to the episode in which God demands that Abraham sacrifice his own son. Stern admits that, if any man among his contemporaries were to act as Abraham did, " we would not hesitate for a moment to treat him as insane" (p. 160)—by which he means, no doubt, to commit him to an institution, whatever the result of the examination might

be. I have mentioned the Abraham question previously, in a different context. Here I wish to take up the same question once more, but within a more specific framework.

What does it mean when a devout psychiatrist declares that he would knowingly and intentionally stand in the way of the fulfilment of God's word? I imagine that there may be those who will find my raising such a question somewhat absurd; I cannot agree. Abraham is the paragon of the faithful. His faithfulness was rewarded (if that was a reward) by his becoming the founder of an allegedly chosen nation. There is no reason for the devout to rule out the possibility that God might again test man by what is no doubt the hardest and the supreme test. If I were devout, and that happened, I would not dare to commit Abraham.

A similar question has been raised as to what man would do if Christ returned; here, however, the devout psychiatrist would not have to feel any scruples. Christ, at least, was endowed with supernatural forces, so that no intention of his could be forestalled by man; but Abraham, once he was locked up in an institution, would be prevented from carrying out an act which, according to the beliefs of Christianity, is the most pious act that man is capable of.

Stern finds an easy way out of the dilemma. He writes: "Whenever in the history of revelation man and God meet face to face, as it were, something happens which is not at all normal. This is the sign of paradox which marks the entire story of revelation. Unlike the God of the philosophers, who is an object of demonstration, the God of revelation in His relationship with man does not proceed *more geometrico,* it is a relationship of love. God loves man with the madness of love, and He tries man's love to the point of madness" (p. 160). I do not want to ask Stern how he has come to know all that, what foundation he can establish to render legitimate his theologizing so extensively (a question, by the way, which has been raised over and over again with regard to Freud, whose right to have any legitimate opinion on God has been disputed).

Perhaps Stern is right about the 'point of madness.' Yet how does he justify committing Abraham? After all, in meeting Abraham at a time when the latter is carrying out the Lord's command, the psychiatrist is indirectly meeting God; indirectly, therefore, his own love of God is being tried. If he wants to be consistent to his own teaching, he must act with that same madness which is appropriate to man in the direct encounter with God. That is, he *has to* let Abraham go scot-free, and pray that God will be merciful again, and substitute a lamb. According to Stern, he will not then be 'mad,' however—which means that Stern will fail the *experimentum crucis,* and behave in the same orderly fashion as those positivists, rationalists, behaviorists and others who are such objects of detestation to him.[23]

It is also striking that Stern indulges in the use of quotations that are more detrimental to him than they are to the opponents against whom he adduces them. Thus, to illustrate the erroneous approach in studies "in which something which is of the supernatural order is boiled down to its psychological substrate" (p. 166), he quotes Pascal's beautiful words about the pure, natural ignorance that all men have initially, and the knowing ignorance of the great men "who, after having traversed all human knowledge, know that they do not know." Those, however, who never reach that state "have a varnish of saturated wisdom." Does not Stern, after all, belong to this latter group? He *knows* that there is a God, that there is a supernatural order, and many more such things. If one reads the late writings of Freud, on the contrary, one will discover that there were very few things that he felt certain he knew, outside of the perceptive realm. Furthermore, he did not hesitate to consider the possibility that science itself might be an illusion.

Freud strikes me, in fact, as a good instance of knowing ignorance, such as benefits the true man of science, who is aware of the relativity and passing character of scientific formulations. Where Freud is rather adamant—and, I believe, a good many men of knowing ignorance are, along with him—is in the area of negative statements. Freud refers to an instance of this: although we do not possess certain knowledge about what the inner substance of the earth consists of, we can be quite sure that it is *not* jam (1933a, p. 48f.). This way of thinking follows the methodology of Nicolas Cusanus, and is quite valid.

Freud, furthermore, did not make positive assertions about anything ultimate, although his writings are filled with comments that appear to reflect a concern with such questions; but he was quite certain about some negative statements concerning the ultimate—such as, for example,

[23] A similar sleight-of-hand technique is used by Stern when he discusses a patient who did not want to have anything to do with a God that permitted the sufferings and brutalities of our times. He writes: "Of all anti-religious arguments, it is the most tragic one, and the most difficult to refute" (p. 169). I think that the record of a God who commands a father to sacrifice his own son should suffice to prove the projective source of the Old Testament. Yet it must be admitted that history does provide each century with burning pyres that should confirm the absence of Providence. It makes no difference whether what is involved are crusades, plagues, inquisitions, or concentration camps.

that there is no personal God of the kind represented in the Scriptures. In my opinion, negative statements about the ultimate are wholly compatible with Pascal's knowing ignorance, they are even the prerequisites thereof.[24]

Another statement I have mentioned before, which Stern even introduces as the "only one perfectly reliable criterion. It is, 'by their fruits you shall know them'" (p. 167)—a quite risky yardstick, after the rise of Protestantism.

After all, what does belong among the fruits by which we shall "know them?" Is it the Inquisition? is it the Thirty Years' War, which reduced the population of Central Europe to a third of its original figure? When Stern so rightly becomes alarmed about the present state and prospect of the Western world, is the cause of this fear really to be sought in atheistic science? Did not the beginning of the decline of the West start when a spiritual cleavage fissured Western society into two camps? And was this cleavage wholly unrelated to ecclesiastical behavior?

Stern should be reminded here of a few lines that he himself wrote: "A purely negative attitude has had, as many Christian writers have pointed out, a devastating effect in the early phases of the social revolution in the last century; Pope Pius XI made the famous remark that the tragedy of the nineteenth century was that the Church lost the working classes" (p. 15f.). Was science responsible for that "tragedy," to which Stern never returns again throughout his book? Of course, I could go on with a long list of the fruits by which "you shall know them," but scholars of the history of the Church are better prepared for such an assignment than I am. It is enough to say that the yardstick that Stern recommends is unsuitable, and may be cited as a manifestation of his magic thinking.[25]

Yet I cannot conclude without a comment that may perhaps seem extraneous to the subject matter. In the present gloomy state in which mankind finds itself, the Churches have hardly any new element of uni-

[24] It is not out of context to quote here a kind of slip made by Stern: "To live as an individual with a psyche without Christ at the center should induce even more anxiety, and I strongly suspect that *our cocksureness* is something like whistling in the dark" (p. 192, my italics).

[25] Evidently Stern would have to limit the "by their fruits you shall know them" measure to a small segment for, if it were generally applied, it would have a devastating effect upon some of his most cherished personal views. In the history of his conversion, he wrote of a perfection that "has been corrupted in time by an act of choice which was made possible by the creation of Freedom" (1951, p. 282). Thus the fruit of freedom was corruption! The ensuing theological entanglements, I trust, have kept a good many ecclesiastical councils debating into the small hours.

fication to offer, so as to help minimize the wave of aggressions that may be unleashed. Even if Catholic theology should, by a miracle, be correct, will the Chinese, will the Indians, will the Mohammedans become baptized? There is not the slightest chance of any such happening. For reasons that cannot be discussed here, I follow those who place their last hopes in science.

No one knows for certain whether this hope is justified; one thing does seem to be certain, however: that, if it should turn out that science *is* incapable of doing any more for the domestication of *homo sapiens* than religion and its institutions have succeeded in doing, then the future becomes truly dark. When I speak of science, I mean, of course, all of its departments, the most important of which, such as psychology and sociology, are still in the early phases of their development. If only enough time is left for science to realize its potential!

One of the things that can be gained from Dr. Stern's book is an insight into the magnitude of the difficulties that man encounters on the road to acquiring mastery over his illusions. To be sure, he is not yet helped sufficiently in that task by science itself. Actually, little is known about the psychology of those feelings that are signified by the term 'faith.' They are ubiquitous: they are to be found in the scientist and in the atheist; and their manifestations vary vastly, of course, on the behavioral level.

They were also in Freud, as can be observed in his letter to Putnam, in which he admits that his reason cannot justify goodness:

> When I ask myself why I have always aspired to behave honorably, to spare others and to be kind wherever possible, and why I didn't cease doing so when I realized that in this way one comes to harm and becomes an anvil because other people are brutal and unreliable, then indeed I have no answer. Sensible this certainly was not (Freud, 1873-1939, p. 308).

How could it be otherwise but that a man who devoted his life to truth and to the welfare of those he loved should also have faith? It may be that the various behavioral outcomes of faith are correlated with levels of sublimation, for science also presupposes a kind of faith, a faith in patterns of some discoverable order within events; a faith that is therefore greatly supported by observation and reason, but remains, I believe, still faith, in the sense that science has not yet achieved, and will never achieve, *absolute* knowledge (cf. Ross, 1958, pp. 526, 537).

In my opinion, Stern is misleading when he differentiates the psychology of science and faith in the following way: "The searching reason of science is a masculine, aggressive principle . . . . It proceeds according to a plan of attack. The world of faith is just the opposite . . . . We have to remain open for God . . . . Reason tackles problems, it is associated with activity. Contemplation beholds mysteries, it is associated with silence" (p. 186). If I understand Stern correctly, he would like to correlate the psychology of science with activity, and that of faith with passivity. The distrust of religious faith that prevails in modern man would then be the result of an anxiety with regard to passivity and of pregenitality, as Stern intimates at another place.

Psychological observation does not confirm these correlations. Defense against passivity may greatly disturb sublimatory processes of any kind. Parents, misunderstanding the present historical stage of the debate between science and religion, sometimes interfere with the child's religious life. I know of instances in which the child has been ridiculed for his belief in God. The result is usually serious damage to the creative potential of the adult.

Freud, it seems to me, was quite fortunate in growing up in an environment that did not interfere with his religious life as a child. He did not have to cope with orthodoxy; instead he went through a phase of intense, apparently spontaneous participation in the reading of the Bible, which he outgrew during the course of his mental development. The result was an apparently high potential of sublimation, a full representation of cultural and moral values, along with unharmed independence of judgment. Such a synthesis of high moral standards with independence of judgment seems to be a particularly difficult task.

To denigrate science at this hour seems to me to be a culturally destructive step. The opponent of science will say that he has not denigrated it, he has merely warned against its excesses. Yet apparently Darwin's theories are also excesses, just as is Freud's theory of personality. Both will be recorded in any future history of science as landmarks, and I cannot call it anything but denigration, when anyone regards either of them as a culturally destructive event.[26]

Freud (1933a) once wrote of the "constitutional incapacity of men

[26] Of course, I now risk being reproached for having denigrated religious institutions. If it should turn out that man can maintain a minimum of civilized behavior only by bowing to monolithic spiritual agencies, this reproach will be correct. Yet, until this is proved, the battle cry *écrasez l'infâme* is as meaningful as it was when it was first uttered.

for scientific research" (p. xi). This may sound paradoxical, when it is said by a man who did so much for science himself. One might think that he considered himself an exception, particularly when one recalls that, two years before, he had remarked in a letter that "only a few people are constitutionally capable of scientific investigation" (Freud, 1873-1939, p. 407). Nevertheless, in his own scientific endeavors, he had noticed in himself a resistance against acknowledging the truth, and even as an old man, upon making a discovery which he considered to be of importance, he broke out with these words: "It is a discovery of which one ought almost to be ashamed, for one should have divined these connections from the beginning and not after thirty years" (Freud, 1873-1939, p. 361),[27] thus acknowledging in himself the same "constitutional incapacity," even though he had acquired a vigorous ability to counteract it. I would compare it, myself, with man's constitutional incapacity to fly. Some heroes of mind and action have made it possible for man to fly more quickly and further than any bird, which is, after all, "constitutionally" capable of flight—and yet there are people who are still afraid of entering an airplane.

I could have cited Freud's remark about man's constitutional incapacity for science when I was discussing the fate of psychoanalysis at the hands of the neo-Freudians. There it is, of course, particularly confounding. The rise of new frames of reference, however, is historically an agonizing process, and it should not perplex us that Freud's step forward was first followed by regressions. After all, despite the victory of Christianity over paganism, the Greek gods still continue to live in the guise of saints, and perhaps even animism still continues to live in the belief in the Devil.[28] Consequently, the impression I may have unintentionally created, of thinking that all good is in the scientist and all weakness in the believer, must be corrected. Barber (1961), in a highly commendable paper, has put together material that impressively demonstrates the 'constitutional incapacity' in the scientist himself.

In him is also to be observed at times a hankering for illusions—in this instance, a clinging to what, through the progress of research, has become an outdated scientific illusion, now inordinately charged with narcissism. On the other hand, the individual believer is capable of extraordinary scientific achievements, as can be observed not only in Newton but also

[27] See also Freud's letter to Putnam, in which he expresses dissatisfaction with his intellectual endowment (Freud, 1873-1939, p. 308).
[28] For the survival of archaic religious beliefs, see Murray (1921).

in Mendel, one of the most illustrious minds of the nineteenth century, a Catholic monk who was vastly superior as a scientist to his contemporary colleagues, many of whom may well have been unbelievers. Yet this supposed constitutional incapacity of the individual is of no significance when the history of science as an objective entity is appraised. Individual incapacity may delay progress; it cannot eliminate it.

It seems that once the basic principle of empirical research was established, the attack of a large number of scientists upon the unknown was enough to make the areas of ignorance crumble away. One scientist may be stopped in his tracks by his illusions; decades later, another (who also has illusions, but in a different area) will successfully tackle the same problem. Reality will intervene, here stimulating research, and there impeding it; yet, in another region, that same impediment may be overcome. Although, as Freud intimates, the individual scientist should be ashamed of his incapacities rather than boastful of his achievements (which are small even under optimal conditions, when compared with what is still unknown), the total output of science—taken as an objective, historical entity—is a glorious page in mankind's history.

It is different with the Churches. While the individual believer may have contributed much to science, may even have been the first one to carry the scientific method into a new field, the Church as a historical entity has had, if anything, a retarding effect. The rise of science had to be achieved in the face of her opposition; she has almost never led or guided or stimulated it; she has almost always limped behind, making concessions *a posteriori*. In order to survive, she must try to absorb as much as possible of man's creative energy into prayer and faith; what was true of the medieval Church should, if she were consistent, be equally true of the Church in the twentieth century.

Indeed, if the New Testament is really God's word, it is ludicrous to perform research in a laboratory, or to build a plant or arm a nation; instead, every good Christian should strive to submerge his mind in prayer, reducing his contact with reality to the minimum necessary for his survival. As a matter of historical fact, however, mankind's creative impulses have been increasingly drawn into research and its application to reality; whatever theological dogma has had to say about faith and science, the historical process has pushed the Churches—and, with them, religion—to the wall, because inherently Church and science are incompatible.

When the historical measure is applied, the scientist has no reason to complain, or to feel pessimistic. He is grateful to those communities that let him do his work as best he can, without interference or threat; a book like Stern's, though it is at heart antiscientific, is really the minimum attack to be expected. And if the concessions that Stern makes are considered seriously, one may even see in Stern's book—at least, in part— a sign of remarkable progress.

Yet, when all the forces that are in motion against science, and particularly mental science, have been taken into account, and when the urgency of the present historical moment is fully grasped, then, of course (always assuming that it is science which will furnish the solution to the present dilemmas), the call for more faith in religion at the expense of the scientific outlook, and the request that certain areas be exempted altogether from scientific investigation, may deserve a less even-handed appraisal. Religion is deeply rooted in the emotional sphere; hard and unpleasant as may be the ethical demands embodied in some religions, still it can be said that it is apparently easier to believe in God than not to. This may once more take us back to Freud's assertion about man's constitutional incapacity with regard to science.

We take it for granted that insight into the structure of reality provides us with the possibility, and under certain conditions with the opportunity, of giving to reality the direction we wish—as, for example, in the mastery that modern man has acquired over physical matter and organic life. If we look at this nexus between insight and mastery, however, as a 'metaphysical accident,' and not as a necessary consequence; or if we assume a world in which insight and mastery are in no way correlated (as actually happens, after all, in certain areas—all our knowledge of earthquakes, for example, does not help us one iota towards taking any action to prevent them), then the insights that man's ingenuity has so far accumulated might still be as true or as false as they are now, but very few scholars would regard them as true, or even as approximations to the truth.[29]

The vast majority of mankind would disregard those insights and even ridicule them, whenever they infringed upon common sense. One of the arguments that will be raised against this theorem will be that, even if what I have called the 'metaphysical accident' were not present, the

[29] I believe that this is one of the reasons why psychoanalytic insights are so easily dropped, refuted, disbelieved, overruled, and so on. Psychoanalytic insights do not furnish the power to bear upon reality in such spectacular and unquestionable and convincing ways as do insights in the natural sciences, in a very large number of instances.

scientist would still be able to make more correct predictions about future events than someone who rejected science, and that in itself would earn him the respect of the community.

It is true that his predictions would be more reliable. He would probably be capable of predicting with fair accuracy which patient will recover and which will die, when there will be good crops and when bad, and other such events of great importance. But the more accurate his predictions were, the more he would be suspected of being responsible for the harmful course that reality might take—for, unfortunately, his predictions would be more often unpleasant than otherwise, and very soon the scientist with the keenest insight would either be put on the stake or forbidden to prophesy.

Even in our scientific times, the scholar who brings bad tidings is sometimes accused of being an 'ill-wisher.' Thus we may recognize that the general 'belief' in science which has had such a profound effect on Western civilization, and which is now spreading all over the world, is rooted, in the final analysis, to the fact that science fulfills (in actuality) old magic wishes.

Whoever possesses a person's counterfeit has power over him. If distrust should spread with regard to the 'metaphysical accident,' science may once again become chained.

Additional Remarks

In a letter to Pfister, Freud called the religious sublimation *die bequemste Form*[30] of sublimation (E. Freud and Meng, 1963, p. 12). In this casual remark, he suggested a quantitative frame of reference with regard to sublimation. Leaving aside the question of energic transformation, it can be stated that the new goal or content cathected in the course of sublimation may be closer to or more distant from the original physical goal. Since the content of religion—particularly in the form of a personal God—is close to infantile and childhood imagery, whereas the abstract nature of scientific conclusions is far more removed from childhood imagery, the psychic work involved in the sublimations of science is *ceteris paribus* greater than in the former.

This, however, cannot be correlated directly with degrees of pleasurable experiences. In individual instances, the religious sublimation or an

[30] *Bequem* is used to denote that which is comfortable or easy, *bequemste* could be translated as "most comfortable."

attempt in that direction may elicit pain and despair, whereas scientific endeavors may, in other instances, lead to great pleasure. This clinical observation, however, would not militate against the formulation Freud intended when writing Pfister. It would be improbable for infantile imagery to come closer to the truth than scientific abstractions.

The relativism of the scientist is the highest form of sublimation since it dispenses with and renounces the feelings of absolute certainty that inhere in early childhood imagination.

Appendix 3

Some Tentative Notes on the Psychology of One Aspect of Japan's History

Shortly after Pearl Harbor, an idea came to me concerning one significant aspect of Japanese history. Subsequent consideration has given me the feeling that the idea may be correct. It concerns the relation, in this sphere, between trauma and repetition compulsion which is well known from clinical observations and which—on the historical plane— is the center of Freud's (1939) *Moses* book. Although Moloney's 1954 study contains the essentials of what I have in mind, nevertheless I think that my approach is sufficiently different from his to justify this appendix.

The reason for my presenting it at this point should not be difficult to grasp. Quite independently of whether I am right or wrong in my hypothesis, it may demonstrate concretely how consequential in principle the evolvement of psychoanalytic anthropic science may be to the mutual understanding of nations.

I must begin by briefly referring to an experience that I had in the Army, where I had to discuss the problems of a large number of subjects (soldiers who had failed in their military service because they were neurotic or delinquent) with their superiors (commissioned and non-commissioned officers). These latter were men from all walks of life;

usually, however, they all tended to be angry and ill-disposed toward these soldiers, who were, in their eyes, a great hindrance to the war effort. Nevertheless, I was almost always able to get across to them an understanding of the particular issues that were significant in the individual instances—something I would not have been able to do without the psychoanalytic approach.

Psychoanalysis provides a linguistic tool that now makes possible a sensible interchange of ideas about man, just as we are able to talk sensibly about matters of the physical world only since the natural sciences have evolved a proper terminology. It is still a question, however, whether psychoanalysis also contains the proper vocabulary for presenting the history of any national group in such a way that even someone to whom the national group may otherwise seem strange and alien, because of differences in ethics, customs, and philosophy, can empathize or identify with it. If this can be done, a formidable barrier separating national groups can at last be removed, aside from the incomparable advantage that is to be gained if a national unit can thus be led to understand its own history better, instead of merely responding to the 'unconscious' motives stemming from its own past.

The principles of psychoanalytic research into history were laid down by Freud (1939) in his book *Moses and Monotheism*. These principles cannot be better justified than by the following quotation from Pirenne (1944):

> History is essentially a continuity . . . which proceeds from generation to generation, so that man cannot escape from it, and which thereby links our times with the most distant epochs [p. ix, my translation].

If Pirenne is right, then Freud's book is also right, at least as far as its methodology is concerned. Yet, the fact is that I do not intend to inquire as to whether or not Freud's application of psychoanalysis to history was correct. In what follows, I take its methodological correctness by and large for granted.

The practical (I shall not say heuristic) value of postulating the principle of relevant coherence for the history of a people as well as that of an individual should not be doubted.[1] Yet I am myself no historian,

[1] Notwithstanding my own convictions regarding psychoanalytic psychology, I am fully aware that nobody can truly foretell at present which of the many psychoanalytic findings will be regarded by later generations as correct, which will be refuted outright, and which, even though in modified form, will find a permanent place in psy-

and thus cannot be regarded as an expert on the history of Japan. This circumstance alone stands in the way of even a resemblance between what follows and a historical, scientific inquiry. I do not wish to do anything else here but to try to determine how far the psychoanalytic principle can carry us, when facts are gathered, in so far as they are available, through the scanning of some basic source material. Japanese history, although it is complicated enough, may be more suitable for such an undertaking than that of many other peoples, since her known history may contain fewer relevant variables, and in any case her official entry into the concert of modern world powers starts relatively later than that of most other major world powers of the modern age.

If Freud's concept of the psychology of history is confirmed and elaborated, the legends, beliefs, and folklore—in short, the totality of a group's tradition—will acquire new prominence. One must expect to discover factors at work in that area similar to those found in the exploration of the *Ur-Phantasien* that an individual carries in himself about himself. These *Ur-Phantasien,* or *Ur-Bilder,* which the individual has formed about himself, are usually difficult to reach. They are often riveted to early recollections which we know to be substitutes in the form of 'screen' or 'cover' memories. These images, although experienced as memories, are actually a composite of real happenings and fantasy, with one or the other prevailing, and to a varying degree.

The notable aspect is that both the objectively true and the imagined part cover items of greater seriousness than those that meet the eye. This discovery should be applied to the traditional story of a nation, in which we should presumably encounter also a composite of real events and fantasy. Since we do not have a fixed rule by which to decide between the fantasy or reality nature of the traditional story, much will depend on the psychologist's art and skill—that is, on his hunches and intuition. Freud, with what may not have been sufficient justification, selected an unusual element of such an early story, and built upon it a significant delineation of Jewish history.

---

chology. The fate of Newton's physics should teach us how futile it is generally to make predictions of this sort. Nevertheless, I am reasonably certain that the future historian's verdict will be that it was Freud's psychological theories that offered the best possible explanation in his time. Of this, however, I am more certain than in regard to the psychoanalytic approach to history. Here is an area in which the later verdict may be rather different. On the other hand, in view of the relative ignorance that still shadows man's understanding of his history, there is also the possibility that this feat of Freud's will be regarded later on as even greater than the many that he performed in the area of pure psychology.

I would not even dare to undertake a similar attempt, particularly in view of the feeling of strangeness that Japanese folklore inevitably evokes in anyone who has grown up in the Occident, thus impeding empathy. Nevertheless, on a purely speculative basis, some features may be pointed out as suggestive of certain trends that may be active at the core of the unconscious of Japanese history.

The principal conclusion that I venture to derive from early Japanese folklore has to do with the substantial effect that the matriarchate may have had. I shall present just one episode of the rich material. The second generation of gods, Izanagi and Izanami, were the parents of the Japanese Islands. Then the goddess Izanami produced the Sun Goddess and the Moon God. She gave birth to many gods, the last one being a son who was the Fire or the Fire God, Ho-musubi. She was burned to death, while she was giving birth to him. Izanagi tried to join his wife in the Land of Darkness, but she had become a putrified mass (Sansom, 1958, p. 30).[2]

The point that I have in mind is an inference by analogy to the type of event which Freud reconstructed or hypothesized as preceding the rise of totemism, and for which he had discovered more specific evidence in Jewish history—namely the occurrence of the murder of a father or his substitute, which, in Japanese history (in prehistoric times?) came to pass in the form of a matricide. I limit myself here to suggesting tentatively that the myth of Izanami, and her death at the birth of her youngest child, reflect an actual murder of a mother figure by the youngest hero son. The youngest is often known in myth as the one who carries out patricide; in such an instance, one may easily think of reality factors that may have served to facilitate such a deed.

The youngest son had known his father only at a time when, presumably, aging had already begun to weaken him. The very aging process in the father had also led to the youngest being treated in a more affec-

[2] It should be noted, however, that some authors maintain that these early legends concerning Shinto deities were strongly influenced by the Chinese. E.g., "The prevalence of paired male and female deities, such as Izanagi and Izanami, may also be the result of conscious selection with the *yin* and *yang* principles in mind" (Tsunoda, 1960, p. 26f.). Even if the godly pair were of Chinese vintage, would this extend also to the theme of the permanent destruction of a female deity? Moreover, even if Chinese influences did become apparent in one or the other element of Japanese folklore, would that militate against the reconstruction of an event that may actually have come to pass in Japanese history? If an apparently foreign element was voluntarily integrated, this may have occurred primarily because it expressed, in a more suitable form than did native folklore, something that was genuinely Japanese.

tionate way than his siblings had been, so that the developing superego may have been more tolerant, reflecting the tolerance with which he had been treated in his youth.[3] Yet the kindness with which he was treated may also have aroused passive longings, which would call for a particularly aggressive defense. It appears less understandable to me why the youngest should have been predestined to carry out matricide.[4] Suffice it to say that, up to a certain point in Japanese history, queens played a prominent role, at just the critical moments in that history. So unique was this factor believed to be, that the Chinese called Kyūshū, the Southwestern Island, on which Japan's organization as a state began, "Queen Country."

Another factor seems quite unusual. According to one ancient source, the divine offspring from whom the imperial line is traced was produced from the mouth of a male god, after he had chewed up the ornaments of a goddess. "Thus the ordinary male and female functions are reversed in establishing the genetic relationship" (Tsunoda, 1960, p. 17). This reversal of creative functions (quite different from Pallas Athene's springing fully clothed from Zeus's head) may likewise point in the direction of the matriarchate.

Yet when and how the events began that led to the establishment of Japanese tradition is as little known as in the instances of other great cultures. The original settlement of the islands in prehistoric times seems to have been brought about peacefully. The aboriginal Ainus were only later forced to withdraw to the two northern islands, by warfare that lasted many centuries. When more is known about the 'repetition compulsion' in the historical process, the fact that the earliest settlement of Japan came to pass without warfare may be regarded as of prime importance, giving the whole of subsequent Japanese history its specific stamp.

The origin of the Japanese state, as far as is known from historical times, took place in Kyūshū, an island which although mountainous and poor on the whole, was destined to be of major importance, probably through its closeness to Korea, from which the extensions of Chinese culture reached Japan. It is assumed that it was the rise of powerful dynasties in China and Korea that caused the Japanese to strive toward

[3] That one does not follow necessarily from the other, Freud (1930a) showed in *Civilization and Its Discontents* (pp. 124-126).

[4] Dr. Angela Selke de Sanchez was kind enough to make the very convincing suggestion that the frequent event of the mother's death being caused by the birth of her last child might have given rise to this element of the myth.

a unified government, for otherwise they might have been overwhelmed by the strong and efficient continental powers.[5]

The expedition of the legendary Emperor Jimmu Tenno (whom the chronicles place in the seventh century B.C.) from Kyūshū probably took place around 350 A.D. He is believed to have had a hard fight with the Ainus or their ancestors in the plains of Yamato, which was to become the area of early centralized government. Interestingly enough, the Chronicles report that later a rebellion started in Kyūshū, and that the court even had to take temporary residence there in order to subdue the rebellious tribes. The perennial problem of Japanese history—the conflict over the Emperor's orbit of power—apparently already existed during its early phases. The Emperor subdued various clans and made their chieftains his vassals, although the individual chieftain preserved a considerable degree of independence.

There is one factor in the Japanese institution of Emperorship that is quite remarkable and, I believe, distinguishes it from its equivalents in other countries. It became so deeply rooted in the very existence of the Japanese State that the one has since been unthinkable without the other. The Japanese emperorship is the oldest political institution of its sort that has reached the present without interruption. At times—and these were not such short intervals—deprived of all political power, in what practically amounted to a state of captivity, reduced to pawns in the power politics of powerful chieftains, some of the emperors were humiliated or even killed, without having any say about their successorship. Yet, strangely enough, the institution of the emperorship—with negligible exceptions—has never been in actual danger, so that direct continuity from the very beginning of Japanese history has been preserved. This is, in my opinion, what makes the Japanese emperorship so remarkable.

As a political institution, it early acquired a form which was independent of its actual functioning. The reduction of the kingship to a nullity by a powerful *major domus* is a frequent theme in history; yet, it

[5] The explanatory value of such external influences upon historical processes of this kind has often been questioned. At least the effect of a precipitating factor may, I presume, be attributed to them. But there is no doubt, that the rise of a superior political organization per se has no relevance to the neighboring territory, unless its inhabitants are equipped to perceive and respond to the change. The key problem in this context would be the psychological state of the inhabitants of Kyūshū who, according to the prevailing hypothesis, felt impelled to achieve an organization similar to that which they had observed on the continent.

has happened just as frequently that the *major domus* has taken over the regalia and made himself the king. This has never happened in the history of Japan, however, so that the present—the 123rd—Mikado claims unbroken descent from the first emperor, who descended from the Sun Goddess.[6]

It is a challenging problem to discover how this unbroken lineage was maintained; in dealing with that problem, one discovers a pattern that may represent the only form capable, in the light of the basic features of human nature and of group life, of achieving such continuity, or its like. Early in the process of imperial organization, a subsidiary power center developed, exercising its functions in a variety of forms, until it finally led to the Bakufu and the Shōgunate, both of which disappeared only in the nineteenth century, with the Restoration. I have called this power center 'subsidiary' because that is how it appears in terms of hierarchy; in terms of actual power and effect, however, it was for the most part supreme although, curiously enough, it remained throughout replaceable, whereas the Imperial institution which it actually dominated survived and persisted unbroken.

Thus this subsidiary—or, perhaps better, substitute—power was a sort of scapegoat against which the aggression of the discontented could turn if need be. To a certain extent, it had to do the dirty work of history, while the emperorship could go through those same events unblemished. It seems to be almost impossible for those who hold power not to abuse it, and not to commit serious blunders, since they are basically blind to the signs of the historical periods in which they are living. Thus, the emperors would have been bound to discredit themselves, had they succeeded in openly maintaining the supreme power position that most of them avowedly or concealedly desired. Yet, on the other hand, in the emperor, the state had an instrument ever available in times of crisis. Thus, when subsidiary power had compromised itself, or various aspirants for government had proven unsuitable, there was always a power present in the background, to step in and keep the state from falling apart.

[6] It is quite curious to observe that an analyst, by making a wrong prediction, contributed what to his mind would be a proof of the Mikado's divine origin: "In order to preserve the rule of a capitalistic oligarchy after a lost war, the Son of Heaven will, indeed, have to prove his divine power" (Alexander, 1942, p. 33). The Japanese emperorship is one of the few institutions which would provide the opportunity to study the prerequisites for enduring governmental institutions, or what makes an institution survive against odds. There is no doubt that the Japanese emperorship is the sort of structure that absorbs ambivalence and uses it for its survival.

However much the emperor's political power may have been reduced, he always held full magical-religious sway. He was the intermediary between the State and Heaven, and it was his task to perform the decisive rites on which the welfare of the country depended. He had to re-establish the equilibrium between the secular world and the cosmos, when a disharmony, capable of leading to earthquakes, floods, and such calamities, had been brought about by human misdeeds. This magical power of the throne, as far as I know, has never been touched or disputed by any other political force; and it may have been appraised by the entire nation as far greater than any secular power.

There have been two extremes in man's attitude to superior extra-secular powers (Freud, 1930a, p. 127). The fetishist, upon being disappointed by the course of events, dismisses his old fetish and sets up a new one, expecting from it the beneficial effects he has sought to bring about. In monotheism, on the other hand, God is irreplaceable; thus we see the Jews assigning the cause for misfortune to their own sinful conduct, rather than to any inefficiency on the part of the heavenly machinery. The scientist, incidentally, proceeds on the one hand like the monotheist, in his unshakable conviction that nature follows laws; on the other hand, he resembles the fetishist in so far as he takes up and drops one method after the other, until he has reached his goal. Indeed, had the Jews applied the scientific method of induction, they would undoubtedly have tried out the religious teachings of their captors.

It is not without piquancy to consider that had they done so, they might have quickly ended their plight. Be that as it may, an unshatterable devotion to an intellectual principle of a high ethical order is properly regarded as the manifestation of a higher, more differentiated psychic organization than that which underlies a fetishistic approach to the transcendental world. In Japan we encounter—to simplify the description of the sociological forms—a fetishistic attitude toward the substitute power, and a monotheistic attitude toward the emperor.

The intense adherence to tradition, characteristic of Japanese culture and reflective of an equally intense desire for predictability, would have required a monotheistic attitude toward the substitute power as well. We shall see that it was the interference by reality—that factor that Freud, following the Greeks, epitomized under the term *ananke*—which over and over again disturbed the possibility of predictability in that area. I would call it a matter of national genius that fetishistic and monotheistic forms and attitudes were able to be so successfully brought into harmony and synthesized. From a certain point of view, this may be regarded as an ideal solution. In order to deal with reality, the fetishistic antitraditional attitude is necessary. However, the structure of the human personality requires, as soon as society is sufficiently differentiated, the monotheistic attitude, unless moral chaos and anarchy are to be the constant, even if only latent, threats to the maintenance of social order.

The mode of appearance of the emperorship leads me to raise the further question of whether this formation can be linked to the matri-archal elements which, I think, can be discovered in Japanese culture and civilization. The emperor is kept in isolation, unapproachable; he is not soiled or contaminated by contact with the seamy side of reality. The emphasis is on his ritualistic functions, which are concretely and directly creative; he is kept politically powerless in the sense of decision-making by the scheming efforts of a dictatorial power whose vigor cannot be disputed. The emperor himself had rather to rely on passive techniques in general. Even when he did become actively engaged in a struggle against the substitute power, he was forced to entrust the carrying out of that stratagem to others. Nevertheless, at certain points, notably at points of crisis, his voice did become effective. The carrier of substitute power had to consider continuously the vicissitudes of the emperor, so that he felt safe chiefly while the emperor was still a child. Among the parties contending for power, the one which held the emperor in custody had the best chance of assuming power.

Elements such as are observed in the Japanese emperorship evoke the ancient image of an all-powerful mother-goddess, who has access to secret magic rites, who is to be feared so long as she is not appeased or rendered powerless, whose existence is not to be questioned, and whose functions can be taken over only by one of her kind, if at all. The possibility of turning, in times of crisis, to this ever-present background power seems to me, if anything, to confirm this image.

I have mentioned previously the fact that Kyūshū was called "Queen Country" by the Chinese. There was, initially, a matrilineal succession; queens are, up to a certain time, not too infrequent in Japanese history. It is worth considering the circumstances under which the actual queen-ship came to an end in Japan. The Empress Shōtoku died in 770. Her history is rich in adventures and surprising events. Here it is important to take note only of her infatuation with Dōkyo, a monk on whom she conferred the highest offices. These great successes apparently whetted his appetite, so that he aspired to become emperor.

Actually, it was he who held supreme power—which in itself ran counter to another tradition of those times, the resting of substitute power in the hands of the Fujiwara family. I assume that the Empress's way-ward sexual behavior, plus her arbitrariness in traditional matters, had destroyed maternal prestige forever, so that, on the death of the succeed-ing Emperor (Shōtoku had died without issue), the council of ministers refused to allow a woman to take the throne, thereby creating a precedent for the future. There occurred only two unimportant instances to the contrary, and these only after 1600.[7]

Nevertheless, the decision to eliminate the queenship does not neces-sarily militate against my general hypothesis. The unsuitable behavior of one woman may interfere with this image of power, whereas a male carrier of power, by punctiliously sticking to the rules, may live up to the style of functioning of maternal power, as outlined above, more satis-factorily than an unruly empress. It would be, in my estimation, a mis-take—particularly in view of the earlier-mentioned element of sex reversal in a Japanese myth—to think that the mother image is necessarily sex-bound.[8]

Officially, the Emperor held all the power; substitute power such as the Shōgun held was only delegated. Yet, how profoundly and appar-ently permanently this power had been delegated at times (it appeared to be almost abdicated or abandoned power) can be seen from the length of time that it took the Americans and other Western powers to find out the true state of affairs.[9] For a long time, they actually took the Shōgun to be the ultimate holder of temporal power, and addressed him as the Emperor.

Does not all this appear like an attempt to buy off the gods? The per-son who has the power is not permitted to exert it—which keeps him free of guilt: if the use of power produces offensive acts, then punishment will fall on the one whose exertion of power has produced the repre-hensible act. The further extension of this hide-and-seek—this game of 'who has the real power?'; that is, 'who reigns and who rules?'—at times took ridiculous forms. Thus it might happen that, in a family which had hereditarily held the place of the Regent, the power of the Regent

[7] See Sansom (1958, p. 90f.; 1931, p. 184f.).

[8] As will be seen later, by a peculiarity of the Japanese political system, matrilinealism became indirectly an important element in imperial succession.

[9] See Satow, 1921, p. 33f.

might be held by the Regent's Deputy, the official Regent having become in his turn a mere figurehead.

The practice of deputy functioning spread at times—as under the Ashikaga Shōgunate—to many other areas of rule (Sansom, 1961, p. 145f.), so that the principle of substitute power finally became in effect a basic characteristic of the structure of Japanese society, perhaps the indispensable adjunct to maintaining any semblance of preserved tradition. I imagine that the deputy at any level, for example, must have felt readier to meet new situations with new solutions than did the figurehead, who officially held a position assigned to him by tradition.

The bearing of tradition on Japanese life and history cannot be overestimated. This impact of the past upon the present may have required extraordinary techniques in order to keep the society in a viable condition. Adherence to tradition and the superego are closely allied. Of course, someone who acts in accordance with tradition may do this for motives that would not at all be approved by a strict superego; yet from the actions of those who serve as superego figures for groups, as well as from the societal demands, one can draw a composite picture of the cultural superego. Then one observes that, despite the heavy impact that the precepts of tradition had on Japanese society in general, and on everyday life in particular, the religious orbit was of an astonishing tolerance and liberality.

The basic rules and precepts of Shintō actually cover rather small areas of conduct; thus—and this may prove most surprising from the Occidental point of view—for long periods, Shintō and Buddhism flourished peacefully side by side. There is one example in particular which shows incisively the basic difference between the Japanese and the Occidental feeling about Godship. In the opening year of the Empress Shōtoku, whom I have mentioned before, a Shintō deity declared its wish to proceed to the capital. Upon arrival there, the symbol of their god was installed in a shrine in which forty Buddhist priests recited masses, and a civilian mark of high distinction was conferred upon the god. "One can hardly imagine," writes Sansom (1931), "a more perfect display of the spirit of compromise than a religious ceremony for the bestowal of civil rank upon one deity in the shrine of another" (p. 183).

In speculating about the structure of the superego of the Japanese, one distinctive feature is to be considered: the relatively late formation of a Japanese script.[10] To be sure, the fact that the population of a country is literate is a rather late achievement of civilization; I suppose that, even at present, the majority of mankind are still illiterate. But it is rather exceptional that the elite, in a community of such differentiation and structuralization as the Japanese community was, should have remained for a long time devoid of a scriptural medium of its own, which finally had to be imported from abroad.

Isakower (1939) has brought forth the great importance of the auditory sphere in the formation and structuralization of the superego. In the instance of Japan, we have a cultural superego that depended for the longest time upon the auditory sphere alone. It seems to me almost a foregone conclusion that the existence or nonexistence of a script must have had a deepgoing bearing not only on the character of any cultural superego, but likewise on the rhythm, speed, and dynamic momentum of its development.

Let us consider two extremes. In an industrialized democracy, such as the United States, one would be surprised to discover the political slogan of the previous year still arousing interest in the following year. Any politician worth his salt will coin a new slogan for each election campaign that he undertakes. The rapidity with which a political ideal vanishes and is replaced, so as to ensure that the political interest of the community is kept awake, is almost fearsome.

The other extreme we find in aboriginal civilizations, in many of which culture has been at a standstill for perhaps many centuries. Why is this so, one asks, considering the irresistible momentum of change prevalent in the Occident? What we observe here, instead, is an exclusively aural process of forwarding the essence of societal wisdom from one generation to the other. Under conditions of great secrecy and pain, during puberty, the group member is initiated into 'the political slogan.' It is understandable that, under such conditions, the chance of change will be greatly reduced. The traditional knowledge having been obtained under difficult conditions of sacrifice and suffering, any significant change would amount merely to its being needlessly wasted.

Children in our society are forced to learn what in primitive society would be regarded as secrets of governmental institutions. Societal knowledge is taken as a matter of course; it loses its mystery, and leaves no

[10] In 405 A.D., Chinese script was introduced at Court, but writing remained the monopoly of a small group. The evolvement of Japanese script took place only in the ninth century. Cf. Sansom (1931, pp. 36, 63, 237).

feeling of awe in the citizen, because of its easy familiarity and access. Furthermore, it seems that a written content lends itself more readily to change and varying interpretation than does a spoken content. We are dealing here with the basic structural properties of sensory systems. Suffice it to say that the precepts of Japanese tradition had been forwarded by the use of the auditory sense for centuries, and it may be that we have to search here for one of the causes of Japan's deep conservatism.[11]

Yet there is another characteristic observable here, which seems contradictory to the one just discussed. When Buddhism entered the Japanese scene, during the eighth century, a comparatively mild crisis ensued, after which it flourished side by side with Shintō. It would be wrong to search, behind the relative ease with which a foreign cult was incorporated, for imitative mechanisms, as is so often done. One observes throughout Japanese history an adherence to their original religion, with an intensity that, of course, varied from period to period —yet, in the end, Shintō proved to be stronger than the newcomer.

The impact of Chinese culture and civilization on Japan is well known; what is remarkable, however, is that, not only in religion, but also in other cultural aspects, these values were not taken over *en bloc,* but were truly digested and transformed into something essentially Japanese. One cannot truly speak, I believe, of the 'intrusion' of Chinese values into Japanese culture, but rather of a Japanese extending of tentacles into Chinese culture, an eager grasping for Chinese values. Sansom, in an instructive comparison between Japan and England, points out that China was far too occupied with her own problems to pursue an aggressive policy toward Japan, and that Japan was therefore spared the fate of the British Isles, which were first occupied by the Roman legions, and then, after their withdrawal, sacked by the barbarians (Sansom, 1958, pp. 39ff.). 'Nothing imposed upon her by force' is the *Leitmotif* of Japan's relation to the continent.

We see a geographical political factor, combining with what may be a psychological one, to create a well defined identificatory pattern. The factors of spontaneity and eagerness in laying hands on Chinese values are quite impressive, so much so that it is clear why Japanese civilization never became a branch of the civilization of China. I wonder whether

[11] The kind of medium through which a culture is transmitted from one generation to another strikes me as having a consequential bearing on the structure of the culture. For many pertinent remarks on this problem, see Rosenzweig (1937).

it was not the firmly and solidly formed core of an aurally fixated cultural superego that made possible the integration of a new and foreign culture without the pitfalls of mere imitation. In view of the real differences between Shintōism and Buddhism, it is noteworthy that the latter could be introduced into Japan to the extent that it was, without cleaving the cultural structure. To be sure, there was rivalry and discussion; the discord, however, remained far different from Europe's history of religious wars.

I shall now turn to some details of Japanese history. Sansom asserts that the absolute power of the early sovereigns, as described in the legends, was an ideal, and not true to fact. The central power in Kamato, where the Kyūshū people established their headquarters, was, he says, neither stable nor absolute, even at the end of the seventh century, although undoubtedly the imperial clan did exercise some authority over other clans powerful enough to control their own land. At that time, then, the court's position was no more than that of *primus inter pares*— except for one function.

The leader of the imperial clan was the intermediary between the people and the gods; because of the ceremonial observances, he thus also held political advantages. This may be the crucial point. The emperor's outstanding position was not so much the result of the material power gathered into his hands, as it was the outcome of a primarily spiritual power. This rooting of the imperial power in spiritual values—merging with a secular power which was not arrogated, but was as genuinely inherent in the emperorship as the spiritual one—represents a societal form of an eminently practical character.

The division of life into spiritual and secular areas, so characteristic of the Occident, was thereby bridged. The papacy originated as a purely spiritual force, yet by arrogating substantial secular power over long periods, it created dissension through its secular claims and its secular interferences. On the other hand, it withheld its decision in important secular matters, so that the priest of the same church could bless the arms of two opposing armies, the faithful being left in the dark as to whose was the rightful side.

By synthesizing the secular and the divine into one symbol, the Japanese state developed an extremely effective instrument of statecraft, by means of which religious dissension could be avoided, and secular unity established, in times of crisis. The accumulation of such formidable power in one center may have been an important factor contributing to that deficit of individual independence and structuralization that has been noted among the Japanese by the historian: the individual exists only as a member of the family, and the family as a member of the State (Charles Eliot in *Japanese Buddhism*, cited from Sansom, 1958, p. 35).

During the course of the seventh century, in conjunction with the spread of Buddhism, a reform movement took place, the highlights of which included Prince Shōtoku's issuance of the famous 'constitution' (604), the proclamation of the doctrine of absolute monarchy (645), the creation of a centralized bureaucracy, the abolition of private title to land, the division between civil and military officials, reform of taxation, introduction of military conscription, and a sexennial redistribution of land.

In all this, there are some aspects which evoke a psychological interest. The reform movement was precipitated by events taking place on the continent. The centrally organized Han and Tang dynasties, in conjunction with the identically organized power in Korea, caused Japan to lose its hold in Korea. A unified and expanding China was a threat to a weak and decentralized Japan, which had nothing of the like to show, its own elite being threatened with division by the rise of Buddhism. Japan had no other precedent but this very continental organization upon which to pattern its own reforms; thus, not only Buddhism but also the new form of organization originated in China.

Nevertheless, as I have already indicated, this time also it was not just a process of copying China, for there are enough deviations from the Chinese model to see in the reforms a characteristically Japanese product. Thus, for example, the Chinese doctrine that the mandate of Heaven did not apply to a sovereign without virtue was not accepted. The national tradition in Japan of basing the sacredness and inviolability of the emperor on descent alone was not changed by the reformers. Furthermore, Japanese hierarchy continued to be founded on birth, and not on talent, as in China. The Japanese emperorship was not contingent, nor was it conditional.

Of great interest is the way in which such a deep-going reform was carried out—a reform, one may say, that in almost any other country would have led to a revolution. Since subjugation of the clans by force was far beyond the limits of imperial power, the following technique was used, in the main because of the efforts of Fujiwara Kamatari, the founder of what was to be the leading family for centuries to come.

The introduction of new principles—such as the abolition of private title to land, which would surely otherwise have precipitated a fight on the part of those who were thus dispossessed—was accomplished by giving the dispossessed governmental functions, with such emoluments that hardly anything was actually changed with regard to the substance of their privileges.

This may make it seem as though the reforms were merely a sham; such a conclusion would be wrong, however. To be sure, the goals laid down in the prescripts were not reached; but a centralized force was established, and a decisive growth and structuralization in organization took place. It may be added that the whole process was started under the reign of an empress, Suiko (592-628); and it may also be repeated that it was stimulated by a historical process that took place on the continent. In fact, it seems questionable whether, without this stimulus from outside, the organizational change would have occurred at all, or at any rate at that time.

The succeeding historical period is characterized by the gradual transfer of political power into the hands of the Fujiwara family. The Japanese, less given to strict classification than the Chinese, created new offices, not foreseen by the various codes but required by practical ends. The office of the Kampaku, a regent, provided dictatorial power. Moreover, a custom became widespread of having the emperor retire to a monastery upon his reaching his majority, and letting a child succeed him.

The Fujiwaras filled most of the influential offices, and acquired huge estates. They saw to it that their daughters married members of the Imperial family; only the husband of a Fujiwara girl could become emperor. (I see in this policy a reflection of matrilineal succession.) Yet although the Fujiwaras were thus the real carriers of power, the family itself never aspired to the throne.

It would be wrong, however, to see in Fujiwara politics nothing more than a struggle for power and supremacy. As a matter of fact "they . . . appear not to have been moved solely by vain personal ambition, but to have truly wished to guide the monarchy in the interest of the state . . . . They seem generally to have produced the kind of capable man the times demanded" (Sansom, 1958, p. 142). Yet their supreme interest in court intrigue, and their manipulation of the emperors, on which the Fujiwaras exhausted their best efforts instead of on such true statesman-

ship as considers the welfare of the whole of the country, would ultimately prove to be one more potent reason for their downfall.

There were many reasons why the reforms of the seventh century did
not fulfill what they had promised, or what they had been intended for.
In the first place, there was the failure of the fiscal system. The custom
of making estates immune to taxation spread so widely that in the end
the reduction of the public domain deprived the Crown of most of its
revenue. By the tenth century, two statesmen were already submitting
memoranda in which the throne was implored to reform abuses that had
become quite apparent. When revolts occurred during the tenth century,
the authority of the throne was great enough to suppress them quickly;
but this was accomplished with the assistance of some leading provincial
families, and no longer by the strength of the Emperor alone.

Curiously enough, it was the custom of Cloister Government that
finally undermined the Fujiwara hold on power. The abdication of the
emperors in favor of a child emperor, who was closely related to the
Fujiwara family through the mother, gave the regent absolute power
over the throne; but in view of the power that the outgoing emperor,
who abdicated and retired to a cloister, had arrogated, the power distribution was in fact significantly changed.

"Whereas a Regent had been able to influence the reigning emperor
because his empress was a Fujiwara daughter, now an abdicated emperor could govern because the emperor was his own son" (Sansom,
1958, p. 201). The cloistered emperor therefore did not feel obliged to
rest his influence on Fujiwara assistance. He drew support from other
families, sometimes of lower rank but greater wealth, and thus a social
change was brought about, around 1200, that led to a relaxation of the
preceding strict hierarchical rule.

Since the system of conscription for military service did not take hold,
the Crown was without military power. Japan had entered a period of
good relations with the continent and of internal peace, and there was
consequently no need for a standing army. Yet, with the decline of land
tenure by the Crown, and the evolvement of a manorial system, with
estates of considerable size being held by powerful landlords who enjoyed fiscal and juridical immunity, a new class arose that boldly stepped
into the existing power vacuum. It was the rise of the warrior class that
caused a change in Japan's political structure.

This warrior class goes back to the time of the early border fighting,
when private bands of warriors defended the country at the north. Such

a band was not quite independent, for it was under the control of a powerful monastery, or of a manorial lord. At the start, these clans were in the service of the existing political power, the Fujiwara family. But in due time, with the extension of their land holdings and the assumption of command over their private armies, the manorial lords put pressure on the governing family until they themselves were able to arrogate political power. Thus a new nobility arose, independent of both the civil authority and the central government, and assumed control over the professional warriors, who felt that they owed their loyalty to their individual masters.

The history of the establishment of Japanese feudalism is long and complicated. Suffice it to say that the country fell into almost complete disorganization under the Fujiwaras, and that it was incumbent upon the military chieftains to restore order when situations of acute crisis occurred. As can be imagined, there was rivalry between various clans; but after long and bloody wars, it was the Minamoto clan that came out victorious and in possession of the supreme power.

The country was given a new political organization, the so-called Bakufu, whose head held the title of Shōgun. Yoritomo, the first Shōgun, moved his capital to Kamakura, three hundred miles away from Kyoto where the Emperor and the Court resided, in order to maintain his independence from the throne, and so as to oversee his vassals and evade the weakening influence of Court living. Thus, from 1185 on, the power was held by military men. The Shōgun depended on the support of the feudal chieftains, and was responsible for their loyalty. His power was determined chiefly by the extent of the land that he could get under his dominion, and the number of followers at his command.

The Bakufu, with its own system of vassalage, which included the stewards and constables whom it had the authority to appoint (the Shōgun himself being the Constable-General and Steward-General), led to a dual administrative system: one by the crown, with only nominal power; the other, military and feudal. The new system quickly proved its efficiency, for the state of disorganization subsided and Japan once more enjoyed internal peace—particularly since the tax system was overhauled, the immunity of the greatest estates was greatly curtailed and the landlords were required to pay one fifth of their yield as a tax for military purposes.

The Bakufu evolved a new ethical and legal code, in conformity with the new political structure. This code was not applied to vassals outside of the Kamakura domain, nor to monasteries, nor to the civilian administration. Furthermore, the Bakufu adhered to simplicity and justice. Not much of the original Chinese model remained by the time of the introduction of feudalism, for Japan had at last evolved a political form that grew spontaneously, so to speak, out of its native soil.

The reformers of the seventh century had tried to fit facts to their scheme, but the founders of feudalism fitted their plans to facts (Sansom, 1931, p. 286), evolving a complex system of rights and duties that put the distribution of land, taxation, and military service into balance. The principles of feudal government were based on trial and error and everyday experience, whereas the early reforms had been founded on theory.

Political power did not, however, stay very long in the hands of the descendants of the first Shōgun. The Hōjō family took over, in the form of a regency, without abolishing the Shōgunate itself. Here is another example of the Japanese tendency to make a separation between the functions of reigning and governing, by the delegation of power. As the Fujiwaras continued to respect the imperial house, even though it had lost political power, so the Hōjō regents respected the Shōgunate, although it, in turn, was no longer a power center. "We have thus," writes Sansom, "in Japan of the thirteenth century, the astonishing spectacle of a state at the head of which stands a titular emperor whose vestigial functions are usurped by an abdicated emperor, and whose real power is nominally delegated to an hereditary military dictator but actually wielded by an hereditary adviser of that dictator" (1931, p. 300). Into the era of the Hōjō Regents fell the two Mongol invasions which, although with the help of the elements, were brilliantly warded off by the Bakufu. The threat was no minor one, if one considers the power and organizational skill of Khubilai, the Great Khan, whose power Japan was the only country in the Far East to withstand. I believe that the Bakufu here proved its mettle, and I wonder whether Japan would have been capable of keeping the invader at bay, if the attack had occurred one hundred years earlier.

One might have expected a success of such proportions on a national scale to contribute greatly to the solidification of the political structure. Yet the actual effect was just the reverse. It seems that the monasteries demanded credit for the defeat of the invaders, and popular feeling supported the view "that what had saved the country was the intercession of the clergy" (Sansom, 1958, p. 454). The expenditures for war and for the maintenance of a strong defense (a third invasion, although it never occurred, was greatly feared) exhausted the country's finances, while the Regents did not have the courage to increase taxation. The Bakufu could not reward its vassals for their great services to the defense of the country; a mercantile class was rising, which also threatened the warrior class; and the Regents themselves became corrupt and lost their earlier bent for even-handed justice.

Writers like Sansom set forth the difficulties that the Bakufu had to face, prior to the Mongol invasion, by way of showing that warfare only added further complications to a situation which was untenable per se. The historian may, of course, be quite right in that assumption, but a political system unencumbered by any particularly onerous responsibilities may prove to be more efficient than one might have expected in the light of its collapse when it was burdened with additional strain.

I have mentioned previously the by no means inconsiderable areas remaining outside direct Kamakura administration. For the purposes of national defense, the Hōjō Regents had to keep in their good graces, and thus were prevented from asserting their full force. Is it not conceivable that, without the necessity of keeping the country on a full-scale war alert for a considerable period of time, the Kamakura government might have extended its area of direct dominion, or achieved what only a much later generation was able to bring about? A civil strife, or any internal belligerent action of significance, would have amounted to national suicide, at a time when Japan was facing an external adversary of such gigantic proportions.

It is impressive, in any case, that Japan was capable of such forceful action against her former teacher, and the fountainhead of her culture. I still feel that it was the Mongol wars that prevented the Hōjō Regents from reducing the power of the other clans to such an extent that their turning against the Bakufu would have been out of the question. It seems that the Bakufu were kept in constant anxiety over a new invasion, and that this alone may have weakened the forcefulness they needed to show in order to be accepted as the strongest among the powerful chieftains. Thus, when discord broke out in the imperial house, and two lines aspired to the throne, the one which was opposed by the Regent found sufficient support even from some Kamakura vassals to defeat the Bakufu. Kamakura was burnt down, and the throne was temporarily able to exercise power. But the return to the former political structure was impossible, and soon new rivalry broke out between the powerful chieftains.

At last, in 1392, the quarrel about the succession was ended, and the Ashikaga clan seemed to have come out victorious from the fight for supremacy. Since their power was not strong enough to keep the vassals in a subordinate position, however, the country was rather an aggregate of many power centers, each of which eagerly kept its eye fixed on the advantage of its own territory, and tried to enlarge its domain by aggrandizement. The court lost all prestige and strength, and the Shōgunate was reduced to a shadowy existence.

Powerful families arrogated to themselves as much power as they could. Sansom (1931) speaks of a truncated feudalism. "The regional hierarchies were complete but the national hierarchy was without an apex" (p. 404). As can easily be imagined, such a state could never remain in equilibrium for a long time. As a matter of fact, what followed was a period of more or less constant warfare, the intervals of relative peace being brought about by the exhaustion of the participants, rather than by any solidification of organization.

Japan was, so to speak, remade. Powerful families were annihilated, and new ones came to power: thus, of the 260 feudal houses in existence around the middle of the fifteenth century, all but a dozen had disappeared by 1600, and other families, fewer in number than previously, had risen at some time from obscurity. Yet these one and a half centuries of turmoil should not be evaluated solely in terms of the destruction that they entailed.

Despite all the destruction, cultural progress did not come to a standstill. Besides the gain in commerce, trade and industry, there took place a removal of class barriers. In the course of the rivalry of the chieftains, a feudalism maturer than before was in the making. The great feudal houses, in order to survive in times of anarchy on the national plane, had to enforce law and order within their own territories. Thus, contrary to all expectation, it was not the decay of law that took place, but rather its growth.

Under the leadership of three great statesmen, Oda Nobunaga (1534-1582), Toyotomi Hideyoshi (1537-1598), and Tokugawa Ieyasu (1541-1616), Japan at last became a unified state. The last-named was the first of the Tokugawa Shōgunate, which was to govern the country until 1868, the year of the official end of Japan's feudalism. At this point there started, with seeming abruptness, what appeared to be an entirely new Japanese history, unconnected with the past, and little more than a replica of Western civilization.

The Tokugawa Shōgunate is, in my opinion, puzzling only in that it came to an end. Its structure was sound, particularly in the light of Japan's preceding history; its relatively long duration speaks per se in favor of its genuine soundness. Nevertheless, I want to interpolate here a general remark. It is certainly true of organic life that a structure, in order to remain the same, has to change constantly. The living cell maintains its identity by constant change—that is to say, a huge number of processes go on incessantly in the preservation of the status quo. If a social structure were to remain in a state of monotonous sameness, it might, similarly, be necessary to institute a multiplicity of social processes such as would constantly undo the effects of this quiescence. In other words, it may be true of societal organisms as well that it is only by constant changes that their identity can be maintained.[12] Perhaps the best way to express this view is by reversing the famous *"Plus ça change, plus c'est la même chose,"* of Alphonse Karr (1849), so as to make it read, *"Plus c'est la même chose, plus ça change."*

Tokugawa Ieyasu made Yedo his headquarters, and it became the military, administrative, economic and cultural metropolis of Japan. He and his successors distributed the feudatories in such a way that no single one, nor any combination, could challenge the Shōgun's power. The sovereign and his nobles were not permitted to own land, but received revenue in kind. The function of the Court was a purely ceremonial one, thus excluding the potential rivalries. Special measures were taken to keep vassals at bay. The so-called 'outside lords'—namely, those who had joined the Tokugawa Shōgun only *after* he had acquired supremacy —were, of course, the potential power centers that might later dispute the Shōgun's dictatorial power. The richest and the most renowned were among them; but their offensive power was ingeniously reduced by their increased obligation to contribute to public undertakings. Furthermore, the requirement that they spend considerable time in Yedo, or leave their families as hostages, made rebellion almost out of the question.

In order to rule out changes, the country was kept practically under martial law. In accordance with the spirit of the Bakufu, the military class was the foremost one, and all other classes were supposed to serve its interests. To ensure maximum protection against even partial changes,

---

12 However, it is questionable whether this law, if correct, can be applied to identity of the ancient empires.

no person in service was permitted to leave his employment without the consent of the overlord, nor was a warrior permitted to become a townsman, or a farmer to work for hire. Class distinctions were regarded as rigid and unchangeable: the social position into which anyone was born was to remain immutable, and he was to stay loyal to one master.

The maintenance of stability and order was explicitly the major pillar of policy and, for that purpose, all intercourse with the outside world was forbidden and severely punished. The edicts established earlier against Christians, who had become quite numerous after Japan's contact with the Portuguese, were carried out now, and the choice among the three main religions (Shintō, Buddhism, Confucianism) was made mandatory. Consequently, since the whole structure of society was in effect based on duty and loyalty, and at this juncture feudalism had engulfed the whole state, Japan had at last reached that condition toward which, it seems, its whole preceding history had been moving.

If one tries to put this history into general terms, one has to consider two main problems. Japan's economy depended entirely on rice: it was a single-staple economy, and therefore extremely sensitive to natural forces. All attempts failed to make Japan's economy more flexible, by basing it on other staples. Moreover, rice functioned for a very long time as Japan's currency. This dual function of rice as the only staple, nationally and locally, and also as the only acceptable currency, may have had unique effects. Be that as it may, the perennial focal problem in Japanese history is: who is to possess the bulk of this commodity, and how is it to be distributed?

A great Japanese statesman of the fourteenth century explained the dynastic warfare of his time by "the claims of an unlimited number of persons on a limited amount of land"; Sansom (1961) adds that, in this statement, "the whole of Japanese history from the beginning down to modern times" is summarized (p. 30).[13]

Those who actually produced the rice had the least to say about it— as seems to have been true, in fact, all over the world, for most of the time since societal organization led to the specialization of functions. The economic aspect of this struggle, however, is of less psychological significance than is what Sansom had to say about the whole of Japanese

[13] See Norman (1940, p. 12) for literature and a short discussion of features typical of Japanese feudalism, in which the revenue of rice, and not direct ownership of land, determined power. He also includes a brief note on decentralized and centralized feudalism in Japan.

political history, which "subsequent to the Reform of 645, may be interpreted as a series of attempts to perpetuate, by one device after another, a complex system of centralized administration with no real power behind it, a system that seemed to work in the metropolis but was quite unsuited to actual conditions in the country and to the temper of the rural magnates" (Sansom, 1958, p. 201f.).

We have set forth in broad strokes this struggle for political power; this game of hidden power behind official power; the vast discrepancy between reigning and ruling; the back and forth of the accumulation of power in a central focus, its subsequent dispersal to a large number of forces, and its gathering once again into one hand—which, however, succeeded only in the seventeenth century in drawing the entire country into its orbit. The end was, at last, a solidly built hierarchical pyramid, whose structure engulfed the whole nation.

What I have set forth of Japan's history up to this point should not be taken as more than a sort of preamble. Its intent is to demonstrate that Japan had become an organism whose total aggressivity was satiated within its orbit, in a way that: (1) left no energy free for discharge centrifugally outside of her borders; (2) did not need any influx of stimulation or energy from outside, in order to keep up her existence; (3) provided satisfactory internal channels for the organized internal discharge of her energy. In short, Japan, after a long detour and after having gone through much turmoil and many tragedies, had, at last, reached a state of true homeostasis.

We shall see that this is perhaps not quite correct, for most authors agree upon the fact that a political change had become necessary, and was actually impending, by the time a new force was, so to speak, artificially introjected into Japanese history with the landing of Commodore Perry in 1853. Whatever the end result might have been, if Japanese development had had an opportunity to proceed in accordance with its own inner dialectics, without disturbance by the West, I think it is reasonably certain that Japan did not *need* any influx from abroad.

Japan had been actively engaged previously in only two foreign adventures. In her early history, during the eighth century, we find her armies in Korea, with a permanent foothold of varying extent in the south. This had to be given up, because of the superior organization of continental empires. From then on, despite frequent, and at times intensive contacts of a cultural and commercial nature with the continent, no belligerent expeditions occurred until the sixteenth century, when, quite suddenly and surprisingly, under the leadership of Hideyoshi, we find a huge expeditionary force making substantial inroads into Korea, and reaching the border of China, with the express intention of conquering that country.

This latter adventure collapsed. I take it to have been the product of the unbalanced mind of a great statesman who, like many of his kind, became a victim of megalomaniac impulses toward the end of his life. Yet his successors had learned their lesson, so that no intention, hardly even any thought, of expansion is to be noticed subsequently. Indeed, not only was any desire to become actively entangled with foreign countries totally lacking; a real aversion to anything foreign is observable, so that any contact with foreigners was strictly prohibited, and an invisible and practically impenetrable wall was drawn around Japan's shores, permitting only an occasional Dutch ship or some Chinese to land at Nagasaki.

It would be wrong, I believe, to speak here of xenophobia; as is well known, a phobia is a well-organized structure designed to ward off strong unconscious wishes. This, I believe, is not applicable to the Japanese 'xenophobia' of the seventeenth and eighteenth centuries, which is rather comparable to the barrier against stimulation (*Reizschutz*) with which sense organs are sometimes surrounded, intensified in this instance to a point where the barrier excludes the penetration of *any* stimulus.

In the light of the necessity of making external stimulation impossible, in order to maintain a permanent homeostasis, the suppression of Christianity—which had made, in a short time, astounding inroads—becomes understandable. Christianity was the only religion propagated in Japan that maintained an active link with foreign countries; its spread required constant reinforcement and support from abroad. Consequently, quite aside from what actually happened, Christianity would have been a thorn in the side of the centripetal hierarchical structure at which the Japanese had arrived in the seventeenth century.

Here I have reached the crucial point of my excursus. In 1853, Commodore Perry's squadron appeared in the Harbor of Ugada; and, with uncanny speed, Japan became a completely westernized state, with a military potential unrivaled in the Far East. She thereupon defeated China and Russia, took possession of British Crown colonies, expelled all Occidental powers from a huge orbit, and for a short time even made the nation that had opened her shores momentarily defenseless, by sinking a substantial part of its fleet, until she in turn succumbed to the ill-fated bombs dropped on Hiroshima and Nagasaki. Can psychoanalysis make any significant contribution to the explanation of this drama, which is altogether unlike anything that had happened until then?

To be sure, the power of this historical process would be more dramatic than it was (and the psychoanalytic explanation I would have to suggest would be all the more convincing) if the Tokugawa Shōgunate had really succeeded in achieving what it had set out to achieve—the establishment of a permanent equilibrium (which I have compared earlier with the modern concept of homeostasis). The fact is that the Shōgunate did come as close to such a state as is imaginable, following the period of the great Empires of early antiquity. Was it certain organizational deficiencies that prevented the Shōgunate from the complete attainment of its goals, or was it the effect of as yet unrecognized forces, which do not let mankind ever come to rest, but keep up the relentless continuation of the historical process? However this may be, historical research has delineated the forces that would eventually have ended the Tokugawa Shōgunate, even without the appearance of Perry's ships.

A variety of causes is claimed. The founders of modern feudalism, Nobunaga and Hideyoshi, began by attacking Japanese Buddhism, which was still further restricted by Hideyoshi. This decline of Japanese Buddhism has as its consequence a rise in the native Shintō religion, and a renaissance of national history and literature. Since it was the imperial house that presided over the Shintō cult, the question "whether loyalty to the throne did not transcend loyalty to a feudal overlord" became acute (Sansom, 1931, p. 510), and thus the Shōgunate itself, quite without intending to, contributed to the growing awareness that the Shōgun was only a delegate for—or, as some began to think— a usurper of Imperial power.

The economic causes for the downfall of Japanese feudalism have been set forth quite ably by Norman, and I shall briefly mention only a few of them: the class of warriors (Samurai) had become parasites, for after the pacification of the country, there remained no social function for them to fill. The Shōgunate had already divorced them completely from agriculture, in which they had been previously active, simultaneously with the disappearance of their military duties. Although a money economy was only gradually replacing the rice economy, the merchant class, which had been officially kept at the bottom of the social hierarchy, and prevented from expansion by the Shōgunate's restrictive measures, succeeded—at least in a few instances—in penetrating into the ruling class, thus causing a breach in the rigid caste system on which feudalism was founded. The plight of the small farmers became unbearable, through the prevailing tax system and the fluctuation of the prices for rice. The prevailing economic uncertainty impoverished even the Samurai, who had to live on a rice stipend. The Bakufu itself became bankrupt, and had to resort to forced loans and currency debasement.

The reasons adduced here, and many more besides, are usually brought into correlation with the political structure of the Bakufu—to wit, Japanese feudalism. Sansom warns against our being too sure about this link, and his discussion shows that the problem is probably far more complex than is usually assumed. If I understand him correctly, the crisis of the nineteenth century was inherently not a political one, and the economic problem of the country could have been solved essentially within the political framework of the Tokugawa Shōgunate (Sansom, 1949, pp. 226-231).[14] Sansom's suggestion is important here, in that it implies that a reform carried out within the Shōgunate might have been feasible. The question I wish to concern myself with has to do with the course that Japan's history might have taken, if the West had not forced the opening of the country.

I conclude from the preceding course of Japan's history that, if the Shōgunate had proven to be inflexible, the ensuing crisis would have forced the Throne to take an active stand, in order to save the country from collapse. Whether the Imperial power would have carried out reforms by its own power, or whether a new power center would have been formed, to which the Throne would have delegated its traditional right, is of no major importance here.

It is conceivable that a sort of state council might have been formed, whose reforms the Bakufu would have been forced to carry out. Such reforms, to be sure, would have been in keeping with the tradition. The Crown would probably have once again taken over the domain; the merchant class would have found its proper place in the hierarchical structure; and contact with foreign countries would have been permitted, within strictly supervised channels, and in accordance with predetermined restrictions. I am well aware of the many objections that can be raised against such a perspective, and of the variety of possible alternatives. Yet I am forced to conclude that, without the emergence of

[14] In this context, Sansom's remarks about the dangers of a one-staple economy, the Shōgunate's awareness of this liability, and its attempts at remedy, are of particular interest.

certain events that were basically foreign to the logic inherent in Japan's history, the actual course that Japan took might never have come to pass.

We shall now turn to those initial events, whose consequences were more fateful for Japan than anything that had gone before. Although it is not necessary for what follows to understand the motives of Japan's antagonist, a few remarks may not be superfluous.

In the first stages of the establishment of American-Japanese relations, the leading role fell to two outstanding Americans, Commodore Perry and Townsend Harris. Both men were sober-minded, practical, energetic, and honest; the general consensus is that no one of their contemporaries would have been able to acquit himself better. Their personalities would seem to be of no relevance here, since they solved their tasks in so ideal a fashion, as far as concerns the country whose emissaries they were. Yet what may be ideal conduct, with regard to personal adjustment and maturity, may nevertheless appear in a quite different light, when it is viewed in terms of world history.

Thus, the actions of these two outstanding men must be evaluated, to begin with, in terms of their service to the American expansionist momentum ("The impulse towards expansion" of which Mahan speaks [1900, p. 4]). One of the central motive forces in American history has been the very opposite of the impulse toward isolation, which was pre-eminent in Japan at the time when the two countries came to clash. This impulse toward expansion, I believe, has never been adequately explained.

At the cradle of American democracy there had stood, after all, men whose minds were not set on adventure and expansion, but on a refuge from tyranny, and a place where a livelihood could be scraped together in a way that was not offensive to God. The outlook of the Pilgrim Fathers may not have been so fundamentally different from that which guided the Japanese. After all is said and done, both wanted above all to work and to be left in peace.

Yet the America of 1854 was of a different temper. Six years earlier, she had reached the shores of the Pacific. California has been only shakily incorporated into the Union, at the time when commercial interests take a great leap 5,000 miles further West; it will take less than another century for her soldiers to occupy the islands. Yet, it was not only the energy potential of expansion that made the two antagonists so different. The sociopolitical structure of the Western democracy was the exact opposite of that of the Eastern dictatorship: in the latter the maximum of power was at the top of the pyramid, in the former at its base; the one was directed entirely by tradition, the other boasted of being unencumbered by it; in the East there was a rigid caste system, in the West a maximum of social fluidity; here a desire to absorb as many foreigners as possible, there their radical exclusion.

That two diametrically different cultures or nations should clash, and that the stronger should defeat the weaker, is a common enough event in the history of mankind. Yet, although the Western power was—at least in terms of physical strength—infinitely stronger than Japan, it faced a difficult task, for its official ideology was based on peace and non-violence. Thus the paradoxical situation emerged in which a powerful nation, seeking compliance from the defenseless, was nevertheless inhibited in imposing its will upon those at its mercy. Considering the way China was treated in the nineteenth century by the Occident, it is safe to say that no European power, in the same situation, would have balked at the use of force.

The momentous expansion of the original Confederation across the continent, within less than one hundred years after its foundation, could perhaps be justified, and the frequent employment of undemocratic means to achieve this feat could perhaps be partly denied and partly vindicated; but here was democracy facing a people with which, either geographically or historically, it had no connection at all, and which was putting up only one demand—to wit, to be left alone. The American people were unaware that, in that year, the beginnings of American imperialism hung in the balance; yet a warlike action might have aroused severe internal criticism. From the writing of a gifted British diplomat, it is clear that the other powers were well aware of the dilemma in which the North American Republic had found itself. The situation could not be better described than in Satow's own words:

> . . . Having accomplished their own independence as the result of a contest in which a few millions of half-united colonists had successfully withstood the well-trained legions of Great Britain . . . , they added to this memory of ancient wrongs a natural fellow-feeling for other nations who were less able to resist the might of the greatest commercial and maritime Power the world has yet seen. While sympathizing with Eastern peoples in the defence of their independent rights, they believed that a conciliatory mode of treating them was at least equally

well fitted to ensure the concession of those trading privileges to which the Americans are not less indifferent than the English.

. . . In China, like the other western states, they had profited by the negotiations which were the outcome of the Opium War, without having to incur the odium of using force in dealing with the obstinate conservatism of Chinese mandarins. For many years their eyes had been bent upon Japan . . . . Warned by the fate of all previous attempts to break down the wall of seclusion that hemmed in the 'country of the gods,' they resolved to make such a show of force that with reasonable people, unfamiliar with modern artillery, might prove as powerful an argument as theories of universal brotherhood and the obligations imposed by the comity of nations [Satow, 1921, p. 42f.].

Here the Briton flings the missile of uninhibited sarcasm at the sister nation that had claimed for itself a position of superior morality. The doctrine of universal brotherhood was made to appear as a hypocritical slogan, which does, to be sure, make certain forms of good conduct necessary, but does not, in practice, exclude the course of Imperial high-handedness so familiar in British history. The great merit of Perry and Harris lay in their succeeding in getting for the United States the most advantageous commercial treaties, and without compromising their homeland—which would certainly have happened, if the United States had become recognized as directly responsible for any warlike action.

Appearances were very carefully preserved; yet the record shows unmistakably that the techniques actually used lay outside of mere persuasion or indoctrination, or indeed of anything worthy of a democracy. How else could one have expected a nation which was proud, and determined to preserve its traditions, whose institutions were hallowed by an age that made the intruding nation appear like a child, to voluntarily (in the true sense of the word) abrogate a cherished and fundamental principle? It was Perry's repeated references to the artillery on his ships, and on the other ships that might follow, that induced compliance.

It is worthwhile to present some material drawn from the Commodore's report itself. The compiler in his introduction refers to "some" who boldly proposed "that Japan had no right to . . . cut herself off from the community of nations; and that what she would not yield to national comity should be wrested from her by force" (Hawks, 1897, p. 96). It is indeed an interesting question whether or not a nation has the right to isolation. Today, I imagine, one would heartily disagree with the compiler's implications, and perhaps there are even those who would find a *casus belli* in any nation's attempt to enforce by threat of attack the conclusion of commercial treaties.[15]

Now Commodore Perry had deliberately landed in Yedo Bay, although he knew that, according to Japanese law and custom, only one harbor was open for foreign ships—to wit, Nagasaki. When this law was brought to his attention by a Japanese emissary, he refused to obey, for obvious reasons, and threatened to use force if the Japanese guard boats that had collected around the American vessels did not disperse immediately (Hawks, p. 269).[16]

A show of arms had the desired result. "This," says the Commodore, "was the first important point gained" (Hawks, p. 269). His policy was "to assume a resolute attitude toward the Japanese government." He had resolved to pursue a policy quite different from those who had been to Japan before this on similar missions.

He would "demand as a right," and not "solicit as a favor, those acts of courtesy which are due from one civilized nation to another" (Hawks, p. 220). He would not put up with anything that "in the least conflicted with his own sense of what was due to the dignity of the American flag" (Hawks, p. 270). We find, marked off here, a frame of reference which was clearly incompatible with the establishment of peaceful relations between these two nations, not only because such terms cannot be adequately delimited, but also because insistence upon any specific interpretation of those terms would inevitably lead to unsolvable contradictions: courtesy to the Japanese throne would have required Commodore Perry's proceeding to Nagasaki, while the dignity of the Japanese flag was seriously offended by the Commodore's having given orders to Japanese vessels in Yedo Bay.

When, on the following day, an even higher dignitary than on the previous occasion once more explained the urgency of Perry's proceeding to Nagasaki, the Commodore threatened even to make an enforced landing in order to present the President's letter to the Emperor, by whom, of course, he meant the Shōgun.[17]

15 It is all the more interesting to cast a glance backward, and to set the common sense judgments of one hundred years ago, with their stress on 'national comity,' alongside the exclusion of Japanese immigration in 1924.

16 It may sound naïve to remind the reader that, already in the eighteenth century, the 'three-mile limit' was recognized between England and the United States.

17 As a matter of fact, Commodore Perry would have been enforcing the delivery of the letter to the wrong person—and later actually did, since the Shōgun possessed only delegated power. The person actually equivalent to the U.S. President would, it seems, have been the Mikado himself.

At last an agreement was reached and the Commodore was permitted to land on shore with his retinue (which he did, under the protection of howitzers kept ready to land), and to meet the representatives whom he considered to be high enough in rank to accept the President's letter. The Japanese stated expressly in their receipt of the letter that this was "in opposition to the Japanese law," and demanded that, now that the American request had been fulfilled, the American squadron should leave. Yet the Commodore moved his ship even closer to Yedo before he left.

On his way to Japan, the following year, Perry was informed of the Shōgun's death, and was asked by the Japanese to delay his return. The objection was declared by the Commodore to be a ruse (the death had actually occurred); even if it were correct, said he, it should be overruled since, in China, government business is not interrupted by the death of an Emperor (Hawks, p. 373f.). We do not know whether the Japanese actually used the incident as an excuse; but there can be no doubt that Perry in this instance definitely offended the "comity of nations," since national mourning is usually respected. In general, there was a noticeable hardening of Perry's attitude. It seems that the success of his previous imperialistic gestures had whetted his appetite, since he ordered what amounted to an occupation ("measures of precaution," Hawks, p. 375) of the island, Lew Chew, further justifying his action by the probability that the Russians, French or English "in their eagerness to anticipate the Americans" would do the same. Here we can observe the full incorporation of imperialistic techniques and rationalizations into American foreign policy.

Upon his return to Japan, Commodore Perry and his squadron were received with great courtesy by the Japanese. When one of his ships was grounded, there was no sign of hostility, but instead a show of readiness to help. However, tension was caused by the Commodore's persistent refusal to accept Ugada (where the Americans had landed the previous year) as the place where the Emperor's answer to his letter would be received, and his insistence that it had to be where he had landed this time, only twenty miles from Yedo. The Japanese were informed that, if his request were refused, the Commodore "would then know what to do" (Hawks, p. 387).

The Japanese desire to negotiate at a place where the Shōgun's city would not be under the direct line of fire of American artillery is understandable. It was a gesture purporting to show a minimum of independence. The Commodore insisted that his refusal to proceed to Ugada was due to the need for safety measures, but I doubt that this was the true reason. It seems that Perry measured his demands in such a way as always to ask for a bit more than the Japanese were willing to give. The previous year, when they had wanted him in Nagasaki, he had insisted on Ugada. This year, when it was they who wished Ugada, he insisted on Yedo.

All these negotiations were conducted with a show of courtesy on both sides and with an exchange of gifts, but the hard hand of the foreigners was constantly felt by the Japanese, if only in the fact that, despite Japanese protests, the Americans consistently took navigational charts and surveys of the waters that they crossed. However, this was done "not only for the convenience of the immediate purpose of the expedition but for the future interests of the United States, and we may add, those of the whole civilized world" (Hawks, p. 384).

The principal aim of Perry's expedition was, of course, the negotiation of a treaty. Japan was in reality a poor country; but, ever since Marco Polo's days, it was believed to be replete with fabulous riches. Since most of the area suitable for colonial exploitation had been preempted, Japan was the last important unit that could be drawn into the American orbit. Of course, there was no idea of making a colony out of Japan, but with a favorable commercial treaty at this point, when no other power had succeeded in obtaining the same, there was a chance of establishing a preferential position in the country's economy.

A letter written by Perry to the Shōgun in an effort to facilitate negotiations is noteworthy. In it, the abusive treatment by the Japanese of shipwrecked American sailors, and how that treatment must be changed, is made the center of the American government's demands. Undoubtedly, the Japanese government would have been all too ready to secure the safety of shipwrecked sailors.

It is discernible in Perry's report, and frequent reference can be found throughout the literature, that the Japanese—or Orientals in general, for that matter—must be expected to use subterfuges, duplicity or other ruses in their negotiations. There are passages of moral indignation, when it becomes apparent, or even when it only seems probable, that the Japanese negotiators have used an excuse, or distorted facts, for purposes of delay.

Yet what must the Japanese student of his own country's history feel and think, when he comes across the following passage, in Perry's letter to the Shōgun: "As an evidence of the friendly intentions of the President, and to pay the highest honor to his Imperial Majesty, he has sent me in command of a number of ships—to be increased by others which are to follow—not only to bear to his Majesty the letter which I have already presented, but to evince, by every suitable act of kindness, the cordial feelings entertained by him towards Japan" (Hawks, p. 409). This one paragraph surely suffices to underline the hypocrisy of which the Japanese administration must necessarily have been aware. Indeed, it almost sounds like a deliberate act of ridicule.

Unfortunately, China, which had suffered terrible blows at that same time in its contacts with the West, and the 'great advantages' she had reaped from her treaty with the United States, were also mentioned in the letter to the Shōgun. Why a country that obviously felt as averse to contact with foreigners as Japan did should have been expected to be favorably impressed by the fact that, in that year, the Chinese export of tea to America would amount to 3,600,000 taels, can hardly be understood. Here the Occidental tradition, with its grave defects in understanding the East, was painfully carried forward: in it, as so often before and since, the conquering nation's value system is held to be implicitly superior to that of the other nation; and, without further deliberation, import and export are held up as indisputable values, which only the uncivilized or uncultured could regard as of secondary importance, or of no importance at all.[18]

The result of Commodore Perry's intervention is well known. He had carried out the mission as successfully as he had planned it.

The way was open for the commencement of trade relations, and it was left to an American equally astute, persistent and patient to effectuate in social reality what Perry had devised within the framework of a treaty. For, as the compiler of Perry's report stated: "It would be a foul reproach to Christendom now to force Japan to relapse into her cheerless and unprogressive state of unnatural isolation." He anticipated liberal commercial treaties "for the upward progress of our common humanity" (Hawks, p. 453).

The man who was perhaps that foreigner who personally had the greatest impact on Japanese history—at least among those who came from

[18] On better grounds, possibly, the compiler praises the Occident over the East, when he compares the brutal performances of Japanese wrestlers with the exhibition of telegraph and railroad by the Americans, both of which occurred on the occasion of a later friendly meeting between the two parties (Hawks, p. 433).

the Occident—was Townsend Harris (1804-1878). His biography is colorful, and invites psychoanalytic study. An inveterate bachelor to the end of his life, he responded poorly to his mother's death, and started to indulge all too freely in the intake of alcohol. The decline of his business, and the ensuing vituperation by his older brother, made him leave New York and travel around the world. Thus when President Pierce in 1855 had to appoint a consul general to Japan, he could have hardly found a man better suited for this post than Townsend Harris, who had been a member of the Chamber of Commerce, President of the New York Board of Education, trustee of a savings bank, and who had sailed as a trading merchant for six years through the South Seas and the China Sea, and had visited New Zealand, the Philippines, China, Ceylon, and India.

One may feel inclined to link his readiness to endure the social isolation and the hardships of solitude which he knew to be waiting[19] (and which he later did have to painfully endure for a long period of time) with the undue attachment to his mother. If this were so, one might be able to examine in this instance how individual psychopathology fits effectively into a historical demand, or how a historical demand draws the fitting psychopathology into its whirlpool. However that may be, Townsend Harris was, like Perry, ideally suited for his mission. Fortunately, we possess his diaries from 1856 to the beginning of 1858; unfortunately, those covering the rest of the time that he spent in Japan (up to 1862) have not yet been found.

Raised by his grandmother in an extreme anti-British way ("Tell the truth, fear God and hate the British" [Griffis, 1896, p. 4]), he had strong feelings against colonialism. The following bitter statement is recorded: "When a British Resident is forced on any Asiatic power, it is only a question of time how long that power shall be permitted to exist" (Harris, p. 73). Yet even though he was free of the spirit of colonialism in the narrower sense, Harris was throughout a child of his times, and convinced of the superiority of the Western world over Asia.

This paternalistic attitude led to direct and indirect threats, such as had been already observed in Perry's approach and, at one juncture in his conduct of negotiations, he reached the point of "Cannon Balls for

---

[19] Cf. his letter to the President of August 4, 1855: "I have a perfect knowledge of the social banishment I must endure while in Japan, and the mental isolation in which I must live, and am prepared to meet it. I am a single man, without any ties to cause me to look anxiously to my old home . . . ." (Harris, 1855-1858, p. 9).

Arguments" (Crow, 1939, pp. 221-227; Harris, p. 496). Yet such threats did not occur only at those times when exasperation about the slowness and dilatoriness of the Japanese reached a peak, so that one might be forced to regard them as exceptional; his negotiations were spiced, quite frequently, with innuendoes of that sort, and when no American ship of war did appear for a long time, Harris seemed to have become panicky about losing face with the Japanese (Harris, p. 350).

Yet, when at last a treaty of the kind that Harris had striven for was concluded,[20] the aggressive component seems to have been gradually replaced by what may even be described as an affectionate feeling for the Japanese nation. Thus when Mensken, his interpreter and secretary, was slain in 1861 by a Japanese, he continued to stay in Yedo and, by not fleeing, prevented reprisals (Crow, p. 265). He later reported that, according to the Japanese, "I have prevented the horrors of war from being brought on them": and, when it became known that he would leave Japan, the government asked the Americans to induce him to stay. Actually, when he left, he was showered with honors; in 1927, his memory was honored by the erection of a monument.

Harris himself "heartily grieved" over the non-revision of the treaties for whose conclusion he had done so much (the other Great Powers took his treaty as a model), for he had anticipated a change, as was stipulated, after half a decade (Griffis, p. 330). However, the treaties deprived Japan of her full power of levying customs duties, and of her full juridical sovereignty, inasmuch as foreigners were to be tried, in both criminal and civil suits, in the consular courts. This was regarded by the Japanese as a grave blow to their national honor; Japan had to wait almost thirty years after the Restoration (until 1894), for a redress of that tort.[21]

I shall select, from the rich material found in Harris's diaries, a few points of psychological interest. His honesty cannot be doubted; his interests from the beginning—and all the more so, with advancing maturity—were not centered on gain or the accumulation of wealth. That can

[20] Harris, of course, did not know what was going on in the Japanese political scene during his negotiations, and many an event which he appraised as the effect of his actions was in reality the product of the drama of internal politics that was simultaneously unfolding.

[21] See Harris, (p. 316f.) for a description of the lack of Japanese resistance to this stipulation. Harris made an interesting slip. In the sentence preceding his expression of surprise about the quick agreement on this point, he wrote that Americans should be "punished if guilty according to Japanese laws," as if he was aware of the inherent injustice of his demand.

be clearly seen in his complaints about having to listen to incessant money talk in the club that he attended upon his return to New York.[22]

And still, if my understanding of finances is correct, a personal characteristic of Harris's, close to greediness in its nature, had grave consequences for the history of Japan. It concerned the rate of exchange between the dollars and *seni*. At the time Harris arrived in Japan, the rate had been stipulated as 1,600 seni to the dollar. The Japanese offered at last a rate of 4,670 to the dollar; but Harris rejected even this offer (Harris, p. 327). On the 6th of June 1857, however, we find an entry recording the fact that, had he paid his account in Japan in accordance with the rate that Perry had accepted, he would have had to pay $1,474 more than he did (which, it seems, would actually have gotten him into an almost impossible financial situation).[23]

Yet the financial arrangement between Japan and the foreign powers wreaked havoc on the Japanese economy, since the differences in the exchange rates of silver and gold between Japan and the occidental powers began to produce a gradual migration of gold abroad, the consequences of which can be readily imagined. It was just these consequences that gave rise to the violent feelings against the treaties and, as a secondary result, aroused the strongest impetus in the fight against the Shōgunate.

If my assumption of a link between the exchange rate demanded by Harris and the loss of gold is correct, it would be an impressive example of how a personal factor can produce reverberations on both the national and international scales. That the Japanese economy would have been exploited in any event by the treaty-seeking powers cannot be doubted, in the light of the fate generally suffered by non-European countries in the nineteenth and early twentieth centuries. The only question would be about the intensity and speed of that process, which was here accelerated by specific economic treaty obligations.

Another rather tragic factor in Harris's dealings with the Japanese government was his relative ignorance of the political structure of Japan. He often thought that the Japanese were lying, using excuses or trying to cheat, in instances when nothing of the kind was true.

It was doubtful whether the United States Government actually had

---

[22] Harris acquired great fame in New York's history: he was the founder of its City College.
[23] When Harris was appointed Consul in China, his salary was $1000 per annum. For a direct reference to salary and currency exchange, see Harris, p. 343.

the right to dispatch a consul general, since the Japanese version of the Perry treaty said that *both* governments had to agree on the necessity of appointing consuls, whereas what the American version said was that such appointments could be made by the United States Government, if *either* of the two governments deemed this necessary (Harris, p. 209n.). There are other instances of Harris's being in error, one of which had particularly tragic consequences: his insistence that foreigners were safe in Japan, so that, when the Japanese government suggested restrictions on their movements, or the necessity of their being protected by guards, he was convinced that this was being demanded only for the sake of spying on foreigners, or of keeping the population and the Westerners separated.

Of what Harris was not aware at all was that the Shōgunate was fighting for its life, and that treaties of the kind that Harris insisted upon would surely mean the downfall of the Shōgunate, if they were ratified and carried out. What may have looked like the subterfuge and prevarication was really nothing more than the desperate attempts, on the part of an administration which was financially and politically bankrupt, to win a breathing spell here or there.

It would be instructive to know whether Harris would have proceeded in a different way, had he known of the tragic events that were in the making because of his appearance and his actions. Perhaps he would have welcomed the idea of making a significant contribution to the end of Japanese feudalism; perhaps he would have been even more forceful than he was. Most of the time, his conscious attitude must have been that any step that would reduce the cultural differences between Japan and the West was to be favored. Yet it bespeaks his greatness that, at least for moments, he was capable of doubting his own dogma. Thus he wrote: "I sometimes doubt whether the opening of Japan to foreign influences will promote the *general happiness* of this people. It is more like the gold age of simplicity and honesty than I have ever seen in any other country" (italics by Harris, p. 429).

This passage, with all its moving implications, is of general significance. Here was one of the best men that the West could send, working hard and selflessly to spread the value system in which he believed, among those whom he believed to be until then ignorant. Yet, in the midst of his work, he was suddenly struck by the possibility that all he was doing was an error; almost prophetically, he seemed to have sensed for a second all the tragedy that would follow in succeeding decades, after he himself would be no more. It is my feeling that such doubts would never have struck a Roman or, before that, a Greek statesman.[24] The doubt probably arose out of the tragic discrepancy between theory and practice that is so characteristic within the Christian orbit, a discrepancy which has perhaps been not quite so extreme or so guilt-arousing in other expanding civilizations.

Whatever the consequences of the West's knocking at Japan's closed doors might have been under more favorable circumstances, the immediate effects did not harbor a blessing, but added further fuel to the disturbances of the moment. The story of the political moves, countermoves, power games, falsehoods, intrigues—all the hallmarks of a society in change—that occurred between Perry's landing and the Restoration of 1868, when Japan started its seeming integration of Western civilization, and made its first step onto the stage of modern world history, is very complex—so complex, indeed, that no one has yet succeeded in making a lucid presentation of it. Suffice it to say that Perry and Harris created an unsolvable dilemma for the Bakufu.

There was one grave necessity, overriding everything else—namely, the complete avoidance of any repetition of China's fate on Japanese soil. The Bakufu was well aware of the process of national disintegration that China had suffered at the hands of the Occident, and the prohibition of the importation of opium was made a special point of Japan's treaty. If China's fate was to be avoided, the Great Powers must not be permitted any excuse for intervention.

The Shōgun's representatives were in fact thrown into consternation, whenever mention was made of those men-of-war that might appear. There was, no doubt, a feeling of dread about the possibility that Japan might be bombarded. This Japanese reaction was like a phobia. One may, of course, counter that such a feeling of dread was all too well justified, and should rather be called a reality anxiety. The reality danger was great, to be sure; but other nations faced similar dangers, and took their chances. Japan's postrestoration history shows more than once that the country was quite ready to run the risk of being bombarded, if need be, and did not shrink from the possibility of suffering such a fate.

Neurotic fears may hide behind and within reality fears. It has been

[24] The distrust of some intellectuals with regard to their own culture, at certain historical junctures, has been generally noted; but Harris was on a political mission that was predominantly ego-syntonic, and his sudden, momentary seizure of doubt is a peculiar phenomenon that deserves further exploration.

noted that soldiers in World War II, if they were told that an area was mined or booby-trapped, became panicky. Of course, the occupation of such an area was dangerous; but experience had already taught that the actual dangers were far less than those under different circumstances—which caused no panic. Apparently, the image evoked by mines and booby-traps is significantly more fear-arousing than that of other and far greater reality dangers. One gets the same impression, watching the Japanese negotiators going into a state of panic at the slightest mention of men-of-war. This fear, the origin of which I do not know,[25] and which cannot be completely explained by Japanese awareness of contemporary events in China, is to be kept in mind, when the Bakufu's overriding desire to pacify the Occident is considered.

On the other hand, the Shōgun knew that a surrender to the 'barbarians' would not be tolerated, either by the feudal class or by the Throne. Therefore, the Bakufu had to play a double game: to accept the West's conditions, and to tell the Imperial house that this was only a delaying action, carried through in order to prepare for the expulsion of all foreigners (Sansom, 1949, p. 294). Of course, one day the bluff would be called, and the Shōgun would fall.

The voices in favor of the foreigners were few, even though it was clear that Japan could not defend herself. Yet, after the Restoration, the resistance was no longer formidable or forbidding; the nation went into a process of Westernization unequalled by anything ever observed anywhere else. There seems to have taken place a more or less sudden 'turn' of the Japanese mind, if this vague term may be temporarily permitted. I have a definite hypothesis about the reasons that brought this about—a turn that transformed a country which, measured in terms of the

---

[25] Tentatively, I would refer this extreme fear of assault from abroad back to Japan's early history, when she was apparently settled without violence. Sansom (1958) summarizes the further course of Japan's history as follows:

"Whether the peaceful or the violent kind of cultural change is more salutary in the long run is a matter of opinion, but there can be little doubt that the most characteristic features of Japanese civilization are due to its development in comparative seclusion, which favored the continuity of tradition and the survival of original elements of strength and perhaps also of weakness in the nation's life" (p. 40).

The English past was quite different, and in her history traumatophobia seems to have less bearing. Japanese history was geared to the discharge of aggression within its own orbit. There is no trace of cowardice to be noted in Japanese history, and this particular traumatophobia—as I seem to sense on this occasion—may be referable to the fact that an aggression was threatening from without, endangering the Emperor's life. I might suggest that the matriarchal implications of the Japanese Throne weakened the resistance to an impending trauma, as if the latter had the unconscious meaning of exposing the mother to the possibility of rape.

Occident, was the most backward, within three decades into a far more modern one than many others that had participated in Occidental development for centuries.

I have in mind the two instances of actual bombings of Japanese cities, and I shall briefly recapitulate the relevant data.

On the 14th of September 1862, an Englishman named Richardson, who was a merchant from Shanghai, was killed by the Japanese. In the company of two other Englishmen, he had been riding along a road, when they met a train of the retainers of an important *daimyō*. They were told to stand aside, but continued their journey along the roadside. When they reached the palanquin, occupied by Shimadzu Saburô, the father of the Prince of Satsuma, several armed men set upon them, and attacked them with their swords. Richardson fell dead from his horse; the others got away with serious wounds.[26]

Several murders of foreigners had already come to pass; but it seems that this was the first time that an English merchant was the victim. In the spring of the following year, the Shōgun was asked for the payment of £100,000 for "allowing an Englishman to be murdered in his territory" (Satow, 1921, p. 72). From the Prince of Satsuma were demanded the trial and execution of the culprit, and the payment of £25,000 as compensation to the relatives of the victim (Satow, 1909, p. 845). The Shōgun, under the pressure of a Court hostile to the 'barbarians,' would have liked to refuse these requests *en bloc;* but an ultimatum backed up by a naval force made the government comply. The money requested from the Shōgun was turned over, with an expression of regret, and intimations were given of the readiness to pay Satsuma's indemnity; the Shōgun's power being limited, he could not arrest or punish the perpetrators, since they were the retainers of a powerful *daimyō,* who did not owe vassalage to the Tokugawas.

To show the difficulties that the Shōgun was facing, it is only necessary to consider that, the same day that he paid the indemnity, he gave orders that arrangements should be made for the closing of all ports to foreigners. This dual policy was apparently designed to appease the immediate wrath of the Western powers, on the one hand, and to make

[26] The episode is recounted in great detail by Satow (1921, p. 52). A different version is found in Murdoch (Vol. 3, p. 728). The Japanese version, in turn, deviates considerably from the English. In evaluating this episode, cognizance must be taken of the fact that, as early as A.D. 297, the following passage about Japanese customs is found in Chinese records: "When the lowly meet men of importance on the road, they stop and withdraw to the roadside" (Tsunoda, p. 7).

a strong antiforeign gesture, on the other, in order to appease the throne and its vociferous supporters, who were hostile to the West. The answer of the British *chargé d'affaires*, which contained a strongly worded refusal and a threat of war, is of interest; it appears to have contained also an indirect offer to the Shōgun to assist him materially in the suppression of the anti-foreign element (Satow, 1921, p. 83).

Here the Shōgun would have had a golden opportunity to reacquire the dictatorial position that his clan had held for over two centuries. That such a possibility was not even so much as considered by the Shōgun shows clearly that, despite all the internal dissension in Japan, and the personal ambitions that motivated groups and their leaders, the total welfare of the country still remained the dominant motive. A mind of lesser character or steadiness might easily have succumbed to that tempting offer of aid.

The Prince of Satsuma, being one of the most prominent of the antiforeign *daimyōs*, refused to comply. The English thereupon sent a squadron to the Bay of Kagoshima. How intense the determination was to get rid of the foreigners in that sector of the country may be seen from the plan of the Satsuma official and his party of forty men, who came on board the English flagship to deliver the *daimyō's* answer to the English demands.[27] They had the intention of making a sudden onslaught upon the British officers and thus taking possession of the flagship. Only the precautions that the British had taken prevented the execution of this bold plan (Satow, 1921, p. 85).

Instead, the British took possession of some foreign-built steamers lying at anchor at Kagoshima. When the Japanese shore batteries opened fire, the occupied ships were burnt, and the bombardment of Kagoshima took place. The next day, a Sunday (gone were the times when Townsend Harris refused to negotiate with the Japanese on a Sabbath!), "the squadron weighed anchor and proceeded down the bay at slow speed, shelling the batteries and town at long range" (August 16, 1863; Satow, 1921, p. 89). Kagoshima was destroyed; the number of lives lost is not known. The English lost eleven men (including the flag captain and the commander).

The second incident concerned the Chōshū clan, which held power over the Straits of Shimonoseki, commonly used by the ships traveling between Yokohama and Nagasaki. That clan, which had hated foreigners

[27] His answer was not without wit. Among other things it said that the Shōgun should not have made treaties "without inserting a clause to prevent foreigners from impeding the passage of the prince along the highroads" (Satow, p. 85).

as much as did the Satsuma clan, had erected batteries on its shores; in June, 1863, an American steamer was fired upon. During the following month, the same thing happened to a Dutch boat and a French one. An American man-of-war was dispatched to retaliate. Four days later, a French Admiral landed a party, and spiked some of the guns. The Straits, however, remained closed; and, in September, 1864 a joint expedition of ships, formed by the British, the Americans, the French and the Dutch, attacked Shimonoseki, and destroyed its guns and forts.[28]

Actions like those of the Great Powers at Kagoshima and Shimonoseki were not unusual in the history of the West's conquest of the East, but what was altogether surprising was the consequences. Within a month after the bombardment of Kagoshima, two high Satsuma officers promised the British *chargé d'affaires* that they would pay the indemnity requested, and would also search for the culprits and execute them.

Something similar happened shortly after the Shimonoseki affair. Chōshū officials readily concluded an agreement to keep the Straits open, and to pay indemnity for the damage caused to foreign ships, the expenses of the expedition, and even the ransom for the town of Shimonoseki. There were, of course, quite a few voices within the orbit of Western civilization that condemned the two naval actions as either immoral, unnecessary or wantonly destructive; some of the antiforeign Japanese also found new food in this for their campaign. But the two clans upon whom the assaults had been thrust, the Satsuma and Chōshū, who had previously been the most ardent and uncompromising foes of the West, now became their best friends and advocates.[29]

Historians are agreed that, without their turn of mind, and their ensuing strong cooperation, the Restoration might not have taken place, at least not with the degree of smoothness that it showed. The government of the early years of the Meiji, so decisive for Japan's Westernization, was dominated by the Samurai of Chōshū and Satsuma (Sansom 1949, p. 30f.). The situation can best be summarized in the following words:

> It was, by a paradox characteristic of the times, the anti-foreign activities of Satsuma and Chōshū that brought to birth a new government

[28] The details of this encounter are not relevant in this context. There is a detailed description by Satow (1921, pp. 105-115), who was an eyewitness of most of the events.

[29] Murdoch recorded: "Some of these desperadoes [Satsuma officers, who had been on the English flagship in order to ambush the foreigners] have since held not merely high office but the very highest offices in Japan" (Murdoch, Vol. 3, p. 734), at a time when Japan had become most friendly to the West.

dedicated to the fullest extension of foreign intercourse. The clans that had uttered the loudest cries of "Expel the Barbarians" were those which led the way in spreading Western ideas throughout Japan. It is not surprising that Japan gained the reputation in the West of being a topsy-turvy land [Sansom, 1949, p. 302].

The aim of this appendix is precisely to question whether we are truly dealing here with a paradox, and whether such sequences can justly be taken as indicating a "topsy-turvy" state of affairs. Sansom (*ibid.*) explains it as the effect of a "valuable lesson" to the two clans, "by showing the futility of the expulsion policy and by preventing the bloodshed and humiliation that would have followed an attempt to carry out the instructions of the court."

There is some doubt in my mind as to whether the Chōshū clan acted in good faith in closing the Straits and responding to the orders of the Court. No other clan responded to the request to expel the foreigners, and it was the Chōshū clan that not so long before had shown its capacity for insubordination, in its plan for taking possession of the Mikado. In closing the Straits, therefore, one may feel certain that they were acting in accordance with their own desires and convictions, and not in response to a request. Those were definitely not years of rational thinking; groups responded to cherished traditions, feelings, biases—that is to say, to the irrational part of the personality prevailing among the principal representatives of the élite. Indeed, it is hardly likely that any group of people 'learns its lesson' that speedily. The punishment that they had to suffer did not militate against the organization of a kind of guerrilla warfare, and there were enough Samurai and Ronins who would have been all too happy individually to ambush foreigners piecemeal. Indeed, a great deal could have been undertaken to deceive the powers, and to carry out the initial determination to wage a war to the finish against the Westerners.

An eye witness has the following observation to report, definitely disproving, it seems to me, the theory of 'the lesson learned.'

> They [the Chōshū people] proved so obliging that we could not help regretting that in order to gain their friendship it had been necessary to come to blows with them. And it is not a little remarkable that neither the Satsuma nor the Chōshū men ever seemed to cherish any resentment against us for what we had done, and during the years of disturbance and revolution that followed they were always our most intimate allies [Satow, 1921, p. 129].

The total absence of resentment, the intimacy, the graciousness—all prove that the assaulted clans had converted hostile feelings into their opposite. Such turns in sentiment are not prompted by rational deliberations, however, for such deliberations, when they are carried to their limits, may instead prompt decisive actions. The person who hates, even when cowed into obedience, still harbors feelings of resentment or spite.

When Satow writes that "the demonstrated superiority of European methods of warfare had converted our bitterest and most determined foes into friends" (Satow, 1921, p. 134), he is describing the effects of a psychological mechanism well known to the psychoanalyst—namely, identification with the aggressor (A. Freud, 1936, pp. 117-131; Moloney, 1954). As is well known, Japan in an incredibly short time incorporated western technique and science to perfection. Such profound changes can only take place when influential and important parts of the *élite* have undergone a personality change such as may well be produced by far-reaching identifications. That the two bombings had specific effects can be seen from the fact that Japan three times carried out surprise assaults, at times before the declaration of war—which makes them all the more similar to the two traumata that Japan herself had to suffer during the 1860's.

During the period of internal reorganization, concluded in 1894, there were already definite signs that Japan was determined to take the West as her model, not only with regard to her internal reorganization, but also with regard to her foreign policy. First, she incorporated some near-by islands (Kurile Islands—1875; Bonin Islands—1876; Ryukyu Islands —1879), which may be regarded as belonging to her geographical or, so to speak, natural orbit. Furthermore, within that same period there also falls the punitive expedition to Formosa, which unquestionably belonged to China, while another aggressive step was directed against Korea. It is worth quoting Latourette (1918) on this point: an armed expedition, he says, "adopted the plan used by Perry with the Shogun's officials and by tactful intimidation obtained a treaty," (p. 26). Japan took the lead in opening Korea to the outside world, repeating actively what she herself had had to submit to earlier (cf. Moloney, 1954).

These various expeditions, it should be noted, were undertaken without great strain or risk. The first great national aggressive effort was the Sino-Japanese war of 1894-1895. Here some of the aspects of military strategy I have referred to previously were already observable, although one cannot be certain whether they were premeditated or merely accidental. It is striking that the Japanese sank a few Chinese ships shortly before declaring war, and in the battle of the Yalu River, which was decisive in its effects, the Chinese ships were taken by surprise while they were engaged in disembarking their troops (T. White, p. 555).

This same technique was brilliantly used in the Russo-Japanese war of 1904-1905, when the Russian fleet was practically defeated before Port Arthur, by a surprise attack taking a few hours from the 8th to the 9th of February, the war itself being declared, however, only on the 10th of February. Haintz, an authority on that war, maintains that the whole outcome of the war depended on the first move, and that Japan would have been beaten from the very beginning, had she not succeeded in carrying out that bold undertaking.

The third instance of this sort was Pearl Harbor, where—again, *before* a declaration of war—the annihilation of the opponent's fleet was successfully carried out. Here the medium was no longer a naval force but aircraft, which is ideally suited for that sort of attack.

In the two wars against China and Russia, Japan carried out her total design brilliantly; in the last war, her war machine collapsed after achieving stupendous successes, and all that she had gained by previous wars was lost.

If one attempts to dissolve this history into psychological sequences, superficial and general as they may be, one must begin by noting that the tendency to discharge aggression against goals outside of the national organism had been always negligible in Japanese history. Under the Tokugawa Shōgunate, aggression had at last found channels of satiation within the national collective, and without causing destruction therein. Aggression had become internalized, and did not appreciably upset the homeostasis; previously, despite the tendency toward internalizing, no permanent nondestructive channels had been found for long periods of time. Over and over again, states of homeostasis had been disturbed by renewed destructive outbreaks, and new forms of nondestructive channelization had had to be found—a process which had finally led to the solid and comprehensive Tokugawa Shōgunate.

Yet these old channels became worn out; the equilibrium was once again disturbed, and an inner reorganization became unavoidable. Whether or not this reorganization, if it had been left to its own inner dialectic, would have led once more to a new equilibrium—characterized by internalized aggressions, turned totally inward—cannot be determined.

The fact is that, instead, Japan was subjected twice to formidable traumata, in the form of devastating aggression by a superior enemy.

Three circumstances seem relevant here, regarding the period before
the traumata took place: (1) The occurrence of the trauma was feared
in a way that is reminiscent of clinical phobias. (2) The aggressor was
alien to Japanese tradition, incomprehensible, nationally dystonic, and
outside the orbit of any possible identification. When Kagoshima and
Shimonoseki were bombed, all defenses against the occurrence of these
traumata had failed, despite consistent efforts, and even the overstraining
of internal resources, for the purpose of averting precisely such an occurrence. (3) The trauma, in the form of aggression, however, did not lead
to chaos, dissolution of structure or any other form of disorganization
(Kardiner, 1941). By an act that looked like an identification, the trauma
was seemingly overcome.

"I will do to you what you have done to me"—this became the underlying principle of that stupendous effort that made the country, on the
surface at least, similar to its erstwhile aggressor and enemy. The impetus
for this process of seeming assimilation, and the momentum with which
it was carried out were derived, it seems to me, from the wish to acquire
the means which would permit an adequate discharge of aggression—
this time against the world outside. The country was liberated from the
compelling necessity of discharging aggression internally. Those acts of
internal aggression that still occurred were more and more designed to
effect the removal of the barriers that stood in the way of external aggressive discharge.

There is an event in Japan's recorded history that strikes me as being
the precursor of the process of seeming identification with the aggressor.
Japan had once before been in danger of being subjugated by an enemy.
I am referring to the attack by the Mongols in 1274 and again in 1281.
It is remarkable that, after Japan had averted the first invasion, she built
a stone rampart along Hakata Bay, where the first landing had taken
place. Each chieftain had to construct one inch of wall for every third
of an acre in his possession. It was to have been completed in six months;
it was accomplished in fact only after five years (Sansom, 1931, p. 316f.).

Construction work in a coastal area for the purpose of defense against
invasion is not very rare, I imagine, any more than is the idea of surrounding with ramparts a limited area, such as a city. But to build a wall
along one part of a shore does not make for a promising defense, unless
an island is rendered otherwise invulnerable by the natural geographical

features along the rest of its shoreline. In Sansom's (1958) words: "This plan had one disadvantage. It was certain to come to the knowledge of the invaders and cause them to look for other landing places along the coast, from which they could turn Japanese positions behind the wall" (p. 448)—which, of course, was exactly what the Mongols did. But what makes the Japanese idea of a coherent stone rampart so noteworthy is the fact that the Chinese had already built a huge wall in order to keep invading nomadic hordes out of their own country.

The idea of countering the Mongols' invasion by an attack against Korea had been initially in the Bakufu's mind, but then dropped. The wall seems to me to be a sign of identification with the aggressor—in this instance, not *qua* aggression, but *qua* the defense that the aggressor had used, when he had himself been the object of aggression and the famous Chinese Wall was built (during the third century B.C.). It is my impression that, in the Japanese idea of a coastal wall, we have an example of the effects of a psychological mechanism, untainted by the interference of realistic or reality factors.[30]

The process of Westernization was not, after all, the first instance of Japan's acceptance of a foreign culture. Long before, she had integrated Chinese civilization, which had been a foreign body when she first came into contact with it. In that instance, however, the foreign culture had not been imposed upon her, although it was probably partly the fear of the superiority of Chinese political organization that had induced the desire for introducing the continental civilization. Chinese culture was, as I have said before, not imitated but assimilated; but even the strong hold that Buddhism gained over Japan did not kill off Shintō, and ultimately it was Buddhism that had to give way to the native cult.

The effects of the inroads of a foreign culture, or of a foreign element, depend on the state of the receiving country. When Shakespeare had his effect on *Sturm und Drang*, the German literary movement of the eighteenth century, there was a group of young authors ready for such stimulus. Shakespeare expressed something that lay dormant in them;

[30] Professor Otto Maenchen raised an objection against this hypothesis because the invaders were Mongols and not Chinese. They called themselves Mongols and were so called by the Japanese. His argument deprives my hypothesis of a fair amount of its credibility. However, the first invasion army is described as having been composed "of 15,000 Mongol and Chinese troops . . . and 8,000 Korean troops of poor quality." There were "about 7,000 Korean sailors together with Chinese seamen" (Sansom, 1958, p. 442). In the second invasion the majority of troops were Chinese (Sansom, 1958, p. 448f.).

in Shakespeare something was concretized that was vaguely, and without explicit form, in the minds of the longing and searching youth. But when the Japanese accepted Western values and techniques and political forms, they were not ready for that type of civilization. It was not the Western world that Japan had been searching or longing for.[31]

It is my belief that, despite the sudden interest in, indeed fervor for everything Western, there was no intention of dropping the Japanese past. The primary loyalty of the Japanese belonged to their own great tradition, and there seems to be evidence that what appeared as love of the West was in reality the path that the Japanese took in order to destroy it. At any rate, the quotation that follows may be taken to indicate that, from the very beginning, the ostensible identification with the aggressor on the part of at least a section of the elite was, in fact, aimed toward his later annihilation.

> Make our country secure by military preparations—encourage and protect the people at home, and then wait for the time of the confusion of Europe which must come eventually sooner or later, and although we have no immediate concern with it ourselves we must feel it, for such an event will agitate the nations of the Orient as well, and hence, since our country is not mixed up in the matter so far as Europe is concerned, we may become the chief of the Orient [Viscount Tani, 1887; quoted after Norman, p. 5].

Thus, I believe, it would be very wrong to speak of imitation, as is so often done, when Japan's Westernization is discussed. Japan played its Western role to perfection, and with an efficiency that cannot be achieved by imitation; yet Western civilization was not really integrated, since the loyalty to traditional cherished values was unquestionable. The answer to the two great traumata of Kagoshima and Shimonoseki was an identification of a kind that could lead to its own abolition.

The identification—if it may be called an identification, under such circumstances—anticipated the destruction of that very object with which the identification had been established, a destruction which would also make that identification no longer necessary. Thus the quasi identification was not carried out by admiration, respect or love, but by destructive forces. The superego permitted identification with the ego dystonic, be-

---

[31] The process of the Westernization of Japan may be somewhat compared with a premature or precocious ego development in ontogenesis (cf. Freud, 1913e, p. 325). In this instance, it meant that the old Japanese core could be preserved.

cause it was done in the service of preserving the old Japanese tradition—altogether, a mechanism of unusual complexity and genius, if we consider that here the identification with the new was designed to make possible the eternal survival of the old.

Japan has often been described as treacherous because of the Pearl Harbor attack, and one can go along with such a description when a people's war spirit is being stirred up. It would not have been wise to remind the American nation then that, in so acting, Japan did nothing but carry forward the tradition of her teachers. Indeed, it is almost certain that Japan's expansionist momentum—for which there is only very little historical tradition,[32] and which broke out more or less suddenly with the Restoration—is patterned in accordance with an important aspect of the history of the West.

The geographical similarity between Japan and England has been noted by many historians. Like the British Islands, the Japanese archipelago is face to face with a huge land mass. England, having finally established herself as a nation, after the incursions of various continental invaders, tried to establish herself as a continental power in the wars of the fourteenth and fifteenth centuries. Her failure in this endeavor necessitated the evolvement of a new technique. From then on, she regularly allied herself with the weaker continental party, thereby preventing the expansion of the stronger—an ingenious method, that was carried out with great subtlety and bloodshed.

Japan, never the victim of an invasion prior to her national establishment, had protected herself against the neighboring continent by isolation. When that had been irrevocably destroyed, the English policy of balancing continental powers could not be applied, for there was only one significant continental power facing Japan—namely, China. Yet, China was now in a position similar to that which Japan had been in, being threatened by Russia, which also had territorial designs on the Japanese islands. An attempt at alliance with China against Russia, or with Russia against China, would have been senseless, even though that sort of alliance would have been in accordance with the tradition of modern European power politics, at the time when Japan took to regarding the subjugation of China as a prerequisite for her own security.

It is psychologically understandable that Japan did not succeed when

[32] For an early example, consider Honda Toshiaki (1744-1821), who suggested how Japan should proceed in order to acquire "the American islands, which are Japan's possession manifestly" (Tsunoda et al., 1960, p. 555).

she tried to inflict the very same trauma that she had passively suffered upon the power or powers that had originally inflicted it upon her. Material factors notwithstanding, the psychological factor ought not to be underestimated. Awe and anxiety could scarcely be eliminated, when the aggression turned *against the originators of the historical process*—which came to an end when Hiroshima and Nagasaki were destroyed by bombs, just as had happened to Kagoshima and Shimonoseki eighty-odd years before.

That awe was felt in Japan's reaction to Roosevelt's death. The Tokyo radio, after announcing the event, broadcast "a few minutes of special music in honor of the passing of this great man"; shortly thereafter, Japan's Premier had this to say:

I must admit that Roosevelt's leadership has been very effective and has been responsible for the Americans' advantageous position today. For that reason I can easily understand the great loss his passing means to the American people and my profound sympathy goes to them (Asbell, 1961, p. 94.)[33]

This response is magnificent; but it reflects the unconscious (probably masochistic) love of or fixation on a hated enemy. It does not portend victory. Western civilization, we must remember, was never integrated, and was never intended to be integrated, by the Japanese people. Hence, a feeling of awe for the representative of that power that had fully integrated Western civilization and was on the verge of proving its material superiority to all the other representatives of it.

Yet, when the bombs fell on Hiroshima and Nagasaki, psychologically that was 'the return of the repressed'; the aggressive discharge directed outside had collapsed, and the aggression now rebounded and reappeared in its original form, this time a thousandfold multiplied, as compared with the primordial traumata of Kagoshima and Shimonoseki.

One may examine the history of the period from Perry's entry into Japan to the end of the second World War, as if it were the history of a traumatic neurosis. To be sure, in the latter, according to Freud, the trauma is abreacted in anxiety dreams, in which the traumatic event is repeated. On the national scale, the trauma was abreacted by inflicting it on others. When the total destruction of two cities occurred in 1945—in a sense, the equivalent of a severe punishment for the attempt at

[33] One may compare with this the vulgar, if not obscene response that Hitler is purported to have made, upon being told of Roosevelt's death.

destruction of an object of partial identification—the idea of aggression was given up altogether. At least, according to recent reports, the Japanese themselves suggested to MacArthur that militarism should be eradicated forever in Japan by extreme constitutional measures.

One may well imagine that the two bombs meant to the Japanese nation a total block to any further attempt at aggressive discharges directed against the outer world. One may even suspect that depression or melancholia would become inescapable under such conditions.[34]

There is, or there should be, agreement that, for human reasons alone, the two bombs should never have been dropped. That it was Japan that was chosen as the victim was all the more tragic, in view of her psychological history.

There is an episode recorded in the memoirs of Joseph Grew (1944) that deserves attention. He was our Ambassador to Japan from 1932 to 1942, approaching his assignment with the greatest conscientiousness and devotion, as well as with a more than serious effort to understand the Japanese mentality and civilization. On April 22, 1934, at a time of relative calm before the period of gradually increasing hostility between the two countries, a Japanese-American Friendship Day was celebrated. It was in commemoration of the eightieth anniversary of the signing of Japan's first treaty by Commodore Perry, and the main ceremony took place at the spot where his ships had stayed most of the time. First, the official party made a short stay at Kakizaka, where Townsend Harris had lived for four years before moving to Yedo. There is (or was, at least) also a monument to Harris, on which the following (partly inexact) excerpt from his diary is engraved:

> Thursday, September 4, 1856. Slept very little from excitement and mosquitoes,—the latter enormous in size. Men on shore to put up my flagstaff. Heavy job. Slow work. Spar falls; break crosstrees; fortunately no one hurt. At last get a reinforcement from the ship. Flagstaff erected; men form a ring around it, and, at two and half P.M. of this day, I hoist the "First Consular Flag" ever seen in this Empire. Grim reflections— ominous of change—undoubted beginning of the end. Query,—if for the real good of Japan?

[34] That this phase did not last long in reality does not necessarily speak against my thesis: the aggressor was once more inconsistent. After inflicting two terrible traumata, and taking away all the spoils of successful imperialism, he did not, after all, touch the core of Japanese tradition, the Emperorship, but instead proved once more to extend a friendly hand for cooperation. I wonder whether MacArthur went through phases of attitude similar to those experienced by Townsend Harris.

Grew reported that, on this occasion, the following conversation took place:

> Admiral Nomura asked me what he meant by "Undoubted beginning of the end." I said he must have meant that this was to be the end of Japanese isolation (I wonder) and that his final observation "Query,—' if for the real good of Japan?" showed that he was thinking of the interests of Japan quite as much as of the interests of his own country [Grew, 1944, p. 1927].

It seems to me that, in this little incident, the crux of the whole problem inherent in Japanese-American relations between 1853 and 1945 becomes apparent in a flash. From the historic-psychological point of view, Admiral Nomura's question should have been unceasingly on the Ambassador's mind. His actual answer was the gentlest way of pulling out of an embarrassing situation, and showed his great ability at repartee; yet it was a hypocritical answer, for Grew could not possibly have thought that such a reply would resolve the problem which appeared to be on the Admiral's mind.

I have tried—but failed—to find out at whose suggestion this inscription had been selected. The tablet was unveiled on October 1, 1927. The monument was erected at the instigation of Viscount E. Shibusawa, Edgar A. Bancroft, the American ambassador, and Henry M. Wolf of Chicago.[35] The accurate tracing of the history of this monument would make an important contribution to social psychology and to the psychology of history.

The inscription, to my mind, contains everything necessary to keep the ambivalence toward the 'barbarians' awake in a subtle way, and never to let the Japanese nation forget that America is and has to be its enemy. But why did the Ambassador refuse empathy with Admiral Nomura? At that moment, East and West clashed silently; a finer ear would have grasped the wealth of implications and innuendos that lay behind the admiral's simple question.

One concluding remark may not be out of place. For the longest period of his existence, man has been ignorant of the causative agencies of his history. If we try to reconstruct what the Romans actually knew about economics, their own history, the history of the peoples they subjugated, we get an appalling picture. As little as we can understand how

---

[35] I am indebted to Mr. Eugene Langston for this and other information, and wish to express my thanks on this occasion.

the armies of the past could have survived without antibiotics, K-rations or maps, so little can we imagine how Rome was able to administer a huge empire without statistics or telegraphy.

Only recently, through the application of scientific methods, has the historian gained knowledge of the multiplicity of causative agents, including the biological, the geographical, the economical, and many others. If I understand Freud correctly, what he said was that, aside from all these factors, there is still one which impinges on the unconscious of the group-member (and it remains an open question whether this concerns every group member—which is not likely—or a certain percentage of the elite), and stems from a deposit left by a concealed, so to speak, 'obnoxious' part of the history of the group.

In my opinion, Freud took a giant step here beyond Spengler. Where Spengler had written the biology of human history, its inescapable course from youth to maturity and death, Freud laid the foundations of its psychology. That the two do not contradict each other does not need to be stressed here. In the individual, the biological and the psychological aspects do not exclude each other; they belong together, and both are needed for even a superficial understanding. It is thus justifiable, I think, to read a people's or a group's history, as if it were the history of an individual—with the goal in mind of discovering what that particular history conceals, what it contains as its 'repressed' content.

It may be bold to speculate about the relevance of this psychological factor. If it is present, I am inclined to attribute the greatest importance to it. We expect a statesman to be well informed about his country, and we mean by that term knowledge of the relevant facts, of the events and factors that have moulded the national past and which can be ascertained by objective methods. But what an accretion of flexibility and range of decision there would be, if the statesman—and the nation he represents and leads—were aware of the *irrational* forces that seek release in the historical process. What an accretion of constructive action, if he also understood the history of the nations with whose representatives he is dealing.

There is a small-scale example in modern history in which a great statesman grasped the psychological peculiarity of his reluctant ally-to-be and, by that grasp, resolved a dangerous impasse.

When Roosevelt met Stalin at Teheran (November 26 to December 3, 1943), his primary aim was to establish the closest possible *rapprochement* between the Western Allies and Stalin in order to guarantee a successful invasion of France. He felt desperate at first, because he was failing to come closer to the Russian, on the emotional level. Nothing seemed to be able to cut the ice, until he resorted to an ingenious stratagem. After a brief warning to Churchill, the following situation evolved:

> I began almost as soon as we got into the conference room. I talked privately with Stalin, I didn't say anything that I hadn't said before, but it appeared quite chummy and confidential, enough so that the other Russians joined us to listen. Still no smile.
>
> Then I said, lifting my hand up to cover a whisper (which of course had to be interpreted) "Winston is cranky this morning, he got up on the wrong side of the bed."
>
> A vague smile passed over Stalin's eyes, and I decided I was on the right track. As soon as I sat down at the conference table, I began to tease Churchill about his Britishness, about John Bull, about his cigars, about his habits. It began to register with Stalin. Winston got red and scowled, and the more he did so, the more Stalin smiled. Finally Stalin broke out into a deep, hearty guffaw, and for the first time in three days I saw light. I kept it up until Stalin was laughing with me, and it was then that I called him "Uncle Joe." He would have thought me fresh the day before, but that day he laughed and came over and shook my hand.
>
> From that time on our relations were personal, and Stalin himself indulged in an occasional witticism. The ice was broken and we talked like men and brothers [Perkins, p. 84f.].

It moves me to discover, in this—now, unfortunately, so remote—corner of recent history, an incident that challenges a comparison with a typical psychoanalytic technique. Anyone who has ever watched Aichhorn in the kind of cat-and-mouse play—which almost inevitably unfolds between an intelligent person (well equipped to be a successful delinquent) and the therapist—will be reminded of him when reading the brilliant (so wise and human at the same time) way in which the statesman patched up a situation that, in the hands of the less skilled, would have led to untold sufferings on the part of those whose welfare was his responsibility.

Roosevelt broke through the isolation of distrust with which his opponent-ally had surrounded himself, by imposing on the object a narcissistic identification. This was the hub of Aichhorn's procedure: to force the recalcitrant delinquent into an emotional tie with the analyst.

That a piece of legitimate psychoanalytic technique was intuitively used by a great mind in a constructive effort to eliminate a block to cordial relations gives me hope that acceptance of Freud's far more inclusive construction of human history may yet have far more wide-reaching effects.

Here it was solely a matter of an interpersonal impasse, and yet differences in national psychology, and an endeavor to bridge those differences, were significant. It is only one step (great as that step may be, in proportion) toward the grasp of those supraindividual forces which are apparently also revealed in the peculiarities of the individual. Much seems to depend on that one step. It may lead to a nation's taking cognizance of where it itself is standing in the maelstrom of human history, and what the unconscious contents are that might otherwise push indomitably toward repetition of the past, thus enforcing a lethal restriction on flexibility; but such advance of knowledge may also lead to a knowledge of the adversary's unconscious, and of the form of repetition toward which he is being dragged indomitably.

It may well be that Freud laid the foundations for an essentially new kind of understanding between nations, although there is not much likelihood that the present age will be able to profit from it. There is, however, a faint hope that later generations will prove to be wiser than we are. After all is said and done, even the delay of the machine age has been overcome. May the delay of psychology not cost mankind too much![36]

[36] Lately a book was published that gives a step by step development of Chōshū's rise to the level of national politics, and its bearing on the Meiji Restoration (Craig, 1961). The author analyzes with admirable lucidity the reasons for this fief's ability to overthrow the Bakufu and the Shōgun. The question of why Chōshū became a fief advocating and supporting the Westernization of Japan unfortunately finds only a very subordinate place in the author's inquiry. He affirms the potential, still inherent in the Tokugawa system, for surviving for a long time; and he asserts that there was no *crise de système* (p. 86). It is noteworthy that he does not regard the Meiji Restoration as a new formation, but rather as the logical outcome of the preceding process of feudalization, which had not been accomplished by the Tokugawa—that is to say, "much of the emperor-centered Meiji nationalism was essentially a form of transmuted Tokugawa loyalty" (p. 144).

When the author closes his book with, "In Japan as in Choshu it is in a large measure to the strength and not to the weaknesses of the traditional society that we must turn to comprehend its modern history" (p. 374), I think that he raises a point that is not alien to Freud's metahistory, in the light of observations made of the individual. It is even quite reminiscent of problems centering on the dichotomy of ego strength and ego weakness (Nunberg, 1939), and I suppose that, for history, too, a discussion would be required regarding a definition of weakness and strength.

What I would have liked to learn from a presentation as excellent as the one in

It was only recently that I came across Richard's pamphlet of 1863 on the destruction of Kagoshima; I recommend its study to the contemporary reader. It would be an excellent lesson in history, in view of what has happened since then. It is impressive to notice how succinctly the author was aware of the historical situation, how soberly and correctly he judged the Japanese. It is not merely a historical analysis, presenting all the pertinent data; it is also inspired by the religious values of Christianity at its best.

Indeed, one of the great unresolved questions is whether morality has a beneficial effect on the course of history, or whether the path of history is indifferent to such sets of values. It may be that the prolonged corruption of community institutions, the conspicuous deviations of the élite from moral standards that, officially at least, are declared to be valid, have a disorganizing effect; but it seems to me that often the equivalent question regarding the intercourse of *national groups* is moot. The *immoral* way in which the American Indians were treated does not appear to have been injurious to the perpetrators, whereas the injustice meted out to the Negroes seems to rebound, so that the future historian, if he prefers to believe in Providence, may even perhaps find occasion to suggest the workings of a Divine retribution in this area.

It is sensible to ask whether the terrible threat of Asia which weighs upon the West at present would be no menace at all, or a menace to a considerably lesser degree, if the West had conducted itself in the nineteenth century in accordance with Christian principles. In the light of this question, it seems reasonable to summarize the content of Richard's pamphlet, even at the risk of repetition. I have not checked the sources that Richard cites; his tract sounds honest and reliable.

The City of Kagoshima had a population of 180,000 inhabitants. The entire town was left a mass of ruins—the city, like all Japanese cities,

---

question, is: (1) whether historical observations confirm the assumption of the working of mechanisms such as a sort of identification with the aggressor; (2) whether the day-to-day record of the historical process confirms the belief that it was because of this mechanism that Satsuma and Chōshū reached the attitudes toward the West which they did evolve shortly before the beginning of the Restoration period.

From the book, neither a clear 'no' nor a clear 'yes' can be derived. If anything, one may gather clues that speak against my hypothesis; but since the author's main interest centers in the vicissitudes of the Bakufu and the Shōgunate, it is perhaps unsuitable to use his book at all as a touchstone for my hypothesis. Still, since it is not proven—after all, by a study which goes into great detail with regard to one of the most significant processes of the Restoration—that my hypothesis is wrong, it gives me a modicum of hope that there may be some truth in it.

having been built of wood. After the first bombardment, which left half of the city buried, a heavy typhoon set in. Nevertheless, the fleet continued its work of destruction the following day. By citing facts, as stated by the responsible British Admiral and diplomat, Richard convincingly refutes the argument which has been raised in the defense of those who were responsible for the destruction of the city—that it was a matter of accident. He stresses the incongruity between the incident that provoked the destruction (one Englishman killed and two wounded), and the number of Japanese whose lives were threatened, as well as those who were actually killed; the lack of warning to the population; the utter innocence of those who were affected by the punitive action.

The author gives important details about the precipitating incident. It was a long established custom in Japan to retire, or to kneel down at the approach of a princely train. The Government, anticipating that this custom was not acceptable to the foreigners, and might lead to incidents of the kind that actually did come to pass, tried to forestall an encounter of foreigners with princely processions, but all measures such as special roads, guardhouses or escorts, were rejected, and the only answer given by the British diplomat was: "I do not understand why a Daimyō should have the road to himself" (p. 6).

Since such princely processions were not short, but rather long, the English party was sufficiently forewarned, and had ample opportunity to leave the road before they came upon the Prince himself, and the Japanese assault occurred. The author asks what the British reaction would be, if "a number of Americans or Frenchmen . . . should insist upon breaking through the barriers and galloping their horses along the line reserved in London, on Lord Mayor's Day," on the plea that "commercial treaties, existing between their respective countries and England, ensure them a free right of way through London at all times" (p. 5).

He refers to the arrogance of which the West had made itself guilty, when he asks rhetorically: "Why should Englishmen, if they force themselves, purely for their own profit, into countries where their presence is not desired, expect that all the social laws and observances of such countries should be set aside for their convenience?" (p. 5).

An equal arrogance is visible regarding the British demands after Richardson had been murdered: apology and £100,000 from the Shōgun and £25,000 from the Daimyō, and the execution "in the presence of one or more of her Majesty's naval officers of the chief perpetrators of the murderous assault" (p. 7). It seems that, in all seriousness, it was ex-

pected that the Daimyō would have his own father publicly hanged—
for the prince whose train led to the assault was the Daimyō's father.
Since the English knew that the Shōgun could not enforce these requests,
and moreover, was not responsible for the behavior of an unruly prince,
the demand for double indemnity was contradictory in itself. Contemporary sources indicate that the Daimyō's representatives behaved in a
civilized and conciliatory way when the British Admiral appeared before
Kagoshima, but that even negotiations were peremptorily refused by the
British.

The author then gives a history of Japan's intercourse with the Occident: her trust and friendly acceptance of the missionaries; the growth
of Christianity in Japan, until conspiracies, political intrigues aiming at
the overthrow of the government, were discovered; not to speak of the
continued feuds between the various monastic orders, and the insatiable
cupidity of the merchants. Thus, the author concludes, the experiences
of the Japanese well justify their isolating themselves and their determination to keep all foreigners from their shores.

Furthermore, the Japanese were informed of what had happened to
India and China. He describes how, in other places, the traders humbly
settled in one or two outlying posts "gradually growing more arrogant
and encroaching, year by year, until at length they bring tremendous
armaments to ravage the coasts, to bombard the cities," etc. (p. 12). He
reports on the incidents in Japan herself, preceding Kagoshima: the
drunken sailors; the flouting of all laws by the purchase and export of
Japanese gold; the ensuing increase in cost of living; and the poverty of
a population, that had seemed to be able to live quite comfortably until
then.

It would lead us too far afield to give a detailed description of the actual
misconduct of foreigners; but the reader can well imagine it, when one
considers the deportment of sailors in foreign ports, and the low level
of those who, at that time, went abroad for the purpose of ruthless and
quick enrichment. It is evident that there was no trace of respect, empathy or understanding in the majority of those who came to Japan.

Richard's reasoning thus leads to an unqualified indictment of the
West. How far he colored his arguments goes beyond my knowledge;
but his presentation strikes me, not only as reflecting accurately what
a small minority in the West felt and thought, but also what the thoughts
of an astute, well informed and unbiased Japanese must have been.
Unavoidably, the conduct of the West must have impressed such a per-

son as a series of atrocities and injustices, and the frequent references to Christianity as nothing more than elements of a hypocritical scheme of considerable mendacity.

If to all this is added the unavoidable nationalism—or rather, the profound integration of certain values of conduct and art that were constantly being offended by the 'barbarians'—we may come close to fathoming the state of rage by which many Japanese must have justifiably been prepossessed.

All the more, therefore, has it seemed necessary to proffer a psychological construct of why just those who had fallen victim to the worst humiliation and torture by the barbaric Occidentals were to become their most ardent supporters.

Appendix 4

Challenges to Freud's Honesty

The appearance of a genius is an event of extreme rarity. Its infrequency is due, at least in part, to the fact that it is contrary to what may be expected in terms of biological structure. We know that man's fundamental biological functions are the same as those of all other organisms: reproduction and self-preservation through adjustment. The function of genius, however, is to create a new world rather than to adjust to its existing habitat—and that in itself appears to set it into contradiction with man's biological nature. It is not surprising, therefore, that genius is more often than not combined with what seems to be severe psychopathology.[1]

If anyone were to refer to such seeming psychopathology in a derogatory way, he would only prove thereby his own ignorance of the nature of genius. But if he should go so far as to imply the presence in a genius of a psychopathology that did *not* exist—and this, to boot, with derogatory intent, even though the evidence to the contrary was readily accessible to him—then he would be adding to his display of ignorance an unforgivable element of ingratitude. The great majority of geniuses

[1] In Aristotle's *Problemata* (Book XXX, 1) one reads: "Why is it that all men who have become outstanding in philosophy, statesmanship, poetry or the arts are melancholic?"

have had to pay with their own deep suffering for the advances they have brought into the world by their creativity. Thus was it, too, with Freud.

If any or all of the allegations against Freud which I am about to discuss were correct, that fact would, nevertheless, not destroy one iota of his greatness, or of the debt that the world owes him. It would mean no more than a problem for scientific inquiry, just as in the lives of other geniuses. This statement has to be made at the start, because it has become almost fashionable among certain groups to decry any attempt one may make to correct an unfavorable picture of Freud—such as so many have become desirous of establishing—as the outcome merely of the reproving analyst's positive transference, and his idiosyncrasy against blemishes upon his ego ideal. In taking up this discussion, I am actually violating a recommendation that I have been told Freud gave to his pupils—namely, to bypass recriminations of just the sort that I shall here refute, and not to honor an undeserving opponent by dignifying him with a reply.[2]

I have also been told that this section would have gained by my deleting any personal remarks in the name of such things as 'equanimity' or 'objectivity'; but I do not see any reason to conceal from the reader the indignation that I felt after checking on the correctness of these allegations.

In what follows I shall deal with two among the several instances, during the last decade, in which allegations of a fairly serious nature have been put forth against Freud's character. I have selected the first chiefly because it was made by a great American scholar, whose prestige may lend more credibility to his assertions than they might otherwise have obtained. The other instance, I have selected for personal reasons as well as for some others.

I should like the reader to keep two things in mind: first, a single quoted paragraph, while short, may contain so many misrepresentations, in such a condensed form, that it may take a few pages to disprove all of them. Second, much of the abuse that has been heaped on Freud has been put in the form of questions, which are in essence rhetorical. I shall discuss such rhetorical questions, in keeping with their own real intent, as assertions.

[2] Cf. Freud (E. Freud and Meng, 1963, p. 31): "Let them yelp, and let us continue on our steep road" (translation mine); cf. also Freud, 1914, p. 40.

I

In his Academic Lecture of 1956, upon reaching his subject matter after a long preamble, Dr. Percival Bailey had the following to say:

Let us begin with Jones's biography which is appearing these days. In its preparation he was obliged to read a great deal. Recently he wrote: "Freud has been regarded as a revolutionary genius who introduced novel and disturbing ideas. The first half of the sentence is undoubtedly true, but the second half needs qualification. As a result of my researches I came to the unexpected conclusion that hardly any of Freud's early ideas were completely new" [Jones, 1954, p. 20]. Then he gives a long list and adds: "This is a formidable list, which I cannot discuss here in detail, and yet it can be shown that there are broad hints of all of them in the writings of previous workers with which Freud was thoroughly familiar." Why was this conclusion so unexpected by Jones? Obviously because he had not read of them previously. But there is another aspect of the matter. Why had Freud left a faithful devoted disciple in such ignorance? Freud tells us, in one of his letters to Fliess, that he stopped reading because he found his own ideas expressed better than he could. Did he wish to save his disciple Jones from such a deception? Or had he forgotten? If so, what motive had he for forgetting? You will pardon me for asking such a question, but I am told that I must learn to think dynamically—that is, in terms of motives. I leave you to speculate on the answers. I remember only that Freud was a very ambitious man [Bailey, 1956, p. 392].

Here the accusation is clearly made that Freud may have deliberately —and with conscious intent to deceive—withheld from a "faithful devoted disciple" information concerning the true sources of his life's work. Yet, before he makes such an accusation, one surely has the right to expect Dr. Bailey—unless he is ready to hold Freud responsible for everything that his pupils wrote—first to evaluate Jones's statement on its own merits. With regard to Jones's surprise at not having found anything "completely new" in Freud's early ideas, one wonders, to begin with, whether Dr. Bailey can think of *any* man who ever thought, wrote, or created something *completely* new. Just as *natura non facit saltus*, so also is man's cultural history, in all its ramifications, a continuum (cf. de Saussure, 1950, p. 36f.). Further, the history of ideas is not everyone's *métier*, and Freud and his pupils may well have had their hands full with more serious problems than the historical analysis of their own ideas, which Freud had, in any case, revised by the time he became acquainted with Jones. Furthermore, Jones asserts that Freud was familiar with the works in which those ideas had been expressed. How did Jones know that? Did he perhaps learn of Freud's familiarity with those books from the citations in Freud's work itself? The passage that Dr. Bailey quotes from Jones might seem important to someone interested in Jones's personality; one is truly at a loss, however, to discover in the Jones quotation the premises from which Dr. Bailey drew his conclusions concerning Freud.

Be that as it may, considering the solemnity of the occasion, the presence of a representative cross-section of his psychiatric colleagues, and the prestige of his own name—for all these reasons, if not in the name of truth itself—one might have expected the speaker to have made quite certain, before putting into words a question which, if answered affirmatively, would gravely denigrate Freud's character, that there was at least some shred of evidence to justify his asking such a question.

Fortunately, Jones did not stop with recording his surprise, but went on to cite the antecedents of Freud's early ideas (which Freud, according to Dr. Bailey, may have concealed from Jones, with the purpose of deceiving him). I shall not enumerate the sources that Jones (1954, pp. 204-207) cited, which Bailey says Freud may have concealed from him.[3] In documenting his "surprise," Jones points out that "the idea of an unconscious mind" was familiar to the nineteenth century, and refers to von Hartmann's *Philosophy of the Unconscious,* which was cited at least once by Freud, who also referred to Schopenhauer and Lipps, it should be noted, as predecessors who had stressed the importance of the unconscious.

Let us assume, however, that Freud had never mentioned any predecessors at all, in terms of their contribution to the development of the concept of the unconscious. It cannot go without notice that his daughter translated Israel Levine's *The Unconscious,* Part One of which is entitled *The Unconscious before Freud,* in which the history of the concept of the unconscious is traced not only to Eduard von Hartmann but also to Leibniz, Schopenhauer, Samuel Butler and Höffding. In case

[3] In general, I would recommend, to any reader who wishes to preserve a negative picture of Freud, that he take care not to go back to the originals on which the accusation supposedly rests, for many a seemingly solid statement has been known to collapse, like a house of cards, under such treatment.

anyone may think that Levine's stress on some of the historical roots of the idea of the unconscious did escape Freud's attention, or that Levine's account may even have been published in the *Internationale Psychoanalytische Bibliothek* without Freud's consent, he may be assured that the last section, on Butler, was translated by Freud himself (Jones, 1954-1957, Vol. 3, p. 224).

Jones cited Meynert as a predecessor of Freud's division of the mind into two classes, and also of "the idea of wish fulfillment in the psychopathological processes." Freud (1900) himself cited Meynert at least six times in his works: once specifically in reference to the division of the mind (primary and secondary ego; p. 250); three times with regard to Meynert's amentia, which Freud used as a paradigm of "wish fulfillment in the psychopathological processes." But let us assume, once again, that Freud had never cited this former teacher of his. In 1932, Maria Dorer published a book, *Historische Grundlagen der Psychoanalyse* (Historical Foundations of Psychoanalysis). In this work she went into great detail about the influence that Meynert's theories had exercised on the development of Freud's fundamental views. The book was favorably reviewed by Heinz Hartmann (1933) in *Imago*, a journal edited by Freud, and there it was expressly recommended to analysts, even though the reviewer did not agree with some of the author's critique.[4]

Next on Jones's list stands Herbart (1776-1841). To be sure, he was cited by Freud only once; and since he aimed at a doctrine of the mechanics of 'mental presentations' (*Vorstellungen*) which rival, inhibit, weaken, or repress one another, he should, it would seem, have deserved more frequent citation by Freud.[5] At last we seem to have

[4] Hartmann (1956) came back to the same set of problems later, and clarified the function of tradition in Freud's work.

[5] I do not want to appear altogether to belabor Bailey's starting point of his Freud critique, since this may make the uninformed suspect that I am begging the question. The well-informed will, I am sure, agree with Kris, who can be instructively quoted here in so far as he casts grave doubt on the adequacy of the primary problem that Bailey raises: "The physiology of the brain which Freud took as his point of departure is as out-of-date as Herbart's mechanistic psychology, which Freud frequently took as his point of departure, as M. Dorer [1932] has convincingly shown. But the terms thus taken over into psycho-analysis have acquired new meanings which often have little to do with their original meanings. It was the stimulus provided by Herbart that caused Freud to be the first to replace Herbart's mechanistic psychology of association with a new one. The question of the origin of the terminology and fundamental assumptions of psycho-analysis . . . has nothing whatever to do with the question of the value of those assumptions and that terminology for psycho-analysis as a science." (Kris, in Freud, 1950, p. 47.)

caught the old master at his sinister game of pulling the wool over faithful Jones's eyes. However, Freud did not hesitate to accept for publication an article by von Karpinska (1914), *Über die psychologischen Grundlagen des Freudismus* (On the Psychological Foundations of Freudism), in which the similarities between psychoanalysis and experimental psychology are stressed. We find, for example, the following sentence: "As a starting point I shall take the deep-going (*tiefgreifende*) analogy that exists between Herbart and Freud which permits us directly to penetrate into Freud's views" (p. 309). How Freud succeeded in withholding this ominous sentence from Jones, who was a member of the editorial board, we shall probably never know.[6]

Dr. Bailey will not, I hope, assert that Freud left Jones ignorant of the influence on his work of Fechner, who is cited by Freud at least eleven times, for Jones himself reports, on this occasion, one of Freud's references to Fechner. Griesinger, who is cited by Freud at least four times, is also quite rightly listed by Jones.

That the sexual drive has been regarded as the prime mover in human behavior by many—"from Plato to Schopenhauer," as Jones says—is certainly an established fact; one wonders, therefore, how Freud succeeded in concealing this from Jones. At any rate, by 1929, A. J. Storfer had already published an article quoting from six passages in which Freud had affirmed the existence of historical connections between his findings and Plato's views, three of these referring directly to his libido theory. Furthermore, there are nine citations by Storfer of writings by others in which the similarities and dissimilarities between Plato and Freud had been discussed. And all these references go back to before 1929!

As to Schopenhauer, Freud himself enumerated in his autobiography three questions on which the philosopher anticipated Freud's findings (1925d, p. 59f.).[7] Besides, a merely superficial scanning of the literature reveals ten articles or other writings that appeared prior to Freud's death, dealing with the question of the relationship between Schopenhauer and

---

[6] It is an open question why Freud did not cite Herbart more frequently. He acknowledged Schopenhauer's priority with regard to repression (Freud, 1925d, p. 59), although Herbart might justifiably have been the one to be cited there. Bernfeld's discovery that Freud, during his high school years, used a psychology textbook that was based on Herbart's work, may be a clue, in so far as knowledge transmitted in this way is later on often not regarded as worthy of quotation.

[7] Freud even wrote of "the large extent to which psycho-analysis coincides with the philosophy of Schopenhauer," and he expressed himself in similar terms with regard to Nietzsche.

psychoanalysis, and at least eight doing the same thing with regard to Nietzsche.

That the pediatrician S. Lindner (1879), whom Jones also quotes to prove his point, was the first to describe the erotic quality of the infant's sucking, was stated by Freud, a fact which should certainly have been known to Bailey, since the reference also occurs in the three essays on sexuality (1905a).[8] Freud even went further. If Dr. Bailey had only been born a few years earlier, he might have heard Freud's 1909 lectures at Worcester, in the fourth of which Freud tried to impress on the audience the fact that, in a paper by Bell (1902), published three years earlier than his own three essays, the main points of the libido theory were anticipated (Freud, 1910e, p. 42).

It may be less well known that, contrary to the usual suppositions, Freud's technique of free association had its precursors, too. Jones quotes from Ludwig Börne (1786-1837), a German writer, and from Sir Francis Galton (1822-1911). He almost certainly obtained the former reference from a paper by Freud, first published anonymously in 1920 (b), but two years later included in a volume of his collected papers, in which Freud discussed very charmingly the influence which, during his youthful years, the perusal of a publication by Börne (1823) must have had on him.

In Galton's paper (1879-1880), we find—again?—one source that Freud seems definitely to have concealed from Jones—assuming, of course, that he had read it and still recalled it. It was Zilboorg (1952) who first demonstrated the historical importance of Galton's paper.[9] I would not be surprised if what actually happened was that Freud *had* read the paper, and had then forgotten about it; but surely no one without an initial bias could draw from such a situation the conclusion that Freud had withheld such information from Jones *deliberately*, and for the sake of *deception*.

How ready Freud was to let the public know about his own predecessors can be observed on another occasion, when he quite spontaneously called attention to a precursor who had gone unnoticed by others— this time with regard to the cathartic method. In 1930 (b), he referred to a passage in Goethe's correspondence, which makes it clear that

[8] Lindner's original article was reprinted in a psychoanalytic journal in 1934.

[9] It cannot be ascertained whether or not Freud did read Galton's paper. (Zilboorg, correctly remarks that this is not a decisive question with regard to the place of Galton's paper in the history of science [p. 494].)

Goethe had performed—about one hundred years before Freud—"a psychological feat" (Goethe, 1785), that may be regarded as a kind of miniature cathartic treatment.

Apparently Freud felt pleased whenever he could find a link between his own work and that of those who had taken part before him in the grand concert of Western cultural life; and it appears to be well documented that, with him, the desire to have historical truth recognized took precedence over whatever ambition he may have possessed to be acclaimed an original discoverer. The pleasure derived from making original discoveries was, of course, great at the beginning, but the concealment of sources would have been out of the question for Freud if only because—quite apart from his moral strictness—by citing predecessors, he would increase the chances for the acceptance of his assertions, most of which violated 'common sense.'

Yet I do not wish to assert that Freud's memory was perfect, or that he was always aware of all the external sources that had had a bearing on his work. I am speaking here of Freud's *character* and its *tendencies*.

His memory surely lapsed, as does that of other human beings, and few have ever reported their own lapses of memory as faithfully as Freud. Bry and Rifkind recently established one source for Freud's wish fulfillment theory of dreams that Freud had overlooked. They quote a passage from *Niels Lyhne,* the Danish novel written by Jens Peter Jacobsen (1847-1885), which contains Freud's basic idea, and which he read (cf. Freud, 1887-1902, p. 128) but never cited (Bry and Rifkind, 1962, p. 21).

Furthermore, the views of the historian often differ from those that Freud may have held, with regard to the validity of ancestral claims. Where the historian looks for similarity, *he* might have stressed that difference which, after all, always goes along with similarity. I should imagine that this would have occurred, for example, with regard to an appraisal of the influence of Meynert—who, I believe, remained within the confines of an organically oriented psychiatry, whereas Freud would have felt inclined to accept proof of ancestry only with respect to psychological formulations.

It is hard to understand how anyone, even someone only half-familiar with Freud's writings, could have any doubts as to the freedom with which he publicly acknowledged the sources of his work. The following quotation from The *Interpretation of Dreams* shows impressively with what degree of precision he appraised his contribution. I am referring to a subsection of the famous Chapter VII of his book on dreams, in some editions titled "The Reconciliation of Contradictions in the Doctrine of Dreams":

> My treatment of the problems of dreams has found room for the majority of these contradictory views [of the authorities that had investigated the psychology of dreams before Freud]. I have only found it necessary to give a categorical denial of two of them—the view that dreaming is a meaningless process and the view that it is a somatic one [Freud, 1900, p. 588].

In this way, he was acknowledging that what was original in his work was the evolvement of a psychic system in which all the findings (except two) that had been made by previous researchers in the field, but which had seemed hopelessly contradictory to each other, had found a logical, understandable, perhaps even necessary place. Those who understand the history of science will know that this state of affairs is true not only of Freud, but also of other "orderers," whom "every science has in the structure of history, one who first framed objective concepts widely enough to reorient its posture" (Gillispie, 1960, p. 202). Of Freud's book on dreams, one may say what the same author says of another among the Western galaxy: "Everything, indeed, or nearly everything that Galileo put together may be found in the writings . . . of some predecessor" (Gillispie, 1960, p. 7). Thus, if Freud was merely an 'ambitious' man, he would have had all the more reason to demonstrate that he was no foreign body in the history of Western ideas. His profusion of quotations, from Empedokles to Arthur Schnitzler, reveals his extraordinary power to synthesize the seemingly disparate.

Looking back now to my starting point, we may say once again that it might have been more to the point if Dr. Bailey had first checked to see whether Jones's surprise was really warranted. As far as I can recall, Jones did not repeat that same expression of surprise in the final form of his Freud biography. In any case, speaking quite generally, one may observe that the distance between Jones's surprise about some questions of the history of psychoanalysis, on the one hand, and giving serious consideration, on the other hand, to the question of possible 'deception' in Freud is not only enormous, it also fails to provide the basis for any illuminating connection with regard to Freud's character.

Dr. Bailey may have forgotten, or he may not have read, what sources of psychoanalysis Jones did have in mind; yet, he was able to recall a passage from Freud's letters to Fliess that struck him as being indicative of a personality capable of ready deception. One may, perhaps, be entitled ordinarily—that is, in the absence of sufficiently strong evidence to the contrary—to surmise the presence of some tendency to insincerity when a scientist stops reading because, as he himself is alleged to have asserted, "he found his own ideas expressed better than he could."

The discrepancy frequently to be found between quality of character and quality of achievement is an interesting psychoanalytic problem at the focus of present-day research; but Dr. Bailey was clearly not motivated by any such research interests, for the purely derogatory aim of his lecture already appears at this point, as can be seen from the fact that Freud never even wrote the sentence which Dr. Bailey erroneously (one may charitably assume) attributed to him.

Further study of the Fliess letters (Freud, 1887-1902) has not led to the discovery of any other passage with regard to Freud's 'not reading' but rather to the following:[10]

I do not want to read, because it stirs up too many thoughts and stints me of the satisfaction of discovery. In short, I am a wretched recluse. Apart from that, I am so exhausted that I must lay the whole thing[11] aside for a while [Oct. 8, 1895; p. 126].

Incidentally, what horrifies me more than anything else is all the psychology I shall have to read in the next few years. At the moment I can neither read nor think. I am sufficiently absorbed in observation. My self-analysis is stagnating again . . . [November 5, 1897; p. 228].

I am deep in the dream book [*The Interpretation of Dreams*] . . . If only one did not have to read! The literature on the subject, such as it is, is too much for me already. The only sensible thing on the subject was said by old Fechner in his sublime simplicity . . . [February 9, 1898; p. 244].

[10] Not trusting my own accuracy in a matter of such grave import—namely, the possibility of an outstanding scholar misquoting a deceased colleague in the process of raising doubts about the latter's honesty—I asked Miss Liselotte Bendix (an experienced librarian, whose help I acknowledge here with thanks) to make a careful check of the English edition of the Fliess letters. She too was not able to discover the sentence that Dr. Bailey attributed to Freud.

[11] Freud uses here, for his own work, the vernacular *Quark,* which is extremely pejorative. Apparently he was in one of those crises so characteristic of the years of his greatest creativity.

I certainly do not think of this version [the part of *The Interpretation* that Freud had sent to Fliess] as final. First I want to get my own ideas into shape, then I shall make a thorough study of the literature on the subject, and finally make such insertions or revisions as my reading will give rise to. So long as I have not finished my own work I cannot read, and it is only in writing that I can fill in all the details [March 24, 1898; p. 249].

The literature (on dreams) which I am now reading is reducing me to idiocy. Reading is·a terrible infliction imposed upon all who write. In the process everything of one's own drains away. I often cannot manage to remember what I have that is new, and yet it is all new. The reading stretches ahead interminably, so far as I can see at present [December 5, 1898; p. 270].

So the dreams will be done . . . . Alas! That the gods should have set up the existing literature on a subject to frighten off the would-be contributor to it! The first time I tackled it I got stuck, but this time I shall work my way through it; there is nothing that matters in it anyway. None of my work has been so completely my own as this [May 28, 1899; p. 281].[12]

And thus Freud ploughed his way through the at least seventy-eight publications cited in the bibliography of the first edition of his *magnum opus,* and wrote that beautiful chapter on "The Scientific Literature on Dreams," a masterpiece of organization and the synthesis of a huge mass of literature into a single unit.

Yet Dr. Bailey, unduly preoccupied with Freud's reading habits, as it seems to me, considered the matter important enough to take it up once again five years later. In 1961, he said: "Sigmund Freud became reluctant to read, as he tells in his letters to Fliess, and rarely referred to what he read: 'I do not want to read, because it stirs up too many thoughts and stints me of the satisfaction of discovery. In Lipps I have rediscovered my own principles quite clearly stated—perhaps rather more so than suits me' " (Bailey, 1961, p. 216).

One sees at once what Dr. Bailey is aiming at, which is why a trust-

---

[12] The following quotation is also of interest here: "This plunging myself up to the neck in psychological literature is depressing. It gives me the feeling that I do not know anything instead of having grasped something new. Another unfortunate thing is that one cannot keep up this reading and note-making activity for more than a few hours a day" (June 9, 1899; p. 283).

ing reader may be more than surprised—indeed, may even be shocked—upon discovering that the two sentences which Bailey has put into direct sequence were actually separated by 136 pages of the printed text and a time interval of over two and a half years. The first sentence will be found in my previous quotation of Freud's letter of October 8, 1895, and needs no further comment. Before quoting the full context of the second sentence, I wish to call the reader's attention to a remark Freud had made about Lipps five days earlier. "I have set myself," he wrote to Fliess, "the task of making a bridge between my germinating metapsychology and what is in the books, and I have therefore plunged into the study of Lipps, whom I suspect [the German word translated as "suspect" is *ahnen*, for which a more appropriate translation would be "have a hunch"] of being the best mind among present-day philosophical writers" (August 26, 1898; Freud, 1887-1902, p. 260f.). On August 31, 1898, he had the following to add:

> The psychology is going better. In Lipps I have rediscovered my own principles quite clearly stated—perhaps rather more so than suited me. "The seeker often finds more than he seeks." Lipps regards consciousness as only a sense organ, the contents of the mind as ideation, and all mental processes as unconscious. In details the correspondence is close too; perhaps the divergence on which I shall be able to base my own contribution, will come later. I have read only about a third of him. I got stuck at the treatment of tone-relations, with which I always had trouble, lacking the most elementary knowledge of the subject because of my stunned acoustic sensibility [Freud, 1887-1902, p. 262f.].

I assume that Dr. Bailey, in alleging that Freud "rarely referred" to his sources, was not aware that Lipps is cited thirty-seven times in Freud's works after 1900.[13]

I have deliberately gone into great detail about what Freud wrote re-

[13] Even if Dr. Bailey always abided by the traditional academic standards with regard to the making of generalizations, that in itself would probably not lift appreciably the measure of his quotations and of their contribution to a discussion. For his seeming modesty (to which he refers when he says: "If I quote others, it is because I also find my ideas better expressed by them" [1961, p. 216]) allows him to introduce one quotation after another, utilizing them uncritically, and often rather indiscriminately, *so long as each quotation contains something detrimental to psychoanalysis.* He thereby reveals a somewhat incredible lack of familiarity with excellent studies (of which I want to refer only to the two by Axelrad [1956, 1962]), which prove incisively that quotations per se are worse than meaningless, unless the validity and relevance of their contents have been scrupulously checked. This is, however, a precaution which Dr. Bailey seems rather rigorously to abstain from—perhaps on principle?

garding his struggle with an unwieldy body of literature. It is an exquisite illustration for a sensitive mind of the pain and agony inherent in the creative process. What a chance Dr. Bailey missed because of paramnesia!

Dr. Bailey also complains that the close examination of Freud's works has cost him "much fruitless travail" (p. 388). I do not know how far he progressed in his studies; he may really have stopped altogether too early —unless he meant it as a joke when he wrote (p. 393): "Although I thoroughly detested my father, I could not then, or since, find any trace in my unconscious of a desire to murder him in order to replace him in my mother's bed."

When Georg Brandes (1842-1927), the great Danish critic and historian of literature, visited Freud, part of their conversation ran as follows: " 'But there is one thing I should like to say to you: I never had any sexual feeling for my mother.' 'But there's no need at all for you to have been conscious of it,' was my [Freud's] reply; 'such processes are unconscious in grown-up people.' 'Oh, so *that's* your idea,' he said; I heard later that . . . he . . . liked to make use of what was for him a new word—'repression' " (Italics by Freud, 1933a, p. 190f.). May I add that candidates risk flunking out at a *bona fide* psychoanalytic institute if they do not know that repression is a function of the unconscious part of the ego—a discovery which Brandes, even though he was not himself a neurologist, had integrated well.

Furthermore, one has the right to expect that anyone who set out to judge Freud and his work would know at least as much about psychoanalysis as a reader of the *Encyclopaedia Britannica* knows, in which Freud wrote that obsessional states can be successfully treated by psychoanalysis (Freud, 1926b, p. 264). Surely, no one who had read that article could seriously reproduce a translator's mistake, as Bailey does in wrongly quoting Freud as having said that psychoanalysis is powerless against obsessions (Bailey, p. 397, n. 1), when Freud, in reality, had spoken of delusions (Freud, 1916-1917, p. 255).[14]

Gillispie (1960) says about Copernicus and the heliocentric theory: "Stock objections blocked assent for about a century and to rehearse them will suggest how strongly his ideas had to swim upstream against

---

[14] The translator's mistake can be found in G. Stanley Hall's translation, published by Boni and Liveright, p. 220. How right Dr. Bailey was when he wrote: "One of the brighter of the younger men recently confessed to me that he could read no other language than English. What a frustrating handicap to overcome!" (1956, p. 391).

the side of common sense" (p. 19). It seems evident that the one hundred years that a correct and meaningful theory may need, in order to be fully fought out by minor or major minds, are not yet over, as far as Freud's theory of personality is concerned.[15]

II

I shall now turn to a book by two authors (Gicklhorn and Gicklhorn, 1960), who investigated Freud's academic career at the University of Vienna.

Since I am burdened with an indirect responsibility for the publication of the Gicklhorns' book, the reader will permit me to try to set the record straight, and to correct some of the authors' many erroneous interpretations of documents which they have published for the first time, as well as to refute their denial of a well-documented episode that took place during Freud's academic career. I have felt induced to do this all the more in view of the friendly review that the Gicklhorns' book has recently received in this country, and particularly since that reviewer took the opportunity to make some general remarks highly adverse to Freud and to psychoanalysts (Sherwood, 1962). For example, he informs us that the contents of the Gicklhorns' publication "differ so materially from the story Freud himself and his pupils would have us believe that we must wonder if the half-truths, distortions, and falsifications are errors or deliberate propaganda" (p. 235).

The reviewer seems to be quite unaware that Freud himself published scarcely anything on this question, and that the Gicklhorns assert repeatedly that the newly published documents have previously been unknown to any of Freud's biographers, and some very relevant ones among them unknown even to Freud. How analysts could have used them previously, therefore, in forming their image of Freud, only the reviewer can explain.

Before making statements such as, "Perhaps it is, then, only natural that his [Freud's] school should continue in its writings to forego the study of reality and take liberties with evidence and proof" (p. 237), the reviewer might have taken into consideration the fact that the collec-

---

[15] The period required for the acceptance of Freud's theories and discoveries may take even longer than a century. René de Messières (1933, p. 50, n. 3) notes that William Harvey's famous discovery of the mechanism of the circulation of the blood (1616) was still being rejected in 1672 at the *Faculté de Paris*, whereas Molière, in his *Le Malade Imaginaire* (1673), took Harvey's side.

tion of these documents and others was undertaken at the initiative of the Sigmund Freud Archives, and that the Archives made a grant previously in order to carry out this project—all of which the authors plainly state in their preface (Gicklhorn and Gicklhorn, 1960, p. xi).

What the reviewer could not know (because the authors did not mention it) is that their attention was called to the need for research on Freud, and that they were introduced to their work about Freud by the late Siegfried Bernfeld (1892-1953), one of Freud's outstanding pupils, and the author of several very incisive essays on selected chapters in Freud's life (Bernfeld 1944, 1946, 1951; Bernfeld and Bernfeld 1944, 1949, 1952). It was he who engaged them to do the spadework for his biographical studies, so rudely interrupted by his untimely death.

From the (unpublished) Bernfeld-Gicklhorn correspondence,[16] it is evident that Bernfeld guided the Gicklhorns step by step, and that, with admirable ingenuity and resourcefulness, for both of which he was renowned, he made a series of constructive suggestions as to what to look for and where to look for it. He made it clear to the Gicklhorns (e.g., in his unpublished letters of May 4 and October 19, 1951), that it was not his intention to idealize Freud, but that he was eager to collect—even from those who had opposed Freud—data for the time up to the year 1906, beyond which the trickle of reliable biographical data becomes a broad stream.

It goes without saying that the Archives were not founded with any idea of honoring or idealizing Freud—since his giant stature has become clear enough, and does not need those honors with which we try to console smallness—but solely out of fear lest irreplaceable documents might be lost and the task of the future biographer rendered unsolvable thereby.

Thus analysts have contributed their share toward living up to the psychoanalytic tradition of serving the truth, and the reviewer's derogatory remarks are wholly unfounded. (He also must have overlooked, by the way, the statement by the Gicklhorns [1960, p. 63] that "an integral part" of their material was on view at the Freud Centenary Exhibit in Chicago.[17])

When the first signs of Dr. Bernfeld's fatal illness were already weak-

[16] This correspondence is in the possession of The Sigmund Freud Archives. I owe thanks to the late Mrs. S. Bernfeld for permission to quote from it.

[17] See Freud Centenary Exhibit (1956) nos. 31-39, pp. 37-40; nos. 49-60, pp. 42-44. Even Prof. J. Gicklhorn's chart (see later), which seems so damaging to Freud, was on exhibit (without correction of its errors, because of the shortness of time).

ening his boundless energy, he recommended Prof. Gicklhorn, who already had to his credit the discovery of two important Freud manuscripts (Freud, 1955, 1956), as well as the many documents collected for the Bernfelds. Under such auspicious circumstances, I did not hesitate, as Secretary of the Sigmund Freud Archives, to propose Prof. Gicklhorn for research to the Archives Board, from whom he received every assistance that he requested. A penetrating historical analysis—clarifying a point that Bernfeld and Jones had both misunderstood—of the first paper that Freud published as a student (Gicklhorn, 1955) seemed to me to justify my recommendation.

Thus, I was astonished when I read Prof. Gicklhorn's writing on Wagner-Jauregg's relationship to Freud (1957), for it was replete with errors, misunderstandings, and unwarranted attacks against Freud's character. Unfortunately, Prof. Gicklhorn died shortly thereafter, and my rebuttal (1958a) was never read by him. I was even more surprised, however, when Mrs. Gicklhorn published a paper (1958), in which she tried to challenge the accuracy, on quite inadequate grounds, of the account of a well-documented episode in Freud's university career, throwing in additional remarks derogatory to Freud, Sachs, and Jones. In the recent book by the Gicklhorns, there are once again so many errors, unproven conclusions, and defamatory statements about Freud, Jones, Sachs, and analysts in general, that I deeply regret having contributed indirectly to this work, and wish to apologize, therefore, not only to the members of the Board of the Sigmund Freud Archives, but also to any other colleagues who are interested in historical truth. The documents published in the book are nevertheless important to biographers of Freud, and I shall now discuss the relevant points, in so far as they have been used by both author and reviewer to present a false picture of Freud's personality and character.

1. *The analysts' alleged condoning of legends about Freud and Freud's alleged condoning of a bribe:* Sachs is called a liar, the inventor of a fairy tale, and Freud is charged with having let himself be deceived by a patient's desire to make herself important (Gicklhorn, 1958)—all because the former reported an episode (Sachs, 1944, p. 78) of which Freud had told him, with respect to the way in which he became an associate professor at the University of Vienna in 1902. The event in question had to do with the donation of a painting to a public gallery by a patient of Freud's, in order to induce the Minister of Education,

Wilhelm Freiherr von Hartel,[18] to submit the decree of appointment (made by the University College of Professors in 1897) to the Emperor for the latter's signature.[19]

The reviewer seems to be in full agreement with the author and, like her, adds expressions of personal disapproval of the behavior of Freud and his followers: "On the one hand—and this throws a strange light on Freud himself and on his biographers—they allowed a legend to grow which has it that the Minister had to be bribed; a grateful patient had to give him a precious *Böckling* [sic!] painting, for a public gallery in order to obtain favors for Freud. Actually, the picture is now known never to have changed hands until it was confiscated by the Nazis, and, in the first place, never belonged to Freud's patient" (Sherwood, 1962, p. 237).

How did Mrs. Gicklhorn prove that this traditional story was wrong? While Sachs and Jones affirmed that the donation was a painting by Böcklin, the Gicklhorns proved, by elaborate inquiries, that no Böcklin had ever been donated to the gallery, and that the painting in question has remained in the possession of the patient's aunt. This is, however, in accordance with Freud's letter to Fliess of March 11, 1902, to which no reference can be found in Mrs. Gicklhorn's 1958 piece; in it Freud described the episode, saying: "I believe that *if* a certain Böcklin had been in her [the patient's] possession *instead* of that of her aunt . : . . I should have been appointed three months earlier" (italics mine; Freud, 1887-1902, p. 343).[20] The content of Freud's letter, however, does confirm the chief point made by Sachs and Jones.

An unbiased reader will, I trust, consider Jones's and Sachs's paramnesia with regard to the painter's name to be pardonable, and call it an error rather than a lie, since the question of who was the painter of the donated painting is of secondary importance. Still, the Archives was interested in his identity, for Freud continued that *"as it is"* (italics

[18] For a summary of von Hartel's career, see footnote 74, at the end of this appendix.

[19] Jones confirmed the fact that Freud had told him of the same incident, although there are differences in the versions given by Sachs and Jones (Jones, 1954-1957, Vol. 1, p. 339f.).

[20] It is clear from this passage that it would be unnecessary to investigate the possibility of a Böcklin donation. Apparently, Sachs and Jones made an error in their recollection of what Freud had told them. No doubt, Freud did speak of a Böcklin in this context; but they seem to have recalled the contents of a *conditional* sentence as though it referred to a *matter of fact*. Sachs published his book prior to the publication of the Fliess letters; Jones, on the other hand, apparently felt so certain that, in writing the biography, he did not consult the Fliess letters to verify this particular point.

mine), the Minister would have to be satisfied with "a modern picture," Böcklin (1827-1901) apparently not being considered modern any longer at that time. The late Valerie Reich succeeded in finding out that it was a painting by Emil Orlik (1870-1932) that was donated by Freud's patient, in 1902, to the gallery in question.

In my rebuttal of Mrs. Gicklhorn's paper (1958b), all this was set forth; I even called the Fliess letter to her attention, for it was apparently unknown to her. In view of Freud's contemporaneous description of the event, and in view of the finding of the 1902 donation deed of Freud's patient, one might think that the matter was closed. But no, in their 1960 book, Mrs. Gicklhorn[21] once again goes through the whole matter, asserting that Jones and Sachs were in error, and 'proving' that it could not have been a Böcklin.[22]

At this point, it seems to me, a conscientious reviewer should have wondered how the author could disregard Freud's own letter in her discussion, clinging instead to her 1958 thesis, and without stating any of her reasons for assuming that an event described in a contemporaneous document—and by someone directly involved—did not happen in reality. Instead, the reviewer uses this nonsense as part of his reason for gratuitously accusing a whole professional group of bad faith.

It is still more surprising when the reviewer (Sherwood, 1962) raises the following rhetorical question, in which is embedded a grave accusation against Freud's character: "Is it not strange that Freud would condone bribery, if not actually solicit it, and is it not strange that in his ignorance of the fight between Faculty and Minister he or his friends knew the right target?" Did the reviewer really raise this question in

[21] Prof. Gicklhorn finished the manuscript in October 1957, and died the following month. Since, in one section, direct reference is made to the material that I have published since then, while in another section an opinion is expressed that differs essentially from one voiced previously by one of the authors (Gicklhorn, 1957), but which comes quite close to my own (Eissler, 1958a), it is evident that Prof. Gicklhorn is not responsible for all parts of the book, and therefore I shall on occasion refer to Mrs. Gicklhorn as the author of the book.

[22] Since all of this has to do with an event which—aside from its present use to denigrate the character of honest people—can hardly be regarded as more than a mere triviality, one will call the whole situation nightmarish. An author tries to prove, by way of an error in a second-hand report on a single detail, that an event in toto never took place—without so much as citing the historical source in which the same event is described without error. When this is called to her attention, she repeats the same fairy tale, this time citing at least part of the document, but again denying the whole event, and still without one word of explanation as to why the document should not be accepted as a valid historical source.

good faith, driven by a psychological or historical interest, and without any defamatory implication?

If he were really interested, I would advise him to do what he should have done before writing his review—namely, to read the Fliess letters, in which he will find that part which Mrs. Gicklhorn, for obvious reasons, left out in her book, and from which he will learn that Professor Exner[23] was the source of information. After 1894, Exner was the powerful representative of the College of Professors in the Ministry, and should therefore have known what delayed the confirmation of Freud's appointment, and what might be done about it. It was he who told Freud about "personal influence which appeared to be at work against me" with von Hartel, and *"advised me to seek a personal counter-influence"* (Freud, 1887-1902, p. 343; italics mine).

My question as to whether or not this reviewer acted in good faith was, I suppose, unnecessary. I am certain that, in attempting to follow his reasoning, the reader must have been reminded of the ancient story, in which a defendant claims never to have borrowed a pot, but to have returned it and at that, undamaged, even though it had a hole when he borrowed it. With similar consistency, Sherwood asserts first that no painting was ever donated, and that the episode was invented by Freud and his followers, and then, in the same breath, that Freud condoned such a donation, and thus condoned a criminal action. *Difficile est satiram non scribere;* and I, for my part, feel compelled to ask: Is the reviewer ignorant of the Aristotelian syllogism; or does he favor Plutarch's *audacter calumniare, semper aliquid haeret?*

Yet, since the episode was not invented, but did actually happen, I also have to discuss the implication of bribery. Mrs. Gicklhorn writes as if the episode, assuming that it did happen, would have signified a bribe. In my rebuttal (1958b), I disputed this interpretation, for facts themselves make it evident that no bribe was involved. First, the Minister was induced to do something that was within the law—if anything, prescribed by the law.[24] Second, no personal gain accrued to the Minister,

[23] Sigmund R. von Exner, Professor of Physiology at the University of Vienna, formerly Assistant at von Brücke's Institute of Physiology, where Freud worked from 1876-1882, and where he started his scientific career (cf. Freud, 1925d, p. 9: ". . . men . . . whom I could respect and take as my models: the great Brücke himself, and his assistants, Sigmund Exner . . .").

[24] In my understanding of the matter, the Minister had the right to withhold confirmation of the appointment. This, however, was against tradition, unless the reasons for withholding were conveyed to the College of Professors; but it seems that no legal procedure was provided that could have been used to compel a Minister to submit an

since the donation was made to a public institution, and at one point Freud made sure that this would be understood by Fliess. Third, as the author now claims—and perhaps rightly so—the value of the donated Orlik painting was minimal. We can thus safely dismiss the matter of the bribe,[25] while still suggesting that Mrs. Gicklhorn may have underestimated the value that the painting had in the donor's, although not necessarily in the Minister's eyes.[26]

I cannot forgo the citation of further documentation, although a reasonable reader may have, by this time, become convinced that Freud was not a spreader of legends when he conveyed to Sachs and Jones an account of the episode in question. According to Freud's letter to Fliess, he told Exner of his friendship with Elise Gomperz, wife of Theodor Gomperz (1832-1912), who was a colleague of von Hartel on the Faculty. Exner approved of her intercession with the Minister (1887-1902, p. 343); yet it evidently did not suffice. The documentary proof of the correctness of this detail becomes irrefragable with the publication of two letters by Freud to Elise Gomperz, dated November 25, 1901 and December 8, 1901 (Freud, 1873-1939, pp. 241-244), in which Freud thanks Mrs. Gomperz for what she has done on his behalf, and again mentions that Exner "knew of my plan to accept your assistance and encouraged me to do so." More can also be found in that letter about von Hartel's behavior. Freud had made his acquaintance four and a half years earlier, when "he professed to have heard 'excellent things' about

appointment for signature to the Emperor, or to force the latter to make the appointment. For example, the Emperor had, between 1895 and 1896, three times refused confirmation even of the duly elected Mayor of Vienna, finally doing so only in 1897. See Billroth (1886, p. 42) about the various ways in which appointments to professorships could come about. The Emperor, as well as the Minister, had the right to accept or to reject any nomination submitted to the College.

[25] Apparently, aside from Mrs. Gicklhorn and the reviewer, only Martin Freud in his Memoirs (1957, p. 74) referred to the episode as a bribe (see Gicklhorn and Gicklhorn, 1960, p. 21f.); yet it is questionable whether he meant this seriously, for at two points he speaks of an "amiable intrigue" (p. 73f.). Sachs called it "a bargain" (1944, p. 78).

[26] Thieme-Becker (1932, p. 51) and Vollmer (1956, p. 522) record four outstanding museums that bought works by Orlik, at least five shows in which he exhibited, and over 110 bibliographic references. In 1900, Richard Muther—in his days the greatest, even though a questionable, authority on the history of painting—published a favorable article on Orlik, which certainly was an excellent recommendation to the public. I owe to Dr. Hans Aurenhammer (Österreichische Gallerie, Vienna) the information that "Orlik was one of the most respected [angesehenst] graphic artists of his time, primarily in Germany." The subject of the Orlik painting was "Church in Auscha." I am indebted to Dr. Otto Kallir (New York) for the information that it was never recorded in the Museum's catalogues. Dr. Aurenhammer informs me that, nevertheless, the painting was probably on exhibition, although the times when it was shown cannot be ascertained any longer.

me"; nevertheless he asserted, when Elise Gomperz spoke to him, that he did not know who Freud was.

When Freud's patient became interested in the matter, the chances of Freud's academic advancement improved immeasurably, since this patient was closely related to three wealthy and powerful Viennese families, and therefore stood high in Vienna's social elite. She herself was a well-known socialite with high prestige. Now a Minister is not only a person who is sought out for the sake of the influence he can exert; he is also a person who seeks connections himself. Thus the patient's interest was, in all probability, a matter of no little concern to the Minister. Of course, she could not impose upon him at their first meeting, but as soon as she had succeeded in getting acquainted with him, "a mutual woman friend" interceded with the Minister on her behalf (Freud, 1887-1902, p. 343). Then the patient herself took up her request with the Minister; it may be on this second occasion that he dropped a remark with respect to his interest in the Böcklin painting, then in the possession of the patient's aunt.[27]

The Gicklhorns try to prove that the so-called Böcklin episode could not have been of any relevance to the confirmation of Freud's professorship, because it had been decided positively previously. In 1958 (p. 16) Mrs. Gicklhorn—without offering any proof—asserted that the decree had already been prepared for the Emperor's signature by that time; in 1960 (p. 23), in order to prove their point, the Gicklhorns set forth the *non sequitur* that the Minister of Education had decided upon the stipulation of advancement in 1898.

One has only to turn again to Freud's letter of December 8, 1901, to Elise Gomperz, to find that the authors are quite wrong. There one can find a literal quotation of a part of a letter that Professor Exner had sent Freud (Freud, 1873-1939, p. 243), in which he let him know that he had spoken to the Minister about Freud, that the Minister had acknowledged

---

[27] I do not see any reason to assume that Freud's professorship was totally dependent upon the donation. It would help the reconstruction if the Minister's relationship to the patient's aunt were known (Sachs's [1944, p. 78] remark about that relationship is not reliable). Had he once before suggested the donation to her, and asked for the niece's support? Or did he try to use the patient as an intermediary to find out what were the chances for such a donation? When the patient had to report that her endeavor had failed, she—I would guess—promised the donation of the Orlik, as a gesture of good will. Is it conceivable that the Minister would have been boorish enough to renege on a service toward which he, even though he had never pledged it, had nevertheless expressed himself as favorably inclined? He certainly would have proven himself to be rather discourteous, aside from his being indefensibly prejudiced, if he had withheld the decree any longer from the emperor's signature.

Elise Gomperz's intercession, and that he (Exner) regarded Freud's advancement as questionable in the near future, and possibly even after a year's lapse.

Since most of the details regarding the painting transaction were known to Freud only second-hand, one may surmise that his patient was trying to ingratiate herself by exaggeration or distortion. However, when we read that the Minister had promised that the patient "would be the first to hear when the matter was completed," and that she came one day "to her appointment beaming and waving an express letter from the Minister" (Freud, 1887-1902, p. 344), we can be certain that Freud read the letter and saw the Minister's signature.

We can also surmise that Freud's professorship had become a matter of secondary importance to the Minister, while his desire to find favor with Freud's patient was primary. At the same time, this very element cuts the ground out from under any probability of a bribe, for a corrupt person would, only in the rarest circumstances, be so insane as to gratuitously provide evidence as incriminating as this letter would have been, if there had been a bribe.

All the details of Freud's letter to Fliess, in so far as they can be documented, have been confirmed. Elise Gomperz *had* spoken to the Minister; Exner *had* reported that this intervention was not sufficient; the patient's aunt *did* possess a Böcklin, and it was *not* donated; the patient herself *did* donate a painting by "a modern painter"—all, just as Freud recorded it.

The whole incident was trivial, and of a kind which, I am sure, happened over and over again—not only in the capital of the Austrian monarchy (based as it was on aristocratic division, and already obsolete, being by that time only seventeen years short of its dissolution), but also in flourishing democratic republics, and even in ancient Athens and Rome. The incident itself makes a good story: it is colorful, it has an angle of humor, and I can well imagine how Freud chuckled in telling it to his friends during later years.

In his letter to Fliess, it is of quite subordinate importance, for the main point he tried to convey to his friend was that he did not get the title of professor solely (or at all) in recognition of his merits as a scientist, but through the use of *Protektion* (which is translated approximately as 'favoritism acquired through connections'—or, in brief, 'pull'). Anyone who has even a superficial knowledge of Imperial Vienna must know of the weight of this factor, as all-important as it was elusive.

In 1902, upon going to Exner, Freud felt humiliated that reality had forced him to 'do as the Romans do,'[28] and his letter to Fliess was tantamount to a confession to a friend who had congratulated him upon what he had mistakenly regarded as a sign of recognition. How happy Freud would have been, if the title he had at last obtained had really been, as Fliess thought, entirely the result of recognition of his work!

2. *Freud's character and the traveling scholarship of 1885.* The reviewer (Sherwood, 1962) writes:

> Freud applied for a travelling scholarship; it stipulated that its holder should continue and expand studies in his special field, and that this should be done at a German language university. What Freud did is well known—he went to Paris; he attached himself to Charcot, who lectured on hysteria and hypnosis, neither of which can be said to have much to do with Freud's specialty, neuropathology . . . . The resultant report to the Faculty (with whom he had quarreled by correspondence during his absence over the monies involved) contains items which the Faculty overlooked with remarkable graciousness, amongst them allegations that Vienna could provide no patient material such as the Salpêtrière, and that he could not expect to learn much essentially new at a German university: be this true or not, it shows neither diplomacy nor tact [p. 236].

The reader could never guess from this that the stipulation of Freud's traveling award was that the candidate should attend a "foreign, *preferably* German university" (Gicklhorn and Gicklhorn, 1960, p. 73; italics mine),[29] without which reservation Freud would never have been able to submit his application, in which he, of course, stated *expressis verbis* that he planned to go to Charcot in Paris. If Sherwood thinks that it was tactless of Freud to state in his report that "Vienna could provide no patient material such as the Salpêtrière," he should have added that this was precisely one of the reasons why Freud had been granted the schol-

[28] How badly Freud felt about having to use 'pull' in a matter in which he was convinced that his own merits warranted the reward can also be seen from his letters to Elise Gomperz, in which, in a seemingly facetious way, he calls himself a "climber," but then, writing in a vein that reflects his bitter, not to say tragic feelings, goes on to exclaim: "May I never be in a position to return it [the favor she had done him]! This is the best expression of gratitude I can think of" (Freud, 1873-1939, p. 242).

[29] Here, again, is an example of the unreliability of the Gicklhorns. On page 10, one reads that "in the charter only *German* universities were provided" (italics by the authors). Were the Gicklhorns so sure that all readers would act as Sherwood did, not finishing the book and thus not reading the charter which they themselves reproduced on page 73?

arship, for Freud had raised that very point in his application to the College of Professors (Gicklhorn and Gicklhorn, 1960, p. 77).

Sherwood might also have shown that, as Freud states in his report, in going to Charcot, he was following a suggestion made by von Brücke,[30] the very man who had vigorously sponsored his candidacy in the decisive meeting of the Faculty (Gicklhorn and Gicklhorn, 1960, p. 83; M. Freud 1957, p. 3). When Sherwood regards it as offensive of Freud to say that "he could not expect to learn much essentially new at a German university" (p. 236), he is misunderstanding the passage, which, by the way, is one of those linguistic gems for which Freud's style has become famous. What Freud actually wrote was that, after "having enjoyed direct and indirect instruction in Vienna from Professors T. Meynert and H. Nothnagel,"[31] he "was bound to reflect that I could not expect to learn anything essentially new at a German university" (M. Freud, 1957, p. 2)—which, in the light of the traditional rivalry between Austria and Germany, was the greatest compliment he could pay, not only to his two teachers, but indirectly to the whole Faculty.[32]

3. *Freud and his alleged negligence of duties at the University of Vienna.* The reviewer summarizes, somewhat inexactly, an important section of the book as follows:

> Freud's efforts to meet his teaching obligations remained sporadic and dubious; courses were announced and cancelled and he went far below the permissible minimum of teaching activity without having his venia legendi (the privilege to teach) revoked. . . . When the time came for Freud to be proposed for an "extraordinary professorship" (something like an associate professor), he was proposed by the college of professors, even though he had neglected his official teaching duties [p. 236].

No reader could even guess from Sherwood's summary that Freud never once cancelled an announced lecture (at least as far as the documents show); that prior to 1917, there were only a few semesters in which he announced in the University catalogue that he would not lecture, which it was his right to do, and which was quite accepted in

[30] Ernst Wilhelm von Brücke (1819-1892), outstanding physiologist; Professor of Physiology at the University of Vienna.

[31] Theodor Meynert (1833-1892) was Professor of Psychiatry in Vienna, and Hermann Nothnagel (1841-1905) Professor of Medicine.

[32] For a disproof of Sherwood's allegation that Freud devoted his work in Paris to topics outside his specialty, see later.

elective courses of little importance to the student body.[33] From the book, the reviewer could not, of course, know with what vigor and tenacity Freud struggled to overcome the obstacles that stood in his way as a lecturer (see below).

The question basically at issue is the following: In 1897, the College of Professors elected Freud Extraordinary Professor; yet the Ministry confirmed the appointment only in 1902. This was an unduly long delay, and, in a previous section I have discussed the events that at last induced von Hartel, the Minister of Education, to comply with the request of the College. In view of the strong anti-Semitic tendencies at the University of Vienna, which had started at least during World War I, if not earlier, and the unfriendly attitude that psychoanalysis met with both within and outside the academic institutions in Vienna, Sachs and Jones were both practically certain that the delay in Freud's appointment was caused primarily by these two factors.[34] It is the merit of the archival studies of the Gicklhorns that documents were found that suggested a hitherto unknown explanation of the first two years of the delay.[35]

To put a rather complicated affair into the simplest terms, in 1897 a disagreement took place between the Ministry and the College of Professors—the former wanting to confirm extraordinary professorships, which were salaried, only in the case of those *Dozenten*[36] who were so closely attached to university institutions that one might consider them to be prospective full professors. Those *Dozenten* who did not fulfill

[33] The reviewer's mistake is probably caused by his confusing columns II and III in Figure 12 of the Gicklhorn book, and by his unawareness that 'to cancel' has a different connotation in English from that of the German *absagen*, in the particular context he is referring to.

[34] The Gicklhorns go far in their castigation of Jones and Sachs for making the reference that they did to anti-Semitism. It is not clear why this error of fifteen years, at best, regarding the onset of the movement is considered by them to be such an outrage. After all, in the last decade of the nineteenth century, Vienna elected a mayor who was widely known for his anti-Semitism; the famous Schönerer affair took place around that time; and Billroth, one of the most famous members of the College of Professors, had once publicly admitted his anti-Semitism—all factors that make the error in timing understandable. Or did the authors want to imply that the University of Vienna was altogether free of anti-Semitism, as the century started to unfold?

[35] However, neither the Gicklhorns nor the reviewer seem to be acquainted with Ernst Kris's excellent introduction and footnotes to the Fliess letters. There the historical situation was quite correctly described: Kris attributed the delay in Freud's academic advancement solely to the policy of the Ministry of Education (Freud, 1887-1902, p. 200, fn. 3).

[36] The academic hierarchy was divided into *Privatdozent, ausserordentlicher* (extraordinary) *Professor, and ordentlicher* (full) *Professor.*

this condition, but nevertheless deserved advancement as a reward for their research or teaching, would obtain only the *title* of Extraordinary Professor, which did not carry a salary. It took from one to two years to get this set-up working, within which time all the *Dozenten*, except Freud, received either one or the other professorship.

The question remains open, therefore, why Freud was not given the title of Professor after the disagreement between the College of Professors and the Ministry was finally straightened out; why, although all other nominees were appointed, Freud was passed over; and why he might well have had to wait even longer, if the 'bribe' had not come to pass. Since the Gicklhorns chose to ignore the information available in the Fliess letter, they had to offer a new theory—that Freud failed in the teaching aspects of his position as a Dozent.[37] As the result of their laborious work in checking thousands of forms and other documents, the Gicklhorns express the certainty that Freud, during the thirty-three semesters between his appointment as *Dozent* and his appointment as Professor (the period of chief significance in this context), lectured during only thirteen semesters.[38]

Not being an archivist myself, I am, of course, not prepared to decide whether the Gicklhorns used proper methods of archival research in their investigation. However, the results of their research, at least as presented in summary form in their Figure 12, deserve criticism. Of the many inaccuracies and contradictions that one can discover in their Table, I want to discuss only two, because these are serious enough to throw into question the creditability of their work per se, quite aside from the frequent ineptitude of their interpretations.

The main part of the table consists of four columns, to one or the other of which each semester of Freud's teaching is assigned: (1) Lectures announced and held; (2) lectures announced and not held; (3) no lectures announced; (4) no information available. The decisive col-

[37] At the Central European universities, anyone who had obtained a doctorate could apply, when he was able to submit evidence of original and significant research in the form of publications, for the highly prized title of *Privatdozent*. A *Dozent* had the obligation to give lectures (throughout the semester) on a topic of his own choosing, within the area in which he had established himself, and he was expected, although not obliged, to continue his research.

[38] Of the twenty semesters missed, three are *prima facie* accounted for, since Freud announced for the summer semesters of 1886 and 1901, and for the winter semester of 1899-1900, that he would not hold lectures, which it was quite legitimate for a lecturer to do. In what follows, I shall discuss only the remaining seventeen 'unaccounted for' semesters. I also wish to emphasize that, whenever the term 'lecture' is used in this section, a *semestral course of lectures* is meant.

umn is column two: lectures announced and not held. A mistake seems to have been made for the summer semester of 1900, which is put into column two, even though Freud (1887-1902, p. 320) wrote of lecturing to an audience of three during that semester. The following mistake—which also betrays a truly disheartening ignorance of the basic events in the history of psychoanalysis—concerns the winter semester of 1915-1916, which is also put in column two, in spite of the fact that, during that semester, Freud held the first part of his *Introductory Lectures*—which, after being translated into all civilized languages, must now exist in book form in seven-place numbers.[39] Furthermore, on November 23, 1915, Freud wrote to Ferenczi that his audience had mounted to over a hundred (Jones, 1954-1957, Vol. 2, p. 218).

Yet there are other points which also speak against the correctness of the authors' findings. When Freud writes to Fliess in March 1899 that he has given up his lectures that year (1887-1902, p. 280), this surely sounds as if not lecturing during a semester was a rather exceptional occurrence for Freud, at least at that time. Furthermore, in the report on Freud submitted to the Ministry after the College had nominated him Professor in 1897, Krafft-Ebing says: "As far as Freud's activity as a teacher is concerned, he has held since 1886 (20 semesters), with rare interruptions, a weekly two-hour lecture per semester . . . . [Was Freud's Lehrtätigkeit betrifft, so hat derselbe seit 1886 (20 Semester) mit seltenen Unterbrechungen ein zweistündiges Semestralcollegium . . . abgehalten] (Gicklhorn and Gicklhorn, 1960, p. 98). Yet, as the Gicklhorns report, the Ministry was well informed about the success or failure of lecturers: there was even, they allege, a special commission within the College of Professors that kept a check on the teaching success (*Lehrerfolge*) of the *Dozenten* (Gicklhorn and Gicklhorn, 1960, p. 158). Krafft-Ebing would have been taking an unwarranted risk, one would think, in misinforming the Minister about Freud's activity as a lecturer. Freud's scientific accomplishments were sufficient to cover about three printed pages in Krafft-Ebing's report (Gicklhorn and Gicklhorn, 1960, pp. 95-98), and a specific reference to lecturing was not really necessary.

There was no need to say anything about the teaching record of the candidate, for in the committee report on the ten *Dozenten*—of whom Freud was one—there is for one (Wertheim), no reference at all to his

[39] It is strangely ironical that, occasionally, the research of archivists, who spend hours in the service of the most rigorous exactness, leads instead to results which even a beginner (as happens in this instance) can easily prove wrong.

teaching, and for another (Biedl) only the fact that he was "a very good teacher" (Gicklhorn and Gicklhorn, 1960, p. 112f.). But all this is a matter only of probabilities and does not provide desirable certainty; I shall therefore take it for granted—against my conviction—that the Gicklhorn statistic is, with exception of the two instances mentioned, correct, and that prior to 1902 Freud did miss about twenty semesters during his lecture assignment.

Now then, what conclusions do the authors draw from this alleged fact? "Freud's total activity as a lecturer," they write, *"proves a surprising indifference and lack of zeal"* (p. 162; italics mine) with regard to his teaching assignments. This conclusion regarding Freud's character is quite surprising and without documentary proof, a failure of methodology that seems somehow to have escaped the reviewer's scrutiny.

How is one to explain the authors' conclusion, since they themselves group the unaccounted semesters under "lectures that were announced [by Freud] but not held *because no students at all or too few students registered"* (italics mine)? So they say, at least on page 162. Yet, on page 158, the heading of the very same group was: "Lectures that, though announced, did not come to pass, either because of lack of audience [*Hörer*], or because of Freud's fault [*Verschulden*]." The authors do not waste a single word on reasons why one must assume either the one or the other, nor on why they themselves transformed this 'either-or' proposition into one that left no other explanation than a defect in Freud's character.

The authors themselves report circumstances that, in my opinion, prove that it was the problem of the famous *tres faciunt collegium* that interfered with the lectures taking place.[40] We find, among the listeners, the names of Freud's friends, such as Breuer and Königstein; registrations occurred often after the official deadline; some of the registrants did not even know the name of Freud's lecture. All this speaks strongly in favor of the authors' suggestion that participants had to be "fetched in" (*heran-*

[40] It seems that a semestral course of lectures became part of the teaching record of a *Dozent* when at least three participants had formally registered for the course and had, at the end of the semester, made their registration valid. This required the students to get the lecturer's signature and present their registration records at the Dean's Office. Thus it is possible that an instructor like Freud, whose lectures were elective—that is, confirmation of attendance was not a prerequisite for graduation—may still, even after having given a semestral series of lectures, have lost official recognition for it, if no three of the students found it worth the trouble to obtain validation of attendance.

holen) (p. 182).[41] Thus we hear of a summer semester when there was, for a long time, only one listener; much later, two more joined (Gicklhorn and Gicklhorn, 1960, p. 183).[42]

That Freud apparently went to such length to safeguard his teaching record would itself disprove the claim of negligence, for Freud was a proud person, with a strong feeling for dignity and decorum. It is reasonable to assume that he felt humiliated at having to ask others to attend his lectures so as to bring the attendance to the minimum of three. Nevertheless, he seems to have done so, at least during a few semesters.

Despite the evidence that the Gicklhorns adduce with respect to Freud's efforts to organize a minimum of participants, they declare him to be at fault on the grounds that *not all the Dozenten* had such trouble, and they conclude with the statement: "It evidently depended on the kind of Freud's lectures which had little attraction for students" (p. 183). In this, they may very well have been right; but it still does not entitle them—or Sherwood—to charge negligence.[43]

I shall cite a passage from a paper by Max Weber, which I do not expect will make any impression on those who share the outlook of the Gicklhorns and the Sherwoods. Weber had the following to say:

> The number of students enrolled is a test of qualification, which may
> be grasped in terms of numbers, whereas the qualification for scholarship
> is imponderable and, precisely with audacious innovators, often debatable
> —that is only natural. Almost everybody thus is affected by the sugges-

[41] This seems to have been a perennial trouble, because I recall that I myself, studying at the University of Vienna four or five decades after Freud's *Dozentur,* was asked to register for courses solely for the purpose of helping a *Dozent* to achieve the minimum of three registrants. As to Freud's time, there is documentary evidence for this state of affairs available. Dumreicher (1878) gave an example of the shrinkage of attendance in the instance of a lecture that had become elective: the original attendance of over 200 students dwindled within three years to 25 for the winter semester, and to four for the summer semester; a few years later, the lecture—even though to be given by the illustrous Billroth—did not come about at all, because of lack of an audience (p. 17). Billroth himself (1886) complains that of 450 students registered for his course, only 50-60 actually attended (p. 8), and he had bitter words about the indolence of most students. Whoever reads Billroth's *Aphorisms,* published shortly after Freud obtained his *Dozentur,* will understand that Freud's initial failure as a teacher—if it happened at all—does not per se require the assumption of negligence as the reason. How very complex the academic situation was in Vienna at that time can be learned from Professor Lasky's publication of 1963.

[42] With their peculiar exactitude, the Gicklhorns say about that semester: "It is not possible that the course came about" (193); on the table, nevertheless, the semester counts as one in which Freud lectured.

[43] For other proofs of Freud's eagerness to lecture, see below.

tion of the immeasurable blessing and value of large enrollments. To say of a dozent that he is a poor teacher is usually to pronounce an academic sentence of death, even if he is the foremost scholar in the world. And the question whether he is a good or a poor teacher, is answered by the enrollments with which the students condescendingly honor him.

It is a fact that whether or not the students flock to a teacher is determined in large measure, larger than one would believe possible, by purely external things: temperament and even the inflection of his voice. After rather extensive experience and sober reflection, I have a deep distrust of courses that draw crowds, however unavoidable they may be. Democracy should be used only where it is in place. Scientific training, as we are held to practice it in accordance with the tradition of German universities, is the affair of an intellectual aristocracy, and we should not hide this from ourselves. To be sure, it is true that to present scientific problems in such a manner that an untutored but receptive mind can understand them, and—what for us is alone decisive—can come to think about them independently, is perhaps the most difficult pedagogical task of all. But whether this task is or is not realized, is not decided by enrollment figures" [Weber, 1919, p. 133f.][44]

Even if Freud does not find grace in the eyes of the Gicklhorns and the Sherwoods, at least those who think that he was a great and honest man may find some consolation in the fact that Max Weber would surely have counted him among the intellectual aristocracy—for his published lectures prove all too well that he was the sort of man to live up to Weber's specifications. All those among his audience whom I have had the privilege of interrogating are agreed on his masterly way of lecturing

---

[44] It is noteworthy that Billroth (1886) took a contradictory view to other passages in the same essay. He wrote: "If he [the Dozent] is unsuccessful as a teacher, it is sad enough for him, as it is always sad for anyone to have to acknowledge that he has chosen a career to which he is unequal" (p. 43).

A passage in one of Freud's letters to his bride deserves citation because of its documentation of what a difficult situation a *Dozent* had to face. In May 1884, that is to say, sixteen months before his appointment as a *Dozent,* Freud spoke with Professor Nothnagel concerning his career. The latter had the following to say about Freud's hopes as a university lecturer: "Now, you must realize how difficult it is to get anywhere with these lectures. As you know, if a man is in an official position, people come flocking to him, whether he is a blockhead or not. But when a man without a position begins lecturing, he may well fare as I did when I started in Breslau. In my first course I had four students. You won't have any more, and will have to wait a long time before a course of this kind pays its way" (Freud, 1873-1939, p. 110f.). The word which appears in the official translation as "blockhead" is, in the original, far stronger and more vivid; in a literal translation, it would be "a horned bull with whom one could break down a wall." In any event, the connotation is one of incredible and outrageous stupidity.

(although there was disagreement with regard to many other qualities); similarly, in view of the clarity and precision of his neurological writings, there is no reason to surmise that the lectures were of a low quality.

The reviewer, following the lead of the authors, creates the impression that the College of Professors showed signs of particular kindness or generosity in not revoking Freud's *Dozentur* because of his alleged negligence or failure. During the course of their argumentation, the authors quote, under the heading "Abstracts from the University Law" (*Auszug aus dem Hochschulgesetz*) (pp. 131-135), what appear to be laws. Actually, their quotations stem from a document which never did become law, since it concerned only propositions, and which they do not identify by sufficient references (thus again failing to fulfill the minimum standards of a scientific publication).

This is all the more surprising since the pertinent decrees have been published, in a text that is understandable even to the layman; from it I shall now set forth those decrees that were in force during Freud's *Dozentur*. It will then become clear that a revocation of the *venia legendi* —quite aside from such an event being an extremely rare occurrence— would have been, in Freud's case, out of the question.

Ministerial decree of December 25, 1866

When a *Dozent* has announced a [semestral] lecture and was ready to hold it, but it was not held solely for the reason that no listeners registered [for it], then he has done his duty as far as concerns the use he has made of the right to hold lectures, and a failure of his announcement [to eventuate] in [an actually held] lecture series [for reasons] outside of his responsibility, cannot contribute to his disadvantage [Beck and Kelle, 1906, p. 184].

In the Ministerial decree of May 20, 1879, an abuse of the law just quoted is discussed, and it is decreed that a *Dozent* shows himself at fault

. . . when circumstances permit the assumption that a *Dozent* did not have the serious intention at all to bring about a lecture [*Kollegium*] but has announced lectures only for the sake of appearance, particularly when such a *Dozent* has not brought about a lecture [*Kollegium*] for years, whereas at the same time the lectures of other *Dozenten* on the same discipline enjoy adequate attendance [Beck and Kelle, 1906, p. 188].

Ministerial decree of February 11, 1888

The *venia docendi* ceases when a *Dozent* has not announced any lectures for four semesters . . . . When a *Dozent* has announced lectures through four subsequent semesters, but actually has not held them, then the *venia legendi,* upon the motion of or after interrogation by the College of Professors, can be declared by the Minister of Education to have ceased to exist [Beck and Kelle, 1906, p. 171].[45]

From these decrees, the contents of which were the equivalents of laws, it is evident that the Ministry had taken into full account the difficulty of obtaining a quorum in the instance of elective lectures, and that only actual neglect or abuse of the *Dozentur* might have given just cause for prosecution.[46] No automatic cessation of the *venia docendi* was provided. Yet, let us assume that the Gicklhorns' Figure 12 is correct, and that the College of Professors did interrogate Freud. Freud would have been able to bring in the fact that Scholz, the chief of a clinic at which Freud had been active, had refused him—contrary to a previous promise—the use of patients for teaching purposes, an incident about which I shall have more to say later; that Meynert had refused him access to the neurological laboratory out of anger over Freud's acceptance of Charcot's new discoveries and theories, for which, aside from Freud's own writings (1925d, p. 16; 1900, p. 437f.), approximate 'documentary' evidence can be found in Wagner-Jauregg's *Lebenserinnerungen*.[47]

Freud could have set forth the limitation imposed upon him by the University itself, in denying him the use of a lecture room, and his pro-

[45] From a footnote, it seems that, between 1888 and 1906, it happened only once that a *Dozent* was suspended for two semesters, because of his having harmed the prestige and dignity of the University. There seem also to have been criminal charges involved, which were tried in court.

[46] Billroth (1886) wrote: "A strict control should be held, however, upon whether or not a *Dozent,* after his *habilitatio,* brings about lectures at all, and one should then also carry out the law that a *Dozent* who does not lecture for three years is separated from the academic community" (p. 48). This quotation shows that: (1) in contrast to the claims of the Gicklhorns, the teaching success of the *Dozenten* was apparently not controlled; (2) the difficulties that Freud met in his teaching endeavors were not unique, but frequent; and (3) some of the academic laws referring to *Dozenten* were not carried out exactly (I have nowhere found any reference to *three* years, as Billroth writes), and had no practical validity.

[47] See Wagner-Jauregg (1950, p. 72): "After his return to Vienna [from Paris] he [Freud] held a lecture in the *Gesellschaft der Ärzte* in which he spoke exclusively of Charcot and praised him in the highest tones. This the Viennese great [men] tolerated badly. Bamberger and Meynert rejected Freud harshly and with that he fell into disfavor with the faculty. He was thus a neurological practitioner without patients."

test to the Dean, which proved futile.[48] Furthermore, Freud could have brought up what the authors themselves describe: his own efforts to obtain permission to lecture at a pediatric outpatient clinic outside the University hospital, where he could have introduced the students to neurological pediatrics, which was not taught at all in Vienna at that time. That this request was rejected by the College of Professors on flimsy grounds can be deduced from the fact that Freud's chief was permitted to lecture at the same place (Gicklhorn and Gicklhorn, 1960, p. 12).

All or some of this must have been known to some members of the College of Professors. In the light of these facts, there cannot have been very many among them who thought that Freud was indifferent or lacking in zeal. Consequently, any attempt to revoke Freud's *venia docendi*—quite aside from the scandal it would have caused, because of its unusual character—would have created a situation highly embarrassing to the University and, by no means, to Freud: the grievances against Scholz's clinic; Meynert's jealousy; the plight of those *Dozenten* who were still seeking a lecture room—all this would have come to light, *and* in the case of a young scientist who had been extraordinarily productive in his field. No, the College of Professors would have been severely criticized even by a conservative Minister of Education, who had the last word in such matters, merely for an attempt to eliminate Freud from the Faculty (and we can now reflect with what ridicule and contempt the University would have burdened itself in the eyes of posterity for actually having expelled a Freud from its staff!).

How inappropriate—not to say bizarre—the Gicklhorns' charges are, how tendentious their misjudgment, can be proven—if such proof is still necessary—by a careful study of the documents they themselves have published. After having constructed, out of nothing, the myth of a Freud unmindful of his duties as a teacher, they had to prove that his supposed neglect was egregious, and to affirm that the Ministry wished preference

---

[48] The authors dispute Freud's statement about the difficulties he met in obtaining a lecture room (Freud, 1925d, p. 16), and claim that there is no documentary proof thereof (Gicklhorn and Gicklhorn, 1960, p. 163), even though the late Dr. Bernfeld wrote them (June 11, 1951) that "Freud reports . . . that he complained to Ludwig, who was then the Dean," and that "Ludwig made promises but nothing happened." I owe thanks to Mrs. Suzanne A. Bernfeld for the information that Dr. Bernfeld referred in that passage to a footnote which Freud added, in 1911, to his *Interpretation of Dreams* (Freud, 1900, p. 168), in which the incident is described in detail. Freud used only the letter L. instead of the Dean's full name (Ludwig was Dean of the Medical Faculty in 1886-87 and in 1891-92).

to be given to those *Dozenten* who had shown appreciable success, *in the first place,* through teaching (Gicklhorn and Gicklhorn, 1960, p. 23).

It is not clear from the documents whether this is true even with regard to appointments to salaried professorships, as can be gathered from the memorandum of the Minister of Education, Count Bylandt (May 1898); in these he explicitly says that the title of Professor should be given to *Dozenten* "for their meritorious teaching *or* scientific activity" (p. 102, italics mine).[49]

As to the authors' certainty of the effect that Freud's alleged neglect of his teaching function had on his promotion, the following circumstance also speaks strongly against their thesis: Exner would not have hesitated at all to let Freud know, when the latter looked him up, that an objective cause might prevent his receiving a titular professorship. From the earlier letter by Freud to Elise Gomperz, one can see that Freud himself was most eager to discover the reason that militated against his advancement. He wrote: "But if the Minister, as one might conclude from Exner's diplomatic hints, really does not want to act on my behalf for some definite reason, isn't one allowed to ask what this reason is?" (Freud, 1873-1939, p. 243).

Exner had dropped the remark that, in "certain circles," the trend of Freud's work was "laughed at." Facetiously, Freud added that if he were told that this was the cause, then he could "consider whether to alter this trend or to renounce the title (*ibid.*). And—we may ask—why did Freud get the title at all, then, more or less suddenly after he had intervened with Exner, even though Exner had let him know that he might have to wait more than one year longer (see above)? No shred of evidence has been found of anyone looking askance at Freud as a teacher, although the customary difficulties that he ran into may have been known initially.

And Freud? In a moving address to the B'nai B'rith Society, in 1926, he described the spiritual loneliness in which he had to live from 1895 on, and the longing he felt to find a group with whom he could talk. Even if someone did not yet know for certain that Freud was a man who

---

[49] It is quite depressing to observe the arbitrary and prejudiced way in which people—who allege that they are using scientific methods—are willing to proceed in order to reach a preconceived goal, and further, how a reviewer will co-operate with them in their objectionable procedure. We are dealing here with an event (Freud's professorship) which per se is of secondary importance; still, it is used for a derogatory statement about Freud, although the very *first* step of the explanation offered by the authors can be disproved by use of *their own documents.*

fulfilled his obligations punctiliously, how could he still believe, after reading that address, that Freud was not interested in giving lectures at that time? When students bypassed the exhilarating possibility of witnessing the first semester of scientific lectures on dream psychology ever held, one cannot reproach them for their misjudgment, any more than one ought to falsify the record, or seek negligence as the answer, where what isolation there was, was clearly *forced upon* a genius far in advance of the common sense of his time. There can be no doubt, therefore, that the Gicklhorns' thesis, while facile enough, has nothing to do with the truth.

4. *The reliability of archival studies.* The reviewer, in agreement with the authors, seems to put his full trust in facts, as "revealed through sifting" of documents (Sherwood, 1962, p. 235). And, no doubt, with regard to the very fact of the publication of documents, there is merit in the Gicklhorns' book. Nevertheless, what the archivist and the reviewer overlook is that, as soon as the meaning of documents begins to be explicated, interpretation also begins. I can demonstrate the effect of interpretation particularly well, because the book contains one section that has appeared previously, but with significantly different conclusions.

In 1957, Prof. Gicklhorn published the report that Wagner-Jauregg wrote in 1919, upon recommending Freud for full professorship. Prof. Gicklhorn, on this occasion, added a number of commentaries. In my rebuttal, I have set forth an interpretation quite different from Gicklhorn's (1958a). In their book, however, where the same topic is taken up (pp. 47-50), I found to my delight that some of my views—without citation, of course—have been incorporated, at least substantially, if not as a whole. One may thus learn that, though *acta loquuntur,* the listening ear also has a bearing on the outcome of archival research.[50]

The authors are in the habit of fashioning their opinions to suit the needs of the given situation. Gicklhorn (1957) reported a parapraxia that happened to Wagner-Jauregg in the last paragraph of his 1919 memorandum on Freud. Instead of making the motion that Freud ought

[50] When the authors rely on their own wits, they come close to the bizarre. As a *curiosum,* I may cite the conclusion that they drew from the fact that the fathers of 65 per cent of those who attended Freud's lectures were merchants: "Here the propaganda of Freud's father among his acquaintances must have been of influence" (p. 179). This ridiculous conclusion might safely be dropped without further investigation. I cite it here mainly because it shows how unreliable the authors' methods are. They do not cite any figures about the general distribution of paternal occupations within the student body. They do not even take the trouble to separate, in their inquiry, Freud's audience before and after the death of his father—which occurred in 1896.

to receive the title of *Professor Ordinarius,* he wrote that Freud ought to receive the title of *Professor Extraordinarius,* which Freud had already received in 1902 (p. 535). Yet Gicklhorn was apparently unaware that this very parapraxia speaks strongly against his interpretation of the document. He replied to my inquiry that the mistake had not been corrected by Wagner, but at the Dean's office (Eissler 1958a). In 1960 (p. 48), however, it is maintained that Wagner himself might just as well have corrected the mistake, which would, of course, greatly reduce the degree of ambivalence that one would have to assume to have been active in the writer, under the other set of circumstances.

More serious is what appears to be Gicklhorn's reliance on the readers' limited knowledge of the pertinent literature. In 1957, he affirmed that Freud behaved toward Wagner-Jauregg in a way which, if true, would have been blameworthy indeed. The occasion is of some interest to the historian. In 1919, a parliamentary commission was appointed to investigate the treatment of war neuroses during the first World War.[51] Now Wagner was at the center of that investigation, before which Freud was called as an expert witness. The situation for Wagner-Jauregg was indeed a dangerous one.

Upon being called before the commission, Freud first read his expert opinion (Freud, 1920c), in which he set forth his scientific criticism of the electric treatment (which, as far as I have been able to learn, was never again used by Army psychiatrists in any country), and cleared Wagner-Jauregg of any possible suspicion. Yet, it would reflect gravely on Freud's character if Gicklhorn were right in claiming, on the basis of an *unpublished* stenographic record (made accessible solely to him) of Freud's oral testimony, that "in a confrontation with Wagner, Freud raised accusations that are today simply incomprehensible" (Gicklhorn, 1957, p. 536).[52]

In my earlier rebuttal, I took exception to this practice of raising allegations against a deceased person, without presenting the complete facts, possession of which would make verification possible. Upon my inquiring as to what Freud's accusations had been, Gicklhorn gave as

[51] The electric treatment recommended at that time had aroused great resentment. As a matter of fact, it had led to instances of death (cf. Freud, 1920c; Jellinek, 1947), a fact the authors preferred to ignore, since they write as if the widespread excitement had been caused by rabblerousers, cowards, or 'goldbricks' (Gicklhorn, 1957 and Gicklhorn, 1960).

[52] Indeed, if that had been the case, Freud would have been deserting and endangering, in a moment of crisis and emergency, not only an innocent scientist, but also an old and deserving friend.

one example Freud's assertion that Wagner did not understand anything of psychology (Eissler, 1958a)—a statement which was not only utterly immaterial to the parliamentary investigation, but would not have been denied even by Wagner himself. In the Gicklhorns' (1960) last publication, however, we read instead that it was Freud whose testimony was attacked by Wagner's assistant, Raimann,[53] in the form of "most vehement invectives" (p. 49). This is what remains, for the time being, of the original grave charge against Freud of "incomprehensible accusations" against Wagner.

5. *On Freud's allegedly negligent attitude toward an academic career.* The reviewer writes: "He [Freud] now practised psychiatry, not neuropathology, in which field he held his teaching appointment. Unlike some of his contemporaries and his senior, Wagner-Jauregg, he did not take the trouble to take additional 'dozenturs' in the field in which he wished to be professor . . ." (p. 236). Since the extension of a *Dozentur* to additional specialties did not require more than a simple application to the College of Professors (Gicklhorn and Gicklhorn, 1960, p. 132), Freud might appear to be particularly careless in not having asked to have his *Dozentur* extended to include psychiatry.

However, the reviewer is here merely repeating a mistake the Gicklhorns have made consistently, even though I had called their attention to it (Eissler, 1958a). Prof. Gicklhorn, who was primarily a biologist, had shown excellent judgment with respect to Freud's biological writings (Gicklhorn, 1955); but he was doomed to error in his conduct of an investigation that called for knowledge of the history of psychiatry.

Nevertheless, one has the right to expect that a book which deals with an episode in the history of psychiatry would at least be reviewed by someone familiar with that field. The Gicklhorns and the reviewer could both have easily avoided the error I have referred to, if they had undertaken to scrutinize the documents involved. In 1899, Wagner submitted a memorandum to the College of Professors, in which he surveyed the academic staff of the department of neuropsychiatry. About Freud, he had the following to say: "Dr. Freud is only *Dozent* in neuropathology and has never occupied himself thoroughly with psychiatry" (Gicklhorn and Gicklhorn, 1960, p. 30). Now, if Sherwood and the Gicklhorns were right in stating that Freud had abandoned his original field and was practising psychiatry, then this would make Wagner either a liar

---

[53] Emil Raimann was Professor of Psychiatry at the University of Vienna; he also wrote a scathing attack upon psychoanalysis (1924).

or an ignoramus; either alternative being out of the question, to my knowledge, I must therefore assume that the authors and the reviewer have both erred.

As a matter of fact, *Studies on Hysteria*, the publication of which may well be said to have initiated modern psychiatry in the narrower sense of the term, was published in 1895. Heinz Hartmann called my attention to the fact that, at that time, the neuroses were not a topic of psychiatry, but of neuropathology.[54] It is easy enough to verify this. The book on hysteria by Charcot (1887) was entitled *Leçons sur les Maladies du Système Nerveux;* and on the frontispiece, where Freud signed as the translator, his title is given as *Dozent für Nervenkrankheiten* (*Dozent* for nerve diseases). A textbook on psychiatry, however, such as that by Rudolf Arndt (1883), who was not only professor of psychiatry but also director of the psychiatric clinic at the University of Greifswald, contained next to nothing about the neuroses, whereas L. Löwenfeld, who worked on neurasthenia and hysteria (1894), and on psychotherapy (1897), called himself a specialist for nerve diseases (*Spezialarzt für Nervenkrankheiten*).

To eliminate any possible doubt, we have only to turn to the first sentence in Binswanger's (1904) monograph on hysteria. It is: "Hysteria is the woe-begotten child of nerve pathology" (*Die Hysterie ist das Schmerzenskind der Nervenpathologie*) (p. 1). The Gicklhorns must have had an inkling of the correct answer, because they write: "From the winter semester 1892/93 on, Freud changes the subject of his lectures and chooses special chapters of *neuropathology* with special consideration of the great neuroses" (1873-1939, p. 157; italics mine).

Both the authors and the reviewer are, nevertheless, certain that Freud impeded his academic advancement by not applying for an extension of the *Dozentur* to include psychiatry. Since such an application, of course, had to contain the proof that the applicant was an expert in the field to which he wanted his *Dozentur* extended, Freud would have had to acquire those skills and experiences that a psychiatrist was sup-

[54] Therefore, the reviewer was also wrong when he thought Freud had not lived up to his obligation in going to study the neuroses under Charcot in Paris. From the report Freud submitted to the College upon his return from Paris (Freud, 1886), it is evident that he believed—apparently wrongly, as we now hear—that he had worked in Paris in the field of neuropathology. Dr. Hartmann also pointed out that, from passages in Freud's lectures on "Psychoanalysis and Psychiatry" (Freud, 1916-1917, pp. 243-256), it is evident that Freud adhered, even then, to the old terminology, and did not consider himself a psychiatrist.

posed to possess at the turn of the century, and which he did not possess, as is proven by Wagner's memorandum.[55] Therefore, in my reply (1958a) to Gicklhorn (1957), I said that, in order to apply for such an extension, Freud would have had to interrupt the research on which he was engaged.[56]

The criticism here becomes glaringly inconsistent. Freud, who had no desire to become a psychiatrist (in the sense of the term as used in the early 1900's), who was engaged in research in the field of neuro-pathology (in the sense the term was used at that time), and who had no other request *vis-à-vis* the College of Professors than to be given a professorship, titular or regular, in the specialty in which he was work-ing, is now castigated (for the third time) for not having extended his *Dozentur* to psychiatry, a field in which he had little practical experi-ence. In disregard of the most elementary facts about the history of mental science, assertions are made reflecting on Freud's character, in contradiction to the historical evidence, and thus seem to be the product either of unrestrained bias or of sheer ignorance.

6. *Freud and the 'love of lucre.'* The reviewer writes of Freud's "in-tent to concentrate on private practice admittedly for the sake of lucre" (p. 236). This statement is apparently intended to summarize scattered remarks that the Gicklhorns had made with respect to Freud's "open avowal that he is mainly concerned with a higher income" (p. 26); of his "attitude directed toward the lucrative"; of the Ministry's not being interested "to procure the professorship for the purpose of collecting higher fees from patients" (p. 28).

As to the 'openness' of the avowal, that very likely stems from letters of Freud, in which he speaks of the urgency with which he would need the professorship, in view of his lack of patients.[57] I ask the reader to

---

[55] Freud served as *Sekundärarzt* for five months in Meynert's Psychiatric Clinic (Jones, 1953-1957, Vol. 1, pp. 64f.). This, besides a short service in a private sani-tarium, was the only psychiatric experience he would have reported. It is evident that this would not have sufficed to apply for an extension of his *Dozentur*, aside from his not yet having published any paper that the College of Professors would have considered a psychiatric one.

[56] In the book, Mrs. Gicklhorn, however, insists on the same error Prof. Gicklhorn had made and, evidently discussing my objection, she turns, without citing my name, against "adherents of Freud, who under no circumstances want to pay heed to historic facts" (Gicklhorn and Gicklhorn, 1960, p. 31).

[57] Freud had already demonstrated quite clearly his ability to endure poverty without faltering. For example, at 27 he had found himself, on one occasion, at the end of the month with, literally, 'no more than a dime to his name'; at 28, he was able to indulge, for the first time, in the luxury of possessing a second necktie (Freud, 1873-1939, pp. 49, 91). When, at 44, he was ready to 'move heaven and earth,' in order to avoid the repeti-

consider that a *Dozent* was not in a position to apply for a professorship; that Nothnagel had voluntarily confided to Freud the secret that he and Krafft-Ebing would propose Freud for nomination to a professorship;[58] and that Freud did not hear a single word about his professorship for five years, and did not undertake anything further during that time. When his *élan vital* was stimulated during his first and so long delayed stay in Rome, and when upon his return to Vienna he found the number of patients threateningly reduced (*eingeschmolzen*) (Freud, 1887-1902, p. 342), he went to Exner (see *ante*).

When Freud undertook this step, he was forty-five years old, had published 47 papers, 7 books (one of which is still considered by some as perhaps the greatest treatise on the mind so far produced in Occidental culture), 9 reviews and 3 articles, on the literature of cerebral palsy, containing a total of 83 reviews and abstracts; he had translated and edited five French tomes.[59] Thus, he had produced, merely in terms of quantity, more in the way of scientific writings than many a full professor, and, let us assume, he may have thought that he could retire from scien-

---

tion of this terrible poverty—and its even more terrible implications for the continuation of his work, on which he has already made great strides—under such circumstances, his decision could be challenged only by the most insensitive and willful detractors.

[58] Cf. Freud (1887-1902, p. 191). Nothnagel did so evidently in recognition of Freud's contribution, *Die infantile Cerebrallähmung* (1897), to his own *Handbuch der speziellen Pathologie*, etc. (See Gicklhorn and Gicklhorn, 1960, p. 97, for Krafft-Ebing's praise of Freud's monograph, comprising 327 pages. "It contains not only a lucid presentation of the anatomical and clinical [aspects of the] subject, perfect in form and content, and the inclusion of the whole world literature, but also connections with the major part of the rest of cerebral pathology and most valuable attempts at reaching a clinical classification and differentiation of as yet highly confusing and ambiguous syndromes.") It is reasonable to assume that Nothnagel felt indebted to Freud for the invaluable contribution he had made to the *Handbuch*. Thus Freud could be certain of the fullest support by Nothnagel, who was one of the most influential persons in the College and Ministry (cf. Gicklhorn and Gicklhorn, 1960, p. 31). Nothnagel committed himself extensively by promising that if the College did not agree with him and Krafft-Ebing, they alone would send the request to the Ministry, adding: "You know the further difficulties" (Freud, 1887-1902, p. 191). Thus Freud was told that the College as well as the Ministry might oppose Nothnagel's move. Can the historian really ignore this evidence of the possibility of a bias against Freud?

[59] For an impressive record of Freud's annual scientific output, see Tyson and Strachey (1956). Freud's work as a translator had, in itself, earned him the gratitude of his profession. I owe thanks to Dr. Grinstein for calling my attention to the historically highly important review of Freud's translation of Charcot's third volume (Charcot, 1887) written by "Dr." Arthur Schnitzler, which ends as follows: "Dr. Freud has carried over the book in such an excellent way that one is hardly reminded anywhere that he has a translation in front of him. He has introduced a work into the German literature which truly enriches it, and has performed a service for which he deserves the gratitude of German physicians and the recognition of critics in equal measure" (Schnitzler, 1887; translation mine).

tific production. Even such a resolve should have had no effect on the decisions as to whether he *deserved* a professorship. After all, the title of professor carried with it *no obligation* for the achievement of further scientific accomplishments; it was an acknowledgement of merits so far accumulated, and no doubt Nothnagel's promise had assured Freud that his merits were considerable.

Let us assume, therefore, that Freud really did go to Exner exclusively for the sake of 'lucre'; the faculty would still have been in debt to him, merely by virtue of the fact that he had written a book, *The Interpretation of Dreams,* that would carry the name and glory of the University of Vienna all around the globe. Furthermore, this book had been written without any assistance from the University (except perhaps for its library—and even that is questionable); even before the book had been completed, Krafft-Ebing—according to the Gicklhorns and Sherwood, probably erroneously—was praising Freud for his idealism, stressing the fact that Freud had achieved so much in science "at the cost" of his practice (Gicklhorn and Gicklhorn, 1960, p. 98).[60]

[60] The Gicklhorns, and Sherwood, in turn, are continuing—I presume inadvertently—a distortion of facts begun by Wilhelm Stekel. In a footnote, Stekel (1931, p. 58n.) had the following to say: "Those who follow the analytic literature, will know of the moving case of a compulsive (obsessional) patient, who was treated for five years, lost his whole fortune in the interim, and for whom a collection had to be made in psychoanalytic circles. Later, a lengthy analysis, because of a paranoiac delusion, was carried out free of charge."

It is evident that Stekel, without daring to bring in Freud's name, is here referring to the Wolf Man. However, it is impossible that Stekel could have read Freud's and Mack Brunswick's papers attentively, for the Wolf Man left Freud's treatment in 1914 a wealthy man; he lost his fortune subsequently through the Russian revolution. I have cited this case earlier as an example of Freud's charitable spirit, and it is, indeed, a strange thing to reencounter it in Stekel's writings as an example of psychoanalytic greediness. I interrogated the Wolf Man once more on this point. He was quite surprised when I informed him of Stekel's comment. With the patient's permission I am able to report that Freud's honorarium during the patient's prewar (World War I) treatment was fifty Kronen per treatment hour, a fee which he was able to pay with ease in view of his great wealth at that time. When he returned to Vienna in 1919 and resumed treatment for a few months, "a piece of the transference which had not hitherto been overcome was successfully dealt with" (1918, p. 122). Freud did not charge a fee, however, and treated the patient with the understanding that, if he should regain his wealth or part thereof, he would reimburse Freud for services rendered. Subsequently, because of the permanence of his limited finances, the patient was not in a position to pay this debt. Freud, of course, never made any request for payment.

Stekel (1931) continues: "The case R. is also tragic. A patient analyzed for 3 years had sacrificed his whole fortune to his analysis, remained unhealed and is today, of course, an embittered opponent of psychoanalysis." The case R. (analyzed by Freud around 1908) was known to many in Vienna. His history was never published. I interviewed his brother in this country, and he had nothing of the sort that Stekel alleges to report. He recalled that his brother had had a disagreement with Freud and therefore left

But did Freud ever *really* intend to change horses in midstream, and to become a practitioner without interest in research? After all, roughly one hundred and sixteen papers and sixteen books were still to be written by him. At least, the 'lucre' was well invested, I hazard to guess, since it insured the realization of a veritable stream of creativity, which did not ever cease to propel the genius forward. He continued his research literally to his last breath, in spite of the tribulations of old age, cancer, about thirty surgical operations, extreme pain caused by the pressure of maxillary prosthesis, the death of a child and of a grandson, beloved beyond description, war, revolution, persecution, and exile. What 'lucre'!

One really has to be unbelievably innocent to overlook the fact that, during the last decade of the century, Freud's office had changed into a research laboratory, and that the dearth of private patients would be followed not only by economic collapse, but also by the collapse of his whole scientific project. One was not permitted to analyze patients in university hospitals or clinics at that time (I doubt that one can do it even now), and his own private office offered Freud the only chance for testing the correctness of the hypotheses that were emerging gradually. When the Gicklhorns and Sherwood continue to lay stress on the supposed contrast between Freud's private practice and his research or teaching, they are simply revealing that they do not understand the historical situation. The allegations and insinuations that one finds scattered throughout the book, to the effect that Freud's private practice *distracted* him from fulfilling his duties toward the University, are arbitrarily constructed, presented without documentation, and, at bottom, quite erroneous.

Further, one should consider the embarrassment and helplessness of a physician practising in a booming city, the number of whose patients at times was threateningly dwindling;[61] one should consider the appre-

treatment, which he continued with somebody else. Nothwithstanding temporary improvement, the patient's disorder took a relentlessly malignant course. There is no doubt that Stekel did not hesitate to state as a fact what he could, at best, have heard as a rumor. I wonder when his footnote will appear among the others in the lexicon of anti-Freudian quotations—if it has not done so yet.

[61] One really has to have achieved an unusual degree of insensitivity to be able to bypass passages such as the following: "I am isolated as you could wish me to be . . . because a void is forming round me. So far I bear it with equanimity. What I find less agreeable is that this year for the first time my consulting room is empty, that I see no new faces for weeks on ends, that I get no new cases for treatment, and that not one of the old ones is finished yet" (Freud to Fliess, May 4, 1896; Freud, 1887-1902, p. 162f.); or: "Otherwise I am resigned. I have enough to live on for a few months yet"

hension that this caused, particularly in the light of Freud's financial responsibilities for his wife, six children, and parents.

The Gicklhorns report that they have heard that a patient gave him a house as a gift. Is it the function of archivists to record gossip? The episode of the impecunious patient I mentioned before, who consulted Freud and then left his office with a substantial amount of money in his pocket (Goetz, 1952), is not gossip, but was reliably witnessed; it is quite probably far more revealing of Freud's 'love of lucre' than the reader may have been led to think, after going through the Gicklhorns' book and its review.[62]

Indeed, in a city in which it was the title of 'Professor' that decided in individual instances, by its presence or absence, whether a physician could survive economically or not, Freud was right in expecting his Alma Mater to reward him with that minimum of recognition after years of dedication to research, at least part of which was regarded by his contemporaries as being of the finest quality, and part of which had the distinctive character of giving a new direction to the thought of mankind.[63]

7. *Freud's psychopathology.* Sherwood (1962) writes: "What is surprising, is that neither he [Freud], nor his psychiatrist biographers recognize quirks of his mind they would instantly spot in a patient" (p. 27). The reviewer probably had in mind such "quirks of mind" as he himself attributed to Freud in his review; yet I do not see that Sherwood has succeeded in giving proof of their existence. When one follows up his allegations, they turn out to be based on wrong claims, misunderstand-

(Freud to Fliess, June 9, 1899; Freud, 1950, p. 283); or: "Nothing is really happening. When I think that I am going to lose four patients between April and May, I cannot feel exactly cheerful. How I am to get through I do not yet know, but I am determined to stick it out" (Freud to Fliess, January 26, 1900; Freud, 1887-1902, p. 308f.).

62 The incident happened in 1904 or 1905, and had to do with a gift of 200 Kronen. (A letter of Freud's, that was auctioned recently shows that in 1907 Freud's hourly honorarium was 30 Kronen [Stargardt, 1964]. Thus Freud may have given the destitute patient the equivalent of about seven hours of his own working time.)

63 The Gicklhorns try hard to justify the fact that Freud obtained few honors in the city to whose fame he had contributed so much. I shall discuss, elsewhere, their inadequate explanation of why Freud was not elected to membership in the Austrian Academy of Sciences; after all, he was elected a Corresponding Member of the Royal Society. Here, I want to add only a few words about Freud's own desires in this respect. Oddly enough, from an unpublished letter, one can be reasonably sure that what Freud wished personally was a distinction of merely local importance—namely, the Austrian Award of Honor for Art and Science, a decoration the Republic had taken over from the Monarchy and which was the highest honor the State awarded for outstanding accomplishments in either field. This wish of Freud's was probably the remnant of an identification with a revered teacher, von Brücke (cf. Jones, 1953-1957, Vol. 3, p. 208f.)

ings, and lack of knowledge with regard to detail, the historic situation and the society in which Freud lived.

Sherwood's reference (p. 236)—following the Gicklhorns—to Freud's quarrel with his chief Scholz,[64] shortly before he was made *Dozent,* may appear to come closest to what he calls "quirks of mind." Yet when we hear that Scholz's patients went hungry, that the ward was unclean, that the patients had to stay in darkness because no gas had been installed (Jones, 1953-1957, Vol. 1, p. 68)—and that Freud's quarrel with his chief was apparently brought about as a result of his fight for the improvement of the patients' condition—we may, after all, surmise that here again a misunderstanding has occurred.

I can well understand that, for many neuropsychiatrists, who have been indoctrinated with the doctrine of 'adjustment,' the idea of contradicting a chief in the name of truth and justice may seem to be a sign of appalling maladjustment. Indeed, it may well be true that it is advisable for the weaker to adjust to his environment, in so far as he may not bear up well under the pressure of conflict with it. Nevertheless, Freud's readiness to risk his own career for the sake of improving the plight of the sick should not serve the mental scientist of the twentieth century as a warrant for turning the prejudices and problems of his own present habitat into a weapon against Freud.

I do not overlook altogether the possibility that the Gicklhorns and the Sherwoods may, after all, be right; it may perhaps be wiser to 'adjust' and not to "disturb the sleep of the world" (Freud, 1914, p. 21). Nevertheless, in the name of science, one has to warn against a view that would declare the Galileos and the Freuds to be maladjusted, solely on the grounds that their genius provoked the hostility of their contemporaries (as well as that of the next two or three generations).

Freud was aware of his own conflicts and peculiarities. Anyone who takes the trouble to read the Fliess letters, the book on *Dreams,* and the recently published letters (Freud, 1873-1939), can hardly miss this.[65] Yet,

[64] *Primarius* Dr. Franz Scholz was chief of Medicine of the fourth section in the *Allgemeine Krankenhaus,* where Freud worked as a kind of resident for fourteen months (1884-1885).

[65] How direly mistaken Sherwood is can be observed not only from Freud's self-analysis, the highlights of which can be learned from a study of the Fliess letters, but also from Freud's letters dating from the preanalytic period. For example, in his letter of February 2, 1886, to his bride, he reported the self-diagnosis of neurasthenia, and described the existence of other nervous symptoms (Freud, 1873-1939, p. 200f.). However, the confession of all the insight obtained in that letter was facilitated by the cocaine Freud had taken that evening. He was aware of this, testifying in this detail, also, to the high degree of his self-observation and of his honesty toward himself and others.

when Freud countered Marie Bonaparte's reference to him as a genius with "Geniuses are unbearable people. You have only to ask my family to learn how easy I am to live with, so I certainly cannot be a genius" (Jones, 1954-1957, Vol. 2, p. 415), he spoke a deep truth; for the phobia-like neurosis from which he suffered in his early years, and the personal peculiarities he enumerated (Freud, 1873-1939, p. 402f.) on the occasion of his correcting the idealized picture Stefan Zweig (1931) had given of him, are truly of no great significance. The psychological problem in Freud's case, if there is one, is the relative absence of significant or severe psychopathology.

One could hardly imagine a more relaxing or soothing occupation than watching the results of the hybridization of peas. Still, the discoverer of the Mendelian laws showed signs, toward the end of his life, of systematized paranoid ideas.[66] To be the first to investigate pregenitality and the oedipus complex is a far more 'dangerous' undertaking than that which Mendel dealt with, and one might well expect conspicuous psychopathology in that sort of Promethean mind.

I have cited Mendel for an additional reason. He is, aside from Freud, the only other "orderer" of a science (in the sense of Gillispie, 1960, p. 202f.) who flourished in Austria; and he, too, did not fare well with the universities. Aside from attending the University of Vienna for only a few semesters, he twice flunked the examinations given there for a teacher's license. His life's achievement, which laid the foundations for modern genetics, was not ridiculed by the professors; it was totally ignored by them. On the other hand, his contact with Karl Nägeli—that is to say, indirectly with the University of Munich—had a bad effect on his work, for the advice he received from him was the worst one could look for, in terms of the progress of his fundamental experiments (Iltis, 1924).[67]

Further, is it not strange that Darwin's work was done outside a university, that Lavoisier worked in a privately financed laboratory, and that Spengler, one of the most original minds of the recent past, remained without university contact? I am inclined to draw the conclusion that universities are not good soil for those original minds that establish

---

[66] This, at least, is the conclusion one feels compelled to draw after the perusal of Gregor Mendel's biography by Iltis (1924), although the author himself denies the existence of disease.

[67] See also Gillispie (1960, p. 328f.), for a revealing remark regarding Nägeli's attitude toward Mendel.

a new science,[68] even when this may come about through the synthesis of previous discoveries. It is of the greatest historical significance that Freud got along famously with the academic institutions, so long as he stayed in the organic area of neuropathology. Only with the beginning of what was later to become known as psychoanalysis does the tension begin.[69]

I wish to demonstrate what I have in mind by means of a hypothetical situation. If Freud had submitted his histological, physiological, and neurological works to the faculty, the College of Professors would probably have voted unanimously in favor of their publication; if he had submitted his psychological papers to a vote, I assume that, on the contrary, an overwhelming majority would have voted *against* their publication.[70]

As in so many other instances, an essential aspect of the historical situation at the medical faculty of the University of Vienna during the decades following 1890—when an insidious but relentless decline was making it slip from its leading position, which was the real crux of the matter—is not revealed in the official documents. Anyone who reads Wagner-Jauregg's *Memoirs* (1950) will be struck by the fact that parts of his manuscript, concerning events in the medical College of Professors, had to be held back from publication. "He [Wagner-Jauregg] shows up," so the editors say, "with sharpness and objectivity the existing abuses [*herrschende Misstände*]" (p. 74). Thus, ten years after his death, there was still much that was not 'fit to print.' If he had not written his *Memoirs*, we would probably never have heard that there were abuses at all.

Further, has archival research yet turned up, for example, the historical details that caused Wagner-Jauregg to write about Josef Breuer that he resigned from his *Dozentur*, "after he was, in his opinion, treated in an undignified way by the College [of Professors]" (p. 72)? The great

---

[68] At least, the way they have been organized in Central Europe; it may be slightly different in the United States, where universities are far more liberal, and even scholars without degrees may become heads of departments. However, recently Foraker (1963, p. 11) in a short letter to *Science*, pointed out that neither Robert Koch nor Edward Jenner would have had any chance, within the present system of organized research, of obtaining the necessary resources for their investigations.

[69] When psychoanalysts make unfriendly remarks about the University of Vienna, they refer historically to the period of Freud's psychological researches, not to the time of his organic research.

[70] In view of Bailey's (1956) "Academic Lecture," one has the right to surmise that a vote on the same question at the Illinois State Psychopathic Institute would probably even now lead to the same result.

Breuer treated in an undignified manner? Who would think this possible, after the College has been introduced to us as a group of the most virtuous men, who spent their days studying law in order to avoid committing any injustice?

The evidence has not yet been found of the true reasons for Breuer's resignation, and he himself is silent about them;[71] but I do not see how one can avoid assuming that Breuer had told Freud the truth with respect to his feeling compelled to resign. As a matter of fact, Freud twice weighed the idea of resigning his *Dozentur* (1887-1902, pp. 190, 280), thus revealing, in my opinion, a tendency to identify with his admired friend. From Wagner's *Memoirs* we also learn one of the factors that would have made it quite precarious for Freud to try to live out that identification to the extent that he might have wished; for, after his resignation, Breuer (so Wagner continued, p. 72) "devoted himself to his extensive and lucrative practice."

Is it possible that Breuer took offense at not being appointed professor and successor to his chief Oppolzer?[72] When Schönbauer writes (1947) that Breuer "retired into private practice after Oppolzer's death" (p. 375), this conclusion gains in probability. (What may have been at stake here was also a professorship, and we thus encounter a further point of identification.)

Indeed, Freud too felt as though he had been treated in an undignified way, when events took a turn that made it look as if the College of Professors or the Ministry had passed him over for five years.[73] He felt the impulse to do what his great friend had done, perhaps also out of loyalty to Breuer. When Freud wrote to Fliess, "Breuer will say I have done myself a lot of harm" (1887-1902, p. 245), it sounds as if such problems as those of idealism versus reality necessities, uncompromising adherence to principle versus 'adjustment' to the powers that be had been discussed between them.

As often happens in instances of developing greatness, Freud also

[71] Breuer, apparently being an unpolemical person, gave as the motive for his leaving the faculty, the duties imposed upon him by his private practice. Wagner's remark makes it clear that this reason must have been of minor importance or a pretense.

[72] Johann von Oppolzer (1808-1871), professor of Internal Medicine at the University of Vienna.

[73] For the contemporary physician practicing in this country, all this fuss about a professorship may not make much sense. The following quotation may at least make it clear that there was no peculiarity of Freud's involved here: "A *Dozent* who does not even become [professor] *extraordinarius* carries in his heart the dagger for the rest of his life" (Billroth, 1886, p. 43).

showed much hotheadedness and rashness, when he had to face the indignities of his time. The sage, as we have come to know him from later portraits, was then only in the making. Breuer could fall back on a lucrative practice when he resigned his *Dozentur,* but Freud was trapped: either he would get his professorship, or he would have to ask others for support.

Be that as it may, the fact that Sherwood used the term 'lucre' in connection with Freud will be considered an indignity of our time by the future historian of science—if he should deign to take notice of it.

One wonders, of course, why the review of the Gicklhorns' book should have been assigned to a person who was apparently not too familiar with the German language, rather poorly informed about the subject matter, certainly ignorant of the basic literature, obviously prejudiced, and ready to abuse his task for a gratuitous attack against the honesty of a whole professional group. I was not particularly surprised when I was told that the review had been accepted because it had been forwarded "by Dr. Percival Bailey in Chicago; and, coming from such a scholarly and outstanding individual . . . [we] thought of it as being certainly completely accurate in every respect" (personal communication from the Editor, quoted with his permission).[74]

[74] Von Hartel, Minister of Education and distinguished classical philologist, has come up so often in the preceding appendix that some readers may be curious to learn a bit more about him. (The following data are culled from Engelbrecht, 1908.) He was born in 1839, not far from Freud's birthplace, in a small Moravian town. He came from straitened circumstances, which did not prevent his obtaining an excellent education. At an early date, he also came into close contact with the high aristocracy, and had the opportunity for extensive travels in his capacity as the teacher of the powerful Count Lanckoronski's son. In 1866 he became Dozent, in 1869 *professor extraordinarius,* in 1871 a member of the Academy of Science, in 1872 full professor, in 1874-1875 Dean of the philosophical faculty. In 1882 the Emperor raised him to hereditary nobility; in 1883 he had the honor of receiving a call to Göttingen, and in 1886 to Heidelberg— but in both instances he declined. In 1890 he was elected *Rector Magnificus* of the University; in 1891 he became member for life in the Upper Chamber (of Parliament). From 1891 to 1896 he was Director of the Imperial Library. In 1893 he organized the 42nd convention of German philologists, whose participants probably owed to von Hartel the unusual honor of being invited to the Imperial Palace. In the same year he received the highest distinction a scholar could receive under the Monarchy—namely, the honorary medal for art and science. In 1896 von Hartel started his career as a civil servant. He was appointed undersecretary (*Sektionschef*) in the Ministry of Education, and from 1900 to 1905 he served as Minister of Education. From 1899 on, he was vice-president of the Academy of Sciences. His career, very much in contrast to that of Freud's, is characterized by an uninterrupted sequence of successes. There were no defeats or crises in his professional development. He died in 1907, sixty-eight years old. The bibliography of his published writings runs to eighty-five numbers.

If it is remembered that he was a self-made man, one has to admire his achievements all the more. His life story is that of an unusually successful man. The fact that he apparently, for a short while, stood in the way of Freud's career may seem to suggest that he was unfavorably disposed to a man *rerum novarum cupidus*. Yet this would not be confirmed by his record, for von Hartel made a decisive contribution to the emancipation of women in Austria, inasmuch as he made women eligible for the *matura* (the prerequisite for university attendance), which permitted them to acquire M.D.'s and Ph.D.'s. In music, he was Wagnerian and patronized Bruckner; in art, he supported the so-called *Secession*, the contemporary modern movement. His organizational talent was combined with farsightedness. Under his leadership, new University institutes sprouted; the medical faculty owed him particular thanks for new hospital buildings which had been overdue for a long time.

Lovers of antiquity are indebted to him for the restoration and preservation of the famous palace of Diocletian in Spalato. Much more could be said in his favor, his notable scholarship being not the least. Ernst Kris, who was the first to recognize that the delay in Freud's professorship had been brought about by the Ministry of Education, suggested in a footnote (Freud, 1887-1902, p. 200) the possibility of anti-Semitism. But that element can assuredly be excluded in von Hartel's case. His biographer reports the following incident: When a commission under his chairmanship gave a prize for eminence in dramatic literature to the Jew, Arthur Schnitzler, he had to answer a parliamentary interpellation; in it, he said that "under his direction the just and the sinners, Christians and Jews, foreigners and natives receive this distinction, since according to the foundation charter it was not the certificate of baptism but the literary achievements that were decisive." (Engelbrecht, 1908, p. 23; translation mine.)

However, the biographical account published after his death contains a passage of relevance in this context. To understand that passage properly, one must know that the Minister of Education occupied one of the most vulnerable positions in the Monarchy, which was a conglomeration of different nationalities. Since every national group insisted upon nationalized schools and their extension, and in addition the clerical parties aimed at the return to a Church-supervised school system, it is understandable that Parliament was in a constant uproar about educational matters. In addition, since von Hartel's appointment was nonpolitical, he could not rely on the assured support of any political group.

This precarious situation evidently forced the Minister to consider politics in his university appointments, so that he sometimes had to impose upon the faculty personalities "deprecated with horror" (*perhorreszierte Persönlichkeiten*) by it (Engelbrecht, 1908, p. 18). Although this does not cover the episode in question, it sharply disproves the Gicklhorns' pet theory of 'unprejudiced' university appointments. However, the biographer records one instance of a political action for which von Hartel was responsible, and which was undoubtedly deleterious. It had to do with a measure that had the effect of reducing the state's responsibility for school matters in favor of the clerical parties (p. 26).

Von Hartel is described as a man of conciliatory temperament, well-versed in the art of diplomacy, who successfully tried to stay in the good graces of the forces in power. The biographer also records that he played an eminent role in the *salons*, which may be taken as further confirmatory evidence of at least one of the details reported by Freud. But from all this, one does not learn why von Hartel should have been opposed to Freud's promotion. To be sure, he was modern in the fields of art and music; but could this very astute diplomat have sensed the fact that in Freud the 'modern' spirit took a turn that would yet prove to be dangerous to the dynasty to which his primary loyalties were attached? *Non liquet*.

Bibliography

Adrian, E. D. (1946). The Mental and the Physical Origins of Behavior. *International Journal of Psycho-Analysis*, 27:1-6.

Aichhorn, A. (1936), Zur Technik der Erziehungsberatung. Die Übertragung. *Zeitschrift für psychoanalytische Pädagogik*, 10:5-74.

────── (1947), Gewaltlose Erziehung. In: *Erziehungsberatung und Erziehungshilfe.* Bern & Stuttgart: Huber, 1959, pp. 134-150.

Alexander, F. (1927), Discussion on Lay Analysis. *International Journal of Psycho-Analysis*, 8:224-230.

────── (1932), *The Medical Value of Psychoanalysis.* New York: Norton, 1936.

────── (1935a), The Logic of Emotions and Its Dynamic Background. *International Journal of Psycho-Analysis*, 16:399-413.

────── (1935b), The Problem of Psychoanalytic Technique. *Psychoanalytic Quarterly*, 4:588-611.

────── (1938), Psychoanalysis Comes of Age. *Psychoanalytic Quarterly*, 7:299-306.

────── (1940a), Psychology and the Interpretation of Historical Events. In: *The Cultural Approach to History*, ed. C. F. Ware. New York: Columbia University Press, pp. 48-57.

────── (1940b), A Jury Trial of Psychoanalysis. *Journal of Abnormal and Social Psychology*, 35:305-323.

────── (1941a), The Psychiatric Aspects of War and Peace. *American Journal of Sociology*, 46:504-520.

────── (1941b), Defeatism Concerning Democracy. *American Journal of Orthopsychiatry*, 11:643-651.

────── (1942), *Our Age of Unreason. A Study of the Irrational Forces in Social Life.* Philadelphia & New York: Lippincott.

────── (1954), Psychoanalysis and Psychotherapy. *Journal of the American Psychoanalytic Association*, 2:722-733.

——— (1956), *Psychoanalysis and Psychotherapy. Developments in Theory, Technique, and Training.* New York: Norton.

———, French, T. M., et al. (1946), *Psychoanalytic Therapy. Principles and Application.* New York: Ronald Press.

——— & Staub, H. (1929), *The Criminal, the Judge and the Public. A Psychological Analysis.* New York: Macmillan, 1931.

Allers, R. (1934), Die neue Zeit und die Heilerziehung. *Der christliche Ständestaat,* 1:15-17.

Andreas-Salomé, L. (1912-1913), *In der Schule bei Freud. Tagebuch eines Jahres 1912/1913.* Zurich: Niehans Verlag, 1958.

——— (1931), *Mein Dank an Freud.* Vienna: Internationaler Psychoanalytischer Verlag.

Ansbacher, H. L. & Ansbacher, R. R., eds. & annot. (1956), *The Individual Psychology of Alfred Adler. A Systematic Presentation in Selections from his Writings.* New York: Basic Books.

Aristotle, *Problems.* The Loeb Classical Library, 2 vols. Cambridge: Harvard University Press, 1953.

Arndt, R. (1883), *Lehrbuch der Psychiatrie für Ärzte und Studierende.* Vienna & Leipzig: Urban & Schwarzenberg.

Asbell, B. (1961), *When F.D.R. Died.* New York: Holt, Rinehart & Winston.

Axelrad, S. (1956), The Straw Couch: Some Misunderstandings of Freudian Theory and Technique. *American Journal of Orthopsychiatry,* 26:408-419.

——— (1962), Infant Care and Personality Reconsidered. A Rejoinder to Orlansky. In: *The Psychoanalytic Study of Society,* 2:75-132. New York: International Universities Press.

Bailey, P. (1956), The Great Psychiatric Revolution, Thè Academic Lecture. *American Journal of Psychiatry,* 113:387-406 (1956-1957).

——— (1961), A Rigged Radio Interview. *Perspectives in Biology and Medicine,* 4:199-265.

Bandler, B. (1960), The American Psychoanalytic Association 1960. *Journal of the American Psychoanalytic Association,* 8:389-406.

Barber, B. (1961), Resistance by Scientists to Scientific Discovery. *Science,* 134:596-602.

Beach, F. A. (1960), Experimental Investigations of Species-Specific Behavior. *American Psychologist,* 15:1-18.

Beck von Mannagetta, L. & von Kelle, C. (1906), *Die österreichischen Universitätsgesetze.* Vienna: Manz.

Bell, J. S. (1902), A Preliminary Study of the Emotion of Love between the Sexes. *American Journal of Psychology,* 13:325.

Bernfeld, S. (1925), *Sisyphos oder die Grenzen der Erziehung.* Leipzig, Vienna & Zurich: Internationaler Psychoanalytischer Verlag.

——— (1932), Die kommunistische Diskussion um die Psychoanalyse und Reichs "Widerlegung der Todestriebhypothese." *Internationale Zeitschrift für Psychoanalyse,* 18:352-385.

——— (1937), Zur Revision der Bioanalyse. *Imago,* 23:197-236.

——— (1941), [Abstract] Über die Beziehungen zwischen der psychoanalytischen und behaviouristischen Begriffsbildung (On the Relation Between Psychoanalytic and Behavioristic Concepts), by Walter Hollitscher. *Psychoanalytic Quarterly,* 10:690.

——— (1944), Freud's Earliest Theories and the School of Helmholtz. *Psychoanalytic Quarterly,* 13:341-362.

——— (1946), An Unknown Autobiographical Fragment by Freud. *American Imago,* 4:3-19.

——— (1951), Sigmund Freud, M.D. 1882-1885. *International Journal of Psycho-Analysis,* 32:204-217.

——— & Bernfeld, S. (1944), Freud's Early Childhood. *Bulletin of the Menninger Clinic,* 8:105-115.

—————— —————— (1949), Freud's Scientific Beginnings. *American Imago*, 6:163-196.
—————— —————— (1952), Freud's First Year in Practice, 1886-1887. *Bulletin of the Menninger Clinic*, 16:37-49.
Bettelheim, B. (1957), Review of *The Life and Work of Sigmund Freud* by Ernest Jones. *American Journal of Sociology*, 62:418-420.
Bibring, E. (1947), The So-called English School of Psychoanalysis. *Psychoanalytic Quarterly*, 16:69-93.
—————— (1954), Psychoanalysis and Dynamic Psychotherapies. *Journal of the American Psychoanalytic Association*, 2:745-770.
Billroth, T. (1886), *Aphorismen zum "Lehren und Lernen der medicinischen Wissenschaften."* Vienna: Gerold.
Binswanger, O. (1904), *Die Hysterie* in *Spezielle Pathologie und Therapie*, ed. H. Nothnagel, Vol. XII, I. Hälfte, Abt. II. Vienna: Hölder, 1904.
Bleuler, E. (1919), *Das autistisch-undisziplinierte Denken in der Medizin und seine Überwindung.* Berlin: Springer, 1927.
Boguslavsky, G. W. (1958), The Effect of Vigilance on the Rate of Conditioning. In: Gantt (1958), pp. 266-269.
Bonaparte, M. (1960), Vitalism and Psychosomatics. *International Journal of Psycho-Analysis*, 41:438-443.
Boring, E. G. (1929), *A History of Experimental Psychology.* New York: Appleton-Century-Croft, 1957.
—————— (1942), William James on Sensation. *American Journal of Psychology*, 55:310-327.
—————— (1942), *Sensation and Perception in the History of Experimental Psychology.* New York: Appleton-Century-Crofts.
—————— (1955), Dual Role of the *Zeitgeist* in Scientific Creativity. *Scientific Monthly*, 80:101-106.
Börne, L. (1823), Die Kunst, in drei Tagen ein Original-Schriftsteller zu werden. *Gesammelte Schriften*, 3 Vols., 1:120-122. Leipzig: Reclam.
Bornstein, B. (1948), Emotional Barriers in the Understanding and Treatment of Young Children. *Journal of Orthopsychiatry*, 18:691-697.
Bouillenne, R. (1962), Man, the Destroying Biotype. *Science*, 135:706-712.
Braceland, F. J., ed. (1955), *Faith, Reason and Modern Psychiatry.* New York: Kenedy & Sons.
Brazier, M. A. B., ed. (1959), *The Central Nervous System and Behavior.* Transactions of the First Conference, Sponsored by the Josiah Macy, Jr. Foundation, New York, N.Y.
Breuer, J. & Freud, S. (1893-1895), Studies on Hysteria. *Standard Edition*, 2:1-305.
Bridger, W. H. (1958), *Pavlovian Concepts and Human Behavior.* In: Gantt (1958), pp. 96-111.
—————— (1960), Signaling Systems in the Development of Cognitive Functions. In: *The Central Nervous System and Behavior*, ed. M. A. B. Brazier. Third Conference, 425-456. New York: The Josiah Macy, Jr. Foundation.
Brody, B. & Grey, A. L. (1948), The Nonmedical Psychotherapist: A Critique and a Program. *Journal of Abnormal and Social Psychology*, 43:178-192.
Broughton, L. R. D. (1927), Vom Leben der Bienen und Termiten. *Imago*, 14:142-146, 1928.
Brown, N. O. (1959), *Life Against Death. The Psychoanalytic Meaning of History.* Middletown, Conn.: Wesleyan University Press.
Browning, N. L. (1961a), Is the Couch on its Way Out? *Chicago Sunday Tribune Magazine*, April 2, Part 3:7-9.
—————— (1961b), The Case for Psychoanalysis: Part of the Puzzle. *Chicago Sunday Tribune Magazine*, April 9, Part 3:24-29.
Brugsch, T. & Lewy, F. H., eds. (1926-1931), *Die Biologie der Person*, 4 Vols. Vienna & Berlin: Urban & Schwarzenberg.

Brun, R. (1936), Sigmund Freuds Leistungen auf dem Gebiet der organischen Neurologie. *Schweizer Archiv für Neurologie und Psychiatrie*, 37:200-207.
――― (1953), Über Freuds Hypothese vom Todestrieb. *Psyche*, 7:81-111.
Brunswick, R. M. (1928), A Supplement to Freud's 'History of an Infantile Neurosis.' *International Journal of Psycho-Analysis*, 9:439-476.
Bry, I. & Rifkind, A. (1962), Freud and the History of Ideas: Primary Sources, 1886-1910. *Science and Psychoanalysis*, 5:6-36.
Bryan, D., ed. (1927), Bulletin of the International Psycho-Analytical Association. *International Journal of Psycho-Analysis*, 8:558-559.
Bühler, K. (1918), *The Mental Development of the Child*. London: Routledge & Kegan Paul, 1949.
――― (1934), *Die Darstellungsfunktion der Sprache*. Jena: Fischer.
Bychowski, G. (1951), Metapsychology of Artistic Creation. *Psychoanalytic Quarterly*, 20:592-602.
Bykov, K. M. (1942), *The Cerebral Cortex and the Internal Organs*. New York: Chemical Publishing Co., 1957.
Caruso, I. A. (1952), *Psychoanalyse und Synthese der Existenz*. Freiburg: Herder, 1952.
Cassirer, E. (1927), *Individuum und Kosmos in der Philosophie der Renaissance*. Studien der Bibliothek Warburg, X, ed. F. Saxl. Leipzig & Berlin: Teubner.
――― (1944), *An Essay on Man. An Introduction to a Philosophy of Human Culture*. New Haven: Yale University Press.
Catherinet, F. M. (1952), Demoniacs in the Gospel. In: *Satan* (1952), pp. 163-177.
Ceithaml, J. J. (1955), Admission to Medical School Then and Now, or Wanted: More Well-Qualified Applicants. *Bulletin of the Alumni Association*, School of Medicine, University of Chicago, 11:3-4, 10.
Chambers, J. A. (1964), Creative Scientists of Today. *Science*, 145:1203-1204.
Chandler, T. (1962), Ikhnaton and Moses. *American Imago*, 19:127-139.
Charcot, J.-M. (1887), Leçons sur les maladies du système nerveux. Tome 3e, Paris; translated by Freud as: *Neue Vorlesungen über die Krankheiten des Nervensystems insbesondere über Hysterie* (1886). Leipzig & Vienna: Toeplitz & Deuticke.
Charron, P. (1601), Traité de la Sagesse. Bordeaux.
Cicero (45 BC), *Tusculan Disputations*. The Loeb Classical Library, Cambridge: Harvard University Press, 1950.
Clark, K. (1950), *Landscape Painting*. New York: Scribner.
Cohen, M. B., Baker, G., Cohen, R. A., Fromm-Reichmann, F. & Weigert, E. V. (1954), An Intensive Study of Twelve Cases of Manic-Depressive Psychosis. *Psychiatry*, 17:103-137.
Cole, L. E. (1953), *Human Behavior Psychology as a Bio-Social Science*. Yonkers-on-Hudson, N.Y.: World Book Company.
Cole, W. G. (1955), *Sex in Christianity and Psychoanalysis*. New York: Oxford University Press.
Coleman, L. L. (1950), Psychologic Implications of Tonsillectomy. *New York State Medical Journal*, 50:1225-1228.
Craig, A. M. (1961), *Chōshū in the Meiji Restoration*. Harvard Historical Monographs XLVII, Cambridge: Harvard University Press.
Crow, C. (1939), *He Opened the Door of Japan. Townsend Harris and the Story of his Amazing Adventures in Establishing American Relations with the Far East*. New York & London: Harper.
Daim, W. (1951), *Umwertung der Psychoanalyse*. Vienna: Herold.
Danzinger, L. & Frankl, L. (1934), Zum Problem der Funktionsreifung. Erster Bericht über Entwicklungsprüfungen an albanischen Kindern. *Zeitschrift für Kinderforschung*, 43:219-254.
Day, F. (1944), The Future of Psychoanalysis and Religion. *Psychoanalytic Quarterly*, 13:84-92.
de Kruif, P. (1926), *Microbe Hunters*. New York: Harcourt, Brace.

Delbridge, C. L. (1916), *How to Make War Impossible*. St. Louis: Delbridge Company.

de Messières, R. (1933), ed. & annot. of *Le Malade Imaginaire* by Molière. Paris: Librairie Larousse.

Dempsey, P. J. R. (1956), *Freud, Psychoanalysis, Catholicism*. Chicago: Regnery.

Denny-Brown, D. (1932), Theoretical Deductions from the Physiology of the Cerebral Cortex. *Journal of Neurology and Psychopathology*, 13:52-67.

De Sanctis, S. (1924), *Religious Conversion. A Bio-psychological Study*. London: Kegan Paul, Trench, Trubner; New York: Harcourt, Brace, 1927.

de Santillana, G. (1955), *The Crime of Galileo*. Chicago: University of Chicago Press.

de Saussure, R. (1950), Psychoanalysis and History. In: *Psychoanalysis and the Social Sciences*, 2:7-64. New York: International Universities Press.

Descour, L. (1922), *Pasteur and His Work*. London: T. Fisher Unwin.

de Toquédec, J. Exorcism and Diabolical Manifestations. In: *Satan* (1952), pp. 178-203.

Deutsch, F., ed. (1959), *On the Mysterious Leap from the Mind to the Body*. New York: International Universities Press.

Deutsch, H. (1944-1945), *The Psychology of Women*. New York: Grune & Stratton, 2 Vols.

Dilthey, W. (1905), *Das Erlebnis und die Dichtung*. Stuttgart: Teubner. Göttingen: Vandenhoeck & Ruprecht, 1957.

Discussion on Lay Analysis (1927), *International Journal of Psycho-Analysis*, 8:174-283.

Dorer, M. (1932), *Historische Grundlagen der Psychoanalyse*. Leipzig: Meiner.

Drabovitsch, W. (1935), Freud et Pavlov. *L'évolution Psychiatrique*, Fasc. 3:21-34.

Dumreicher, Freiherr von, J. (1878), *Über die Nothwendigkeit von Reformen des Unterrichts an den medizinischen Facultäten Österreichs*. Vienna: Hölder.

Dykman, R. A. & Gantt, W. H. (1958), Cardiovascular Conditioning in Dogs and in Humans. In: Gantt (1958), pp. 171-195.

Edelstein, E. J. & Edelstein, L. (1945), Asclepius, A Collection and Interpretation of the Testimonies, 2 Vols. In: *Publications of the Institute of the History of Medicine*. The Johns Hopkins University, Second Series, Texts and Documents, Vol. II. Baltimore: The Johns Hopkins Press.

Eder, M. D. (1962), The Myth of Progress. *British Journal of Medical Psychology*, 35:81-89.

Editorial (1943), Psychoanalysis and the Scientific Method. *Journal of the American Medical Association*, 122:811-812.

Editorial (1960), Experiment in Medical Education. *Bulletin of the Alumni Association, School of Medicine, University of Chicago*, 16:2.

Ehrenberg, R. (1923), *Theoretische Biologie*. Berlin: Springer.

Einstein, A. (1934), Active Pacifism. In: *Ideas and Opinions*. New York: Crown Publishers, 1954, p. 110f.

Eisenstadt, S. N. (1961), The Causes of Disintegration and Fall of Empires: Sociological and Historical Analyses. *Diogenes*, 34:82-107.

Eissler, K. R. (1958a), Julius Wagner-Jaureggs Gutachten über Sigmund Freud und seine Studien zur Psychoanalyse. Entgegnung auf Professor Josef Gicklhorns wissenschaftsgeschichtliche Notiz. *Wiener Klinische Wochenschrift*, 70:401-407.

———— (1958b), Kritische Bemerkungen zu Renée Gicklhorns Beitrag "Eine mysteriöse Bildaffaire." *Wiener Geschichtsblätter*, No. 3.

Engelbrecht, A. (1908), Wilhelm Ritter von Hartel. *Biographisches Jahrbuch für Altertumskunde*, Vol. 31. Leipzig: Reisland.

Federn, E. (1960), Die therapeutische Persönlichkeit, erläutert am Beispiel von Paul Federn und August Aichhorn. *Schweizerische Zeitschrift für Psychologie und ihre Anwendung*, 19:117-131.

Federn, P. (1928), Psychoanalyse und Medizin. *Das Psychoanalytische Volksbuch*, eds. E. Federn & H. Meng. Berlin & Stuttgart: Huber, 1957, pp. 76-83.

———— (1943), Psychoanalysis of Psychoses. In: *Ego Psychology and the Psychoses*, ed. & introd. E. Weiss. New York: Basic Books, 1952, pp. 117-165.

Feigl, H. (1958), The "Mental" and the "Physical." In: *Minnesota Studies in the Philosophy of Science, Vol. II: Concepts, Theories, and Mind Body Problem*, eds. H. Feigl, M. Scriven & G. Maxwell. Minneapolis: University of Minnesota Press, pp. 370-497.

Feldman, A. B. (1959), *The Unconscious in History*. New York: Philosophical Library.

Feldman, S. S. (1949), Review of *Sigmund Freud, An Introduction* by Walter Hollitscher. *Psychoanalytic Quarterly*, 18:92.

Fenichel, O. (1938-1939), *Problems of Psychoanalytic Technique*. New York: Psychoanalytic Quarterly, 1941.

———— (1945), Nature and Classification of the So-Called Psychosomatic Phenomena. *The Collected Papers of Otto Fenichel*, 2 Vols., second series, pp. 305-323, New York: Norton, 1953-1954.

———— (1946), Abstract of "On the Concepts of Psychological Health and Illness" by Walter Hollitscher. *Psychoanalytic Quarterly*, 15:128.

Ferenczi, S. (1926), Contra-Indications to the 'Active' Psycho-Analytical Technique. In: *Further Contributions to the Theory and Technique of Psycho-Analysis* by S. Ferenczi, compiled by J. Rickman, London: Hogarth Press, 1950, pp. 217-230.

———— (1933), Confusion of Tongues between the Adults and the Child. *International Journal of Psycho-Analysis*, 30:225-230 (1949).

Flugel, J. C. (1953), The Death Instinct, Homeostasis and Allied Concepts. Some Problems and Implications. *International Journal of Psycho-Analysis*, 34(Supplement):43-73.

Foraker, A. G. (1963), If Robert Koch Had Applied for a Research Grant. *Science*, 142:11.

Ford, C. S. & Beach, F. A. (1951), *Patterns of Sexual Behavior*. New York: Harper.

Ford, J. C. (1953), May Catholics Be Psychoanalyzed? *The Vincentian*, April 1953.

Freedman, D. A. (1957), Letter to the Editor. *American Journal of Psychiatry*, 113:846-847 (1956-1957).

French, T. M. (1933), Interrelations Between Psychoanalysis and the Experimental Work of Pavlov. *American Journal of Psychiatry*, 12:1165-1203.

Freud, A. (1936), *The Ego and the Mechanisms of Defense*. New York: International Universities Press, 1957.

————, ed. (1946), Bulletin of the International Psycho-Analytical Association. *International Journal of Psycho-Analysis*, 27:170-186.

————, ed. (1948), Bulletin of the International Psycho-Analytical Association. *International Journal of Psycho-Analysis*, 29:260-274.

———— (1950), Probleme der Lehranalyse. In: *Max Eitingon in Memoriam*. Jerusalem: Israel Psychoanalytic Society, pp. 80-94.

———— (1951), August Aichhorn. *International Journal of Psycho-Analysis*, 32:51-56.

Freud, E. & Meng, H., eds. (1963), *Sigmund Freud—Oskar Pfister Briefe 1909-1939*. Frankfurt: Fischer.

Freud, M. (1957), *Glory Reflected*. London, Sydney, Melbourne & Wellington: Angus & Robertson.

Freud, S. (1873-1939), *Letters of Sigmund Freud (1873-1939)*. Ed. E. Freud. New York: Basic Books, 1960.

———— (1877), Beobachtungen über Gestaltung und feineren Bau der als Hoden beschriebenen Lappenorgane des Aals. *Sitzungsberichte der Akademie der Wissenschaften, Wien* (Math.-Naturw. Kl.), Abt. III, 75:15.

———— (1886), Report on My Studies in Paris and Berlin. *International Journal of Psycho-Analysis*, 37:2-7 (1956).

———— (1887-1902), *The Origins of Psycho-Analysis. Letters to Wilhelm Fliess, Drafts and Notes: 1887-1902*. Eds. M. Bonaparte, A. Freud & E. Kris. New York: Basic Books, 1950.

BIBLIOGRAPHY

———— (1888-1889), Introduction to H. Bernheim's *Die Suggestion und ihre Heilwirkung. Collected Papers*, 5:11-24.

———— (1891a), *On Aphasia.* London: Imago, 1953.

———— (1891b), Hypnose. In: *Therapeutisches Lexikon für Praktische Ärzte*, ed. A. Bum. Vienna & Leipzig: Urban & Schwarzenberg, pp. 724-732.

———— (1893a), Some Points in a Comparative Study of Organic and Hysterical Paralyses. *Collected Papers*, 1:42-58.

———— (1893b), Charcot. *Standard Edition*, 3:11-23.

———— (1895), Project for a Scientific Psychology. In: Freud (1887-1902), pp. 355-445.

———— (1897), Die infantile Cerebrallähmung. In: *Spezielle Pathologie und Therapie*, ed. H. Nothnagel, Vol. IX, II. Teil, II. Abt. Vienna: Hölder.

———— (1900), The Interpretation of Dreams. *Standard Edition*, 4 & 5.

———— (1901), The Psychopathology of Everyday Life. *Standard Edition*, 6.

———— (1904), Freud's Psychoanalytic Procedure. *Standard Edition*, 7:249-254.

———— (1905a), Three Essays on the Theory of Sexuality. *Standard Edition*, 7:130-243.

———— (1905b), Jokes and Their Relation to the Unconscious. *Standard Edition*, 8:9-238.

———— (1905c), Psychical (or Mental) Treatment. *Standard Edition*, 6:283-302.

———— (1905d), Psychische Behandlung (Seelenbehandlung). *Gesammelte Werke*, 5:287-315. London: Imago, 1942.

———— (1905e), Fragment of an Analysis of a Case of Hysteria. *Standard Edition*, 7:7-122.

———— (1905f), On Psychotherapy. *Standard Edition*, 7:257-268.

———— (1907a), Prospectus for "Schriften zur angewandten Seelenkunde." *Standard Edition*, 9:248-249.

———— (1907b), Delusions and Dreams in Jensen's *Gradiva. Standard Edition*, 9:7-95.

———— (1907c), Obsessive Actions and Religious Practices. *Standard Edition*, 9:117-127.

———— (1909a), Analysis of a Phobia in a Five-Year-Old Boy. *Standard Edition*, 10:5-149.

———— (1909b), Notes Upon a Case of Obsessional Neurosis. *Standard Edition*, 10:155-249.

———— (1910a), 'Wild' Psycho-Analysis. *Standard Edition*, 11:221-227.

———— (1910b), Leonardo da Vinci and a Memory of His Childhood. *Standard Edition*, 11:63-137.

———— (1910c), The Psycho-Analytic View of Psychogenic Disturbance of Vision. *Standard Edition*, 11:211-218.

———— (1910d), Prospects of Psycho-Analytic Therapy. *Standard Edition*, 11:141-151.

———— (1910e), Five Lectures on Psycho-Analysis. *Standard Edition*, 11:9-55.

———— (1911a), Formulations on the Two Principles of Mental Functioning. *Standard Edition*, 12:218-226.

———— (1911b), Psycho-Analytic Notes on an Autobiographical Account of a Case of Paranoia (Dementia Paranoides). *Standard Edition*, 12:9-82.

———— (1911c), The Handling of Dream-Interpretation in Psycho-Analysis. *Standard Edition*, 12:91-96.

———— (1912a), Recommendations to Physicians Practising Psycho-Analysis. *Standard Edition*, 12:111-120.

———— (1912b), Types of Onset of Neurosis. *Standard Edition*, 12:231-238.

———— (1913a), The Claims of Psycho-Analysis to Scientific Interest. *Standard Edition*, 13:163-190.

———— (1913b), On Beginning the Treatment. *Standard Edition*, 12:123-144.

———— (1913c), The Theme of the Three Caskets. *Standard Edition*, 12:291-301.

———— (1913d), Introduction to Pfister's *The Psycho-Analytic Method. Standard Edition*, 12:329-331.

———— (1913e), The Disposition to Obsessional Neurosis. A Contribution to the Problem of Choice of Neurosis. *Standard Edition*, 12:317-326.

———— (1913f), Observations and Examples from Analytic Practice. *Standard Edition*, 13:193-198.

———— (1913g), Totem and Taboo. *Standard Edition*, 13:1-161.

———— (1914a), On the History of the Psycho-Analytic Movement. *Standard Edition*, 14:7-66.

———— (1914b), On Narcissism: An Introduction. *Standard Edition*, 14:73-102.

———— (1915), Instincts and Their Vicissitudes. *Standard Edition*, 14:117-140.

———— (1916-1917), *Introductory Lectures on Psycho-Analysis. Standard Edition*, 15, 16.

———— (1917b), A Metapsychological Supplement to the Theory of Dreams. *Standard Edition*, 14:222-235.

———— (1917c), A Difficulty in the Path of Psycho-Analysis. *Standard Edition*, 17:137-144.

———— (1917d), Mourning and Melancholia. *Standard Edition*, 14:243-258.

———— (1918), From the History of an Infantile Neurosis. *Standard Edition*, 17:7-122.

———— (1919a), On the Teaching of Psycho-Analysis in Universities. *Standard Edition*, 17:171-173.

———— (1919b), 'A Child is Being Beaten.' A Contribution to the Study of the Origin of Sexual Perversions. *Standard Edition*, 17:179-204.

———— (1919c), Lines of Advance in Psycho-Analytic Therapy. *Standard Edition*, 17:159-168.

———— (1920a), Beyond the Pleasure Principle. *Standard Edition*, 18:1-64.

———— (1920b), A Note on the Prehistory of the Technique of Analysis. *Standard Edition*, 18:263-265.

———— (1920c), Memorandum on the Electrical Treatment of War Neurotics. *Standard Edition*, 17:211-215.

———— (1921), Group Psychology and the Analysis of the Ego. *Standard Edition*, 18:69-143.

———— (1923a), The Ego and the Id. *Standard Edition*, 19:12-66.

———— (1923b), Two Encyclopaedia Articles, (A) Psycho-Analysis. *Standard Edition*, 18:235-254; (B) The Libido Theory, *ibid.* 18:255-259.

———— (1923c), A Seventeenth-Century Demonological Neurosis. *Standard Edition*, 19:72-105.

———— (1923d), Remarks on the Theory and Practice of Dream-Interpretation. *Standard Edition*, 19:109-121.

———— (1924a), A Short Account of Psycho-Analysis. *Standard Edition*, 19:190-209.

———— (1924b), The Economic Problem of Masochism. *Standard Edition*, 19:159-170.

———— (1924c), The Dissolution of the Oedipus Complex. *Standard Edition*, 19:173-179.

———— (1924d), The Loss of Reality in Neurosis and Psychosis. *Standard Edition*, 19:183-187.

———— (1924e), Neurosis and Psychosis. *Standard Edition*, 19:149-153.

———— (1924f), Letter to Le Disque Vert. *Standard Edition*, 19:290.

———— (1925a), A Note upon the 'Mystic Writing-Pad.' *Standard Edition*, 19:227-232.

———— (1925b), Negation. *Standard Edition*, 19:235-239.

———— (1925c), Preface to Aichhorn's *Wayward Youth*. *Standard Edition*, 19:273-275.

———— (1925d), An Autobiographical Study. *Standard Edition*, 20:7-74.

———— (1925e), Some Psychical Consequences of the Anatomical Distinction between the Sexes. *Standard Edition*, 19:248-258.

———— (1925f), The Resistance to Psychoanalysis. *Standard Edition*, 19:213-222.

———— (1925g), Moral Responsibility for the Content of Dreams. *Standard Edition*, 19:131-134.

——— (1926a), The Question of Lay Analysis. *Standard Edition*, 20:183-250.
——— (1926b), Psycho-Analysis. *Standard Edition*, 20:263-270.
——— (1926c), Inhibition, Symptom and Anxiety. *Standard Edition*, 20:87-172.
——— (1926d), Dr. Reik and the Problem of Quackery. A Letter to the *Neue Freie Presse. Standard Edition*, 21:247-248.
——— (1927a), Postscript (to the Question of Lay Analysis). *Standard Edition*, 20: 251-258.
——— (1927b), The Future of an Illusion. *Standard Edition*, 21:5-56.
——— (1927c), Fetishism. *Standard Edition*, 21:152-157.
——— (1928), Dostoevsky and Parricide. *Standard Edition*, 21:177-194.
——— (1930a), Civilization and Its Discontents. *Standard Edition*, 21:57-145.
——— (1930b), Address Delivered in the Goethe House of Frankfurt. *Standard Edition*, 21:208-212.
——— (1930c), Introduction to the Special Psychopathology Number of *The Medical Review of Reviews. Standard Edition*, 21:254-255.
——— (1931), Libidinal Types. *Standard Edition*, 21:217-220.
——— (1932), My Contact with Josef Popper-Lynkeus. *Collected Papers*, 5:295-301.
——— (1933a), *New Introductory Lectures on Psycho-Analysis*. New York: Norton.
——— (1933b), Why War? *Collected Papers*, 5:273-287.
——— (1937a), Analysis Terminable and Interminable. *Collected Papers*, 5:316-357.
——— (1937b), Constructions in Analysis. *Collected Papers*, 5:358-371.
——— (1939), *Moses and Monotheism*. London: International Psycho-Analytical Library, Hogarth Press, and Institute of Psycho-Analysis, 1951.
——— (1940a), *An Outline of Psychoanalysis*. New York: Norton, 1949.
——— (1940b), Abriss der Psychoanalyse. In: *Gesammelte Werke*, 17:63-138. London: Imago.
Fromm, E. (1950), *Psychoanalysis and Religion*. The Terry Lectures, New Haven: Yale University Press.
——— (1959), *Sigmund Freud's Mission*. New York: Harper.
Galton, F. (1879), Psychometric Facts. *The Nineteenth Century*, 5:425-433.
——— (1879-1880), Psychometric Experiments. *Brain*, 2:149-162.
Gantt, W. H. (1944), *Experimental Basis for Neurotic Behavior. Origin and Development of Artificially Produced Disturbances of Behavior in Dogs*. New York: Hoeber.
——— (1952), The Conditional Reflex Function as an Aid in the Study of the Psychiatric Patient. In: *Relation of Psychological Tests to Psychiatry*, eds. P. Hoch & J. Zubin. New York: Grune & Stratton, pp. 165-188.
——— (1953), The Physiological Basis of Psychiatry: The Conditional Reflex. In: *Basic Problems in Psychiatry*, ed. J. Wortis. New York: Grune & Stratton.
——— (1957), Pavlovian Principles and Psychiatry. In: *Progress in Psychotherapy*, 2:140-146. Eds. J. N. Masserman & J. L. Moreno. New York & London: Grune & Stratton.
———, ed. (1958), *Physiological Bases of Psychiatry*. Springfield, Ill.: C. C Thomas.
——— & Hoffmann, W. (1940), Conditioned Cardio-Respiratory Changes Accompanying Conditioned Food Reflexes. *American Journal of Physiology*, 129:360.
Gardiner, M. (1960), A Note on Accreditation. *Bulletin of the Philadelphia Association for Psychoanalysis*, 10:56-58.
——— (1962), The Seven Years of Dearth. *Bulletin of the Philadelphia Association for Psychoanalysis*, 12:168-170.
Gemelli, A. (1955), *Psychoanalysis Today*. New York: Kenedy & Sons.
Gengerelli, J. A. (1957), The Limitations of Psychoanalysis. Dogma or Discipline? *Saturday Review*, March 23.
Gibbon, E. (1776), *The Decline and Fall of the Roman Empire*. Abridgement by D. M. Low, 3 Vols. New York: Washington Square Press, 1962.
Gicklhorn, J. (1955), Wissenschaftliche Notizen zu den Studien von S. Syrski (1874) und S. Freud (1877) über männliche Flussaale. *Sitzungsbericht der Öster-*

reichischen Akademie der Wissenschaften (Mathem.-Naturw. Kl.), Abt. I, Bd. 164, Heft 1 and 2.

———(1957), Julius Wagner-Jaureggs Gutachten über Sigmund Freud und seine Studien zur Psychoanalyse. *Wiener Klinische Wochenschrift,* 69:533-537.

———& Gicklhorn, R. (1960), *Sigmund Freuds akademische Laufbahn.* Vienna & Innsbruck: Urban & Schwarzenberg.

Gicklhorn, R. (1958), Eine mysteriöse Bildaffäre. Ein kritischer Beitrag zur Freud-Forschung in Wien. *Wiener Geschichtsblätter,* 13(73):14-16.

Gillispie, C. C. (1960), *The Edge of Objectivity.* Princeton, N.J.: Princeton University Press.

Gitelson, M. (1951), Psychoanalysis and Dynamic Psychiatry. *A.M.A. Archives of Neurology and Psychiatry,* 66:280-288.

———(1959), A Critique of Current Concepts in Psychosomatic Medicine. *Bulletin of the Menninger Clinic,* 23:165-178.

———(1962), Communication from the President about the Neoanalytic Movement. *International Journal of Psycho-Analysis,* 43:373-375.

Glover, E. (1927), Discussion on Lay Analysis. *International Journal of Psycho-Analysis,* 8:212-220.

———(1945), Examination of the Klein System of Child Psychology. In: *The Psychoanalytic Study of the Child,* 1:75-118. New York: International Universities Press.

———(1961), Some Recent Trends in Psychoanalysis. *Psychoanalytic Quarterly,* 30:86-107.

———(1964), Freudian or Neofreudian. *Psychoanalytic Quarterly,* 33:97-109.

Goethe, J. W. (1785), Letter to Charlotte von Stein, 5 September. In: *Goethes Werke. Sophienausgabe,* Abt. IV, 7:87. Weimar: Böhlau, 1891.

———(1810), Zur Farbenlehre. Historischer Theil, Vol. 1, *Sophienausgabe,* Abt. II, Vol. 3. Weimar Böhlau, 1893.

———(1819), Eines verjährten Neptunisten Schlussbekenntnis. Abschied von der Geologie. *Goethes Werke,* Abt. II, 13:314, Weimar: Böhlau, 1904.

———(1826), Zahme Xenien. *Goethes Werke,* 5(1):134, Abt. I, Weimar: Böhlau, 1893.

———(1827), Den Vereinigten Staaten. Zahme Xenien IX, 742-753. In: *Goethes Sämtliche Werke. Jubiläums-Ausgabe* in 40 Vols. 4:127. Stuttgart & Berlin: Cotta.

———(1828), In: *Gespräche mit Goethe in den letzten Jahren seines Lebens,* by Johann Peter Eckermann, ed. H. H. Houben. Leipzig: Brockhaus, 1910, 10th edition.

Goetz, B. (1952), Erinnerungen an Sigmund Freud. *Neue Schweizer Rundschau,* 20: 3-11.

Goldman, H. B. & Crain, I. (1957), Psychologic Aspects of Tonsillectomy. *New York State Journal of Medicine,* 57:232-238.

Greenacre, P. (1950), Discussion of John N. Rosen's Paper "The Optimum Conditions for the Treatment of Schizophrenic Psychosis by Direct Analytic Therapy," read to The New York Psychoanalytic Society on June 13, 1950.

———(1956), Re-evaluation of the Process of Working Through. *International Journal of Psycho-Analysis,* 37:439-444.

———(1958), Toward an Understanding of the Physical Nucleus of Some Defence Reactions. *International Journal of Psycho-Analysis,* 39:69-76.

Grew, J. C. (1944), *Ten Years in Japan.* New York: Simon & Schuster.

Griffis, W. E. (1960), *Townsend Harris, First American Envoy in Japan.* Boston & New York: Houghton, Mifflin.

Grotjahn, M. (1960), *Psychoanalysis and the Family Neurosis.* New York: Norton.

Gustav, L. & Wolf, K. (1937), Kinderpsychologische Experimente mit bedingten Reflexen. *Zeitschrift für Kinderforschung,* 46:307-336.

Haintz, O. (1937), *Der Russisch-Japanische Krieg von 1904-1905.* Berlin: Stilke.

Hall, R. (1959), The Scholar and the Craftsman in the Scientific Revolution. In:

Critical Problems in the History of Science, ed. M. Claggett. Madison: University of Wisconsin Press, pp. 3-23.

Harris, T. (1855-1858), *The Complete Journal of the First American Consul and Minister to Japan*, ed. & introd. by M. E. Cosenza. Rutland, Vermont, & Tokyo, Japan: Tuttle, 1959.

Hartmann, H. (1927), *Die Grundlagen der Psychoanalyse*. Leipzig: Thieme.

—— (1933), Review of Dorer (1932). *Imago*, 19:135-137.

—— (1939), Ego Psychology and the Problem of Adaptation. New York: International Universities Press, 1958.

—— (1947), On Rational and Irrational Activity. In: *Psychoanalysis and the Social Sciences*, 1:359-392. New York: International Universities Press.

—— (1948), Comment on the Psychoanalytic Theory of Instinctual Drives. *Psychoanalytic Quarterly*, 17:368-388.

—— (1950), Comments on Psychoanalytic Theory of the Ego. In: *The Psychoanalytic Study of the Child*, 5:74-96. New York: International Universities Press.

—— (1952), The Mutual Influences in the Development of Ego and Id. In: *The Psychoanalytic Study of the Child*, 7:9-30. New York: International Universities Press.

—— (1955), Notes on the Theory of Sublimation. In: *The Psychoanalytic Study of the Child*, 10:9-29. New York: International Universities Press.

—— (1956), The Development of the Ego Concept in Freud's Work. *International Journal of Psycho-Analysis*, 37:425-438.

—— (1958), Comments on the Scientific Aspects of Psychoanalysis. In: *The Psychoanalytic Study of the Child*, 13:127-146. New York: International Universities Press.

—— (1959), Psychoanalysis as a Scientific Theory. In: *Psychoanalysis, Scientific Method and Philosophy*: A Symposium, ed. S. Hook. New York: Grove Press, pp. 3-37.

—— (1960), *Psychoanalysis and Moral Values*. The Freud Anniversary Lecture Series. New York: International Universities Press.

—— & Betlheim, S. (1924), Über Fehlreaktionen bei der Korsakoffschen Psychose. *Archiv für Psychiatrie und Nervenkrankheiten*, 72:278-286. Reprinted in part in *Organization and Pathology of Thought*, ed. & transl. D. Rapaport. New York: Columbia University Press, 1951, pp. 288-310.

—— & Kris, E. (1945), The Genetic Approach in Psychoanalysis. *The Psychoanalytic Study of the Child*, 1:11-30. New York: International Universities Press.

—— Kris, E. & Loewenstein, R. M. (1951), Some Psychoanalytic Comment on "Culture and Personality." In: *Psychoanalysis and Culture. Essays in Honor of Géza Róheim*, eds. G. B. Wilbur & W. Muensterberger. New York: International Universities Press.

Hawks, F. L. (1857), *Narrative of the Expedition of an American Squadron to the China Seas and Japan, performed in the Years 1852, 1853, and 1854, under the Command of Commodore M. C. Perry, United States Navy*. New York: Appleton.

Hebb, D. O. (1949), *The Organization of Behavior. A Neuropsychological Theory*. New York: Science Editions, 1961.

—— (1960), The American Revolution. *American Psychologist*, 15:735-745.

Hediger (1959), Wie Tiere schlafen. *Medizinische Klinik*, 54:938-946.

Heider, F. (1926), Thing and Medium. In: *Psychological Issues*, Monograph 3: *On Perception and Event Structure, and the Psychological Environment, Selected Papers* by F. Heider. New York: International Universities Press, 1959, pp. 1-34.

—— (1930), The Function of the Perceptual System. In: *Psychological Issues*, Monograph 3: *On Perception and Event Structure, and the Psychological Environment, Selected Papers* by F. Heider. New York: International Universities Press, 1959, pp. 35-60.

Hendrick, I. (1955), Presidential Address: Professional Standards of the American

Psychoanalytic Association. *Journal of the American Psychoanalytic Association,* 3: 561-599.

—— (1961), The Birth of an Institute. In: *The Birth of an Institute,* ed. I. Hendrick. Freeport, Maine: The Bond Wheelwright Company, pp. 1-94.

Hermann, I. (1926), Modelle zu den Ödipus- und Kastrationskomplexen bei Affen. *Imago,* 12:59-69.

—— (1933), Zum Triebleben der Primaten. *Imago,* 19:113-125.

Herzog, R. (1931), Die Wunderheilungen von Epidauros. Ein Beitrag zur Geschichte der Medizin und der Religion. *Philologus,* Suppl. Band 22, Heft III. Leipzig: Dieterich'sche Verlagsbuchhandlung.

Hilgard, E. R. & Marquis, D. G. (1940), *Conditioning and Learning.* New York: Appleton-Century-Croft, 1961, revised, 2nd edition.

Hollitscher, W. (1938), Über einen Weg einige psychoanalytische Begriffe in die Behaviouristik einzuführen. *Unity of Science Forum,* October, 17-21.

—— (1939a), Über die Beziehungen zwischen der psychoanalytischen und behaviouristischen Begriffsbildung. *Zeitschrift für Psychoanalyse,* & *Imago,* 24:398-416.

—— (1939b), The Concept of Rationalization (Some Remarks on the Analytical Criticism of Thought). *International Journal of Psycho-Analysis,* 20:330-332.

—— (1940), Über die Begriffe der psychischen Gesundheit und Erkrankung. *The Journal of Unified Science (Erkenntnis),* 8:314-351.

—— (1942), Review of *A Long-Term Study of the Experimental Neuroses in the Sheep and Dog* by O. D. Anderson & R. Parmenter. *International Journal of Psycho-Analysis,* 23:183-184.

—— (1943), On the Concepts of Psychological Health and Illness. *International Journal of Psycho-Analysis,* 24:125-140.

—— (1947a), *Sigmund Freud, An Introduction, A Presentation of his Theory, and A Discussion of the Relationship between Psycho-Analysis and Society.* New York: Oxford University Press, International Library of Sociology and Social Reconstruction.

—— (1947b), *Über die Begriffe der psychischen Gesundheit und Erkrankung. Eine wissenschafts-logische Untersuchung.* Vienna: Gerold.

—— (1960a), *Die Natur im Weltbild der Wissenschaft.* Vienna: Globus Verlag.

—— (1960b), Freud's Psychoanalyse. Zu H. K. Wells neuem Buch. In: *Die Volksstimme,* Vienna, Sept. 24.

Hull, C. L. (1929), A Functional Interpretation of the Conditioned Reflex. *Psychological Review,* 36:498-511; The Dilemma of the Conditioned Defense Reaction, *ibid.,* 509-511.

—— (1939), The Problem of Stimulus Equivalence in Behavior Theory. *Psychological Review,* 46:9-30.

Humboldt, A. (1845-1850), *Kosmos, Entwurf einer physischen Weltbeschreibung,* 3 Vols. Stuttgart & Tübingen: Cotta.

Hutchins, E. & Gee, H. H. (1961), The Study of Applicants, 1959-60. *Journal of Medical Education,* 36:289-304.

Iltis, H. (1924), *Life of Mendel.* New York: Norton, 1932.

Isakower, O. (1939), On the Exceptional Position of the Auditory Sphere. *International Journal of Psycho-Analysis,* 20:340-348.

Jaspers, K. (1923), *Allgemeine Psychopathologie.* Berlin: Springer.

—— (1949), *Strindberg und Van Gogh. Versuch einer pathologischen Analyse unter vergleichender Heranziehung von Swedenborg und Hölderlin.* Bremen: Storm.

Jellinek, S. (1947), *Dying, Apparent Death and Resuscitation.* Baltimore: Williams & Wilkins.

Jensen, P. (1906), *Das Gilgamesch-Epos in der Weltliteratur,* Vol. 1: *Die Ursprünge der alttestamentlichen Patriarchen-, Propheten-, und Befreier-Sage.* Strassburg: Trübner.

Jones, E. (1908), Rationalization in Every Day Life. In: *Papers on Psycho-Analysis.* London: Baillière, Tindell & Cox, 1918, pp. 8-15.

———— (1927a), Discussion on Lay Analysis. *International Journal of Psycho-Analysis,* 8:174-198.

———— (1927b), Review of *Die Frage der Laienanalyse* by S. Freud. *International Journal of Psycho-Analysis,* 8:86-92.

———— (1953-1957), *The Life and Works of Sigmund Freud,* 3 Vols. New York: Basic Books.

———— (1954), The Early History of Psychoanalysis. *Journal of Mental Science,* 100: 198-210.

———— (1956), *Sigmund Freud, Four Centenary Addresses.* New York: Basic Books.

———— (1959), *Free Associations. Memories of a Psycho-Analyst.* New York: Basic Books.

———— Strachey, J. & Rickman, J. (1927), Abbreviated Report of the Sub-Committee on Lay Analysis. *International Journal of Psycho-Analysis,* 8:559-560.

Josephson, M. (1928), *Zola and His Time.* New York: Garden City Publishing Co.

Jowett, B., tr. (1937), *The Dialogues of Plato,* 2 Vols. New York: Random House.

Jung, C. G. (1907), The Psychology of Dementia Praecox. *Nervous and Mental Disease,* Monograph Series No. 3, 1936.

———— (1963), *Memoirs, Dreams, Reflections.* Recorded and edited by A. Jaffé. New York: Pantheon.

———— & Riklin, F., ed. (1910-1911), *Correspondenzblatt der internationalen psychoanalytischen Vereinigung.* Zurich-Selnan: Leemann & Co. (6 issues, from July 1910 to August 1911).

Justin, (1960), *Menschen und Paragraphen (Die Versuchung). Die Weltwoche,* No. 1395:24 (Aug. 5).

Kallen, H. (1937), Psychoanalysis. In: *Encyclopedia of the Social Sciences,* 12:580-588. New York: Macmillan.

Kannengiesser, A., comp. tr. & ed., (n.d.), *Dreihundert ausgewählte Briefe Friedrichs des Grossen.* Leipzig: Reclam.

Kardiner, A. (1941), *The Traumatic Neurosis of War.* Washington, D.C.: National Research Council, Psychosomatic Medicine Monographs II-III.

Kardos, L. (1962), *Grundfragen der Psychologie und die Forschungen Pavlovs.* Budapest: Verlag der Ungarischen Akademie. Berlin: Deutscher Verlag der Wissenschaften.

Kaufman, M. R. (1951), Psychoanalysis in Medicine. *Bulletin of the American Psychoanalytic Association,* 7:1-12.

Kempf, E. S. (1958), The Conflicting Conditioned Self-determining Attitude. In: Gantt (1958), pp. 127-170.

Kempis, T. à (1441), *The Imitation of Christ.* Melbourne, London & Baltimore: Penguin Books, 1954.

Kety, S. S. (1960), A Biologist Examines the Mind and Behavior. *Science,* 132:1861-1870.

Kierkegaard, S. (1843), *Furcht und Zittern.* Jena: Diederichs, 1923.

Kinsey, A. C., Pomeroy, W. B. & Martin, C. E. (1948), *Sexual Behavior in the Human Male.* Philadelphia & London: Saunders.

———— ———— ———— & Gebhard, P. (1953), *Sexual Behavior in the Human Female.* Philadelphia & London: Saunders.

Klein, G. S. (1956), Perception, Motives and Personality. In: *Psychology of Personality. Six Modern Approaches,* ed. J. L. McCary. New York: Logos Press, pp. 123-199.

Kline, M. (1953), *Mathematics in Western Culture.* New York: Oxford University Press.

Knight, R. (1953), The Present Status of Organized Psychoanalysis in the United States (Presidential Address, American Psychoanalytic Association). *Journal of the American Psychoanalytic Association,* 1:197-221.

Kohlbrugge, J. H. F. (1913), *Historische-kritische Studien über Goethe als Natur-forscher*. Würzburg: Kobitz.

Korff, H. A. (1923-1958), *Geist der Goethezeit*, 5 Vols. Leipzig: Koehler & Arnelang.

Koyré, A. (1957), *From the Closed World to the Infinite Universe*. Harper Torchbooks. New York: Harper, 1958.

Kris, E. (1939), *On Inspiration*. In: Kris (1952), pp. 291-302.

—————— (1946), The Function of Drawings and the Meaning of the "Creative Spell" in a Creative Artist. In: Kris (1952), pp. 151-169.

—————— (1947), The Nature of Psychoanalytic Propositions and Their Validation. In: *Freedom and Experience*, eds. S. Hook & M. R. Konwitz. New York: Cornell University Press. Also in: *Psychological Theory*, ed. M. H. Marx. New York: Macmillan, 1957, pp. 322-351.

—————— (1950), Introduction. In *The Origins of Psycho-Analysis*. Letters to Wilhelm Fliess, Drafts and Notes: 1887-1902, by Sigmund Freud. New York: Basic Books, 1954, pp. 1-47.

—————— (1952), *Psychoanalytic Explorations in Art*. New York: International Universities Press.

Kroeber, A. L. (1944), *Configurations of Culture Growth*. Berkeley & Los Angeles: University of California Press.

Kubie, L. S. (1934), Relation of the Conditioned Reflex to Psychoanalytic Technique. *Archives of Neurology and Psychiatry*, 32:1137-1142.

—————— (1948), Instincts and Homeostasis. *Psychosomatic Medicine*, 10:15-30.

—————— (1952), The Independent Institute. *Bulletin of the American Psychoanalytic Association*, 2:205-208.

—————— (1954), The Pros and Cons of a New Profession: A Doctorate in Medical Psychology. *Texas Reports on Biology and Medicine*, 12:125-170.

—————— (1958a), Pavlov, Freud, and Soviet Psychology. *Monthly Review*, March 9.

—————— (1958b), *Neurotic Distortion of the Creative Process*. Lawrence Porter Lectures, Series 22, University of Kansas.

—————— (1959), Pavlov, Freud and Soviet Psychiatry. *Behavioral Science*, 4:29-34.

Kuhn, T. S. (1962), The Structure of Scientific Revolutions. *International Encyclopedia of Unified Science*, Vol. 2, No. 2. Chicago: University of Chicago.

Langer, W. L. (1958), The Next Assignment. *American Historical Review*, 63:283-304.

La Piere, R. T. (1959), *The Freudian Ethic: An Analysis of the Subversion of American Character*. Des Moines, Iowa: Duell, Sloan & Pierce.

—————— & Farnsworth, P. R. (1936), *Social Psychology*. New York, Toronto & London: McGraw-Hill, 3rd edition, 1949.

Lashley, K. S. (1929), *Brain Mechanism and Intelligence. A Quantitative Study of Injuries to the Brain*. Chicago: University of Chicago Press.

Lasswell, H. D. (1930), *Psychopathology and Politics*. London: Cambridge University Press.

Latourette, K. S. (1918), *The History of Japan*. New York: Macmillan, 1957.

Le Corbeiller, P. (1946), Stars, Proteins, and Nations. *Atlantic Monthly*, 178 (December 6):78-83.

—————— (1947), Man in Transit. *Atlantic Monthly*, 179:57-62.

Leeming, B. The Adversary. In: *Satan* (1952), pp. 19-39.

Lesky, E. (1963), Probleme medizinischen Unterrichtes in der Zeit Billroths. *Wiener Klinische Wochenschrift*, 75:221-224.

Levine, I. (1923), *The Unconscious. An Introduction to Freudian Psychology*. New York: Macmillan. Transl. into German by Anna Freud, *Das Unbewusste*, Leipzig, Vienna & Zurich: Internationaler Psychoanalytischer Verlag, 1926.

Lewin, B. D. & Ross, H. (1960), *Psychoanalytic Education in the United States*. New York: Norton.

Lewin, K., ed. (1926), Vorbemerkungen über die psychischen Kräfte und Energien und über die Struktur der Seele. *Psychologische Forschung*, 7:294-329.

———— & Lippit, R. (1938), An Experimental Approach to the Study of Autocracy and Democracy: A Preliminary Note. *Sociometry,* 1:292-300.

————, ———— & White, R. K. (1939), Patterns of Aggressive Behavior in Experimentally Created 'Social Climates.' *Journal of Social Psychology,* 10:271-299.

Lewis, J. (1946), *The Ten Commandments.* New York: Freethought Press Association.

Liddell, H. (1950), The Role of Vigilance in the Development of Animal Neurosis. In: *Anxiety,* eds. P. H. Hoch & J. Zubin. New York: Grune & Stratton, pp. 183-196.

Lindner, S. (1879), Das Saugen an den Fingern, Lippen, etc. bei den Kindern (Ludeln). *Journal der Kinderheilkunde* (N.F.), 14:68. Reprinted in *Zeitschrift für psychoanalytische Pädagogik* (1934), 8:117-138.

Linn, L. (1958), Some Comments on the Origin of the Influencing Machine. *Journal of the American Psychoanalytic Association,* 6:305-308.

Loewenstein, R. M. (1951), *Christians and Jews. A Psychoanalytic Study.* New York: International Universities Press.

———— (1956), Some Remarks on the Role of Speech in Psychoanalytic Technique. *International Journal of Psycho-Analysis,* 37:460-468.

Loewi, O. (1953), *From the Workshop of Discoveries.* Porter Lectures, Series 19. Lawrence: University of Kansas Press.

Loomie, L. S., Rosen, V. R. & Stein, M. H. (1958), Ernst Kris and the Gifted Adolescent Project. In: *The Psychoanalytic Study of the Child,* 13:44-57. New York: International Universities Press.

Lorenz, K. (1935), Companionship in Bird Life. In: *Instinctive Behavior,* tr. & ed. C. H. Schiller. New York: International Universities Press, 1957, pp. 83-128.

———— (1952), *King Solomon's Ring.* London: Methuen.

———— (n.d.), *So kam der Mensch auf den Hund.* Wien: Verlag Dr. G. Dorotha-Schoeler.

Löwenfeld, L. (1894), *Pathologie und Therapie der Neurasthenie und Hysterie.* Wiesbaden: Bergmann.

———— (1897), *Lehrbuch der Gesammten Psychotherapie.* Wiesbaden: Bergmann.

Lowenfeld, H. (1941), Psychic Trauma and Productive Experience in the Artist. *Psychoanalytic Quarterly,* 10:116-130.

Luria, A. R. (1923), Psychoanalyse und Marxismus. Author's Abstract, *Internationale Zeitschrift für Psychoanalyse,* 9:543.

———— (1925), Die Psychoanalyse in Russland. *Internationale Zeitschrift für Psychoanalyse.* 11:395-398.

———— (1926), Die moderne russische Physiologie und die Psychoanalyse. *Internationale Zeitschrift für Psychoanalyse,* 12:40-53.

Mach, E. (1875), Grundlinien der Lehre von den Bewegungsempfindungen. Leipzig: Engelmann.

Mahan, A. T. (1900), *The Problem of Asia and its Effect upon International Policies.* Boston: Little, Brown.

Mainage, T. (1915), La Psychologie de la Conversion. Paris: Beauchesne & Gabalda.

Mann, T. (1936), Freud and the Future. *International Journal of Psycho-Analysis,* 37:106-115 (1956).

Marquis, D. P. (1931), Can Conditioned Responses be Established in the Newborn Infant? *Journal of Genetic Psychology,* 39:479-492.

Mauthner, F. (1924), *Der Atheismus und seine Geschichte im Abendlande,* 4 Vols. Stuttgart & Berlin: Deutsche Verlags-Anstalt.

McLaughlin, P. J. (1957), *The Church and Modern Science.* New York: Philosophical Library.

Mehlberg, H. K. (1958), *The Reach of Science.* Toronto: University of Toronto Press.

Meijer, A. F., ed. (1922), Niederländische Vereinigung für Psychoanalyse, Jahresbericht 1921. *Internationale Zeitschrift für Psychoanalyse,* 8:112.

Mendelson, M. (1960), *Psychoanalytic Concepts of Depression*. Springfield, Ill.: C. C Thomas.

Menninger, K. A. (1954), The Homeostatic Regulatory Function of the Ego. *Journal of the American Psychoanalytic Association*, 2:67-106.

Merton, R. K. (1959), On the Paper of Rupert Hall. In: *Critical Problems in the History of Science*, ed. M. Clagett. Madison: University of Wisconsin Press, pp. 24-29.

Miller, G. A., Galanter, E. & Pribram, K. H. (1960), *Plans and the Structure of Behavior*. New York: Holt.

Millis, W. (1931), *The Martial Spirit*. The Literary Guild of America. Cambridge: Riverside Press.

Mitscherlich, A. (1963). *Auf dem Weg zur vaterlosen Gesellschaft*. Munich: R. Piper & Co.

Moloney, J. C. (1954), *Understanding the Japanese Mind*. New York: Philosophical Library.

Morris, L. (1947), *Postscript to Yesterday. America: The Last Fifty Years*. New York: Random House.

Mueller, W. F., ed. (1958), *Aufstieg und Untergang der Grossreiche des Altertums*. Stuttgart: Kohlhammer.

Müller-Braunschweig, C. (1927), Discussion on Lay Analysis. *International Journal of Psycho-Analysis*, 8:231-238.

Murdoch, J. (1903-1926), *A History of Japan*, 3 Vols. London: Routledge & Kegan Paul; Vols. 1 and 2 (3rd impression) 1949. Vol. 3 rev & ed. by J. H. Longford, 1926.

Murray, M. (1921), *The God of the Witches*. Garden City, N.Y.: Doubleday.

Muther, R. Emil Orlik. *The International Studio*, 11:159-164.

Myerson, A. (1933), Discussion of the Paper by Thomas M. French. *American Journal of Psychiatry*, 12:1201-1202.

Neuburger, M. (1906), *Geschichte der Medizin*. Stuttgart: Enke.

Nietzsche, F. (1876-1878), Menschliches, Allzumenschliches. Ein Buch für freie Geister. *Gesammelte Werke*, Vol. 8. Munich: Musarion Verlag.

———— (1882), Die fröhliche Wissenschaft. *Gesammelte Werke*, Vol. 12. Munich: Musarion Verlag.

———— (1886), Menschliches, Allzumenschliches. Ein Buch für freie Geister. *Gesammelte Werke*, Vol. 9:92. Munich: Musarion Verlag.

Norman, H. E. (1940), *Japan's Emergence as a Modern State, Political and Economic Problems of the Meiji Period*. New York: Institute of Pacific Relations.

Nunberg, H. (1930), The Synthetic Function of the Ego. In: *Practice and Theory of Psychoanalysis. A Collection of Essays*. New York: Nervous and Mental Disease Publishing Co., 1948, pp. 120-136.

———— (1938), Psychological Interrelations Between Physician and Patient. New York: Nervous and Mental Disease Monographs, No. 74, 1948.

———— (1939), Ego Strength and Ego Weakness. In: *Practice and Theory of Psychoanalysis*. New York: Nervous and Mental Disease Monographs, 1948, pp. 185-198.

———— & Federn, E. eds. (1962), *Minutes of the Vienna Psychoanalytic Society*, 3 Vols. (1962-   ). New York: International Universities Press.

Oberndorf, C. P. (1912), A Case of Hallucinosis Induced by Repression. *Journal of Abnormal Psychology*, 6: 438-448.

———— (1948), *Which Way Out? Stories Based on the Experience of a Psychiatrist*. New York: International Universities Press.

———— (1953), *A History of Psychoanalysis in America*. New York: Grune & Stratton.

Ogburn, W. F. & Nimkoff, M. F. (1940), *Sociology*. New York: Houghton, Mifflin.

Olinick, S. L. (1954), Some Considerations of the Use of Questioning as a Psychoanalytic Technique. *Journal of the American Psychoanalytic Association*, 2:57-66.

———— (1957), Questioning and Pain, Truth and Negation. *Journal of the American Psychoanalytic Association*, 5:302-324.

Orr, D. W. (1942), Is There a Homeostatic Instinct? *Psychoanalytic Quarterly,* 11:322-335.

Osgood, C. E. (1953), *Method and Theory in Experimental Psychology.* New York: Oxford University Press.

Ostow, M. & Scharfstein, B. A. (1954), *The Need to Believe. The Psychology of Religion.* New York: International Universities Press.

Pavlov, I. P. (1903), Experimental Psychology and Psycho-pathology in Animals. In: Pavlov (1928), pp. 47-60.

———— (1906), Scientific Study of the so-called Psychical Processes in the Higher Animals. In: Pavlov (1928), pp. 81-96.

———— (1910-1911), The Food Centre. In: Pavlov (1928), pp. 147-155.

———— (1916a), The Reflex of Purpose. In: Pavlov (1928), pp. 275-281.

———— (1916b), An Analysis of some Complex Reflexes in the Dog; and the Relative Strength and Tension of Several Centres. In: Pavlov (1928), pp. 255-260.

———— (1917), The Reflex of Freedom. In: Pavlov (1928), pp. 282-286.

———— (1919), How Psychiatry may Help us to Understand the Physiology of the Cerebral Hemispheres. In: Pavlov (1928), pp. 287-293.

———— (1923), The Latest Successes of the Objective Study of the Highest Nervous Activity. In: Pavlov (1928), pp. 329-338.

———— (1925a), The Inhibitory Type of Nervous Systems in the Dog. In: Pavlov (1928), pp. 363-369.

———— (1925b), Normal and Pathological States of the Hemispheres. In: Pavlov (1928), pp. 353-362.

———— (1926), *Conditioned Reflexes. An Investigation of the Physiological Activity of the Cerebral Cortex.* New York: Oxford University Press, 1927.

———— (1928), *Lectures on Conditioned Reflexes. Twenty-Five Years of Objective Study of the Higher Nervous Activity (Behaviour) of Animals,* tr. W. H. Gantt. New York: International Publishers.

———— (1930), Trial Excursion of a Physiologist in the Field of Psychiatry. In: Pavlov (1941), pp. 39-43.

———— (1932a), Physiology of the Higher Nervous Activity. In: Pavlov (1941), pp. 86-94.

———— (1932b), Contributions to the Physiology of the Hypnotic State in the Dog. In: Pavlov (1941), pp. 75-82.

———— (1932c), Concerning Human and Animal Neuroses. In: Pavlov (1941), pp. 83-85.

———— (1932d), Essay on the Physiological Concept of the Symptomatology of Hysteria. In: Pavlov (1957), pp. 516-541.

———— (1935a), Experimental Pathology of the Higher Nervous Activity. In: Pavlov (1957), pp. 459-480.

———— (1935b), The Conditioned Reflex. In: Pavlov (1941), pp. 166-185.

———— (1941), *Conditioned Reflexes and Psychiatry.* Tr. & ed. W. H. Gantt. New York: International Publishers.

———— (1956), *Pawlowsche Mittwochkolloquien. Protokolle und Stenogramme Physiologischer Kolloquien,* 3 Vols. Berlin: Akademie Verlag.

———— (1957), *Experimental Psychology and Other Essays.* New York: Philosophical Library.

Penfield, W. (1937), *The Cerebral Cortex and Consciousness.* The Harvey Lectures Series XXXII. Baltimore: Williams & Wilkins, pp. 35-69.

Penrose, L. S. (1953), Psycho-Analysis and Experimental Science. *International Journal of Psycho-Analysis,* 34(Suppl.):74-82.

Perkins, F. (1946), *The Roosevelt I Knew.* New York: Viking Press.

Peters, H. F. (1962), *My Sister, My Spouse. A Biography of Lou Andreas-Salomé.* New York: Norton.

Pfister, O. (1927), *Analytische Seelsorge. Einführung in die praktische Psychoanalyse. für Pfarrer und Laien.* Göttingen: Vandenhoeck & Ruprecht.

———— (1944), *Christianity and Anxiety*. New York: Macmillan, 1948.
Piaget, J. (1935), *The Origins of Intelligence in Children*. New York: International Universities Press, 1952.
———— (1937), *The Construction of Reality in the Child*. New York: Basic Books, 1954.
Pirenne, J. (1944), *Les Grands Courants de L'histoire Universelle*, Vol. 1, *Des Origines à l'Islam*, 3rd edition, 1945. Neuchâtel: Editions de la Baconnière. Paris: Albin Michel.
Pius XII (1952), Moral Limits of Medical Research and Treatment. *The Catholic Mind*, 51:305-313 (1953).
———— (1953), Psychotherapy and Religion. *The Catholic Mind*, 51:428-435.
Plato, *Republic*. In: *The Dialogues of Plato*, tr. B. Jowett, 2 Vols., 1:591-879. New York: Random House, 1937.
Plé, A. (1952), Saint Thomas Aquinas and the Psychology of Freud. *Dominican Studies*, 5:1-34.
Plutarch, *The Lives of the Noble Grecians and Romans*. New York: The Modern Library, n.d.
Racker, H. (1956), On Freud's Position Towards Religion. *American Imago*, 13:97-121.
Rado, S., Grinker, R. R., Sr., & Alexander, F. (1963). Editorial, *AMA Archives of General Psychiatry*, 8:527-529.
Raimann, E. (1924), *Zur Psychoanalyse*. Berlin & Vienna: Urban & Schwarzenberg.
Rangell, L. (1959), The Nature of Conversion. *Journal of the American Psychoanalytic Association*, 7:632-662.
Rank, O. (1924). *The Trauma of Birth*. New York: Harcourt Brace, 1929.
———— & Sachs, H. (1913), Die Bedeutung der Psychoanalyse für die Geisteswissenschaften. *Grenzfragen des Nerven-und Seelenlebens*, XCIII, ed. L. Loewenfeld. Wiesbaden: Bergmann.
Rapaport, D. (1951a), *Organization and Pathology of Thought*. Austen Riggs Foundation Monograph No. 1. New York: Columbia University Press.
———— (1951b), The Autonomy of the Ego. *Bulletin of the Menninger Clinic*, 15:113-123.
———— (1958), The Theory of Ego Autonomy: A Generalization. *Bulletin of the Menninger Clinic*, 22:13-35.
Raymond, M. J. (1956), Case of Fetishism Treated by Aversion Therapy. *British Medical Journal*, 22:854-857.
Reich, W. (1927), Discussion on Lay Analysis. *International Journal of Psycho-Analysis*, 8:252-255.
Reik, T. (1927), Discussion on Lay Analysis. *International Journal of Psycho-Analysis*, 8:241-244.
———— (1935), *Surprise and the Psychoanalyst: on the Conjecture and Comprehension of Unconscious Processes*. London: Kegan Paul, Trench, Trubner; New York: Dutton, 1937.
Richard, H. (1863), *The Destruction of Kagosima and Our Inter-Course with Japan*. London: Walford & Hodder.
Richter, C. P. (1958), The Phenomenon of Unexplained Sudden Death in Animals and Man. In: Gantt (1958), pp. 112-123.
Rosenbaum, M. (1954), Freud-Eitingon-Magnes Correspondence. Psychoanalysis at the Hebrew University. *Journal of the American Psychoanalytic Association*, 2:311-317.
Rosenzweig, F. (1937), *Kleinere Schriften*. Berlin: Schocken Verlag/Jüdischer Buchverlag.
Ross, N. (1958), Psychoanalysis and Religion. *Journal of the American Psychoanalytic Association*, 6:519-539.
Rostand, J. (1958), *Error and Deception in Science*. New York: Basic Books, 1960.
Rusk, H. A. (1961), A Career in Medicine. *New York Times*, April 21, p. 54.
Sachs, H. (1919), The Unconscious in Shakespeare's "Tempest." In: *The Creative Unconscious*. Cambridge, Mass: Sci-Art Publishers, 1951, pp. 243-323.

———— (1933), The Delay of the Machine Age. *Psychoanalytic Quarterly*, 2:404-424.

———— (1944), *Freud, Master and Friend*. Cambridge: Harvard University Press.

Salter, A. (1941), *Conditioned Reflex Therapy*. New York: Capricorn Books, 1961.

Sanders, B. G. (1949), *Christianity After Freud. An Interpretation of the Christian Experience in the Light of Psycho-Analytic Theory*. London: Bles.

Sansom, G. B. (1931), *Japan, A Short Cultural History*. London: Cresset Press.

———— (1949), *The Western World and Japan. A Study in the Interaction of European and Asiatic Cultures*. New York: Knopf, 1958.

———— (1958), *A History of Japan to 1334*. Stanford: Stanford University Press.

———— (1961), *A History of Japan 1334-1615*. Stanford: Stanford University Press.

Sarton, G. (1927-1948), *Introduction to the History of Science*. Carnegie Institute of Washington. Baltimore: Williams & Wilkins.

———— (1952), Science and Morality. In: *Moral Principles of Action, Man's Ethical Imperative*, planned & edited by R. N. Anshen. Science of Culture Series Vol. VI. New York & London: Harper, pp. 436-452.

———— (1955), *Six Wings: Men of Science in the Renaissance*. Bloomington: Indiana University Press, 1957.

Satan (1952), New York: Sheed and Ward. Based upon Satan (1948), *Les Etudes Carmélitaines*, Desclée de Brouwer, n.p. ed. Père Bruno de Jésus-Marie, O.c.D.

Satow, E. M. (1909), Japan. In: *The Cambridge Modern History*, Vol. XI: The Growth of Nationalities. Cambridge: Cambridge University Press, pp. 823-865.

———— (1921), *A Diplomat in Japan*. London: Seeley, Service.

Schapiro, M. (1956), Leonardo and Freud: An Art-Historical Study. *Journal of the History of Ideas*, 17:147-178.

Schilder, P. (1921), Über die kausale Bedeutung des durch Psychoanalyse gewonnenen Materiales. *Wiener Klinische Wochenschrift*, 34:355-356.

———— (1933), Psychoanalyse und Biologie. *Imago*, 19:168-197.

———— (1935), Psychoanalysis and the Conditioned Reflexes. In: *Mind: Perception and Thought in Their Constructive Aspects*. New York: Columbia University Press, 1942, pp. 153-172.

———— (1940), The Influence of Psychoanalysis on Psychiatry. *Psychoanalytic Quarterly*, 9:216-228.

Schiller, F. (1795a), Die Weltweisen. In: *Schillers Sämtliche Werke*, Säkular-Ausgabe, 16 Vols., 1:256-258. Stuttgart & Berlin: Cotta, 1904.

———— (1795b), Letter to Goethe of October 16, 1795. In: H. H. Borcherdt, *Briefwechsel zwischen Schiller und Goethe in den Jahren 1794 bis 1805*, 2 Vols., 1:118. Berlin, Leipzig, Wien & Stuttgart: Deutsches Verlagshaus, Boug, 1914.

Schneirla, T. C. (1959), An Evolutionary and Developmental Theory of Biphasic Processes underlying Approach and Withdrawal. *Nebraska Symposium on Motivation*, pp. 2-42. Lincoln: University of Nebraska Press.

Schnitzler, A. (1887), Review of: *Neue Vorlesungen über die Krankheiten des Nervensystems, insbesonders über Hysterie von J. M. Charcot*. Autorisierte deutsche Ausgabe von Dr. S. Freud. *Internationale Klinische Rundschau*, 1:20.

Schönbauer, L. (1947), *Das Medizinische Wien*. Vienna: Urban & Schwarzenberg.

Schopenhauer, A. (1819), Objectivation des Willens im thierischen Organismus. Ergänzungen zu Die Welt als Wille und Vorstellung. *Sämmtliche Werke*, 2:981-1009. Leipzig: Grossherzog Wilhelm Ernst Ausgabe, Inselverlag.

Schrötter, K. (1912), Experimentelle Träume. *Zentralblatt für Psychoanalyse und Psychotherapie*, 2:638-646. Reprinted in condensed form in: *Organization and Pathology of Thought*, ed. & tr. D. Rapaport. New York: Columbia University Press, 1951, pp. 234-248.

Schur, M. (1955a), Comment on the Metapsychology of Somatization. In: *The Psychoanalytic Study of the Child*, 10:119-164. New York: International Universities Press.

———— (1955b), Constitutional Aspects of Psychosomatic Disorders. *Samiksa*, 9:104-115.

Schwing, G. (1940), *A Way to the Soul of the Mentally Ill.* New York: International Universities Press, 1954.

Scott, J. P. (1962), Periods in Behavioral Development. *Science,* 138:949-958.

Sèchehaye, M.-A. (1947), *Symbolic Realization: A New Method of Psychotherapy Applied to a Case of Schizophrenia.* New York: International Universities Press, 1951.

———— (1950), *Reality Lost and Regained: Autobiography of a Schizophrenic Girl.* New York: Grune & Stratton, 1951.

Sheen, F. J. (1949), *Peace of Soul.* New York: Perma Books, 1955.

Sherwood, S. (1962), Review of *Sigmund Freuds akademische Laufbahn im Lichte der Dokumente,* by Josef Gicklhorn & Renée Gicklhorn. *Diseases of the Nervous System,* 23:235-237.

Simmel, E. (1926), The "Doctor-Game," Illness and the Profession of Medicine. *International Journal of Psycho-Analysis,* 7:470-483.

———— (1940), Sigmund Freud: The Man and His Work. *Psychoanalytic Quarterly,* 9:163-176.

Smith, V. E. (1955), The Study of Man: An Essay in Reconstruction. In: Braceland (1955), pp. 145-179.

Spengler, O. (1917-1922), *The Decline of the West.* New York: Knopf, 1939.

Stargardt, J. A. (1964), *Autographen aus Allen Gebieten.* Katalog 567, No. 447.

Stekel, W. (1911), *Die Sprache des Traumes.* Munich-Wiesbaden: Bergmann.

———— (1931), Die Technik der Psychoanalyse. *Psychoanalytische Praxis,* 1:1-13; 49-64; 113-123; 169-179.

Stern, K. (1951), *The Pillar of Fire.* New York: Harcourt, Brace.

———— (1954), *The Third Revolution. A Study of Psychiatry and Religion.* Garden City, N.Y.: Image Books, 1961.

———— (1955), *Some Spiritual Aspects of Psychotherapy.* In: Braceland (1955), pp. 125-140.

———— (1962), Anything can be Reduced to the Irrational—but does it Help? Review of *Psychoanalysis and Religion* by Gregory Zilboorg. *New York Times Book Review,* May 6, pp. 6, 18.

Stone, L. (1954), The Widening Scope of Indications for Psychoanalysis. *Journal of the American Psychoanalytic Association,* 2:567-594.

———— (1961), *The Psychoanalytic Situation. An Examination of Its Development and Essential Nature.* The Freud Anniversary Lecture Series. New York: International Universities Press.

Storfer, A. J. (1929), Beiträge zur psychoanalytischen Bibliographie (Plato und Freud. Musik. Asthma. Ibsen). *Die Psychoanalytische Bewegung,* 1:67-73.

Strachey, J. (1958), Editor's Introduction to Papers on Technique. *Standard Edition,* 12:85-88.

———— (1959), Editor's Note, The Question of Lay Analysis by S. Freud. *Standard Edition,* 20:179-181.

Straus, E. (1935), *Vom Sinn der Sinne. Ein Beitrag zur Grundlegung der Psychologie.* Berlin: Springer.

Strauss, A. (1955), Unconscious Mental Processes and the Psychosomatic Concept. *International Journal of Psycho-Analysis,* 36:307-319.

Szasz, T. A. (1959), Psychiatry, Psychotherapy and Psychology. *AMA Archives of General Psychiatry,* 1:455-463.

Taubes, J. (1957), Religion and the Future of Psychoanalysis. In: *Psychoanalysis and the Future, A Freud Centenary Memorial,* foreword by B. Nelson. New York: National Psychological Association for Psychoanalysis, pp. 136-142.

Tawney, R. H. (1926), *Religion and the Rise of Capitalism.* New York: Harcourt, Brace.

Tax, S., ed. (1960), *The Evolution of Life, Its Origin, History and Future.* Chicago: University of Chicago Press.

The Freud Centenary Exhibit (1956), Catalogue. New York City: Tri-Arts Press.

The Problem of Medical and Lay Psychotherapy (1950), A Symposium. *American Journal of Psychotherapy,* 4:419-456.

Thieme-Becker (1932), *Allgemeines Lexicon der Bildenden Künstler,* ed. Vollmer, Vol. 26. Leipzig: Seemann.

Thorpe, W. H. (1956), *Learning and Instinct in Animals.* Cambridge, Mass.: Harvard University Press.

Tillich, P. (1950), Anxiety-Reducing Agencies in Our Culture. In: *Anxiety,* eds. P. H. Hoch & J. Zubin. New York: Grune & Stratton, pp. 17-26.

―――― (1951), *Systematic Theology,* Vol. 1. Chicago: University of Chicago Press.

Tolstoy, L. (1884), The Death of Ivan Ilyich. In: *The Death of Ivan Ilyich, and other Stories.* New York: New American Library, 1960.

Toynbee, A. (1949), Can Western Civilization Save Itself? *Commentary,* 7:103-110.

Tsunoda, R., de Bary, W. T. & Keene, D., compilers. (1960), *Sources of Japanese Tradition.* New York: Columbia University Press.

Turkel, H. (1962), Outmoded? Has Psychoanalysis Actually Outlived its Usefulness? *New Medical Materia,* 4:49.

Tyson, A. & Strachey, J. (1956), A Chronological Hand-List of Freud's Works. *International Journal of Psycho-Analysis,* 37:19-33.

Van Ophuijsen, J. H. W. (1927), Discussion on Lay Analysis. *International Journal of Psycho-Analysis,* 8:279-281.

Vollmer, H., ed. (1956), *Allgemeines Lexicon der Bildenden Künstler des XX. Jahrhunderts.* 3rd Vol. Leipzig: Seemann.

Von Berger, A. (1896), Chirurgie der Seele. Partly reprinted in: *Die Psychoanalytische Bewegung,* 4:73-76, 1932.

Von Karpinska, L. (1914), Über die psychologischen Grundlagen des Freudismus. *Internationale Zeitschrift für Psychoanalysis,* 2:305-326.

Von Mayer, J. R. & Popper-Lynkeus, J. (1875), Two Letters. In: *Autographen aus der Sammlung Karl Geigy-Hagenbach, Basel* (catalogue of auction). Marburg: Stargardt, 1961.

Vowles, D. M. (1961), Neural Mechanisms in Insect Behaviour. In: *Current Problems in Animal Behaviour,* ed. W. H. Thorpe & O. L. Zangwill. Cambridge: Cambridge University Press, pp. 5-29.

Waelder, R. (1934), Ätiologie und Verlauf der Massenpsychosen. Mit einem soziologischen Anhang; über die geschichtliche Situation der Gegenwart. *Imago,* 21:67-91 (1935).

―――― (1936), The Problems of the Genesis of Psychical Conflict in Earliest Infancy. *International Journal of Psycho-Analysis,* 18:406-473 (1937).

―――― (1956), Freud and the History of Science. *Journal of the American Psychoanalytic Association,* 4:602-613.

―――― (1960), *Basic Theory of Psychoanalysis.* New York: International Universities Press.

―――― (1963), Historical Fiction. *Journal of the American Psychoanalytic Association,* 11:628-651.

Wagner-Jauregg, J. (1950), *Lebenserinnerungen.* Ed. & compl. L. Schönbauer & M. Jantsch. Vienna: Springer.

Weber, M. (1904-1905), *The Protestant Ethic and the Spirit of Capitalism* (tr. T. Parsons). London: Allen & Unwin, 1930.

―――― (1919), Science as a Vocation. In: *From Max Weber: Essays in Sociology,* tr., ed. & introd. H. H. Gerth & C. W. Mills. New York: Oxford University Press, 1946, pp. 129-156.

Weiss, E. (1933), A Recovery from the Fear of Blushing. *Psychoanalytic Quarterly,* 2:309-314.

―――― (1942), Emotional Neurosis and Acting Out. *Psychoanalytic Quarterly,* 11:477-492.

Wells, H. K. (1956), *Ivan P. Pavlov. Toward a Scientific Psychology and Psychiatry.* New York: International Publishers.

———— (1960), *Freud. A Pavlovian Critique.* New York: International Publishers.

Werner, H. (1940), *Comparative Psychology of Mental Development.* New York: International Universities Press, 1957.

Wernicke, C. (1900), *Grundriss der Psychiatrie in klinische Vorlesungen.* Leipzig: Thieme.

White, A. D. (1895), *A History of the Warfare of Science with Theology in Christendom.* New York: Braziller, 1955.

White, L., Jr., (1962), *Medieval Technology and Social Change.* Oxford: Clarendon Press.

White, T. (1895), *The War in the East.* Philadelphia & St. Louis: Ziegler.

Wobbermun, G. (1928), Die Methoden der religionspsychologischen Arbeit. In: *Handbuch der biologischen Arbeitsmethoden,* Abt. IV: Methoden der experimentellen Psychologie, Teil C/I, Methoden der angewandten Psychologie, 1:1-44. Berlin & Vienna: Urban & Schwarzenberg.

Wohl, R. P. & Trosman, H. (1955), A Retrospect of Freud's Leonardo. *Psychiatry,* 18:27-39.

Zangwill, O. L. (1961), Lashley's Concept of Cerebral Mass Action. In: *Current Problems in Animal Behavior,* ed. W. H. Thorpe & O. L. Zangwill. Cambridge: Cambridge University Press, pp. 59-86.

Zetzel, E. R., ed. (1963), 122nd Bulletin of the International Psycho-Analytical Association. *International Journal of Psycho-Analysis,* 44:384-386.

Zilboorg, G. (1943), *Mind, Medicine, Man.* New York: Harcourt, Brace.

———— (1951), *Sigmund Freud, His Exploration of the Mind of Man.* London & New York: Scribner's.

———— (1952), Some Sidelights on Free Associations. *International Journal of Psycho-Analysis,* 33:489-495.

———— (1953a), Love in Freudian Psychoanalysis. In: Zilboorg (1962a), pp. 117-139.

———— (1953b), Scientific Psychopathology and Religious Issues. In: Zilboorg (1962a), pp. 104-116.

———— (1955), Some Denials and Assertions of Religious Faith. In: Braceland (1955), pp. 99-121.

———— (1958), Psychiatry's Moral Sphere. In: Zilboorg (1962a), pp. 189-194.

———— (1962a), *Psychoanalysis and Religion.* Ed. & introd. M. S. Zilboorg. New York: Farrar, Straus & Cudahy.

———— (1962b), The Sense of Guilt. In: Zilboorg (1962a), pp. 169-188.

Zimmer (1951), *Philosophies of India.* New York: Pantheon Books.

Zuckermann, S. (1932), *The Social Life of Monkeys and Apes.* New York: Harcourt, Brace.

Zweig, S. (1931), *Mental Healers: Franz Anton Mesmer, Mary Baker Eddy, Sigmund Freud.* New York: Viking Press, 1933.

INDICES

Name Index

Compiled by Harold Collins.

Subject Index

Compiled by Harold Collins.

Child analysis
    educators' need for understanding of, 216
    impending disappearance of, 215
    lack of medical analysts equipped for, 214
    purported "injury" to child's mind in, 215
    replacement of classical forms of, 213
    specific character of, as contrasted with adult, 213
    use in testing genetic reconstructions, 214
    value for adult analysts of experience in, 215n.
Childhood, unhappiness characteristic of, 212
Christian ethics, Freud's characterization of, 28
Church
    attitude toward psychoanalysis, 247
    dominance of, and later development of science, 221
    prestage of truly religious attitude, 275
    psychoanalysis, and antiscientific bastions of, 254
Church doctrine, concept of soul in, and systemic psychology, 255
Civilization
    decline and fall of current, 223, 228
    disorder and, 222
    Spengler on "biological" necessity of death of, 227
    universal concern about future of Western, 406
Common sense, conflict with ideas of Copernicus, 515-516
Communism, as antipsychological, 299
Conclusions, based on psychological observation of nonpsychological entities, 429
Conditioned reflex
    and vegetative functions, 331-332
    establishment of, 309-310
    role of cortex in, 342n.
    theory of, 311-312
    two meanings of, 332n.
Conscience, residue of historical development, 157
Conservatism, relationship of aural tradition to, 454
Contradictions, basic difference between religious and scientific, 431-432
Conversion
    and denial of reality, 269
    despair as key to, 167

    nature and incidence of, 266
    psychological conditions for, 268
"Core events," 50-51
"Correctional emotional experiences," as therapeutic technique, 95
Cosmic experience, nature of, 275
Creativity
    adaptability and vulnerability of, 14
    and adolescence, 180-181
    and illness, 19
    and personality structure, 18, 19
    bases for psychological theory of, 158
    continuing enigma of, 14
    humanities' contribution to understanding of, 20
Criticism
    "constructive" and "unconstructive," viii
    part and whole, x
    styles of, vii-ix
Culture
    metapsychology of, and anthropic sciences, 159
    metapsychology of, and psychoanalytic anthropic research, 158
    structure and medium of transmission, 455n.

Death instinct
    origins of Freud's concept of, 156
    rejection by most psychoanalysts of, 156
Defenses, weakening through aging, 22
Depression of the aged, cause of, 21
Disease
    activating effect on psychic elements, 115
    as death in miniature, 111
    as integral part of life, 111
    chemical and physical processes as medicine's keys to, 207
    dehumanized by scientific medicine, 112
    molecular level of medicine's understanding of, 207
    necessity to physician of experience of, 160
    physician's attitude toward relationship of mind to, 140
    predisposition to recovery from, 118
    psychogenic origins of, 111
Dreams
    Freud's early emphasis on interpretation of, 75
    responsibility for, 264
Drives, Freud's early division into ego- and object-, 156